ISSUES IN
K-12 EDUCATION

SELECTIONS FROM CQ RESEARCHER

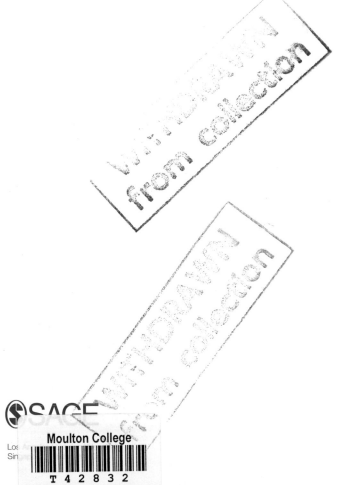

⑤SAGE

For information:

SAGE Publications, Inc.
2455 Teller Road
Thousand Oaks, California 91320
E-mail: order@sagepub.com

SAGE Publications Ltd.
1 Oliver's Yard
55 City Road
London EC1Y 1SP
United Kingdom

SAGE Publications India Pvt. Ltd.
B 1/I 1 Mohan Cooperative Industrial Area
Mathura Road, New Delhi 110 044
India

SAGE Publications Asia-Pacific Pte. Ltd.
33 Pekin Street #02-01
Far East Square
Singapore 048763

Printed in the United States of America

Library of Congress Cataloging-in-Publication Data

Issues in K-12 education : selections from CQ researcher.
    p. cm.
Includes bibliographical references.
ISBN 978-1-4129-8007-4 (pbk.: alk. paper)
  1. Early childhood education. 2. Education, Elementary. 3. Education, Secondary. I. Sage Publications, inc.

LB1139.2.I88 2010
370.973—dc22   2009033511

This book is printed on acid-free paper.

09   10   11   12   13   10   9   8   7   6   5   4   3   2   1

Acquisitions Editor:	Diane McDaniel
Associate Editor:	Deya Saoud
Editorial Assistant:	Ashley Conlon
Production Editor:	Laureen Gleason
Typesetter:	C&M Digitals (P) Ltd.
Cover Designer:	Candice Harman
Marketing Manager:	Christy Guilbault

Contents

ANNOTATED CONTENTS   ix

PREFACE   xv

CONTRIBUTORS   xvii

ISSUES IN JUSTICE, EQUITY, AND EQUALITY

**1. Racial Diversity in Public Schools:
Has the Supreme Court Dealt a Blow
to Integration?**   1

    Should school systems promote racial
      diversity in individual schools?   5

    Should school systems seek to promote
      socioeconomic integration in individual
      schools?   6

    Is the focus on diversity interfering
      with efforts to improve education
      in all schools?   9

    Background   10

      The 'Common School'   10

      'Elusive' Equality   14

      'Diversity' Challenged   16

    Current Situation   18

      'Resegregation' Seen   18

      Legal Options Eyed   19

    Outlook   20

      'Minimal Impact'?   20

    Notes   21

    Bibliography   22

**2. No Child Left Behind: Is the Law
Improving Student Performance?**   25

    Has No Child Left Behind raised student
      achievement?   28

    Are too many schools being labeled
      "in need of improvement"?   29

    Is No Child Left Behind improving
      the quality of teaching?   32

    Is No Child Left Behind adequately
      funded?   34

    Background   37

      Federal Reforms   37

      Achievement Gaps   40

    Current Situation   41

      States Push Back   41

      Teachers' Union Sues   41

      War of Words   43

    Outlook   43

      Reform Unlikely?   43

    Notes   44

    Bibliography   45

**3. Special Education: Do Students With
Disabilities Get the Help They Need?**   49

    Should the federal government spend
      more to educate disabled students?   52

    Does the availability of federal funding
      for special education encourage the
      overdiagnosis of learning disabilities?   55

Has IDEA increased discipline problems in
   public schools? 57
Background 60
   IDEA Aids States 60
   Escalating Costs 60
   Revamping the Law 61
Current Situation 63
   Paying the Bill 63
Outlook 64
   Reauthorization Fight? 64
   Support from both presidential candidates 67
Notes 67
Bibliography 68

4. **Fixing Urban Schools: Has No Child
   Left Behind Helped Minority Students?** **71**
   Has the No Child Left Behind law helped
      urban students? 74
   Should governments make schools more
      racially and economically diverse? 76
   Are teachers prepared to teach successfully
      in urban classrooms? 78
Background 79
   Educating the Poor 79
   Two Tracks 81
   Minority Schools 84
   Poor in School 86
Current Situation 88
   Congress Divided 88
   Retooling NCLB? 89
Outlook 90
   Agreeing to Disagree 90
Notes 90
Bibliography 92

5. **Charter Schools: Will They Improve or
   Hurt Public Education?** **95**
   Are charter schools harming the
      traditional public school system? 100
   Do charter schools foster innovation and
      achievement? 101
   Should private companies be allowed
      to run charter schools? 103
Background 107
   Born on a Napkin 107
   States Climb Aboard 108
   Creative Resources 109
   Seeking Accreditation 110

Current Situation 111
   Federal Support 111
   Vouchers Link 111
   Steps Forward and Back 113
Outlook 113
   Just a Fad? 113
Notes 114
Bibliography 115

6. **Home Schooling Debate: Is the Movement
   Undermining Public Education?** **119**
   Should the government regulate
      home schooling? 123
   Should the public-school system
      support home schooling? 125
   Does home schooling threaten the
      fundamental American concept
      of universal public education? 127
Background 130
   'Common Schools' 130
   Rise of Reformers 130
   States' Rights 131
Current Situation 133
   Nationwide Movement 133
   Into the Mainstream? 134
Outlook 136
   'Saber Rattling' 136
   Limited Growth? 137
Notes 137
Bibliography 138

7. **Single-Sex Education: Do All-Boy and
   All-Girl Schools Enhance Learning?** **141**
   Does single-sex education enhance
      learning? 144
   Do single-sex schools reinforce gender
      stereotypes? 145
   Do single-sex schools help or hurt
      the goal of gender equity? 146
Background 147
   'Tide of Coeducation' 147
   Gender Equity 150
   Single-Sex Revival 153
Current Situation 155
   Starting New Schools 155
   Revising Federal Rules? 156
Outlook 159
   A New Era? 159

Notes 159
Bibliography 161

8. **Religion in Schools: Should the
   Courts Allow More Spiritual Expression?** **163**
   Are barriers to prayer in schools
       too rigid? 165
   Are Christian groups "sneaking"
       religion into schools? 167
   Should taxpayer-supported vouchers
       help parents send their children to
       private or religious schools? 169
   Background 172
   Colonial Intolerance 172
   'Common' Schools 173
   Court Decisions 173
   Conservative Christians 175
   Current Situation 175
   Limits on Prayer 175
   Voucher Battles 176
   Outlook 177
   Bush's Impact 177
   Notes 180
   Bibliography 180

ISSUES IN TEACHING AND LEARNING

9. **Students Under Stress: Do Schools
   Assign Too Much Homework?** **183**
   Are students today under more
       academic pressure than in past
       generations? 186
   Are schools assigning too much
       homework? 188
   Are high-stakes tests putting too much
       pressure on students? 190
   Background 193
   Schooling Expands 193
   Different Visions 194
   Cold War Fears 194
   Bulging Backpacks? 195
   Current Situation 198
   Reevaluating Homework 198
   Testing the Tests 200
   Outlook 201
   Learning to Teach 201
   Notes 202
   Bibliography 204

10. **Gender and Learning: Are There
    Innate Differences Between the Sexes?** **207**
    Is there really a gender gap in
        math and science? 212
    Are there "innate differences" between
        males and females in math and science
        aptitude? 214
    Is enough being done to encourage
        women in science and math? 216
    Background 220
    Women in Science 220
    Growing Sexism 221
    'Weak-minded' Women 222
    Gender-Equity Fight 222
    Current Situation 225
    Discrimination or Choice? 225
    More Women Scientists 226
    Outlook 226
    Crisis Ahead? 226
    Notes 227
    Bibliography 229

11. **AP and IB Programs: Can They
    Raise U.S. High-School Achievement?** **233**
    Are AP and IB programs effective? 236
    Should AP and IB be more broadly
        available? 238
    Can advanced high-school courses
        close the achievement gap? 240
    Background 242
    It's Not Academic 242
    Starting Small 246
    Reform Movement 247
    States Back AP, IB 248
    Current Situation 249
    States Resist 249
    Outlook 252
    Challenge for All? 252
    Notes 252
    Bibliography 254

12. **Teaching Math and Science:
    Are Students Being Prepared
    for the Technological Age?** **257**
    Are U.S. students proficient in
        math and science? 261
    Are U.S. math and science curricula
        adequate? 263

Are U.S. math and science teachers
  well trained? 265
Background 267
  Wake-up Call 267
  The 'New Math' 268
  'A Nation at Risk' 268
  Setting Standards 270
Current Situation 272
  Congress OKs Testing 272
  Improving Teachers 272
  What Works? 274
  Revisiting the Standards 274
  Evolution Debate 275
Outlook 275
  Funding Questioned 275
Notes 276
Bibliography 278

13. **Reading Crisis? Do Today's Youth
    Read Less Than Past Generations?** 281
  Do young people read less than
    in the past? 284
  Is there a literacy crisis? 286
  Will harm be done if new technologies
    crowd out traditional reading? 288
Background 290
  Breaking the Code 290
  Reading Truce? 294
Current Situation 296
  Boys, Teens Lag 296
  Online Literacy 297
  Cuts in Reading Programs 299
Outlook 300
  Future of Reading 300
Notes 301
Bibliography 302

14. **Video Games: Do They
    Have Educational Value?** 305
  Does playing video
    games improve literacy? 309
  Are video games addictive? 312
  Do video games prepare young people
    for the future job market? 313
Background 317
  Pinball Precursor 317
  Equity Gap? 318
  Gender Gap Narrows 319

Current Situation 322
  Big Business 322
  Social Networking 323
  Libraries Log On 323
  Saying Less? 323
Outlook 324
  Testing the Hypothesis 324
Notes 325
Bibliography 327

ISSUES IN SCHOOL ENVIRONMENT

15. **Teacher Shortages: Should States
    Ease Certification Standards?** 329
  Should "fast-track" or alternative-
    certification programs be used
    to reduce teacher shortages? 332
  Would raising teacher pay or overhauling
    the teacher-compensation
    system solve the teacher-shortage
    problem? 334
Background 337
  Early Reforms 337
  First Shortages 337
  Lowering Standards 339
Current Situation 342
  Revamping ESEA 342
  States' Efforts 343
Outlook 344
  Bush's Plan 344
Notes 346
Bibliography 347

16. **Discipline in Schools:
    Are Zero-Tolerance Policies Fair?** 351
  Have zero-tolerance policies made
    schools safer? 354
  Is racism responsible for high
    suspension rates among
    minorities? 357
  Should students have more legal rights
    in discipline cases? 359
Background 360
  Rise of Zero Tolerance 360
  Violence and Bullying 364
  Teacher Education 365
Current Situation 365
  'Scarlet Letter' 365

SAVE Act 369
State Proposals 369
Outlook 369
Zero Tolerance? 369
Notes 370
Bibliography 372

17. **Zero Tolerance: Is Mandatory
Punishment in Schools Unfair?** **375**
Are zero-tolerance policies effective? 378
Are zero-tolerance policies
constitutional? 380
Are zero-tolerance policies fairly and
consistently applied? 381
Background 383
'We Need to Get Tough' 383
'Broken-Windows' Approach 385
Is Violence Declining? 385
Current Situation 388
Alternative Schools 388
Amending IDEA 390
Zero-Zero Tolerance 392
Outlook 393
Ebb and Flow 393
Notes 394
Bibliography 394

18. **Bullying: Are Schools Doing
Enough to Stop the Problem?** **397**
Is bullying a serious problem? 400
Is enough being done to curtail bullying? 403
Are school anti-bullying
programs effective? 405

Background 406
Early Research 406
Changing Society 409
Learned Behavior 410
Current Situation 411
Christian Opposition 411
Federal Law 414
Outlook 415
Going to Court 415
Notes 416
Bibliography 417

19. **Cheating in Schools:
Are High-Stakes Tests to Blame?** **421**
Are students today more dishonest
than earlier generations? 424
Should schools adopt honor codes
to reduce cheating? 426
Should educators be more aggressive
in stopping cheating? 427
Background 431
Ancient Crib Sheets 431
Values Confusion 433
Feminism and Multiculturalism 433
Current Situation 434
High-Stakes Testing 434
Defending the Tests 436
Preventive Measures 438
Character Education Gains Supporters 438
Outlook 438
More Cheating? 438
Notes 440
Bibliography 440

Annotated Contents

ISSUES IN JUSTICE, EQUITY, AND EQUALITY

Racial Diversity in Public Schools:
Has the Supreme Court Dealt a Blow to Integration?

Fifty years after the Supreme Court outlawed racial segregation in public schools, a new ruling has raised doubts about how far local school boards can go to integrate classrooms. The court's 5-4 ruling in cases from Seattle and Louisville bars school districts from using race as a factor in individual pupil assignments. Like many other school districts, the two school systems used racial classifications to promote diversity in the face of segregated housing patterns. But parents argued the plans improperly denied their children their school of choice because of race. Dissenting justices said the ruling was a setback for racial equality. In a pivotal concurrence, however, Justice Anthony M. Kennedy said schools still have some leeway to pursue racial diversity. Meanwhile, some experts argue that socio-economic integration — bringing low-income and middle-class students together — is a more effective way to pursue educational equity.

No Child Left Behind:
Is the Law Improving Student Performance?

More than three years have passed since President Bush signed the No Child Left Behind Act. The controversial legislation mandates "highly qualified" teachers in every classroom and holds schools that accept federal funds accountable for raising the achievement of all students, particularly those with disabilities, those from low-income families and racial and ethnic minorities and those with limited English proficiency. Supporters call the law an evolutionary change in education policy while critics call it a revolutionary federal incursion into states' historic domain that makes too many unfunded demands. Eight school districts and the nation's largest teachers' union have sued the Department of Education over the law's funding provisions, and legislators in several states have introduced bills seeking exemptions from the law. Supporters, meanwhile, worry that No Child Left Behind is not being enforced stringently enough and is in danger of being diluted.

Special Education: Do Students With Disabilities Get the Help They Need?

The Education for All Handicapped Children Act was passed in 1975 after the courts ruled that states must provide a "free appropriate public education" to children with physical, mental or emotional problems. Under the law, renamed the Individuals with Disabilities Education Act (IDEA), the federal government is required to help local school boards pay for the special-education services needed by students with disabilities. Although the law has produced many successes in integrating the nation's 6 million disabled children into public schools, troubling problems remain. The dropout rate for disabled students is far higher than for non-disabled students. And countless disabled children, especially from low-income, minority or rural communities, are not receiving the full benefits of the law.

Fixing Urban Schools: Has No Child Left Behind Helped Minority Students?

African-American and Hispanic students — largely in urban schools — lag far behind white students, who mostly attend middle-class suburban schools. Critics argue that when Congress reauthorizes the 2002 No Child Left Behind Act (NCLB), it must retarget the legislation to help urban schools tackle tough problems, such as encouraging the best teachers to enter and remain in high-poverty schools, rather than focusing on tests and sanctions. Some advocates propose busing students across district lines to create more socioeconomically diverse student bodies. But conservative analysts argue that busing wastes students' time and that permitting charter schools to compete with public schools will drive improvement. Meanwhile, liberal analysts point out that

successful charter programs are too costly for most schools to emulate, and that no one has yet figured out how to spread success beyond a handful of schools, public or private.

Charter Schools: Will They Improve or Hurt Public Education?

A decade after the birth of the charter school movement, reform activists and mainstream educators disagree over whether these experimental public schools are a promising innovation or a damaging distraction. The nation's nearly 2,700 charter schools operate in 39 states, enjoying freedom from many traditional regulations. But they must deliver concrete results in a specified period or risk being shut down. Charters vary as much in their instructional approaches as they do in their genesis, facilities, quality and political constituencies. Yet, the evidence remains inconclusive as to whether they are boosting student achievement. The evolving movement remains divided between critics, who see it as the first step in dismembering America's public education system, and those who see it as the system's last best hope.

Home Schooling Debate: Is the Movement Undermining Public Education?

The number of U.S. children educated at home has nearly tripled in the last 10 years, as mainstream parents have embraced a movement once considered the domain of aging hippies and religious fundamentalists. Advocates say home schooling is the best way to assure a high-quality education and want it exempted from federal and state accountability requirements. But critics warn that removing children from the public schools threatens an essential pillar of democracy while depriving students of vital contact with children and adults from other backgrounds. And school officials complain that when home schooling doesn't work, parents "dump" their children back in the public schools, which are then blamed for the home-schoolers' poor performance.

Single-Sex Education: Do All-Boy and All-Girl Schools Enhance Learning?

The Bush administration wants to make it easier to establish all-boy or all-girl public schools. While there is a long tradition of private single-sex schools in the United States, there are probably fewer than two dozen single-sex public schools. Advocates of single-sex education believe it represents a valuable educational option, especially for girls, who they say flourish away from boys' teasing. But critics say the approach offers no real social or educational benefits for girls or for boys. Federal law currently casts doubt on the legality of single-sex public schools. The law bars single-sex programs unless comparable services are available to boys and girls alike. The Department of Education is considering revising its regulations to soften that provision, reversing three decades of federal policy.

Religion in Schools: Should the Courts Allow More Spiritual Expression?

In the past half-century, the U.S. Supreme Court has consistently ruled against religious observance in public schools, citing the First Amendment wall between church and state. But civil liberties groups point with concern to renewed efforts by conservative Christian groups and others to foster religion in schools by distributing Bibles, posting the Ten Commandments and allowing student-led prayers. While conservatives say the barriers to spiritual expression in public schools are too rigid, liberals warn that conservatives are "sneaking" religion into the schools. President-elect George W. Bush says he supports student-led prayer as well as controversial taxpayer-funded school vouchers for religious and other private schools. But his greatest impact on religion in schools ultimately may come from his appointments of new Supreme Court justices.

ISSUES IN TEACHING AND LEARNING

Students Under Stress: Do Schools Assign Too Much Homework?

The average homework load for first- through third-graders has doubled over the past two decades, even though research shows homework doesn't benefit such young children. Indeed, some schools require preschoolers to tackle academic subjects like reading and writing. In response a parents' movement has arisen — mainly in middle- and upper-income suburbs — protesting excessive homework and other forms of academic pressure, including so-called high-stakes testing. Parents say the added pressure robs children of needed play and family time and can cause stress, sleep deprivation, depression

and family strife. Some schools have responded by limiting homework for the youngest children and downplaying stress-causing programs, such as academic honor rolls. At the same time, however, U.S. high school students spend less time in class than students in most other countries, and their homework loads remain far below the two hours per day that research shows is optimal for college-bound students.

Gender and Learning: Are There Innate Differences Between the Sexes?

Harvard President Lawrence Summers ignited a firestorm recently when he suggested more men than women are scientists because of differences between males and females in "intrinsic aptitude." Many scientists — both men and women — expressed outrage at Summers' remarks and blamed any lag in math among girls mainly on discrimination and socialization. They point out that girls have closed the gap in average scores on most standardized math tests in elementary and high school. Today women constitute almost half of college math majors and more than half of biology majors. But Summers's supporters say he courageously raised a legitimate question for scientific inquiry. Indeed, in recent years some researchers have been pursuing a scientific explanation for the discrepancies in math and science aptitude and achievement among boys and girls and have found differences, including biological ones.

AP and IB Programs: Can They Raise U.S. High-School Achievement?

More than 25 percent of first-year college students need remedial courses. Concern about the ability of American high-school graduates to handle college-level work has led some schools to offer Advanced Placement (AP) and International Baccalaureate (IB) programs. Engaging students in more challenging coursework appears to boost learning and achievement, although there is little research on the effects of AP and IB programs. Higher-income students are much more likely to be offered AP and IB classes or other challenging learning experiences than students from disadvantaged educational or socio-economic backgrounds. Over the past decade, most school reform has focused on the elementary grades, but a growing number of states are now concentrating on improving the college readiness of their high-school students. But critics say the effort is wasted if younger students aren't given adequate preparation for high school.

Teaching Math and Science: Are Students Being Prepared for the Technological Age?

Americans have always been leaders of technological innovation. The good news today is that more students are taking higher-level math and science than ever. But their performance on international math and science tests has been lackluster, raising questions about their ability to face the unforeseen challenges of a technological age. Educators agree that students need more math and science, but they disagree vociferously about how the two subjects should be taught. The new No Child Left Behind Act requires school systems to develop educational standards for core subjects and to test how well students are meeting those standards. Meanwhile, attracting qualified teachers remains a critical problem throughout the nation.

Reading Crisis? Do Today's Youth Read Less Than Past Generations?

The number of Americans who read for pleasure has been dropping for decades, and now recent data show the lowest levels ever, especially among Americans ages 15 to 24. At the same time, reading scores among teenagers are dropping. Some literacy experts are declaring the situation a crisis. They warn that with fewer fluent, habitual readers, America may soon lack not only the skilled workers needed for an information-based economy but also the informed voters crucial to democracy. Others dismiss such views as alarmist, arguing the data don't capture the large amount of online reading today, especially by young adults. Technology experts also note that computers and video may be simply changing the form of literacy needed today, just as the printing press and typewriter did in ages past. While book reading formed the core of 20th-century literacy, in the 21st century literacy is more likely to mean writing blogs and instant messages as well as skimming online video and audio, along with text, to gather information.

Video Games: Do They Have Educational Value?

More than three-quarters of American youths have video-game consoles at home, and on a typical day at least 40 percent play a video game. Some academic scholars claim playing games is good for literacy, problem-solving, learning to test hypotheses and researching information from a variety of sources. Others say gaming may be good for understanding technical information but not for reading literature and understanding the humanities. Enthusiasts claim gaming is preparing young people for the knowledge-based workplace. Critics worry that it's making kids more socially isolated, less experienced in working with others and less creative. Experts remain divided about whether addiction to games is widespread and whether violent games produce violent behavior. Increasingly, researchers are studying why games are so engrossing, and some are urging educators to incorporate games' best learning features into school programs.

ISSUES IN SCHOOL ENVIRONMENT

Teacher Shortages: Should States Ease Certification Standards?

Severe teacher shortages are expected over the next 10 years, mainly because of widespread teacher retirements, swelling school enrollments and the trend toward smaller classes. Education experts and policy-makers are bitterly divided over how to offset the shortages, which will primarily affect inner-city and rural schools and hard-to-staff subjects such as math and science. Most of the states now permit "fast-track" certification programs that can turn out teachers in as little as four weeks. And some districts issue emergency teaching certificates to people with little or no teaching experience. But critics fear that alternative-certification initiatives are lowering teacher-quality standards. They say that raising salaries and giving teachers the professional recognition and support they deserve is the only way to reduce shortages while maintaining quality.

Discipline in Schools: Are Zero-Tolerance Policies Fair?

More than a decade after a string of deadly school shootings focused attention on student discipline, the search continues for effective methods to curb classroom misconduct. Zero-tolerance policies, widely adopted during the 1990s, have led to skyrocketing suspension and expulsion rates in many school districts, sparking criticism that get-tough conduct codes are ineffective at stopping misbehavior and harmful to the education process.

Civil-rights and child-advocacy groups say such codes have led to too many cases of harsh punishment for relatively minor violations, sometimes sending youngsters out on the street where they get into worse trouble. Critics also charge that black students are far more likely to be punished for similar misconduct than whites under the zero-tolerance approach. Meanwhile, a provision in the federal No Child Left Behind law, which requires states to identify "persistently dangerous schools," is the subject of sharp debate as the law moves toward possible reauthorization this year.

Zero Tolerance: Is Mandatory Punishment in Schools Unfair?

A series of schoolyard mass killings in recent years has prompted school officials and lawmakers to impose mandatory punishments for a multitude of misbehaviors, many of them seemingly minor. Proponents credit tough disciplinary policies with driving school crime rates down. But critics question their effectiveness and worry about the impact the policies are having on individual rights. And civil rights advocates say the policies are being used to kick out minority, disabled and academically challenged students who might drag down standardized test scores. But the latest school violence — the shooting of a Michigan first-grader on Feb. 29 by another 6-year-old — left little doubt that zero-tolerance policies will remain in force.

Bullying: Are Schools Doing Enough to Stop the Problem?

The nation received a shocking wake-up call about bullying when investigators revealed that the Columbine killers and other school shooters had been repeatedly bullied by classmates. On a typical school day today three out of 10 American youngsters are involved in bullying as perpetrators, victims or bystanders, and an estimated 160,000 children skip school for fear of being harassed. Bullied students are more prone to suicide, depression and poor school performance; bullies have a far higher likelihood of committing crimes as adults. At least 16 states have passed laws requiring schools to provide anti-bullying programs, but many states and school districts have been slow to act. Their reluctance may stem in part from opposition by conservative Christians, who argue that anti-bullying legislation and programs aimed at reducing sexually oriented teasing promote homosexuality and impinge on Christian students' freedom of speech.

Cheating in Schools: Are High-Stakes Tests to Blame?

Cheating is at or near an all-time high in schools and colleges. In addition to cheating on tests, students are plagiarizing from on-line term-papers mills. Many educators say the intense pressure created by high-stakes tests fosters cheating by students who worry that college admission, or graduation, hangs on the outcome of a single test. Moreover, teachers are cheating too, test critics say, because test results often determine whether schools retain their accreditation, whether educators get fired or get raises — and even whether local real estate values go up or down. Exasperated ethicists ask whether educators are doing everything they possibly can to curtail cheating and instill core values, while others think implementing honor codes in more schools and curtailing high-stakes tests might help solve the problem.

Preface

Are students being prepared for the technological age? Can AP and IB programs raise U.S. high-school achievement? Do schools assign too much homework? These questions — and many more — are at the heart of K–12 education. How can instructors best engage students with these crucial issues? We feel that students need objective, yet provocative examinations of these issues to understand how they affect students, teachers and schools today and will for years to come. This collection aims to promote in-depth discussion, facilitate further research and help readers formulate their own positions on crucial issues. Get your students talking both inside and outside the classroom about *Issues in K–12 Education*.

This first edition includes nineteen up-to-date reports by *CQ Researcher*, an award-winning weekly policy brief that brings complicated issues down to earth. Each report chronicles and analyzes executive, legislative and judicial activities at all levels of government. This collection is divided into three distinct areas — issues in justice, equity and equality; issues in teaching and learning; and issues in school environment — to cover a range of issues found in most foundational or introductory education courses.

CQ RESEARCHER

CQ Researcher was founded in 1923 as *Editorial Research Reports* and was sold primarily to newspapers as a research tool. The magazine was renamed and redesigned in 1991 as *CQ Researcher*. Today, students are its primary audience. While still used by hundreds of journalists and newspapers, many of which reprint portions of the reports, the *Researcher's* main subscribers are now high school, college and public libraries. In 2002, *Researcher* won the American Bar Association's coveted Silver Gavel award for magazine excellence for a series of nine reports on civil liberties and other legal issues.

Researcher staff writers — all highly experienced journalists — sometimes compare the experience of writing a *Researcher* report to drafting a college term paper. Indeed, there are many similarities. Each report is as long as many term papers — about 11,000 words — and is written by one person without any significant outside help. One of the key differences is that writers interview leading experts, scholars and government officials for each issue.

Like students, staff writers begin the creative process by choosing a topic. Working with the *Researcher's* editors, the writer identifies a controversial subject that has important public policy implications. After a topic is selected, the writer embarks on one to two weeks of intense research. Newspaper and magazine articles are clipped or downloaded, books are ordered and information is gathered from a wide variety of sources, including interest groups, universities and the government. Once the writers are well informed, they develop a detailed outline, and begin the interview process. Each report requires a minimum of ten to fifteen interviews with academics, officials, lobbyists and people working in the field. Only after all interviews are completed does the writing begin.

CHAPTER FORMAT

Each issue of *CQ Researcher,* and therefore each selection in this book, is structured in the same way. Each begins with an overview, which briefly summarizes the areas that will be explored in greater detail in the rest of the chapter. The next section chronicles important and current debates on the topic under discussion and is structured around a number of key questions, such as "Does corporate social responsibility really improve society?" or "Does corporate social responsibility restrain U.S. productivity?" These questions are usually the subject of much debate among practitioners and scholars in the field. Hence, the answers presented are never conclusive but detail the range of opinion on the topic.

Next, the "Background" section provides a history of the issue being examined. This retrospective covers important legislative measures, executive actions and court decisions that illustrate how current policy has evolved. Then the "Current Situation" section examines contemporary policy issues, legislation under consideration and legal action being taken. Each selection concludes with an "Outlook" section, which addresses possible regulation, court rulings and initiatives from Capitol Hill and the White House over the next five to ten years.

Each report contains features that augment the main text: two to three sidebars that examine issues related to the topic at hand, a pro versus con debate between two experts, a chronology of key dates and events and an annotated bibliography detailing major sources used by the writer.

ACKNOWLEDGMENTS

We wish to thank many people for helping to make this collection a reality. Tom Colin, managing editor of *CQ Researcher,* gave us his enthusiastic support and cooperation as we developed this edition. He and his talented staff of editors and writers have amassed a first-class library of *Researcher* reports, and we are fortunate to have access to that rich cache. We also wish to thank our colleagues at CQ Press, a division of SAGE and a leading publisher of books, directories, research publications and Web products on U.S. government, world affairs and communications. They have forged the way in making these readers a useful resource for instruction across a range of undergraduate and graduate courses.

Some readers may be learning about *CQ Researcher* for the first time. We expect that many readers will want regular access to this excellent weekly research tool. For subscription information or a no-obligation free trial of *CQ Researcher,* please contact CQ Press at www.cqpress.com or toll-free at 1-866-4CQ-PRESS (1-866-427-7737).

We hope that you will be pleased by this edition of *Issues in K–12 Education.* We welcome your feedback and suggestions for future editions. Please direct comments to Deya Saoud, Senior Associate Editor, SAGE Publications, 2455 Teller Road, Thousand Oaks, CA 91320, or deya.saoud@sagepub.com.

—The Editors of SAGE

Contributors

Thomas J. Billitteri is a *CQ Researcher* staff writer based in Fairfield, Pennsylvania, who has more than 30 years' experience covering business, nonprofit institutions and public policy for newspapers and other publications. He has written previously for *CQ Researcher* on "Domestic Poverty," "Curbing CEO Pay" and "Mass Transit." He holds a BA in English and an MA in journalism from Indiana University.

Charles S. Clark, a senior editor at the Association of Governing Boards of Universities and Colleges, has written on education for *Teacher* magazine, *Phi Delta Kappan, Educational Leadership* and the National Center on Education and the Economy. He is a former *CQ Researcher* staff writer, *Washington Post* editorial writer and *National Journal* managing editor. He graduated with a BA in history from McGill University.

Marcia Clemmitt is a veteran social-policy reporter who previously served as editor in chief of *Medicine & Health* and staff writer for *The Scientist.* She has also been a high-school math and physics teacher. She holds a liberal arts and sciences degree from St. John's College, Annapolis, and a master's degree in English from Georgetown University. Her recent reports include "Climate Change," "Health Care Costs," "Cyber Socializing" and "Prison Health Care."

Rachel S. Cox is a freelance writer and contributing writer to *CQ Researcher.* She also writes for *The Washington Post* and is a former associate editor of *Preservation* magazine. She holds an AB in English from Harvard University. She lives in Washington, D.C., with her husband and two school-age sons.

Sarah Glazer, a New York freelancer, is a regular contributor to *CQ Researcher*. Her articles on health, education and social-policy issues have appeared in *The New York Times, The Washington Post, The Public Interest* and *Gender and Work,* a book of essays. Her recent *CQ Researcher* reports include "Increase in Autism" and "Stopping Genocide." She graduated from the University of Chicago with a BA in American history.

John Greenya is a freelance writer in Washington, D.C., who has written for *The Washington Post, The New Republic, The New York Times* and other publications. He teaches writing at George Washington University and is the author of several books, including *Silent Justice: The Clarence Thomas Story* and *P.S. A Memoir,* written with the late Pierre Salinger. He holds an AB in English from Marquette University and an MA in English literature from The Catholic University.

Brian Hansen joined the *CQ Researcher* after reporting for the *Colorado Daily* in Boulder and the Environment News Service in Washington. His awards include the Scripps Howard Foundation Award for Public Service Reporting. His *Researcher* reports include "Kids in Prison" and "Nuclear Waste Disposal." He holds a BA in political science and an MA in education from the University of Colorado.

Joan Hennessy is a freelance writer in Laurel, Maryland, who specializes in education policy. She previously was a reporter and editor at the *Florida Times-Union* in Jacksonville. She holds a master's degree from the University of Maryland School of Journalism and a bachelor of fine arts from Loyola University in New Orleans.

Kenneth Jost graduated from Harvard College and Georgetown University Law Center. He is the author of the *Supreme Court Yearbook* and editor of *The Supreme Court from A to Z* (both CQ Press). He was a member of the *CQ Researcher* team that won the 2002 ABA Silver Gavel Award. His previous reports include "School Desegregation," "Black Colleges" and "Affirmative Action."

Kathy Koch specializes in education, youth and social-policy issues. She was one of several *CQ Researcher* writers who won the 1999 Society of Professional Journalists Award for Excellence for a 10-part series on health issues. Kathy has worked as a daily newspaper reporter in South Florida and as a freelancer in Asia and Africa for the *Christian Science Monitor, USA Today* and other publications. She also covered environmental legislation for *CQ Weekly.* She received a journalism degree from the University of North Carolina at Chapel Hill.

Barbara Mantel is a freelance writer in New York City whose work has appeared in *The New York Times,* the *Journal of Child and Adolescent Psychopharmacology* and *Mamm Magazine.* She is a former correspondent and senior producer for National Public Radio and has won several journalism awards, including the National Press Club's Best Consumer Journalism Award and Lincoln University's Unity Award. She holds a BA in history and economics from the University of Virginia and an MA in economics from Northwestern University.

Patrick Marshall is a freelance writer in Bainbridge Island, Washington, and former opinion page editor of *The Oakland Tribune.*

1

Racial Diversity in Public Schools

Has the Supreme Court Dealt a Blow to Integration?

Kenneth Jost

White enrollment at Seattle's Ballard High School is above previous guidelines five years after a racial-diversity plan was suspended because of a legal challenge. The Supreme Court's June 28 decision invalidating racial-balance plans in Seattle and Louisville, Ky., bars school districts from using race for student-placement decisions but may permit some race-conscious policies to promote diversity.

From *CQ Researcher*, September 14, 2007.

annah MacNeal's parents were glad to learn of an opening at the popular magnet elementary school near their upscale neighborhood in eastern Louisville, Ky. When they applied in mid-August for Hannah to enroll as a fourth-grader at Greathouse/Shryock Elementary, however, school system officials said she could not be admitted.

The reason: Hannah is white.

Only six weeks earlier, the U.S. Supreme Court had ruled that Jefferson County Public Schools (JCPS) — which includes Louisville — was violating the Constitution by assigning students to schools on the basis of their race.

Hannah's stepmother, Dana MacNeal, was surprised and upset when she learned Hannah would have been admitted to the school if she had been black. And she was all the more upset when JCPS Student Placement Director Pat Todd insisted on Aug. 14 that the Supreme Court ruling allowed the school system to continue maintaining separate attendance zones for black and white students for Greathouse/Shryock and two of the system's other three magnet elementary schools.

The school system's lawyers were surprised as well to learn of the policy. After the MacNeals decided to fight the decision keeping Hannah in her regular elementary school, officials agreed to enroll her at Greathouse/Shryock and scrap the racially separate boundary zones beginning in 2008.[1]

"Of course, they backed off from the position, knowing they were wrong," says Louisville attorney Ted Gordon, who represented

1

School Racial-Balance Plans in Louisville and Seattle

T*he Supreme Court's June 28, 2007, ruling on the school racial-diversity plans in Seattle and Jefferson County (Louisville) bars the use of racial classifications in individual pupil assignments but appears to permit some "race-neutral" policies aimed at racial diversity.*

Jefferson County (Louisville) (98,000 students; 35 percent African-American)

History: County was racially segregated before *Brown v. Board of Education* ruling; court-ordered desegregation plan in 1975 called for crosstown busing between predominantly African-American West End and mainly white neighborhoods in eastern suburbs; court order dissolved in 2000; school board adopts pupil-assignment plan with use of racial classifications to promote diversity; assignment plan still in effect after Supreme Court decision, pending new plan expected for 2009-2010 academic year.

Details: Plan classifies students as "black" or "white" (including Asians, Hispanics and others); guidelines call for each elementary, middle or high school to have between 15 percent and 50 percent African-American enrollment; residence-based system assigns students to school within residential "cluster"; most West End neighborhoods assigned to schools outside area; student applications for transfer from assigned school evaluated on basis of several factors, including effect on racial makeup; under Supreme Court decision, individual transfer requests will no longer be denied on basis of race.

Seattle (45,000 students: 58 percent "non-white")

History: No history of mandatory segregation, but racially identifiable neighborhoods: predominantly black south of downtown, predominantly white to the north; racial-balance plan with crosstown busing voluntarily adopted in 1978; school choice introduced in 1990s, with race as one "tiebreaker" to distribute students among oversubscribed schools; school board suspended the plan in 2002 because of legal challenge; Supreme Court ruling held plan invalid.

Details: Ninth-graders permitted to apply to up to three of district's 10 high schools; tiebreakers used for applications to oversubscribed schools; sibling preference was most important factor, race second; race used if school's enrollment deviated by specified percentage from overall racial demographics: 40 percent white, 60 percent non-white.

the MacNeals in the latest round in his long-running battle to overturn Jefferson County's school racial-diversity policies. "They have to follow the law."

The Supreme Court's fractured ruling struck down pupil-assignment policies adopted in 2000 limiting African-American enrollment at any individual school in Jefferson County to between 15 percent and 50 percent of the student body. The ruling also rejected the Seattle school system's use of race as a "tiebreaker" for assigning students to high schools; the plan had been suspended in 2002 because of the litigation.[2] (*See box, above.*)

In response to the MacNeals' case, Todd's office drew up new boundary zones for the four magnet elementary schools that were approved by the school board on Sept. 10. For the longer term, officials are trying to find ways to

maintain a measure of racial balance in the 98,000-student school system under the Supreme Court decision, which bars the use of racial classifications in individual pupil assignments but appears to permit some "race-neutral" policies aimed at racial diversity. (*See box, p. 3.*)

"We are going to do our best to achieve it," says JCPS Superintendent Sheldon Berman. "We are deeply committed to retaining the qualities of an integrated environment."

The court's June 28 decision dealt a blow to hundreds of school systems around the country that have adopted voluntary race-mixing plans after court-ordered desegregation plans lapsed in recent years.

Five of the justices — led by Chief Justice John G. Roberts Jr. — said using racial classifications in pupil assignments violated the Equal Protection Clause of the 14th Amendment. That is the same provision the court cited a half century earlier in the famous *Brown v. Board of Education* (1954) ruling that found racial segregation in public schools unconstitutional.[3]

In a strong dissent, the court's four liberal justices — led by Stephen G. Breyer — said the ruling contradicted previous decisions upholding race-based pupil assignments and would hamper local school boards' efforts to prevent "resegregation" in individual schools. But one of the justices in the majority — Anthony M. Kennedy — joined the liberal minority in endorsing racial diversity as a legitimate goal. Kennedy listed several "race-neutral" policies, such as drawing attendance zones or building new schools to include students from different racial neighborhoods, that schools could adopt to pursue the goal.

The ruling drew sharp criticism from traditional civil rights advocates. "It's preposterous to think the 14th Amendment was designed to permit individual white parents to strike down a plan to help minority students have better access to schools and to prevent school districts from having integrated schools that are supported by a majority of the community," says Gary Orfield, a longtime civil rights advocate and director of the Civil Rights Project at UCLA's Graduate School of Education and Information Sciences.

Ted Shaw, president of the NAACP Legal Defense Fund, said the ruling blocks school boards from using "one of the few tools that are available" to create racially diverse schools. "The court has taken a significant step away from the promise of *Brown*," says Shaw. "And this

Racial Classifications Barred But Diversity Backed

The Supreme Court's June 28 decision in *Parents Involved in Community Schools v. Seattle School District No. 1* invalidating pupil-assignment plans in Seattle and Louisville bars school systems from assigning individual students to schools based on their race. In a partial concurrence, however, Justice Anthony M. Kennedy joined with the four dissenters in finding racial diversity to be a legitimate government interest and in permitting some race-conscious policies to achieve that goal.

Roberts (plurality opinion)

Scalia   Thomas   Alito

"Racial balancing is not transformed from 'patently unconstitutional' to a compelling state interest simply by relabeling it 'racial diversity.' "

Kennedy (concurring in part)

". . . [A] district may consider it a compelling interest to achieve a diverse student body. Race may be one component of that diversity. . . . What the government is not permitted to do . . . is to classify every student on the basis of race and to assign each of them to schools based on that classification."

Breyer (dissenting)

Stevens   Souter   Ginsburg

"The plurality . . . undermines [*Brown v. Board of Education's*] promise of integrated primary and secondary education that local communities have sought to make a reality. This cannot be justified in the name of the Equal Protection Clause."

Credits: AFP/Getty Images/Paul J. Richards (Alito, Kennedy, Roberts, Souter, Scalia, Thomas); Getty Images/Mark Wilson (Ginsburg, Stevens); AFP/Getty Images/ Brendan Smialowski (Breyer)

comes on top of the reality that many school districts are highly segregated by race already."

Conservative critics of race-based school policies, however, applauded the ruling. "I don't think school districts should be drawing attendance zones or building

Southern Schools Least Segregated, But Slipping

Schools in the South were the least segregated in the nation in the 1970s and '80s, a distinction they maintained in the 2005 school year. But Southern schools have been resegregating steadily since 1988.

Change in Black Segregation in Southern Schools, 1954-2005

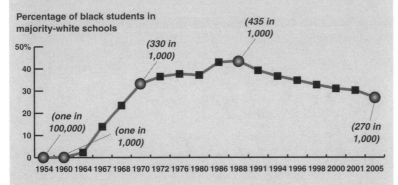

Percentage of black students in majority-white schools

(one in 100,000)

(one in 1,000)

(330 in 1,000)

(435 in 1,000)

(270 in 1,000)

50%
40
30
20
10
0

1954 1960 1964 1967 1968 1970 1972 1976 1980 1986 1988 1991 1994 1996 1998 2000 2001 2005

Source: Gary Orfield and Chungmei Lee, "Historic Reversals, Accelerating Resegregation, and the Need for New Integration Strategies," Civil Rights Project, UCLA, August 2007

schools for the purpose of achieving a politically correct racial mix," says Roger Clegg, president of the Center for Equal Opportunity, which joined in a friend-of-the-court brief supporting the white families that challenged the Seattle and Louisville school policies.

"A lot of parents out there don't like it when their students are treated differently because of race or ethnicity," Clegg adds. "After these decisions, the odds favor those parents and those organizations that oppose school boards that practice racial or ethnic discrimination."

School officials in Louisville and Seattle and around the country are generally promising to continue race-mixing policies within the limits of the court's decision. "School boards are going to have to do the hard work to find more tailored ways of approaching diversity in their schools," says Francisco Negrón, general counsel of the National School Boards Association.

The evidence in Louisville and nationally suggests, however, that the goal will be hard to achieve. In Louisville, nine schools are now outside the district's 15/50 guidelines, with several having more than 55 percent African-American enrollment, according to Todd. "If the board wants to continue to maintain

diversity, we've already had some significant slippage at some selected schools," he says.[4]

Nationally, a new report by the UCLA Civil Rights Project concludes that African-American and Latino students are increasingly isolated from white students in public schools. Overall, nearly three-fourths of African-American students and slightly over three-fourths of Latino students attend predominantly minority schools. Both figures have been increasing since 1980, the report says.[5] (*See graphs, p. 5.*)

Critics of race-based pupil assignments are unfazed by the trends. "We're past guidelines, we're past quotas and we need to move on," says Gordon of the Louisville statistics. He calls instead for an array of reforms focused on schools with high concentrations of low-income students.

"All other things being equal, I like racially diverse schools," says Abigail Thernstrom, a senior fellow at the conservative Manhattan Institute and a former member of the Massachusetts Board of Education. "But I do not think it works from any angle to have government entities — whether they are federal courts or local school boards — try to engineer diversity."

Supporters of racial-balance plans argue that diversity in the classroom helps boost academic achievement for minority students without adversely affecting achievement for white students. Opponents dispute those claims. (*See sidebar, p. 15.*)

The debate over diversity also highlights a secondary dispute over the widespread practice of "tracking" — the offering of separate courses for students based on ability or previous achievement. Supporters say the practice matches curriculum to students' needs and abilities, but critics say it results in consigning already disadvantaged students — including a disproportionate number of African-Americans — to poor-quality education. (*See sidebar, p. 12.*)

Meanwhile, some experts and advocates are calling for shifting the focus away from race and instead trying

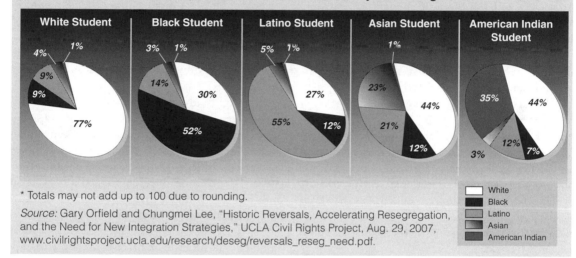

White Students Are Racially Isolated

Segregation remained high in 2005-06 for all racial groups except Asians. White students remained the most racially isolated, although they attended schools with slightly more minority students than in the past. The average white student attended schools in which 77 percent of their peers were white. Meanwhile, more than half of black and Latino students' peers were black or Latino, and fewer than one-third of their classmates were white.

Racial Composition of Schools Attended by the Average . . .

| White Student | Black Student | Latino Student | Asian Student | American Indian Student |

White Student: 4%, 1%, 9%, 9%, 77%

Black Student: 3%, 1%, 14%, 30%, 55%, 52%, 12%

Latino Student: 5%, 1%, 27%, 12%

Asian Student: 1%, 23%, 44%, 21%, 12%

American Indian Student: 35%, 44%, 3%, 12%, 7%

* Totals may not add up to 100 due to rounding.

Source: Gary Orfield and Chungmei Lee, "Historic Reversals, Accelerating Resegregation, and the Need for New Integration Strategies," UCLA Civil Rights Project, Aug. 29, 2007, www.civilrightsproject.ucla.edu/research/deseg/reversals_reseg_need.pdf.

Legend: White, Black, Latino, Asian, American Indian

to promote socioeconomic integration — mixing low-income and middle- and upper-class students. Richard Kahlenberg, a senior fellow with the left-of-center Century Foundation who is most closely associated with the movement, says policies aimed at preventing high concentrations of low-income students will produce academic gains along with likely gains in racial and ethnic diversity.

"Providing all students with the chance to attend mixed-income schools can raise overall levels of achievement," Kahlenberg writes in a report released on the day of the Supreme Court decision.[6]

As the debate over diversity in public-school classrooms continues, here are the major questions being considered:

Should school systems promote racial diversity in individual schools?

School officials in Lynn, Mass., a former mill town 10 miles northeast of Boston, take pride in a pupil-assignment system that has helped maintain racial balance in most schools even as the town's Hispanic population has steadily increased over the past decade. "We work very hard to promote integration and cultural diversity so that our children are able to get along with each other," says Jan Birchenough, the administrator in charge of compliance with the state's racial-balance law.

But attorney Chester Darling says Lynn's policy of denying any transfer requests that would increase racial imbalance at an individual school "falls squarely within" the kinds of plans prohibited by the Supreme Court decision in the Louisville and Seattle cases. "It can't be race-neutral if you use the word race," says Darling, who is asking a federal judge in Boston to reopen a previously unsuccessful suit filed by parents challenging the policy.[7]

Critics of race-based assignment plans hope the Supreme Court decision will persuade or force school districts like Lynn's to drop any use of racial classifications in pupil placement. "Most school districts will look at the decision's bottom line, will consider that the Louisville and Seattle plans were not sloppily done, and yet at the end of the day were declared unconstitutional," says Clegg of the Center for Equal Opportunity. "This cost the school boards a lot of time and money, and they're going to have to pay the other side's lawyer."

But school board officials say the court's fractured ruling leaves room for local systems to consider race in trying to create racial and ethnic mixing in individual schools. "Race is still not out of the question," says Negrón of the school boards' association. "A plurality of the court said certain things that are not the law of the land. What the majority has done is invalidate these particular programs, but certainly left the door wide open to the use of race — which continues to be a compelling government interest."

Apart from the legal issue, supporters and opponents of racial-diversity plans also disagree on their educational and other effects. "There's a consensus in the academic world that there are clear educational benefits, and the benefits aren't just for minority students," says UCLA Professor Orfield.

Conversely, "racial isolation leads to reduced achievement," says Negrón.

Critics of racial-diversity policies, however, say those benefits are unproven and the logic of the claimed cause-effect relationship unconvincing. "There is very little empirical evidence," says Thernstrom, the Manhattan Institute fellow.

"I don't think how well you learn or what you learn depends on the color of the skin of the person sitting next to you," says Clegg. "Students in overwhelmingly white schoolrooms in Idaho and in overwhelmingly African-American classrooms in Washington, D.C., can each learn."

Critics cite as one concrete disadvantage the time spent on buses when students are transported out of their neighborhoods for the sake of racial balance. "There's no educational benefit there, and it's a waste of their very precious time," says Thernstrom. The travel burdens also hamper student participation in extracurricular activities and parental involvement, the critics say.

In traditional desegregation plans, those burdens typically fell for the most part on African-American students, who were transported out of their

neighborhoods to schools in predominantly white areas. Busing was "usually a one-way street" for African-Americans, says James Anderson, head of the department of educational-policy studies at the University of Illinois, Champaign-Urbana.

In recent years, however, school-choice policies in some communities have meant increased busing for whites as well as minority students. Negrón cites the example of Pinellas County (Clearwater), Fla., which has a universal-choice program allowing students to enroll in any school in the county and providing transportation if requested. "It is a cost," Negrón says. "But school districts are finding that it depends on the facts and circumstances."

Civil rights advocates counter that racial isolation imposes much more serious costs for minority students. "The consequences of segregation of African-American students in public schools — and it is increasingly true for Latino students — have been concentration of poverty, deprivation of resources and a host of other problems that do impact on the quality of education," says the Legal Defense Fund's Shaw.

Like many of the critics, Thernstrom stops short of absolute opposition to any race-conscious school policies. "I don't mind" redrawing attendance zones for racial mixing, she says, "but I don't think we should be starry-eyed about what it's going to achieve."

Michael Rosman, president of the Center for Individual Rights, says schools should try to prevent "racial isolation" in individual schools "if it is shown to have deleterious educational effects."

But Illinois Professor Anderson says school boards should take affirmative steps to "take advantage" of diversity. "We could build wonderful, intellectually rich environments where kids really do have an exchange of ideas and an exchange of cultures and come out of that with a cosmopolitan sense of culture that is unique," he says. "How can you be global," he adds, "yet at the same time so parochial?"

Should school systems seek to promote socioeconomic integration in individual schools?

The consolidated school system in Wake County, N.C. — encompassing the rapidly growing Research Triangle Park area (near Raleigh and Durham) — made nationwide news in 2000 by dropping the use of racial guidelines in favor of socioeconomic-integration policies. The "Healthy School" assignment guidelines call for limiting individual schools to no more than 40 percent enrollment of students receiving free or reduced-price lunches or 25 percent enrollment of students performing below grade level.

Seven years later, the policies are a bragging point for the school system and exhibit No. 1 for advocates of socioeconomic integration. "Classrooms that are balanced from a diversity point of view are important to maintaining academic performance," says Michael Evans, the school system's communications director, citing the district's declining achievement gap for African-American, Hispanic and low-income students.

Some Wake County parents are not sold, however. Dave Duncan, the one-time president of the now largely inactive advocacy group Assignment by Choice, discounts the claimed academic gains by pointing to the relatively small percentage of students assigned under the guidelines and the comparable academic gains statewide. The school system "used the diversity issue as a smoke screen when there is criticism or opposition to the way they do the student-assignment process," Duncan says.

As the most prominent advocate of socioeconomic integration, the Century Foundation's Kahlenberg acknowledges varied results in districts with such policies. But he strongly argues that the policy of mixing students by socioeconomic background offers educational benefits in its own right and practical advantages for districts trying to promote racial diversity without running afoul of the Supreme Court's new limits on race-based assignments.

Non-Racial Approaches to Integration

Some 40 school districts around the country are seeking to diversify enrollment in individual schools through socioeconomic integration—typically, by setting guidelines for the percentage of students eligible for free or reduced-price lunch. Here are some of the districts taking such approaches, as drawn from a report by the Century Foundation's Richard Kahlenberg, a strong advocate of the policies.

School District Enrollment: Percentage of whites (W), African-Americans (B), Hispanics (H), Asian-Americans (A)

Berkeley, Calif. (9,000: 31% W, 29% B, 17% H, 8% A)

Socioeconomic and racial diversity guidelines were adopted in 2004 to replace a voluntary racial-integration plan, plan being phased-in one grade at a time; in 2005-06, eight of 11 elementary schools were within 15% of the districtwide average of 40% of students receiving subsidized lunches; most parents (71%) still receive first choice of schools.

Brandywine, Del. (11,000: 54% W, 39% B, 3% H, 4% A)

The district — comprising parts of Wilmington and surrounding suburbs — was granted an exception in 2001 by state Board of Education to law mandating neighborhood schools; plan limits subsidized-lunch enrollment to between 16% and 73%; plan credited with maintaining racial diversity; some evidence of academic gains in higher grades.

Cambridge, Mass. (6,000: 37% B, 35% W, 15% H, 11% A)

Plan adopted in 2001 to replace race-conscious "controlled choice" system says individual schools should be within 15 percentage points of districtwide percentage of free/reduced lunch students; race remains a potential factor in assignments; racial diversity maintained, socioeconomic diversity increased; limited evidence finds academic gains for low-income students, no negative effect on middle-income students.

Charlotte-Mecklenburg, N.C. (129,000: 42% B, 36% W, 14% H, 4% A)

School board dropped racial-desegregation effort, adopted public school choice plan after school system was declared "unitary" in 2001, or no longer a dual system based on race; plan gives some priority to low-income students in schools with concentrated poverty, but transfers to higher-performing schools are permitted only if seats are available; plan seen as unsuccessful in creating racial or socioeconomic integration.

La Crosse, Wis. (7,000: 20% minority)

Was first district to adopt socioeconomic integration policy in 1991-92 in response to influx of Hmong refugees; plan used redrawn attendance zones and busing to spread low-income students among elementary schools and two high schools; plan largely survived political battle in 1992-93 that included recall of several school board members; plan touted as success, but enrollments at most elementary schools have been and still are outside guidelines.

(Continued)

"There's a wide body of research that the single, best thing you can do for low-income kids is to give them the opportunity to attend a middle-class school," says

(Continued)

School District   *Enrollment: Percentage of whites (W), African-Americans (B), Hispanics (H), Asian-Americans (A)*

Manatee County, Fla. (*42,000: 60% W, 20% H, 15% B, 4% other*)
District south of Tampa Bay has had limited success with a plan adopted in 2002 admitting students to schools based on maintaining socioeconomic balance: Only 10 elementary schools were within guidelines in 2005-06; among 14 schools with above-average low-income enrollment, only four showed adequate academic gains.

McKinney, Tex. (*20,000: 64% W, 21% H, 11% B, 3% other*)
Dallas suburb adopted socioeconomic-balance policy in 1995 by redrawing attendance zones; low-income students perform better on statewide tests than low-income students statewide; some opposition to longer bus rides, but plan said to have broad support.

Minneapolis, Minn. (*36,000: 41% B, 28% W, 16% H, 10% A*)
Desegregation suit settled in state court in 2000 with agreement to adopt four-year experiment to encourage socioeconomic integration; plan provides transportation for low-income students to suburban schools; also requires wealthier magnet schools in Minneapolis to set aside seats for low-income students; 2,000 low-income students attended suburban schools over four-year period; legislature voted to extend program after end of experiment.

Omaha, Neb. (*47,000: 44% W, 32% B, 21% H*)
School board adopted plan aimed at socioeconomic integration after system was declared unitary in 1999; low-income students given preference in weighted lottery for admission to magnet schools; 2006 proposal to expand plan to recently annexed neighborhoods prompted backlash in state legislature, but education groups won passage of 2007 bill to establish goal of socioeconomic diversity throughout metropolitan area.

Rochester, N.Y. (*33,000: 64% B, 22% H, 13% W*)
Managed-choice plan adopted in city in 2002 includes socioeconomic-fairness guidelines; vast majority of elementary school students (83%) are economically disadvantaged; plan seen as likely to have limited effect unless interdistrict choice program is established between city and suburbs.

San Francisco (*55,000: 32% Asian, 22% H, 13% B, 9% W*)
Student-assignment plan adopted in 2001 replaced racial-desegregation scheme with plan aimed at socioeconomic diversity; seven-part definition includes SES (socioeconomic status), academic achievement, language, other factors; plan seen as fairly successful in balancing schools by SES, less so in producing racial diversity; district is consistently top-performing urban district in state.

Wake County (Raleigh), N.C. (*136,000: 54% W, 27% B, 10% H, 5% A*)
Guidelines adopted in 2000 replacing racial guidelines limit schools to 40% free/reduced lunch, 25% reading below grade level; policies credited with maintaining racial diversity; role in academic gains questioned; school-zone changes due to growth draw criticism from some families.

Sources: Richard D. Kahlenberg, Century Foundation, "Rescuing Brown v. Board of Education: Profiles of Twelve School Districts Pursuing Socioeconomic School Integration," Century Foundation, June 28, 2007, www.tcf.org; news accounts.

Kahlenberg. Despite some well-publicized exceptions, schools with "concentrated levels of poverty" tend to have more student-discipline problems, lower caliber teachers and principals and less parental involvement than predominantly middle- or upper-class schools, he explains. Socioeconomic integration, he says, results in higher academic achievement for low-income students and no adverse effect on others as long as there is "a strong core of students with middle-class background."

Kahlenberg says socioeconomic integration is also likely to produce some racial and ethnic mixing since the poverty rate among African-Americans and Latinos is higher than among whites. In educational terms, however, he says socioeconomic diversity is more valuable than racial diversity because the academic gains of mixing by class and income appear to be well established, while the claimed gains of race mixing are in dispute.

Traditional civil rights advocates like the Legal Defense Fund's Shaw do not quarrel with socioeconomic integration but insist that it is "not an adequate substitute for racial integration."

Orfield agrees that socioeconomic integration is "a good idea" but quickly adds, "You can't achieve racial integration very well by using social and economic integration."

"If you talk to districts that have relied solely on that, it doesn't reach all of the students that they need to reach," says Negrón at the school boards association.

For their part, conservatives raise fewer objections to mixing students by socioeconomic background than by race, but they worry the practice may merely be a pretext for racial classifications. "It has fewer constitutional problems," says Thernstrom. "It is less politically controversial."

"It's better than race-based student assignments," says Clegg at the Center for Equal Opportunity. "But if you're using socioeconomic status simply as a proxy for race, many of the same policy and legal problems remain."

Thernstrom is unconvinced, however, of the claimed academic benefits. "There are no proven results from it," she says. She scoffs at what she calls "the notion that if you sit next to somebody, differences [in values] are going to somehow melt away."

In any event, Clegg says he opposes either racial or socioeconomic mixing if it requires assigning students to schools distant from their homes. "Neighborhood schools are the preferable means of assignment," he says, "because you're not having to pay for busing and you're not having to put children on long bus rides, which keep them from engaging in extracurricular activities."

Kahlenberg disagrees. "I haven't heard anyone make a convincing case that from an educational perspective the best way to assign students is the place where their parents can afford to live," he says. "That's the way we do it, but there's no argument that's the best way to educate kids in our society."

From opposite perspectives, however, both Orfield and Thernstrom agree that socioeconomic integration engenders some of the same kinds of opposition that racial integration does. "You do have a lot of middle-class flight as a result," Thernstrom says. "It's not really more popular than racial integration," Orfield says.

Despite the resistance, Kahlenberg believes the policy would fulfill a fundamental goal of public education in the United States. "Most people believe at least in theory that education is the way for kids of any background to do well," he says. "As long as we have economically segregated schools, that promise is broken."

Is the focus on diversity interfering with efforts to improve education in all schools?

As he wrapped up his legal challenge to the Louisville pupil-assignment plan before the Supreme Court, attorney Gordon depicted the case as a choice between "diversity" and "educational outcome."

"For me," Gordon told the justices during the Dec. 4 arguments, "I would use all these millions of dollars. I would reduce teacher-student ratio. I would give incentive pay to the better teachers. I would [build] more magnet schools, more traditional schools."

"We presuppose that we're going to have bad schools and good schools in this country," he continued. "I don't think we can no [sic] longer accept that."

Gordon describes himself as a civil rights liberal, but his argument parallels the views of conservatives like Clegg. "School districts should be worrying less about the racial and ethnic mix than about improving the education that's offered at all schools," Clegg says.

"If you're just focusing on racial diversity, as it's called, for its own sake without trying to assess whether you're improving the educational outcomes," says Rosman, "then you're detracting from the overall goal of achieving educational excellence. In some instances, that's happened."

"The solution is to reduce the gap, the racial gap, the ethnic gap, the socioeconomic gap," says Thernstrom. "Then kids will be looked at as just kids without any kind of assumptions made about, you know, are they like me?"

Traditional civil rights groups and advocates insist that diversity and educational reform complement rather than conflict with each other. In any event, they say, the push for diversity is neither so strong nor so extensive as the critics contend.

"We haven't had any federal policy of promoting diversity since 1981," says Orfield, referring to the first year of Ronald Reagan's presidency. "We haven't had any new lawsuits to integrate schools for a long time. Ever since 1980, most desegregation plans have had voluntary choice and magnet schools, and almost all of them are part and parcel of educational reform plans."

John Trasviña, president and general counsel of the Mexican American Legal Defense and Educational Fund (MALDEF), calls the claimed conflict between diversity and educational quality "a diversion." Referring to educational reform, he says, "We aren't doing that either. It's always easy to say let's address some other issue. When it comes to do that, it's not done."

Diversity advocates dispute critics' suggestion that racial or economic integration has been pursued solely for its own sake with no attention to improving educational quality. "I don't think anybody ever thought that school integration by itself was a sufficient policy," Orfield says.

"The whole reason for economic integration is to promote academic achievement and raise the quality of schooling," says Kahlenberg. "No one has figured out how to make separate schools for rich and poor work well, certainly not for poor kids."

Orfield and Kahlenberg also dismiss concerns that the transportation costs entailed in some diversity plans take scarce dollars from other, more promising school-improvement initiatives. "We've spent billions and billions of dollars on low-income schools, which hasn't produced a lot of results," Kahlenberg says.

Orfield is even blunter about recent efforts to reduce the racial gap. "It's been a failure," he says. Desegregation and anti-poverty programs of the 1960s and '70s did narrow the racial-achievement gap, Orfield writes in the recent UCLA Civil Rights Project report. But he says "most studies" find that President Bush's No Child Left Behind law — which specifically calls for narrowing the achievement gap between white and minority pupils — has had "no impact" on the disparities so far.[8]

From opposite perspectives, Thernstrom and Trasviña lay out demanding agendas for schools to try to close the racial gap. "I want more learning going on," says Thernstrom. "You need really good schools. The day should be longer, the teachers should be better, the principals should have more authority.

"Our kids aren't learning enough in school," she continues. "That will level the playing field."

"We clearly need to improve the quality of our schools," says Trasviña. He calls for steps to reduce the dropout rate and to channel more students into so-called STEM courses (science, technology, engineering and math). But diversity helps, not hurts reform efforts, he says.

"While it is true that simply putting children of different backgrounds in seats in the same classroom does not necessarily improve the classroom experience by itself, [diversity] adds to it," Trasviña says. "And it adds to the political will to make sure that people understand that these are our schools."

BACKGROUND

The 'Common School'

The idea of free, universal public education has been espoused in the United States since the Revolutionary Era and still holds a central place in American thought as a tool for personal development and social cohesion. But the ideal of equal educational opportunity for all has never

been obtained in practice. Even as education became more nearly universal in the 20th century, African-Americans and other racial and ethnic minorities faced blatant discrimination that was only partly alleviated by landmark court rulings outlawing legally mandated segregation.[9]

George Washington and Thomas Jefferson were among the nation's early leaders to call in general terms for mass public education, but the educational "system" of the early 19th century consisted of private academies, rural district schools and a handful of "charity" schools in cities. Horace Mann, the so-called father of American public education, used his appointment as Massachusetts' first commissioner of education in 1837 to advocate the "common school" — publicly supported and open to all. As University of Wisconsin educational historian William Reese explains, Mann saw education as a way to restore social harmony at a time of social tensions between rich and poor and between native-born and immigrants. Others saw the same connection. His fellow New Englander Alpheus Packard wrote in the 1840s of the "sons of wealth and poverty" gaining mutual respect by sitting side by side in a public school.[10]

Abolitionist Mann's vision had no practical meaning, however, for African-American slaves before the Civil War and only limited significance for their descendants for decades after slavery was abolished. Both before and after the Civil War, the vast majority of African-Americans "lived in states that were openly and explicitly opposed to their education," according to the University of Illinois' Anderson.

After emancipation slaves who had learned to read and write became teachers in rudimentary schools, aided by Northern missionaries and philanthropists and some sympathetic white Southerners. With the end of Reconstruction, however, Southern leaders "pushed back the gains that had been made," Anderson says. In a racially segregated system in the early 20th century, per capita spending for black pupils in the South amounted to one-fourth to one-half of the amount spent on whites.[11]

Education was becoming nearly universal for white Americans, even as racial segregation became entrenched for African-Americans and, in many places, for Mexican- and Asian-Americans.[12] Elementary school attendance was nearly universal by the 1920s. High schools — once viewed as fairly selective institutions — began doubling

CHRONOLOGY

Before 1950 *Free, universal public education is enshrined as American ideal and advances in practice, but African-Americans, Hispanics and Asian-Americans are consigned to separate and unequal schools in much of the country.*

1950s-1960s *Racial segregation in public schools is ruled unconstitutional, but desegregation is slow.*

1954, 1955 Supreme Court's unanimous decision in *Brown v. Board of Education* (1954) outlaws mandatory racial segregation in public schools; a year later court says school districts must dismantle dual systems "with all deliberate speed" (*Brown II*). "Massive resistance" in South stalls integration.

1964, 1965 Civil Rights Act of 1964 authorizes Justice Department to file school-desegregation suits; Title I of Elementary and Secondary Education Act provides targeted aid to school districts for low-income students.

1968 Supreme Court tells school districts to develop plans to dismantle dual systems "now."

1970s-1980s *Busing upheld as desegregation tool but draws strong protests in North and West as well as South; Supreme Court, Justice Department withdraw from desegregation cases.*

1971 Supreme Court unanimously upholds federal courts' power to order crosstown busing to desegregate schools.

1973 Supreme Court rejects federal constitutional right to equal school funding; one month later, New Jersey supreme court is first to sustain funding-equity suit under state constitution.

1974 U.S. Supreme Court, 5-4, bars court-ordered desegregation between inner cities and suburbs; decision is first in series of closely divided rulings that limit desegregation remedies.

1983 U.S. Department of Education report "A Nation at Risk" paints critical picture of rising mediocrity in U.S. schools, shifts agenda away from equity issues.

1990s *Racial isolation increases for African-Americans, Latinos; "reverse discrimination" suits by white students backed in some federal courts, fail in others.*

1991 La Crosse, Wis., becomes first school district to aim to balance enrollment by students' income status: "socioeconomic integration."

1995 Supreme Court signals federal courts to wrap up desegregation cases; lower courts respond by generally granting "unitary" status to school systems seeking to be freed from desegregation orders.

1998, 1999 Federal appeals courts in Boston, Richmond, Va., bar racial preferences in public school admission.

2000-Present *Socioeconomic integration advances; Latinos become largest ethnic minority; Supreme Court ruling bars racial classifications in pupil assignments.*

2000 Wake County (Raleigh), N.C., becomes largest school district to try socioeconomic integration.

2001 President George W. Bush wins congressional approval of No Child Left Behind Act, requiring school districts to meet achievement benchmarks, including closing racial gap.

2001-2005 White families challenge racial-diversity plans in Seattle and Louisville, Ky; federal courts back school districts, ruling plans are "narrowly tailored" to achieve "compelling" interest in diversity.

2005, 2006 Bush nominates John G. Roberts Jr. and Samuel A. Alito Jr. to Supreme Court; both win Senate confirmation, strengthening conservative majority on court.

2007 Supreme Court ruling in Louisville and Seattle cases limits use of race in pupil assignments, but five justices say race-neutral measures can be used to promote compelling interest in diversity; school boards vow to try to maintain racial diversity; advocates push socioeconomic integration on legal, political grounds.

'Tracking' Leads to Racial Separation in Classes

But grouping students by ability has wide support.

Ballard High School sits on a spacious campus in an overwhelmingly white suburban neighborhood in the eastern end of Jefferson County, Ky. As part of Jefferson County Public Schools' racial balance policies, however, Ballard's attendance zone includes neighborhoods on the opposite side of the county in Louisville's predominantly African-American West End section.

By drawing students from the West End, the school achieved around 25 percent black enrollment in the 2006-07 academic year. But despite the measure of racial balance in overall enrollment, Ballard students say blacks and whites are less than fully integrated inside. "Kids naturally separate," remarks Ben Gravel, a white 12th-grader, as he arrives at school on Aug. 13 for the opening of a new school year.

At Ballard — and in schools around the country — the racial separation is especially pronounced in the classroom itself. African-American students are disproportionately enrolled in less challenging, "low-track" classes and underrepresented in higher-track classes, such as advanced placement (AP) courses and international baccalaureate (IB) programs. In 2006, for example, African-Americans comprised about 13 percent of graduating high school seniors but only 6 percent of the total number of students who took advanced placement exams administered by the College Board.[1]

The widespread practice of tracking — or "ability grouping" as supporters prefer to call it — has been a contentious issue within education circles for more than two decades. "Detracking" advocates have had occasional success in pushing reforms, but the practice has persisted — in part because of strong resistance from parents of students enrolled in higher-track courses.[2]

Supporters say the practice matches curricular offerings to students' abilities and achievement level. "It doesn't make sense to the average person that you would put a non-reader in the same English classroom as some kid who's reading Proust," says Tom Loveless, director of the Brown Center on Educational Policy at the Brookings Institution in Washington.

Critics say the practice simply keeps already-disadvantaged students on a path to lower academic achievement. "If you have classes that are structured to give kids less of a challenge, those kids tend to fall farther behind," says Kevin Welner, an associate professor at the University of Colorado's School of Education in Boulder.

Civil rights advocates say the enrollment patterns reflect what they call "segregation by tracking." In her critique of the practice, Jeannie Oakes, director of urban schooling at UCLA's Graduate School of Education and Information Studies, cited research evidence indicating that African-American and Latino students were more likely to be assigned to low-track courses than white students even when they had comparable abilities or test scores.[3]

in enrollment each decade after 1890 thanks to a declining market for child labor and the growing enforcement of new compulsory education laws. Secondary school enrollment increased from 50 percent of 14-17-year-olds in 1920 to nearly 95 percent of that age group by the mid-1970s. Meanwhile, the average school year was also increasing — from 144 days in 1900 to 178 days in 1950. And per capita investment in education rose during the same period from 1.2 percent of national income to 2 percent.

The Supreme Court's 1954 decision in *Brown* outlawing racial segregation in public schools capped a half-century-long campaign by the NAACP to gain a measure of equal educational opportunity for African-Americans.[13] The legal campaign — directed by the future Supreme Court justice, Thurgood Marshall — was waged at a deliberate pace even as many black students and families were agitating for better schools at the local level. The eventual decision seemed far from inevitable beforehand. Only after 1950 did the NAACP decide to ask the court to abolish segregation rather than try to equalize the separate school systems. And the justices were closely divided after the first round of arguments in 1952; they joined in the unanimous ruling

"I wouldn't use the phrase 'segregation by tracking.' A lot of it is self-tracking," counters Abigail Thernstrom, a senior fellow at the conservative Manhattan Institute and co-author of a book on the educational gap between white and minority students. "Is it terrible that we have so few Latino and black students who are prepared to take the most educationally rigorous courses?" she adds. "Of course, it's terrible."

Welner acknowledges minority students often choose low-track courses, but faults school systems instead of the students. Minority parents and students often lack the information needed to understand the different course offerings, he says. And students "sometimes don't want to be the only minority in the high-track class," he says.

Loveless acknowledges the critics' complaints about low-track classes, but says the solution is to reform not to abolish them. "Let's fix the low-track classes," he says. Despite the critics' doubts, he says many private, charter and parochial schools have developed low-track curricula that more effectively challenge students than those often found in public schools.

"If we know how to create a high-track class, why would we then create a separate set of classes that don't have those opportunities?" Welner asks. "Why would we let students opt for a lesser education?"

Sixth graders study science as part of the international baccalaureate curriculum at Harbour Pointe Middle School in Mukilteo, Wash.

AP Photo/The Herald/Elizabeth Armstrong

Loveless says under a random-assignment system, high-achieving students "would lose quite a bit," middle range students "would lose a bit" and lowest-achieving students "would probably benefit a little bit" — mainly by reducing the concentration of students with behavioral issues in low-track classes.

Welner disagrees that high-achieving students are necessarily harmed by reforms. "Good detracking doesn't take anything away from these kids," he says. "The high achievers are not only holding their own but are doing better after the reform."

Despite the recurrent clashes at the local level, Loveless predicts that tracking will continue to be a widespread practice. "Polls are very clear," he says. "Parents, teachers and students favor ability grouping. Those are three important constituency groups."

---

[1] College Board, "Advanced Placement: Report to the Nation 2006," p. 11 (www.collegeboard.com). For background, see Marcia Clemmitt, "AP and IB Programs," *CQ Researcher*, March 3, 2006, pp. 193-216.

[2] For opposing views, see Tom Loveless, *The Tracking Wars: State Reform Meets School Policy* (1999); Jeannie Oakes, *Keeping Track: How Schools Structure Inequality* (2d ed.), 2005.

[3] *Ibid.*, pp. 230-231.

---

in 1954 only after a second round of arguments and shrewd management of the case by the new chief justice, Earl Warren.*

The high court's "remedial" decision one year later in *Brown II* directed school districts to desegregate "with all deliberate speed." Many Southern politicians lent support to a campaign of "massive resistance" to the ruling by diehard segregationists. A decade after *Brown*, fewer than 5 percent of black students in the South were attending majority-white schools; more than three-fourths were attending schools with 90 percent minority enrollment.[14] In 1968, an evidently impatient Supreme Court declared that school districts had to develop plans to dismantle dual systems that promised "realistically" to work — and to work "now." Three years later, a new chief justice, Warren E. Burger, led a unanimous court in upholding the authority of local federal courts to order school districts to use

---

* California, home to the nation's largest concentration of Asian-Americans and the second-largest concentration of Mexican-Americans after Texas, had abolished racial segregation in schools by law in 1947.

More Blacks and Latinos Attend Poorest Schools

The vast majority (79 percent) of white students attend schools where less than half the student body is poor, compared with 37 percent of black students and 36 percent of Hispanics. For schools where at least 91 percent of the students are poor, whites made up just 1 percent of the student body compared with 13 and 15 percent, respectively, for blacks and Hispanics.

Distribution of Students in Public Schools by Percentage Who Are Poor, 2005-2006

Percent Poor	Percentage of each race				
	White	Black	Latino	Asian	American Indian
0-10%	20	5	7	23	17
11-20%	17	5	5	14	6
21-30%	16	7	7	12	8
31-40%	14	9	8	11	9
41-50%	12	11	9	9	11
51-60%	9	11	10	8	11
61-70%	6	12	11	6	11
71-80%	3	13	12	6	10
81-90%	2	14	14	6	8
91-100%	1	13	15	4	9

* Totals may not add up to 100 due to rounding.

Source: Gary Orfield and Chungmei Lee, "Historic Reversals, Accelerating Resegregation, and the Need for New Integration Strategies," Civil Rights Project, UCLA, August 2007

Total number of students (in millions)	
White	28
Black	8
Latino	10
Asian	2
American Indian	1

cross-neighborhood busing as part of a desegregation plan.[15]

'Elusive' Equality

The campaign to desegregate schools stimulated broader efforts in the late 20th century to equalize educational opportunity at national, state and local levels. Initially, desegregation advanced in the South and to a lesser extent in other regions. But integration eventually stalled in the face of white opposition to busing, ambivalence among blacks and Supreme Court decisions easing pressure on local school districts to take affirmative steps to mix white and black students. School funding reform efforts produced some

results, but as the 21st century began educational equality remained — in Professor Reese's word — "elusive."[16]

The Supreme Court's unanimity in school race cases broke down in the 1970s, and a continuing succession of closely divided decisions reduced districts' obligations to develop effective integration plans. In one of the most important rulings, the justices in 1974 divided 5-4 in a case from Detroit to bar court-ordered desegregation between predominantly black inner cities and predominantly white suburban districts. Three years later, the court essentially freed school districts from any obligation to prevent resegregation after adopting a racially neutral assignment plan. The decisions coincided with widespread opposition to busing for racial balance among white families in many communities, most dramatically in Boston in the 1970s, where police escorts were needed for buses taking pupils from predominantly black Roxbury to predominantly white South Boston.

African-American students and families, meanwhile, had mixed reactions to desegregation generally and busing in particular, according to Professor Anderson. In many districts, desegregation meant the closing or transformation of historically black schools that had provided a good education for many students. In the South, desegregation also often meant the loss of black principals and teachers. And busing was a "one-way street" for African-Americans: most plans entailed the transportation of black students away from their neighborhoods to a mixed reception at best in predominantly white communities.

From the start, the NAACP and other civil rights groups had viewed desegregation not only as a goal in its own right but also — and perhaps more importantly — as an instrument to equalize educational opportunities for black and white pupils. In the heady

Do Racial Policies Affect Academic Achievement?

Most studies find beneficial effects from integration.

When the Supreme Court outlawed racial segregation in schools in 1954, it relied heavily on research by the African-American psychologist Kenneth Clark purporting to show that attending all-black schools hurt black students' self-esteem. Over time, the court's reliance on Clark's study drew many critics, who questioned both the research and its prominent use in a legal ruling.

A half-century later, as they considered challenges to racial-diversity plans in Seattle and Louisville, Ky., the justices were deluged with sometimes conflicting research studies on the effects of racial policies on educational achievement. Among 64 friend-of-the-court briefs, nearly half — 27 — cited social science research. Most found beneficial effects from racial integration, but a minority questioned those claims.

The National Academy of Education, a select group of education scholars, created a seven-member committee to evaluate the various studies cited in the various briefs. Here are the committee's major conclusions from the research, released on June 29 — one day after the court found the school districts' plans unconstitutional:

Academic achievement. White students are not hurt by desegregation efforts or adjustments in racial composition of schools. African-American student achievement is enhanced by less segregated schooling, although the magnitude of the influence is quite variable. The positive effects for African-American students tend to be larger in the earlier grades.

Near-term intergroup relations. Racially diverse schools and classrooms will not guarantee improved intergroup relations, but are likely to be constructive. The research identifies conditions that need to be present in order for diversity to have a positive effect and suggests steps schools can take to realize the potential for improvement.

Long-term effects of school desegregation. Experience in desegregated schools increases the likelihood over time of greater tolerance and better intergroup relations among adults of different racial groups.

The critical-mass question. Racial diversity can avoid or mitigate harms caused by racial isolation, such as tokenism and stereotyping, particularly when accompanied by an otherwise beneficial school environment. Some briefs suggest a minimum African-American enrollment of 15 percent to 30 percent to avoid these harms, but the research does not support specifying any particular percentage.

Race-neutral alternatives. No race-neutral policy is as effective as race-conscious policies for achieving racial diversity. Socioeconomic integration is likely to marginally reduce racial isolation and may have other benefits. School choice generally and magnet schools in particular have some potential to reduce racial isolation, but could also increase segregation.

Source: Robert L. Linn and Kevin G. Welner (eds.), "Race-Conscious Policies for Assigning Students to Schools: Social Science Research and the Supreme Court Cases," National Academy of Education, June 29, 2007 (www.naeducation.org/Meredith_Report.pdf).

days of the civil rights era, Congress had put educational equality on the national agenda in 1965 by passing a law as part of President Lyndon B. Johnson's "war on poverty" to provide federal aid targeted to poor children.[17] By the end of the century, however, Title I of the Elementary and Secondary Education Act was seen as having produced mixed results at best — in part because allocation formulas shaped by the realities of congressional politics directed much of the money to relatively well-to-do suburban districts.

Meanwhile, advocates of educational equity had turned to the courts to try to reduce funding disparities between school districts — with mixed results.[18] The Supreme Court ruled in 1973 that funding disparities between

districts did not violate the federal Constitution. One month later, however, the New Jersey Supreme Court became the first state tribunal to find differential school funding to run afoul of a state constitutional provision. Over the next three decades, school funding suits resulted in court rulings in at least 19 states finding constitutional violations and ordering reforms. But funding disparities persisted. In a wide-ranging survey in 1998, *Education Week* gave 16 states a grade of C- or below on educational equity between school districts.[19]

At the same time, school policymakers were focusing on clamorous calls to improve educational quality stimulated by the publication in 1983 of a report by the Reagan administration's Department of Education sharply

Minnijean Brown, 15, one of the Little Rock Nine, arrives at Central High School on Sept. 25, 1957, guarded by soldiers sent by President Dwight. D. Eisenhower. Brown and eight other African-American students desegregated the Arkansas school three years after the Supreme Court's landmark *Brown v. Board of Education* ruling.

criticizing what was depicted as rising mediocrity in U.S. schools. The debate generated by "A Nation at Risk" brought forth all manner of proposals for imposing educational standards, revising curricula or introducing competition within public school systems or between public and private schools. The debate diverted policymakers' attention to some extent from diversity issues and led many white parents to worry more about their own children's education than about educational equity or diversity.[20]

By the end of the 1990s, federal courts were all but out of the desegregation business, and racial isolation — "resegregation" to civil rights advocates — was on the rise. In a trio of cases in 1991, 1993 and 1995, the Supreme Court gave federal courts unmistakable signals to withdraw from superintending desegregation plans. School districts that sought to be declared "unitary" — or no longer dual in nature — and freed from desegregation decrees, like Jefferson County, invariably succeeded. By 2001, at least two-thirds of black students and at least half of Latino students nationwide were enrolled in predominantly minority schools. And after narrowing in the 1980s, the educational-testing gaps between white and black students began to widen again in the 1990s. In 2000, the typical black student scored below about 75 percent of white students on most standardized tests.[21]

'Diversity' Challenged

Even as courts reduced the pressure on school districts to desegregate, hundreds of school systems adopted voluntary measures aimed at mixing students of different racial and ethnic backgrounds. Some plans that made explicit use of race in pupil assignments drew legal challenges from white families as "reverse discrimination." Meanwhile, several dozen school systems were adopting — and achieving some success with — diversity plans tied to socioeconomic status instead of race. Support for socioeconomic integration appeared to increase after the Supreme Court's June 28 decision in the Seattle and Louisville cases restricting the use of race in pupil assignments but permitting race-neutral policies to achieve diversity in the classroom.

School boards that voluntarily sought to achieve racial and ethnic mixing claimed that the policies generally improved education for all students while benefiting disadvantaged minorities and promoting broad political support for the schools. Many plans — like those in Seattle and Louisville — explicitly considered race in some pupil assignments, and several drew legal challenges. In November 1998 the federal appeals court in Boston struck down the use of racial preferences for blacks and Hispanics for admission to the prestigious Boston Latin School. Then in fall 1999, the federal appeals court in Richmond, Va., ruled in favor of white families challenging race-based policies in two districts in the Washington, D.C., suburbs. The rulings struck down a weighted lottery that advantaged blacks and Hispanics in Arlington County, Va., and a transfer policy in Montgomery County, Md., that limited students from changing schools in order to maintain racial balance.[22]

The idea of socioeconomic integration first gained national attention when the midsized town of La Crosse, Wis., redrew attendance zones in the early 1990s to shift students from an overcrowded, predominantly affluent high school to the town's second high school in the blue-collar section with a growing Hmong population. In Kahlenberg's account, the plan survived concerted political opposition, produced measurable educational progress and now enjoys widespread support. Cambridge, Mass., substituted socioeconomic integration policies for racial busing in 1999 after the federal appeals court ruling in the Boston Latin case. Wake County, N.C., similarly dropped its racial balancing plan in 2000 in favor of an assignment plan

Is racial diversity in the classroom essential to a good education?

YES   Janet W. Schofield
Professor of Psychology,
University of Pittsburgh

Written for *CQ Researcher*, September 2007

Education in a democratic society serves three basic purposes. It provides students with workforce skills, prepares them to function as thoughtful and informed citizens in a cohesive country and enriches their lives by awakening them to new knowledge, perspectives and possibilities. Racial diversity in schools and classrooms enhances the attainment of each of these goals.

The ability to work effectively with individuals from diverse backgrounds is a fundamental workplace skill, as the well-known report "What Work Requires of Schools," issued by President George H.W. Bush's administration, points out. Yet, many students never develop this skill because our country's neighborhoods, social institutions and religious organizations are often highly segregated. Racially diverse schools provide a milieu essential to the development of this crucial skill.

Racially diverse schools also have a vital role to play in developing fair-minded citizens and in promoting social cohesion. Research demonstrates that in-school contact with individuals from different backgrounds typically reduces prejudice, a fundamentally important outcome in our increasingly diverse society. In addition, students who attend diverse schools are more likely than others to choose diverse work and residential settings as adults, thus promoting social cohesion.

Racially diverse schools also enrich students' understanding and expand their perspectives by placing them in contact with others whose views and life experiences may be very different. Just as visiting a foreign country is a much richer and more powerful experience than reading about it, interacting with students from different backgrounds brings their perspectives and experiences alive in a way not otherwise possible.

Even individuals who discount the arguments above must acknowledge that heavily segregated minority schools disadvantage the very students most in need of an excellent educational environment. Such schools typically have relatively impoverished curricular offerings, great difficulty recruiting experienced teachers and high teacher-turnover rates, all of which may help to explain why research suggests that attending such schools typically undermines students' achievement relative to similar peers in more diverse schools.

Racial diversity in and of itself does not guarantee a good education, but as a recent report by the National Academy of Education suggests, it creates preconditions conducive to it. In our increasingly diverse democracy, the educational cost of segregated schools is too high for majority and minority students alike.

NO   Abigail Thernstrom
Senior Fellow, Manhattan Institute
Co-author, No Excuses: Closing the
Racial Gap in Learning

Written for *CQ Researcher*, September 2007

Racially diverse classrooms are desirable — of course. But are they essential to a good education? Absolutely not. If they were, big-city school districts would be stuck providing lousy educations for America's most disadvantaged children into the indefinite future. A large majority of students in 26 out of the 27 central-city districts with a public school population of at least 60,000 are non-white. The white proportion in these districts averages 16 percent. Thus, big-city schools will not be racially "diverse" unless we start flying white kids from Utah into, say, Detroit.

Or rather, they will not be racially "diverse" according to the Seattle school board's definition in the racial balancing plan the Supreme Court condemned last term. Seattle had divided students into only two racial groups: white and non-white. If schools were half-Asian, half-white, that was fine; if they were 30 percent white with the rest Asian, they weren't sufficiently "diverse," and educational quality would be somehow lacking.

What racial stereotyping! Do all non-white students express the same non-white views — with all white students having a "white" outlook? In fact, why is racial diversity the only kind that counts for those concerned about the group clustering in certain schools? What about a social class or religious mix?

And on the subject of racial stereotyping, do we really want to embrace the ugly assumption that black kids are incapable of learning unless they're hanging around some white magic? Good inner-city schools across the country are teaching the children who walk through the door. In excellent schools, if every one of the students is black — reflecting the demography of the neighborhood — the expectations for educational excellence do not change. And happily, there are no compelling studies showing enormous positive gains for black students when they attend schools with large numbers of whites.

Good education is not confined to academic learning. But there is no evidence that schools engaging in coercive racial mixing build a lifelong desire to "socialize with people of different races," as Seattle assumed. Visit a school lunchroom! Racial and ethnic clustering will be very much in evidence.

Those who insist school districts should turn themselves inside out to engineer racial diversity haven't a clue as to the limits of social policy. And they demean the capacity of non-Asian minority kids to learn, whatever the color of the kid in the seat next to them.

tied to free or reduced-lunch status to comply with the rulings by the Richmond-based appeals court in the Arlington and Montgomery County cases. By 2003, Kahlenberg claimed some 500,000 students nationwide were enrolled in school systems that used economic status as a factor in pupil assignments.[23]

However, the main school districts that had adopted racial balancing plans stuck with them despite legal challenges. Seattle adopted its "open choice" plan in 1998 — some two decades after it had become the largest school district in the nation to voluntarily adopt a racial busing plan. The ad hoc group Parents Involved in Community Schools filed its suit challenging the use of race as a "tiebreaker" in pupil assignments in July 2000. That same year, Jefferson County Public Schools adopted its controlled choice plan after a federal judge freed the system from a desegregation decree dating to 1975. Parent Crystal Meredith challenged the race-based assignments in April 2003. Federal district judges upheld the plans — in April 2001 in the Seattle case and in June 2004 in the Jefferson County case. The 4th U.S. Circuit Court of Appeals in Cincinnati then upheld the Jefferson County plan in July 2005. The Seattle case followed a more complicated appellate route. The school district suspended the plan after an initial setback in 2002, but eventually the 9th U.S. Circuit Court of Appeals in San Francisco upheld the plan in October 2005.

The Supreme Court's decision to hear the two cases immediately raised fears among civil rights advocates that the conservative majority fortified by President George W. Bush's appointments of Chief Justice Roberts and Justice Samuel A. Alito Jr. would strike down the plans. Questions by Roberts and Alito during arguments on Dec. 4, 2006, left little doubt about their positions. The high-drama announcement of the decision on June 28 lasted nearly 45 minutes with Roberts, Kennedy and Breyer each delivering lengthy summaries of his opinion from the bench.

"The way to stop discrimination on the basis of race," Roberts declared as he neared his conclusion, "is to stop discriminating on the basis of race."

Breyer was equally forceful in his dissent. "This is a decision that the court and this nation will come to regret," he said.

Almost immediately, however, Kennedy's pivotal concurrence began to draw the closest scrutiny as advocates and observers tried to discern what alternatives remained for school boards to use in engineering racial diversity. The National School Boards Association urged local boards to continue seeking diversity through "careful race-conscious policies." Administrators in Seattle and Louisville said they planned to do just that.

But Clegg of the Center for Equal Opportunity said school systems would be better off to drop racial classifications. "At the end of the day, these two plans didn't pass muster," he said. "And the impact will be to persuade other school districts that this is not a good idea."[24]

CURRENT SITUATION

'Resegregation' Seen

The Louisville and Seattle school systems are in the opening weeks of a new academic year, with few immediate effects from the Supreme Court decision invalidating their previous pupil-assignment plans. Officials in both districts are working on new pupil-assignment plans to put into effect starting in fall 2009, with racial diversity still a goal but race- or ethnic-based placements no longer permitted.

Both school systems, however, are reporting what civil rights advocates call "resegregation" — higher percentages of African-American students in predominantly minority schools. Critics of racial-diversity policies object to the term, arguing that segregation refers only to legally enforced separation of the races. Whatever term is used, a new report documents a national trend of "steadily increasing separation" in public schools between whites and the country's two largest minority groups: Latinos and African-Americans.

The report by the UCLA Civil Rights Project shows, for example, that the percentage of black students in majority-white schools rose from virtually zero in 1954 to a peak of 43.5 percent in 1988 before beginning a steady decline. In 2005 — the most recent year available — 27 percent of black students attended majority-white schools.

Meanwhile, the proportion of African-Americans attending majority-minority schools has been slowly increasing over the past two decades — reversing gains in integration in the 1960s and '70s — while the percentage of Latino students in majority-minority schools has grown steadily since the 1960s. In 2005, 73 percent of black students were in majority-minority schools, and more than one-third — 38 percent — were in "intensely segregated" schools with 90 to 100 percent minority enrollment. For Latinos, 78 percent of students were in majority-minority schools.

By contrast, Asian-Americans are described in the report as "the most integrated" ethnic group in public schools. In 2005, the average Asian student attended a school with 44 percent white enrollment — compared to 30 percent white enrollment for the average black student and 27 percent white enrollment for the average Latino. The report attributed the higher integration for Asians to greater residential integration and relatively small numbers outside the West.

Seattle was already experiencing increasing racial isolation after suspending its previous placement plan, which included race as one "tiebreaker" in pupil assignments. "There has been a decline in racial diversity since suspension of the plan," says Seattle Public Schools spokeswoman Patti Spencer.

In Louisville, nine schools now have African-American enrollment above the previous guideline limit of 50 percent — most of them in predominantly black neighborhoods in Louisville's West End or the heavily black areas in southwestern Jefferson County. Black enrollment in some schools in the predominantly white East End has declined, though not below the minimum figure of 15 percent in the previous guidelines.

The 15/50 guidelines remain "a goal," according to Student Placement Director Todd. "We're trying to prevent as much slippage as possible."

In Seattle, outgoing Superintendent Raj Manhas told reporters after the Supreme Court ruling that the school district would look at "all options available to us" to try to preserve racial diversity in the schools.[25] The new superintendent, Maria Goodloe-Johnson, is an African-American who was sharply critical of racial policies in her previous position as superintendent in Charleston, S.C. Since taking office in Seattle in July, however, Goodloe-Johnson has not addressed racial balance, according to Spencer.[26]

Opponents of the race-based policies say school districts should refocus their efforts. "Where school districts should focus is on education standards, not creating a specific racial mix of students," says Sharon Browne, a staff attorney with the Pacific Legal Foundation, the conservative public interest law firm that supported the legal challenges in Louisville and Seattle.

"The guidelines are gone," says attorney Gordon in Louisville. "They're past tense."

In Seattle, Kathleen Brose, the longtime school activist who founded Parents Involved in Community Schools to challenge the use of race for high school placements, says diversity is "important," but parental choice is more important. "The school district has been so focused on race," she adds, "that, frankly, I think they forgot about academics."

Legal Options Eyed

School boards around the country are re-examining their legal options for promoting diversity. At the same time, they are bracing for new legal challenges to their diversity plans that, so far, have not materialized.

The National School Boards Association plans to provide local boards with advisories on what policies can be used under the Supreme Court's decision to promote racial balance. But General Counsel Negrón expects few changes as a result of the ruling.

"School districts are not going to be changing their policies drastically to the extent that they will be abandoning their choices of diversity or integration as their goal, if that's what they've chosen to do," Negrón says. "School districts are going to comply with the law as they understand it. And there's a lot of room in Justice Kennedy's concurrence for school districts to be creative and innovative."

Barring any consideration of race, Negrón adds, "was just not what the decision stood for."

Pacific Legal Foundation attorney Browne, however, worries that school districts are not complying with the ruling. "We are very disappointed that there are school districts who are ignoring the decision by the U.S. Supreme Court and continuing to use race [in pupil assignments]," she says.

Browne says school districts should have begun developing contingency plans for assigning students on a non-racial basis after the oral arguments in the Seattle and Louisville cases in December indicated the court would find both plans unconstitutional.

The Louisville and Seattle cases themselves are still pending in lower federal courts, with winning lawyers in both cases asking the courts to order the school boards to pay attorneys' fees.

In Seattle, the firm of Davis Wright Tremaine is seeking $1.8 million in attorneys' fees despite having previously said that it was handling the parents' case pro bono — for free. "Congress specifically and explicitly wrote into the law that if the government is found to have violated citizens' civil rights, then the prevailing party should seek fee recovery," explained Mark Usellis, a spokesman for the firm. The school system reported spending $434,000 in legal fees on the case.[27]

Louisville solo practitioner Gordon is asking to be paid $200 per hour for the "hundreds of hours" he devoted to the case plus a bonus for the national impact of the case. Without specifying a figure, he also wants to be reimbursed for spending his own money on expenses and court costs. Meanwhile, plaintiff Crystal Meredith is asking for $125,000 in damages, which she attributes to lost wages, invasion of privacy and emotional distress.[28]

Gordon says he received several complaints from parents whose applications for transfers for their children had been denied on the basis of limited capacity at the school they had chosen. Gordon says he suspected school officials were actually denying the transfers on racial grounds, but the MacNeals' case was the only "smoking gun" he found.

The Pacific Legal Foundation is following up on "many inquiries" received from parents since the Supreme Court ruling, according to Browne, but no new cases have been filed. She declined to say where the complaints originated. The foundation has suits pending in California courts against the Los Angeles and Berkeley school districts over race-based policies.

If any new legal challenges are filed, Negrón expects federal courts will defer to local school boards' decisions, for the most part. "The [Supreme Court] didn't tell us exactly what to do," he explains. "School districts will be trying their best to come up with something that meets the requirements of the law and at the same time meets their educational interest in regard to diversity."

OUTLOOK

'Minimal Impact'?

In striking down the Seattle and Jefferson County racial-balance plans, Chief Justice Roberts cited figures from the two school districts showing that the policies actually affected relatively few students — only 52 pupils in Seattle and no more than 3 percent of the pupil assignments in Jefferson County. The "minimal impact," he wrote, "casts doubt on the necessity of using racial classifications."

Writing for the dissenters, however, Justice Breyer cast the stakes in broader terms by citing the growing percentage of black students in majority non-white schools nationwide. The Louisville and Seattle school boards, Breyer said, were asking to be able to continue using tools "to rid their schools of racial segregation." The plurality opinion, he concluded, was "wrong" to deny the school boards' "modest request."

Two months after the ruling, civil rights advocates are continuing to voice grave concerns that the decision will hasten what they call the resegregation of public schools nationwide. "We're going to have a further increase in segregation of American schools," says UCLA's Orfield. "School districts are going to have to jump through a whole series of hoops if they want to have some modest degree of integration."

Legal Defense Fund President Shaw fears new challenges not only to pupil-assignment plans but also to mentoring and scholarship programs specifically targeting racial minorities. "Our adversaries are not going to go away," says Shaw. "They're going to continue to attack race-conscious efforts to address racial inequality."

Opponents of racial-balance plans either discount the fears of increased racial isolation or minimize the harms of the trend if it materializes.

"I don't think there will be dramatic consequences from these decisions," says Rosman of the Center for Individual Rights. School systems with an interest in racial diversity "will find a way to do that legally," he says. "For schools that use race explicitly, it will still be a contentious matter."

"There's going to be less and less focus on achieving politically correct racial and ethnic balance and more focus on improving education," says the Center for Equal Opportunity's Clegg. "That's where the law's headed, and that's where policy's headed. We ought to be worrying less about integration anyhow."

For his part, the Century Foundation's Kahlenberg stresses that the number of school districts with race-conscious policies — guesstimated at around 1,000 — is a small fraction of the nationwide total of 15,000 school systems. Many of the districts that have been seeking racial balance will likely shift to socioeconomic integration, he says, "because that's a clearly legal way to raise academic achievement for kids and create some racial integration indirectly."

In Louisville, the county school board did vote on Sept. 10 to broaden its diversity criteria to include socioeconomic status. "Race will still be a factor," Superintendent Berman said, "but it will not be the only factor."[29] Meanwhile, Student Placement Director Todd says Jefferson County's use of non-contiguous school attendance zones to mix students from different racially identifiable neighborhoods is likely to be continued.

In his concurring opinion, Justice Kennedy suggested "strategic site selection" as another permissible policy to promote racial diversity — placing new schools so they draw students from different racial neighborhoods. The suggestion may prove impractical in many school districts. Jefferson County opened one new school this fall — in the rapidly growing and predominantly white eastern end, far removed from the African-American neighborhoods in the West End. As Breyer noted in his opinion, many urban school systems are unlikely to be building new schools because they are losing not gaining enrollment.

Changing demographics and changing social attitudes are inevitably bringing about changes in the schools. Within a decade or so, demographers expect white students will no longer comprise a majority of public school enrollment. And, as Abigail Thernstrom notes, young people have different attitudes toward race than their parents or grandparents.

"In terms of racial attitudes, we're on a fast track," Thernstrom says. "Young kids are dating across racial and ethnic lines. America is changing in very terrific ways and has been for some time. I expect that change to continue."

But University of Wisconsin educational historian Reese cautions against expecting racial issues to disappear. "It's like a never-never land to imagine that racial issues can somehow disappear," he says. "It's a nice thing to say that we should live in a kind of perfect world, but we don't. I can't imagine that it will disappear. It couldn't have disappeared in the past, and it won't disappear in the future."

NOTES

1. For coverage, see Chris Kenning, "Separate attendance zones voided," *The* [Louisville] *Courier-Journal*, Aug. 29, 2007, p. 1A.

2. The decision is *Parents Involved in Community Schools v. Seattle School District No. 1*, 552 U.S. _ _ _ (2007); the companion case was *Meredith v. Jefferson County Public Schools*. For a detailed chronicle of the cases, see Kenneth Jost, "Court Limits Use of Race in Pupil Assignments," in *The Supreme Court Yearbook 2006-2007*, http://library.cqpress.com/scyb/.

3. For background, see Kenneth Jost, "School Desegregation," *CQ Researcher*, April 23, 2004, pp. 345-372.

4. See Chris Kenning, "JCPS sees change in racial makeup," *The* [Louisville] *Courier-Journal*, Sept. 2, 2007, p. 1A.

5. Gary Orfield and Chungmei Lee, "Historic Reversals, Accelerating Resegregation, and the Need for New Integration Strategies," UCLA Civil Rights Project (formerly based at Harvard University), August 2007, pp. 29, 35.

6. Richard D. Kahlenberg, "Rescuing *Brown v. Board of Education*: Profiles of Twelve School Districts Pursuing Socioeconomic School Integration," June 28, 2007, p. 3.

7. For coverage, see Peter Schworm, "AG Urges Court to Uphold Lynn Plan," *The Boston Globe*, July 18, 2005, p. B4.

8. Orfield and Lee, *op. cit.*, pp. 7-8. For background, see Barbara Mantel, "No Child Left Behind," *CQ Researcher*, May 27, 2005, pp. 469-492.

9. Background drawn in part from William J. Reese, *America's Public Schools: From the Common School to "No Child Left Behind"* (2005); R. Freeman Butts, *Public Education in the United States: From Revolution to Reform* (1978).

10. Reese, *op. cit.*, pp. 10-11, 25-26.

11. For background, see James Anderson, *The Education of Blacks in the South, 1860-1935* (1988). See also Heather Andrea Williams, *Self-Taught: African American Education in Slavery and Freedom* (2003).

12. For background, see "School Desegregation," *op. cit.*, p. 350 (Latinos), pp. 356-357 (Asian-Americans), and sources cited therein.

13. Some background drawn from James T. Patterson, Brown v. Board of Education: *A Civil Rights Milestone and Its Troubled Legacy* (2001).

14. For data, see *ibid.*, pp. 228-230.

15. The decisions are *Green v. County School Board of New Kent County*, 391 U.S. 430 (1968), and *Swann v. Charlotte-Mecklenburg County Board of Education*, 402 U.S. 1 (1971).

16. Reese, *op. cit.*, p. 246. For background on later school desegregation cases, see Patterson, *op. cit.*

17. For background, see H. B. Shaffer, "Status of the War on Poverty," in *Editorial Research Reports*, Jan. 25, 1967, available at *CQ Researcher Plus Archive*, http://library.cqpress.com.

18. Background drawn from Kathy Koch, "Reforming School Funding," *CQ Researcher*, Dec. 10, 1999, pp. 1041-1064.

19. The decisions are *San Antonio Independent School District v. Rodriguez*, 411 U.S. 1 (1973), and *Robinson v. Cahill*, 62 A.2d 273 (N.J. 1973).

20. For background, see Charles S. Clark, "Attack on Public Schools," *CQ Researcher*, July 26, 1996, pp. 649-672.

21. See Patterson, *op. cit.*, p. 214 n.19, p. 234.

22. The decisions are *Wessmann v. Gittens*, 160 F.3d 790 (1st Cir. 1998); *Tuttle v. Arlington County School Board*, 195 F.3d 698 (4th Cir. 1999), *Eisenberg v. Montgomery County Public Schools*, 197 F.3d 123 (4th Cir. 1999). For coverage, see Beth Daley, "Court Strikes Down Latin School Race Admission Policy," *The Boston Globe*, Nov. 20, 1998, p. A1; Jay Mathews, "School Lottery Loses on Appeal," *The Washington Post*, Sept. 26, 1999, p. C1 (Arlington County); Brigid Schulte, "School Diversity Policy Is Overruled," *ibid.*, Oct. 7, 1999, p. A1 (Montgomery County).

23. See Richard D. Kahlenberg, *All Together Now* (2003 ed.)., p. xiii.

24. Quoted in Andrew Wolfson, "Desegregation Decision: Some Find 'Sunshine' Amid Rain," *The* [Louisville] *Courier-Journal*, June 29, 2007, p. 6K.

25. Quoted in Jessica Blanchard and Christine Frey, "District Vows to Seek Out Diversity Answers," *Seattle Post-Intelligencer*, June 29, 2007, p. A1.

26. See Emily Heffter, "First Day of School for Chief," *Seattle Times*, July 10, 2007, p. B1.

27. See Emily Heffter, "Law firm wants school district to pay $1.8M," *Seattle Times*, Sept. 6, 2007, p. B5.

28. Chris Kenning and Andrew Wolfson, "Lawyer in schools case seeks fees, bonus," *The* [Louisville] *Courier-Journal*, July 29, 2007, p. 1A.

29. Quoted in Antoinette Konz, "Schools adopt guidelines for assignment plan," *The* [Louisville] *Courier-Journal*, Sept. 11, 2007.

BIBLIOGRAPHY

Books

Frankenberg, Erika, and Gary Orfield (eds.), *Lessons in Integration: Realizing the Promise of Racial Diversity in American Schools,* **University of Virginia Press, 2007.**

Twelve essays by 19 contributors examine the educational and social effects of desegregation and the disadvantages to students in segregated schools. Orfield is co-director of the Civil Rights Project, UCLA Graduate School of Education and Information Studies (formerly, the Harvard Civil Rights Project); Frankenberg is a study director for the project. Includes notes, 46-page bibliography.

Loveless, Tom, *The Tracking Wars: State Reform Meets School Policy,* **Brookings Institution Press, 1999.**

The director of the Brown Center on Educational Policy at Brookings depicts tracking as a traditional educational practice and detracking as "a gamble" that may hurt rather than help students in low-achievement schools. Includes detailed notes.

Oakes, Jeannie, *Keeping Track: How Schools Structure Inequality* **(2nd ed.),** *Yale University Press,* **2005.**

The director of urban schooling at UCLA's Graduate School of Education and Information Studies updates the landmark critique of tracking that launched a detracking reform movement after its publication in 1985. Includes detailed notes.

Patterson, James T., Brown v. Board of Education: *A Civil Rights Milestone and Its Troubled Legacy,* **Oxford University Press, 2001.**

An emeritus professor of history at Brown University gives a compact account of the landmark school desegregation case and a legacy described as "conspicuous achievement" along with "marked failures."

Reese, William J., *America's Public Schools: From the Common School to "No Child Left Behind," Johns Hopkins University Press,* **2005.**
A professor of educational-policy studies at the University of Wisconsin-Madison provides an accessible overview of the history of U.S. public education from Horace Mann's advocacy of the "common school" through 20th-century developments.

Thernstrom, Abigail, and Stephan Thernstrom, *No Excuses: Closing the Racial Gap in Learning, Simon & Schuster,* **2003.**
The authors decry the persistent achievement gap between white and black students but discount the importance of racial isolation in schools as a cause. Includes extensive statistical information, notes. Both authors are senior fellows with the Manhattan Institute; Abigail Thernstrom is vice chair of the U.S. Civil Rights Commission, Stephan Thernstrom a professor of history at Harvard.

Articles

Simmons, Dan, "A Class Action: Leaders Tried to Rein In Effects of Poverty in Public Schools; Voters Were in No Mood for Busing," *La Crosse* **(Wis.)** *Tribune,* **Jan. 21, 2007, p. 1.**
The story and an accompanying sidebar ("Balance by Choice") examine the history and current status of the La Crosse school district's 15-year experiment with socioeconomic integration.

Reports and Studies

Kahlenberg, Richard D., "Rescuing *Brown v. Board of Education:* **Profiles of Twelve School Districts Pursuing Socioeconomic School Integration,"** *Century Foundation,* **June 28, 2007, www.tcf.org.**

The 42-page report describes the mixed results of socioeconomic integration in 12 school systems, with lengthy treatment of three: La Crosse, Wis.; Cambridge, Mass.; and Wake County (Raleigh), N.C. For a book-length treatment, see Kahlenberg, *All Together Now: Creating Middle-Class Schools through Public School Choice* (Brookings Institution Press, 2001).

Linn, Robert L., and Kevin G. Welner (eds.), "Race-Conscious Policies for Assigning Students to Schools: Social Science Research and the Supreme Court Cases," *National Academy of Education,* **June 29, 2007, www.naeducation.org/Meredith_Report.pdf.**
The 58-page report details social-science research on the effects of racial diversity in schools and finds "general support" for the conclusion that the overall academic and social effects of increased racial diversity are "likely to be positive."

Orfield, Gary, and Chungmei Lee, "Historic Reversals, Accelerating Resegregation, and the Need for New Integration Strategies," *UCLA Civil Rights Project,* **Aug. 29, 2007, www.civilrightsproject.ucla.edu.**
The 50-page report finds "accelerating isolation" of African-American and Latino students in public schools and recommends a variety of measures to counter the trend, including an attack on housing segregation, socioeconomic integration of schools and congressional initiatives "to require and/or to support racial progress."

On the Web

The *Courier-Journal* has an extensive compilation of articles, photographs and information on the course of school desegregation in Louisville and Jefferson County (www.courier-journal.com/desegregation). Current coverage can be found on the Web sites of Seattle's two newspapers, the *Seattle Times* (http://seattletimes.nwsource.com/html/education/) and the *Seattle Post-Intelligencer* (http://seattlepi.nwsource.com/).

For More Information

American Educational Research Association, 1430 K St., N.W., Suite 1200, Washington, DC 20005; (202) 238-3200; www.aera.net. National research society encouraging scholarly research in efforts to improve education.

Center for Individual Rights, 1233 20th St., N.W., Suite 300, Washington, DC 20036; (202) 833-8400; www.cir-usa.org. Nonprofit public-interest law firm opposed to racial preferences.

Center for Equal Opportunity, 7700 Leesburg Pike, Suite 231, Falls Church, VA 22043; (703) 442-0066; www.ceousa.org. Think tank devoted to equal opportunity and racial harmony.

Century Foundation, 41 E. 70th St., New York, NY 10021; (212) 535-4441; www.tcf.org. Public-policy institution promoting methods for socioeconomic integration in education.

Mexican American Legal Defense and Educational Fund, 634 S. Spring St., Los Angeles, CA 90014; (213) 629-2512; www.maldef.org. Protects and promotes the civil rights of Latinos living in the United States.

NAACP Legal Defense and Educational Fund, 99 Hudson St., Suite 1600, New York, NY 10013; (212) 965-2200; www.naacpldf.org. Serves as legal counsel on issues of race, with emphasis on education, voter protection, economic justice and criminal justice.

National School Boards Association, 1680 Duke St., Alexandria, VA 22314; (703) 838-6722; www.nsba.org. Seeks to foster excellence and equity in public education by working with school board leadership.

Here is contact information for the school districts involved in the Supreme Court decision, *Parents Involved in Community Schools v. Seattle School District No. 1:*

Jefferson County Public Schools, VanHoose Education Center, 3332 Newburg Rd., P.O. Box 34020, Louisville, KY 40232-4020; (502) 485-3949; www.jefferson.k12.ky.us.

Seattle School District No. 1, 2445 Third Ave. South, Seattle, WA 98134; (206) 252-0000; www.seattleschools.org.

No Child Left Behind

Is the Law Improving Student Performance?

Barbara Mantel

2

President Bush visits with students in St. Louis, Mo., on Jan. 5, 2004, the second anniversary of the No Child Left Behind Act. Bush has called the sweeping overhaul of federal education policy the start of "a new era, a new time in public education." But today the bipartisan legislation is under heavy criticism from Republicans and Democrats alike. Besides seeking exemptions from parts of the law, legislators are pressing Congress for more money to implement the act.

From *CQ Researcher*,
May 27, 2005.

Politics indeed makes for strange bedfellows: There was President Bush standing on a Boston stage flanked by four jubilant legislators, two Republicans and two Democrats, including liberal lion Sen. Edward M. Kennedy of Massachusetts. The occasion was the signing on Jan. 8, 2002, of the No Child Left Behind Act — a sweeping, bipartisan overhaul of federal education policy.

Cheering crowds greeted Bush and the four lawmakers that day as they touted the new law on a whirlwind, 12-hour tour of three states, with the president calling the legislation the start of "a new era, a new time in public education."

Kennedy, who played a key role in negotiating the bill's passage, told Bush: "What a difference it has made this year with your leadership."[1]

The law is actually the most recent reauthorization of the Elementary and Secondary Education Act (ESEA), which since 1965 has tried to raise the academic performance of all students.

"This legislation holds out great promise for education," said education researcher G. Gage Kingsbury, director of research at the Northwest Evaluation Association, in Lake Oswego, Ore. "But it also has strong requirements and includes a host of provisions that have never been tried on this scale before."[2]

No Child Left Behind (NCLB) increases the reach of the federal government into the management of local schools and raises the stakes for schools, districts and states. It increases funding for schools serving poor students, mandates "highly qualified" teachers in every classroom and holds schools that accept federal funds accountable

Few States Make the Grade on Teacher Quality

Only three states — Connecticut, Louisiana and South Carolina — received a grade of A for their efforts to improve teacher quality, according to a 2005 assessment by Education Week. In every state except New Mexico, more than 50 percent of secondary teachers majored in the core academic subject they teach. But only eight states had more than 75 percent of secondary school teachers who majored in their core subject.

Rating State Efforts to Improve Teacher Quality

Wash. C- 53%
Mont. D+ 62%
N.D. D 65%
Minn. D+
N.H. 72% 58%
Vt. D- 65%
Maine D
Ore. C- 58%
Idaho C 56%
Wyo.
S.D. D 57%
Wis. B- 79%
Mich. D 54%
N.Y. B- 74%
Mass. C 70%
Calif. B- 82%
Nev. C 57%
Utah D+ 61%
Colo. C 75%
Neb. C+ 71%
Iowa C 69%
Ill. C
Ind. B+ 61%
Ohio B+ 73%
Pa. C 72%
A-
R.I. C- 77%
Conn. 91%
Ariz. D- 62%
N.M. B- 48%
Kan. C+ 64%
Mo. B- 61%
W.Va. B- 59%
Va. B 66%
N.J. B- 74%
Texas C- 53%
Okla. B 53%
Ark. B+ 89%
Tenn. C+ 57%
Ky. 60%
N.C. B 76%
Del. C 55%
Md. C+ 68%
La. A 93%
Miss. C- 58%
Ala. C 65%
Ga. C 61%
A- 74%
S.C.
D.C. D 81%
Fla. C 67%

Alaska D- 53%

Hawaii C- 62%

● Overall grade for efforts to improve teacher quality

% Percent of secondary teachers who majored in the core academic subject they teach

Source: Education Week

for raising the achievement of all students. Schools that don't meet state benchmarks two years in a row are labeled "in need of improvement" and suffer sanctions.

Most significantly, NCLB sets a deadline: By 2014 all students must be grade-level proficient in reading and math — as evidenced by their scores on annual tests in grades 3-8, and once in high school. (*See sidebar, p. 27.*)

But more than three years after its passage, the bipartisan accord that produced the bill appears badly frayed. Kennedy now says No Child Left Behind "has been underfunded, mismanaged and poorly implemented and is becoming the most spectacular broken promise of this Republican administration and Congress. America's children deserve better."[3]

In the states, politicians from both parties are equally unhappy, including GOP legislators from some "red states" that overwhelmingly supported Bush in last year's presidential election. "I wish they'd take the stinking money and go back to Washington," said state Rep. Steven Mascaro, R-Utah.[4]

"We have to fight back," Gov. John Baldacci, D-Maine, said. "We have to tell them we're not going to take it any more."[5]

It hasn't been just talk. In early May, Utah's Republican governor signed legislation giving precedence to the state's education policies when they conflict with NCLB, and in the past year and a half more than 30 states have introduced bills that would release them from some of the law's requirements.

The ABCs of NCLB

Here are the basic provisions of the No Child Left Behind Act, which spells out its standards and requirements in more than 1,000 pages of regulations:

Standards and Testing — As in the previous version of the law, each state must adopt challenging standards for what its students should know and be able to do. Academic standards must contain coherent and rigorous content and encourage the teaching of advanced skills. States must also develop tests aligned to the standards and establish cutoff scores that classify student achievement as basic, proficient or advanced. What has changed is the amount of testing states must do. Beginning in September 2005, states must test children annually in grades 3-8 and once in high school. Previously, schoolchildren had to be tested only four times in grades K-12.

Public Reporting — For the first time, states must publicly report their test results, with student scores broken down into four subgroups: economically disadvantaged students; major racial and ethnic groups; students with disabilities and students with limited English proficiency. States must report each school's progress in raising student performance and the difference in teacher qualifications in high-poverty versus low-poverty schools.

Accountability — All students must reach proficiency in reading and math by 2014. States must establish annual benchmarks for their schools, with special emphasis on closing achievement gaps between different groups of students. Since 1994 states had been required to make "adequate yearly progress" (AYP) in raising achievement, but there was no firm timetable or deadline for students reaching proficiency. Now if a school does not make AYP, the state and district must develop a two-year plan to help the school improve.

Sanctions — If a school receiving Title I funds — designed to improve the performance of low-income students — does not make AYP in raising student performance for two years in a row, the state must designate it a school "in need of improvement."[1] Most states are applying this rule to all schools in a Title I district, even those that do not take Title I money. Students in these schools must be given the option of transferring out, and if a school fails to achieve its AYP for three consecutive years, it must pay for tutoring, after-school programs and summer school for those low-income students who remain. After four years, the state must restructure the school.

Teachers — For the first time, teachers must be "highly qualified," meaning they have a college degree and are licensed or certified by the state. Newly hired middle-school teachers must have a major or pass a test demonstrating their knowledge in the subjects they teach. Veteran teachers can do the same or demonstrate their competency through an alternative system developed by each state.

[1] About 55 percent of the schools in the nation's 100 largest districts were eligible for Title I funds in the 2001/2002 school year; http://nces.ed.gov/pubs2003/100_largest/table_05_1.asp.

Besides seeking exemptions from parts of the law, legislators are pressing Congress for more money to implement the act. Much of the controversy stems from the fact that Congress has appropriated $27 billion less than it authorized for the law's implementation.

But the act's supporters say enough money is being provided, pointing out that federal funding for public education has increased by more than 30 percent since the NCLB was enacted. "The education reforms contained in the No Child Left Behind Act are coupled with historic increases in K-12 funding," according to the Web site of Sen. Judd Gregg, R-N.H., who made the whirlwind trip with Bush and Kennedy three years ago.[6]

Nevertheless, in April the National Education Association, the nation's largest teachers' union, sued the Department of Education on the grounds that the act is not properly funded. In addition, Connecticut also is threatening to sue, estimating that NCLB will cost the state an extra $41.6 million dollars in the next few years. The atmosphere has gotten so disagreeable at times that Secretary of Education Margaret Spellings angrily called Connecticut officials "un-American."

Part of the states' resentment stems from the fact that Congress provides only 8 percent of total funding for public education — $501.3 billion in the last school year — but since the 1960s has passed laws giving the Department of Education increasing powers over the nation's 96,000 schools.[7] The NCLB is the most far reaching yet.

Supporters of the act say it represents an evolutionary change, while critics say it is a revolutionary incursion of the federal government into the historic domain of the states.

"I don't know any educator or parent who doesn't think our schools should be accountable," said state Rep. Margaret Dayton, R-Orem. "The question is: To whom should they be accountable? Under No Child Left Behind our local schools are accountable to Washington, D.C., and here in Utah, we think our schools should be accountable to the parents and the communities where they are."[8]

Even supporters acknowledge that NCLB's provisions have been overwhelming for states without the administrative staff to implement the law.

In 2004, No Child Left Behind became "a significant force affecting the operations and decisions of states, school districts and schools," according to the Center on Education Policy, an independent advocate for public education.[9] For example, the law has compelled states and school districts to step up efforts to test students in more grades and put "highly qualified" teachers in every classroom. In addition, for the first time entire school districts have been labeled "in need of improvement."

However, as the law's requirements take hold, the debate about its fairness and efficacy has been escalating. Besides the debate over funding, critics argue that the law is too rigid and that too many schools — even good schools — are being told they need to improve. This has sparked widespread opposition to President's Bush's proposal to extend the law's annual testing requirements to high school students. (*See "At Issue," p. 42.*)

On the other side of the debate, many of NCLB's staunchest defenders worry that the Department of Education has become too flexible in implementing the law, citing a recent relaxation of requirements for testing disabled students and department approval of what some see as lax state plans to ensure that veteran teachers are "highly qualified."

And voices from all sides call for more guidance and technical support to localities from the Department of Education.

As the public discussion grows louder leading up to the law's reauthorization fight in 2007, coalitions have begun to form. The American Association of School Administrators, the Children's Defense Fund, the Learning Disabilities Association of America, the National Education Association and several other groups joined together last fall to call for significant revisions in the law. Proponents — including the Citizens' Commission on Civil Rights, the National Alliance of Black School Educators, Just for Kids, the Education Trust and the Business Roundtable — formed their own coalition, called the Achievement Alliance, to vigorously defend the law.

Here are some of the questions parents, educators, children's advocates, lawmakers and researchers are asking:

Has No Child Left Behind raised student achievement?

The goal of the NCLB law is to ensure that by 2014 all children are at grade-level proficiency in reading and math. The law requires states to measure student achievement by testing children in grades 3-8 every year, and once in high school.

But each state determines its own academic standards, the courses taught, the standardized tests used and the cutoff scores that define a student as proficient. Thus, the rigor varies between the states, making it impossible to compare one state to another. Colorado may have reported 87 percent of its fourth-graders proficient in reading in 2003 and Massachusetts 56 percent, but no one knows what that says about the relative achievement of their students.[10]

It is possible, however, to look at student achievement within a state and ask, for example, how this year's fourth-graders compare to last year's.

With a growing number of states administering annual tests, researchers have conducted some preliminary studies. They all show that student achievement, for the most part, is improving.

The Center on Education Policy surveyed states and a sampling of school districts and reported that 73 percent of states and 72 percent of districts said student achievement is improving. In addition, states and districts were more likely to say that achievement gaps between white and black students, white and Hispanic students, and English-language learners and other students were narrowing rather than widening or staying the same.[11]

Similarly, the Council of the Great City Schools, a coalition of 65 of the nation's largest urban school systems, reported that while math and reading scores in urban schools remain lower than national averages, they are rising and achievement gaps are narrowing.[12]

The Education Trust, a nonprofit advocate of school reform, also analyzed proficiency rates since No Child Left Behind took effect. It found that in most states it studied, achievement scores of elementary school students had risen, and achievement gaps had narrowed. But when the Trust looked at middle and high schools, the results were more mixed. While the majority of states in the study reported an increase in the percentage of proficient students, there was much less success in narrowing achievement gaps.[13]

Delaware is a case in point. The state has made some of the largest strides in raising achievement and narrowing gaps among elementary students. For instance, the gap in Delaware between the percentage of reading-proficient white and Hispanic fifth-graders narrowed from 31 points in 2001 to less than five points in 2004, and for African-American students, the gap narrowed from 22 points to 16.[14] But in middle schools, achievement gaps have actually widened.

"It is a little harder to get a reform groundswell in middle schools and high schools," says Delaware's Secretary of Education Valerie Woodruff. "In math, for example, we don't have enough well qualified teachers at the middle school level."

The fundamental question is how much of the documented improvement is a result of No Child Left Behind. Daria Hall, a policy analyst at the Education Trust, says it is a significant amount. Educators "are using the standards to develop a challenging curriculum for all students," she says. "They are using assessment results to inform their instruction in the classroom." NCLB, Hall says, gives administrators leverage to make needed changes.

Diane Rentner, project coordinator at the Center on Education Policy, is hearing something different. The center did not specifically ask state and district officials if they thought the law was responsible for achievement gains. But Rentner says district officials later said they "were almost offended that No Child Left Behind would be viewed as this great catalyst of change because they felt like they had been working for years to improve student achievement."

"Our math curriculum has been completely reviewed from K-12 and in the majority of cases exceeds state standards," says Margo Sorrick, an assistant superintendent in Wheaton, Ill. For instance, the district now requires three years rather two years of math for high school graduation. "These changes have nothing to do with No Child Left Behind," says Sorrick.

But the law does shine a new light on those reforms. Now that states must report their progress in raising student achievement, the press routinely covers the release of so-called state report cards. Stiffening graduation requirements, revising the curriculum and replacing staff at the worst schools have taken on more urgency, Rentner says. "We jokingly say the news media have become the enforcer of the law," she adds.

But trying to figure out the law's exact impact is still all but impossible. Besides the difficulty of teasing out the roles of pre- and post-NCLB reforms, there are gaps in the data. Most states started testing students only six or seven years ago, and many changed their tests, making before-and-after comparisons unreliable.

Several experts also warn that initial gains in achievement scores may be deceptive. Brian Stecher, a senior social scientist at the RAND Corporation, a nonprofit research organization, says that on new, high-stakes tests teachers often feel pressure to coach students in test-taking skills and to teach the material emphasized on the test. "That can allow you to get initially a relatively big gain in scores," Stecher says, "and then the increase tapers off."

That's of particular concern to states because the pace of recent improvement is not fast enough to ensure 100 percent student proficiency by 2014. "Progress needs to be accelerated," Hall says bluntly.

Are too many schools being labeled "in need of improvement"?

Holding states accountable for student achievement is central to No Child Left Behind. The law gives states a firm goal and a firm deadline, and to reach it each state must come up with annual benchmarks. In Wisconsin, for instance, 67.5 percent of a school's students must be proficient in reading this school year, 87 percent six years later and finally 100 percent in 2014.[15]

But it's not enough for a school to look at its students as a single, undifferentiated block. NCLB requires schools to divide students into subgroups — ethnic, racial, low-income, disabled and English-language learner — and each must meet the proficiency benchmarks as well.

Thousands of Schools Missed Progress Targets

Eleven thousand public schools — or nearly 12 percent of the nation's 96,000 public schools — failed in 2004 for the second year in a row to meet "adequate yearly progress" (AYP) targets set by the No Child Left Behind law. Such schools are labeled "in need of improvement" and must offer all students the right to transfer; after missing AYP for three consecutive years, they must offer low-income students supplemental services, like after-school tutoring. After four years, the state must restructure the school.

Number of Public Schools Needing Improvement
(based on failure to meet "adequate yearly progress" targets)

Wash.	166
Mont.	40
N.D.	21
Minn.	71
N.H.	71
Vt.	28
Maine	50
Ore.	328
Idaho	71
Wyo.	64
S.D.	106
Wis.	51
Mich.	450
N.Y.	713
Mass.	381
Neb.	N/A
Iowa	66
Pa.	333
Calif.	1626
Nev.	122
Utah	16
Colo.	129
Kan.	21
Ill.	694
Ind.	77
Ohio	487
R.I.	39
Mo.	40
W.Va.	37
Conn.	134
Ky.	130
Va.	113
N.J.	520
Ariz.	184
N.M.	124
Okla.	146
Ark.	305
Tenn.	165
N.C.	160
Del.	43
Texas	199
Miss.	132
Ala.	83
Ga.	413
S.C.	208
Md.	256
La.	75
D.C.	79
Fla.	965
Alaska	179
Hawaii	138

Source: Education Week

Schools also must test at least 95 percent of students in a subgroup, meet state-determined attendance requirements and improve high school graduation rates.

Schools that meet all of these targets are deemed to have made "adequate yearly progress" (AYP). But if a school misses just one target it doesn't make AYP, and the district and state must create a two-year intervention plan. Options include reducing class size, providing extra help for disadvantaged students and increasing professional development for teachers. Local and state officials decide on the details, and the federal government provides extra funding.

Sanctions prescribed by the law, however, kick in when a school doesn't make AYP for two consecutive years. Such schools, if they take Title I funds, are labeled "in need of improvement" and must offer all students the right to transfer; after missing AYP for three consecutive years, they must offer low-income students supplemental services, like after-school tutoring. After four years, the state must restructure the school.

This system of accountability is among the most contentious elements of NCLB. While praising the overall goals of the law, the National Conference of State Legislatures called the system rigid and overly prescriptive.

Is Testing Crowding Out Art and Recess?

Testing required by the No Child Left Behind Act is taking a toll on education, says George Wood, an Ohio high school principal and director of The Forum for Education and Democracy. "School people are no fools," Wood wrote in the 2004 book *Many Children Left Behind*. "Tell them what they will be measured on, and they will try to measure up."

"Test preparation crowds out much else that parents have taken for granted in their schools," Wood said. Recess for elementary school students, nap time for kindergartners and music and art for middle school students are some of the things being eliminated from the school day, he contends, along with reductions in class time for social studies and creative writing.

Diane Rentner, project coordinator at the Center on Education Policy, says the cutbacks haven't been too bad so far. "It's not huge, it's not a revolution yet," she says. In a March 2005 survey of school districts, the center found "a slight movement toward cutting down on other subjects to focus on reading and math," Rentner says.

More than two-thirds of districts reported that instructional time on subjects other than math and reading had been reduced minimally or not at all. However, 27 percent of the districts reported that social studies class time had been reduced somewhat or to a great extent, and close to 25 percent said instruction time in science, art and music had been reduced.

While the center's findings don't support a revolutionary shift in class time, Rentner still calls the trend worrisome and expects that as state proficiency benchmarks rise, there may be additional pressure on schools to focus more time on reading and math. "It would be sad if there were no arts in the schools, and students didn't learn civic education," she says.

Rentner also points out another potentially troubling survey result: The poorer the school district, the more likely it was to require schools to allot a specific amount of time to math and reading. "You could jump to the next conclusion that low-income kids are receiving a less rich curriculum," Rentner says. While that might be necessary in the short term to bring kids closer to proficiency in math and reading, Rentner hopes that it doesn't have to continue.

It is this impact on low-income and minority schools that most concerns Wood. An opponent of NCLB, Wood calls for a moratorium on high-stakes testing until more research shows it to have some link to student success after leaving high school.

But Daria Hall, a policy analyst at the Education Trust, which generally supports the goals and methods of No Child Left Behind while criticizing the government's implementation of the law, says that's the wrong response. "We don't deny that focusing so much on math and reading means that other subjects might not receive the attention they deserve," says Hall. But that doesn't have to happen, she says, citing schools, many in poor districts, that have integrated math and reading instruction into their other subjects.

"So, for example, there is no need to give short shrift to social studies," she claims. "We can teach the content of social studies while at the same time covering state standards on reading." The same can be done, she says, with math and science.

But it's not something that one teacher or even one school can do alone, Hall adds. "There needs to be research from the U.S. Department of Education on how to effectively integrate standards across the curriculum," she says. "It needs to really be a systemic effort."

Too many schools, it said, are being labeled "in need of improvement," and the law, therefore, "spreads resources too thinly, over too many schools, and reduces the chances that schools that truly are in need can be helped."[16]

Last year, 11,008 public schools — nearly 12 percent of the nation's total — were identified as needing improvement.[17] Critics of the law see that number rising dramatically. "Essentially, all schools will fail to meet the unrealistic goal of 100 percent proficient or above,"

wrote testing expert Robert Linn, "and No Child Left Behind will have turned into No School Succeeding."[18]

But Keri Briggs, senior adviser to Acting Deputy Secretary of Education Raymond Simon, strongly disagrees. "We have identified schools that have beat expectations; there are several in many states," says Briggs. "We know it's possible."

Critics, however, say the accountability system has several flaws, such as not recognizing progress made by schools that start with large numbers of low-performing students. A school that significantly raises the percentage of students reading at proficiency, for example, would still not make AYP if that percentage remains below the state benchmark. Such schools "should be given credit," says Scott Young, a senior policy specialist at the National Conference of State Legislatures.

But the law does provide a so-called safe harbor alternative for these schools: If a subgroup of students falls short of the benchmark, the school can still make AYP if the number below the proficiency level is decreased by 10 percent from the year before. But according to Linn, that's something even the best schools would have difficulty accomplishing. "Only a tiny fraction of schools meet AYP through the safe-harbor provision because it is so extreme," Linn wrote.[19]

After protests from both Republican and Democratic governors, Secretary Spellings announced in April she would appoint a panel to consider allowing states to use a "growth model" to reward schools whose students make significant progress but that still miss AYP. Such a model would follow individual students as they move from grade to grade. By contrast, the current system compares the current fourth-grade class, for example, with last year's fourth-graders.

Kingsbury, at the Northwest Evaluation Association, likes the growth-model idea but says goals and timetables are needed. Otherwise, Kingsbury explains, "there is no guarantee students will end up at a high level of proficiency when they graduate."

Another frequent complaint is that the accountability system is too blunt an instrument. "The problem," says Patricia Sullivan, director of the Center on Education Policy, "is the lack of distinction between the school that misses by a little and the school that misses by a lot." The school that misses the benchmark for one subgroup for two consecutive years is identified as needing improvement just like the school that misses the benchmark for several subgroups. Both face the same sanction: All students would have the option to transfer.

Since urban schools tend to be more diverse and have more subgroups, it is harder for them to make AYP. But the Education Trust's Hall says those who complain care more about the adults working in urban schools than the kids. "Is it fair to expect less of schools that are educating diverse student bodies?" Hall asks. "Is it fair to those students? Absolutely not."

The Department of Education has signaled its willingness to compromise, to a degree. Many districts have complained that requiring all students with disabilities to be grade-level proficient by 2014 is unfair and unrealistic. The law does allow 1 percent of all students — those with significant cognitive disabilities — to take alternative assessments. Secretary Spellings recently declared that another 2 percent — those with persistent academic disabilities — could take alternative tests, geared toward their abilities and not necessarily at grade level. States would have to apply to the Department of Education in order to use this option.

The reaction from educators was muted. Betty J. Sternberg, Connecticut's education commissioner, said, "The percentages are fine. They help us. The problem may be in the details of what they are requiring us to do to have access to the flexibility."[20]

But advocates for disabled students worry that the department is backpedaling. Suzanne Fornaro, board president of the Learning Disability Association of America, is particularly concerned about students with learning disabilities: "If the changes result in lowering expectations, they might result in decreasing a student's access to the general curriculum and high-quality instruction."

Is No Child Left Behind improving the quality of teaching?

Teaching quality may be the single most important in-school factor in how well students learn. While it's difficult to know precisely what makes effective teachers, there are some common yardsticks, including mastery of their subject area. Yet government surveys show that, "One out of four secondary classes (24 percent) in core academic subjects are assigned to a teacher lacking even a college minor in the subject being taught." (*See map, p. 26.*) That figure rises to 29 percent in high-minority schools and 34 percent in high-poverty schools.[21]

No one blames teachers. It's rarely by choice that teachers are assigned to a subject out of their field. But NCLB requires a "highly qualified" teacher in every classroom by the end of the 2005/2006 school year. Highly qualified teachers must have a bachelor's degree, be licensed or certified by the state and demonstrate that they know each subject they teach. New teachers can qualify by either passing a state test or having completed a college major in their subject area. Veteran teachers have a third option: an alternative evaluation created by each state, known by the acronym HOUSSE (high objective uniform state standard of evaluation).

Most states are likely to claim success by the deadline. Many say they are already close. But whether teaching actually will have changed is less certain. In "Quality Counts 2005," a report by *Education Week*, researchers graded states on their efforts to improve teacher quality, looking at the amount of out-of-field teaching allowed, the quality of the state certification process and the amount and quality of professional development. (*See map, p. 26.*) Only three states got As, 14 got Bs and the rest received Cs and Ds.[22]

No Child Left Behind's ability to alter the picture may be limited, critics say. They point to the problems rural and urban schools are having recruiting and retaining skilled teachers and to many states' less-than-rigorous HOUSSE plans.

"I love my job. I know how kids learn," says Jon Runnalls, Montana's "Teacher of the Year" in 2003, "and for someone to come and say that now I'm not highly qualified, that's a slap in the face." Runnalls has taught middle school science for 31 years, but his college degree is in elementary education with an emphasis in science. According to NCLB, he'd have to go back to school, take a state test or pass the state's alternative evaluation. But Montana doesn't have a test, and its HOUSSE plan has not yet been approved by the Department of Education. It's really not a plan at all; it simply says that a veteran certified teacher is, by default, highly qualified.

Not surprisingly, Montana reports 98.8 percent of its classes are taught by highly qualified teachers.

Ten other states, like Montana, don't evaluate veteran teachers, arguing that the state certification process is a rigorous enough hurdle. But even many of the states that do have more elaborate HOUSSE plans have faced criticism.

Most states use a system in which veteran teachers accumulate points until they have enough to be considered highly qualified. "The most prevalent problem is that states offer too many options that veteran teachers can use to prove they are highly qualified — options that often have nothing to do with content knowledge," says

Kate Walsh, president of the National Council on Teacher Quality. While states give points for university-level coursework, states also give them for sponsoring a school club, mentoring a new teacher and belonging to a national teacher organization. Teachers also get points for experience.

But according to Walsh, "The purpose of HOUSSE is to ensure that teachers know their content, not to count the number of years in the classroom."[23]

Even with the flexibility offered by the HOUSSE option, some schools in rural and urban areas are struggling to meet the law's requirements, although the Department of Education has given rural districts a three-year extension. After studying a rural district in Alabama that offered a $5,000 signing bonus to new teachers, researchers from the Southeast Center for Teaching Quality noted: "Central office staff told us that to ensure the bonus worked, they could only require recipients work two years. Most teachers take the bonus, serve their two years and leave." Urban districts the researchers studied struggled to find experienced teachers prepared to work with few resources and students with diverse learning and emotional needs.[24]

As a result, rural and urban schools are more likely to assign teachers to instruct in multiple subjects, often outside their field. These schools are also more reliant on teachers who have entered the profession through some alternative route, usually with little or no classroom experience. No Child Left Behind says such teachers are highly qualified if enrolled in an intensive induction and mentoring program and receiving high-quality professional development.

But Tom Blamford, an associate director at the National Education Association, says the quality of these programs is often poor. "We know what it takes to change classroom practice," Blamford says. "It has to do with knowledge, coaching, feedback and more knowledge, and it's a cyclical process. It's very rare that professional development meets those standards." Usually, he says, it's someone standing in front of a group of teachers lecturing them.

What rural and urban schools need to do, according to Scott Emerick, a policy associate at the Southeast Center for Teaching Quality, is use federal funds more effectively to improve working conditions, design better professional-development programs and devise sophisticated financial incentives to attract and retain teachers. But Emerick says they often don't know how, and the federal government is not providing enough guidance.

"These districts need on-the-ground assistance beyond accessing a federal Web site that tells you what other people are doing," he says.

Is No Child Left Behind adequately funded?

The funding question is so contentious it has divided former congressional supporters of the law and prompted both Republican and Democratic state lawmakers to introduce bills exempting their states from portions of the law.

The issue also has generated nearly two-dozen studies from think tanks, lobbying groups, school districts and states. Their conclusions about the adequacy of funding range from modest surpluses to shortfalls of millions, and in a few cases, even billions of dollars.

Beneath the competing claims are radically different estimates of the costs of implementing the law. Researchers can't even agree on what costs should be included, let alone their size. Adding to the problem, said a study, "is the evolving nature of the regulations, guidance and other advisories issued by the U.S. Department of Education."[25]

After reviewing the studies, the National Conference of State Legislatures concluded a shortfall is more likely and released a report in February calling for change. "We would ask Congress to do one of two things," says senior policy specialist Young. "Either increase funding to levels that would allow states to meet the goals of the law or provide states waivers from having to meet requirements where there is insufficient funding."

In response, the Education Department embraced the studies projecting plenty of funds. "The perpetual cry for more money . . . simply does not comport with the facts: Since taking office, President Bush has increased education funding by . . . 33 percent," said a department press release.

To understand the debate, it is helpful to break down the costs of implementing the law into two categories: complying with the letter of the law versus bringing students to grade-level proficiency by 2014, which several states claim may be much more costly.

To comply with the letter of the law, states must establish academic standards, create assessments, monitor schools' progress, help schools needing improvement, pay for students to transfer and receive tutoring and place a highly qualified teacher in every classroom. Connecticut recently called its estimate of these costs "sobering." The state said that through fiscal 2008 it would have to spend $41.6 million of its own money to comply with the law.[26] Minnesota said its cost would be $42 million.[27]

Other states go even further. They say doing what's explicitly called for in the law will not be enough to bring 100 percent of students to proficiency in reading and math by 2014. In order to reach that goal, several states say they'll have to do much more. "It might involve after-school services and making sure children are well nourished," Young says. "Early-childhood education is a big one, essential to preventing the achievement gap from occurring."

Ohio commissioned a study that adopted an expanded notion of costs and included summer school, an extended school day and intensive in-school student intervention. The study calculated the annual cost of fully implementing NCLB at $1.5 billion; the additional federal funding that Ohio receives through the law, however, is only $44 million.[28]

The authors of the Ohio study acknowledged, "the task of assigning costs to the requirements of No Child Left Behind presents a formidable challenge."[29] Their assumptions, and the assumptions of other state studies, have come under attack.

A report in *Education Next*, a journal devoted to education reform, last spring accused the state studies of gross exaggeration. The authors, including the chairman of the Massachusetts Board of Education, contended that while there may be a shortage of money to evaluate schools and help those that need intervention, the gap can be filled by giving states more flexibility to shift existing federal money around. And it concludes, "No one — neither critics nor supporters of NCLB — really has any idea what it would cost to bring all students to proficiency by 2014, or even if it can be done at all."[30]

Accountability Works, a nonprofit research and consulting firm, goes a step further, concluding there is "little solid evidence that NCLB is insufficiently funded." In fact, the firm concluded some states might even have surpluses.

Echoing *Education Next*, Accountability Works said the reports claiming NCLB provides insufficient funding contain significant flaws. "Often, expenditures that are not required by NCLB are included in the calculations,"

CHRONOLOGY

1950s-1960s *A legal challenge and federal legislation initiate an era of education reform.*

1954 In *Brown v. Board of Education*, the Supreme Court decides "separate educational facilities are inherently unequal."

1958 Congress passes National Defense Education Act in response to the Soviet launch of *Sputnik*.

1965 President Lyndon B. Johnson signs Elementary and Secondary Education Act (ESEA) providing funds to school districts to help disadvantaged students.

1966 Congress amends ESEA to add Title VI, establishing grants for the education of handicapped children.

1966 Sociologist James S. Coleman's "Equality of Educational Opportunity" report concludes that disadvantaged black children learn better in well-integrated classrooms, helping to launch an era of busing students to achieve racial balance in public schools.

1968 Congress amends ESEA to add Title VII, called the Bilingual Education Act.

1970s-1980s *Studies criticize student achievement, and the standards movement gains momentum.*

1975 Coleman issues a new report concluding busing had failed, largely because it had prompted "white flight."

1980 U.S. Department of Education is established, ending education role of Department of Health, Education, and Welfare.

1983 National Commission on Excellence's "A Nation at Risk" report warns of a rising tide of mediocrity in education and recommends a common core curriculum nationwide.

1989 President George H.W. Bush convenes nation's governors in Charlottesville, Va., for first National Education Summit, which establishes six broad objectives to be reached by 2000.

1989 National Council of Teachers of Mathematics publishes *Curriculum and Evaluation Standards for School Mathematics*.

1990s-2000s *Congress requires more standards, testing and accountability from the states.*

1994 President Bill Clinton signs the Goals 2000: Educate America Act, which adopts the goals of the first National Education Summit. The act creates the National Education Standards and Improvement Council with the authority to approve or reject states' academic standards. The council, however, becomes ineffective after Republicans take control of Congress during midterm elections and object to the increasing federal role in education. . . . Clinton later signs Improving America's Schools Act of 1994, requiring significantly more testing and accountability than the original ESEA.

Jan. 8, 2002 President George W. Bush signs No Child Left Behind Act, increasing funding to states while also increasing federal mandates and sanctions to an unprecedented degree. States must increase student testing, place "highly qualified" teachers in every classroom and meet state-determined annual targets for student proficiency in reading and math. By 2014, all students must be 100 percent proficient. Title I schools not meeting annual targets must offer transfers to students and provide supplemental services, like tutoring.

April 7, 2005 Secretary of Education Margaret Spellings announces her willingness to provide some flexibility to states in meeting the requirements of No Child Left Behind.

April 19, 2005 Republican-dominated Utah legislature passes a bill giving priority to state educational goals when those conflict with No Child Left Behind and ordering officials to spend as little state money as possible to comply with the federal law.

April 20, 2005 The nation's largest teachers' union and eight school districts in Michigan, Texas and Vermont sue the Department of Education, accusing the government of violating a No Child Left Behind Act provision that states cannot be forced to spend their own money to meet the law's requirements.

Are Schools' Graduation Rates Accurate?

The No Child Left Behind Act holds schools accountable not just for student achievement but also for graduation rates. High schools must raise their graduation rates if they are to make adequate yearly progress. Increasing the percentage of graduates is a worthy goal, but it serves another purpose as well. The requirement is designed to prevent schools from improving achievement scores by encouraging their lowest-performing students to leave.

The system depends, of course, on accurate reporting. But researchers say that high school graduation rates reported by most states are just not believable.

The problem: States don't really know how many kids are dropping out of school.

States "consistently underestimate the number of dropouts, thereby overstating the graduation rates, sometimes by very large amounts," says Jay P. Greene, a senior fellow at the Manhattan Institute for Policy Research. In a recent report, Greene called some states' rates "so improbably high they would be laughable if the issue were not so serious."[1]

Although a few school districts have been accused of falsifying dropout data, researchers don't believe deception is at the root of the problem. Rather, they say the cause is more benign: Most schools don't know what happens to students who leave. Did a student transfer to another school? Move to another state? Or really drop out? Trying to answer those questions may be a secretary or clerk who often has other responsibilities as well.

"You basically have to do detective work," says Christopher Swanson, a senior research associate at The Urban Institute's Education Policy Center. "That takes time, effort and resources that may not be available to the school." Swanson says schools don't have an incentive to distinguish dropouts from transfers if it means that the graduation rates they report will be lower as a result.

Even states with sophisticated systems to track individual students over time — and there are a handful — can still report inflated graduation numbers. Texas, which reported an 84.2 percent graduation rate for its Class of 2003, counts as graduates students who have left school and either received or are working toward a General Educational Development certificate (GED).[2] No Child Left Behind prohibits the practice.

Both Swanson and Greene have developed methods for estimating how many students are actually graduating that do not rely on dropout data. Instead, they use two pieces of basic information they say are less subject to manipulation: the number of students enrolled in high school and the number of graduates. Their formulas differ, but both researchers come up with similar graduation rates that are far lower than those published by the states.

For example, South Carolina reported a high school graduation rate of 77.5 percent for the class of 2002[3]; Greene calculated the rate as 53 percent.[4] California reported a 2002 graduation rate of 87 percent; Greene put it at 67 percent. Indiana reported a graduation rate of 91 percent; Greene says it was 72 percent.

To fix the problem, Greene would like to see all states assign each student a unique identifying number for tracking their school careers, with reasonable definitions of who is a dropout and who is a graduate and an auditing program to ensure the quality of the data.

"Starbucks knows exactly what sells," Greene says. "Wal-Mart knows what inventory it has in every store. Schools have no idea."

Some states are developing such systems, but doing so will be time-consuming and costly. In the meantime, some critics of the current reporting methods want the Department of Education to require states to estimate graduation rates using methods similar to Greene's or Swanson's. "The department's role does not end with the collection of data," the Education Trust says. "It must ensure that state calculations are accurate, complete and accessible to the public."[5]

However, federal education officials believe the responsibility lies elsewhere. While the Department of Education will provide technical assistance to states as they create more sophisticated systems for tracking students, it believes that the quality of the data is the states' responsibility. "Anytime there is a problem in the states, parties are always prone to point the finger," says Deputy Assistant Secretary for Policy Darla Marburger. "And folks point the finger at the U.S. Department of Education. But it is not really a problem in our house."

---

[1] Jay P. Greene, "Public High School Graduation and College Readiness Rates: 1991-2002," Education Working Paper No. 8, Manhattan Institute for Policy Research, p. 2, February 2005.

[2] www.tea.state.tx.us/peims/standards/wedspre/index.html?r032.

[3] Education Trust, "Telling the Whole Truth (or Not) About High School Graduation," December 2003, p. 4.

[4] Greene, *op. cit.*, Table 1.

[5] Education Trust, *op. cit.*

the report said. "In other cases, such studies included expenditures that were required by prior federal law."[31]

Given the huge range of estimates and the fact that some of the repercussions of the law are just beginning to be felt, it may take years for the true costs of implementation to become clear.

But one thing is clear: State education departments are often overwhelmed. Many don't have the staff or the expertise to effectively carry out No Child Left Behind's requirements: creating data systems to monitor each school's adequate yearly progress; putting teams together to help schools in need of improvement and, as more fail, to restructure schools; and evaluating outside suppliers of tutoring services. Many states have never had to do these things, on this scale, before, and the alarm has been sounded not only by the states but also by private researchers and even the Government Accountability Office.

The Department of Education's Briggs says the federal government is helping. "We have held conferences where we have tried to bring states together to learn together."

But many states say the problem is rooted in past state budget cuts and resulting staff reductions. The extra money provided by NCLB is being used to create assessment tests or reduce class size, with little left over to hire administrative staff. That's the case in Idaho, says Allison Westfall, public information officer at the state Department of Education. "We have a very small Title I staff — we're down to five people now — who are often on the road visiting schools," she says. "So we've had to bring in people from other departments, and we're stretched really thin." And there are no plans to hire.

"This lack of capacity — not a lack of will — on the part of most states is the single, most important impediment to achieving the gains of No Child Left Behind," said Marc Tucker, president of the National Center on Education and the Economy, a research group. On average, state education departments have lost 50 percent of their employees in the past 10 years, he says, calling it "the hidden issue."[32]

BACKGROUND

Federal Reforms

On April 11, 1965, President Lyndon B. Johnson returned to the Texas school he had attended as a child to sign the nation's first comprehensive education law, the Elementary and Secondary Education Act. "As president of the United States," he declared, "I believe deeply no law I have signed or will ever sign means more to the future of America."[33]

The primary assumption in ESEA — enacted as part of Johnson's War on Poverty — was that higher-quality education would move poor students out of poverty.

With ESEA, the federal government began to address the causes of the achievement gap. In the process, the federal role in education policy — until then a strictly local affair handled by the nation's 15,000 independent school districts — expanded dramatically. ESEA's signature program, Title I, initially allocated more than $1 billion a year to school districts with high concentrations of low-income students. To administer the program, federal and state education bureaucracies grew, as did the federal and state roles in local school districts.

During the next decade, minority achievement improved marginally, but dissatisfaction with public education grew faster, as did resentment over federal infringement on local education affairs. In 1981, President Ronald Reagan took office vowing to abolish the U.S. Department of Education.

The next year, Reagan and Secretary of Education Terrell Bell appointed the National Commission on Excellence in Education to report on the quality of public education. Eighteen months later, the commission's explosive report, "A Nation at Risk," declared, "the educational foundations of our society are presently being eroded by a rising tide of mediocrity that threatens our very future as a Nation and a people."[34]

The report focused on how poorly American students compared with students from other countries; the steady decline in science scores; a drop in SAT scores; the functional illiteracy of too many minority students; and complaints from business and military leaders about the poor quality of U.S. high school graduates.

To overcome the problems, the report called for rigorous and measurable academic standards, establishment of a minimum core curriculum, lengthening of the time spent learning that curriculum and better teacher preparation.

"A Nation at Risk" marked the beginning of a movement for national standards and testing. Over the next

'These Are the Very Weakest Programs Offered'

*A*rthur E. Levine, president of Teachers College, Columbia University, led a four-year assessment of the 1,200 university programs that prepare most of the nation's school principals and administrators. Released in March 2005 by Levine's Education Schools Project, the study, "Educating School Leaders," says most university-based preparation programs for administrators range in quality from "inadequate to appalling." Levine recently discussed the report with writer Barbara Mantel.

CQ: Does No Child Left Behind make the issue of how we train school leaders more urgent?

AL: No Child Left Behind demands assessment; it demands effective curricula that will move students to achievement of standards and requires that all students achieve those standards. Principals and superintendents have to lead that transformation of the schools, which requires a very different set of skills and knowledge from their predecessors.

CQ: What is your overall characterization of university-based programs that train school administrators?

AL: The quality is very weak. These are the very weakest programs offered by America's education schools. While a relatively small proportion could be described as strong, the majority vary in quality from inadequate to appalling.

CQ: Do most principals and superintendents come through these programs?

AL: I can't give you numbers on superintendents. For principals, it is 89 percent.

CQ: In what areas do these programs fall short?

AL: First of all, the curriculum for the master's degree is irrelevant to the job of being a principal, appearing to be a random grab bag of survey courses, like Research Methods, Historical and Philosophical Foundations of Education and Educational Psychology.

CQ: Your report also talks about admission standards.

AL: The standardized test scores for students in leadership programs are among the lowest of all students at graduate schools of education, and they're among the lowest in all academe. But the larger problem is that the overwhelming majority of students in these programs are in them primarily for a bump in salaries. All 50 states give salary increases for educators who take master's degrees or graduate credits. So people want quickie programs and easy degrees. There is a race to the bottom among programs as they compete for students by dumbing down the curriculum, reducing the length of the program, cutting the number of credits required to graduate and lowering expectations of student performance.

CQ: Your report also says the degrees offered don't make sense.

decade, seven groups received federal financing to develop standards for what students should know, including the National Council of Teachers of Mathematics, the National History Standards Project and the National Standards in Foreign Language.[35]

In September 1989, President George H.W. Bush — the self-described "education president" — convened an education summit in Charlottesville, Va. Ignoring traditional Republican reluctance to actively involve Washington in education policy, Bush teamed with the president of the National Governors' Association — Democratic Gov. Bill Clinton, who had been active in education reform in his home state of Arkansas.

"The movement gained momentum with the 1989 education summit," wrote Andrew Rudalevige, an associate professor of political science at Dickinson College, in Carlyle, Pa.[36] Bush and the governors set broad performance goals for American schools to reach by the year 2000. It was hoped that all children would attend preschool, that 90 percent of all high school students would graduate, that all students would be proficient in core subjects, that U.S. students would be first in the world in science and math, that every adult would be literate and every school free of drugs and violence.

In 1994, President Clinton signed the Goals 2000: Educate America Act, which adopted the summit's ambitious

AL: Generally the master's degree is considered preparation for principalship and the doctorate for a superintendency. Why does anybody need a doctorate to be a superintendent? A doctorate is a research degree. What does that have to do with running a school system?

CQ: What are some of your key recommendations?

AL: States and school boards should eliminate salary increases based on taking degrees. Or they can give people raises based on master's degrees but require that the field be germane to their work. If you're a math teacher, I can understand giving an increase in salary for taking a degree in mathematics or advanced teaching skills. Number two: close down failing programs. States can clean this up if they want to. They are in charge of the authorization of university programs and the licensure of school administrators. But I would like to see universities try first before the states step in.

CQ: How much time would you give the universities to do this?

Arthur E. Levine, president, Teachers College, Columbia University

AL: I would give universities two years to clean up their house, and then the state has an obligation to step in if they fail to do that.

CQ: What other recommendations do you have for universities?

AL: Eliminate the current master's degree and put in its place something I've been calling a master's of educational administration, which would be a two-year degree combining education and management courses, theory and practical experience. The doctor of education degree (EdD) would be eliminated. It has no integrity and no value. The PhD in education leadership should be reserved for the very tiny group of people who wish to be scholars and researchers in the field.

CQ: And your last recommendation?

AL: There is a tendency of universities to use these programs as cash cows. They encourage these programs to produce as much revenue as possible by reducing admission standards, using adjuncts and lowering academic standards for graduation in order to get enough cash to distribute to other areas. Universities need to stop doing that.

agenda and provided federal funds to help states develop standards. The real sea change came later that year, Rudalevige wrote, when reauthorization of ESEA "signaled a nationwide commitment to standards-based reform."[37] The law required states to develop content and performance standards, tests aligned with those standards and a system to measure a school's "adequate yearly progress" in bringing all students to academic proficiency. But there was no deadline, and it took several years for the Education Department to develop the accompanying regulations and guidelines. By 1997, only 17 states were fully complying with the law, according to Krista Kafer, senior education policy analyst at the Heritage Foundation.[38]

In January 2001 former Texas Gov. George W. Bush became president, having made education a centerpiece of his campaign. Three days after his inauguration, he proposed what became the blueprint for No Child Left Behind. Its standards-and-testing strategy wasn't new, but accountability provisions were. They significantly raised the stakes for states, local districts and schools.

The proposal called for annual testing in grades 3-8, school and state report cards showing student performance by ethnic and economic subgroups, a highly qualified teacher in every classroom and sanctions for schools not showing progress in bringing students to proficiency.

Gov. Jon Huntsman, R-Utah, prepares to sign a state measure on May 2, 2005, defying the No Child Left Behind Act, aided by a Provo elementary school student. In the past year and a half, more than 30 states have introduced bills that would release them from some of the law's requirements.

Congress finally passed NCLB after nearly a year of intense debate and political horse-trading, which included the elimination of private school vouchers, increases in funding and, significantly, addition of a provision requiring that all students reach proficiency in math and reading in 12 years.

"The political compromises written into No Child Left Behind make the regulatory process crucial," said Rudalevige.[39] That's because the law grants the secretary of Education the power to grant waivers and interpret the rules and, until the bill is reauthorized, determine the flexibility states will have to meet their goals.

Achievement Gaps

Most educators say the best thing about No Child Left Behind is its focus on minorities and low-income students.

"When you say to a school that you expect every subgroup of kids to meet standards," says Delaware Education Secretary Woodruff, "that really makes schools pay closer attention to all kids." It is now possible, for instance, to track how minority and low-income students perform on state tests at each school and to calculate the achievement gaps between them and their peers. The fundamental goal of No Child Left Behind is to close these gaps while raising the achievement of all students, which has been the goal of education reforms for decades.

But to get a sense of how students have been performing historically, researchers must look to national data, because state testing is too new.

To get that information, the U.S. Department of Education has been measuring American students' achievement levels since 1969 through its National Assessment of Educational Progress (NAEP). NAEP periodically administers what it calls a "trend assessment" to a nationally representative sample of students at ages 9, 13 and 17 and breaks down the results for white, black and Hispanic students.

The data show that black and Hispanic students have made long-term gains, thus narrowing the achievement gap. From 1971 to 1999 for example, the last year for which data are available, the difference between the average reading scores of 13-year-old white and black students shrank from 39 points to 29 points. In math, the gap plummeted 14 points — from 46 points to 32 points.[40]

However, most of the reductions in the achievement gap occurred during the 1970s and 1980s, as minorities made notable gains while white students' average achievement increased slightly or not at all. Then, in the 1990s, the gap stopped shrinking; in fact, in many cases it grew. Black and Hispanic students continued making modest gains in math and Hispanic students in reading, but those improvements no longer exceeded those of whites.[41]

"When achievement goes up for all groups," the Center on Education Policy noted, "African-American and Hispanic students must improve at a faster rate than others for the gap to close."[42]

While still smaller than decades ago, the achievement gap remains quite large. For instance, the 32-point difference in math scores for black 13-year-olds and their white peers in 1999 is the equivalent of roughly three grade levels.[43]

"What, then, are the most probable explanations for the achievement gap?" asked the Center on Education Policy in a report examining minority achievement. "A complex combination of school, community and home factors appear to underlie or contribute to the gap," it answered.[44]

CURRENT SITUATION

States Push Back

Mounting state resistance to NCLB — including its level of funding and strict achievement timetables — has led to a mini-revolution in the states.

In 2004, legislatures in 31 states introduced bills challenging aspects of the law.[45] This year, so far, 21 states have either introduced or reintroduced legislation, and the numbers are likely to grow if more states decide to test Education Secretary Spellings's promise to take a "common sense" approach to enforcing the law.[46]

In Colorado, Republican state Sen. Mark Hillman proposed allowing school districts to opt out of No Child Left Behind if they forgo Title I funds; he suggested a tax increase to replace the lost federal funds. In Idaho, two Republican state senators introduced legislation demanding that predominantly rural states be exempt from the law. In Maine, Democratic state Sen. Michael Brennan sponsored a bill directing the state's attorney general to sue the federal government if federal funding is insufficient to implement No Child Left Behind.

Despite the blizzard of proposals, only three states actually passed legislation. The Republican-dominated Utah legislature passed a bill on April 19 — and the governor signed it on May 2 — allowing schools to ignore NCLB provisions that conflict with state education laws or require extra state money to implement. Spellings has warned that Utah could lose $76 million of the $107 million it receives in federal education funding.

"I don't like to be threatened," an angry state Rep. Mascaro told *The New York Times*.[47]

Raul Gonzales, legislative director at the National Council of La Raza, which advocates for Hispanic-Americans, agrees that money is tight in states still suffering from a four-year-long budget crisis.[48] "States are trying to implement this law on the cheap," Gonzales says, "because there isn't really enough money."

For example, under the law states are allowed to test English-language learners for up to three years in their native language, but most states don't have reading tests in native languages. "We're not accurately measuring what kids can do because we're using the wrong tests," he says.

Perry Zirkel, a professor of education and law at Lehigh University, in Bethlehem, Pa., says the states' resistance to the law is still mostly "sparks, not fire." He points out that New Mexico, Virginia and Utah are the only states to pass legislation.

"Despite all the talk," Zirkel says, "I don't think there has been sufficient momentum to convince the majority of the public that No Child Left Behind is, on a net basis, a bad law."

Moreover, a coalition of Hispanic, African-American and other educators have voiced concerns that the Utah legislature's effort to sidestep provisions of the federal law might allow minority students to fall through the cracks.[49]

Teachers' Union Sues

One day after the Utah legislature made its move, the NEA and eight school districts in Michigan, Texas and Vermont sued the Department of Education, contending it is violating an NCLB provision that says states cannot be forced to use their own money to implement the law:

"Nothing in this Act shall be construed to authorize an officer or employee of the Federal Government to mandate, direct, or control a State, local education agency, or school's curriculum, program of instruction, or allocation of State or local resources, or mandate a State or any subdivision thereof to spend any funds or incur any costs not paid for under this Act."

"We don't disagree when the Department of Education says federal funding has increased," explains NEA spokesman Dan Kaufman. "We just don't believe that the funding has been enough for the types of really strict, comprehensive things that it requires states to do." The teachers' union would like to see Congress appropriate the full amount it authorized when passing the bill. So far, it is $27 billion short.

"We . . . look forward to the day when the NEA will join us in helping children who need our help the most in classrooms, instead of spending its time and members' money in courtrooms," the Department of Education said in response.[50]

The lawsuit was filed in the U.S. District Court for the Eastern District of Michigan, which has jurisdiction over one of the school districts joining the suit. The suit asks the court to declare that states and school districts

AT ISSUE

Should annual testing be extended to high school?

YES   Bob Wise
President, Alliance for
Excellent Education

Written for *The CQ Researcher*, May 5, 2005

Achieving the national goal of building a better educated, more competitive work force for the 21st century requires effective tools. With two-thirds of high school students either dropping out or graduating unprepared for college, the majority of our nation's young people need more support than they are currently getting from their secondary schools and teachers. An increased number of required tests at the high school level could help to leverage the academic assistance many students require, if those tests are designed and implemented appropriately.

Last fall, President Bush set off a major debate when he proposed extending the reading and math tests required by the No Child Left Behind Act for third- through eighth-graders and in one year of high school to students in grades nine, ten and eleven. "We need to be sure that high school students are learning every year," he said.

At the Alliance for Excellent Education, we believe all children deserve an excellent education that prepares them for the economic and social challenges that follow high school. And we agree with the president that our schools must be held accountable for providing that high-quality education. Testing students during their high school years has the potential to provide needed data about their progress — as a whole, and by gender, race and ethnicity — and could allow us to better measure the effectiveness of the schools supposed to be preparing all of our young people to become productive members of American society.

But tests should help schools understand and address the needs of their students. If we are going to hold schools accountable for their students' ability to perform at high academic levels, we must also give them the resources necessary to provide the additional, targeted instruction that many teens need to become proficient in reading, writing, math and other subjects.

To be taken seriously by students, tests need to be relevant. High school tests should be aligned to the expectations of colleges and employers and provide both educators and students with a gauge to measure progress toward a successful transition to postsecondary education, technical training or rewarding jobs.

Finally, the federal government should fully cover the cost of designing and administering the exams, thus ensuring that states can adequately and effectively implement the tests they are required to give.

Tests alone won't make a difference. But as a part of a toolkit designed to improve the nation's graduation and college-readiness rates, they are worthy of our consideration.

NO   Paul Houston
Executive Director, American
Association of School Administrators

Written for *The CQ Researcher*, April 27, 2005

High school reform should not focus on a test but rather on what is being learned. I recently visited the Olathe, Kan., school district to learn more about a series of programs called 21st Century Schools, which have been implemented in all the high schools. These are "vocational" schools. In other words, they are focused on the future work life of students, and the programs are very rigorous and produce great results. But more important, the programs are meaningful, engaging and hands on, using the students' motivation to create a vehicle for excellence.

As I walked through Olathe Northwest High School, I saw students and teachers engaged in hard work. In one classroom, they were constructing a "battlebot," a robot that is used in gaming to battle other robots — with the last one running being the winner. The students were looking forward to taking their creation to a national competition later this year. While this sounds fun (some may say "frivolous"), what is really happening is that students are experiencing deep learning about metallurgy, structures, engines, insulation and a hundred other things I didn't understand. They were excited and knowledgeable about what they were doing — and about how much fun they were having with the learning process.

There were about a dozen students who stayed after the bell to talk with me, and every one of them plans to attend college and study engineering. There is no shortage of engineering candidates in Olathe. I asked them why they liked what they were doing, and the answer was simple. One told me he got to use what he was learning in class. "Telling me that calculus is good for me isn't very meaningful," he said. "Now I see how I can use it."

I would suggest to those who want to reform high schools that the place to start is in places like Olathe, where the school district has figured out that the best way to get students to learn more is to give them engaging, imaginative work that creates meaning for them. And we must give schools adequate resources to provide state-of-the-art opportunities for students to receive hands-on learning.

Those who are interested in reform should focus on getting schools the resources they need to do the job and then challenging them to make schools interesting and engaging places. Reform will not be achieved by mandating more testing. Education has always been about the whole child, and unless we take that into consideration, the current effort to reform high schools will be just as unsuccessful as the others that preceded it.

do not have to spend their own funds to comply with NCLB and that failure to comply for that reason will not result in a cutoff of federal education funds.

Some legal experts say that, regardless of its merits, the lawsuit could be dismissed on procedural grounds. First of all, the teachers' union may not have the legal standing to bring suit because it doesn't have a direct stake in the outcome, even though its members do. The experts also say the court could rule that the lawsuit is premature, and that NCLB does not specify that there is a right to sue.

Moreover, several legal experts said, courts typically don't want to take on messy political debates. Just deciding the facts and determining the costs of No Child Left Behind would be extremely complex.

"The courts' view is that if you have problems with this law, then go lobby Congress to change it," Lehigh's Zirkel says. In fact, the lawsuit may actually be an indirect way to lobby Congress, he adds, and it may be more effective because it's more public.

War of Words

Zirkel says Connecticut's threat to sue may also be an indirect attempt at lobbying Congress. In early April, Connecticut Attorney General Richard Blumenthal announced he would sue the Department of Education on grounds that the federal government's approach to the law is "illegal and unconstitutional."[51] Connecticut's argument is essentially the same as the teachers' union's, but the state — which has a direct stake in the outcome — has better legal standing, Zirkel says. Blumenthal has estimated the annual testing required by the law would create an additional financial burden for the state, which now tests students every other year.

While a few school districts have sued the government over the law, Connecticut would be the first state to do so, but as of May 25, Blumenthal had yet to act.

Meanwhile, the state's dispute with the Education Department has become very public. "We've got better things to spend our money on," Connecticut Education Commissioner Sternberg said in explaining her opposition to annual testing. "We won't learn anything new about our schools by giving these extra tests."[52]

But Secretary Spellings clearly will not compromise on annual testing, consistently calling it one of the "bright lines" of NCLB. She and Sternberg have been having a war of words, with Spellings calling the law's opponents "un-American" and Sternberg demanding an apology.

Spellings also has accused Connecticut of tolerating one of the nation's largest achievement gaps between white and black students. Sternberg has said the huge gap was due to the extraordinary performance of white students in Connecticut's affluent suburbs.

The two finally met in mid-April, but the meeting was inconclusive.

OUTLOOK

Reform Unlikely?

If the NEA's lawsuit and Connecticut's threat to sue are indirect ways of lobbying Congress, their timing may be off.

Jeffrey Henig, a professor of political science and education at Columbia University's Teachers College, says some constituents in prosperous suburban school districts are beginning to grumble as well-regarded schools fail to make "adequate yearly progress" because one or two subgroups of students miss proficiency targets.

"But I don't think it has really gelled into clear, focused pressure on Congress to reform the law," Henig says, adding that the situation could change if more schools fall into that category.

But lawmakers are extremely reluctant to revisit the law before it comes up for reauthorization in 2007, Henig says. Moderate Democrats are committed to the law's focus on raising achievement levels for minority, low-income and disabled students, he says, and they fear that any reworking could result in easing the pressure on states to shrink the achievement gap. And a core group of Republicans is committed to the law's tough accountability provisions. Both groups, Henig says, would prefer "to hold to the legislation and to placate any dissatisfied groups through the regulatory process."

The Department of Education has already amended the law's regulations, guidelines and enforcement. For instance, in 2003 and 2004 it allowed English-language learners to be tested in native languages for their first three years, gave rural districts more time to place highly qualified teachers in classrooms and allowed some flexibility on testing participation rates.

In April, Spellings — then in her new job as secretary for just three months — told states they could apply to test a greater portion of disabled students using alternative assessments. In addition, Spellings said she would grant states flexibility in other areas if they could show they were making real progress in closing achievement gaps and meeting proficiency targets.

But Young of the National Conference of State Legislatures says states are trying to decipher what she means. "There is no indication of what that flexibility would include," he says, "and there is no indication of how states would be judged by these indicators."

So far, Spellings is holding firm on annual testing, but she did grant North Dakota a waiver temporarily allowing new elementary school teachers to be rated highly qualified without taking a state test.

"The Department of Education is really feeling the heat and is trying to compromise," says educational consultant Scott Joftus, former policy director at the Alliance for Excellent Education.

The department also has allowed some states to lower the cutoff point for proficiency on their student assessment tests and to use averaging and other statistical methods to make it easier for schools to make adequate yearly progress. Young calls it gaming the system and expects it to continue unless Congress reforms No Child Left Behind.

In 2007, when the law comes up for reauthorization, Congress could negotiate changes, but the process could take years. Last time, it took two-and-a-half extra years.

NOTES

1. Dana Milbank, "With Fanfare, Bush Signs Education Bill," *The Washington Post*, Jan. 9, 2002.

2. Northwest Evaluation Association, "The Impact of the No Child Left Behind Act on Student Achievement and Growth: 2005 Edition," April 2005, p. 2.

3. http://kennedy.senate.gov/index_high.html.

4. Sam Dillon, "Utah Vote Rejects Parts of U.S. Education Law," *The New York Times*, April 20, 2005.

5. "Governor worried about costs of Bush education reform law," The Associated Press State & Local Wire, April 26, 2005.

6. http://gregg.senate.gov/forms/myths.pdf.

7. www.ed.gov/nclb/overview/intro/guide/guide_pg11.html#spending.

8. National Public Radio, "Talk of the Nation," May 3, 2005.

9. Center on Education Policy, "From the Capital to the Classroom: Year 3 of the No Child Left Behind Act," March 2005, p. v.

10. *Ibid.*, p. 4.

11. *Ibid.*, p. 1.

12. Council of the Great City Schools, "Beating the Odds: A City-By-City Analysis of Student Performance and Achievement Gaps on State Assessments," March 2004, pp. iv-vi.

13. The Education Trust, "Stalled in Secondary: A Look at Student Achievement Since the No Child Left Behind Act," January 2005, p. 1.

14. University of Delaware Education Research and Development Center, "Awareness To Action Revisited: Tracking the Achievement Gap in Delaware Schools, State of Delaware Report," March 2005, p. 2.

15. www.dpi.state.wi.us/dpi/esea/pdf/wiaw.pdf.

16. National Conference of State Legislatures, "Task Force on No Child Left Behind: Final Report," February 2005, p. vii.

17. http://edcounts.edweek.org.

18. Center for the Study of Evaluation, "Test-based Educational Accountability in the Era of No Child Left Behind," April 2005, p. 19.

19. *Ibid.*, p. 14.

20. Susan Saulny, "U.S. Provides Rules to States for Testing Special Pupils," *The New York Times*, May 11, 2005, p. A17.

21. The data are from 2000, the most recent available. See The Education Trust, "All Talk, No Action: Putting an End to Out-of-Field Teaching," August 2002, p. 4.

22. Education Week Research Center, "Quality Counts 2005," January 2005, p. 92. www.edweek.org/rc/index.html.

23. National Council on Teacher Quality, "Searching the Attic," December 2004, p. 12.

24. Southeast Center for Teaching Quality, "Unfulfilled Promise: Ensuring High Quality Teachers for Our Nation's Students," August 2004, pp. 8-9.

25. Augenblick, Palaich and Associates, Inc. "Costing Out No Child Left Behind: A Nationwide Survey of Costing Efforts," April 2004, p. 1.

26. Connecticut State Department of Education, "Cost of Implementing the Federal No Child Left Behind Act in Connecticut," March 2, 2005, p. iii.

27. Center on Education Policy, *op. cit.*

28. Ohio Department of Education, "Projected Costs of Implementing The Federal 'No Child Left Behind Act' in Ohio," December 2003, p. vi.

29. *Ibid.*

30. James Peyser and Robert Castrell, "Exploring the Costs of Accountability," *Education Next,* spring 2004, p. 24.

31. Accountability Works, "NCLB Under a Microscope," January 2004, p. 2.

32. Joetta L. Sack, "State Agencies Juggle NCLB Work, Staffing Woes," *Education Week,* May 11, 2005, p. 25.

33. www.lbjlib.utexas.edu/johnson/archives.hom/speeches.hom/650411.asp.

34. www.ed.gov/pubs/NatAtRisk/risk.html.

35. For background, see Kathy Koch, "National Education Standards," *The CQ Researcher,* May 14, 1999, pp. 401-424, and Charles S. Clark, "Education Standards," *The CQ Researcher,* March 11, 1994, pp. 217-240.

36. www.educationnext.org/20034/62.html.

37. *Ibid.*

38. Heritage Foundation, "No Child Left Behind: Where Do We Go From Here?" 2004, p. 2.

39. www.educationnext.org/20034/62.html.

40. National Center for Education Statistics, "Trends in Academic Progress: Three Decades of Student Performance," 2000, p. 39.

41. *Ibid.,* p. 33.

42. Center on Education Policy, "It takes more than testing: Closing the Achievement Gap," 2001, p. 2.

43. *Ibid.,* p. 1.

44. *Ibid.,* p. 3.

45. National Conference of State Legislatures, "No Child Left Behind Quick Facts: 2005," April 2005.

46. www.nea.org/lawsuit/stateres.html.

47. Dillon, *op. cit.*

48. For background, see William Triplett, "State Budget Crisis," *The CQ Researcher,* Oct. 3, 2003, pp. 821-844.

49. Dillon, *op. cit.*

50. U.S. Department of Education, "Statement by Press Secretary on NEA's Action Regarding NCLB," April 20, 2005, p. B1.

51. Sam Dillon, "Connecticut to Sue U.S. Over Cost of School Testing Law, *The New York Times,* April 6, 2005.

52. Michael Dobbs, "Conn. Stands in Defiance on Enforcing 'No Child'," *The Washington Post,* May 8, 2005, p. A10.

BIBLIOGRAPHY

Books

Meier, Deborah, and George Wood, eds., *Many Children Left Behind: How the No Child Left Behind Act Is Damaging Our Children and Our Schools,* Beacon Press, 2004.
Meier, the founder of several New York City public schools, and Wood, a high school principal and the founder of The Forum for Education and Democracy, and other authors argue that the law is harming the ability of schools to serve poor and minority children.

Peterson, Paul E., and Martin R. West, eds., *No Child Left Behind: The Politics and Practice of School Accountability, Brookings Institution Press,* 2003.
Peterson, director of the Program on Education Policy and Governance at Harvard, and West, a research fellow in the program, have collected essays that examine the forces that gave shape to the law and its likely consequences.

Rakoczy, Kenneth Leo, *No Child Left Behind: No Parent Left in the Dark, Edu-Smart.com Publishing,* 2003.

A veteran public school teacher offers this guide to parents for becoming involved in their children's education and making the most out of parent-teacher conferences in light of the new law.

Wright, Peter W. D., Pamela Darr Wright and Suzanne Whitney Heath, *Wrightslaw: No Child Left Behind,* *Harbor House Law Press,* **2003.**
The authors, who run a Web site about educational law and advocacy, explain the No Child Left Behind Act for parents and teachers.

Articles

Dillon, Sam, "New Secretary Showing Flexibility on 'No Child' Law," *The New York Times,* **Feb. 14, 2005, p. A18.**
Education Secretary Margaret Spellings has shown a willingness to work with state and local officials on No Child Left Behind, saying school districts need not always allow students in low-performing schools to transfer to better ones if it caused overcrowding.

Friel, Brian, "A Test for Tutoring," *The National Journal,* **April 16, 2005.**
Friel examines the controversy surrounding some of the outside tutoring firms providing supplemental services to students under provisions of No Child Left Behind.

Hendrie, Caroline, "NCLB Cases Face Hurdles in the Courts," *Education Week,* **May 4, 2005.**
Hendrie describes the hurdles facing the National Education Association's lawsuit against the Department of Education.

Ripley, Amanda, and Sonja Steptoe, "Inside the Revolt Over Bush's School Rules," *Time,* **May 9, 2005.**
The authors examine efforts by states to seek release from aspects of No Child Left Behind and the teachers' union's lawsuit against the federal government.

Tucker, Marc S., and Thomas Toch, "Hire Ed: the secret to making Bush's school reform law work?

More bureaucrats," *Washington Monthly,* **March 1, 2004.**
The authors discuss staffing shortages at state departments of education that are slowing implementation of No Child Left Behind.

Reports and Studies

Center on Education Policy, From the Capital to the Classroom: Year 3 of the No Child Left Behind Act, **March 2005.**
The center examines the implementation of No Child Left Behind at the federal, state and local levels and points out positive and negative signs for the future.

Citizens' Commission on Civil Rights, Choosing Better Schools: A Report on Student Transfers Under the No Child Left Behind Act, **May 2004.**
The commission describes the early efforts to implement the school-choice provision of No Child Left Behind, calling compliance minimal.

National Conference of State Legislatures, Task Force on No Child Left Behind: Final Report, **February 2005.**
The panel questions the constitutionality of No Child Left Behind and calls it rigid, overly prescriptive and in need of serious revision.

Northwest Evaluation Association, The Impact of No Child Left Behind Act on Student Achievement and Growth: 2005 Edition, **April 2005.**
The association reports the percentage of proficient students is rising on state tests but also notes the disparity between the achievement growth of white and minority students.

Southeast Center for Teaching Quality, Unfulfilled Promise: Ensuring High Quality Teachers for Our Nation's Students, **August 2004.**
The center finds that rural and urban schools don't have the skills and training to recruit and retain highly qualified teachers and offers recommendations for change.

For More Information

Achieve, Inc., 1775 I St., N.W., Washington, DC 20006, (202) 419-1540; www.achieve.org. A bipartisan, nonprofit organization created by the nation's governors and business leaders that helps states improve academic performance.

Alliance for Excellent Education, 1201 Connecticut Ave., N.W., Suite 901, Washington, DC; (202) 828-0828; www .all4ed.org. Works to assure that at-risk middle and high school students graduate prepared for college and success in life.

Center on Education Policy, 1001 Connecticut Ave., N.W., Washington, DC 20036; (202) 822-8065; www .cep-dc.org. Helps Americans understand the role of public education in a democracy and the need to improve academic quality.

Council of the Great City Schools, 1301 Pennsylvania Ave., N.W., Suite 702, Washington, DC 20004; (202) 393-2427; www.cgcs.org. A coalition of 65 of the nation's largest urban public school systems advocating improved K–12 education.

Editorial Projects in Education, 6935 Arlington Rd., Suite 100, Bethesda, MD 20814; www.edweek.org. A nonprofit organization that publishes *Education Week, Teacher Magazine,* edweek.org and *Agent K–12.*

Education Commission of the States, 700 Broadway, Suite 1200, Denver, CO 80203; (303) 299-3600; www .ces.org. Studies current and emerging education issues.

The Education Trust, 1250 H St., N.W., Washington, DC 20005; (202) 293-1217; www2.edtrust.org/edtrust. An independent nonprofit organization working to improve the academic achievement of all students.

National Conference of State Legislatures, 7700 East First Pl., Denver, CO 80230; www.ncsl.org. A bipartisan organization serving the states and territories.

Northwest Evaluation Center, 5885 Southwest Meadows Rd., Suite 200, Lake Oswego, OR 97035; (503) 624-1951; www.nwea.org. A national nonprofit organization dedicated to helping all children learn.

Southeast Center for Teaching Quality, 976 Airport Rd., Suite 250, Chapel Hill, NC 27514; (919) 951-0200; www.teachingquality.org. A regional association dedicated to assuring all children have access to high-quality education.

U.S. Department of Education, No Child Left Behind Web site, www.ed.gov/nclb/landing.jhtml?src=pb. Describes the provisions of the No Child Left Behind law.

Wrightslaw, www.wrightslaw.com. Provides information about effective advocacy for children with disabilities, including "Wrightslaw: No Child Left Behind."

3

Special Education

*Do Students With Disabilities
Get the Help They Need?*

Kathy Koch

Alex Wright, 3, who suffers from cerebral palsy, rides a Go-Bot to play "Ring Around the Rosie" at the University of California-Stanford University Health Care Rehabilitation Technology and Therapy Center in Palo Alto, Calif.

KRT Photos/Anna Marie Dos Remedios

From *CQ Researcher*,
November 10, 2000.

Rose, a bright-eyed fifth-grader living in a small Pacific Northwest town, is a high-achiever who wants to go to college and have a career. She was elected class secretary and has served on the student council.

But she is not your typical pony-tailed youngster. Rose has cerebral palsy. She cannot walk unassisted and has limited use of her hands. She uses a motorized wheelchair and special word-prediction software on her computer that helps her complete written assignments.

The software was developed with funds from the Individuals with Disabilities Education Act (IDEA), enacted 25 years ago to help local schools pay for the special equipment, instructors and services that students with disabilities need to attend public school.

Before IDEA was enacted, about 1.7 million handicapped children like Rose were denied access to public schools. Another 2.5 million were relegated to institutions largely offering substandard educations.

But passage of the law has enabled millions of disabled youngsters to be educated at public expense, either in regular classrooms or in special settings at public or private schools serving the disabled. Today, 6.3 million students between ages 3 and 21 — with disabilities ranging from stuttering to attention deficit disorder to severe emotional disturbance — receive free public educations.

By nearly all accounts, the law has been highly successful at educating children once turned away at the schoolhouse door as "untrainable" or because their wheelchairs were considered a fire hazard.

State Programs Are Underfunded

The centerpiece of the Individuals with Disabilities Education Act (IDEA) is the grant program for states. Appropriations for the states more than doubled from 1996 to 2000. But the annual funding during that period was at least $10 billion below the amount needed to fully fund the program.

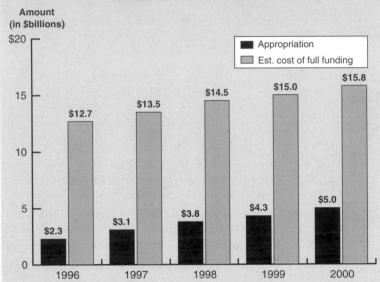

IDEA Funding for States
Recent Appropriations vs. Cost of Full Funding

Amount (in $billions)

Legend:
- ■ Appropriation
- ▨ Est. cost of full funding

Year	Appropriation	Est. cost of full funding
1996	$2.3	$12.7
1997	$3.1	$13.5
1998	$3.8	$14.5
1999	$4.3	$15.0
2000	$5.0	$15.8

Source: Congressional Research Service, CRS Report for Congress, Richard N. Apling, "Individuals with Disabilities Education Act: Full Funding of State Formula," Dec. 28, 1999.

"It's been a true success story," says Diane Shust, manager of federal relations for the National Education Association (NEA). More disabled children have access to the classroom and are graduating from high school and attending college than at any time in history, she points out. "We do this better than any other country in the world."

And since the law was changed in the 1990s to require schools, whenever possible, to integrate disabled students into regular classrooms, more disabled students than ever are being taught the same academic curricula as mainstream students. Before, they were often segregated in separate rooms and taught a less challenging curriculum.

During all these changes, teachers have learned a great deal about how to help students with disabilities learn better.

"Today we have a whole cadre of professionals who have dedicated their professional lives to providing better educational services for disabled youngsters," says Bruce Hunter, director of public policy for the American Association of School Administrators (AASA).

Congress passed the law, originally called the Education for All Handicapped Children Act, in 1975 at the request of state governments. The states sought the law because they were having trouble complying with court orders to provide a "free and appropriate education" to all children — regardless of their handicaps or the cost. Renamed the IDEA in 1990, the law provides federal grants to states to help local school boards pay for the extra services needed by disabled students.

Despite the success of integrating millions of disabled students into the public schools, educators say many problems still remain in the program, including:

- A dropout rate for disabled students twice that of regular students.
- Inequities in services received by disabled children from low-income, minority or rural areas compared with children of middle-class parents.
- Students in overcrowded classrooms being diagnosed as learning-disabled just because they haven't been taught to read properly and need remedial help.
- Relegating children with behavior problems to special-ed classes — misbehavior often caused by an inability to read — with slowed-down curricula taught by often unqualified teachers.
- Putting low-achievers in special-ed classes in order to boost a school's overall test scores, since some states don't count special-ed students' standardized test scores in the same pool as general-ed students.
- Diagnosing students' learning disabilities belatedly, when they are too far behind to ever catch up to their peers.

- Chronic shortages of qualified special-ed teachers, a job that requires extra time and paperwork sometimes without additional pay.
- Underfunding by local, state and federal governments, causing constant short supplies of aides, materials and other special services required by law.

In addition, according to a recent National Council on Disability (NCD) report, many states have simply ignored the IDEA. The report found "widespread and persistent" non-compliance. "Enforcement is too often the burden of parents who must invoke formal complaint procedures and request due process hearings to obtain the services and supports their children are entitled to under law," the NCD said.[1]

The report could have been referring to the recent class-action suit filed by parents of disabled minority children in East Palo Alto, one of California's poorest school districts. The judge in the case called the lack of special-ed services "appalling and disturbing." In an unprecedented settlement announced last January, the school district agreed to completely revamp its special-ed system.

"What has disturbed me since I've been in this office is that in many cases the state and local education authorities are not taking responsibility for these children," Judith E. Heumann, assistant secretary for special education and rehabilitative services at the Department of Health and Human Services, told lawmakers recently. "Instead, the parents [who seek services for their children] are being identified as problem parents."[2]

"The one constant factor throughout two and a half decades is that federal [enforcement] efforts over several administrations have been inconsistent and lacking any real teeth," said Lilliam Rangel-Diaz, an NCD board member. "There have been no consequences for states that have disregarded the law and devastating

Educating Students With Disabilities

More than 95 percent of the 5.7 million U.S. students with disabilities ages 6-21 were served in regular school buildings in 1996-97. Of the remaining students, about 3 percent attended separate public or private day schools and 2 percent were served in either residential facilities or homebound/hospital environments.

Learning Environment	Number of students	Percentage
Regular Class	2.65 million	46.2
Resource Room	1.53 million	26.7
Separate Class	1.29 million	22.4
Public Separate School Facility	129,578	2.3
Private Separate School Facility	61,260	1.1
Public Residential Facility	22,479	0.4
Private Residential Facility	14,828	0.3
Homebound/Hospital Placement	38,526	0.7
Total Children	**5.7 million**	**100%**

* Percentages do not add up to 100 due to rounding.

Source: U.S. Department of Education, "Twenty-first Annual Report to Congress on the Implementation of the Individuals with Disabilities Education Act," 1999

consequences for the students with disabilities and their families who have been denied the protections of the law."

Paul Marchand, chairman of the Consortium for Citizens with Disabilities, a coalition of 100 organizations representing the disabled, says, "Some school systems are doing a superior, superior job educating disabled students, and others are resisting all the way. And there is a pile of schools that fall in between those extremes."

For instance, he says, "A significant portion of our schools is still inaccessible to children in wheelchairs or on crutches because they don't have elevators or ramps."

But while some parents of disabled students say their children's needs are being ignored, school administrators complain the law is cumbersome and restricts their ability to run schools efficiently.

The IDEA has also turned out to be far more expensive than anyone ever imagined. As special-ed enrollments have skyrocketed, so has the court-ordered list of services schools must provide for disabled students. For instance, the Supreme Court recently ruled that schools must pay for any medical services — except those provided by a medical doctor — needed for a disabled child to attend school. "We now have kids coming to classes in ambulances," says the NEA's Shust.

"Some of these high-cost kids can quickly bankrupt a small town's school district," she says, citing a rural Maine school district that offered to relocate the family of one high-cost disabled student to a larger nearby school district. "It would have been cheaper for them to relocate the family than provide them with appropriate services," she says.

The Education Department estimates that local, state and federal governments spend $51 billion for special education. The federal government provides $5 billion of that.

Because local and state funding has not kept pace with the increased costs of educating disabled students, schools often have borrowed money from general education funds, creating friction between the parents of disabled and non-disabled students.

As special education eats up an ever-increasing portion of the state and local education money pie, the price tag threatens to spiral even higher. In California, for instance, where diagnoses of autism have jumped significantly in the past decade, the number of school-age children requiring special education jumped 54 percent from 1986 to 1998.

The IDEA's authorization expires in 2002, and the newly elected Congress will be revisiting the law in the coming months.

As lawmakers, educators and parents consider the law's future, these are among the questions they will be asking:

Should the federal government spend more to educate disabled students?

Under IDEA, Congress provides states with grants to help defray some of the cost of educating special-ed students. The law says that for each disabled child, the grants may total up to 40 percent of the average amount schools spend to educate a student.

But even at the 40 percent level, the grants would only provide around 20 percent of the actual cost of educating a special-ed student, because such children cost twice as much as regular students to educate.

However, Congress has never funded IDEA at the 40 percent rate. "The federal government gets an 'F' in arithmetic in this instance," Sen. Gordon H. Smith, R-Ore., told the Senate on Sept. 26.[3] In fact, the current federal share of 12.6 percent is the highest it's ever been. The last time it was anywhere near this high was in 1979, when the federal share reached 12.5 percent, according to Education Department statistics.

"The underfunding of special education by both federal and state governments has really hurt local education programs," says the AASA's Hunter. After the law was passed, he says, local school districts "almost overnight had to absorb costs equal to about 20 percent of their local budgets."

"Congress needs to ensure that the federal government lives up to the promise it made to students, parents and schools over two decades ago," said Rep. Bill Goodling, R-Pa., chairman of the House Education Committee. (See "At Issue," p. 65.) In fact, if the federal government would fully fund IDEA, he insists, school districts would have the local funds necessary to build new schools, hire new teachers, reduce class size and buy more computers — the biggest items on the Clinton administration's education wish list.[4]

Congressional authorizers have long favored higher funding for IDEA, but appropriators balk, citing the law's budget-busting potential. The Congressional Research Service (CRS) estimates that at today's enrollment rates, it would cost an additional $15.8 billion per year — three times more than the current $5 billion appropriation — to fund IDEA at the 40 percent level.[5]

Nonetheless, last May 3 the House voted 431-3 to bring the federal share up to the 40 percent level over the next 10 years by increasing IDEA funding by $2 billion a year. A Senate committee followed suit on Sept. 20.[6] But those votes were largely symbolic, because congressional appropriators have proposed only raising IDEA funding for one year — 2001 — by $1.6 billion.

Congressional Republicans are quick to point out, however, that current record-high IDEA appropriations follow four years of major IDEA increases, in which funding jumped $2.6 billion, and the federal share increased from 5 percent to 12.6 percent.

"Republicans have done a much better job of making special education a high priority," points out House Education Appropriations Subcommittee Chairman John E. Porter, R-Ill.

But even Porter, who says he favors full funding of IDEA, notes that providing the full 40 percent "would take massive amounts of money — and it can't be done overnight."

Others insist the 40 percent formula was only an upward ceiling or goal, not an obligation, a point brought out during floor debate on the original bill.

In fact, both Republicans and Democrats historically have had serious doubts about the law's potentially exorbitant price tag. Maine Democrat Edmund Muskie, then-chairman of the Senate Budget Committee, said during the 1975 floor debate on the bill, "We need to understand clearly that large out-year authorizations, such as those included in this bill, do not mean that we will necessarily spend at those levels."[7]

And Republican President Gerald Ford complained when he reluctantly signed the bill into law that the sponsors were "falsely raising the expectations" of advocates for the disabled by recommending "excessive and unrealistic" authorization levels.[8]

Such expectations indeed seem to have been raised. For decades, school officials have complained bitterly that because the federal government has not lived up to its "promise," school districts have had to either raise local property taxes or spend increasing amounts of general education funds to educate the ever-burgeoning ranks of special-needs children.

In fact, a 1997 study by the Economic Policy Institute (EPI) found that over the last 30 years, instead of increasing overall education spending, school districts apparently shifted money earmarked for regular students to programs for the disabled. Between 1967 and 1991, the share of total school spending going to regular education dropped from 80.1 percent to 58.5 percent, while the share going to special education rose from 3.6 percent to 17.8 percent, the EPI found.[9]

Hunter says as a result, the needs of regular-ed students have been pitted against the needs of special-ed students. "Do you add an AP-English course that will help 25 kids go on to college," he asks, "or do you use that money to provide services for three disabled kids, who may or may not even graduate?"

If the federal government fully funded IDEA, it would reduce such "resource competition," quieting some of the special-ed backlash that results, says Marchand of the Consortium for Citizens with Disabilities. "Washington has created an inappropriate and unfair conflict between children with disabilities and children without," said Sen. Smith.

Marchand and others call the 40 percent formula an unfunded federal mandate. "Congress doesn't mind mandating the responsibility, but they sure do mind mandating the appropriations," says Dan Fuller, director of federal programs for the National School Boards Association (NSBA).

But others say the IDEA is a voluntary grant program, created at the request of state officials who were finding it prohibitively expensive to provide court-ordered education for all disabled children. "It's not a federal mandate, because states don't have to abide by the IDEA unless they seek the federal grants," says a congressional staffer. Besides, he adds, educating children is the responsibility of state and local governments, and the resource competition problem could be avoided if they would increase overall education spending, rather than diverting general-ed funds to pay for special education.

Yet Republicans say that if the federal government would fully fund IDEA, local school districts could afford Clinton administration education priorities, like smaller classes, more teachers and school construction. They have tried unsuccessfully to redirect funds from Clinton pet projects into special education. But Democrats have argued that Congress should fund both special-ed and administration priorities.

"We should not rob Peter to pay Paul [without] changing the bottom line," said Rep. Robert C. Scott, D-Va.[10]

However, Wendy Burns, an advocate for the Disability Rights Education and Defense Fund (DREDF) in Berkeley, Calif., cautions against getting full 40 percent funding too quickly. "A lot of states lack the infrastructure to properly administer that amount of IDEA dollars and provide training and oversight," she says. "It would overwhelm the system if Congress approved it tomorrow."

Others fear that a huge increase in funds for special education will further increase the resentment toward general-education parents, possibly causing an even greater backlash.

Rooting Out Cheaters While Ensuring Fairness

Educators and testers must perform a tricky balancing act when it comes to testing students with disabilities. They must decide what kind of special accommodations the students should receive and how challenging the tests should be — without being unfair to the non-disabled students taking the same tests.

But educators also must root out cheaters — students who claim non-existent learning disabilities in order to get an unfair advantage or schools that exempt students with disabilities from taking standardized tests.

Before the Individuals with Disabilities Education Act (IDEA) was overhauled in 1997, disabled students were routinely exempted from statewide achievement tests. Because faculty raises and school funding are often tied to test results, some high-scoring schools were caught wrongly classifying low-achievers as exempt special-ed students so they would not drag down overall school scores. Now the law requires that all disabled students, to the extent possible, be assessed along with the general student body.

Currently, some states are giving disabled students the regular statewide achievement tests, sometimes with special accommodations and sometime without. A blind student, for instance, may be allowed to have a test read to him or provided in Braille, or a dyslexic student may get time and a half.

New York has dramatically increased participation rates of special-ed students on its Regents' exam, with "phenomenal results," says Bill East, executive director of the National Association of State Directors of Special Education. "There's a lot of hope that students with disabilities will perform much better than we ever dreamed they could."

Some states are struggling to create alternative tests for disabled students who cannot take the statewide tests, even with accommodations. Others are considering giving them tests designed for students in a lower grade level.

"Probably a substantial part of the current special-ed population should be required to take some reasonable version of the state tests," says Chester E. Finn Jr., president of the Thomas B. Fordham Foundation, a conservative education think tank. "But for a smaller fraction, such as the profoundly retarded, it makes no sense."

Meanwhile, critics say a small percentage of affluent parents of non-disabled kids realize that getting extra time on the college entrance exams can increase scores by as much as 100 points. So some parents are trying to get their children diagnosed as "learning disabled," one of the most nebulous disability categories under IDEA and one that now makes up more than half of all disabilities claimed under the act.

A diagnosis of learning disability can include, among other things, such "invisible" disabilities as attention deficit hyperactivity disorder (ADHD), which some say is greatly overdiagnosed. The controversial condition is characterized by inattentiveness, impulsivity and hyperactivity.

A *Los Angeles Times* investigation found that the number of students receiving extra time to complete the Scholastic Aptitude Test (SAT) due to a learning disability jumped more than 50 percent in recent years, with most of the growth coming from exclusive private schools and public schools in mostly affluent, white suburbs along the Boston-New York-Washington corridor.[1]

The paper calculated that while only about 2 percent of students nationwide get special accommodations for the SAT, 10 percent of New England prep school students get such special treatment. Those receiving accommodations are much more likely to be male, white and from families earning more than $100,000.

The paper also found that the practice has spread to similar communities on the West Coast. San Francisco psychologist Jane McClure, who tests learning-disabled students, says parents who bring their teens to her for testing say, "I don't think he has a learning disability. I just want him to have every advantage possible."[2]

College Board President Gaston Caperton said, "We are concerned about people taking advantage of it who are not

Likewise, other advocates for the disabled say that even if IDEA funding were substantially increased, strings should be attached to ensure that the money is used for education. "We very much favor Congress fully funding IDEA," Marchand says. "But where would this huge influx of money go?" Without restrictions on how the money could be spent, it might "get buried and lost in general-education budgets or in property tax cuts."

In recent years, he points out, "IDEA funding doubled, but we haven't seen education services for kids with disabilities improve significantly as a result."

really qualified to, but have been smart enough to step around the rules. And, secondly, that people who are not as [economically] advantaged have equal access to accommodations."[3]

Because a complete psychological and educational evaluation for an ADHD diagnosis can cost thousands of dollars, children diagnosed with the disorder are disproportionately middle and upper class. In fact, the *Times* found that none of the 1,439 students from 10 inner-city Los Angeles high schools got extra time or other accommodations on their SATs. "Something is out of whack," said Perry Zirkel, a Lehigh University professor of education law, pointing out that disabilities generally increase with poverty.[4]

Special educators, who are already understaffed, resent requests by wealthy parents to test their high-achieving 17-year-olds — who happen to be due to take the SAT — for learning disabilities. "We are normally dealing with kids functioning at the fourth-grade level," said Greg Missigian, head of special education at Monroe High School in North Hills, Calif., where there are 400 special education students. "Why in the world are we testing [these] kids when we have so many more who are legitimate?"

Most special accommodations are given to students with well-documented learning disabilities, according to Steve Kotten, the College Board's associate director for students with disabilities. But about five years ago, when the percentage of those getting accommodations on the SAT began to outstrip the increase in students taking the exam, a board panel reviewed the procedures for allowing extended time and recommended that students be required to document a history of disability.

Since the new criteria were adopted, requests for accommodations have declined, Kotten says, and the growth rates of students receiving special treatment have leveled off.

Wendy Burns, an advocate for the Berkeley, Calif.-based Disability Rights Education and Defense Fund, thinks instances of parents playing the system are overblown. "Most parents only want accommodations that will level the playing field for their child," she says.

Special Treatment

A higher percentage of students who got extra time on the SAT, citing learning disabilities, were male, white and wealthy, compared with those who took the test the usual way.

Male

45%

60%

White

56%

58%

Family income above $100,000

11%

19%

☐ No special treatment
☐ Received extra time

Source: College Board

Going through the hassle of demanding special services for a child from a recalcitrant school bureaucracy is not easy, she says. "I'd rather have a root canal without Novocaine than sit in one of those meetings begging for services and being told there simply isn't money or staff to provide them," she says.

---

[1] Kenneth R. Weiss, "New Test-Taking Skill: Working the System," *Los Angeles Times*, Jan. 9, 2000.

[2] Quoted in *Ibid.*

[3] *Ibid.*

[4] *Ibid.*

Does the availability of federal funding for special education encourage the overdiagnosis of learning disabilities?

Some members of Congress oppose increasing IDEA spending because they think the program provides financial incentives to over-identify children as needing special-ed services. Such overidentification, argued Rep. Ron Paul, R-Texas, "unfairly stigmatiz[es] many children and, in a vicious cycle, lead[s] to more demands for increased federal spending on IDEA."[11] Some lawmakers are especially wary of increases because children with learning disabilities now make up 51 percent of those receiving special-ed services. Unlike more obvious physical disabilities that require wheelchairs or crutches, learning disabilities — defined as difficulty reading and calculating — are invisible, and thus more susceptible to allegations of overdiagnosis.

"The intent of the original law was to ensure that those with physical disabilities receive a free and appropriate public education," Colorado State Board of Education member Patti Johnson told a House Education oversight subcommittee hearing on Sept. 29 on the use of behavioral drugs in schools. "But those children are now being shortchanged because such a large percentage of special-education funds are being diverted to vague psychiatric diagnoses."

The panel focused on whether federal incentives are contributing to skyrocketing diagnosis rates for the learning disability attention deficit hyperactivity disorder (ADHD), an "invisible" and controversial condition characterized by uncontrollable inattentiveness, hyperactivity and impulsiveness. Increasing numbers of American schoolchildren are taking powerful stimulant medications for ADHD, and some doctors think it is being grossly overdiagnosed.[12]

Witnesses told the panel that in 1990, after heavy lobbying by parents of children with ADHD, the definition of learning disabilities covered by IDEA was amended administratively to include attention deficit disorders. Five years later, the use of Ritalin, the most popular drug for treating childhood ADHD, had shot up sixfold. And by 1998, the number of children identified in the IDEA category that includes ADHD had increased nearly fourfold.

In addition, lawmakers said, parents are complaining that some school administrators will not allow their children to remain in school unless they take Ritalin, which calms hyperactive children and helps them focus on their schoolwork. Lawmakers said they fear that federal incentives may be prompting such actions by administrators.

"When the federal government provides billions of dollars in incentives, it is expected that the local administrators and teachers will follow the money," said an angry Rep. Bob Schaffer, R-Colo. "Without a doubt, we are subsidizing the aggressive pursuit of disabilities, and it's resulting in overdiagnoses of these conditions."

Johnson agreed with Schaffer, contending that, "So-called learning disorders have, sadly, become a way

for financially strapped schools to make ends meet." She quoted a 1996 letter from the Illinois State Board of Education criticizing a school superintendent for not participating in Medicaid programs for disabled students. The letter said, "The potential for dollars is limitless" from the program. Johnson claimed the program has become a "lucrative cash cow" for many schools.

But the Education Department's Heumann told the panel that IDEA funds are not nearly significant enough to encourage schools to over-identify students as disabled. The current federal grant of $827 per child, she said, is only a fraction of the approximately $12,000 a year it costs to educate a special-ed child.

"How can that small amount of IDEA funds possibly be an incentive for us to overidentify kids as needing special services?" asks AASA's Hunter.

Moreover, he says, the $2 billion that Medicaid reimburses schools for medical services they provide for special-ed students is "only a drop in the bucket" compared with the increasing cost of such services that school districts are now required to provide.

Supreme Court decisions in 1984 and in 1999 concluded that districts must pay for any medical services, except those provided by a medical doctor, needed for a special-ed student to attend school. "We now have teachers being forced to change diapers and suction lungs" in school districts where school nurses have been eliminated or cut back due to cost-cutting, says the NEA's Shust.

David Egnor, a senior policy consultant for the Council for Exceptional Children (CEC), contends that rather than milking Medicaid to help them pay for medical services, far too few schools are tapping into the funds. "If a kid is eligible for Medicaid, he ought to be getting Medicaid services," Egnor says. "But only half the kids who are eligible for Medicaid ever get onto the Medicaid roles, and only half of those kids ever access any actual Medicaid services."

Heumann also denies that the IDEA encourages the use of Ritalin or any other medication. "Increasing the number of children who take behavioral drugs does not increase the amount of funds a school district gets under IDEA," she insisted.

Besides, she said, to eliminate even the possibility that IDEA might be encouraging overidentification of disabilities, the state-grant formula was amended in 1997. Now any extra IDEA funds are distributed based on total student population and poverty rates, rather than on how many disabled students are identified in a school district.

Heumann said rather than too much money being thrown at special-ed programs, not enough is being spent to reduce classroom size and properly train teachers to work with children with disabilities, especially behavior-related disabilities. "Teachers and administrators are not being provided with the proper training to teach these children appropriate positive behavior," Heumann said. "As a result, these children are either dropping out of school or are being inappropriately suspended or expelled."

If students are being overidentified as learning disabled, Heumann said, it's not because teachers are seeking additional federal funds for them. More likely, they are seeking one-on-one academic help, she said. In today's crowded classrooms, sometimes a special-ed program is the only way to get extra help for struggling students, she said.

The AASA's Hunter agrees. "If a kid isn't a good reader by the age of 6, they hang a special-ed label on him to get him individual help," he says. "Unfortunately, almost no special-ed teacher knows how to teach reading."

Heumann and Hunter's observations were borne out by an in-depth examination of California's burgeoning special-ed population by the *Los Angeles Times*. The newspaper found that tens of thousands of students were placed in special education because they were never taught to read properly. "[Special-ed] is where children who weren't taught well go," said G. Reid Lyon, a neuropsychologist who directs reading research at the National Institutes of Health.[13]

Rep. Schaffer bristled at the idea that overcrowded classrooms and insufficient resources may lead to children being inappropriately labeled as needing special education, which could in some cases lead to the child being put on stimulant medications.

"I find [this] abhorrent," Rep. Schaffer said. "In no case should lack of resources or lack of preparedness by the teachers become the basis for drugging children — never."

Has IDEA increased discipline problems in public schools?

Under the IDEA, disabled students who misbehave get special due-process protections designed to prevent schools from unfairly removing them from class. Advocates for the disabled say such protections are necessary, given the history of schools excluding disabled children just because they were "difficult" or expensive to educate.

But administrators complain that such special protections prevent them from effectively disciplining IDEA students. "School officials' hands are tied by the double standard of disciplining special-ed kids one way and regular kids another way," says the NSBA's Fuller. Such a lack of flexibility "can cause increased discipline problems," he says.

Under IDEA, "Schools are subject to a dangerous dual-discipline system that handcuffs them from removing violent students," Sen. John Ashcroft, R-Mo., wrote recently.[14]

The NEA's Shust is quick to point out that, contrary to some misconceptions, disabled students are not any more disruptive than regular students. "In fact, disabled students are more than likely to be the victims of violence or bullying by the other students than they are to be the ones causing the trouble," she says.

"If you took all the special-ed children out of the classrooms," Heumann adds, "you'd still have discipline problems."

However, Shust points out, the law does make it more difficult to deal with disabled students when they do cause problems.

Originally, the law's "stay put" provision had proved the most troublesome. It required that an IDEA student who broke a school rule remain in the classroom while the school followed due-process procedures, such as parental notification and an administrative hearing. But the provision stirred resentment and controversy because it ran counter to federal safe-school laws like

> "School officials' hands are tied by the double standard of disciplining special-ed kids one way and regular kids another way." Such a lack of flexibility "can cause increased discipline problems."
>
> — *Dan Fuller*
> *Director of Special Programs*
> *National School Boards Assn.*

the Gun-Free Schools Act, which requires an immediate one-year expulsion of any student bringing a weapon to school.

"IDEA overrides state and federal zero-tolerance-for-firearms laws," says Julie Lewis, an NSBA lawyer. "They contradict one another. This policy is creating a lot of problems."[15]

Ashcroft tells the story of a disabled Missouri grade-schooler who announced that he was going to bring a knife to school "and cut the bus driver's throat." Under most school zero-tolerance rules, any student making such a threat would be suspended. But under IDEA, unless the boy actually shows up with a knife, he cannot be suspended, because he had already been suspended once that year, Ashcroft says.

Betty Chong, assistant superintendent for special services in Missouri's Cape Girardeau school district, says holding disabled students to a laxer discipline standard in school does not prepare them for post-graduation life, where they will be held to the same behavior standards and laws as all other adults. "When do they learn how to be law-abiding citizens?" she asks.

In the wake of a spate of school shootings, the IDEA was amended in 1997 to allow more flexibility in disciplining special-ed students who bring a weapon to school. But the new provisions are still controversial. For one thing, the new law is extremely complicated, Shust says. "I'm a lawyer, and I can't understand the discipline provisions," she says.

Nonetheless, she applauds one change — the "stay put" provision was amended to allow administrators to immediately remove a gun-carrying child from the classroom while pursuing due-process procedures. Now a disabled child can be suspended for up to 10 days, during which time the school must determine whether the offense was caused by his disability.

If the behavior was not caused by the child's disability, he can be expelled for a year — just like other students. But unlike other misbehaving students, special-ed youngsters are entitled to receive continued education in an alternative program during the expulsion. In many states, mainly in the South, no such alternative services are available for non-disabled students.

"The problem is that it's almost impossible to prove the negative — that an action was not the result of a disability," Hunter says. "All the child's lawyer needs to do is claim that the child was being teased for his disability and thus was feeling angry that day."

If the behavior did result from a student's disability, the child can be suspended for 10 days while officials determine whether he continues to pose a danger. If so, the school can expel the student indefinitely, but must provide alternative instruction, and the expulsion must be reviewed every 45 days.

The 45-day reviews ensure that schools will not "just kick the student out and forget about him," says the NCD's Rangel-Diaz. But the policy rankles both parents of regular-curriculum kids expelled without alternative services or periodic reviews, and administrators who must pay for the extra services.

Rangel-Diaz and other advocates for the disabled say much of the controversy would evaporate if schools provided alternative education for all expelled students — disabled or otherwise. But Congress seems inclined to do the opposite. A provision approved by the Senate last May, sponsored by Sens. Ashcroft and Bill Frist, R-Tenn., would require disabled students who bring firearms to school to be treated the same as non-disabled students, regardless of whether or not the action resulted from their disability. Thus, if the student's state is not required to provide educational services during the expulsion period, neither child would receive services.

Egnor of the Council for Exceptional Children says the problem with the discipline amendment is that schools think it is their only option in dealing with a gun-carrying IDEA student. Rather than getting into the complicated 45-day review process, he says, schools need only call in the parents and immediately rewrite the individualized education plan (IEP) created for the child so that he can be removed and educated in an alternative setting.

"It would be extremely rare for there to be a parent who insists that their child go back into the classroom if he has carried a gun to school or is considered dangerous," Egnor says. "The lawyers are the ones insisting that the schools get into a formal, litigious proceeding."

Other critics of IDEA, like South Texas special-ed teacher Jesse Jesness, say it makes teachers and administrators wary of lawsuits, which may then lead them to forsake discipline in favor of behavior-modification

CHRONOLOGY

1970s-1980s *Federal courts hold states responsible for providing a free public education to all retarded and handicapped children. Congress passes landmark law providing grants to help states pay for educating handicapped children.*

Oct. 7, 1971 Federal court requires Pennsylvania to provide free public education to all retarded children (*Pennsylvania Association of Retarded Citizens v. Commonwealth of Pennsylvania*).

Aug. 1, 1972 Federal judge orders District of Columbia to offer educational facilities to all handicapped and emotionally disturbed children (*Mills v. Board of Education, District of Columbia*).

Nov. 29, 1975 President Gerald R. Ford signs Education for All Handicapped Children Act authorizing state grants to help give all handicapped children a "free appropriate education."

June 28, 1982 Supreme Court adopts lax education standard for handicapped children (*Hendrick Hudson Board of Education v. Rowley*).

July 5, 1984 Supreme Court rules that school districts must provide medical services needed by disabled children to attend school (*Irving Independent School District v. Tatro*).

April 29, 1985 Supreme Court rules that parents of disabled students may be reimbursed for private tuition costs if public schools fail to offer appropriate education (*Burlington School Committee v. Department of Education of Massachusetts*).

Sept. 24, 1986 Congress establishes grant incentives aimed at assuring special education for handicapped children beginning at age 3.

1990s-Present *Many school systems bring students with disabilities into regular classrooms. Congress overhauls*

IDEA to deal with discipline issues after a rash of school shootings.

Oct. 15, 1990 Congress renames 1975 law as Individuals with Disabilities Education Act (IDEA), and refuses to include attention deficit hyperactivity disorder (ADHD) as an eligible disability.

1991 Education Department directs schools to include ADHD as a covered IDEA disability, possibly sparking an explosion in Ritalin prescriptions.

Nov. 9, 1993 Supreme Court says lower courts may order school systems to reimburse parents of learning-disabled children for private-school costs even if school does not meet all federal requirements (*Florence County School District Four v. Carter*). Ruling opens door to a new wave of litigation by parents.

1994 Gun-Free Schools Act requires one-year expulsion of any student caught with a firearm at school; the law conflicts with the IDEA's provisions on disciplining disabled students.

June 4, 1997 Congress reauthorizes IDEA giving school districts more flexibility to deal with disabled students who bring weapons to school. If also requires schools to teach and test disabled students according to the regular curriculum, to the extent possible.

March 3, 1999 Supreme Court rules that the IDEA requires public school districts to pay for one-on-one continuous nursing care for some disabled students during the school day. The National School Boards Association estimates the ruling could cost schools $500 million to provide care for 17,000 severely disabled students.

Feb. 18, 2000 Commission on Civil Rights hears that teachers and administrators use zero-tolerance policies to expel learning-disabled students to raise overall test scores.

Nov. 29, 2000 Twenty-fifth anniversary of IDEA.

drugs. "If you try to discipline a child, parents sue. Then the schools become reluctant to punish," he writes. "[So teachers] end up recommending drugs to control behavior.[16]

"History will remember us as the generation that believed it was kinder to drug our children than to spank them or make them run laps," Jesness writes.[17]

The Education Department's Heumann told the House education oversight panel in September that it's not IDEA that causes discipline problems but overcrowded classrooms and poorly trained teachers who haven't taught kids to read properly. "Kids who can't read get bored and cause discipline problems," she said.

BACKGROUND

IDEA Aids States

Before IDEA, America had a spotty record when it came to educating the handicapped. Separate schools for blind or deaf children were common in the mid-20th century, and about a dozen states specifically excluded handicapped children from public schools, usually on the grounds that wheelchairs were fire hazards. Only about half the states required local school districts to educate so-called "trainable" pupils.

At the time, courts generally upheld local school systems' power to exclude handicapped children. The Illinois Supreme Court ruled in 1958, for example, that the state's compulsory-education law did not require a public education for a mentally impaired child.[18]

But in the 1960s and '70s, when millions of disabled youngsters still were not attending school or receiving an education addressing their special needs, a handicapped-rights movement sprouted and grew, demanding an equal education for disabled Americans.

Then two federal court rulings forever altered the special-ed law landscape. In 1971, a three-judge federal court approved a settlement requiring Pennsylvania school districts to provide a free public education to all retarded children.[19] A year later, a federal judge in Washington ordered the District of Columbia to provide free education to all retarded, handicapped and emotionally disturbed children. It was the first time a judge held that handicapped children had a constitutional right to a public school education.[20]

It didn't take long for states to realize how expensive it would be to provide such services, and they asked Congress for help. Congress responded with the 1975 law, guaranteeing an education to all handicapped youngsters and providing federal assistance to local school districts to do so. To qualify for federal aid under the law, states had to ensure that school districts provided a "free appropriate public education" to all handicapped youngsters, and that "to the maximum extent appropriate" the handicapped children be educated with non-handicapped kids.

School districts also had to develop an IEP for each handicapped student, specifying yearly educational goals and steps to meet those goals. Parents were to be consulted in drawing up the plans and were allowed to contest them or their child's placement, either in court or administrative hearings.

Escalating Costs

Given how Republicans are at the forefront today in arguing for increasing IDEA funding, it is ironic that, when the law first passed, Republican President Ford signed it reluctantly, fearing it would cost too much.[21]

Ford's concerns foreshadowed the program's escalating costs, as the courts have progressively broadened the definition of what schools must provide under the law. In its first ruling on the law, the U.S. Supreme Court in 1982 tilted in favor of schools providing only minimal services. The court said a school must only provide sufficient services for a disabled student to receive some — not necessarily the maximum — benefit from his education.[22]

Three years later, however, when the Burlington, Mass., school system proposed an IEP for a learning-disabled boy that provided only minimal services, the parents rejected it as inadequate and enrolled him in a special private school. A federal appeals court later ruled that the school system must pay the boy's tuition, a decision eventually upheld by the Supreme Court.

The ruling opened the door to a new wave of litigation by parents. Some educators say it also led to wealthier, mostly white parents suing to get public funding for their children to attend private schools specializing in treating learning disabilities. The practice is particularly common, they say, in a handful of states with sizable ethnic populations or with large, failing, urban public school systems.

For instance, during the 1996-97 school year, nearly half of the 76,000 students nationwide who went to private school using IDEA funds lived in California,

New Jersey or New York. Each of those three states placed more than 10,000 disabled students in private schools, unlike most other states, which placed far fewer disabled students in private schools. Texas, for instance, placed only 67 IDEA-funded students in private schools that year.

Aside from such anomalies, the general push has been to mainstream disabled students in regular classes. In the mid-1980s, the Reagan administration launched a controversial program to integrate disabled students, especially students with mild learning disabilities, into regular classrooms. The policy was aimed at preventing children with disabilities from being trapped in special-education classes for their entire schooling.

However, the disabilities community initially opposed the policy, arguing that it minimized the problems faced by learning-disabled students and that some would not thrive in mainstream classrooms.

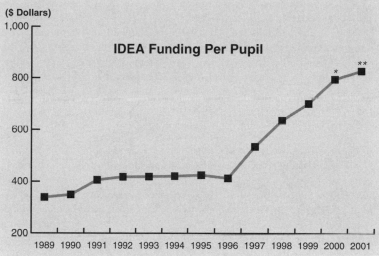

Per-Pupil Spending Doubled

The per-pupil amount provided by the government through special-education grants to the states under the Individuals with Disabilities Education Act (IDEA) more than doubled from 1989 to 2000.

IDEA Funding Per Pupil

($ Dollars)

* Estimated
** Estimated at president's budget request level

Source: Congressional Research Service, CRS Report for Congress, Richard N. Apling, "Individuals with Disabilities Education Act: Full Funding of State Formula," Dec. 28, 1999

But states and local school systems — citing research that most disabled children do better in mainstream classrooms — pushed for what came to be called "inclusion" by the end of the decade. The movement continued to gain momentum, even after the Bush administration eased the federal push toward inclusion.

Revamping the Law

Congress has revised IDEA several times. In 1986, it expanded the law's coverage to provide special-education services to disabled children beginning at age 3, after educators and advocacy groups told Congress that the earlier disabled children could be identified, the more effective the interventions would be.[23]

During a 1990 review of the law, Congress renamed it the Individuals with Disabilities Education Act, reflecting the popular move away from use of the term "handicapped." It also added a new program to help disabled youths make the transition from school to the outside world, and required the Education Department

to study whether ADHD should be included as a disability covered by the law.

School administrators and national education groups opposed the move, fearing that the definition of ADHD was so vague and the diagnosis rate was escalating so rapidly that public schools would be swamped by requests for special services.

Under IDEA, learning-disabled students are entitled to free special services, like separate classes, extra help from learning specialists, laptop computers, tape recorders and tailored homework assignments. They also can receive extra time on standardized achievement and college entrance exams, or be given those exams orally if their disabilities are severe enough. According to the National Institutes of Health (NIH), public schools may have spent as much as $3 billion for extra services for ADHD students in 1995.[24]

But parents of ADHD children were concerned that their youngsters would be disadvantaged by their invisible learning disabilities and lobbied Congress heavily to make ADHD eligible for IDEA services. Then civil

Testing in College Strains the System

Providing testing accommodations for learning-disabled students in college raises additional questions about logistics, consistency and fairness.

Some faculty members complain that college administrations treat learning disabilities differently from physical disabilities. Elevators and wheelchair ramps needed for physically disabled students are readily provided by college administrations, they say, but classroom professors often must provide the extra time, proctors and space needed to test learning-disabled students.

The logistics can be a nightmare, according to Wendy M. Williams and Stephen J. Ceci of Cornell University in Ithaca, N.Y. They point out that the lengthier nature of college-level exams can mean that the learning-disabled students require several extra hours to take tests. They also are often entitled to distraction-free settings with proctors who can give them individual help.[1]

The two professors of human development say it is almost impossible during hectic exam weeks to find extra rooms available for a five-hour stretch or busy teaching assistants — who must take exams themselves — willing to set aside five hours to proctor such exams.

They also complain that too few institutions are asking whether accommodating learning-disabled students penalizes students without special needs, or those who have undiagnosed learning disabilities. How, Williams and Ceci ask, do you ensure fairness to all students amid dramatic increases in the rate of certain disabilities, like ADHD, that resist precise definition, are not easily observed or measured and are not well understood by experts?

"We are convinced that some diagnoses of learning disability are incorrect," they wrote, noting that they see more learning disabilities diagnosed among children from wealthy families. "What about students with undiagnosed special needs, whose parents could not afford professional evaluations?" they asked.

But even if a student is correctly diagnosed as learning disabled, they question the scientific basis for the specific accommodations that are demanded. "Is it simply a wish list made up by high school counselors or private doctors hired by upper-middle-class parents?" they ask.

David Egnor, a senior policy consultant for the Council for Exceptional Children, says the solution is to "develop assessments that cater to a wide range of kids' abilities and needs without going through this farce of providing accommodations."

---

[1] Wendy M. Williams and Stephen J. Ceci, "Accommodating Learning Disabilities Can Bestow Unfair Advantages," *The Chronicle of Higher Education*, Aug. 6, 1999.

rights groups weighed in with fears that an ADHD label might be used to stigmatize minorities and segregate them into separate classrooms. In the end, Congress refused to include ADHD as an eligible disability.

Undeterred, the ADHD parents launched a massive letter-writing campaign to the Education Department. In 1991 the department issued a "Policy Clarification Memorandum" directing schools to include ADHD as a covered IDEA disability. Some educators argue that the policy change helped spark an explosion in Ritalin production and prescriptions during the 1990s.

In 1997, Congress again overhauled IDEA, following three and a half years of difficult negotiations between disability advocates and education groups. By that time, the number of disabled students had risen to 10 percent of the student population, and safety and discipline issues were at the forefront of the congressional debate.

Besides strengthening the discipline portions of the law, the rewrite required school officials to justify why a disabled child will not participate with regular students in academic, non-academic and extracurricular activities. Previously, school officials only had to explain why students would participate in regular classes and activities.

The revision also required schools testing non-English-speaking children for disabilities to determine the extent to which the disability was due to special needs or to a lack of English skills. It also mandated that disabled students be tested along with non-disabled students in statewide achievement tests. And it allowed school districts to use 20 percent of any federal increase in IDEA funds for general education purposes.

"In our 1997 amendments, we focused the law on the quality education a child with disabilities is to receive rather than upon process and bureaucracy," said Rep. Goodling. As a result, he said, IEPs are developed with the general curriculum in mind, and students with disabilities are taking district and statewide achievement tests in greater numbers. "Both of these improvements mean children with disabilities will receive a higher-quality education."

"On this [25th] anniversary, we are now moving in the right direction both in how we present the program and also in the amount of funding that we are providing," he said.

At the same time, the population of disabled students has changed dramatically from that envisioned by Congress when it passed the original legislation, thinking it was not much more than a wheelchair-access law.

"It's just amazing the range of disabilities that school systems have been able to accommodate," said Marsha Fields, former executive director of the National Association of State Directors of Special Education.[25]

"We now have students in the regular classrooms who once would have been institutionalized or would not have lived as long as they do today," Shust says.

CURRENT SITUATION

Paying the Bill

Since the Republicans took control of Congress in 1995, they have sparred with the Clinton administration over increasing IDEA funding. Clinton has consistently sought billions of new dollars for school construction, new teachers and after-school programs, while requesting only nominal increases for IDEA.

But Republicans, Democrats and special-ed advocates agree that Clinton "lowballed" special-ed not because he didn't want it increased, but because he knew the Republicans would increase it without his having to ask for it. So he figured he could use IDEA funding as a bargaining chip to get his other pet projects funded.

"He knows it's a high priority for us, so he puts it at a low priority and 'plus-ups' other accounts," says Rep. Porter. "Then when we get down to final negotiations at the end of the year, the president has a huge advantage, especially in a year like this one, which is an election year and members want to get home to campaign."

In the process, Clinton has tossed the Republicans a popular campaign-year issue, Porter says. "By running a cynical budget instead of an honest budget about what his real priorities are, Clinton has handed this issue to the Republicans," he says. Republicans oppose additional spending for Clinton's new education programs, insisting that if Congress would increase IDEA funding, local school districts would be able to fund Clinton's pet projects. "Let the local school districts decide," Porter says.

Thus, whenever education-related budget or appropriations bills have worked their way through Congress in recent years, the two parties have played a tug-of-war over funding for IDEA or school construction and new teachers.

"It's all just politics," says Marchand of the Consortium for Citizens with Disabilities. "Our kids are being used as political footballs. We are tremendously disappointed in both political parties and in the White House. It's a nasty game they are playing."

He pointed out that no president — from Ford to Clinton — has ever requested substantial new dollars for IDEA. He credits Rep. Goodling — a former schoolteacher who made IDEA funding his battle cry for years — with the increases that have occurred since 1996.

Marchand dismisses as "inflated election-year rhetoric" the House vote last May to fully fund IDEA within the next 10 years. Educators were equally insulted. "That vote was the biggest bag of election-year manure," the AASA's Hunter says. "It was a really cynical trick they played on the school districts, because they knew the appropriators would not provide the funds."

Congressional negotiators have been wrangling for weeks over the 2001 spending bill for the Education Department and agreed tentatively to raise IDEA funding for state grants by $1.6 billion for the one year. The measure was deadlocked over other issues when Congress recessed for the election, and the entire package could unravel when lawmakers return Nov. 13, depending on the outcome of the election. But education lobbyists were confident that the IDEA portion of the bill would remain intact.

Hunter says that if the Congress were really serious about fully funding IDEA, it would set it up as a mandatory appropriation, which — like entitlements — does not have to be approved by the Appropriations committees every year.

The NEA also has called for IDEA to become an entitlement program, as have other organizations, saying that the current period of record surpluses and economic good times is the best time to push for such a change.

"It's something whose time has absolutely come," the NSBA's Fuller says. "We've given the appropriators 25 years to do the right thing."

The Consortium for Citizens with Disabilities favors a mandatory IDEA appropriation because it believes it would help the program reach full funding sooner. But the group says increasing funds only for the state grants, known as Part B, will overwhelm funding for other "woefully under-funded" parts of the law. The other sections provide funds for training teachers and parents, developing handicapped-friendly technological aids and identifying disabled infants and toddlers. Keeping such portions properly funded, he says, could help prevent some severe disabilities from developing in the first place and provide teachers with the expertise to properly educate the disabled.

"Without proportionate funding for these other programs, throwing more money into Part B won't work," Marchand says.

But Chester E. Finn, Jr., president of the conservative Thomas B. Fordham Foundation, says making IDEA an entitlement is the dead-wrong approach to fixing the IDEA funding problems. "The sky would be the limit with regard to the endless proliferation of services and the overidentification of kids as disabled," he says.

And, of course, appropriators like Porter strongly oppose making IDEA an entitlement. "Entitlements are cop-outs," he says. "It's our job to determine what our priorities are. You've got to take responsibility for what happens."

Besides, he asks, "What happens when you get into a tough fiscal situation, and you're running huge deficits? Can you control entitlements?" The answer, he says, is only if you have the will to do so, "but nobody ever does."

Nonetheless, Fuller responds, "disabled students still need to be educated, even in hard times."

OUTLOOK

Reauthorization Fight?

Looking to the future, the AASA's Hunter says, "There's been enormous progress. Our biggest remaining problems are lack of money and personnel."

But others say major reform of the program is needed. A conference in Washington this month cosponsored by the Fordham Foundation and the more liberal Progressive Policy Institute (PPI) will discuss ways to overhaul the IDEA.

"You hear a lot of cheerleading about IDEA as folks celebrate the 25th anniversary of the law," says Andy Rotherham, director of education policy at the PPI. "But as soon as you look at it below the cosmetic level, nobody is happy with it. It's time to give the issue some fresh thinking."

One reason the law needs review, he says, is the danger of a major backlash developing over financing the program. That's especially likely to come from very small school districts and states where autism — which often requires one teacher per student and can cost up to $100,000 a year — is skyrocketing.

In California, autism diagnoses rose 273 percent and diagnoses of autism-related disorders skyrocketed 1,966 percent from 1987 to 1998. Maryland reported a 513 percent rise from 1993 to 1998, and dozens of other states have reported increases of 300 percent or more. In some U.S. communities, autism-spectrum disorders have increased from one in 10,000 in 1978 to one in 300 in 1999.

"The California Department of Developmental Services, which administers IDEA, says it fears the autistic children will bankrupt the system," says Burns of the Disability Rights Education and Defense Fund.

Besides financing, the Fordham-PPI conference will examine how to make the program more cost-effective, using such techniques as reducing litigation costs and compliance paperwork. "Perhaps the program could be less compliance-based and more results-based," Rotherham says.

Prevention is another way to make the program more cost-effective, says Fordham's Finn. "A huge fraction of learning-disabled children have reading disabilities," he says. "And a substantial number of those could have been prevented by proper reading instruction."

Increasingly, studies are beginning to tentatively link some learning disabilities with chemical, heavy metal and pesticide pollution. And at least 17 controlled, double-blind studies conducted in the United States, Canada, Europe and Australia over the last 25 years have shown a strong connection between children's ADHD and certain allergenic foods, food additives and artificial food dyes.[26]

Should Congress fully fund the Individuals with Disabilities Education Act?

YES

Rep. Bill Goodling, R-Pa.
From a statement before the House Committee on Education and the Workforce, April 11, 2000

This act will set us on a course for reaching the commitment Congress made 24 years ago to children with special-education needs... to provide [them] access to a quality public education and to contribute 40 percent of the average per pupil expenditure to assist states and local school districts with the excess costs of educating such children.

Achieving full funding of IDEA has been one of my highest priorities.... I know from my years as an educator that failing to fund [the act] not only hinders the ability of schools to provide children with disabilities with an appropriate education but also prevents all students from receiving a quality education.

....The Congressional Research Service estimates that over $15 billion would be needed to fund fully [the act]. The fiscal 2000 appropriation... was $4.9 billion, leaving states and local school districts with an unfunded federal mandate of more than $10 billion.

I do not want to belittle the efforts we have made over the past four fiscal years since Republicans took control of Congress — a dramatic $2.6 billion funding increase for IDEA that amounts to a 115 percent increase in the federal share....

However, this pace is much too slow. Currently we fund only 12.6 percent of the national average per-pupil expenditure to assist with the excess expenses of educating children with disabilities. We must take aggressive action to meet the 40 percent funding goal. [The act] sets a schedule to meet the 40 percent commitment by the year 2010.... This bill will authorize increases of $2 billion each year to ensure that our commitment becomes a reality within 10 years....

Congress needs to ensure that the federal government lives up to the promise it made to students, parents and schools over two decades ago. If we had met that commitment, local school districts would have the local funds necessary to build new schools, hire new teachers, reduce class size and buy more computers.

In my district, the York City School District receives $363,557. If IDEA were fully funded, this school district would receive $1.4 million — an increase of $1.08 million.... York city would have approximately $1.1 million in additional funds to spend on other pressing educational needs.

....Can you imagine what these school districts could fund when they no longer have to pay for, with local funds, the unpaid federal share of IDEA?

NO

Rep. Ron Paul, R-Texas
From a statement on the House floor, May 4, 2000

While I share the goal of devoting more resources to educating children with learning disabilities, I believe that there is a better way to achieve this laudable goal than increasing spending on an unconstitutional, failed program that thrusts children, parents and schools into an administrative quagmire.

Under the system set up by [IDEA], parents and schools often become adversaries, and important decisions regarding a child's future are made via litigation. I have received complaints from a special-education administrator in my district that unscrupulous trial lawyers are manipulating the IDEA process to line their pockets.... Of course, every dollar a local school district has to spend on litigation is a dollar the district cannot spend educating children.

IDEA may also force local schools to deny children access to the education that best suits their unique needs in order to fulfill the federal command that disabled children be educated "in the least restrictive setting".... Many children may thrive in a mainstream classroom environment; however, some children may be mainstreamed solely because school officials believe it is required by federal law, even though the mainstream environment is not the most appropriate for that child.

On May 10, 1994, Dr. Mary Wagner testified before the Education Committee that disabled children who are not placed in a mainstream classroom graduate from high school at a much higher rate than disabled children who are mainstreamed. Dr. Wagner quite properly accused Congress of sacrificing children to ideology.

....Instead of increasing spending on a federal program that may actually damage the children it claims to help, Congress should return control over education to those who best know the child's needs: parents.... I have introduced the Family Education Freedom Act (HR 935), which provides parents with a $3,000 per child tax credit to pay for K-12 education expenses. My tax credit would be of greatest benefit to parents of children with learning disabilities because it would allow them to devote more of their resources to ensure their children get an education that meets the child's unique needs....

....[T]he best means of helping disabled children is to empower their parents with the resources to make sure their children receive an education suited to their child's special needs instead of an education that sacrifices that child's best interest on the altar of the "Washington-knows-best" ideology.

Do Charter Schools Discriminate?

Charter schools — small, regulation-free, experimental academies within the public school system — often operate in conflict with federal laws prohibiting discrimination against disabled students.

"Square peg, round hole," said Eric Premack, director of the Charter Schools Project at the Institute for Education Reform in Sacramento, Calif., referring to how special-ed students sometimes simply don't fit in at charter schools.[1]

In fact, the notoriously bureaucratic federal law mandating the inclusion of disabled students in public education, the Individuals with Disabilities Education Act (IDEA), is anathema to the core premise of the charter school movement — often serving select populations.

Charter schools are publicly funded institutions run by individuals, parents or for-profit corporations under a contract granted by a local or state school board. The contract — or charter — allows them to operate free from many local, state and federal regulations, like curriculum requirements and teacher-salary scales, as long as the schools meet certain performance criteria. About 1,400 charter schools have opened nationwide since the early 1990s, when states began jumping on the charter-school bandwagon.[2]

But state laws authorizing charter schools roam all over the map on the issue of disabled students. "It's quite a mixed bag," says Paul Marchand, chairman of the Consortium for Citizens with Disabilities and director of the Association of Retarded Citizens. Some state laws require charter schools to abide by federal and state anti-discrimination laws, while others are silent on the issue, he says.

Plus, some charter-school laws directly conflict with the IDEA. For instance, a charter might allow a school to hire uncertified teachers, while the IDEA requires that certified teachers and specialists teach certain special-ed students.

And even when schools say they will not discriminate, in practice many apparently do, according to a study conducted by Nancy J. Zollers, assistant professor of teacher education at Boston College, and a group of colleagues. They found that some for-profit charter schools in Massachusetts had failed to live up to the "inclusive models" promised in their presentations to the public.

For instance, the Seven Hills Charter School in Worcester, Mass., run by Edison Schools Inc., rejected two disabled boys who had won admission to the school through a lottery, the study found. "Being free of hiring mandates is one thing," Zollers wrote. "Being free of special-education obligations is quite another."[3] Zollers added, "The behavior of these [for-profit] charter school operators...is reminiscent of school practices before passage of the 1975 federal law."

The Council for Exceptional Children passed a resolution in 1999 stating that charter schools should not discriminate against disabled students in their admissions policies based solely on a student's disability.

Marchand says he could imagine instances in which a charter school could be exempted from admitting certain disabled students. For instance, he says, "A school that caters to high-achieving math and science students could not serve a mentally retarded student," he says. But if a charter school has open enrollment or holds admission lotteries open to all students, it cannot then refuse to admit a disabled student who wins a lottery slot, he says, "It would be discrimination if he was excluded solely because of his disability," he says.

Some educators fear that the growing charter-school movement is a precursor to the privatization of education. Corporations have expressed intense interest in entering the $700 billion education market. But advocates for the disabled fear that for-profit companies will skim off only the cheapest-to-educate students, leaving behind the higher-cost disabled students in the public schools.

Zollers argues that until the federal government establishes rules for charter schools with regard to the inclusion of disabled students, "special-education students will remain vulnerable."

---

[1] Lynn Schnaiberg, "Spec. Ed. Rules Pose Problems For Charter Schools," *Education Week*, Feb. 19, 1997.

[2] For background, see Kathy Koch, "Are Charter Schools the Answer?" *The CQ Researcher*, April 9, 1999, pp. 292-293, and Charles S. Clark, "The Growing Movement Toward Charter Schools, *The CQ Researcher*, July 26, 1996, p. 656.

[3] Nancy J. Zollers, "Schools Need Rules When It Comes To Students With Disabilities," *Education Week*, March 1, 2000.

The conference will examine ways to include prevention as a major component of the IDEA program. "Right now, the program only focuses on accommodation and compensation," Finn says. The conference papers will be published early next year, as a primer for the new Congress as it gears up to reauthorize IDEA in 2002.

Hunter predicts that the next authorization process will be more contentious than the last one. "This time we're not going to hold hands and sing Kumbaya," he says. "We'll state our disagreements openly instead of trying to paper them over."

The 1997 reauthorization was a compromise worked out behind closed doors by representatives from education organizations and advocacy groups for the disabled.

Some say unless the system is reformed, the number of students identified as learning disabled will only increase, especially as more states end social promotion and impose strict accountability measures, tying school test scores to teacher and principal pay raises. That could create even more pressure for schools to shunt poor-performers into special-ed classes. Even though the 1997 law required special-ed students to be tested along with regular students during statewide assessments, many districts have not yet implemented that provision.

The result will be "chaos and more lawsuits," especially in the more dysfunctional school districts, predicted Kevin Feldman, director of reading and early intervention for Sonoma County, Calif., and a member of a California task force that studied the link between reading problems and special-education diagnoses.[27]

The NEA hopes the law can be amended to reduce paperwork. Once a school has completed the federal, state and local IDEA requirements, the typical IEP for a student can be 35 to 40 pages long, says Shust, who admits that much of the paperwork results from districts' fear of litigation rather than from the actual requirements of the law. Nevertheless, she says, "Our members would much rather spend time teaching the students than filling out paperwork."

Support from both presidential candidates

During the presidential campaign, both candidates, Republican Gov. George W. Bush of Texas and Democratic Vice President Al Gore, called for dramatic increases in the IDEA state grants program. Bush also proposed tripling the $11 million spent each year researching technologies to aid the disabled and creating a new $5 billion incentive fund to help states teach students to read by the third grade. Gore promised the largest IDEA funding increases ever and proposed "funding pools" to help small school districts pay for very high-cost disabled students. He also would fund more special-ed training for general-ed teachers.

With both candidates making such promises, some education advocates say the prospect for IDEA becoming an entitlement look brighter than ever. "This is a once-in-a-lifetime situation," says Edward Kealy, executive director of the Washington, D.C.-based Committee for Education Funding. "We've got the money and the political will lined up. For the first time ever, it's become an idea that you don't dismiss out of hand."

Regardless of the funding situation, Marchand and other disability advocates see continuing improvements in education for the disabled and in the acceptance of disabled persons in society, now that 25 years of growing-pain wrinkles have been ironed out.

"I see a much greater acceptance of people with disabilities in our society," he says, "simply because a substantial proportion of the nation's young citizens will have grown up sitting next to kids with disabilities."

Bill East, executive director of the National Association of State Directors of Special Education, predicts that the next 10 years will bring greatly improved support services from the federal government for the IDEA program.

"I also foresee great increases in the numbers of students with disabilities who are leading successful, adult lives thanks to the IDEA," he says.

NOTES

1. "Back to School on Civil Rights: Advancing the Federal Commitment to Leave No Child Behind," National Council on Disability, Jan. 25, 2000.

2. Testimony at House Education Oversight Subcommittee hearing, Sept. 29, 2000.

3. Statement during floor debate on a bill to provide full funding for IDEA, Sept. 26, 2000.

4. Statement during House Education Committee debate on the bill, April 11, 2000.

5. Richard N. Apling, "Individuals with Disabilities Education Act: Full Funding of State Formula," Congressional Research Service, Dec. 28, 1999.

6. See David Nather, "Funding for Special Education Gets Increase From Panel," *CQ Weekly,* Sept. 23, 2000.

7. Apling, *op. cit.*

8. Roberta Weiner and Maggie Hume, "...and education for all — Public Policy and Handicapped

Children," Education Research Group, Capitol Publications, p. 21.

9. Richard Rothstein, "Where's the Money Going?" Economic Policy Institute, 1997.

10. Statement during House Education Committee consideration of a resolution urging full funding of IDEA, June 4, 1998.

11. Statement on the House floor during consideration of increased funding for IDEA, May 4, 2000.

12. For background, see Kathy Koch, "Rethinking Ritalin," The *CQ Researcher,* Oct. 22, 1999, pp. 905-928.

13. Richard Lee Colvin and Duke Helfand, "Special Education a Failure on Many Fronts," *Los Angeles Times,* Dec. 12, 1999.

14. Sen. John Ashford, "Should disabled students be disciplined differently under zero-tolerance policies?" in Kathy Koch, "Zero Tolerance," *The CQ Researcher,* March 10, 2000, p. 201.

15. For background, see Koch, *Ibid.*

16. Jesse Jesness, "Some Reflections on Ritalin," Intellectual Capital.com

17. *Ibid.*

18. For background, see Kenneth Jost, "Learning Disabilities," The *CQ Researcher,* Dec 10, 1993, pp. 1081-1104.

19. *Pennsylvania Association of Retarded Citizens v. Pennsylvania,* 343 F.Supp. 279 (E.D. Pa. 1972). See The New York Times, Oct. 9, 1971, p. A1.

20. *Mills v. Board of Education,* 348 F.Supp. 866 (D.D.C. 1972). See *The Washington Post,* Aug. 2, 1972, p. C1.

21. For background, see 1975 *CQ Almanac,* p. 651.

22. *Hendrick Hudson Board of Education v. Rowley,* 458 U.S. 176 (1982).

23. See 1986 *Congressional Quarterly Almanac,* pp. 270-272; 1990 *Congressional Quarterly Almanac,* pp. 616-617.

24. Quoted in the final report of the NIH Consensus Development Conference on the Diagnosis and Treatment of Attention Deficit Hyperactivity Disorder, Nov. 16-18, 1998.

25. Quoted in Jost, *op. cit.*

26. For background, see Koch, "Rethinking Ritalin," *op. cit.,* pp. 916-917, and Kathy Koch, "Parents of Autistic Children Blame Mercury Poisoning," in "Vaccine Controversies," The *CQ Researcher,* Aug. 25, 2000, pp. 641-672.

27. Quoted in Colvin and Helfand, *op. cit.*

BIBLIOGRAPHY

Books

Kelman, Mark, and Gillian Lester, *Jumping the Queue, An Inquiry into the Legal Treatment of Students with Learning Disabilities,* Harvard University Press, 1997.
The authors trace the evolution of special protections for disabled students, pointing out that early lawsuits to include disabled students in public education occurred after school desegregation in 1954. The authors discuss what to do about the phenomenal growth in the diagnosis of learning disabilities and the problems created by students being entitled to special services and disciplinary tactics.

Yell, Michael L., *The Law and Special Education,* Merrill, 1998.
This comprehensive manual for teachers and administrators outlines what is required under federal law when dealing with disabled students.

Articles

Colvin, Richard Lee, and Duke Helfand, "Special Education a Failure on Many Fronts," *Los Angeles Times,* Dec. 12, 1999.
An in-depth investigation by two newspaper reporters found that thousands of students were placed in special-education classes in California because they were never taught to read properly. Teachers in overcrowded classrooms admitted that getting a floundering student labeled as learning-disabled and sending him to special-ed classes was often the only way to get him extra help.

Sack, Joetta L., "Presidential Candidates Focus on Spec. Ed.," *Education Week,* July 12, 2000.

The reporter outlines the different positions of the presidential candidates on funding for special education.

Schnaiberg, Lynn, "Spec. Ed. Rules Pose Problems For Charter Schools," *Education Week*, Feb. 19, 1997.

The author discusses how the notoriously bureaucratic Individuals with Disabilities Education Act (IDEA) often conflicts with state charter-school laws, which promote regulation-free, experimental academies within the public school system, often serving select populations.

Weiss, Kenneth R., "New Test-Taking Skill: Working the System," *Los Angeles Times*, Jan. 9, 2000.

Using College Board statistics, reporter Weiss found that the number of students receiving extra time to complete college entrance exams due to a learning disability jumped more than 50 percent in recent years, with most of the growth coming from exclusive private schools and public schools in mostly wealthy, white suburbs on the East Coast.

Zollers, Nancy J., "Schools Need Rules When It Comes To Students With Disabilities," *Education Week*, March 1, 2000.

An assistant professor of teacher education at Boston College studied whether for-profit charter schools in Massachusetts were living up to the "inclusive models" they promise in their presentations to the public.

Reports and Studies

Apling, Richard N., "Individuals with Disabilities Education Act: Full Funding of State Formula," Congressional Research Service, Dec. 28, 1999.

The CRS estimates that at today's enrollment rates, it would cost an additional $15.8 billion per year — three times more than the current $5 billion appropriation — to fund IDEA at the 40 percent ceiling envisioned by Congress in 1975 when it passed the law.

National Council on Disability, "Back to School on Civil Rights: Advancing the Federal Commitment to Leave No Child Behind," Jan. 25, 2000.

The report on the progress of the IDEA found "widespread and persistent" state non-compliance with the law. Parents are often forced to invoke formal complaint procedures and request due-process hearings to obtain the services their children are entitled to under law, the report said.

Rothstein, Richard, "Where's the Money Going?" Economic Policy Institute, 1997.

An EPI study found that over the last 30 years school districts apparently shifted money earmarked for regular students to programs for the disabled. Critics say the result is that regular-ed students' parents have been pitted against special-ed students' parents.

U.S. Department of Education, "To Assure the Free Appropriate Public Education of All Children with Disabilities," 21st Annual Report to Congress on the Implementation of the Individuals with Disabilities Education Act.

The 250-page annual report discusses progress being made under the IDEA, including statistical breakdowns on the kinds of disabilities IDEA students have, how old they are and in what kinds of settings they are being educated.

For More Information

Consortium for Citizens with Disabilities, 1730 K St., N.W., Suite 1212, Washington, DC 20006; (202) 785-3388; www.c-c-d.org. A coalition of national consumer, advocacy, provider and professional organizations that advocates for federal legislation and regulations that assure that the 54 million children and adults with disabilities are fully integrated into society.

Council for Exceptional Children, 1920 Association Dr., Reston, VA 20191-1589; (703) 620-3660; www.cec.sped.org. The council, founded in 1922, is the largest professional organization dedicated to improving educational outcomes for students with disabilities and gifted students.

Disability Rights Education and Defense Fund, 2212 Sixth St., Berkeley, CA 94710; (510) 644-2555; www.dredf.org. Founded in 1979 by people with disabilities and parents of children with disabilities, the DREDF is dedicated to protecting and advancing the civil rights of people with disabilities through legislation, litigation and technical assistance.

Learning Disabilities Association of America, 4156 Library Road, Pittsburgh, PA 15234; (412) 341-1515; www.ldan-atl.org. Founded in 1963, LDA is the largest advocacy group for children and adults with learning disabilities.

National Association of State Boards of Education, 1012 Cameron St., Alexandria, VA 22314; (703) 684-4000; www.nasbe.org. NASBE, the national organization of state-level education policy-makers, advocates inclusion policies for students with disabilities.

National School Boards Association, 1680 Duke St., Alexandria, VA 22314; (703) 838-6722; www.nsba.org. A federation of state school board associations that monitors legislation and regulations affecting the funding and quality of public education.

Fixing Urban Schools

Has No Child Left Behind
Helped Minority Students?

Marcia Clemmitt

4

Philadelphia police officers guard West Philadelphia High School on March 12, 2007, where a teacher was attacked by three students three days earlier. Experts suggest that a "behavior gap" between black and white students parallels the academic achievement gap between high- and low-performing students.

"I didn't go to school much in elementary, and they saw me as a bad girl" who skipped class, says Jeanette, a Houston high-school student who dropped out several times but is struggling to get a diploma. After her parents divorced when she was in grade school, she fell into a pattern typical of urban students, repeatedly "switching schools," sometimes living with her mother, sometimes her father and sometimes with an aunt who "didn't make us go to school" at all.[1]

In middle school, Jeanette began taking drugs but later got involved in sports, which motivated her to try, sometimes successfully, to keep up her grades and stay off drugs. Some teachers have tried hard to help her, but like many troubled urban kids, she pulls back. "If I need help . . . I don't say anything. . . . They have to ask me." Still, Jeanette is determined to avoid the fate of her parents, who dropped out of school when they had her. At the time, her mother was only 13. "I don't want to live like them. I want to have a better life," she says.

Jeanette typifies the daunting challenge that urban schools face in promoting academic achievement among children whose lives have been disordered and impoverished.

Most middle-class families with children have moved to the suburbs, leaving urban schools today overwhelmingly populated by low-income, African-American and Hispanic students. "Nationally, about 50 percent of all black and Latino students attend schools in which 75 percent or more of the students are low-income, as measured by eligibility for free and reduced-price lunch," according to the Center for Civil Rights at the University of North Carolina.

From *CQ Researcher*, April 27, 2009.

Minority Districts Often Get Less Funding

In 28 states, school districts with high-minority enrollments received less per-pupil funding (shown as a negative number, top map) than districts with low-minority levels. For example, in Illinois, the highest-minority districts received an average of $1,223 less per student than the lowest-minority districts. In 21 states, the highest-minority districts received more per pupil (shown as a positive number, bottom map), than the districts with the lowest-minority enrollments. For example, in Georgia, the highest-poverty districts received $566 per student more than the lowest-poverty districts.

Minority Funding Gaps by State, 2004

States where high-minority districts received less funding than low-minority districts

	-$2,000+
	-$1,001 to -$2,000
	-$500 to -$1,000
	-$1 to -$500

States where high-minority districts received more funding than low-minority districts

	$0 to $500
	$500 to $1,000
	$1,001 to $2,000
	$2,000+

Note: Hawaii is not shown because data are not available.

Source: Funding Gaps 2006, The Education Trust, 2006

Only 5 percent of white students attend such high-poverty schools.[2] (*See graph, p. 77.*)

These schools, mostly urban, aren't making the grade, even in the context of lagging achievement in American schools overall.

Although states show significant variations, nationwide "71 percent of eighth-graders are not reading at grade level," and the percentage shoots up to between 80 and 90 percent for students of color, says former Gov. Bob Wise, D-W.Va., now president of the Alliance for Excellent Education, a broad-based coalition that advocates for academically stronger high schools.

Furthermore, of the approximately 15,000 U.S. high schools, 2,000 — mostly in cities — account for half of the nation's school dropouts, says Wise.

When President George W. Bush joined Massachusetts Sen. Edward M. Kennedy and other congressional Democrats to enact the No Child Left Behind Act (NCLB) in 2002, a key aim was requiring states to report achievement scores for all student groups. That ensured that lagging scores of low-income and minority students wouldn't be masked by having only state or district overall average scores reported.[3]

This year, Congress is expected to provide funding to keep the law in operation, but there's considerable disagreement about where federal education law should go next, and lawmakers may wait until next year to consider revisions (*see p. 88*).

NCLB's test-score reporting requirements "make it more possible to look at whether schools are doing well just for more affluent students or for poor students" as well, and that's valuable, says Jeffrey Henig, professor of political science and education at Columbia University's Teachers College.

But some supporters, including President Bush, say the NCLB has done more than just improve data-gathering, arguing that the law itself has pushed achievement upward. "Fourth-graders are reading better. They've made more progress in five years than in the previous 28 years combined," he said on March 2.[4]

Many education analysts disagree with that rosy assessment. The small improvement in fourth-grade reading and mathematics scores is part of a long-term trend, which began years before NCLB was even enacted, said Harvard University Professor of Education Daniel M. Koretz. "There's not any evidence that shows anything has changed" since NCLB, he said.[5]

And for urban schools, the post-NCLB picture is especially grim.

Of the non-achieving schools in New York state, for example, 90 percent are in cities and 80 percent in the state's five biggest cities, says David Hursh, an associate professor of teaching and curriculum at the University of Rochester's Margaret Warner Graduate School of Education.

The gap between average reading scores of black and white fourth-graders narrowed by only one point on the 500-point National Assessment of Educational Progress test (NAEP) between 2002 and 2005, and the narrowing appears to be part of a long-term trend, since it narrowed by three points between 1998 and 2005. Between 2002 and 2005, the reading-score gap between white and black eighth-graders actually widened, from 25 points to 28 points.[6]

The continuing severe achievement gap, newly highlighted by NCLB's data-reporting requirements, leaves lawmakers and educators scratching their heads about what to do next.

Some analysts say lagging achievement in urban schools demonstrates that poor families in poor

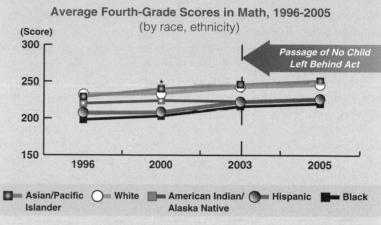

All Racial/Ethnic Groups Improved on Test

Fourth-graders in all racial and ethnic groups began modestly improving in math on the National Assessment for Educational Progress several years before passage of the No Child Left Behind Act.

Average Fourth-Grade Scores in Math, 1996-2005
(by race, ethnicity)

Legend: Asian/Pacific Islander, White, American Indian/Alaska Native, Hispanic, Black

Passage of No Child Left Behind Act

* Some data for 1996 and 2000 not available

Source: U.S. Department of Education, National Center for Education Statistics

communities require much more intense interventions than middle-class students, including better teachers and longer school days as well as improved health care, nutrition and parenting education.

A public school enrolling mainly middle-class white students has a one in four chance of producing good test scores, across years and in different subject matter, according to Douglas N. Harris, assistant professor of education policy at the University of Wisconsin, Madison. A school with a predominantly low-income minority population has a 1-in-300 chance of doing so.[7]

Experts blame the poor outcome on the fact that urban schools, like all schools, are staffed and organized to provide substantial extra help to only 15 percent of students and curriculum enrichment to another 15, while "the students in the middle are supposed to take care of themselves," says Robert Balfanz, associate research scientist at the Johns Hopkins University Center on the Social Organization of Schools and associate director of the Talent Development High School program, a reform initiative in 33 schools nationwide. The formula for extra help fits most suburban schools, "but in urban schools 50 to 60 percent, and sometimes up to

80 percent, of the kids are 'high-needs,' defined as English-as-a-second-language students, special-education students or students below grade level or with severe attendance problems.

"We're not set up to respond when that many kids need one-on-one tutoring, monitoring of their attendance on a daily basis, [or] people calling up to say, 'Glad you came today,' " Balfanz says.

One of the biggest problems is the kind of "student mobility" experienced by Jeanette, the Houston dropout.

"Homelessness is much underreported," says James F. Lytle, a professor at the University of Pennsylvania and former school superintendent in Trenton, N.J. "Statistics are based on who's in shelters and on the streets. But 20 to 30 percent of our kids were living in 'serial households' on a day-to-day basis," or moving about from parents to grandparents to relatives to friends — not living in the same house all the time.

Inner-city schools have a 40 to 50 percent student-mobility rate, which means up to half the students change schools at least once a year because of parents losing or changing jobs, evictions and other factors, says Columbia University's Henig. That disrupts students' ability to keep up with work and build relationships with the adults in a school.

In addition, city students miss school for a wide range of reasons, including high asthma rates; lack of school buses, forcing kids to get to school on their own, often through unsafe neighborhoods; and family responsibilities, like caring for younger siblings.

"Imagine the teacher's dilemma in a classroom where the population is different every day," says Balfanz.

But some conservative analysts argue that a large proportion of high-needs students is still no reason for schools to fail.

"Schools frequently cite social problems like poverty . . . and bad parenting as excuses for their own poor performance," said Jay P. Greene, a senior fellow at the Manhattan Institute, a conservative think tank. "This argument that schools are helpless in the face of social problems is not supported by hard evidence. . . . The truth is that certain schools do a strikingly better job than others," including public, private and charter schools.[8]

Some educators say one solution for low-quality urban schools is establishing publicly funded "charter" schools and awarding vouchers for private-school tuition.[9] When choice is expanded, "urban public schools that once had a captive clientele must improve the education they provide or else students . . . will go elsewhere," said Greene.[10]

But others argue that lessons from successful urban schools, including charters, demonstrate that raising low-income students' achievement requires resources and staff commitment that may be tough for the nation to muster.

"Teachers in high-poverty urban schools are as much as 50 percent more likely to . . . leave than those in low-poverty schools," in part because of the intensity of the work, according to researchers at the University of California, Santa Cruz.[11]

A second-grade teacher fluent in Spanish who reported working 10 hours a day, six days a week said she'd probably stop teaching when she had children: "It's too time-consuming and energy-draining," she said.[12]

"None of the teachers in our sample could conceive of being a successful urban teacher without an extraordinary — perhaps unsustainable — commitment to the work," the researchers commented.[13]

Not just schools but communities must help in the effort to improve students' performance.

"There ought to be a parade through the heart of town" every time a student achieves an academic goal, says Hugh B. Price, a fellow at the Brookings Institution, a liberal think tank. "We need to wrap and cloak kids in this message of achievement." That's how the military successfully trains soldiers, Price says. "They will praise anything that's good."

Schools and communities also have a role in helping parents better equip their children for school, says Mayor Douglas H. Palmer of Trenton, N.J., president of the National Conference of Democratic Mayors. "You don't have to be rich to talk to your child, help her build vocabulary and learn to reason and negotiate," as psychologists recommend, he says. "We can help parents with these skills."

As educators and lawmakers debate the next steps to improving urban schools, here are some of the questions being asked:

Has the No Child Left Behind law helped urban students?

NCLB was intended to improve overall academic achievement and raise achievement for minority and low-income students, in particular, mainly by requiring more student testing, getting schools to report test data separately for student groups including minorities and the poor and requiring schools to employ better-qualified teachers.

The law, scheduled for reauthorization this year, gets praise for focusing attention on the so-called achievement gap between minority and low-income students and their middle-class counterparts. But critics say the legislation doesn't do enough to assure that low-performing urban schools get the excellent teachers they need.

Student achievement also has improved slightly under the law, some advocates point out. "Is NCLB really paying off? The answer is yes," U.S. Chamber of Commerce Senior Vice President Arthur J. Rothkopf told a joint House-Senate committee hearing on March 13. While current testing data is still "abysmal," it nevertheless "represents improvement from where this nation was" before the law.

The law has benefited urban schools by raising reading scores for African-American and Hispanic fourth- and eighth-graders and math scores for African-American and Hispanic fourth-graders to "all-time highs." Achievement gaps in reading and math between white fourth-graders and African-American and Hispanic fourth-graders also have diminished since NCLB, he noted.[14]

NCLB's data-reporting requirements have "lifted the carpet" to reveal two previously unrecognized facts about American education — "the continuing under-performance of the whole system and the achievement gap" for low-income and minority students, says Daniel A. Domenech, senior vice president and top urban-education adviser for publisher McGraw-Hill Education and former superintendent of Virginia's vast Fairfax County Public Schools.[15]

And while some critics complain that NCLB gave the federal government too much say over education — traditionally a state and local matter — "there needs to be a strong federal role for these kids" in low-income urban schools "because they have been left behind," says Gary Ratner, a public-interest lawyer who is founding executive director of the advocacy group Citizens for Effective Schools. "States and localities have not stepped up."

Now NCLB "has got the country's attention," and when Congress reauthorizes the law, "the federal role can be redirected to focus on Title I schools" — those serving a large proportion of disadvantaged students — "and do more of the things that professional educators support," Ratner says.

NCLB's requirement that every school "have very qualified teachers is good," says Gary Orfield, a professor of social policy at the Harvard Graduate School of Education and director of The Civil Rights Project.

But critics argue that NCLB doesn't put muscle behind the high-quality teacher requirement and sets unrealistic goals and timetables for school progress.

NCLB actually "incentivizes teachers to leave failing schools," the last thing lawmakers intended, says Jennifer King-Rice, an economist who is associate professor of education policy at the University of Maryland, College Park. "Teachers say, 'I can't produce the AYP [average yearly progress] results' " the law calls for in low-performing schools with few resources and, frustrated, go elsewhere, she says. Nevertheless, it's still unclear whether and how the government can enforce the qualified-teacher rule. (*See graphs, p. 76.*)

The law provides no additional funding to help schools meet the teacher-quality goal, said Richard J. Murnane, professor of education and society at the Harvard Graduate School of Education. "Teaching in these schools is extremely difficult work," and "very few school districts provide extra pay or other inducements to attract talented teachers to these schools.[16]

"As a result, all too often these schools are left with the teachers other schools don't want," he continued. "And the teachers who do have options exercise seniority rights to leave . . . as soon as they can."[17]

The achievement targets set by NCLB are panned by many. The main goal schools must meet is moving kids over a standardized-testing threshold from "basic" or "below basic" understanding of reading and math to a "proficient" level or above. But focusing on that narrow goal as the key measure by which schools are judged created bad incentives to game the system, many analysts say.

Rather than concentrating on raising overall achievement or trying to give the most help to students who score lowest, many schools concentrate "on students who are on the bubble" — those who need to raise their scores by only a few points to move into the "proficient" range — and "forget the others," says Patrick McQuillan, an associate professor of education at Boston College's Lynch

Minority Enrollment and Teacher Quality

In Illinois, 88 percent of the schools that were virtually 100 percent minority ranked in the lowest quartile of the state's Teacher Quality Index (graph at left). By comparison, only 1 percent of the all-minority schools ranked in the highest quartile (right). High-quality teachers have more experience, better educations and stronger academic skills. Similar patterns are found in most other states.

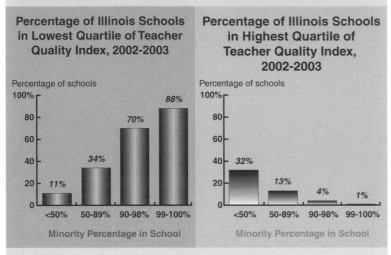

Percentage of Illinois Schools in Lowest Quartile of Teacher Quality Index, 2002-2003

Percentage of Illinois Schools in Highest Quartile of Teacher Quality Index, 2002-2003

Source: "Teaching Inequality: How Poor and Minority Students Are Shortchanged on Teacher Quality," The Education Trust, June 2006

an historically black school for women.

Teachers in training are taught that students are individuals with a wide variety of learning styles, and that no single assessment can define a student, says Peterson. The NCLB's excessive focus on a single measurement of achievement "leaves the teacher in an awful position" she says. "You need to keep the job, but when you are actually completing that form" stating the single score "for a third-grader, you're asking, 'Is that all there is to this child?'"

Should governments make schools more racially and economically diverse?

Today, most African-American and Latino students attend urban schools with a high concentration of low-income students and very few white classmates.

Some advocates argue that the country has backtracked to an era of separate but unequal schools and say government programs aimed at creating more racially and socioeconomically diverse schools are good tools for narrowing the achievement gap. Opponents of government interference with children's attendance at neighborhood schools argue that with residential neighborhoods increasingly segregated by race and income, school integration is unrealistic, and that governments should focus instead on improving achievement in urban schools.[18]

"The effort to get the right racial balance is misguided" and represents a kind of "liberal racism — a belief that black children need to be in school with white children to learn," says Stephan Thernstrom, a history professor at Harvard University and a fellow at the conservative Manhattan Institute.

If integration "can be managed naturally, that's fine, but there is no clear correlation that can be drawn from data" showing it's important for closing the achievement gap, Thernstrom says. He rejects as incomplete

School of Education. Schools that succeed at pushing the scores of "bubble" students up by a few points are deemed successful, according to current NCLB standards, even if they leave the neediest students even farther behind, he says.

The law's pronouncement that 100 percent of U.S. students will test at the "proficient" level is simply unrealistic, some critics say.

"We've never fully funded education in the United States," and achievement continues to lag far below the "proficient" level, especially for low-income students, says Domenech. So "let's not kid around and say that by 2014" all students will be academically proficient, he says. "That's like saying, 'I'm going to push you out the window, and I know you can fly.'"

Furthermore, NCLB's focus on a handful of standardized tests as the sole measures of children's progress puts teachers in an ethical bind that "definitely lowers their morale," says Marshalita Sims Peterson, an associate professor of education at Atlanta's Spelman College, and flawed studies that suggest integration does make a big difference. Furthermore, "if you need a white majority to learn," learning will soon be impossible in America, since Hispanic, Asian and African-American populations are growing faster than the current white majority, he notes.

Racial concentration is not the same as segregation and doesn't stand in the way of achievement, said his wife, Manhattan Institute Senior Fellow Abigail Thernstrom. School districts are powerless to change housing demographics, making it highly unlikely that racial concentration of students ever could be ended, she said.[19]

Some school districts are attempting to integrate lower-income and higher-income students, rather than integrating schools based on race. But Abigail Thernstrom argued that giving children a longer commute to schools outside their neighborhoods, for any reason, simply wastes time better spent in the classroom. "Busing doesn't raise the level of achievement," she told C-SPAN. "Now they're going to start busing on the basis of social class. And I have a very simple view of that. Stop moving the kids around and teach them."[20]

Meanwhile, some charter schools — such as the Knowledge Is Power Program (KIPP), begun in Houston — are making great strides in reducing the urban achievement gap, and for the most part those schools are not racially integrated, wrote *New York Times Magazine* features editor Paul Tough last year.

Most of the 70 schools that make up the three charter networks he observed have "only one or two white children enrolled, or none at all," he noted. Leaders of the networks, all of them white, actually intend to educate their students separately from middle-class students, according to Tough. However, unlike those who've argued that schools can be "separate but equal," the successful high-intensity charter schools aim for "separate but better." Their founders argue that

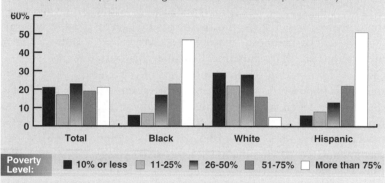

Blacks, Hispanics Attend High-Poverty Schools

Black and Hispanic students are more likely to be concentrated in high-poverty schools than white students. Forty-seven percent of black and 51 percent of Hispanic fourth-graders were in the highest-poverty schools in 2003 vs. 5 percent of white fourth-graders. By contrast, only 6 percent of black and Hispanic fourth-graders were in the lowest-poverty schools compared with 29 percent of whites.

Percentage of Fourth-Graders in High-Poverty Schools
(Based on proportion eligible for free or reduced-price lunch)

Poverty Level: ■ 10% or less ▨ 11-25% ▨ 26-50% ▨ 51-75% ☐ More than 75%

Source: "The Condition of Education 2004 in Brief" National Center for Education, June 2004

"students who enter middle school significantly behind grade level don't need the same good education that most American middle-class students receive; they need a better education," he said.[21]

But many advocates argue that data show a proven way to improve education for thousands of low-income students rather than for the handful that attend the highly successful charter schools is integration of minority and poor students with middle-class children.

School desegregation by race "has clear academic benefits," wrote R. Scott Baker, an associate professor of education at Wake Forest University. Data from Charlotte, N.C., show that the longer both black and white students spent in desegregated elementary schools, the higher their standardized test scores in middle and high school. Research also suggests that "where school desegregation plans are fully and completely implemented," local housing also becomes more integrated.[22]

In the 1960s and '70s some federal courts mandated programs to help urban minority families move to middle-class white suburbs. Long-term data from those cases show that children who moved did better than those who stayed behind, according to Howell S. Baum, a professor of urban studies and planning at the University of Maryland. In St. Louis, 50 percent of the black students who moved to the suburbs graduated from high school, compared to 26 percent of those who remained in the high-minority, low-income urban schools.[23]

Many policy analysts agree that segregating low-income children in some public schools "perpetuates failure," wrote the Century Foundation's Task Force on the Common School. Nevertheless, there is an "equally durable political consensus that nothing much can be done about it." The panel argued that this must change: "Eliminating the harmful effects of concentrated school poverty is the single most important step that can be taken for improving education in the United States."[24]

"Dozens of studies" dating back to the 1960s "find that low-income children have . . . larger achievement gains over time when they attend middle-class schools," said the panel.[25]

"The tragedy right now is that places that were once forced to [integrate their schools] now aren't allowed to," says Orfield of The Civil Rights Project. "That will be seen as a cosmic blunder" for white Americans as well, he said. "We're not preparing ourselves for the multiracial society and world" of the 21st century.

Are teachers prepared to teach successfully in urban classrooms?

Urban schools have high teacher turnover, low test scores and many reported discipline problems. Furthermore, most of America's teaching force still consists of white, middle-class women, while urban schoolchildren are low-income minorities, creating a culture gap that may be hard to bridge.

Consequently, some analysts argue that today's teachers aren't prepared to teach successfully in urban classrooms for a variety of reasons, from discipline to second-language issues. Others, however, point to sterling examples of teachers and schools that do succeed and argue that the real problem is teachers not following good examples.

Fifth-grade teacher Rafe Esquith, at the Hobart Elementary School in central Los Angeles, routinely coaches his urban Korean and Central American-immigrant students to top standardized-test scores. Furthermore, his classes produce Shakespearean plays so impressive they've been invited to perform with Britain's Royal Shakespeare Company, said Abigail Thernstrom.[26]

But despite Esquith's success, "nobody copies him," even in his own school, said Thernstrom. "I went to the fifth-grade [classroom] next door [to Esquith's] one day," and "it was perfectly clear nothing was going on." When Thernstrom suggested the teacher might copy Esquith's methods — which include beginning class as early as 6 a.m. and working with students at his home on weekends — he remarked that "it's an enormous amount of work."[27]

Today, around the country, "we do have shining examples" of schools that succeed at urban education, says Timothy Knowles, executive director of the University of Chicago's Center for Urban School Improvement and a former deputy school superintendent in Boston.

Ratner, of Citizens for Effective Schools, agrees. "I spent time in an elementary school in Chicago a few years ago where all the teachers were teaching reading," even at the upper grades, equipping students with the vocabulary and comprehension skills needed for future academic work, he says. "They had a good principal, and they were showing that it can be done."

But while successful urban schools and classrooms are out there, many education analysts say the know-how and resources needed to spread that success to millions of students are sorely lacking.

Some individual schools are closing the achievement gap for needy students, but "very few, if any" entire school districts have had equivalent success, says Knowles.

Charter schools also haven't seen their successes spread as widely as many hoped.

Out of Ohio's "300-plus charter schools," for example, "some . . . are indeed excellent, but too many are appalling," wrote analysts Terry Ryan and Quentin Suffran of the conservative Thomas B. Fordham Foundation in a recent report.[28]

There are reasons for that, said Mark Simon, director of the Center for Teacher Leadership at Johns Hopkins University, in Baltimore. "Teaching lower-class kids well is tougher than teaching middle-class kids." Furthermore, "it is surprising how little we know about teaching practices that cause students to succeed, particularly in high-poverty schools."[29]

"You have poverty in many districts, but in urban schools you have a concentration of it" that makes teaching successfully there much harder than in middle-class suburbs, says Timothy Shanahan, professor of urban education at the University of Illinois at Chicago and president of the International Reading Association. Schools are traditionally set up to deal with 15 to 20 percent of a student body having very high needs, says Shanahan. But urban schools usually have 50 percent or more of their students needing special attention of some kind, "and that's a huge burden on the teachers," he says.

"Literally, we have 5-year-olds who come into the Chicago school system not knowing their own names," he says. "I know local neighborhoods with gang problems, where the kids are up all night. Their mothers are hiding them under the bed to protect them from shootings in the street. Then teachers can't keep them awake in class."

The nation's rapidly growing Hispanic population is heavily concentrated in urban schools. That new phenomenon presents another tough obstacle for the urban teaching force, because "older teachers know nothing about working with non-native English speakers," says McQuillan of Boston College.

Not just language but race complicates urban-school teaching. As many as 81 percent of all teacher-education students are white women.[30]

"Those most often entering teaching continue to be white, monolingual, middle-class women," wrote Jocelyn A. Glazier, assistant professor of education at the University of North Carolina at Chapel Hill.[31]

Many teachers, especially white women, shy away from making tough demands on African-American students, according to a survey of urban community leaders by Wanda J. Blanchett, associate professor of urban special education at the University of Wisconsin, Milwaukee. "Especially with African-American males, you hear the teachers say, 'Oh, he is such a nice kid.' But . . . this irks me when teachers baby their students to death instead of pushing. . . . I get that a lot when you have white teachers who have never worked with black students from the urban environment."[32]

Many entering education students at Indiana University-Purdue University, in Indianapolis, balked at the school's fieldwork and student-teaching venues, which were in urban schools, wrote Professor Christine H. Leland and Professor Emeritus Jerome C. Harste. "They saw our program's urban focus as an obstacle to their career goals" of teaching in schools like the suburban ones most had attended.[33]

Some viewed urban students as an alien race they didn't want to learn to know. "Students rarely felt the need to interrogate their underlying assumption that poor people deserve the problems they have" or "spent any time talking or thinking about issues such as poverty or racism," Leland and Harste wrote. After student teaching, however, some students changed their plans and applied to become urban teachers.[34]

Race is a taboo subject in America, which some analysts say compounds urban teachers' difficulties. Many teacher-preparation programs center on an effort not to see or at least not to acknowledge race differences, according to Glazier. But "by claiming not to notice [race], the teacher is saying that she is dismissing one of the most salient features of a child's identity."[35]

"Many teachers believe that if they recognize a student's race or discuss issues of ethnicity in their classroom, they might be labeled as insensitive and racist," wrote Central Michigan University graduate student in education Dreyon Wynn and Associate Dean Dianne L. H. Mark. But white teachers' deliberate color-blindness ignores students "unique culture, beliefs, perceptions, [and] values," blocking both learning and helpful student-teacher relationships, Mark and Wynn argue.[36]

BACKGROUND

Educating the Poor

American education has long struggled with providing equal education for the poor, racial minorities and non-English-speaking immigrants. Until recently, however, even people who never made it through high school could usually find a good job. A new, global, technical economy may be changing that.

In the earliest years in the United States, schooling wasn't widespread. A farm-based economy made extensive education unnecessary for most people. In 1805, more than 90 percent of Americans had completed a fifth-grade education or less, and education for richer people was often conducted by private tutors.[37]

CHRONOLOGY

1950s–1960s *Concerns grow over student achievement and racially segregated schools.*

1954 Supreme Court rules in *Brown v. Board of Education* that separate schools are inherently unequal.

1965 Title I of the new Elementary and Secondary Education Act (ESEA) targets the largest pool of federal education assistance to help schools serving disadvantaged students.

1966 Sociologist James S. Coleman's "Equality of Educational Opportunity" report concludes that disadvantaged African-American students do better in integrated classrooms.

1969 National Assessment of Educational Progress (NAEP) tests launched but report statewide average scores only, allowing states to mask lagging achievement among poor and minority students.

1970s–1980s *Latinos are becoming most segregated minority in U.S. schools. "Magnet schools" are established. School integration efforts gradually end.*

1973 Supreme Court rules in *San Antonio Independent School District v. Rodriguez* the Constitution does not guarantee equal education for all children. . . . In *Keyes v. School District No. 1*, the court bans city policies that segregate Denver schools.

1990s–2000s *Steady gains in African-American students' test scores over the past two decades begin to taper off by decade's end. . . . Poverty concentrates in cities. . . . Governors lead efforts to raise education standards.*

1990 New Jersey Supreme Court rules in *Abbott v. Burke* the state must provide more funding for poor schools than for richer ones.

1991 Minnesota enacts first charter-school law.

1994 In reauthorizing ESEA, Congress requires states receiving Title I funding for disadvantaged students to hold them to the same academic standards as all students.

1995 Knowledge Is Power Program charter schools launched in Houston and New York City. . . . Boston creates Pilot School program to research ideas for urban-school improvement.

1999 Florida establishes first statewide school-voucher program.

2000 Countywide, income-based school integration launched in Raleigh, N.C.

2002 Cambridge, Mass., schools begin integration based on income.

2002 No Child Left Behind Act (NCLB) requires states to report student test scores "disaggregated" by race, income and gender to avoid masking the failing scores of some groups. . . . U.S. Supreme Court rules in favor of Ohio's school-voucher program, which allows public funding for tuition at Cleveland parochial schools. . . . State takes over Philadelphia's bankrupt school system, allows private companies to run some schools.

2005 Hoping to halt isolation of the lowest-income students in inner-city schools, Omaha, Neb., tries but fails to annex neighboring suburban districts.

2006 Department of Education admits that few students in failing city schools receive the free tutoring NCLB promised and that no states have met the 2006 deadline for having qualified teachers in all classrooms. . . . Government Accountability Office finds that nearly one-third of public schools, most in low-income and minority communities, need major repairs.

2007 Gov. Deval L. Patrick, D-Mass., puts up $6.5 million to help schools lengthen their hours. . . . Democratic Mayor Adrian Fenty, of Washington, D.C., is the latest of several mayors to take control of schools. . . . New York City Schools Chancellor Joel Klein says he will fire principals of schools with lagging test scores. . . . Teachers' unions slam report calling for all high-school seniors to be proficient in reading and math by 2014. . . . Houston school district calls for state to replace NCLB-related standardized periodic testing on math and reading with traditional end-of-course subject-matter exams.

State legislatures were just beginning to debate whether to establish free tax-funded schools for all children.[38] Nevertheless, even in those early days, some religious and other charitable groups considered it a moral duty to educate the poor. In New York City, for example, the Association of Women Friends for the Relief of the Poor opened a charity school in 1801. By 1823 the group was providing free elementary education for 750 children, with some public assistance. Similar charity schools sprang up in most other major cities.

But as all states began establishing public education systems — between the late 18th and the mid-19th century — questions over equality in education arose, first for black students and later for immigrants. "When public schools opened in Boston in the late 18th century, black children were neither barred nor segregated," wrote Derrick Bell, a visiting professor at the New York University School of Law. "But by 1790, racial insults and mistreatment had driven out all but three or four black children."[39]

Later, some black families joined with white liberals to form black-only schools in Massachusetts and in other states. But complaints about poor conditions and poor teaching in those schools led others to sue for integrated education.

Even in the early 19th century, some courts were bothered by race-based inequities in education, said Bell. A federal court struck down a Kentucky law directing that school taxes collected from white people would maintain white schools, and taxes from blacks would operate black schools. "Given the great disparities in taxable resources" this would result in an inferior education for black children, the court said.[40]

Around the 1820s, waves of non-English immigration began, raising new controversies over educating poor children of sometimes-despised ethnicities.

Before 1820, most U.S. immigrants were English, and a few were Dutch. But between 1820 and 1840 Irish immigrants became the first in a long parade of newcomers judged inferior by the predominantly English population. A rising tide of immigration in the late 19th and early 20th centuries included many non-English-speakers — Italians, Germans, Chinese, Russians, Poles and many others — who posed new challenges for schools and were looked down on by many citizens.

The new immigrants generally clustered in cities, the economic engines of the time, and overcrowded city schools were charged with integrating them into American life. Critics charged that the urban schools used rigid instruction and harsh discipline to control classrooms bursting with 60 or more children, many of whom spoke no English.

Two Tracks

In the economy of the early 20th century, however, there remained little need for most students to learn more than basic reading and writing, so the failure of poor urban schools to produce many graduates wasn't seen as a problem.

In current debates over U.S. education, "people aren't looking at education historically" and therefore expect American schools to do things they were never designed to do, says Ratner of Citizens for Effective Schools.

"We consciously decided to have a two-track system," he says. In the early 20th century, education experts generally agreed that "in the industrial age there are lots of immigrants and poor people, and most are going to work on the assembly line, so how about if we create an academic track and a general/vocational track" mostly for the poor?

The school system that we have "was never set up to educate all students to the levels of proficiency now being asked for," Ratner says.

"I graduated exactly 40 years ago, and then about half the kids — 52 percent — were graduating," says Wise of the Alliance for Excellent Education. "And the non-graduates could still get good jobs."

But today "the fastest-growing sectors of the economy require two years of post high-school training," says Daniel J. Cardinali, president of Communities In Schools, a dropout-prevention group that helps school districts bring services like tutoring and health care to needy students.

Calls in the 1990s for higher academic standards by groups like The Business Roundtable brought widespread attention to the problems of low student achievement, especially in low-income schools.

Today few question the premise that all students should attain higher levels of literacy, mathematical problem-solving and critical thinking. Many who work in schools argue that simply setting higher standards isn't nearly enough, however, especially for urban schools where most students already are behind grade level.

Dropouts' Problems Often Begin Early

Clear warning signs appear, such as skipping class

With the baby-boom generation on the verge of retirement, sustaining the American workforce and economy depends on having a cadre of new young workers to replace them, says former Gov. Bob Wise, D-W.Va., now president of the Alliance for Excellent Education. But with jobs in the fastest-growing economic sectors now requiring at least a high-school diploma and, often, two years or more of post-high-school training, coming up with an adequately trained new workforce won't be easy, Wise says.

The annual graduation rate has risen from a little over 50 percent per year in the late 1960s to 73.9 percent in 2003. If it's to rise higher, however, the improvement must come among poor and minority students, mostly in urban schools, who are far less likely than others to earn diplomas.[1]

For example, while about two-thirds of all students who enter ninth grade graduate four years later, on-time graduation rates for minority and low-income students, especially males, are much lower. In 2001, for example, only about 50 percent of African-American students and 51 percent of Latino students graduated on time, compared to 75 percent of white students and 77 percent of Asian and Pacific Islanders.[2]

Students with family incomes in the lowest 20 percent dropped out of school at six times the average rate of wealthier students.[3]

In about a sixth of American high schools, the freshman class routinely shrinks by 40 percent or more by the time students reach senior year. For the most part, those schools serve low-income and minority students. Nearly half of African-American students, 40 percent of Latino students and 11 percent of white students attend high schools where graduation is not the norm. A high school with a majority of students who are racial or ethnic minorities is five times more likely to promote only 50 percent or fewer freshmen to senior status within four years than a school with a white majority.[4]

Meanwhile, the earning power of dropouts has been dropping for three decades. For example, the earnings of male dropouts fell by 35 percent between 1971 and 2002, measured in 2002 dollars. Three-quarters of state prison inmates and 59 percent of federal inmates are dropouts. In 2001, only 55 percent of young adult dropouts were employed. Even the death rate is 2.5 times higher for people without a high-school education than for people with 13 years or more of schooling.[5]

But if the consequences are known, the cures may be harder to pinpoint.

Many educators say dropping out starts early. "Disengagement doesn't start in the ninth grade. It starts in fifth," says James F. Lytle, a University of Pennsylvania professor and former superintendent of the Trenton, N.J., public schools. For on-track students in middle-class schools, "middle school has the most interesting, exciting stuff in class" — science experiments, readings about interesting people in history and studies "of how the world works" — he says.

But once students are judged to be reading behind grade level, as happens with many urban fifth-graders, middle schools turn to "dumbed-down remedial work" that's below students' real intellectual level and leaves them bored and dispirited, Lytle says. It doesn't have to be that way, he says. "But I wish that educational courseware was farther down the road" of providing ways to combine skills teaching with subject matter that is at students' actual age level.

As standards rise, for example, "ninth-graders are increasingly placed in introductory algebra classes . . . despite skill gaps in fundamental arithmetic," wrote Balfanz and Ruth Curran Neild, research scientists at the Johns Hopkins University Center on the Social Organization of Schools.

But few resources exist to help kids catch up, "nor are there many curriculum materials that specifically target the spotty skills of urban ninth-graders," the Johns Hopkins researchers said. And when students reading behind grade level enter middle and high school, their "secondary-certified English teachers" — educated to teach high-school-level literature and composition — "are generally unprepared" to diagnose reading problems or to teach the comprehension strategies and background vocabulary they need. Science and history teachers are even less prepared to help, Balfanz and Neild said.[41]

"Kids disengage early," says Lalitha Vasudevan, an assistant professor at Columbia University's Teachers College who works in an education program for young African-American males who've been diverted from jail and are mostly dropouts. "Often, early on, they've had teachers say things to them that they interpret as, 'You don't really care that I'm here,' " she says.

Dropping out "is not a decision that is made on a single morning," says a report from the Bill & Melinda Gates Foundation. In an extensive survey of dropouts, researchers found that "there are clear warning signs for at least one-to-three years" before students drop out, such as frequently missing school, skipping class, being held back a grade or frequently transferring among schools.[6]

Some key factors cited by the dropouts in the Gates study: Schools don't respond actively when students skip class and don't provide an orderly and safe environment. "In middle school, you have to go to your next class or they are going to get you," said a young male dropout from Philadelphia. "In high school, if you don't go to class, there isn't anybody who is going to get you. You just do your own thing."[7]

Lytle says cities could also establish post-dropout academies, like the Dropout Recovery High School he started in Trenton, which helped increase that city's graduation numbers.

"Rather than defining the whole problem as stopping dropouts, we can also reach out to those who already have," he says. "There are a slew of people around" who are out of school and would like to go back, from teenage mothers caring for their children to 60-year-olds, he says. "They need a school that is built around their lives. I simply don't understand why urban districts haven't been more imaginative" about this.

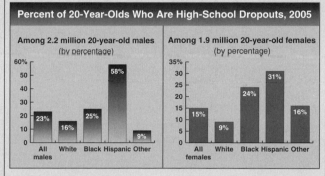

Majority of Dropouts Are Hispanic, Black

More than 50 percent of 20-year-old male high-school dropouts are Hispanic or African-American (graph at left). By comparison, 55 percent of the females are black or Hispanic (graph at right).

Percent of 20-Year-Olds Who Are High-School Dropouts, 2005

Among 2.2 million 20-year-old males (by percentage)
- All males: 23%
- White: 16%
- Black: 25%
- Hispanic: 58%
- Other: 9%

Among 1.9 million 20-year-old females (by percentage)
- All females: 15%
- White: 9%
- Black: 24%
- Hispanic: 31%
- Other: 16%

Source: "The Costs and Benefits of an Excellent Education for All of America's Children," Teachers College, Columbia University, January 2007

[1] Nancy Martin and Samuel Halperin, *Whatever It Takes: How Twelve Communities are Reconnecting Out-of-School Youth,* American Youth Policy Forum, www.aypf.org/publications/WhateverItTakes/WITfull.pdf.

[2] *Ibid.*

[3] *Ibid.*

[4] Robert Balfanz and Nettie Legters, "Locating the Dropout Crisis," Center for Social Organization of Schools, Johns Hopkins University, June 2004.

[5] Martin and Halperin, *op. cit.*

[6] John M. Bridgeland, John J. DiIulio, Jr. and Karen Burke Morison, *The Silent Epidemic: Perspectives of High School Dropouts,* Bill & Melinda Gates Foundation, March 2006.

[7] Quoted in *ibid.*

Retooling the school system to support higher standards may seem daunting, but "a quick walk through history" shows that it wouldn't be the first time the United States has made heroic efforts on education, says Wise. For example, "after World War II, you had soldiers coming home in need of better skills, and you had the GI Bill" to help them continue their educations.

Then "in the civil rights era we said, 'We believe that every child should be able to enter school,' and that happened," Wise says. "Now we're saying that every child should graduate."

For a time, the civil rights era seemed to be accelerating growing academic parity in learning, at least between black and white students. Following World War II, standardized test scores for black students began moving

The 'Behavior Gap' Between Black and White Students

Many educators blame a system that's middle-class and white-centered

Data from around the country indicate that black students, especially males, are cited much more often for disciplinary infractions than whites. The resulting "behavior gap" parallels the much-talked-about academic achievement gap.

Many analysts blame the phenomenon in part on a "culture clash" between black students, many poor, and an education system that's white-centered and middle-class. But there's little agreement about exactly what the gap means and what to do about it.

"You find the gap in all schools," including wealthy ones, says Clara G. Muschkin, a researcher at the Duke University Center for Child and Family Policy. Nevertheless, some evidence suggests there may also be a behavior gap between richer and poorer students, which accounts for just under a third of the black-white gap, Muschkin says.

In North Carolina schools, the racial gap "is persistent at all the grades" but is widest in seventh grade, says Muschkin. About 30 percent of black seventh-graders and 14 percent of whites have at least one disciplinary infraction reported during the school year.

African-American male students have the highest rates of suspensions and expulsions in most metropolitan areas around the country, according to Denise L. Collier, a doctoral candidate in education at California State University, Los Angeles. In New York, for example, where African-American males are 18 percent of the student population, they account for 39 percent of school suspensions and 50 percent of expulsions. In Los Angeles, black males make up 6 percent of the population but account for 18 percent of suspensions and 15 percent of expulsions.[1]

Some educators say that many urban African-American students don't learn at home the kinds of communication behaviors that are the norm for the middle class, and that this lack of background accounts for much of the gap.

"Americans of a certain background learn . . . early on and employ . . . instinctively" techniques like sitting up straight, asking questions and tracking a speaker with their eyes in order to take in information, said David Levin, a founder of the Knowledge Is Power Program (KIPP) charter schools, which serve mainly black and Hispanic students in several cities.[2]

When students in one Levin class were asked to "give us the normal school look," they responded by staring off into space and slouching, recounted *New York Times Magazine* editor Paul Tough in an article last year on successful urban charter schools. "Middle-class Americans know intuitively that 'good behavior' is mostly a game with established rules; the KIPP students seemed to be experiencing the pleasure of being let in on a joke," Tough observed.[3]

Behavior like a proper in-school work ethic has to be taught "in the same way we have to teach adding fractions with unlike denominators," said Dacia Toll, founder of the Amistad Academy charter school in New Haven, Conn. "But once children have got the work ethic and the commitment to others and to education down, it's actually pretty easy to teach them."

The academic gap that puts many black students in remedial instruction as they move through school may worsen the problem, says Robert Balfanz, associate research scientist at the Johns Hopkins University Center on the Social Organization of Schools. "In traditional remedial

closer to white students' scores. The years from the 1960s to the '80s saw fully half of the black-white academic achievement gap eliminated, says The Civil Rights Project's Orfield.

In the late '80s, however, the progress of African-American students in closing the gap stalled, and between 1988 and 1994, average test scores for black students actually began falling.[42]

Minority Schools

U.S. schools briefly became more integrated after the civil rights battles of the 1950s and '60s, but shifting instruction, I assume you know nothing, so I teach the times table" and basic reading skills like letter sounds, he says. "But the majority of kids behind can actually read at a basic level. What they're missing is comprehension skill, vocabulary. So they get bored and frustrated."

Middle-class education majors student-teaching in urban schools found that using books about topics their students personally had encountered — including home-lessness, racism and poverty — decreased discipline problems, even though the teachers initially resisted the books as inappropriate for children, according to Professor Christine H. Leland and Professor Emeritus Jerome C. Harste of Indiana University-Purdue University, Indianapolis. Once the student teachers broached the tough subject matter, they began reporting "fewer discipline problems . . . the children listened carefully and engaged in thoughtful discussions when they perceived that the issues being discussed were worth their attention."[4]

Many African-American student discipline problems involve "defiance" issues such as acting threatening or making excessive noise rather than activities like drug use or leaving the classroom without permission, according to University of Virginia Assistant Professor Anne Gregory.[5]

Seventy-five percent of African-American disciplinary referrals were for "defiance" behaviors in a study Gregory cites, many more than for other ethnic groups. That may suggest that teachers judge African-American students' behavior more "subjectively" than that of other students, Gregory says. Based on their past feelings of being restricted and excluded, some African-American students may be more likely to act out when they perceive that teachers are being unfair, Gregory suggests.

"If I was this little Caucasian boy or this preppy girl, she wouldn't talk with me that way. I am like the opposite. I am this little thug . . . I mean, she don't know," one student in Gregory's study said of a teacher perceived to be unfair.[6]

Avoiding excessive discipline battles in urban schools requires a seemingly contradictory set of characteristics that not everyone can muster, said Franita Ware, a professor of education at Spelman College, a historically black school for women in Atlanta. Teachers who succeed tend to be "warm demanders," those whom "students believed . . . did not lower their standards" but also "were willing to help them."[7]

"Sometimes I mean-talk them in varying degrees of severity," one teacher told Ware. But "sometimes you have to go back and say, 'What was really going on with you when I yelled at you? I'm just so sorry.' "[8]

Often the adult is the provocateur in the behavior situation, even if they don't realize it, such as when a student finds the nurse's office door locked at 3:02 and starts pounding on it, says James F. Lytle, a professor at the University of Pennsylvania and former school superintendent in Trenton, N.J.

"A lot of it is just the way you talk to people — respect," Lytle says. "Many are so accustomed to being denigrated. The kids have so little that the protection of one's ego is very important."

---

[1] Denise L. Collier, "Sally Can Skip But Jerome Can't Stomp: Perceptions, Practice, and School Punishment (Preliminary Results)," paper presented at the American Educational Research Association annual meeting, San Francisco, Calif., April 2006.

[2] Quoted in Paul Tough, "What It Takes To Make a Student," *New York Times Magazine*, Nov. 26, 2006, p. 51.

[3] *Ibid.*

[4] Christine H. Leland and Jerome C. Harste, "Doing What We Want to Become: Preparing New Urban Teachers," *Urban Education*, January 2005, p. 67.

[5] Anne Gregory, "Justice and Care: Teacher Practices To Narrow the Racial Discipline Gap," paper presented at the American Educational Research Association annual conference, San Francisco, Calif., April 2006.

[6] Quoted in *ibid.*

[7] Franita Ware, "Warm Demander Pedagogy: Culturally Responsive Teaching that Supports A Culture of Achievement for African-American Students," *Urban Education*, July 2006, p. 427.

[8] Quoted in *ibid.*

---

housing patterns have caused the concentration of poor, minority and non-English-speaking students in urban schools to rise for the past 25 years.

"One thing that's not fully understood is that, through a long historical process, we've concentrated our most needy students in a small subset of schools and districts" in rural and, mostly, urban areas, vastly increasing the burden those schools face in raising academic achievement, says Balfanz.

In its landmark 1954 *Brown v. Board of Education* ruling, the Supreme Court declared it illegal to intention-ally segregate schools by race.[43] In 1964, Congress passed the Civil Rights Act, outlawing discrimination in any

AP Photo/Mike Derer

Edwin Bradley listens to his fifth-grade daughter Antoinette read at the South Street School library in Newark, N.J. One of the poorest in the state, the school district has been encouraged under a new program to support parental involvement in an attempt to improve student performance.

institution that received federal funds, including schools.[44] As a result, more schools accommodated lower-income students along with middle-class students, white students and students from other ethnic groups.

The civil rights era lasted a scant 20 years, however, and housing patterns and new waves of immigration soon led to concentrations of poor and minority students in many urban school districts again.

As early as 1974, the Supreme Court effectively set limits on how far racial integration of students could go. The court ruled in *Milliken v. Bradley* that the remedy to racial segregation in Detroit could not include moving children to schools in the surrounding suburbs.[45]

Then, in the 1980s, federal efforts to desegregate schools effectively ended. During the presidency of Ronald Reagan (1981-1988), the U.S. Justice Department backed off forcing states to comply with desegregation mandates. Two Supreme Court decisions in the early 1990s effectively declared the goal of black-white school integration had been addressed, as the court ruled that school districts could be excused from court-ordered busing if they had made good-faith efforts to integrate, even if they had not fully complied with court orders.[46]

At the same time, however, Hispanic students were becoming a new minority that concentrated in schools with bigger academic challenges than others, such as teaching English-language learners.

The segregation of Latino students soared during the civil rights era. In 1973, in *Keyes v. School District No. 1*, the Supreme Court outlawed policies in Denver that had the effect of segregating Hispanic and African-American children into separate schools. In ensuing years, however, this somewhat complex ruling was only spottily enforced, according to civil rights advocates.[47]

Today Latinos "are America's most segregated minority group," said Orfield. The average Latino student goes to a school that is less than 30 percent white, has a majority of poor children and an "increasing concentration" of students who don't speak English.[48]

Poor in School

Until around the 1970s, children of all races and classes attended urban schools, and their average achievement levels didn't draw the same alarmed attention as today. Urban sprawl and white flight from cities over the past three decades have not only increased the number of urban schools with high minority populations but also increased the concentration of urban poverty as well, increasing the burden on urban schools.

"Sprawl is a product of suburban pulls and urban pushes," said the University of Maryland's Baum. "Families move to the suburbs for good housing, open space. They leave cities to avoid bad schools, threats to safety . . . contact with other races and poor public services."[49]

Furthermore, minority children are more concentrated in urban areas than the general population, largely because white families with children move to suburbs while childless whites are more likely to remain in the city, said Baum. Nationally, in nearly all school districts with more than 25,000 students, interracial contact has declined since 1986.[50]

Even more than ethnic minorities, poor people have concentrated in cities, says Balfanz. Over the past 20 years, even in periods when overall poverty has dropped, "the cities have gotten poorer and the concentration of poverty there deeper."

Between 1960 and 1987, the national poverty rate for people in central cities rose from 13.4 percent to 15.7 percent. At the same time, the poverty rate for rural residents fell by one-half and for suburban residents by one-third. By 1991, 43 percent of people with incomes below the federal poverty line lived in central cities.[51]

Would raising teacher pay help struggling schools?

YES — Patty Myers
Technology Coordinator,
Great Falls (Montana) Public Schools

From testimony on behalf of the National Education Association
before U.S. Senate Committee on Finance, March 20, 2007

NO — Jay P. Greene
Senior Fellow, Manhattan Institute

Posted on the Web, 2006

Ensuring a highly qualified teacher in every classroom is critical to closing achievement gaps and maximizing student learning. No single factor will make a bigger difference in helping students reach high academic standards. . . .

Unfortunately, difficulty in attracting quality teachers and high turnover rates severely hamper the ability to maintain a high-quality learning environment. Approximately one-third of the nation's new teachers leave the profession during their first three years, and almost one-half leave during their first five years. And turnover in low-income schools is almost one-third higher than the rate in all schools.

The teaching profession has an average national starting salary of $30,377. Meanwhile, computer programmers start at an average of $43,635, public accounting professionals at $44,668 and registered nurses at $45,570.

Annual pay for teachers has fallen sharply over the past 60 years in relation to the annual pay of other workers with college degrees. The average earnings of workers with at least four years of college are now over 50 percent higher than the average earnings of a teacher. Congress should reward states that set a reasonable minimum starting salary for teachers and a living wage for support professionals working in school districts. NEA recommends that all teachers in America enter the classroom earning at least $40,000 annually.

NEA also supports advancing teacher quality at the highest-poverty schools by providing $10,000 federal salary supplements to National Board Certified Teachers. Congress also should fund grants to help teachers in high-poverty schools pay the fees and access professional supports to become certified.

Often schools with the greatest needs and, consequently, the most challenging working conditions have the most difficulty retaining talented teachers. . . . Many hard-to-staff schools are high-poverty inner-city school or rural schools that, as a consequence of their location in economically depressed or isolated districts, offer comparatively low salaries and lack [the] amenities with which other districts attract teachers.

NEA strongly supports federal legislation with financial incentives for teaching in high-poverty schools, such as the Teacher Tax Credit Act introduced in the 109th Congress. The bill would provide a non-refundable tax credit to educators who work at schools that are fully eligible for federal Title I funds for disadvantaged students and would help hard-to-staff schools retain the quality teachers they need to succeed.

The common assertion that teachers are severely underpaid is so omnipresent that many Americans simply accept it as gospel. But the facts tell a different story.

The average teacher's salary does seem modest at first glance: about $44,600 in 2002 for all teachers. But when we compare it to what workers of similar skill levels in similar professions are paid, we find that teachers are not shortchanged.

People often fail to account for the relatively low number of hours that teachers work. Teachers work only about nine months per year. During the summer they can either work at other jobs or use the time off however else they wish. Either way, it's as much a form of compensation as a paycheck.

The most recent data indicate that teachers average 7.3 working hours per day, and that they work 180 days per year, or about 1,314 hours. Americans in normal 9-to-5 professions who take two weeks of vacation and another 10 paid holidays put in 1,928 hours. This means the average teacher's base salary is equivalent to a full-time salary of $65,440.

In 2002, elementary-school teachers averaged $30.75 per hour and high-school teachers $31.01 — about the same as architects, civil engineers and computer-systems analysts. Even demanding, education-intensive professions like dentistry and nuclear engineering didn't make much more per hour.

Some argue that it's unfair to calculate teacher pay on an hourly basis because teachers perform a large amount of work at home — grading papers on the weekend, for instance. But people in other professions also do off-site work.

Many assume that teachers spend almost all of the school day teaching. But in reality, the average subject-matter teacher taught fewer than 3.9 hours per day in 2000. This leaves plenty of time for grading and planning lessons.

It is well documented that the people drawn into teaching these days tend to be those who have performed least well in college. If teachers are paid about as well as employees in many other good professions, why aren't more high performers taking it up?

One suspects that high-performing graduates tend to stay away because the rigid seniority-based structure doesn't allow them to rise faster and earn more money through better performance or by voluntarily putting in longer hours. In any case, it's clear that the primary obstacle to attracting better teachers isn't simply raising pay.

"The nation's student population is two-thirds middle class (not eligible for federally subsidized lunches), yet one-quarter of American schools have a majority of students from low-income households," according to The Century Foundation.[52]

Among the burdens urban schools bear are poverty-related learning deficiencies children bring to school with them, regulations and economic barriers that limit urban-school resources, and a historical role as job providers in inner cities.

A large body of research shows that many low-income parents interact with their children in ways that hinder them in school, wrote Tough last year in *The New York Times Magazine*. For example, professional parents speak to their young children about two-and-a-half more times in an hour than poor parents do and encourage them verbally about six times more often than they discourage them; low-income parents discourage their children about three times as often as they encourage them, he said.

Unlike poor parents, middle-class parents also encourage their children to question, challenge and negotiate. In short, "in countless ways, the manner in which [poor children] are raised puts them at a disadvantage" in a school culture, Tough noted.[53]

For a variety of reasons, urban schools also have a much harder time keeping good teachers. "Many thousands — perhaps millions — of urban students don't have permanent, highly qualified teachers, ones with the skill to communicate important stuff to kids," says Kitty Kelly-Epstein, a professor of education at the Fielding Graduate University in Santa Barbara, Calif. In California, at least, state rules force some urban school districts to rely on temporary teachers because not enough applicants have required certifications, she says. "There never has been a time when low-income schools were fully staffed," she says.

With joblessness high in cities, especially for minority applicants, it's also "not uncommon" for school districts to be the major job source in the area, according to Johns Hopkins University Associate Professor of Education Elaine M. Stotko and colleagues. In a tradition that dates back to patronage systems in the early 20th century, urban politicians often interfere with schools' hiring the best managerial and teaching candidates by pressuring them to hand out jobs "as political favors."[54]

The Supreme Court is due to rule by the end of June in two race-based integration cases. With a new conservative majority, the court is widely expected to rule in favor of the white parents who are seeking to end race-based school integration in Seattle and Louisville, Ky. Decisions against the school districts could end many similar programs around the country, many of which were court-ordered in the past.[55]

But some school districts still worry that schools with high concentrations of minority and poor students harm achievement. Over the past several years, a few districts, including Raleigh, N.C., and Cambridge, Mass., have experimented with integrating students by socioeconomic status. In 2000, for example, the school board in Wake County, N.C., which includes Raleigh and its suburbs, replaced its racial integration system with the goal that no school should have 40 percent of students eligible for free or reduced-price lunch.[56]

Raleigh's effort was simpler politically than most, because the school district contains both the area's low-poverty and high-poverty schools. If the higher-income suburbs had been outside the district, political push-back would have made the program a tougher sell.

Some early Raleigh results look promising. On the state's 2005 High School End of Course exams, 63.8 percent of the low-income students passed, as did 64.3 percent of its African-American seniors, compared to pass rates in the high-40 and low 50-percent range for the state's other urban districts.[57]

CURRENT SITUATION

Congress Divided

The No Child Left Behind Act (NCLB), enacted in 2002, is intended to push American schools to raise achievement for all students, including low-income and minority children. As such, it represents one more step down a road that Congress embarked on in its 1994 reauthorization of the Elementary and Secondary Education Act — exerting federal influence to ensure that all students meet higher academic standards.

With NCLB up for reauthorization, Congress is struggling to figure out its next steps, with little apparent agreement on the horizon. With the press of other business, and strong disagreements in Congress about the education law, it's not clear that it will be reauthorized this year. The new congressional Democratic majority has already begun to hold hearings, however.

U.S. businesses have become increasingly involved in education policy, and many business leaders are urging Congress to continue and strengthen federal efforts to raise academic standards and provide incentives for states and localities to extensively retool their school systems to improve student achievement.

"Unless we transform the American high school, we will limit economic opportunities for millions of Americans," declared Microsoft Chairman Bill Gates at a Senate Health, Education, Labor and Pensions Committee hearing on March 7 [58]

Meanwhile, a group of conservative congressional Republicans has introduced legislation that would replace most of the NCLB achievement and reporting requirements that determine funding with block-grant funding that states could get whether they met NCLB standards or not. The measure would restore states and localities to their traditional role as prime overseers of schools, said Rep. Peter Hoekstra, R-Mich., who sponsored the legislation. "President Bush and I just see education fundamentally differently," he said. "The president believes in empowering bureaucrats in Washington, and I don't." [59]

But many congressional Democrats argue that a strengthened federal hand in education is warranted, partly because NCLB data now clearly reveal that the state-run systems of old have left so many poor and minority children disastrously behind.

Rep. George Miller, D-Calif., and Sen. Kennedy, key supporters of NCLB and chairs of the House and Senate committees that govern it, have both held pre-authorization hearings this year. Both say they're committed to increasing resources for struggling schools in a new bill, especially by supporting the hiring and training of more and better teachers.

"We know the law has flaws, but we also know that with common-sense changes and adequate resources, we can improve it by building on what we've learned," said Kennedy in a statement.

Retooling NCLB?

Education analysts have no shortage of changes to suggest.

President Bush is looking at "tinkering" with NCLB in a reauthorization, but Democrats are "interested in something broader," says Cardinali of Communities in Schools. "The [current] law is too fixated on academics," he says. After

The Knowledge Is Power Program (KIPP) charter school in the Bronx, N.Y., boasts the highest test scores in the area. Although most KIPP schools are not racially integrated, they are reducing achievement gaps between black and white students.

30 years of experience helping students get additional services they need like tutoring and health care, "we've learned that student services are a critical component," he says.

"The brutal truth is that there is only one institution in America where you can get to kids in a thoughtful way — the school," he says. "Let's make that the center" where parents and children can get needs met that are critical for learning readiness. "Are we trying to make public education something it's not? No. It's a holistic view" of what it takes to educate a child.

One gap the University of Chicago's Knowles would like to see rectified: In NCLB's reporting requirements "the unit of analysis is the kid, the school and the district, and there's a stunning absence there if we really believe that instruction is at the heart of learning." Research indicates, he says, that individual classroom teachers may be the strongest in-school influence on student achievement.

However, "Democrats' strong ties to labor" helped keep teacher accountability out of the bill, he says.

In addition, "higher ed has been given pretty much a free pass," Knowles says. A future bill should focus attention on which education schools are producing the best-quality teachers.

Low-achieving schools shouldn't be punished, but given the tools to do better, says Knowles. Supports like teacher development and well-integrated extra services like social workers, closely targeted on high-need schools, are a "precondition" for improvement, he says.

Another key: additional flexibility for leaders of low-achieving schools to hire and fire and set policy and schedules. Principals say, "Yeah, you give me the hiring and firing of teachers and I'll give you the better results," and they're correct, says Knowles.

Reporting data for accountability isn't the problem. It's the very narrowly focused reporting requirement, many analysts say.

"Replace the overreliance on standardized testing with multiple measures," such as attendance figures and accurate dropout rates, says the University of Rochester's Hursh.

The federal government should also support strong, unbiased research on what improves instruction, especially in the middle- and high-school years, which are federally funded at a tiny fraction of the level of elementary schools and colleges, says Wise of the Alliance for Excellent Education. "No state or local district has the money for this," he says.

OUTLOOK
Agreeing to Disagree

There's growing agreement that schools should be educating all students to a higher standard. However, there's still disagreement about how much and what kind of help schools would need to do it.

An ideal outcome would be for institutions that are the most lasting presence in cities, such as business groups like the Chamber of Commerce, local hospitals and colleges to take ownership of urban education to drive change, says Balfanz of Johns Hopkins. A movement in that direction may be beginning, he says. "For awhile, there were mainly rhetorical reports," but today groups like the Chamber of Commerce are producing more potentially useful policy work, he says.

"The climate is shifting" toward the conclusion that everyone needs a diploma, says Balfanz. "You can't even find an employer who says, 'I'll hire people who aren't high-school graduates.' " So when students drop out, "it just feeds the next generation of poverty," he says.

There's currently an opportunity to revise NCLB in a way that helps low-achieving schools, says the University of Chicago's Knowles. Nevertheless, "people have already formed hard opinions," and debate could turn solely partisan, he says.

Lawmakers must aim for a delicate balance on federal initiatives, says Columbia's Henig. Federal interventions must aim at "making local processes work," since local on-the-ground actions are ultimately what make or break schools, he says.

The University of Pennsylvania's Lytle fears that privatization may be on the verge of overwhelming education, with potentially disastrous consequences for low-income families.

"I think the K-12 education business is in the process of deconstructing," he says. "The middle class is looking outside the schools" to private tutoring companies and Internet learning for academics. "More and more, for them, schools are amounting to expensive child care." Some states are aggressively pioneering "virtual" online charter schools and charters granted to home-schoolers, he says.

"The cost side and the efficacy side of education are on a collision course, and I think Congress will end up endorsing fairly radical experimentation" with vouchers, for example, Lytle says. "They'll say, 'There's no evidence that reducing class size or other expensive measures helps, so let's let American ingenuity work. Where does that leave urban kids? Out of luck," Lytle says. "You've got to be pretty sophisticated to make market forces work for you."

But "there's been progress in the last decade with whole-school reform," says Balfanz. "The big question now is how we [change] whole school districts. "It's a big job but within human capacity," he says.

NOTES

1. Quoted in Judy Radigan, "Reframing Dropouts: The Complexity of Urban Life Intersects with Current School Policy," paper presented at the Texas Dropout Conference, Houston, Oct. 6, 2006.

2. "The Socioeconomic Composition of the Public Schools: A Crucial Consideration in Student Assignment Policy," University of North Carolina Center for Civil Rights, Jan. 7, 2005, www.law.unc.edu/PDFs/charlottereport.pdf.

3. For background, see Barbara Mantel, "No Child Left Behind," *CQ Researcher*, May 7, 2005, pp. 469-492.

4. Quoted in David J. Hoff and Kathleen Kennedy Manzo, "Bush Claims About NCLB Questioned," *Education Week*, March 9, 2007, www.edweek.org.

5. Quoted in *ibid.*

6. "The Nation's Report Card: Reading 2005," U.S. Department of Education Institute of Education Sciences, www.nationsreportcard.gov.

7. Douglas N. Harris, "Ending the Blame Game on Educational Inequity: A Study of 'High-Flying' Schools and NCLB," Education Policy Studies Laboratory, Arizona State University, March 2006.

8. Jay P. Greene, "Education Myths," The American Enterprise Online, American Enterprise Institute, August 2006.

9. For background, see Charles S. Clark, "Charter Schools," *CQ Researcher*, Dec. 20, 2002, pp. 1033-1056; Kenneth Jost, "School Vouchers Showdown," *CQ Researcher*, Feb. 15, 2002, pp. 121-144.

10. Greene, *op. cit.*

11. Brad Olsen and Lauren Anderson, "Courses of Action: A Qualitative Investigation Into Urban Teacher Retention and Career Development," *Urban Education*, January 2007, p. 5.

12. Quoted in *ibid.*, p. 14.

13. *Ibid.*

14. Arthur J. Rothkopf, "Elementary and Secondary Education Act Reauthorization: Improving NCLB To Close the Achievement Gap," testimony before the Senate Committee on Health, Education, Labor, and Pensions and the House Committee on Education and Labor, March 13, 2007.

15. For background, see Kenneth Jost, "Testing in Schools," *CQ Researcher*, April 20, 2001, pp. 321-344.

16. Richard J. Murnane, "Improving the Education of Children Living in Poverty," unpublished paper, Jan. 25, 2007.

17. *Ibid.*

18. For background, see Kenneth Jost, "School Desegregation," *CQ Researcher*, April 23, 2004, pp. 345-372.

19. Quoted in "Center on Race and Social Problems Commemorates *Brown v. Board of Education*," University of Pittsburgh School of Social Work, May 7, 2004.

20. Quoted in Brian Lamb, "No Excuses: Closing the Racial Gap in Learning," transcript, "Booknotes," C-SPAN, Feb. 1, 2004.

21. Paul Tough, "What It Takes To Make a Student," *The New York Times Magazine*, Nov. 26, 2006, p. 70.

22. R. Scott Baker, "School Resegregation: Must the South Turn Back?" *Journal of Southern History*, November 2006, p. 993.

23. Howell S. Baum, "Smart Growth and School Reform: What If We Talked About Race and Took Community Seriously?" *Journal of the American Planning Association*, winter 2004, p. 14.

24. "Divided We Fail: Coming Together Through Public School Choice," Task Force on the Common School, The Century Foundation Press, 2002, p. 3.

25. *Ibid.*, p. 13.

26. Quoted in Lamb, *op. cit.*

27. *Ibid.*

28. Terry Ryan and Quentin Suffren, "Charter School Lessons from Ohio," *The Education Gadfly*, Thomas B. Fordham Foundation, March 15, 2007, www .edexcellence.net.

29. Mark Simon, "What Teachers Know," *Poverty & Race*, September/October 2004, www.prrac.org.

30. Dreyon Wynn and Dianne L. H. Mark, "Book Review: Educating Teachers for Diversity: Seeing With a Cultural Eye," *Urban Education*, May 2005, p. 350.

31. Jocelyn A. Glazier, "Moving Closer to Speaking the Unspeakable: White Teachers Talking About Race," *Teacher Education Quarterly*, winter 2003.

32. Wanda J. Blanchett, "Urban School Failure and Disproportionality in a Post-*Brown* Era," *Remedial and Special Education*, April 2005, p. 70.

33. Christine H. Leland and Jerome C. Harste, "Doing What We Want to Become: Preparing New Urban Teachers," *Urban Education*, January 2005, p. 60.

34. *Ibid.*, p. 62.

35. Glazier, *op. cit.*

36. Wynn and Mark, *op. cit.*

37. For background, see Wayne J. Urban and Jennings L. Wagoner, *American Education: A History* (2003);

Stanley William Rothstein, *Schooling the Poor: A Social Inquiry Into the American Educational Experience* (1994).

38. For background, see Kathy Koch, "Reforming School Funding," *CQ Researcher*, Dec. 10, 1999, pp. 1041-1064.

39. Derrick Bell, *Silent Covenants:* Brown v. Board of Education *and the Unfulfilled Hopes for Racial Reform* (2004), p. 88.

40. *Ibid.*, p. 91.

41. Ruth Curran Neild and Robert Balfanz, "An Extreme Degree of Difficulty: The Educational Demographics of Urban Neighborhood High Schools," *Journal of Education for Students Placed at Risk*, spring 2006, p. 135.

42. V. W. Ipka, "At Risk Children in Resegregated Schools; An Analysis of the Achievement Gap," *Journal of Instructional Psychology*, December 2003, p. 294.

43. The case is *Brown v. Board of Education of Topeka*, 347 U.S. 483 (1954).

44. For background, see Jost, "School Desegregation," *op. cit.*; Gary Orfield and John T. Yun, "Resegregation in American Schools," The Civil Rights Project, Harvard University, June 1999, www.civilrightsproject .harvard.edu/research/deseg/reseg_schools99.php.

45. The case is *Milliken v. Bradley*, 418 U.S. 717 (1974).

46. Ipka, *op. cit.* The cases are *Board of Education of Oklahoma City v. Dowell*, 498 U.S. 237 (1991) and *Freeman v. Pitts*, 498 U.S. 1081 (1992).

47. Gary Orfield and Chungmei Lee, "Racial Transformation and the Changing Nature of Segregation," The Civil Rights Project, Harvard University, January 2006, www.civilrightsproject. harvard.edu; *Keyes v. School District No. 1*, Denver, Colorado, 413 U.S. 189 (1973).

48. Gary Orfield and Susan E. Eaton, "Back to Segregation," *The Nation*, March 3, 2003, p. 5.

49. Baum, *op. cit.*

50. *Ibid.*

51. Neild and Balfanz, *op. cit.*, p. 126.

52. "Divided We Fail," *op. cit.*, p. 17.

53. Tough, *op. cit.*

54. Elaine M. Stotko, Rochelle Ingram and Mary Ellen Beaty-O'Ferrall, "Promising Strategies for Attracting and Retaining Successful Urban Teachers," *Urban Education*, January 2007, p. 36.

55. Patrick Mattimore, "Will Court Put Integration on Hold?" *San Francisco Examiner*, Dec. 8, 2006, www .exaaminer.com. The cases — argued on Dec. 4, 2006 — are *Meredith v. Jefferson County Board of Education*, 05-915; and *Parents Involved in Community Schools v. Seattle School District No. 1*, 05-908.

56. Richard Kahlenberg, "Helping Children Move from Bad Schools to Good Ones," The Century Foundation, 2006, www.tcf.org/list.asp?type= PB&pubid=565.

57. *Ibid.*

58. Quoted in Michael Sandler, "Minding Their Business," *CQ Weekly*, April 2, 2007, p. 952.

59. Quoted in Jonathan Weisman and Amit R. Paley, "Dozens in GOP Turn Against Bush's Prized 'No Child' Act," *The Washington Post*, March 15, 2007, p. A1.

BIBLIOGRAPHY

Books

Kozol, Jonathan, *The Shame of the Nation: The Restoration of Apartheid Schooling in America*, Three Rivers Press, 2006.
A longtime education writer and activist reports on his five-year journey to closely observe 60 schools in 11 states. He describes almost entirely resegregated urban schools with dilapidated buildings, dirty classrooms and a dearth of up-to-date textbooks.

Rothstein, Richard, *Class and Schools: Using Social, Economic, and Education Reform to Close the Black-White Achievement Gap*, Economic Policy Institute, 2004.
A research associate at a think tank concerned with low- and middle-income workers and families argues that raising the achievement of urban students requires public policies that address students' multiple social and economic needs.

Thernstrom, Abigail, and Stephan Thernstrom, *No Excuses: Closing the Racial Gap in Learning*, Simon & Schuster, 2004.

A husband and wife who are senior fellows at the conservative Manhattan Institute for Public Policy Research argue that charter schools and the No Child Left Behind Act's focus on holding schools accountable for poor student achievement can close the achievement gap for urban students.

Articles

Boo, Katherine, "Expectations," *The New Yorker*, Jan. 15, 2007, p. 44.

A reform-minded superintendent closes Denver's lowest-achieving high school, hoping its students will accept the offer to enroll in any other city school, including some with mainly online classes. Mostly Latinos from the city's poorest families, the displaced students struggle with losing their old school, which has provided many with a sense of community, and with new choices that confront them, as well as the ever-present choice of dropping out.

Moore, Martha T., "More Mayors Are Moving To Take Over School System," *USA Today*, March 21, 2007, p. A1.

Albuquerque's mayor is among those who believe they could run schools better than their local school boards.

Saulny, Susan, "Few Students Seek Free Tutoring or Transfers From Failing Schools," *The New York Times*, April 6, 2006, p. 20.

The No Child Left Behind Act promises free tutoring for many students in low-achieving schools, but few of those students' families know about the option or have been able to enroll their children in good-quality tutoring programs.

Tough, Paul, "What It Takes To Make a Student," *The New York Times Magazine*, Nov. 26, 2006, p. 44.

A handful of charter schools are making strides against the achievement gap. But largely because low-income and minority students arrive at school with smaller vocabularies and far less knowledge about how to communicate with adults and behave in a learning situation, the work requires extra-long school hours and intense teacher commitment.

Reports and Studies

Beating the Odds: An Analysis of Student Performance and Achievement Gaps on State Assessments: Results from the 2005-2006 School Year, Council of the Great City Schools, April 2007.

A group representing 67 of the country's largest urban school districts examines in detail the recent performance of urban students on state tests.

Divided We Fail: Coming Together Through Public School Choice, Task Force on the Common School, The Century Foundation, 2002.

Basing its discussion on the idea that race- and class-segregated schools have proven a failure, a nonpartisan think tank explores the possibility of encouraging cross-district integration of low-income and middle-income students by methods like establishing high-quality magnet schools in cities.

Engaging Schools: Fostering High School Students' Motivation to Learn, Committee on Increasing High School Students' Engagement and Motivation to Learn, National Research Council, 2003.

A national expert panel examines methods for re-engaging urban high-school students who have lost their motivation to learn, a problem they say is widespread but solvable.

Bridgeland, John M., John J. DiIulio, Jr., and Karen Burke Morison, *The Silent Epidemic: Perspectives of High School Dropouts*, Bill & Melinda Gates Foundation, March 2006.

Nearly half of high-school dropouts say they left school partly because they were bored. A third of the students left because they needed to work, and more than a fifth said they left to care for a family member.

Levin, Henry, Clive Belfield, Peter Muennig and Cecilia Rouse, "The Costs and Benefits of an Excellent Education for All of America's Children," *Teachers College, Columbia University*, January 2007; www.cbcse.org/media/download_gallery/Leeds_Report_Final_Jan2007.pdf.

A team of economists concludes that measures to cut the number of school dropouts would pay for themselves with higher tax revenues and lower government spending.

For More Information

Achieve, Inc., 1775 I St., N.W., Suite 410, Washington, DC 20006; (202) 419-1540; www.achieve.org. An independent bipartisan group formed by governors and business leaders to promote higher academic standards.

Alliance for Excellent Education, 1201 Connecticut Ave., N.W., Suite 901, Washington, DC 20036; (202) 828-0828; www.all4ed.org. A nonprofit research and advocacy group seeking policies to help at-risk high-school students.

The Center for Education Reform, 1001 Connecticut Ave., N.W., Suite 204, Washington, DC 20036; (202) 822-9000; www.edreform.com. A nonprofit advocacy group that promotes school choice in cities.

The Century Foundation, 41 E. 70th St., New York, NY 10021; (212) 535-4441; www.tcf.org. Supports research on income inequality and urban policy.

Citizens for Effective Schools, 8209 Hamilton Spring Ct., Bethesda, MD 20817; (301) 469-8000; www .citizenseffectiveschools.org. An advocacy group that seeks policy changes to minimize the achievement gap for low-income and minority students.

Council of the Great City Schools, 1301 Pennsylvania Ave., N.W., Suite 702, Washington, DC 20004; (202) 393-2427; www.cgcs.org. A coalition of 67 urban school systems dedicated to improving urban schools.

Education Next, Hoover Institution, Stanford University; www.educationnext.org. A quarterly journal on education reform published by a conservative think tank.

The Education Trust, 1250 H St., N.W., Suite 700, Washington, DC 20005; (202) 293-1217; www2.edtrust .org. Dedicated to closing the achievement gap in learning and college preparation for low-income and minority students.

National Center for Education Statistics, 1990 K St., N.W., Washington, DC 20006; (202) 502-7300; http:// nces.ed.gov. A Department of Education agency that provides statistics and analysis on U.S. schools, student attendance and achievement.

5

Charter Schools

Will They Improve or Hurt Public Education?

Charles S. Clark

Capital City Public Charter School/Dave Philhower

Field trips to Rock Creek Park and the National Zoo are fundamental to the program at Capital City Public Charter School, in Washington, D.C. Nearly 680,000 pre-K–12 students attend charter schools in 39 states and the District — slightly more than 1 percent of the 47 million students in traditional public schools. Educators disagree over whether charters — launched 10 years ago in Minnesota — are a promising innovation or a damaging and costly distraction.

From *CQ Researcher*, December 20, 2002.

Forget your preconceived notions of dilapidated inner-city public schools. At the Capital City Public Charter School, occupying rented quarters above a CVS drugstore on once-infamous 14th Street in Washington, D.C., the brick building is new, the school well-lighted and clean.

Every morning at 8, when the 180 pre-K through seventh-grade students step off the elevator, abuzz with enthusiasm, they are greeted by Principal Karen Dresden, the city's charter school Principal of the Year last year. Dresden's charges represent 17 zip codes around the city and diverse racial groups. Four hundred children are on the school's waiting list.

As a charter school, Capital City is a nonprofit, publicly funded experimental school governed by a board, mostly parent volunteers, including many of the school's founders. It is one of 2,696 charter schools established nationwide since the first one opened its doors 10 years ago in St. Paul, Minn. Charter schools are given freedom from most regulations in return for a promise to meet performance goals or lose their charters, usually granted for five-year intervals.

One of Capital City's founders is Anne Herr, a State Department analyst who heads the Board of Trustees. She says starting the school was a "leap of faith" motivated only in part by some parents' dissatisfaction with the traditional public schools their children attended. "The overall motivation was the excitement of starting something new," Herr recalls, though she admits that they might never have started "if we had known all the issues we were going to encounter."

Most States Permit Charter Schools

Since the early 1990s, 39 states and the District of Columbia have passed laws allowing the creation of charter schools, according to the Center for Education Reform, a pro-charter school group that rates state charter laws according to their strengths. Three states — New Hampshire, Tennessee and Iowa — have enabling laws but no charter schools.

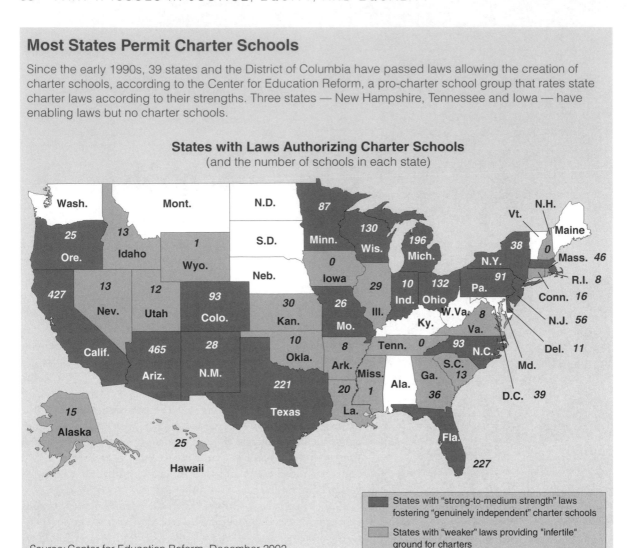

States with Laws Authorizing Charter Schools
(and the number of schools in each state)

- States with "strong-to-medium strength" laws fostering "genuinely independent" charter schools
- States with "weaker" laws providing "infertile" ground for charters

Source: Center for Education Reform, December 2002

Capital City built its instructional regime around two increasingly popular programs: Outward Bound's field-trip-heavy Expeditionary Learning, and a pupil-management approach called the Responsive Classroom, which emphasizes developing social skills and a positive attitude toward selves, school and others.

"It's a real opportunity for teachers to exercise leadership and build the school," Dresden says, adding that their pay and benefits are comparable or better than those in traditional D.C. public schools, even though, she admits, "they do work a little harder." All the teachers boast strong

elementary-education experience, but were not required to jump through all the "hoops and paperwork" of getting locally certified, she says.

Tuition is free at Capital City, which receives public funds based on the normal student-weighted formula — a per-pupil amount, enhanced for special-education students and those with limited English.

Unlike regular public schools, however, charters must find alternative facilities. Financing the lease on the current building — and purchasing a larger one to move into next year — required negotiating loans and revenue bonds from area banks, personally backed by a board member. "Our board has the ideal membership for a startup," Dresden says. "They have backgrounds in banking, facilities, grant-writing, law and architecture. You might think it would be good for board members to know education, but we need their expertise in lots of areas that I'm not as strong in."

Across the country, nearly 680,000 pre-K–12 students attend charter schools in 39 states and the District of Columbia — slightly more than 1 percent of the 47 million students attending traditional public schools. Depending on each state's enabling law, charter schools can be authorized by local school districts, state governments or special chartering boards. Their sponsors include universities, social-service agencies, YMCAs, Boys and Girls Clubs and, increasingly, private, for-profit corporations. Instructional themes range from agriculture to the Montessori method to online learning.

Surveys show that families who choose charter schools want small, effective schools that are responsive to special needs, offer a structured environment and operate flexibly.[1] Yet the charter school movement is bipartisan and philosophically broad. Educational liberals value charters for the freedom to experiment, while conservatives stress the freedom for families to move out of failing schools.

Some enthusiasts see charter schools as opportunities to create laboratories of innovation whose potential has yet to be tapped. "This is a revolution in public education, like democracy was a revolution in how people are governed," says Joe Nathan, director of the Center for School Change at the University of Minnesota. "We're seeing far more sophistication in how charters are set up."

Ron Wolk, founder of *Education Week*, predicts that as charter schools become more popular, they will attract private-school students back into the public system.

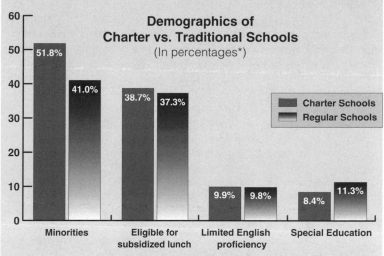

Charter Schools Do Not 'Skim'

Contrary to what critics say, charter schools serve a diverse population, according to an Education Department survey. More than half of charter students are minorities. Charter and traditional public schools serve about the same percentage of poor and non-English speakers, but charters serve slightly fewer students with disabilities.

Demographics of Charter vs. Traditional Schools
(In percentages*)

Charter Schools
Regular Schools

Minorities: 51.8% / 41.0%
Eligible for subsidized lunch: 38.7% / 37.3%
Limited English proficiency: 9.9% / 9.8%
Special Education: 8.4% / 11.3%

* Data for charter schools from 1998-1999; for regular public schools, 1997-1998.

Source: RPP International study, "The State of Charter Schools 2000: Fourth-Year Report," U.S. Department of Education, January 2000, pp. 30-38.

Others see them as an alternative to the public-school status quo. "The current system rewards good teaching by promoting teachers out of the classroom, which promotes mediocrity," says M.S. "Mike" Kayes, project director of the Phoenix-based National Charter School Clearinghouse, a Department of Education-funded group that supplies information on charter schools. "Public education's failures are systemic and institutionalized, so it's not enough to find a new manager. You have to throw off the yoke of how teachers are hired and rewarded."

But critics point out that a disproportionate number of charter schools are set up in ailing urban districts, making many low-income families with at-risk children the guinea pigs for sketchily funded experimentation. Joan Devlin, associate director of educational issues at the American Federation of Teachers (AFT), says even with some successes, charter schools are "a distraction" from reforming mainstream public schools.

Freedom and Headaches: An Educator's Plunge

Taking the plunge into charter schools brings veteran educators freedom — and new headaches. "There was a shocking realization when I went from being in the instructional arena to the business arena in one fell swoop," says Linda Proctor Downing, a former magnet high-school director who started four unique charter schools in Phoenix. "Though I had been an educator for 20 years, I really hadn't understood how hard people in the district bureaucracy have to work to keep instructional programs running day to day."

Downing is now in her sixth year running the nonprofit operation — Arizona Agribusiness and Equine Center (AAEC) — where nearly 300 high school students ride horses and do ranching chores while studying anatomy, physiology, genetics and mathematics.

The Arizona Department of Education funds the schools, housed on community college campuses, but fundraising is always a necessity. Downing is currently in the throes of planning new fundraising to expand the equestrian programs at the two newest centers, started six months ago. "It was an eye-opener that the business aspect meant being on call 24 hours a day, seven days week," she says.

The flexibility Downing has in running the school is reflected in her approach to paying teachers. "We have no salary scale, and we pay what the market demands, with no two similar salaries," she explains. "We hire the best person we can find from an industry, often people whom the school system wouldn't hire because they lack secondary certification."

"We recently stole a biochemist from the local neurological institute," Downing adds. "In my previous school, I had no say in hiring, firing or discipline. Now I can collaborate with staff members and set up an interview team." She can offer job candidates smaller class loads than traditional schools.

The downside to the operation's small size and flexibility is that outside auditors "are a lot harder on us than they are on traditional schools," Downing says. "We're so small that they can spend more time looking at us." The auditors have been impressed both with her students' scores on standardized tests and with the high number of college-level credits they earn from the community colleges — the average student graduates with a 3.43 grade point average and 46 college credits. "Some students have actually received their community college degrees before they get their diploma from us," Downing says.

The program's intimate size also means "we know every kid and parent in the school," Downing says. Parents and children sign an agreement promising to strive for good grades and good attendance; the school promises zero tolerance for

"Charter schools can be good tools if they're carefully done," Devlin says, noting they must be accountable and that their pupils must be required to perform well on the same achievement tests traditional schools are required to give. "And they must be open to all."

Unionized teachers claim that charter schools are a thinly veiled effort to eliminate teachers' unions. Most charter schools do not offer prevailing wages and hours, points out Deanna Duby, a senior policy analyst at the National Education Association (NEA). "They're trying to get rid of union contracts," she says. "They're saying, 'Give us some money and leave us alone, and we'll take care of things.'"

"The majority of our 2.7 million members would just as soon have charter schools go away," Duby says. "They're a sign that we're not doing our job, but many feel that the competition is not fair because if you took away all the regulations [mainstream teachers] work under, we could be creative like charters, too."

In fact, Devlin argues, the tendency of many charters to employ teachers "at will" — without tenure or long-term contracts — is why teacher turnover at the schools is so high: about 60-80 percent. "I'm not saying bureaucracy isn't burdensome, but it is not generally what impedes change and progress," she adds. "It's no longer true that unions prevent school principals from hiring who they want or firing incompetent teachers. You just have to show 'just cause' rather than being capricious."

Many administrators and teachers'-union members worry that charter schools are difficult to govern, organize and regulate, like the Los Angeles charter school that reportedly bought its director a sports car.[2] And authorities revoked the license of Gateway Academy — a chain of California charter schools — after it was discovered misbehavior. "Parents have immediate access to me by phone."

Managerial flexibility stands as a key attraction for entrepreneurial educators. As a Massachusetts charter principal told a researcher for the Thomas B. Fordham Foundation, "When we get a résumé, we call the number, and we can hire the person on the spot if we like them." Another principal explained that his school "expected more of teachers and paid them less, a guarantee that those who took the job really were imbued with the mission of the school."[1]

Some principals boasted of being able to fire a lunch caterer for late deliveries or take students on a field trip with just two days' notice. Others exulted at being freed from the budget syndrome common in traditional schools, in which funds not specifically earmarked are spent haphazardly at the end of the year merely to avoid "losing" them — having them withheld the following year.

Teachers also like the opportunities charter schools offer for in-depth lessons. Dave Philhower, a fourth-grade teacher at the Capital City Public Charter School in Washington, D.C., has taken his students to the National Zoo more than 30 times to study animals and help write children's-level exhibit labels. At his previous teaching job in the suburbs, "I would never have had the release time or an administration so supportive," he says.

The risks of experimentation, however, are high for charter schools, because they have such high profiles, and the financing is often dicey. "In the charter arena, we don't get a

AAEC students Aaron Fontes and Tiana Orberson display their biotech project, "Screening Desert Plants as Potential Antibiotics," at the Future Farmers of America annual competition in Louisville, Ky.

second chance," Downing says. " If you don't get it right the first time, you're likely to end up in the newspaper."

---

[1] Quoted in Bill Triant, "Autonomy and Innovation: How Do Massachusetts Charter School Principals Use Their Freedom?" Thomas B. Fordham Foundation, December 2001.

that some of its 14 schools were teaching Islam, charging parents tuition and hiring convicted felons.[3] The irregularities at Gateway were discovered when a reporter found students praying with their Muslim teachers at a school in Sunnyvale.[4]

Moreover, some studies of student achievement have shown that charter-school test-score gains have been minimal. "If the schools are not effective, they should be curtailed or abandoned," say two Western Michigan University professors.[5]

So far, the Capital City Public Charter School is passing with flying colors. Each year, auditors from the D.C. Public Charter School Board evaluate the school based on students' performance on the Stanford 9 and other standardized tests, as well as non-academic measures like attendance and fulfillment of the school's management plan. During its first year, Capital City reported the highest reading scores of the district's 33 charter schools.

Far less fortunate were the students, staff and parents of three other charter-schools closed by the D.C. Board of Education last June. The World Public Charter School was cited for problems ranging from failing to provide individualized education plans for special-education students and not verifying students' residency to failing to conduct employee background and health checks or supply textbooks.

Nonetheless, charter schools nationwide are on the upswing. President Bush's landmark No Child Left Behind Act proposes new funding and organizational help for charter schools.

"The Clinton administration supported charters as a policy option, but our approach is more entrepreneurial advocacy," says Undersecretary of Education Eugene W. Hickok.

"Charter schools are not just an important part of public education, they are an essential part."

As the charter school movement enters its second decade, here are some of the key issues being debated:

Are charter schools harming the traditional public school system?

In suburban Long Island, N.Y., a group of parents have formed the Coalition to Oppose Charter Schools in Glen Cove. "We want to keep our community desirable," said spokeswoman Gloria Wagner. "The connotation of a charter school is, 'The [traditional public] schools are lousy and are not meeting the needs of our children.' [If charter schools are allowed here], our property values will go down, our taxes will increase to keep the standards up."[6]

In Worcester, Mass., Mark Brophy, president of the local teachers' union, blasted charter schools as "a conspiracy to implode public education" by siphoning away funds needed by traditional schools.[7]

In Indianapolis, officials this fall complained that when four new charter schools opened, the school district lost $1.5 million, mostly because the charters attracted many private-school students.[8] And a recent survey of 49 school districts with charter schools, commissioned by the U.S. Education Department, found that at least half of the districts reported negative budgetary impact.[9]

The financial impact on mainstream schools varies by state, says Paul Houston, executive director of the American Association of School Administrators, in Arlington, Va. "It depends on how closely tethered the charters are to district funds," he says. "In some states, the laws burden districts with oversight and monitoring responsibilities without providing new funds. And superintendents gripe that when charters go belly up, the districts have to sweep up the pieces of a problem they had no role in creating."

A school district's overhead costs are largely fixed, regardless of the number of students, until it reaches "a certain breaking point," Houston adds. So if charter schools reduce the number of children in the mainstream district from, say, 3,000 to 2,800, the district loses the funds for those 200 children who left — but without reducing its overhead. "[Thus], you indirectly impact the kids left in the system, because you still have to maintain buildings and provide services."

But Ted Kolderie, a former journalist and Minnesota citizen activist who helped launch the charter movement, dismisses the siphoned-funds complaint. "You have an established industry that sees change occurring, has trouble changing and tries to stop it," he says. "The complaints are self-interested, though they're not couched that way."

Under the charter school concept, "The money moves, and we finance kids," Kolderie says. "That requires districts to think. All of these assertions come when they think inside the box."

Undersecretary Hickok acknowledges "more than a scintilla of truth" to the problem of rigid overhead costs. "Having said that, I remind my friends in school systems that the issue is not funding or managing their systems, but educating children," he says. "Yes, you've got management challenges, but if families feel their children are not getting an education," it is not the district's job to thwart them.

Critics also complain that the charter movement risks re-segregation and the "Balkanization" of public education, tearing the fabric of communities in ways that have had negative consequences in other countries. For example, after New Zealand abolished its national education department in 1989, the subsequent formation of autonomous schools chosen by parents produced overcrowded, homogenized, re-segregated schools that pick their students rather than vice versa, according to Edward B. Fiske, an education consultant, and Helen F. Ladd, a professor of public policy studies and economics at Duke University.[10]

Charter school proponents say that while the Balkanization charge is logical on the surface, it doesn't hold up to scrutiny. "Neighborhood schools based on housing patterns made sense years ago, but we're now in a crisis in the urban schools," says Jeanne Allen, president of the pro-charter school Center for Education Reform, "and if traditional schools are not serving students, then we must be willing to let them leave."

In fact, neighborhood schools have been losing appeal in some areas, including wealthy suburbs where students attend a variety of alternatives to the local public schools, ranging from religious institutions to college-prep private schools.

Chester E. Finn Jr., charter supporter and president of the Thomas B. Fordham Foundation, says public-school choice offers a "dizzying proliferation of hybrid forms — virtual schooling, home schooling in the morning with charter schooling in the afternoon, public schools outsourced to private firms." Balkanization "implies that having a public school system is our foremost object of concern, but my concern is whether the public is being educated. That can be done in a wide variety of ways."

Indeed, charter proponents say fears that charter schools contribute to re-segregation were not borne out in a recent Education Department survey. It showed that charter schools had 52 percent minorities, compared with 40 percent in traditional public schools, that both sectors had about 39 percent of students in the federal lunch program, and both had about 10 percent with limited English proficiency. The traditional public schools, however, had slightly more special-education students (about 11 percent vs. about 8 percent in charter schools).[11]

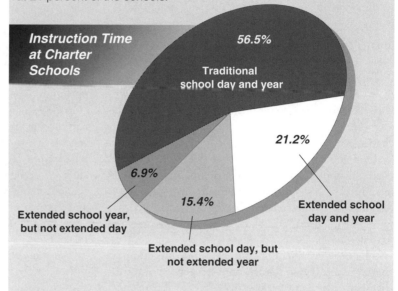

Many Charter Schools Offer Extended Days

More than 40 percent of all charter schools go beyond the traditional school day or year, according to the Center for Education Reform, a pro-charter school group. Both extended days and years are offered at 21 percent of the schools.

Instruction Time at Charter Schools

56.5%
Traditional school day and year

21.2%
Extended school day and year

6.9%
Extended school year, but not extended day

15.4%
Extended school day, but not extended year

Source: Center for Education Reform, October 2002, based on 481 responses from 2,357 charter schools surveyed in September 2001

Many strong public-education advocates do not think charter schools threaten the public schools. "Charters exist because many people want to get out of the bureaucratic environment they're mired in, not because they want to avoid the principles and values of public education," says Wendy Puriefoy, president of the Public Education Network (PEN), an association of community organizations known as local education funds (LEFs), dedicated to improving public schools.

Do charter schools foster innovation and achievement?

After 10 years of the charter school movement, evaluators must still rely largely on anecdotal evidence of innovations and shifting reports of rising or falling test scores — the same complexities and lack of consensus that frustrate discussions of traditional schools.

Skeptics argue that for all the lofty rhetoric about charters being laboratories of innovation that would inspire mainstream schools, mixed results have forced advocates to lower their sights. "The claim was that the schools would be innovative and educators would roll it out on a larger scale," says the NEA's Duby. "We don't hear that now. Instead, you hear, 'Charters provide choice.' That's fine if the schools are innovative and offer something kids can't get in mainstream schools. But if it's just another choice, we're not supportive."

Proponents like Undersecretary Hickok point out that charters were the first to bring in dress codes and instructional programs that weave art and music into the teaching of reading and math. Charters pioneered longer school days and school years and have spotlighted "niche curriculums," such as Core Knowledge and Open Court/Direct Instruction, recently adopted in the Sacramento, Calif., public schools, says the Center for Education Reform's Allen. "The point is not to take one innovation — because the whole charter approach is innovation — but to start with the premise of what can be done differently."

Education scholar Paul Teske found that charter schools deliver innovations more than twice as fast as traditional schools. Among their many innovations: before-and-after-school programs, extra tutoring, high-technology in classes, teacher development, teacher participation in policymaking, pre-K programs, parental contracts and gifted-and-talented programs.[12]

In the Education Department's recent 49-district survey, half of the school leaders with charter schools in their districts reported becoming more customer-oriented, increasing their marketing efforts, tracking students who leave and improving communication with parents. Most districts implemented new programs, or even created new schools with programs like those of the charters.[13]

One superintendent reported that after a second charter school opened in his district, he lost $1 million in state aid. "It's spreading an already-thin budget even thinner," he told researchers, adding that if another charter school opened in his district, he might have to close a school.

The superintendent said he felt competition from the charter schools, even though only 1.3 percent of the district's students had switched to them. He also acknowledged, however, "We're better because of charters. I hate to say it, but we're more aware of the importance of what parents say and have become more customer-service oriented. We're willing to fix anything that parents leave for, like scheduling or busing. The charter schools stole our students; we will steal them back."

As a result of competition from the charter schools, the superintendent implemented several new educational programs, remodeled school buildings, included parents in the hiring process for new principals, encouraged team teaching and directed elementary schools to divide themselves into smaller units, or "families," to increase the sense of community. In addition, he announced that he expected district students to outperform charter school students on future achievement tests and created a new accountability system for district personnel to reinforce that objective.

"There are specialized charter high schools, such as schools for the arts, particularly in urban areas where they're working at reforms," PEN's Puriefoy says. "Urban schools in the standards-based-reform era are like emergency rooms are to medicine. They don't work under antiseptic conditions, and they have people coming in off the streets, but you have the same basic issues of medicine. Urban schools are the real laboratories of learning for public education as a whole."

"In most transitions, the early years are shaky," activist Kolderie says. People complained because "the early automobile was slower than the train, or because the first telephone had a range of only two miles. We never before had a system of autonomous schools. And even when charter schools are using proven learning models, they're still new, in that the organizations created are single-unit operations."

As for student achievement in charter schools, conclusions are complicated because there are no uniform tests or year-to-year data. In the late 1990s, the Phoenix-based Goldwater Institute, a free-market think tank, studied reading scores at Arizona charter and mainstream schools. "Students enrolled in charter schools for two and three consecutive years have an advantage over students staying in [traditional schools] for the same periods of time," the institute said.[14]

But more recent studies are less glowing. In a review released in September by the Brookings Institution's Brown Center on Education Policy, charter school students in four of the 10 states studied scored significantly below those from similar public schools. The study relied on 1999-2001 data from students in grades 4, 8 and 10 in 376 charter schools. Contrary to expectations, students in the urban charter schools scored higher than those in suburban or rural charter schools, and those from larger schools did better than those from small schools.[15]

Similar findings are reflected in an AFT report released in July. It found negative test-score growth in charter schools in six states — North Carolina, Texas, Michigan, Louisiana, Ohio and Pennsylvania — and mixed results elsewhere. Positive results were found only in New Jersey and Connecticut.

The AFT evaluators also concluded that charter teachers feel less empowered to make changes in their workplaces than those in traditional buildings and hold mixed feelings about administrators and governance structures. They said charters encourage innovation but are less effective at changing instruction; that charters help isolate students by race and class; are not accountable financially and neglect special-needs students.[16]

The proliferation of charter schools in Michigan prompted studies by Western Michigan University's Center for Evaluation. "Some districts may be encouraged to improve, but others are launched on a terminal cycle of decline," wrote researchers Michael Mintrom and David N. Plank. "When assessing students' standardized-test scores, no evidence suggests that charter schools are doing better than their traditional counterparts in the same districts."[17]

The North Carolina Center for Public Policy Research and scholars writing for the National School Boards Association both gave thumbs-down reviews of charters.[18]

Not surprisingly, charter advocates question the methodology of some of these studies, calling them biased. "Charter schools are all different," says the Center for Education Reform's Allen. "You have to look at how often the state tests, when the schools opened and whom they serve.

"If you look at individual students' scores, not masked by averages, performance is better at 80 percent of the schools," Allen continues. "With oversight boards and audit groups dropping by more frequently than with traditional schools, charter schools are the most scrutinized movement since desegregation. Yet you find a very optimistic picture, succeeding against all odds."

She points out that more than 50 years of longitudinal trends show that Philadelphia's public schools are failing. "We know more about traditional schools," she notes. "Charters know they are under the gun, but tests are expensive. Many of the schools are serving non-traditional, special-ed, at-risk kids, so they struggle to demonstrate progress. But most are, in fact, doing well by any other measures."

For instance, Allen says, charter school mobility rates are stable (charter kids tend to stay put), high-school graduation rates are at 95-99 percent and 63 percent have waiting lists.

Surveys show rates of student, teacher and parental satisfaction in charter schools triple those of traditional public schools. Finn and his colleagues say parents rate charter schools better on class size, individual attention, school size, teaching quality, parent involvement, curriculum, extra help, enforcing standards, accessibility, discipline, basic skills and safety. Traditional schools rated the same or better only on facilities.[19]

"We have a whole menagerie of charter schools," the Fordham Foundation's Finn says. "Many are fabulous, but there are too many bad and mediocre ones. Some get better, others don't."

The University of Minnesota's Nathan, who notes Minnesota has many prized and influential charter schools, says, "The generic thing called 'charter school' is like the word 'business.' Some are effective, some are not. Some shouldn't have been approved.

"But the key is whether the ineffective ones are closed," he continues. "A lot more charter schools have closed than district schools. More close for business reasons than academic ones, and the ones that do poorly in business also do poorly academically."

Kayes of the National Charter School Clearinghouse argues that the low socioeconomic status of many charter-school students makes it imperative that charters be examined with "more-sophisticated value-added" assessments. "If you're getting high-school kids who come in reading at the sixth-grade level, and if, at the end of one year, they're at the seventh- or eighth-grade level, that's phenomenal," he says.

Parents who choose charter schools for their children tend to be more involved with their kids' educations, Kayes says, and charters tend to be two-thirds to three-fourths smaller than traditional schools. "But improving student performance is absolutely what's needed. If these schools only do as well as their traditional counterparts, then why bother?"

Should private companies be allowed to run charter schools?

In Florida, three-fourths of all new charter school seats are being created by private corporations. Companies like Chancellor-Beacon Academies, based in Coconut Grove, work with developers to build new facilities with small classes. By contracting with counties to receive $2,000 less per student than a traditional school district, they pay teachers less than traditional schools, but they offer them stock options, and, in theory, save taxpayers money.[20]

According to the Center for Education Reform, 19 such companies or their nonprofit subsidiaries — called "educational management organizations" (EMOs) — are operating some 350 schools around the nation, many of them charters. They include nationwide companies like

C H R O N O L O G Y

1970s *Lawmakers and educators experiment with public-school choice programs.*

1971 St. Paul and Minneapolis, Minn., offer the first public choice program in alternative "open" and "free" schools, followed by similar schools in Scarsdale, N.Y., Philadelphia, Pa., and Arlington, Va.

1980s *Nation decides U.S. schools need reform.*

1983 National Commission on Excellence in Education publishes dire warnings about declining quality of U.S. education in "A Nation at Risk" report.

1988 National labor, education and civic leaders hatch idea for charter schools — a concept scribbled on a napkin at Minneapolis foundation conference.

1990s *Charter school movement expands to 36 states and the District of Columbia.*

1991 Minnesota enacts first charter school law.

1992 First charter school opens in St. Paul, Minn. California enacts second charter law.

1993 Charter school laws are enacted in Colorado, Georgia, Michigan, New Mexico and Wisconsin.

1994 Federal government backs charter schools in reauthorization of the 1965 Elementary and Secondary Education Act (ESEA). . . . Arizona enacts one of the nation's most far-reaching charter school laws.

1995 Abandoning earlier opposition, National Education Association (NEA) launches five-year effort that results in four NEA charter schools.

1996 Congress passes District of Columbia School Reform Act granting chartering authority to the D.C. Board of Education and D.C. Public Charter School Board.

1998 ESEA amended with Charter School Expansion Act, which increases federal funding and support.

2000s *Charter school movement continues to expand.*

2000 In presidential campaign, both Republican George W. Bush and Democrat Al Gore promise huge expansion of charter schools; Bush talks of $3 billion in loan guarantees, Gore vows to triple number of schools by 2010.

August 2000 Harvard University's John F. Kennedy School of Government and Ford Foundation award $100,000 to Minnesota for its charter school law, to be used for nationwide advocacy.

Oct. 26, 2000 National Council of La Raza, a nationwide advocacy group for Hispanics, announces it has raised $6.7 million to develop a network of Latino-oriented charter schools.

Nov. 14, 2000 Bill & Melinda Gates Foundation gives nonprofit Aspire Public Schools $3 million to create network of small charter schools, part of larger efforts to create smaller schools.

Jan. 8, 2002 President Bush signs No Child Left Behind Act, requesting $300 million in funding for charter schools and guaranteeing that charters can continue to report their yearly progress to their sponsors, rather than the local school board.

April 29-May 3, 2002 President Bush proclaims National Charter Schools Week. "Charter schools embody the principles of President Bush's No Child Left Behind plan — marrying strict accountability for results, greater options for parents and families, and more freedom and flexibility than traditional public schools," Education Secretary Rod Paige says.

June 19-22, 2002 Education Department convenes fourth national charter school conference in Milwaukee.

June 27, 2002 U.S. Supreme Court rules in favor of Ohio's school voucher program, which allows public-school kids to attend parochial schools in Cleveland, using public education funds for their tuition; some charter school advocates are pleased.

Nov. 5, 2002 GOP election gains boost advocates for voucher programs in Texas, South Carolina and Colorado, in addition to those in effect in Florida, Ohio and Wisconsin.

Edison Schools and National Heritage Academies. In Ohio, White Hat Ventures LLC, founded by a millionaire industrialist and private-voucher advocate, runs a sixth of the state's 91 charter schools. In New York state, companies run half the charter schools, and in Michigan, two-thirds.[21]

To some public-school purists, such public-private partnerships represent a disturbing trend. "It's based on deception," says the NEA's Duby. "The law says a public school can't be for-profit, so they set up a nonprofit foundation. The big corporate guys believe there is money to be made, so some are diving in to take over the charter movement. It will be interesting to see how many mom-and-pop charters will survive and to what degree the movement will become for-profit."

Critics also scoff at the notion that a "cookie-cutter" design from a large corporation can meet the individual needs of kids and families in diverse neighborhoods. "Education is hard," Duby says. "Learning occurs through day-to-day interaction. Corporations can't come in and say, 'We've got magic.' Which kids? Which environment? On what day? Too often they make decisions based on a test score here, a number there. But it's more complex than you think."

Paul Hill, a University of Washington professor and longtime researcher on public schools, warns that schools may not develop a strong sense of "internal accountability" if they do not control such crucial items as their own budget and curriculum. Authorizers who have a positive opinion of an EMO "may be less likely to look critically at each school affiliated with that EMO during both the application and oversight processes."[22]

The companies deny any deception. "We're not in the business of dummy organizations," says Vickie Frazier-Williams, vice president of community and board relations for Chancellor-Beacon Academies. "Every state law is different. Some allow a for-profit to own, run and operate a public school; others require a nonprofit. It's difficult to keep up with changes. But friendly school boards look to us, research us and invite us in."

As for actually earning a profit, Frazier-Williams points out that her company receives a fixed 10-12 percent of a district's payments, so proceeds from any efficiencies are channeled back into the schools. "The profit comes from growing in many different places," she says. "Charters are the toughest model

because the parents vote with their feet. We have to please them."

She also dismisses the common charge that companies try to create cookie-cutter, or "McCharter" schools. "Maybe that happens in the early days, but every child, school and community is different, and each principal sets a different tone," Frazier-Williams says. Chancellor-Beacon partners with land developers to build new schools in overcrowded districts. The school boards consist of parents who all live in the same development, as opposed to traditional school boards, which usually are elected from all parts of a school district.

Marc Egan, director of the Voucher Strategy Center at the Alexandria, Va.-based National School Boards Association, says a local school board — which normally is elected — should be the agency that grants charters. A publicly accountable board must decide whether a school meets the public's needs — not a university or a nonprofit that may be a dummy front, he says.

"What is their motivation? To please some financiers 2,000 miles away?" Egan asks. "You can't eliminate public accountability from how the taxpayer education dollar is being spent."

Undersecretary Hickok disagrees. "School boards, as originally structured, are democratic. But what could be more democratic than parents voting with their feet?"

Finn points out that, technically, under most state constitutions, state governments are charged with educating children — not just local school boards.

"Schools we have now are gypping so many kids and have no prospect of turning around," Finn says. "It's unjust to say we must keep these kids trapped in schools that are not doing what they say they are."

Finn also calls the fear of profit-taking a "red herring." Regular schools contract with private companies to provide lunch and bus services, computers, textbooks, building maintenance and tutoring, he points out. "So a non-trivial part of the budget flows into the coffers of for-profits," he says. "Does that make [those companies] a front? People who don't like choice or charters are trying to get people agitated into thinking EMOs are evil."

Allen also defends the companies. "Anyone who wants to make a quick buck doesn't go into education," she says. "And there is a philanthropic edge to even the most for-profit companies, though there are exceptions. The key is what the company is doing for kids. You can't

Are Charter Schools Failing Special Education?

When Patricia Chittams removed her learning-disabled son from the World Public Charter School, in Washington, D.C., she said he wasn't receiving the extra help he needed.

"They provided no special-education services, no matter how much we wrote and begged," said Chittams. "They did nothing."[1]

Ultimately, the city school board closed World Public and another local charter school, charging — among other problems — that they had failed to provide adequate special-education services.

Some parents and educators fear that the nation's 2,700 charter schools, because of their experimental, regulation-exempted structure, may be neglecting children with disabilities.[2] "Its hard to say that the charter school movement has been beneficial to special-education students," says National School Boards Association (NSBA) spokesman Marc Egan.

Others argue that the charter school model allows schools to better serve children with disabilities. "If you're a charter school that serves the deaf or the blind, then you get an economy of specialization, and you can really concentrate on serving those kids' needs," says Herbert J. Walberg, a scholar at the Hoover Institution and charter school board member.

Government assessments of the prevalence of special-education programs at charter schools have produced seemingly contradictory results. A Department of Education study completed in 1999 found that special-education students made up 8.3 percent of the charter school student population, compared to 11.2 percent at regular public schools. However, the same report also cited findings indicating that charter schools enroll special-education students at a slightly higher rate than their regular counterparts.[3] In conclusion, the Education Department researchers say in most areas data on charter schools and special education "are scant."[4]

And since charter schools are authorized by 39 different state laws, it's difficult to broadly assess their impact. "The federal government is not collecting data on charter schools and special education because the states are responsible for monitoring [them]," says Eileen Ahearn, program director at the National Association of State Directors of Special Education.

While charter schools do not have to comply with many federal and state regulations, they are not exempt from federal laws prohibiting discrimination against the disabled or handicapped. "The laws say [public] schools must provide special-education services to students with disabilities," says Lynda Van Kuren, spokeswoman for the Council for Exceptional Children. "Therefore, it is incumbent on charter schools to provide those services."

A 1975 federal law — now called the Individuals with Disabilities Education Act (IDEA) — says no student can be denied admission or participation in any school program receiving federal financial assistance.[5] Federal funds make up about 7 percent of overall public school monies. "Charter schools are public schools, they're receiving tax dollars and they cannot deny admission to any student," says Egan of the NSBA.[6]

Yet some charter school programs have logged a disproportionate number of special-education-related complaints. For instance, Arizona — which with 465 charter schools has more than any other state — recently revealed that its charter schools accumulate special-education complaints at a rate six times higher than traditional public schools.[7]

"Recently there seems to be an increasing number of hearings requested [under IDEA] regarding charter schools," Ahearn says. Charter schools must accept every

fire the Miami-Dade County teachers' union, but you can fire Edison."

Houston, of the school administrators' group, says he is "more open" to giving EMOs a shot than are many of his colleagues. "Some do a better job than critics say, but they're not the ultimate solution. They're not a cash cow, and some of them may exclude high-cost, special-education kids."

In October, the General Accounting Office, the investigative arm of Congress, released a report saying there is no evidence to prove or disprove EMOs' claims of raising student achievement, because none of the data provided had scientific rigor. Rep. Chaka Fattah, D-Pa., who requested the study, warned Congress to "be leery" of private education companies.

student that applies or hold a lottery if there are more applicants than the school can accommodate.[8]

However, Ahearn is not aware of any federal lawsuits challenging charter schools' treatment of special-ed students. She attributes the lack of complaints to the availability of official avenues of complaint under IDEA.

Advocates for the disabled say some charter schools are "weeding out" the harder-to-educate special-education students. They might be avoiding special-ed students because they score more poorly on standardized tests, and educators are under increasing pressure to show improvement on test scores.[9] Egan admits that he has no hard statistics on how widespread the practice is. "We have some concerns that charter schools may only be admitting children with less-severe disabilities, because they are less costly to educate and provide for," he says.

Charter advocates argue that federally mandating special-education services at charter schools only makes them less effective. "The whole idea of charter schools is to get away from bureaucratic regulation from the federal and state governments," Walberg says. "Special education — because of these bureaucratic and burdensome categories like IDEA — causes a real burden for charter schools. The federal regulations should be loosened."

Because most charter schools are smaller than their traditional public-school counterparts, they may lack the facilities and staff to meet every child's special needs. "You have this huge inefficiency of these federal and state programs. It's a way that the forces of the status quo can prevent charter schools from thriving," Walberg adds.

For some, charter schools offer a middle ground between federally mandated inclusion and non-traditional public schooling. At the CHIME charter school in Los Angeles, Principal Julie Fabrocini and her colleagues integrate children with special needs into mainstream classrooms, a process required by IDEA. "Being a charter school affords us more opportunities to more thoroughly integrate kids with disabilities, because we start from the ground up and bring in staff and faculty who are of like mind," she says. "We want schools to [reflect] an accurate representation of the community, and we want to stop an institutionalized perspective for people with disabilities."

In the end, until more legitimate research is done, the jury is still out on whether the disabled are being adequately served by charter schools. "The data collection is still being done to see what exactly the charter school movement has given to special education," adds Egan.

Walberg agrees: "It's nearly impossible to answer the question of how well charter schools are serving special-education students because charters are very heterogeneous. What we have right now are arguments rather than evidence."

— Benton Ives-Halperin

---

[1] Justin Blum, "Revoked Charter Schools Still Open; Facilities Appealing D.C. Board's Order," *The Washington Post*, May 6, 2002, p. B1.

[2] Center for Education Reform, www.edreform.com/pubs/chglance.htm.

[3] See Thomas A. Fiore and Lessley M. Harwell, "Integration of Other Research Findings with Charter Schools and Students With Disabilities: A National Study," U.S. Department of Education, 2000.

[4] *Ibid.*

[5] From the "Twenty-Third Annual Report to Congress on the Implementation of the Individuals with Disabilities Education Act," Office of Special Education Programs, Department of Education, May 14, 2002.

[6] For background, see Kathy Koch, "Special Education," *The CQ Researcher*, Nov. 10, 2000, pp. 905-928.

[7] Pat Kosan, "Charter Schools Exceed in Special Ed Complaints," *The Arizona Republic*, Dec. 10, 2002.

[8] Eileen Ahearn, "Public Charter Schools and Students With Disabilities," Educational Resources Information Center, June 2001.

[9] Maria L. La Ganga, "Charter School's Scores Up, So Why Is Board Unhappy?" *Los Angeles Times*, March 18, 2001, p. A1.

BACKGROUND

Born on a Napkin

The roots of the charter school movement date to the early 1970s, when the "hippie" movement was trickling down to the high-school level. Reformers in St. Paul, Scarsdale, N.Y., Philadelphia and Arlington, Va., began setting up experimental "free schools" within public schools.

Later, as the national pendulum swung toward a "back to basics" educational approach, the Reagan administration in 1983 released its landmark "A Nation at Risk" report, warning of a rising tide of "mediocrity" in America's public schools. Though educators of all leanings took the harsh report seriously, many felt it was an effort to pave the way for a "school choice" movement that might include taxpayer-supported private-school vouchers.

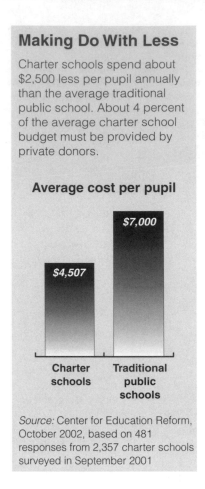

Making Do With Less

Charter schools spend about $2,500 less per pupil annually than the average traditional public school. About 4 percent of the average charter school budget must be provided by private donors.

Average cost per pupil

$7,000

$4,507

Charter schools   Traditional public schools

Source: Center for Education Reform, October 2002, based on 481 responses from 2,357 charter schools surveyed in September 2001

By the late '80s, California had considered legislation that would have required school districts to offer alternative programs if at least 20 parents expressed an interest. Minnesota, at the behest of then-Gov. Rudy Perpich, enacted two laws that permitted public-school transfers across district lines. And Philadelphia began experimenting with "chartering" new educational structures within districts. Meanwhile, overseas, the British Parliament enacted the 1988 Education Reform Act, which allowed schools to opt out of their local district to join a national network.[23]

But many say the official birth of American charter schools occurred at a 1988 Minneapolis Foundation education conference, where the charter-school concept was scribbled on a napkin by a group of seven education and civic leaders: then-AFT President Albert Shanker; Sy Fiegel,

a veteran of the East Harlem school-choice plan; Barbara Zohn, president of the Minnesota Parent Teacher Student Association; Elaine Salinas, the Twin Cities education program officer for the Urban Coalition; Kolderie, of the Citizens League in Minneapolis; Ember Reichgott, a Democratic state senator from Minneapolis; and the University of Minnesota's Nathan.[24]

The advocates, Nathan says, shared a worldview as ambitious as that of early women's-suffrage activist Susan B. Anthony. Shanker dubbed the schools as "charter" institutions, borrowing the name from a book by New England educator Ray Budde, who drew on the idea of Renaissance kings giving charters to explorers to find new worlds.[25] Former Education Secretary Lamar Alexander, then-chairman of the National Governors' Association, first proposed allowing charter schools to trade exemptions from regulations for improved results.

States Climb Aboard

Minnesota passed the nation's first charter school law in 1991. Initially, it was opposed by Gov. Arne Carlson and the Minnesota teachers' unions, whose members called the idea "insulting." The NEA told Congress it was "unalterably opposed" to charters; later it would launch its own charter schools.

The Minnesota program began modestly by authorizing eight charter schools, but a year later only one — the City Academy in St. Paul — had opened its doors.

In 1992, California became the second state to authorize charter schools. Republican Gov. Pete Wilson signed charter-school legislation after a competing voucher initiative was defeated at the ballot box. Five more states followed suit in 1993, and in 1994 Arizona enacted one of the country's most activist, free-market-oriented charter-school laws. Arizona's campaign was led by then-state legislator Lisa Graham Keegan, who later became the state's superintendent of education. The same year, Congress authorized experiments with charter schools when it reauthorized the Elementary and Secondary Education Act.[26]

The charter school movement has now spread to 39 states and the District of Columbia, stressing all or parts of four basic theories, according to University of Washington researcher Hill. Some states, like Georgia, pursued innovation/experimentation strategies. Others — California and Colorado — pursued a more traditional, standards-based reform approach. Michigan and Massachusetts adopted a "new supply of schools" strategy, emphasizing broadening the array of operators. The state with the most charter schools, Arizona, used a "competition/market strategy," which gives parents the widest choices possible.[27]

Charter bills were more likely to pass in Republican-controlled states, according to researcher Bryan C. Hassel.[28] In Georgia and Colorado, the governors wanted to keep school boards in charge of charter schools, while governors in Massachusetts and Michigan saw them as a way to bypass the school boards and teachers' unions.

In some states, strange political bedfellows pushed the legislation through. The charter school bill in New York, for example, was stalled due to opposition from teachers' unions and the state education commissioner. To get the law enacted during a December 1998 lame-duck session, Republican Gov. George Pataki formed an alliance with black leaders from the Urban League, the Rev. Floyd Flake (a former Democratic congressman), Edison Schools and some business leaders.

Most charter schools are in urban areas, "where it's easier to make the argument that you need to do this," says the AFT's Devlin. There is less pressure for such schools in wealthy suburbs, she says, where the public schools are performing relatively well. Some charter laws included specific provisions designed to prevent racial resegregation.

However, charter schools are popular in the suburbs in Colorado, New Jersey and Connecticut, "where proponents have overcome fear of 'unwanted competition' among mainstream educators," one researcher says.[29]

The resulting mosaic of charter schools and related laws is notable for its variations. Minnesota's charter schools, for example, have 43 different sponsoring organizations. In California, 75 percent of charter schools require contracts for parental involvement. And in Indianapolis, the mayor has most of the authority to authorize new charters.

Union opposition, for the most part, has evolved from efforts to block legislation to proposals for charter reforms, such as requirements that the schools hire certified teachers, allow collective bargaining, obtain school board approval, ban contracts with for-profit companies and impose uniform student testing.[30]

But Wolk, of *Education Week*, says unions seeking to reform charters must not remain enamored with "a

bureaucracy that can't tolerate deviation or inconsistency." "The Boston teachers' contract alone is six-inches deep with rules that have accreted over the years," he says. "It's OK to have regulations to ban racial and ethnic discrimination, but most of the regulations are just more paperwork."

Creative Resources

The biggest challenge facing budding charter schools has been the shortage of facilities. In Massachusetts, five of the 14 schools set to open in 1994 still had no buildings lined up, five months before the school year was to start. One charter school temporarily used a motel; recess was held in the parking lot.[31]

Charter schools have found homes in office buildings, warehouses, old parochial schools, strip malls and storefronts, says Jon Schroeder, director of the St. Paul-based National Charter Friends Network. Even so, he points out, they must abide by local building codes, since health and safety regulations cannot be waived. Some states provide "transition impact aid" to help charter founders locate appropriate facilities, while other states offer unused public school buildings. The federal government now supplies some funds for charter facilities.

A variety of organizations have sprung up around the country dedicated to helping charter schools secure buildings and other necessities. "We sponsor job fairs for recruiting teachers and help bring in experts on internal systems," says Shirley Monastra, executive director of the District of Columbia Public Charter School Resource Center. The group also meets informally with representatives of other resource centers in several states. Plus, California State University has launched a Charter School Development Center, while the Walton Family Foundation circulates accountability methods in several states.

Outsourcing is a common practice. According to the Education Department, 54 percent of charter schools obtain legal services from a non-district provider, 59 percent do so for insurance, 46 percent for payroll and 42 percent for social services.[32]

Funding levels for charter schools differ by state, and some argue that they are underfunded. In Washington, D.C., the per-pupil funding rate is 100 percent, which means that charter schools receive 100 percent of what traditional schools receive. But New Jersey charter schools only receive 90 percent of that, Monastra says.

A recent survey by the Center for Education Reform found that the average per-pupil cost in charter schools is $4,507 — significantly less than the $7,000 average in traditional public schools.

However, a study of charter school funding conducted by the AFT found that in some cities, like Boston, charters were actually receiving $1,800-$2,000 more than mainstream schools, Devlin says.[33] She notes that there are more elementary-level charter schools than high schools because high schools have many higher fixed expenses, such as biology labs.

But the University of Minnesota's Nathan insists the AFT is wrong. "There is substantially less money in virtually every charter school," he says. And, many states and cities provide a financial cushion to shield districts from the impact of per-pupil funds lost to charter schools.

"The unions want to keep the competition starving," the Thomas B. Fordham Foundation's Finn says. "The public systems are abysmally awful at handling contraction. If they lose 25 kids, they should get rid of a teacher or close a classroom or building instead of insisting that costs are rising."

Some union locals have challenged the constitutionality of charter schools in court, but such lawsuits have been rejected in California, Colorado, Michigan, Minnesota and New Jersey, according to Schroeder of the National Charter Friends Network. A suit by the Ohio Federation of Teachers challenging the diversion of public funds to charter schools is still pending. In California, the affluent Sequoia Union District sued the state to avoid paying $1 million for facilities required by a state-sponsored local charter school because the district never approved the school. A judge ruled in late August that Sequoia must provide the facilities.[34]

"Charter schools are facing challenges and need capital," says Puriefoy of the Public Education Network. "It's as if General Motors announced a new line of cars but would not provide new capital."

Funding charter schools, says the NEA's Duby, should not mean that teachers give up their pension plans. "Yes, the schools are freed from the bureaucracy of the central office, but many are also freed of [the requirement that they provide] support services, such as buses, food and special education. They find themselves spread thin, and many may be more in need of union support."

Seeking Accreditation

Being free and experimental, most charter schools have forgone the traditional accreditation process, designed to assure officials and the public that a given school meets basic standards in its instructional program and physical plant. Some charters, to reassure parents that their children's charter-school credits will be transferable, apply for accreditation with one of the Education Department's six approved regional accrediting bodies. In the early years, the absence of standardized testing was a major obstacle to accreditation, but the Center for Education Reform reports that 98 percent of charter schools now require at least one standardized test.

Many charter school operators feel they need their own accreditation methods, if only to weed out failing schools to avoid tarring the entire movement. Kayes, of the National Charter School Clearinghouse, says some schools are accredited by the Arizona-based Association for Performance-Based Accreditation, while others are working with the Washington-D.C.-based American Academy for Liberal Education. But some regional bodies exclude charters without certified teachers, which Kayes calls "unreasonable."

This fall, California offered a new accreditation program using team visits, conducted jointly over two years by the California Network of Educational Charters and the Western Association of Schools and Colleges. The program was implemented as Democratic Gov. Gray Davis was imposing new regulations on charter schools after revelations about abuses at some schools, and central district officials complained they lacked the resources to properly monitor charter schools.[35]

Similar complaints last winter about the burden of quality control prompted the Pennsylvania School Boards Association and 100 school districts in the Keystone State to sue a group of "virtual" charter schools that had enrolled some 5,100 K-12 students in an online learning program. The suit claimed the schools drain funds from the public schools and were not sufficiently accountable.[36]

However, some observers fear that the accreditation trend — as well as new demands of the No Child Left Behind Act and the academic-standards movement — could force conformity and standardization on charter schools, says Minnesota activist Kolderie. "Some of the most interesting charter schools have no courses and no employees; they break convention," he says.

Others are concerned about the tendency of some charter schools to engage in religious or quasi-religious instruction. In San Bernardino County, Calif., a charter school was recently disciplined for teaching Christianity.[37] And a charter school in Yuba River, Calif., which features the philosophical Waldorf teaching method, was hit with a lawsuit in 2001 accusing it of practicing religion.[38]

The religion question is a difficult one, says the Fordham Foundation's Finn. "We want to teach character — meaning values, ethics and morals — but not religion," he says. "Some educational programs look to some like religion — they light candles and have rites and rituals. But it's not God or theologically based prayers.

"There's plenty of goofy stuff at charters, even at the progressive schools that practice constructivist nonsense that might work well for some but works badly for others, particularly the disadvantaged."

CURRENT SITUATION

Federal Support

The Bush administration has requested an all-time high of $300 million for charter schools for fiscal 2003.

In June, Education Secretary Rod Paige presided over a charter school conference in Milwaukee that drew record attendance and energized the movement with plans to form new, national, charter school alliances, according to Undersecretary Hickok.

Charter advocates, for the most part, are pleased by the boost charter schools received in the No Child Left Behind Act. The law's requirement that all students demonstrate "adequate yearly progress" in proficiencies toward state standards in core subjects may actually be easier for charter schools, says an analysis by the Center for Education Reform, because they have experience with contracts. But unlike the traditional public schools, notes Schroeder of the National Charter Friends Network, new accountability requirements will be overseen by the schools' authorizers and sponsors, rather than by the school districts. "Time will tell how that will work, and to what extent the existing accountability plans for charters will be incorporated into the overall state plans."

Kayes of the National Charter School Clearinghouse notes that when the time comes for failed schools to be identified under the No Child Left Behind Act, one option would be to turn them into neighborhood charter schools.

Vouchers Link

The November elections, in which Republicans routed Democrats in many parts of the country, were seen as a boon to the school-choice movement in general. Among the winners, 52 percent favor school choice and only 35 percent oppose it, says the Center for Education Reform. Moreover, Republican gains in Congress and in the Florida, Ohio and Wisconsin legislatures were seen as a plus for the related school-voucher movement.[39]

Vouchers are considered more radical than charters, in that many voucher proposals permit public funds to be used for education at private schools, including parochial institutions. Republicans are more inclined toward vouchers than Democrats, even though support for charter schools is evident in both parties. "The parties differ in motivation," the AFT's Devlin says. "Some advocates on the right view charter schools as the camel's nose under the tent for vouchers. Liberal Democrats see them as the moat protecting public schools from vouchers."

Undersecretary Hickok argues that critics create a "false dichotomy" between vouchers and charter schools. "The American public needs to have choice in the broadest sense, and we hope vouchers are part of it," he says.

With vouchers, public funds can be used for tuition at religious schools, as the Supreme Court ruled in a "straightforward decision" last June, Hickok adds, as long as the purpose of the program is secular education. "This administration has its faith-based initiative in play here. So if a school has a secular instructional purpose, that doesn't mean religious people can't be providers."

Allen of the Center for Education Reform sees a variety of education reforms moving on parallel tracks, all responding to different deficiencies of public education. "The voucher is the more direct, immediate service," she says. "Most in education reform say the system for too long was impervious to change and has failed to educate most kids to the levels we need it to. So there's a significant need for choice, but there's no one-size-fits-all approach."

Do charter schools help public education?

YES
Jeanne Allen
President, Center for Education Reform

Written for the *CQ Researcher*, December 2002

Since their inception, charter schools have been committing to opening their doors to children who would not normally have a chance. Success for charters means success for all of education. Researchers who have studied the effect of charters on public education found:

- In California, charter schools are more effective than traditional public schools at improving academic achievement for low-income and at-risk students; in Chicago, charter schools performed better on 80 percent of student performance measures; in Arizona, a statewide study of 60,000 youngsters found charter pupils outperforming traditional public school students.
- Higher proportions of disadvantaged and special-needs students attend charter schools — the antithesis of "skimming the cream" from the public schools, as critics allege. Charters enrolled a larger percentage of students of color than all public schools in the charter states. In 1998-99, the most recent year for which data are available, charter schools were more likely than all public schools to serve black students (24 percent vs. 17 percent) and Hispanic students (21 percent vs. 18 percent).
- Academic accountability: Performance is intensively reviewed by authorizers and parents who must annually renew their commitment to a school.
- Parent and teacher satisfaction surpasses that of parents and teachers in traditional public schools.

Critics contend charter schools do no better than traditional ones, citing some "bad apple" stories or low-grade research. Seven percent of all charters that ever opened have been shut down for failing to meet their goals. Yet 11 percent of all public schools are failing, and there are no provisions for closure.

Charter schools are improving education by sparking improvements in the traditional system — leading schools and districts to alter behavior or improve offerings.

Charters offer at-risk programs and state-of-the-art education. They provide arts and music education, Core Knowledge, Montessori, Back to Basics or other thematic instruction; double the reading instruction; raise the expectations; set innovative discipline policies and ensure parental buy-in. Teachers get wide latitude, and more time is spent teaching.

They educate but do not over-label special-needs children. With 80 percent of the funds normally allotted for education, they are still expected to perform, and perform better — and they do. Some people ask why this can't be done in the regular public school system. The answer is quite simple: Educational change doesn't happen without pressure.

NO
Joan Devlin
Associate Director, Educational Issues Department, American Federation of Teachers (AFT)

Written for the *CQ Researcher*, December 2002

In 1988, when former AFT President Albert Shanker first embraced the idea of charter schools, he envisioned them as laboratories of innovation that would offer new curricula and teaching strategies, eliminate burdensome red tape and improve student achievement.

But today, good charter schools are few and far between. A recent AFT report found that most charters have not lived up to their promise to raise student achievement and promote innovation. Of current charter schools, more than half:

- Fail to raise student achievement compared to traditional public schools in the same area;
- Fall far short of meeting expectations to bring innovation into the classroom and the public school system at large;
- Tend to sort children by socioeconomic status; and,
- Spend more money on administration and less on instruction than other public schools.

Charter schools' staunchest defenders may try to dismiss the AFT report as an aberration, but recent independent research — in states like California, North Carolina and Texas — confirms AFT's findings that charter schools are not leading to innovation or higher student achievement, and, in fact, too often are failing to keep pace with the public schools.

States bear some of the blame for the failure of charter schools. Few states provide adequate oversight, leading to mismanagement and fraud. In Ohio, the Coalition for Public Education has filed a suit charging that Ohio's charter-school program violates the state constitution. And California newspapers assert that state's charter schools have used taxpayer dollars to hire convicted felons, buy a sports car for a school official and commit other offenses. More than half of the nation's charter schools are in Arizona, California, Florida, Michigan, Ohio and Texas, yet these states have open-ended charter school laws that allow such abuses to continue unchecked.

Ardent charter school supporters focus on the few positives, while ignoring or distorting the main body of research and will certainly continue to push for more charters and less oversight. That would be a mistake. To date, the charter experiment is a disappointment at best. Charter schools serve only as a distraction from effective reforms that are raising achievement in communities around the country: smaller class sizes, better early childhood education and greater emphasis on putting well-qualified teachers into every classroom. Policymakers owe it to the public to examine the existing research before they give charter schools a blank check for expansion.

But the Public Education Network's Puriefoy argues that the goal of charters is to give parents and communities "a point of entry" into improving the public education system. *Education Week's* Wolk doesn't agree that charters are "a stalking horse for vouchers." Instead, he feels they are "the best defense against vouchers."

Like the early civil rights movement, there is plenty of vigorous disagreement within the school-choice movement, the University of Minnesota's Nathan says. [Former Supreme Court Justice] "Thurgood Marshall didn't agree all the time with Martin Luther King Jr.," he says. "In any major movement, there are major disagreements.

"I don't think vouchers are a good idea," he continues. Just as there are limits on freedom of speech, so there must be limits on school choice. Schools must be open to all kinds of kids, and voucher advocates want to be sectarian and pick and choose kids."

Steps Forward and Back

Charter schools in the nation's largest school district got a boost this October when newly installed New York City public schools Chancellor Joel Klein announced plans to create additional charter schools. He vowed create a "more welcome environment" for the experimental schools, of which there are currently only 18. The students who go to charter schools only receive two-thirds of the amount traditional school students receive.[40]

In November in Los Angeles, the second-largest system, a newly reconfigured group of school reform activists and academics announced plans to set up 100 charter schools. Members of the Los Angeles Alliance for Student Achievement want to form a "shadow" public school system, run by a nonprofit corporation, to create a more college-bound school culture.[41]

But in Boston, the Massachusetts Department of Education canceled plans to open six additional charter schools next fall, saying that 11 charter schools in the city is enough, given current budget constraints. Ohio, Texas and California also have introduced new curbs on charters.[42]

OUTLOOK

Just a Fad?

No one said the road to a nation of charter schools would be smooth. In Douglas County, Colo., the oldest charter school went through five principals in eight years.[43] Nearly 7 percent of new charter schools fail, according to a recent Center for Education Reform survey — fewer than the 11 percent of public schools the center claims are failing.

"Yes, the closings are wasteful," Kayes of the Charter School Clearinghouse acknowledges, "but what plan do the mainstream schools have for improving?"

Researcher Hassel says the implementation problems and "political compromises" that some charter advocates have been forced to accept "have severely hampered the ability of charter school programs to live up to their promise."[44] For example, 14 states rewrote their charter laws between 1997 and 1998.

The Fordham Foundation's Finn predicts more charter schools will be established in the coming decade, and more data will be available for evaluating them. But the foundation is shifting its focus from the quantity of charter schools to the quality.

Undersecretary Hickok is concerned about losing the movement's "entrepreneurial spirit" to the institutionalization of charter schools. "It could get co-opted" by bureaucracy, he says.

But he is confident the Education Department will help charter schools reach out to disengaged parents and communities. "We can create interest on the part of parents a generation or two removed, for whom there is the possibility of a different kind of community," he says.

Charter schools have a "mixed track record" that in many ways is a distraction for public education, says Houston of the school administrators' association. "They are neither a huge threat nor a landmark innovation," he says. "But if the laws are structured right, administrators should be able to use them for reforms, to leverage and embrace an array of options for improvement."

The movement is "here to stay, at least in the short term, so we will participate," says the NEA's Duby.

"The vista looks promising in terms of the viability of charter school policy innovation," writes Sandra Vergari, an assistant professor of educational administration and policy studies at the State University of New York at Albany. "Symbolically, politically and substantively, the reform appears to hold more long-term significance than the typical fad in educational policy and administration."[45]

But she also asks whether charters might meet individual interests, while not necessarily meeting collective interests.

Indeed, as Kayes points out, there is a proposal in Arizona to create a same-sex charter school for grades 4-8. "We wouldn't say it would be best for all communities or parents, but it would be an alternative," he says.[46]

Puriefoy of the Public Education Network believes charter schools will help create a more varied public education system that uniformly imposes higher expectations, helps students meet standards and gives them choices. There should be "fair and multiple assessments" for both students and adults, she adds, but they will be administered differently in different areas of the country.

"We're headed toward significant progress" she says, "but when charter schools reach a certain scale, they too will encounter what feels like bureaucratic roadblocks."

Movement co-founder Kolderie stresses the long-term view. Nearly 20 years after the warnings in "A Nation at Risk," he says, "No one thinks reform has been done, and there's not a lot of reasons to believe it will be done, even with the big hammer of accountability" in the No Child Left Behind Act.

"We're still in the process of creating the schools we need now," Kolderie says. "To rely exclusively on changing the schools we've long had will not work, and it is an unacceptable risk to take with other people's children."

The AFT's Devlin is more wary. "Charters vary in quality, have little impact on the body of knowledge of what children should learn and will have little impact on how 21st-century schools should be organized," she says. "But they're not necessarily a bad idea, and we don't see them going away. Their founders are discovering what we've always known — that running a good school is really hard work."

NOTES

1. Survey by RPP International, U.S. Department of Education, cited in Paul T. Hill and Robin J. Lake, *Charter Schools and Accountability in Public Education* (2002), p. 37.

2. Joe Mathews, "Charter Schools Embracing Standards to Improve Image," *Los Angeles Times*, Oct. 14, 2002.

3. "Charter Schools Take Root," *The San Francisco Chronicle*, Oct. 6, 2002.

4. Jessica Brice, "Assembly sends charter school reform bill to governor," The Associated Press, Aug. 30, 2002.

5. Gary Miron and Christopher Nelson, "What's Public About Charter Schools?" *Education Week*, May 15, 2002.

6. Kate Zernike, "Suburbs Face Test as Charter Schools Continue to Spread," *The New York Times*, Dec. 18, 2000.

7. Paul E. Peterson and David E. Campbell (eds.), *Charters, Vouchers & Public Education* (2001), p. 203.

8. Caroline Hendrie, "Accredited Status Taking on Cache in Charter Schools," *Education Week*, Oct. 23, 2002.

9. RPP International, "Challenge and Opportunity: The Impact of Charter Schools on School Districts," U.S. Department of Education, June 2001, pp. 41-42.

10. Peterson, *op. cit.*, p. 77.

11. RPP International study, January 2000, "The State of Charter Schools 2000: Fourth-Year Report," U.S. Department of Education.

12. Peterson, *op. cit.*, p. 205.

13. RPP International, "Challenge and Opportunity," *op. cit.*, pp. 41-42.

14. See Lewis Solmon, Kern Paark and David Garcia, "Does Charter School Attendance Improve Test Scores?" Goldwater Institute, March 2001, p. 23.

15. See www.brookings.edu, Sept. 3, 2002.

16. "Do Charter Schools Measure Up? The Charter School Experiment After 10 Years," American Federation of Teachers, July 2002; http://www.aft.org/edissues/downloads/charterreport02.pdf

17. Peterson, *op. cit.*, p. 52.

18. Thomas L. Good, *et al.* "Charting a New Course: Fact and Fiction about Charter Schools," National School Boards Association, October 2000.

19. Chester E. Finn, Jr., Bruno V. Manno and Gregg Vanourek, *Charters Schools in Action: Renewing Public Education* (2000), p. 272.

20. See Kent Fischer, "Public School Inc.," *The St. Petersburg Times*, Sept. 15, 2002.

21. Sandra Vergari (ed.), *The Charter School Landscape* (2002), p. 266.

22. Hill and Lake, *op. cit.*, p. 75.

23. Bryan C. Hassel, *The Charter School Challenge* (1999), p. 4.

24. Vergari, *op. cit.*, p. 18.

25. Ray Budde, *Education by Charter: Restructuring School Districts* (1988).

26. For background, see Charles S. Clark, "Attack on Public Schools," *The CQ Researcher*, Aug. 2, 1996, pp. 649-672, and Kenneth Jost, "Private Management of Public Schools," *The CQ Researcher*, March 25, 1994, pp. 265-288.

27. Hill, *op. cit.*, p.17.

28. Hassel, *op. cit.*, p. 27.

29. See Jain Pushpam, "The Approval Barrier to Suburban Charter Schools," Thomas B. Fordham Foundation, September 2002.

30. See "AFT On the Issues," www.aft.org/issues/charterschools.

31. Hassel, *op. cit.*, p. 113.

32. Peterson, *op. cit.*, p. 42.

33. See American Federation of Teachers, "Venturesome Capital: State Charter School Finance Systems," December 2000, online at www.aft.org/charterfinance/venturesome/chapter4.pdf

34. Bruno V. Manno, "Yellow Flag," *Education Next*, winter 2003, p. 16.

35. Mathews, *op. cit.*

36. Michael A. Fletcher, "Rocky Start in 'Cyber' Classrooms," *The Washington Post*, Feb. 26, 2002.

37. Mathews, *op. cit.*

38. "The Spirit of Waldorf Education," *Education Week*, June 20, 2001.

39. See Kenneth Jost, "School Vouchers Showdown," *The CQ Researcher*, Feb. 15, 2002, pp. 121-144, and Kathy Koch, "School Vouchers," *The CQ Researcher*, April 8, 1999, pp. 281-304, and "GOP's Election Gains Give School Vouchers a Second Wind," *The Wall Street Journal*, Nov. 11, 2002, p. B1.

40. Abby Goodnough, "Chancellor Speaks Up for Charter Schools," *The New York Times*, Oct. 17, 2002.

41. Caroline Hendrie, " 'Shadow' Idea in the Works," *Education Week*, Nov. 27, 2002.

42. Megan Tench, "State Rolls Back Number of Boston Charter Schools," *The Boston Globe*, Nov. 11, 2002.

43. "Charter School Field Plagued by Burnout," *Education Week*, Dec. 6, 2000.

44. Hassel, *op. cit.*, p. 14.

45. Vergari, *op. cit.*, p. 273.

46. For background, see Kenneth Jost, "Single-Sex Education," *The CQ Researcher*, July 12, 2002, pp. 569-592.

BIBLIOGRAPHY

Books

Finn, Chester E., Jr., Bruno V. Manno and Gregg Vanourek, *Charter Schools in Action: Renewing Public Education*, Princeton University Press, 2000.
A think tank president, former assistant Education secretary and a charter school specialist at an Internet education firm summarize arguments for and against charter schools and express hopes the movement will save public education.

Hassel, Bryan C., *The Charter School Challenge: Avoiding the Pitfalls, Fulfilling the Promise*, Brookings Institution Press, 1999.
An education consultant examines the politics, policy debates and operational challenges facing the charter school movement, with a focus on developments in Colorado, Georgia, Massachusetts and Michigan.

Hill, Paul T., and Robin J. Lake, *Charter Schools and Accountability in Public Education*, Brookings Institution Press, 2002.
A research professor of public affairs and a public-policy center director at the University of Washington show how charter schools differ from public schools. They explore the unique and controversial accountability systems that give charters their freedom but put them at risk of funding cutoffs.

Nathan, Joe, *Charter Schools: Creating Hope and Opportunity for American Education*, Jossey-Bass, 1999.
This compendium by one of the charter movement's founders offers a history of the charter school movement and numerous interviews with successful charter school

operators. He proposes a new charter school role for teachers' unions.

Peterson, Paul E., and David E. Campbell, eds., *Charters, Vouchers & Public Education*, Brookings Institution Press, 2001.
Two leaders at Harvard University's Program on Education Policy and Governance assembled 15 scholarly essays on charter schools, vouchers, school choice and civic education, with evidence for the prospective success of each. They include lessons learned from New Zealand and a discussion of related U.S. constitutional issues.

Schorr, Jonathan, *Hard Lessons: The Promise of an Inner-City Charter School, Ballantine Books*, 2002.
A journalist and former teacher provides an eyewitness account of the early frustrations of a fledgling charter school in economically struggling Oakland, Calif.

Vergari, Sandra, ed., *The Charter School Landscape*, University of Pittsburgh Press, 2002.
Fourteen essays by scholars examine a history of the movement and highlight differences among approaches in several states and Canada.

Reports and Studies

***American Federation of Teachers*, "Do Charter Schools Measure Up? The Charter School Experiment After 10 Years," July 2002; www.aft.org/edissues/downloads/charterreport02.pdf**
This study by one of the nation's largest teachers' unions found the vast majority of charter schools have failed to fulfill their promise to bring greater achievement and innovation into the classroom. The report concluded that policymakers should not expand charter school activities until their effectiveness or viability is proven.

***Center for Education Reform*, "Public-Private Partnerships: A Consumer's Guide," 2002.**
A school-choice advocacy group compiled profiles of 19 educational-management companies, for-profit and nonprofit, now working in 350 schools.

***U.S. Dept. of Education*, "The State of Charter Schools 2000: Fourth-Year Report," January 2000.**
This fourth-year report of the Education Department's National Study of Charter Schools describes charter schools operating in the 1998-99 school year and addresses broad policy issues concerning the charter school movement and its potential effect on America's system of public education.

Good, Thomas L., *et. al.*, "Charting a New Course: Fact and Fiction about Charter Schools," *National School Boards Association*, October 2000.
In this skeptical examination, three scholars observe that charter districts "appear to be a strange hybrid of tradition grafted onto conservative values and parental hostility toward public education."

Lockwood, Anne Turnbaugh, "Charter Districts: Much Fuss, Little Gain," *American Association of School Administrators*, November 2001.
An issues analyst at the association examines charter schools in three states, some of which are managed by private companies.

Pushpam, Jain, "The Approval Barrier to Suburban Charter Schools," *Thomas B. Fordham Foundation*, September 2002.
A University of Maine scholar examines suburban school districts in Colorado, Connecticut and New Jersey, all of which have high proportions of charter schools, to deduce why charters are relatively rare in suburbia.

For More Information

American Association of School Administrators, 1801 N. Moore St., Arlington, VA 22209-1813; (703) 528-0700; www.aasa.org. An association of chief school executives, administrators and teachers of school administration, which promotes opportunities for minorities, women and the disabled in educational administration and organization.

American Federation of Teachers, 555 New Jersey Ave., N.W., Washington, DC 20001; (202) 879 4400; www.aft .org. The 780,000-member AFT is the nation's second-largest teachers' union.

Center for Education Reform, 1001 Connecticut Ave., N.W., Suite 204, Washington, DC 20036; (202) 822-9000; (800) 521-2118; www.edreform.com. An independent advocacy organization founded in 1993 to support those seeking fundamental reforms to public schools.

Charter Friends National Network, 1295 Bandana Blvd., Suite 165, St. Paul, MN 55108; (651) 644-6115; www .charterfriends.org. Established in 1996 by the Center for Policy Studies, in cooperation with Hamline University, the network promotes quality charter schools.

National Charter School Clearinghouse, 3900 East Camelback Road, Suite 312, Phoenix, AZ 85018; (602) 954 1414; www.ncsc.info. Funded by a U.S. Education Department grant, the center runs an interactive Web site, publishes a monthly newsletter and disseminates policy information to advance the charter school movement.

National Education Association, 1201 16th St., N.W., Washington, DC 20036; (202) 833-4000; www.nea.org. The union of more than 2.7 million educators from preschool to university graduate programs promotes the interest of the teaching profession and monitors legislation and regulations at state and national levels.

National School Boards Association, 1680 Duke St., Alexandria, VA 22314; (703) 838-6722; www.nsba.org. Federation of state school board associations concerned with funding of public education, local governance and quality of education programs.

Thomas B. Fordham Foundation, 1627 K St., N.W., Suite 600, Washington, DC 20006; (202) 223-5452; www.edexcellence.net. A grant-making and research organization that supports education-reform issues at the national level, with a particular focus on projects in Dayton, Ohio.

Home Schooling Debate

Is the Movement Undermining Public Education?

Rachel S. Cox

School begins with the Pledge of Allegiance at the Shapiro home in Tempe, Ariz. Denise Shapiro and her husband Aaron, a chiropractor, decided to home school to raise "very smart" children but also "biblically, morally responsible adults." At least 850,000 U.S. children are home schooled, nearly triple the number a decade ago. Public-school officials worry home schooling undercuts public education and limits students' exposure to children and adults with diverse backgrounds.

From *CQ Researcher*,
January 17, 2003.

6

When Jane and George Liddle's first child turned 4, they began to think about her formal schooling. Living in the affluent San Francisco Bay Area community of Los Gatos, near Silicon Valley, they had access to some of California's best public schools.

But every Sunday when they attended services at the Saratoga Federated Church, they couldn't help but notice how happy — and successful — the home-schooled children of fellow church members seemed to be.

"At first, I said to myself, 'I will never do this,'" recalls Jane, who was a stockbroker until Caroline was born. "But we saw so many professional, well-educated people who made the choice [to home school] for educational reasons, as well as personal, philosophical ones."

Today, Caroline, nearly 6, starts her day by spending an hour or two working with her mother on language arts and math skills. After family devotions, they move to a classroom set up in a separate building on the rural property to study history and social studies. Two days a week, Caroline and her younger brother, William, 3, visit a home-school co-op to study and play with nearly 60 other children in class-like groupings overseen by their 12 moms.

Jane Liddle concedes that home schooling works for her family for practical as well as philosophical reasons: The extra cost — mainly for books and other educational materials — is minimal. And with the local elementary school some distance away, she appreciates not having to spend two hours each day in her car or making Caroline ride the bus. Home schooling also improves her

AP Photo/East Valley Tribune, Andy Sawyer

Rise of Home-Schooled Students

The number of U.S. children home schooled nearly tripled during the 1990s, according to estimates by the U.S. Department of Education. Home-schooling advocates, however, say 2 million children now are home schooled.

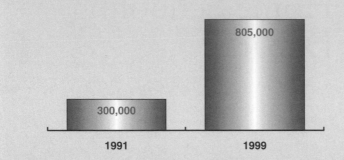

805,000

300,000

1991   1999

Sources: U.S. Department of Education, National Center for Education Statistics, "Parent Survey of the National Household Education Surveys Program, 1999," July 2001; "Issues Related to Estimating the Home-Schooled Population in the United States with National Household Data Survey," September 2000. The next Department of Education report on home schooling is scheduled for release in early 2004.

quality of life. "I spend such incredible time with my children," she says, "and at night when my husband is home, we really are a family. We avoid a lot of the distractions of popular culture and the pressures to arrange lots of after-school activities. We're not just chasing our tails all the time."

She also believes that, at least for now, home schooling offers the best possible educational experience. "I've learned that you can really shoot the moon with your child. I'm right there with her in the learning process. I know what keeps her challenged and what sabotages her. You can customize. You figure out what works for your child."

The Liddles' approach has grown increasingly popular over the last two decades, as a movement once considered the domain of aging hippies and religious fundamentalists increasingly has been embraced by the mainstream. But school districts complain that when parents give up on home schooling, they "dump" their children back on the public schools, which are then held accountable for the home-schoolers' performance, even if the student is lagging behind his in-school peers. Moreover, critics warn that removing children from the

public schools may threaten an essential pillar of democracy, while depriving children of vital contact with other children and adults from diverse backgrounds.

Brian D. Ray, director of the National Home Education Research Institute in Salem, Ore., and a leader in the field, concedes that even as recently as five years ago home-schoolers were considered "kind of weirdo." People thought home-schoolers were all "granola eaters or Bible thumpers," he says. "But now, almost anyone you run into on the street will consider it. It's more common to find support groups, resources are more available and there's less peer pressure against it."

In 1999, the U.S. Education Department estimates, about 850,000 of the nation's 50 million children, ages 5 through 17, were being schooled at home — or 1.7 percent.[1] Ray puts the number at between 1.6 million and 2 million — roughly 2 percent of the school-age population — but his figures are generally considered high.

One thing is certain: The movement has experienced robust growth. Only 30 years ago, few children were being home schooled.[2] By 1991, the Department of Education estimated that up to 300,000 school-age children were being educated at home.[3] Thus, according to the department's own conservative estimates, the number of home-schooled children has nearly tripled in just 10 years.[4]

Most home-schooled children come from urban, two-parent families, the study found, with one wage earner and two or more children. The parents are often well educated — a quarter have at least a bachelor's degree — and 36 percent have household incomes above $50,000 per year. White families outnumber minorities by three to one.

Parents say they home-school for five main reasons: to give their children a better education, for religious reasons, to avoid a poor school environment, for family reasons and to instill "character/morality."[5] (*See chart, p. 124.*)

"The core reasons for home schooling are very deep and stable," says Ray, who has studied the movement since the mid-1980s. "They want their children to learn to read, write and do arithmetic, along with some science and history. They want to individualize the curriculum for each child, meet special interests or needs, provide a safe learning environment and guided social interactions for their kids, nurture strong family ties and transmit certain values and beliefs to their children."[6]

In the 1980s, he notes, the proportion of families choosing home schooling for religious reasons skyrocketed, after tax-code changes forced many religious schools to close.

Critics long have asserted that schooling children at home impedes socialization because home-schooled kids don't learn to get along with their peers in group settings, nor are they exposed to children and adults from different backgrounds. But advocates scoff at the notion.

"I have nothing kind to say about the sort of socialization that occurs in schools," says Holly Albers, an economist in Washington, D.C., who home-schooled her two sons for several years when they were youngsters. "The children are thrown into single-age, often very large groups with no meaningful interactions with adults."

To expose their children to a wide variety of contacts, Albers and other parents organize social and educational activities with other home-schoolers and adults, who often serve as tutors in subject areas that other parents are weak in. As a result, she says, home-schoolers tend to have three advantages: closer family and sibling relationships, more friendships with different ages and genders and more friendships with adults. "There's much more positive socialization for children at home," she says.

In fact, studies appear to refute the argument that home-schoolers are poorly socialized. As early as 1986,

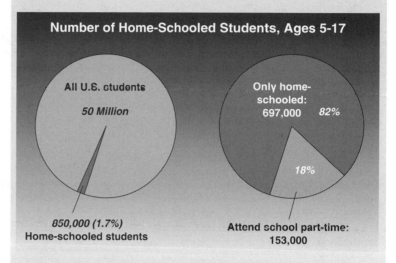

Few Students Are Home-Schooled

About 850,000* of the nation's 50 million school-age children were home schooled in 1999, according to the U.S. Department of Education. More than three-quarters were taught only at home.

Number of Home-Schooled Students, Ages 5-17

All U.S. students
50 Million

850,000 (1.7%)
Home-schooled students

Only home-schooled:
697,000 **82%**

18%

Attend school part-time:
153,000

*Home-schooling advocates say the current number may be as high as 2 million.

Note: Students are considered to be home schooled if their parents say they are home schooled, they attend public or private school for less than 25 hours a week and they were not home-schooled due to a temporary illness.

Source: U.S. Department of Education, National Center for Education Statistics, "Parent Survey of the National Household Education Surveys Program," 1999.

John Wesley Taylor, a doctoral candidate at Andrews University, in Berrien Springs, Mich., found that half of the home-schooled children surveyed scored 47 percent higher than the average conventionally schooled child on a well-validated self-concept scale. "This answers the often-heard skepticism suggesting that home-schoolers are inferior in socialization," he concluded.[7]

Home-schoolers win academic kudos as well. In 2000, for instance, home-schooled children took home the top three trophies in the prestigious Scripps Howard National Spelling Bee, just a week after other home-schoolers won four of the top 10 spots at the National Geographic Society's geography bee.[8] And Buchanan, Mich., home-schooler Jeff Joyce recently scored a perfect 1600 on the College Board's Scholastic Assessment Test (SAT) — a feat accomplished by less than 0.5 percent of the students who take the test each year.[9]

Home Schooling Means Business

Supplying instructional materials for home-schooling families has turned into a $700 million cottage industry, according to Jean C. Halle, chief executive officer of Calvert School Education Services.[1]

For decades the Baltimore-based company, founded in 1906, was the only major institution offering "correspondence courses" for the children of military families, missionaries and other itinerants. In the 1960s, however, they were joined by Christian publishers, whose market share soon exploded, as did the number of religiously motivated home-schooling families.

Today, three major religiously oriented suppliers sell Bible-themed textbooks in all disciplines: Bob Jones University Press, Alpha Omega Publications, of Chandler, Ariz., and Pensacola, Fla.-based A Beka Books. "We have over 100,000 home-schooled pupils using our books," A Beka Sales Manager Eric Fears told *Education Week*.

In addition to books and online curricula, many companies offer testing, record-keeping and teacher consultations as well as class rings, diplomas and caps and gowns.

The growth of the Internet opened national and even global markets to local providers. Core Curriculum, a Florida company offering both Christian and secular curricula, started as a family business in 1989. By 2002 it had reached $1.4 million in revenues, according to Operations Vice President Alexis Thompson, mostly over the Internet.

The rise of publicly funded cyber schools — which allow students to work at home supported by certified teachers — has opened a new market for online curricula providers

William J. Bennett, the outspoken former Secretary of Education under President Ronald Reagan, has joined the ranks of online curriculum providers. The proponent of classical education and author of the best-selling *Book of Virtues* heads K12 Inc., which sells its K-5 curricula to publicly funded cyber schools in nearly a dozen states.

Although he questioned cyber learning in his 1999 book *The Educated Child*, saying there is "no good evidence that most uses of computers significantly improve learning," two years later he had changed his views: "There's tremendous promise for technology."[2]

Bennett's company is a subsidiary of Knowledge Universe, Inc — the $1.75 billion educational-products firm established by disgraced junk bond financier Michael Milken.[3]

In fact, when University of Maryland researcher Lawrence M. Rudner assessed the performance of more than 20,000 K-12 home-schooled students on standardized tests in 1999, their median scores were typically in the 70th to 80th percentile. "The achievement-test scores of this group of home school students are exceptionally high," Rudner concluded.[10]

But Rudner's study, which was funded and widely disseminated by home-schooling advocates, was criticized for failing to acknowledge the narrowness of its sample. The data were gathered exclusively from parents who used the testing services of Bob Jones University, the fundamentalist Christian institution in Greenville, S.C., notorious for its history of racial discrimination. "This data simply cannot be used to reliably compare home-schoolers' achievement levels with those of the general population or to describe the demographics of home-schoolers," scholars Kariane Mari Welner and Kevin G. Welner noted.[11]

Few educators doubt the potential of a customized education when a single adult is working with one child. "There's no doubt that the one-on-one work that parents can do if they're smart or well trained is amazing," says June Million, a spokeswoman for the National Association of Elementary School Principals (NAESP). But home-schooling advocates don't always tell the whole story, she suggests. "The part I never see are the ones who have returned to school after home schooling, and they're behind. It's not always a success."

NAESP President Paul Young agrees. "If families want to work hard at home schooling and do it for the right reasons, they do very well. Others aren't well informed, don't follow through and get frustrated," he says.

When home schooling fails, the problem usually lands in the lap of the public schools, says Young, who is principal at West Elementary School in Lancaster, Ohio. "When the parents realize they can't do it, the kids come back to public school, and then we're held responsible.

Until recently, Bennett was a popular speaker at home-schooling conventions because of his endorsement of values-centered, family-based education. But his decision to sell K12 curricula to publicly funded cyber schools has made him a little less welcome. Many home-schoolers say that with public money come regulations, and regulation for cyber-school parents — some of whom are also home schoolers — could lead to regulation for all home-schoolers.

"We home-schoolers need to let other home-schoolers and the general public know that Bennett's commitment to using public money in this way runs counter to what most home-schoolers want and would undermine the very nature of home schooling as we know it," home schooling columnists and advocates Larry and Susan Kaseman wrote in a recent issue of *Home Education Magazine*.[4]

K12's requests to exhibit as a curriculum vendor at home-schooling conferences have been rejected by home-schooling organizations in at least three states, according to the Kasemans. The Christian Home Education Association of California canceled Bennett as its keynote speaker last year "because of the linkage between K12 and publicly funded programs."

Alpha Omega Publications

Suppliers of educational materials for home schoolers typically offer both secular and religiously oriented products, including Bible-themed textbooks.

[2] "All Things Considered," National Public Radio, Feb. 28, 2001.

[3] Stephen P. Pizzo, "Master of the Knowledge Universe," *Forbes ASAP*, Sept. 10, 2001.

[4] Larry and Susan Kaseman, "How William Bennett's Public E-Schools Affect Homeschooling," *Home Education Magazine*, November-December 2002; online at www.home-ed-magaine.com/HEM/196/ndtch.html.

[1] Mark Walsh, "Home School Enrollment Surge Fuels 'Cottage' Industry," *Education Week*, June 5, 2002.

In some cases these kids have been just running in the street, and the parents are not held accountable for what their children were supposed to be learning."

In addition to its concerns about the lack of adequate socialization, the NAESP worries that home schooling can deny children the full range of curriculum experiences and materials and expose students to unqualified instructors. In addition, the group says home schooling can create an extra burden for administrators responsible for enforcing compulsory-attendance laws; prevent effective assessment of statewide academic standards; violate health and safety regulations and prevent the accurate diagnosis of learning disabilities or other conditions requiring special attention.

"The public schools' greatest concern is to make sure kids are actually learning," says Julie Underwood, general counsel of the National School Boards Association (NSBA). "There are very strong religious-right organizations

that support very conservative [home-schooling] curricula."

Even dedicated home-schoolers acknowledge that home schooling is not right for everyone. "It does require a full-time, at-home parent," Albers says, "and it is *relentless* for that parent."

As educators, parents and policy-makers struggle with the peculiar mix of personal and public decision-making that home schooling entails, these three questions frequently are being debated:

Should the government regulate home schooling?

"Dog Bites System," read *The Rocky Mountain News* headline, when a Colorado man successfully certified his miniature schnauzer, Missy, as progressing nicely in the third grade while being schooled at home.[12]

Under Colorado's home-schooling law, parents must file a notice of intent with a local school district, then

Parents' Reasons for Home Schooling

Nearly half of all parents home-school because they think they can do a better job than the local public schools. High percentages of parents also were motivated by religious reasons and poor school environments.

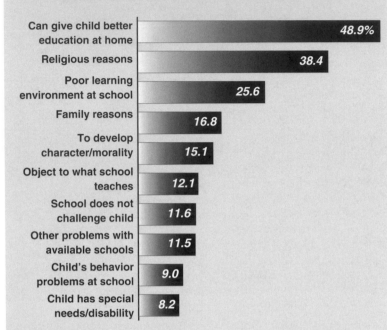

Parents' Main Reasons for Home Schooling

Reason	Percentage
Can give child better education at home	48.9%
Religious reasons	38.4
Poor learning environment at school	25.6
Family reasons	16.8
To develop character/morality	15.1
Object to what school teaches	12.1
School does not challenge child	11.6
Other problems with available schools	11.5
Child's behavior problems at school	9.0
Child has special needs/disability	8.2

Note: Percentages do not add to 100 because respondents could give more than one reason.

Source: U.S. Department of Education, National Center for Education Statistics, Parent Survey of the National Household Education Surveys Program, "Homeschooling in the United States: 1999," July 2001; new data are now being collected for the next comprehensive report on home schooling, due in early 2004.

Thanks to adroit lobbying by home-schooling networks, which have access to Republican lawmakers through their links with politically savvy religious conservatives, home schooling is legal in every state, but requirements for eligibility and evaluation vary widely. Thus, policymakers and educators are debating whether local school districts should regulate home schooling more stringently.

"With home schooling now firmly entrenched on the American education scene," New Jersey attorney David Rubin writes, "the legal battleground has shifted in recent years to defining the rights and responsibilities of school districts and home-schooling families."[13]

Many public educators believe that stricter regulation — including testing — is needed to ensure that home-schooled children are being adequately educated.[14] "Kentucky is very lax on its home-school rules," says Martha Lewis, principal of Benton Elementary in rural Marshall County, Ky. "Most of the students that I have seen being home-schooled are ones whose parents get disgruntled with the public school about something. They are weak students who have poor attendance. When they come back, they are even further behind."

Requiring home-schooled students to be tested would help teachers and administrators when home-schoolers return to school, or when they take some courses in public schools, the NSBA's Underwood says. "In some states, there are no regulations, so public school [teachers and officials] are quite frustrated," she says. So when kids enter or return to school, "They don't know if they're really ready. They don't have any information."

Public educators were particularly concerned when President Bush's recently enacted No Child Left Behind

the student must be tested or evaluated to show progress every other year, starting in the third grade. Dog owners Nick and Cheryl Campbell "evaluated" Missy using an evaluation form they found on the Internet, but no one from the school district ever tried to speak to Missy.

"I did it to make a point" about the laxness of the state's oversight of home-schoolers, said Campbell, who was distressed because a 10-year-old neighbor being home schooled had not yet learned to read.

Act exempted home-schooled students from the new testing requirements it imposed on public-school students. The new law imposes serious financial consequences on schools where students test poorly. Thus, administrators want to make sure that all students are keeping up — including returning home-schoolers.

"When children return to school, that school is held responsible for their performance," says Young of the principals' association. "We need more specific testing requirements so there's some accountability."

"You could have multiple forms of testing," Underwood notes. "It wouldn't have to be standardized testing."

However, to home-schooling advocates like Robert Ziegler, spokesman for the Home School Legal Defense Association, (HSLDA) any regulation is too much. Choosing how to educate one's children is a constitutionally protected parental right, he says. "There should be no regulation of how parents educate their children," he says.

To others, like home-schooling researcher Ray, it is unreasonable to regulate a practice that receives no public financing. "Home-schoolers don't use a single tax dollar," Ray says. "What about children in private schools? Private schools have no regulation. Why do this to us, and not do it to private schools?"

Ray says he doesn't know of "any research suggesting that if you test them, they will do better."

"If the issue is quality in education," Ziegler says, "the argument could be made that heavy government involvement is not a guarantor of success."

Ziegler says stories of children who leave school and are not being educated are irrelevant to debates about regulating home schooling. "It's important to distinguish between home-schoolers and dropouts," he says. "The horror stories are not typical."

Home-schooling parents also point out that children schooled at home can progress at their own pace, so students who might be stigmatized as learning disabled in the public school system often blossom when allowed to pursue their own interests at home on their own schedule. Imposing a state-mandated testing or evaluation regimen would negate these benefits, they say.

Home-schooling advocates often attribute professional educators' efforts to regulate home schooling to their vested interests in keeping the numbers of schoolchildren,

teachers and administrators high. "Big-government types have had a monopoly on education," Ziegler says. For teachers' unions like the American Federation of Teachers (AFT), he says, "It's a dollars-and-cents issue. Fewer jobs, fewer teachers in the union."

But Alex Wohl, AFT's director of public affairs, counters: "The number of home-schooled students is so small that it would never interfere with our membership, even if it were a focus, which it's not."

Should the public-school system support home schooling?

In 1999, when 13-year-old Megan Angstadt wanted to play basketball on her local middle-school's team in Williamsport, Penn., her parents obtained a one-year exception to the school-district policy excluding home-schoolers from extracurricular activities. To assure her participation the following year, they enrolled her in Western Pennsylvania Cyber Charter School, a distance-learning public school. They hoped to take advantage of a state law allowing charter school students to participate in extracurricular activities elsewhere if their charter school does not offer them.[15]

But the school district refused to let Megan rejoin the team. Her parents sued, contending her rights had been violated. But the district court questioned whether Megan's interest in participating in extracurricular activities rose to the level of a constitutionally protected right.

In a change from earlier generations, home-schooling parents like the Angstadts increasingly are augmenting their children's social and educational experiences by seeking access to public-school programs.[16]

And extracurricular activities are not the only public-school resources home-schoolers want to use. According to the 1999 Education Department study, about 18 percent of home schoolers attend public school part time, 11 percent use public-school books or materials and about 6 percent participate in extracurricular activities.[17]

States usually allow local school boards to decide whether or not to honor home-schoolers' requests to take selected courses and join extracurricular activities.

"We do not permit this type of smorgasbord participation in our state," says Robert Heath, principal of W.C. Sullivan Middle School in Rock Hill, S.C. "I believe

Alpha Omega Publications

Minorities make up only about a quarter of the nation's home-schooled students, compared with 36 percent of the children in public and private schools. Critics say home-schooled students don't have a chance to mix with students and adults from other backgrounds. Advocates respond that music, sports and other outside-the-home activities provide ample opportunities for mixing.

this to be appropriate, as our students must earn the right to participate in extracurricular activities through grades, behavior and so forth."

New Jersey attorney Rubin says many school districts deny such requests for a variety of reasons, including administrative inconvenience, lack of state aid and equity *vis-à-vis* other private-school students who would be denied the same opportunities.[18]

Legal challenges to school-district policies prohibiting home-schoolers' participation have generally been defeated. As in Megan's case, courts in Oklahoma, New York, Montana and West Virginia have held that school-district policies or state interscholastic athletic association rules that exclude home-schoolers do not violate the equal-protection rights of home-school or private-school students.[19]

However, a Massachusetts Superior Court ruled in 1995 that home-schooled high-school students may participate in interschool athletics on the grounds that distinguishing between in-school and home-schooled students "was not rationally related to a legitimate state purpose."[20]

When stymied in the courts, home-schooling advocates have turned to the legislative arena. As of spring 2002, 14 states had laws or policies granting home-schoolers access to public-school activities, and several states have legislation pending.[21]

In Oregon, Washington, California, Texas and other states, some public-school districts have gone so far as to design tax-funded school-at-home programs. Local school districts receive all or part of the usual per-pupil funding, while students work off-campus and connect with the schools via computer or at learning centers with computer labs, libraries or science labs. Working closely with parents, teachers at the learning centers may offer curriculum guidance, teach some classes and provide testing and evaluation services.

"Many public educators and the families who send their children full time to public schools . . . look askance at these programs," says Patricia D. Lines, a senior fellow at Seattle's Discovery Institute and longtime observer of home-schooling. " 'It's not fair,' complained a public-school parent, "'for them to want the best of what the public school has to offer without enduring their less-popular aspects.' "[22]

In addition, many home-schoolers are wary of governmental involvement in parent-directed education, viewing it as a Trojan horse by which the state and its employees can gain control over their children's education. "Home-schoolers who get tax dollars for educational expenses will be held accountable by the state, and regulations on them will increase," *Home Education Magazine* warned recently.[23]

"When regulations are increased for some home-schoolers, the increased regulations are very likely to be applied to all home-schoolers, regardless of whether they are accepting tax money (or enrolling in a public e-school)," wrote home-school advocates Larry and Susan Kaseman.

Moreover, many home-schoolers also fear that accepting public-school services will force them to give up the religious orientation of their home program.[24]

But Lines believes the Trojan-horse analogy may, in fact, work the other way around, with home-schoolers subtly reforming the way public schools do business.

"When public schools open their doors to home-schooling families, they must operate in a very different way," she says in a recent study of school-family partnerships. "Rather than losing control over home schooling, it seems more likely that home-schoolers' ideas will influence public practices and curriculum."

Working with home-school families, she says, can force the public schools to adopt "a radically new service orientation toward families." Because home-schooling parents are unlikely to send their children to a conventional school, public educators will attract home-schoolers "only if they are sensitive to their needs, preferences and goals."[25]

Does home schooling threaten the fundamental American concept of universal public education?

One of the primary goals of American public education is to teach citizens how to knowledgeably participate in a democratic society. "The public doesn't realize that is one of the crucial goals of our democracy," says the NSBA's Underwood.

Without a well-educated citizenry, democracy cannot work and might not survive, she says. "Public education makes democracy work well. If people don't recognize that and support it, we're always at risk of losing it."

Home-schooling advocates argue that public-school students have no corner on citizenship, however. "Children do not have to be in the same type of school for them to be productive, kind, free-thinking citizens," says Ray, of the National Home Education Research Institute.

Indeed, home-schooling families tend to be more civically active than the norm, some experts say. A 1999 study based on Education Department data found that home-schoolers were active participants in the political process. "We have reason to believe that the organizations and practices involved in private and home schooling, in themselves, tend to foster public participation in civic affairs," the authors concluded.[26]

Ziegler, of the Home School Legal Defense Association (HSLDA), scoffs at the idea that home-schooling, a tiny fraction of the nation's students, undercuts public education's citizenship goals. "To the degree that having children home-schooled undermines the schools' effectiveness, the government needs to revisit how it structures its public schools."

Others ask how the public-school system can claim to be promoting citizenship and democracy if it is failing to adequately educate all students. The public-school system has "failed us," says California home-school parent Jane Liddle.

Underwood acknowledges that the public schools aren't perfect. "They're run by local elected officials," she says. "Sometimes wacky things happen."

Some supporters of the home-schooling movement, however, believe the public-education system is more focused on producing good workers for U.S. industry than on producing good citizens. Former New York City schoolteacher John Taylor Gatto represents an extreme view of the corporate-influenced goals of state-supported schooling. His massive new book, *Underground History of American Education*, details his vision of the "deliberate transformation of American schooling, corporation-driven, which took place between 1890 and 1920, to . . . subordinate family and individual goals to the needs of 'scientific,' corporate and political managers."[27]

Others see the public schools as an authoritarian "enemy" determined to undermine family values. Much of the home-school movement's literature refers to "government-controlled" or "state-run" schools and reveals grave doubts that any government-controlled agency can operate beneficently, even if the government is a democracy.

Ray himself, in a recent home-schooling guidebook, cast the public schools and their supporters as enemies. "An increasing number of parents are recognizing the battle that is being waged for their children's hearts and minds — a battle that is played out in their education," he wrote.[28]

Educators worry that the home-schooling trend also could jeopardize the role of public education as "the great equalizer in a democracy," in the words of Michael Roberts, a spokesman for the National Parent-Teachers Association. In school, children learn to get along with others from all minorities and all economic backgrounds, he points out, and after graduation they enter the working world equipped with the same basic education. Thus, a public education is designed to, theoretically, give each

CHRONOLOGY

19th Century *The notion of the "common school" takes hold. Despite resistance, secular schools that are free and open to all become the norm.*

1837 Massachusetts legislators create the first state board of education, centralizing control of common schools at the state level. The first secretary, Horace Mann, awakens public to need for educational reform, establishes first teachers' colleges.

1852 Massachusetts passes first compulsory-education law, requiring children 8-14 to attend school at least 12 weeks a year — unless they were too poor. By 1900, all the northern states follow suit.

1900s-1930s *Progressive Movement replaces rote learning with learning by doing and concern for developmental psychology.*

1896-1904 Educator and philosopher John Dewey runs University of Chicago's Laboratory Schools to demonstrate his view of the classroom as a miniature society in which children learn to act democratically.

1918 Mississippi becomes last state to adopt compulsory education.

1920s Supreme Court rulings define the boundaries of state power over education, validating parents' right to have some choice.

1940s-1950s *Conservative critics assert progressive education and bureaucratic control have weakened education, usurped parental authority.*

1953 Launching of *Sputnik* by the Soviet Union focuses Cold War fears on teaching of science and math.

1960s-1970s *Unrest sparked by the Civil Rights Movement and Vietnam War inspires skepticism toward schools and other institutions.*

1964 Educator John Holt explains his theories of child-directed learning in *How Children Learn*.

1977 Holt launches *Growing Without Schooling* magazine for the rising number of parents choosing to "unschool" their children.

1979 Educational researcher Raymond S. Moore argues in *School Can Wait* that children suffer from early schooling, laying the foundation for later advocacy of home schooling.

1980s *Home-schooling movement organizes. Increasing numbers of Christian families join the movement; state and local networks form to fight court battles, lobby for favorable legislation and share educational resources.*

1983 "A Nation at Risk," a scathing Department of Education critique of public education, appears to confirm home-schoolers misgivings. Washington state attorney Michael Farris launches Home School Legal Defense Association.

1990s-Present *Movement gains credibility and diversity.*

1992 Novelist David Guterson (*Snow Falling on Cedars*) helps create program of courses and activities for home-schoolers.

1999 Home School Legal Defense Association breaks ground in Purcellville, Va., for Christian-oriented Patrick Henry College for home-schooled students.

2000 Home-schoolers win top three places in Scripps Howard National Spelling Bee.

2001 Department of Education places number of home-schooled children at an estimated 850,000.

May 2002 Patrick Henry College graduates its first class of 14.

July 2002 California Department of Education sparks a furor when it warns that "home schooling cannot legally be used as a substitute for public-school education."

child a "level playing field" when it comes to economic opportunity and their ability to achieve success. "If we move away from that, that's detrimental."

Because home-schooling is not an option for poor families in which both parents must work, it tends to attract students from wealthier families, which usually are the most vocal in demanding that public schools perform better.

Home schooling "undermines public education's singular potential to serve as a democratic institution promoting the common good," writes Christopher Lubienski, an assistant professor of education at Iowa State University. He notes that powerful, well-organized groups are encouraging parents, especially Christian parents, to remove their children from public schools — a movement he says includes organizations with mailing lists of millions of families and a radio show with 5 million listeners (James Dobson's "Focus on the Family"). "In view of the influential groups promoting moral mandates for home schooling," Lubienski continues, home schooling should be viewed as "organized exit from public schools."[29]

He sees the growth of the home-schooling movement as the result of active and affluent parents pursuing "the best possible advantages for their own children even if it means hurting other children's chances."

By withdrawing wealthier children from the public schools, "Home schooling is a social threat to public education," Lubienski said. "It is taking some of the most affluent and articulate parents out of the system. These are the parents who know how to get things done with

Most Home-Schooling Families Are White

Minorities make up only 25 percent of home-schooled children, compared to 36 percent of students in traditional schools. A quarter of home-schoolers' parents have at least a bachelor's degree.

Characteristic	Home-Schoolers Percent	Not Educated At Home Percent
Race/ethnicity		
White, non-Hispanic	75.3	64.5
Black, non-Hispanic	9.9	16.1
Hispanic	9.1	14.1
Other	5.8	5.2
Number of children in the household		
1 child	14.1	16.4
2 children	24.4	39.9
3 or more children	61.6	43.7
Number of parents in the household		
2 parents	80.4	65.5
1 parent	16.7	31.0
Non-parental guardians	2.9	3.5
Parents in the labor force		
2 parents, 1 in labor force	52.2	18.6
2 parents, both in labor force	27.9	45.9
1 parent in labor force	11.6	28.0
No parent in labor force	8.3	7.5
Household income		
$25,000 or less	30.9	33.5
25,001-50,000	32.7	30.3
50,001-75,000	19.1	17.1
75,001 or more	17.4	19.2
Parents' highest education level		
High-school diploma or less	18.9	36.8
Voc/tech degree/some college	33.7	30.2
Bachelor's degree	25.1	16.3
Graduate/professional school	22.3	16.7

Source: National Center for Education Statistics, Parent Survey of the National Household Education Surveys Program, "Homeschooling in the United States: 1999."

administrators."[30] Indeed, he writes, "Home schooling is not only a reaction to, but a cause of, declining public schools."

"Even self-described liberal, middle-class mothers who profess a loyalty to the idea of equality of educational opportunity are willing to negate such ideals in practice if, by doing so, they can increase educational advantages for their own children," Lubienski writes.

While home schooling involves less than 2 percent of the public-school population now, Underwood says, it is "one of a series of threats to public education," along with efforts to privatize schools and to provide vouchers and tax credits for private-school tuition.[31] "The underlying threat is a lack of public support for the importance of an educational system that serves all children."

But others point to recent polls indicating that support for the public schools is on the rise. In 2001, the annual *Phi Delta Kappan*/Gallup poll registered the highest level of public satisfaction with local schools in the poll's 33-year history, with 51 percent grading them A or B — an 11-point increase over the 1990 rating.[32]

"Schools have clearly gotten better — there is no doubt about it," said poll director Lowell C. Rose. "The 1990s have been a decade of improvement in public schools, and the upward trend reflects the steady increase in regard people have for the public schools."

Moreover, the poll also showed a major rise in public acceptance of home schooling: 41 percent of respondents called it "a good thing," up from only 15 percent in 1985; similarly, 54 percent called it "a bad thing," down from 73 percent in 1985.

"We're starting to win the battle," Ziegler says. "This may be one reason that the establishment is fighting back."

BACKGROUND

'Common Schools'

Although home schooling is widely regarded as a new phenomenon, that attitude "is simply a reflection of the bias of our times," writes Linda Dobson, a home-schooling parent and a prominent writer on the subject. Until the middle of the 19th century, when America began transforming from an agrarian to industrial society, Dobson writes, education occurred largely at home.[33]

Nonetheless, there were many education alternatives in the young United States. In Colonial New England villages, primary schools enjoyed public support, while in the agricultural South, where households were more isolated and self-sufficient, education was almost exclusively a family responsibility. In the middle states, some public schools coexisted with church-sponsored or philanthropically established schools. West of the Allegheny Mountains, the tradition of state-mandated education began with the Ordinance of 1787, which reserved a plot of land in every prospective township for schools.

But the notion of universal education in publicly supported institutions is relatively new. In 1827, the Massachusetts legislature ordered towns of more than 500 families to furnish public instruction in American history, algebra, geometry and bookkeeping, in addition to reading, writing and arithmetic. In 1837, following a campaign to document and publicize the state's dire educational conditions, Horace Mann became the first secretary of the Massachusetts Board of Education and launched the "common school," overseen by the state and paid for by taxpayers. The same year, Michigan established a state-supported and -administered system of education.

The controversies that surrounded common schools — whether the state can rightfully levy school taxes and "usurp" parental rights by assuming authority over children's education — continue to this day. Nevertheless, Connecticut and Rhode Island quickly followed in Massachusetts's footsteps. In addition, as the practice spread, the range of educational opportunities expanded to include high school and college.

Rise of Reformers

The early 20th century brought educational reforms inspired by the Enlightenment views of French philosopher Jean Jacques Rousseau, who viewed education not as the imparting of knowledge but as the drawing out of what resides in the child naturally. Foremost among the reformers was American philosopher-educator John Dewey, who saw the classroom as a miniature society in which the values and methods of democracy were to be nurtured and practiced.

From the soil of this "progressive" tradition sprang modern reformers who first put forward the notion that education should be "child-centered." In 1959, A.S. Neil, founder of the controversial Summerhill school in England, published *Summerhill: A Radical Approach to Childrearing*, which called for freedom, not coercion, in schools and enjoined teachers always to be on the side of the child. In addition, revolutionary thinker Ivan Illich, in his 1971 book, *DeSchooling Society*, analyzed the corrupting effects of institutionalized education, whereby the pursuit of grades and diplomas comes to replace actual learning.

"We like to say that we send children to school to teach them how to think," Reformer John Holt wrote in the preface to his classic, *How Children Learn*. "What we do, all too often, is to teach them to think badly, to give up a natural and powerful way of thinking in favor of a method that does not work well for them and that we rarely use ourselves."[34]

In 1977, Holt founded the magazine *Growing Without Schooling*, which became a Bible of sorts for families who chose to help their children learn free from the strictures of the classroom — an approach that came to be known as "unschooling."

Meanwhile, in books such as *Better Late than Early: A New Approach to Your Child's Education* and *School Can Wait*, educators like Raymond and Dorothy Moore argued that pushing children into a school setting too early could have dire educational and emotional consequences. The Moores saw the home as a better learning environment than the school. To support their cause, they left academia and created the Hewitt-Moore Research Foundation in Washougal, Wash., to support home-schooling families.

Criticism of the public schools also came from other ideological directions. Reacting to the rise of the counterculture, some home-school advocates, and others, protested the spread of "cultural relativism," which espoused that right and wrong are not absolute, but are relative to the cultural identity of an individual, and "humanistic" teaching that suggested man, not God, should be society's central concern.

In 1983, in response to plummeting standardized test scores, economic strains and disciplinary troubles in the schools, the National Commission on Excellence in Education released "A Nation at Risk," an alarming

Home-Schooling Highlights

- *About 850,000 students nationwide — 1.7 percent of U.S. students, ages 5 to 17 — were being home schooled in 1999, the most recent year for which government data are available. One out of five were enrolled part-time in a public or private school.*

- *About 75 percent of home-schoolers are white, compared to 65 percent of children who are not schooled at home.*

- *The parents who home school had household incomes in 1999 similar to those of parents who didn't home school, but parents who home school were more highly educated.*

- *Parents' most common reasons for home schooling were to give their child a better education, religious convictions and because of a poor learning environment at school.*

Source: U.S. Department of Education, National Center for Education Statistics, Parent Survey of the National Household Education Surveys Program, "Homeschooling in the United States: 1999," July 2001.

assessment of U.S. public education that seemed to confirm the misgivings of critics on both the right and the left.

Meanwhile, the ranks of home-schoolers kept growing. In the 1980s, according to Dobson, changes in tax regulations forced smaller Christian schools to close down by the hundreds. Faced with a choice between "government" schools and home schooling, thousands of parents chose to educate their children at home.

"In the mid-1980s, the number of Christian schools exploded," says Ray of the National Home Education Research Institute. "By the time the '90s rolled around, Christian schools were the majority."

States' Rights

In 1852, Massachusetts became the first state to make education compulsory for all children. Mississippi was the last state to do so, in 1918. Ever since, defining the limits on the power of the states to require and regulate education has been a subject for the courts.

"The right of the states to require education under the Constitution is well accepted, but the extent to which that right may be exercised is not unlimited," says education attorney Rubin. The U.S. Supreme Court defined the boundaries of state power in several cases dating back to the 1920s, he points out. "While not dealing specifically

Colleges Praise Home-Schooled Applicants

Twenty years ago, when Harvard University admitted Grant Colfax, a home-schooled high-achiever from California, the achievement earned him an appearance on Johnny Carson's legendary "Tonight Show."

Today, an estimated 30,000 home-schooled students enter college each year, many at top schools after being actively recruited. Stanford University admitted four out of 15 home-schooled applicants in 1999 — a 27 percent acceptance rate, or more than double the rate of the entire applicant pool.[1]

"Home schoolers are the epitome of Brown students," Dean Joyce Reed wrote recently in the Brown University alumni magazine. "They are self-directed, they take risks and they don't back off."[2]

Colleges and universities generally require home-schooled students to provide a description of their academic work, results from standardized tests — usually the SAT or ACT — and personal recommendations. About a third of the colleges require graduates of "non-accredited" schools to provide GED, or high-school equivalency, test scores, according to the National Center for Home Education, the lobbying arm of the Home School Legal Defense Association."[3]

Some colleges require home-schooled students to take more achievement tests — such as the subject-oriented SAT II tests — than they require of regular high-school seniors. Not long ago, Georgia generated a national flap when it began requiring home-schooled applicants to the state university to take eight SAT IIs.

The more-stringent requirements were set aside after researchers found that home-schooled students "ran every organization at the University of Georgia," says Sean Callaway, director of college placement and internships in the Center for Urban Education at Pace University, in New York City. Callaway oversees e-mail contacts between home-schoolers and admissions officials set up by the National Association for College Admissions Counseling.[4]

But financial-aid issues can pose problems for home-schooled applicants to state universities, Callaway says. Recent changes in federal rules have created conflict between state and federal regulations. "It's different in every state," Callaway says. "Washington state is very friendly [to home-schoolers]; New York state is very unfriendly."

How do home-schoolers fare at college? Systematic research into the question "really needs to be done," Callaway says. But, like other research on home schooling,

---

with the right of home instruction, these cases form the constitutional backdrop against which home-instruction cases are viewed."

In 1923 in *Meyer v. Nebraska*, the high court struck down a state law prohibiting the teaching of a modern language other than English to students who had not completed the eighth grade. Ruling that the law violated the defendant's right to teach, the student's right to learn and the parents' rights to choose what their children would be taught, the court said such rights are protected by the due-process clause of the 14th Amendment. At the same time, however, the court recognized the "power of the State to compel attendance at some schools and to make reasonable regulations for all schools."

Two years later, in *Pierce v. Society of Sisters*, the Supreme Court ruled that an Oregon statute compelling attendance at public school without providing for a private-school alternative "unreasonably interferes with the liberty of

parents and guardians to direct the education of children under their control."

States' rights in controlling education came up again in *Farrington v. Tokushige* in 1927. Here the Supreme Court applied the due-process clause of the Fifth Amendment to strike down stringent laws regulating Hawaii's private schools. "The *Farrington* court acknowledged there was a right to regulate private schools, but that right could not be so extensive as to effectively eliminate the alternatives offered by private schools," Rubin commented.[35]

In 1972, the Supreme Court again squarely confronted the issue of state vs. parental power in *Wisconsin v. Yoder*, affirming a Wisconsin Supreme Court's ruling that reversed the conviction of Amish parents for violating the state's compulsory-attendance law. The court held that the conviction had violated the parents' First Amendment right to the free exercise of religion. But the court emphasized that to trigger constitutional protection, the it's complicated by the difficulty of finding a controlled sample. Anecdotal evidence suggests that home-schooled students do well, however.

"Students from a home-schooled background are almost always in the top half of our applicant pool," says Ken Huus, associate dean of admissions at Indiana's Earlham College, which averages three new home-schooled students per year. "They represent themselves extremely well in personal interviews, tend to be very well read and tend to excel in our learning environment."

"To stereotype [home-schoolers] as being high achievers is a pretty accurate description," Susan Christian, director of admissions at Rider University in New Jersey, told *The New Jersey Times*. "Of the group I've seen over the years, I can't recall too many that weren't exceptional."[5]

Maryalice Newborn, the mother of five home-schooled children, says the experience made the transition to college especially easy. "For my children, going from home-schooling high school to college was just a continuation, and not a paradigm shift, like it is for so many institutionalized high-school students. They are already well acquainted with searching for their own answers and finding their own experts."

Heather Herrick graduates last June from the 14-member inaugural class of Patrick Henry College, and receives a handshake from school President Michael Farris. The Christian-oriented school in Purcellville, Va., serves home-schooled students and currently has 193 students enrolled. Farris is the founder of the Home School Legal Defense Association.

---

[1] Cafi Cohen, *Homeschoolers' College Admissions Handbook* (2000), p. 6.

[2] Web site for Homeschool.com, www.homeschool.com/articles/CollegesWantYou/default.asp.

[3] Cohen, *op. cit.*, p. 11.

[4] To join, send an e-mail to listserv@list.pace.edu and ask to be placed on the HSC-L list.

[5] Robert Stern, "Home Schooled, College-Bound," *The New Jersey Times*, April 8, 2002, p. A1.

---

parental interest must be religious rather than philosophical or personal, and it reaffirmed a strong state interest in compulsory education.

In the 1980s, home-schooling advocates turned their attention to the legislative arena. While only two states had home-schooling statutes or regulations in 1980, 37 states had adopted such laws by 2001.[36] States without such statutes still allow home schooling when families designate themselves as private schools or religious schools, according to the Home School Legal Defense Association.

CURRENT SITUATION

Nationwide Movement

By the 1990s — when the pioneering families who launched the movement began their second generation

of home schooling — the world of home schooling had changed dramatically.

Earl Stevens, a Portland, Maine, parent who home-educated his son, remembers how in the 1980s he and a friend, Eileen Yoder, decided to publish a newsletter and create the Home Education Support Network of Southern Maine. It became a model for loosely organized networks of families throughout the country. "I published the newsletter to connect people," he recalls.

He remembers it as a fun and wonderfully harmonious time. For about a dozen years, the network's 200 families and 400-500 kids gathered for activities ranging from baseball to theater productions. "There was always something happening," he recalls. "We were a totally non-directed group. There was never a meeting, never a hierarchy, never a conflict." And dealing with the state of Maine, he said, was a simple matter. "You just had to translate [what your child had accomplished] into a form they could understand."

AP Photo/The Tennessean, Michael Clancy

Members of the Music City Monarchs, a home-schooled baseball team in Mt. Juliet, Tenn., get ready for practice. Advocates of home schooling say sports, music lessons and other outside activities provide home-schooled students with diverse contacts with other students. About 18 percent of home-schoolers take classes or extracurricular activities at public schools.

Today, home-schooling organizations — some formal and some informal — exist in every state. They not only organize softball and basketball games and talent shows but also act as powerful lobbying networks. In addition, the loosely organized groups of families who practice "unschooling" have been joined by more hierarchical, religiously motivated organizations whose families generally prefer a more school-like, top-down approach to teaching and learning.

In 1983 Michael Farris, an attorney in Olympia, Wash., and former executive director of the state's conservative Moral Majority chapter, launched the Home School Legal Defense Association to assist home-schoolers. His nine children grew to maturity schooled primarily by his wife, Vicki, who told reporters that her "first and highest goal for our kids is to love our Lord."[37]

The HSLDA grew in size and influence. By 1993, with headquarters in Purcellville, Va., outside Washington, D.C., the group claimed more than 37,000 dues-paying members, some 90 percent of whom described themselves as evangelical or fundamentalist Christians.[38] That year, Farris ran unsuccessfully for lieutenant governor of Virginia, a move that cemented his ties with the Republican Party.

In 1994, the HSLDA and its home-schooling network demonstrated their political clout by defeating an amendment to the federal Elementary and Secondary Education Act that might have required home-schooling parents in some states and districts to be certified as teachers.

In 1999 the group broke ground for Patrick Henry College in Purcellville. The first students enrolled the next year. The school offers both conventional classroom instruction and an apprenticeship program in government affairs, effectively bringing volunteer workers to the HSLDA.

Today, with a staff numbering close to 60, HSLDA boasts more than 76,000 members, according to spokesman Ziegler.

Other Christian proponents of home schooling have developed veritable home-based industries around their home-schooling experiences and beliefs. For example, Christian Life Workshops, run by Gregg Harris and his family, of Gresham, Ore., centers on organizing seminars to spread the word about Christian home schooling. They also publish and sell home-schooling aids and a magazine.[39]

While conservative Protestant home-schoolers may be more entrepreneurial and media savvy than most, they are only one face of the home-schooling population, notes Mitchell L. Stevens, an associate professor of sociology at Hamilton College in Clinton, N.Y., who studied the home-schooling world for 10 years. "Other home-schoolers have built a decidedly ecumenical home education," he writes. "They have done so according to the rules and with the resources of 'alternative' America: that fragile organizational network left after the ebb of liberal causes of the 1960s and 1970s. This is the world of alternative schools, progressive not-for-profits, food co-ops and the occasional surviving commune that carry on the egalitarian ethos of the student movements and the counterculture.[40]

"Both groups have managed to create lively, talkative, durable causes," Stevens observes, "but one version of home education is larger and wealthier and more handily directs the national conversation on home schooling." That group, Stevens says, is the Christian-based wing of the movement.

Into the Mainstream?

Many mainstream Americans now view home schooling as a reasonable and realistic option, and increasing

Does home schooling promote the public good?

YES
Brian D. Ray, Ph.D.
*President, National Home Education
Research Institute*

NO
Christopher Lubienski
*Assistant Professor, Historical, Philosophical
and Comparative Studies College of Education,
Iowa State University*

Written for *The CQ Researcher*, January, 2003

Research, experience and a philosophy of freedom show that home schooling promotes the public good because increasing the number of well-educated, socially stable and civically active individuals advances the public good.

Americans agree that several things benefit society. First, freedom of choice applies to directing the upbringing and education of one's own progeny, as the Supreme Court has affirmed. Second, having authentic educational choices is itself a democratic institution that protects citizens from government controlling knowledge and thought. Choice makes society richer and more diverse. Socially well-adjusted and educated citizens who are industrious and civically involved benefit society. Finally, particular values and principles, such as those listed above, as well as respectfulness and tolerance of others' beliefs and those embodied in the Constitution and Declaration of Independence, advance the common good. Research shows that home schooling promotes these things.

Research also shows home-schooled students score 15 to 30 percentile points above their peers in public schools on academic achievement tests, are above average in their social and psychological well-being and are involved in sports and community activities. Home-educated adults perform well in college and leadership activities and tend to be independent and critical thinkers who are gainfully employed. Home-school parents are more civically active than average.

Studies also show home schooling is accessible to a wide array of people. A rising tide of African-American and Hispanic families is flowing into home-based education and away from the public-good school experiment they discern can never make good on its promises. Many can afford the average $500 per student per year while saving taxpayers the burden of over $7,000 per public-school student.

Home-schooled young adults, regardless of their political, religious, economic or ethnic backgrounds, affirm values and behaviors that promote the common good. I have taught in public and private schools and in the home-school world and been a professor of education at the undergraduate and graduate levels. While 87 percent of Americans attend public schools, illiteracy, drug abuse, and incarceration rates climb and the battles over funding, power and defining "the common good" that riddle these schools continue. Meanwhile, an ever-increasing number of parents will successfully home school one child at a time, for his or her personal good and the furtherance of the public good.

Written for *The CQ Researcher*, January, 2003

The accelerated movement toward home schooling reflects a serious threat to the collective good — a threat encouraged by organized efforts to withdraw from common endeavors such as public education. Home schooling necessarily encourages individuals to focus on their own child, and diminishes concern for the education of other people's children. By emphasizing only personal benefits, the incentives inherent in home schooling essentially privatize the purpose of education. Home schooling fragments the public good into individual concerns that deny the public's interest in the education of all children.

Some argue that such individualization is not only appropriate but preferable in terms of the educational responsiveness home schooling can offer each child. In the aggregate, such a system better approximates the public good than does any bureaucracy, according to this logic.

Of course, home schooling is not an option available to all. While that is no reason to oppose home schooling, it raises questions about the factors that distinguish which child is home schooled and which are not. Home-schooling parents are by definition active and involved, having the means and initiative to guide their children's learning.

While home schooling may have beneficial effects on their own children's academic achievement, their withdrawal from the community's educational endeavors is a double loss for everyone else. Schools depend on such parents to demand accountability and results; if the channels for citizen participation in such institutions are not effectively exercised, atrophy occurs — making concerns about bureaucratic pre-eminence a self-fulfilling prophecy. Moreover, children from articulate and involved families would likely enhance the peer effect in the classroom, where children learn not just from a teacher, but from each other. Thus, while home schooling might produce a handful of academically elite individuals, it may also undermine the capacity to effectively educate the rest.

Home schooling advances from a thin conception of the public good premised on negative notions of liberty: freedom from others, rather than freedom — indeed, responsibility — to be involved with other members of the community. Such an orientation negates the public's legitimate interest in how children are educated. Families necessarily act to reproduce their values, while individual autonomy depends on free and informed choice within a broader social context. Such conditions are reflected more in a school attended by people from other families and backgrounds, than in a single family.

Mark Thiessen/National Geographic Society

Moderator Alex Trebek looks on as the winner of the National Geographic Bee, Calvin McCarter, right, displays his winning answer. The home-schooled 10-year-old from Jenison, Mich., won a $25,000 scholarship.

numbers of families are home schooling longer, according to Ray, of the National Home Education Research Institute. "In the early years, the numbers were highly disproportionate, with the great majority in grades K-4, or K-6," Ray says. "Now there's a clear trend of home schooling growing in the upper grade levels."

In August 2001, a *Time* cover story on home schooling's arrival in the mainstream, with a picture of a smiling, stereotypically American-looking family, asked: "Is Home Schooling Good for America?" In a wide-ranging, mostly anecdotal account of the phenomenon, the article stressed the diversity of the movement, with a constituency much like the rest of America and including representatives of all political and ethnic backgrounds. It even included a slightly tongue-in-cheek guide to becoming a home-schooler, with a short paragraph describing "How do I design a curriculum?[41]

Web sites and Web-based businesses have proliferated offering curriculum guidance representing a broad range of educational approaches. (*See sidebar p. 122.*) Curriculum fairs for home-schoolers are commonplace and well attended. Bookstores have separate sections for home schooling. Amazon.com lists the titles of more than 1,500 home-schooling books. And in pop culture's ultimate acknowledgement of home schooling's rise to mainstream status, IDG Books added *Home Schooling for Dummies* to its popular how-to series.

But not all observers agree that the choice to home school has become so simple. "It's not mainstream yet," says Sean Callaway, director of college placement and internships in the Center for Urban Education at Pace University in New York City. "A lot of home-school families are in a very, very vulnerable position even when they're doing very well." Callaway, who home-schooled his children off and on for about eight years, has lectured widely on the subject. "You run the risk of having a social-service worker knock on your door. Anyone can accuse you of educational child abuse. It does tend to make people defensive."

Callaway believes that the most useful way to view home-schooled students is as an anarchic school system in which 20 percent of the private-school kids in America are enrolled.

"It's just another way to educate kids, and it works in some situations and not in others," he says. "You have high-end kids and low-end kids. There are both high schools and home schools where the choices are inappropriate, high schools and home schools with a very, very narrow vision."

OUTLOOK
'Saber Rattling'

With the Republican Party in control of both Congress and the White House, the concerns of home-schoolers will likely find a sympathetic ear on Capitol Hill. "The trend has been to increasingly recognize parents' rights and authority," says Ray of the National Home Education Research Institute.

At the same time, he says, state legislatures are increasingly calling for more testing and more regulation. "Out of the blue, it's been happening more and more," Ray says. "I don't know why."

Among the recent trouble spots, from home-schoolers' perspective, are California, where the state superintendent decided that individual families could no longer qualify as private schools, the arrangement under which they had been allowed to home-school for years.

In Pennsylvania and Illinois, local school superintendents have been "rather aggressive" in trying to ascertain whether home-schooling families are operating according to state regulations, says Ziegler of the Home School

Legal Defense Association, adding that the government "saber rattling" has included the issuance of pretrial notifications to some families.

In early 2002, Connecticut state Rep. Cameron Staples, D-New Haven, co-chairman of the legislature's Education Committee, introduced legislation to strengthen state Department of Education home-schooling guidelines by requiring parents to give local school districts copies of their teaching plans, including subjects, materials and a schedule of at least 900 hours of instruction per year. They also were required to obtain an independent assessment of their child's performance. But after a public outcry from home-schooling supporters, he agreed to kill the bill.

And in North Dakota, the House Education Committee is considering a bill — introduced on Dec. 30, 2002, at the request of the superintendent of public instruction — that would require home-schooled students to meet the same math, reading and science requirements as public-school students.[42]

"Some states have pretty strict regulations, others much more freedom," Ziegler says. "We're always working" for more freedom.

Limited Growth?

Advocates predict the home-schooling population will continue growing. "It will continue to grow in absolute numbers and percentage of population," says Ray of the National Home School Research Institute. But, he adds, the movement is also self-limiting. "How many families could or would live on one income? How many are willing to spend that much time with their children? How many believe they can afford to pay property taxes plus the additional expense of home schooling?"

As the movement continues to grow, public-school supporters worry that increasing accountability and assessment in the public schools — without a corresponding increase in accountability of home-schoolers — will create a pronounced educational dichotomy.

"There will be an increasing gap between regulation of public schools and of home schools," says Underwood of the National School Boards Association.

The now-dormant school-voucher issue, meanwhile, could play a role in home schooling. "Probably a minority of home-schooling families strongly want vouchers," Ray says, although vouchers potentially could provide funds for families to underwrite home-schooling costs. But the HSLDA

and other home-schooling organizations are wary of accepting state funds. "State-level leaders tend to warn, 'If you take money, there will be strings attached,' " Ray explains.

But Underwood sees commonalities, and thinks the voucher issue will be back on the federal table this year. "The underlying similarity is greater parental control," she says. "In states where home-schooling parents are treated as private schools, it throws up concerns about [parents] keeping children home and keeping the [voucher] money."

For their part, public-school supporters see the trend toward home schooling as part of the broad drive toward privatization of traditionally governmental functions that began after Ronald Reagan's election to the presidency in 1980.

"Like private school, home schooling is a good option for some," says Ohio elementary-school principal Young. But, he adds, "If it just drives privatization, it would be a drastic mistake for our country."

NOTES

1. Stacey Bielick, Kathryn Chandler and Stephen P. Broughman, "Homeschooling in the United States: 1999," U.S. Department of Education, National Center for Education Statistics, July 2001.

2. J. Gary Knowles, Stacey E. Marlow and James A. Muchmore, "From Pedagogy to Ideology: Origins and Phases of Home Education in the United States, 1970-1990," *American Journal of Education*, Feb. 1992, p. 196.

3. Nola Kortner Aiex, "Home Schooling and Socialization of Children," *ERIC Digest*, ERIC Clearinghouse on Reading, English and Communication, 1994, www.ed.gov/databases/ERIC_Digests/ed372460.html.

4. For background, see Charles S. Clark, "Home Schooling," *The CQ Researcher*, Sept. 9, 1994, pp. 769-792.

5. Greg Toppo, "850,000 Kids are being taught at home, study finds," *USA Today*, Aug. 6, 2001, p. 5D.

6. For background, see Joan Hennessey, "Teaching Math and Science," *The CQ Researcher*, Sept. 6, 2002, pp. 697-720.

7. Quoted in Aiex, *op. cit.*, which offers a summary of such findings.

8. Noreen S. Ahmed-Ullah, "Home-schoolers find vindication in contests," *The Chicago Tribune*, June 21, 2001.

9. See "Home Schooled Michigan Teen Receives Perfect SAT Score," *The Associated Press*, June 1, 2001.

10. Lawrence M. Rudner, "Scholastic Achievement and Demographic Characteristics of Home School Students in 1998," *Education Policy Analysis Archives*, March 23, 1999.

11. Kariane Mari Welner and Kevin G. Welner, "Contextualizing Homeschooling Data: A Response to Rudner," *Education Policy Analysis Archives*, April 11, 1999.

12. Nancy Mitchell, "Dog Bites System When She Receives Progress Certificate," *The Rocky Mountain News*, April 30, 2002, p. 4A.

13. David Rubin, "Home Schooling, Religion and Public Schools: Striking a Constitutional Balance," National School Boards Association, August 2001.

14. For background on testing, see Kenneth Jost, "Testing in Schools," *The CQ Researcher*, April 20, 2001, pp. 321-344.

15. For background, see Charles S. Clark, "Charter Schools," *The CQ Researcher*, Dec. 20, 2002, pp. 1033-1056.

16. *Ibid.*

17. Toppo, *op. cit.*

18. Rubin, *op. cit.*

19. Thomas W. Burns, "Home Schoolers: Eligibility to Participate in Public School Extracurricular Activities," *Inquiry and Analysis*, May/June 2002, p. 6.

20. *Ibid.*

21. *Ibid.*, p. 7.

22. Patricia D. Lines, "When Home Schoolers go to School: A Partnership Between Families and Schools," *Peabody Journal of Education*, January-February 2000, p. 134. Lines has served as a senior research analyst for the U.S. Department of Education and director of the Law and Education Center at the Education Commission of the States.

23. http://www.home-ed-magazine.com/HEM/196/ndtch.html downloaded (11/12/02).

24. See Lines, *op. cit.*, p. 133.

25. *Ibid.*, p. 159.

26. Christian Smith and David Sikkink, "Is Private Schooling Privatizing?" *First Things 92* (April 1999), www.firstthings.com/ftissues/ft9904/smith.html.

27. Online at www.JohnTaylorGatto.com.

28. Brian D. Ray, *2002-2003 Worldwide Guide to Homeschooling* (2002), p. 1.

29. Christopher Lubienski, "Whither the Common Good? A Critique of Home Schooling," *Peabody Journal of Education*, April 2000, p. 207.

30. Quoted in John Cloud, "Home Sweet School," *Time*, Aug. 27, 2001, p. 46.

31. For background on vouchers, see Kenneth Jost, "School Vouchers Showdown," *The CQ Researcher*, Feb. 15, 2002, pp. 124-144

32. Catherine Gewertz, "Public Support for Local Schools Reaches All-Time High, Poll Finds," *Education Week*, Sept. 5, 2001.

33. Linda Dobson, "A Brief History of American Homeschooling," *Homeschoolers' Success Stories*, http://www.geocities.com/homeschoolers_success_stories/part1.html11/6/2002.

34. John Holt, *How Children Learn* (1964, revised 1982), p. xi.

35. Rubin, *op. cit.*

36. *Ibid.*

37. Mitchell L. Stevens, *Kingdom of Children: Culture and Controversy in the Homeschooling Movement* (2001), p. 3.

38. *Ibid.*, p. 123.

39. *Ibid.*, p. 115.

40. *Ibid.*, p. 7.

41. Cloud and Morse, *op. cit.*, p. 46.

42. Robert A. Frahm, "Home School Bill Killed," *The Hartford Courant*, March 15, 2002, p. B1.

BIBLIOGRAPHY

Books

Guterson, David, *Family Matters: Why Homeschooling Makes Sense, Harcourt Brace*, 1992.
The public-school teacher who went on to author the best-seller *Snow Falling on Cedars* explains his belief that home schooling is better.

Holt, John, *How Children Learn*, *Perseus*, 1964, revised 1983.

Holt's clear explication of his theory of children as natural learners played a key role in the growth of home schooling.

Ray, Brian D., *2002-2003 Worldwide Guide to Homeschooling*, *Broadman & Holman Publishers*, 2002.

One of home schooling's most prolific advocates details the benefits he sees in allowing parents to tailor daily school-work to their children's interests and abilities.

Stevens, Mitchell L., *Kingdom of Children: Culture and Controversy in the Homeschooling Movement*, *Princeton University Press*, 2001.

After 10 years of research, a sociology professor analyzes growth and change within the home-schooling movement.

Van Galen, J., and M.A. Pitman, eds., *Home Schooling: Political, Historical and Pedagogical Perspectives*, *Ablex Publishing*, 1991.

This collection of academic articles usefully covers home schooling from a variety of angles.

Articles

Peabody Journal of Education, Vol. 75, January/February 2000.

Several scholarly articles on home schooling offer explanatory theories and historical analyses, describe specific educational programs and assess educational methods.

Archer, Jeff, "Unexplored Territory," *Education Week*, Dec. 8, 1999.

Archer surveys scholarly research on home schooling, providing useful insights into the pitfalls of studying a highly politicized subject.

Cloud, John, et al., "Home Sweet School," *Time*, Aug. 27, 2001, p. 46.

This cover story points out that today's home-schooling parents are a diverse group of parents who are getting results — and putting pressure on public schools.

Knowles, J. Gary, et al., "From Pedagogy to Ideology: Origins and Phases of Home Education in the United States, 1970-1990," *American Journal of Education*, February 1992, p. 196.

University of Michigan researchers analyze the history of the home-schooling movement.

Lyman, Isabel, "Homeschooling: Back to the Future," *Cato Policy Analysis No. 294*, Jan. 7, 1998.

A home-schooling parent and educator offers a short, useful summary of the case for home schooling.

Ray, Brian D., "Customization Through Homeschooling," *Educational Leadership*, Vol. 59, No. 7, April 2002.

A home-schooling scholar details the benefits of parents tailoring schoolwork to their children's interests and abilities.

Reports and Studies

Bielick, Stacey, et al., "Homeschooling in the United States: 1999," *U.S. Department of Education, National Center for Educational Statistics*, July 2001.

This is the most detailed study to date of the U.S. home-schooling population.

Bauman, Kurt J., "Home Schooling in the United States: Trends and Characteristics," *Education Policy Analysis Archives*, Vol. 10, No. 26, May 16, 2002.

A Census Bureau demographer argues that home schooling may have significant impacts on the educational system.

Rubin, David, and Perry Zirkel, "Home Schooling in Religion and Public Schools: Striking a Constitutional Balance," *NSBA Council of School Attorneys*, August 2001, available at www.nsba.org/pubs/index.cfm.

This National School Boards Association report analyzes the case law and constitutional issues involved in defining the legal context for home schooling.

Rudner, Lawrence M., "Scholastic Achievement and Demographic Characteristics of Home School Students in 1998," *Education Policy Analysis Archives*, Vol. 7, No. 8, March 23, 1999, available at http://epaa.asu.edu/epaa/v7n8.

This study found the test scores of more than 20,000 home-schoolers to be exceptionally high. Demographic data also are analyzed.

Welner, Kariane Mari and Kevin G., "Contextualizing Homeschooling Data: A Response to Rudner," *Education Policy Analysis Archives*, Vol. 7, No. 13, April 11, 1999, Available at http://epaa.asu.edu/epaa/v7n13.html.

The Welners warn that Rudner's data are skewed because they came solely from Bob Jones University.

For More Information

Home Education Magazine, P.O. Box 1083, Tonasket, WA 98855; (800) 236-3278 or (509) 486-1351; www .home-ed-magazine.com. Library Journal's *Magazines for Libraries* describes the magazine as "informative and commonsense."

Home School Legal Defense Association, P.O. Box 3000, Purcellville, VA 20134; (540) 338-5600; www.hslda.org. HSLDA provides information on state laws and legislative activity that affect home schooling and legal assistance to home-schooling families. Its lobbying arm, the National Center for Home Education, works to protect parents' right to home school.

National Association of Elementary School Principals, 1615 Duke St., Alexandria, VA 22314; (703) 684-3345; www.naesp.org. The NAESP's mission is to "lead in the advocacy and support for elementary and middle level principals and other education leaders in their commitment to all children.

National Home Education Research Institute, P.O. Box 13939, 925 Cottage St. N.E., Salem, OR 97309; (503) 364-2827; www.nheri.org. NHERI publishes the peer-reviewed journal *Home School Researcher,* undertakes research and provides information and consultation nationally and internationally.

National School Boards Association, 1680 Duke St., Alexandria, VA 22314-3493; (703) 838-6722; www.nsba .org. The foundation's mission is "to foster excellence and equity in public education through innovation in school board leadership and community engagement." It expresses concern that home schooling may expose children to substandard educations and undercut public education.

Practical Homeschooling **magazine**, P.O. Box 1190, Fenton, MO 63026; (800) 346-6322; www.home-school .com. The Christian-oriented publication offers practical tips on home schooling as well as a daily Bible-reading plan.

The Teaching Home: **A Christian Magazine for Home Educators**, P.O. Box 20219, Portland, OR 97294; (503) 253-9633; www.teachinghome.com. Publishers Pat and Sue Welch say: "Our purpose has always been to provide information, inspiration and support to Christian home-school families and Christian home-school state and national organizations . . . to the honor and glory of the Lord God."

7

Single-Sex Education

Do All-Boy and All-Girl Schools Enhance Learning?

Kenneth Jost

The Jefferson Leadership Academies provide single-gender education to boys and girls from low-income families in Long Beach, Calif. The Bush administration wants federal regulations to make it easier for school districts to experiment with single-sex education, now offered in only 13 schools nationwide.

From *CQ Researcher*, July 12, 2002.

P arents, friends and guests strain for a clear view as the graduates file in, resplendent in white academic gowns. Some of the members of this New York City high school class of 2002 are smiling broadly. Others are more solemn as the familiar strains of "Pomp and Circumstance" waft through the packed auditorium.

With the audience seated and the welcome delivered, the 34 graduates are introduced one by one in a slide show, along with the names of the colleges that all but one of the seniors will be attending in the fall.

The college acceptance record is unique for a New York City public school in one of the city's marginal neighborhoods. Even more unusual, all of the graduates are girls — self-described "pioneers" in a six-year-old experiment aimed at improving learning and boosting self-confidence by giving the girls a school of their own, away from the competition and distraction of adolescent boys.

"What a wonderful gift," exclaims Principal Kathleen Ponze, "when the girls come here and we say, 'This is all for you.' "

Welcome to The Young Women's Leadership School of East Harlem: TYWLS, pronounced "Twills" by students and faculty.[1] Founded in 1996, it is one of the success stories being cited by a growing number of advocates of single-sex education as examples for public school systems around the country seeking to improve education for girls and boys alike.

"Single-sex education works better," says Leonard Sax, a family physician and psychologist in Poolesville, Md., near Washington,

141

Same-Sex Schools Target Minority Students

Only 13 public schools in the United States currently operate all or some of their classes on a single-sex basis, according to education experts. Virtually all serve minority communities.

Charter School of San Diego San Diego, Calif. Founded: 2000 Enrollment: 40 girls and 40 boys	The 1,300-student school for grades 7-12 offers single-sex classes in grades 7 and 8. Boys and girls are more comfortable asking questions and interacting in single-sex classrooms, says Director Mary Bixby.
Jefferson Leadership Academies Long Beach, Calif. Founded: 1999 Enrollment: 1,120 boys and girls, grades 6-8	Parents in this low-income community felt that coeducational classes provided too many distractions for students, prompting the conversion to single-sex classes.
Lewis Fox Middle School Hartford, Conn. Founded: 1995 Enrollment: 80 boys and girls in 7th and 8th grades	Students in the single-sex program (total school enrollment is 900) perform 15-20 percent better on standardized tests than citywide averages.
Maria Mitchell Elementary School Denver, Colo. Founded: 1998 Enrollment: 60 4th- and 5th-grade students; 540 total enrollment	Principal Reginald Robinson says the program works because 4th- and 5th-graders are "too inquisitive" about the opposite sex to concentrate on classwork.
Moten Elementary School Washington, D.C. Founded: Fall of 2001 Enrollment: 362 boys and girls, grades 4-6	When this inner-city school switched to single-sex classes and revamped its curriculum, students' standardized test scores rose by an average of 40 percentage points.
Paducah Middle School Paducah, Ky. Founded: 2001 Enrollment: 30 boys and 18 girls in 6th grade	Although performance has not been measured for the pilot program, all 6th- and 7th-graders will attend single-sex classes in the future.

D.C. and founder of the fledgling National Association for the Advancement of Single-Sex Public Education. "Kids who attend single-sex schools not only do better academically but also have a better attitude toward school and a better outlook on life."

After sitting in on three classes at TYWLS in May, Secretary of Education Rod Paige enthused, "Visiting this school fortifies my already strong belief that these kinds of schools should be available for parents."[2]

Paige is giving the idea more than lip service. He has ordered a rewrite of federal regulations to make it easier for school districts to experiment with single-sex schools and classes. The Education Department will also be in charge of doling out money that Congress added to President Bush's education-reform package for school districts to pay for those experiments.

Support for single-sex education is far from unanimous, however. Coeducational schools have predominated in U.S. public education for more than a century — and appear to be popular among the vast majority of students from kindergarten through college. Experts are divided on the claimed academic benefits of single-sex education. And many women's and civil rights groups fear that the movement diverts attention and resources from improving public schools for the vast majority of students or risks undercutting the federal law — known

Philadelphia High School for Girls Philadelphia, Pa. Founded: 1848 Enrollment: 1,400 girls, grades 9-12	The magnet school is open to exceptional applicants citywide and sends 95 percent of its graduates to college. Half of the students are from homes with family incomes below the poverty line.
Robert Coleman Elementary School Baltimore, Md. Founded: 1993 Enrollment: Pre-K - 5th grade	After Principal Hattie Johnson separated classes by gender at the predominantly minority school, test scores rose to among the highest in Baltimore and discipline problems all but vanished.
San Francisco 49ers Academy Palo Alto, Calif. Founded: 1997 Enrollment: 90 boys and 90 girls	Boys and girls' schools operate separately at this middle school. Although classes are single-sex, recess and extracurricular activities are coeducational.
The Young Women's Leadership School New York, N.Y. Founded: 1996 Enrollment: 365 students, grades 7-12	The Harlem school sends almost 100 percent of its students to four-year colleges; 59 percent are Latina, 40 percent African-American.
Thurgood Marshall Elementary School Seattle, Wash. Founded: 2000 Enrollment: 356 boys and girls, grades K-5	After Principal Ben Wright instituted single-sex classes, test scores rose and discipline problems declined. The students are 97 percent minority, and 80 percent receive subsidized lunches.
Western High School Baltimore, Md. Founded: 1844 Enrollment: 1,050 girls	More than 80 percent African-American, Western boasts the third-highest SAT scores in Baltimore and a college acceptance rate of 99 percent in 2001.
Young Women's Leadership School Chicago, Ill. Founded: 2000 Enrollment: 300 girls, grades 7-12	With a curriculum focused on leadership, science and technology, the school serves a student body that is over 80 percent minority, and 65 percent of the students come from poor families.

as Title IX — that prohibits sex discrimination in schools or colleges receiving federal funds.

"I understand that the Harlem girls' school is doing very well, and it should be," says Nancy Zirkin, director of public policy and government affairs at the American Association of University Women (AAUW). "But what is the collateral damage done by pulling kids out and focusing on one school and leaving the other ones behind? I would think it would not improve public schools."

The movement for single-sex education follows a decades-long debate about how well girls are doing in public schools, and a more recent debate over boys' performance as well.[3] A 1992 AAUW report charged that

schools were "shortchanging" girls by "depriving [them] of classroom attention, ignoring the value of cooperative learning and presenting texts and lessons in which female role models are conspicuously absent."[4]

More recently, some experts and advocates have complained that schools shortchange boys by starting them at school at an age when they are developmentally behind girls and then constraining their natural instincts toward physical activity and healthy competition. "As competitiveness and individual initiative are discouraged, classroom discipline loosened and outlets for natural rambunctiousness eliminated, schoolboys tend to tune out," writes Christina Hoff Sommers in her book *The War Against Boys*.[5]

The answer to both problems, single-sex education advocates say, is simple: Let boys be boys and girls be girls. "The solution is to let boys and girls attend separate classes, so that you can take advantage of the sex differences" in learning styles, Sax says.

Others say that the supposed differences between boys and girls are being exaggerated. "There are much greater differences among girls and among boys than there are between girls and boys," say education experts Patricia Campbell and Ellen Wahl.[6]

For the present, the United States offers relatively few places to test the opposing arguments, especially in the public school setting. Only a dozen or so public schools are known to be offering single-sex enrollment or classes. Parochial and private schools were once predominantly single-sex, but are far less so today. In higher education, the number of women's schools has declined sharply over the past four decades, and men's colleges have all but disappeared: Only three remain. (*See story, p. 154.*)

Perhaps surprisingly, academic experts on both sides of the debate say that increasing the number of single-sex schools or classes would be beneficial, at least in terms of research. "We see some of these studies with large samples indicating some positive effect from single-sex schooling," says Rosemary Salomone, a professor at St. John's University School of Law in Jamaica, N.Y. "We won't know unless we permit the programs to survive."

"Anyone who says the research is definitive either way is not accurate," says David Sadker, a professor of education at American University in Washington and a skeptic of single-sex education. "There's still a lot to learn."

Meanwhile, TYWLS founder Ann Rubenstein Tisch is convinced the school provides an invaluable option. "I know that some of our students, our stars, would have done well in any school," says Tisch, a former television reporter turned education activist. "But I also know that there are many others who would never, never have made it were it not for the environment that we offer them. There's got to be something to it."

As the debate over single-sex education continues, here are some of the questions being considered:

Does single-sex education enhance learning?

Australian researcher Kenneth Rowe examined the academic records of some 270,000 high school seniors in an effort to identify what factors really make a difference in students' learning. One of his key findings, according to a press release, was that both girls and boys attending single-sex schools scored 15-22 percentile points higher than their counterparts in coeducational schools.

Advocates of single-sex education in the United States point to the big differential as the strongest proof yet that separating boys and girls improves learning for both genders. "That's enormous," Sax says.

But Rowe, principal research fellow with the Australian Council on Education Research, himself insists that Sax and others are distorting his findings. In his formal paper, Rowe explained that the differences between single-sex and coeducational schools "pale into insignificance" compared to differences attributable to teacher training and ability. Today, Rowe says bluntly that the single-sex school debate amounts to "little more than epistemological claptrap."[7]

The advocates of single-sex education claim its benefits derive in part from biological realities. Boys' and girls' brains develop differently, they say — differences especially significant for learning in early years. Then, as they get older, boys and girls distract each other from academics because of normal social and sexual development.

"If you put a 15-year-old boy next to a 15-year-old girl, his mind is not going to be on geometry, or Spanish or English," Sax says. "It's going to be on that girl sexually. He's got the hormones of a grown man, but the brain of a 10-year-old."

In earlier years, Sax and others say, girls typically begin to read at a younger age and are also less distractible in the classroom. Advocates of single-sex education say these differences set up a dynamic unhelpful for boys' learning.

"To the extent that boys experience school in a competitive way and some boys aren't learning to read as readily, their response is to say that reading is girls' stuff, not boys' stuff," says Christopher Wadsworth, executive director of the International Boys' School Coalition. "That can lead to an attitude that is not conducive to development."

In addition, girls'-school advocates say, single-sex education helps girls overcome the male sexism that still exists in public schools. "Girls are at center stage with only girls in the audience," says Meg Milne Moulton, co-executive director of the National Coalition of Girls' Schools. "They get 100 percent of the attention."

"No girl in a single-sex school is able to say, 'I can't do it because no girl can do it' — because there is some girl who is doing it," adds Cornelius Riordan, a professor of sociology at Providence College.

Critics of single-sex education say these claims are largely unsubstantiated. "People think it helps girls' self-esteem or makes boys calmer," the AAUW's Zirkin says. "This is anecdotal. This is pulling things out of the air. There is not the scientifically based research for anybody to make an informed decision."

Academics on both sides of the issue want more and better studies. "There is not definitive research," says Sadker, of American University.

Riordan, however, insists that although the subject is "overpoliticized and underresearched," the research favors single-sex schooling. "All of the studies consistently show small positive effects for boys and girls," he says. "The effects are stronger for girls than for boys, and the positive effects are always larger for disadvantaged students."

Riordan cites a study he published more than a decade ago comparing boys and girls from the 1972 and 1982 graduating classes at American single-sex or coeducational Catholic high schools. After adjusting for ability and background, Riordan found that minority girls and minority boys in single-sex schools did better — about the equivalent of one grade year — than minority girls or boys respectively in coeducational schools. Girls from more representative cross-sections also did better in single-sex schools, but boys' scores were slightly higher in coeducational schools.[8]

Today, Riordan has refined his argument. In a paper presented in various forums over the past several years, he says, "only females of low socioeconomic status are likely to show significant gains (along with boys) in single-sex schools."

Riordan posits a dozen "theoretical rationales" for why single-sex schools have positive effects — including such hypothetical advantages as reduced sex bias in teacher-student interactions, reduced sex differences in curricula and more successful role models for girls. But, he points out, the fact that attendance at a single-gender school today requires an affirmative decision by students and parents — which he calls "a pro-academic" choice — is perhaps the single most important factor contributing to the positive effects.

"That student realizes, 'I'm going to go to a school where it's not business as usual,'" Riordan explains. "'I'm going to have to work.'"

Critics of single-sex education say all the more explicitly that any benefits are most likely attributable to other factors. "A lot of the effects are [due to the fact that] they're good schools, not because they're single-sex," Sadker says.

"The elements that make for good schools would work whether it's single-sex or coed," Zirkin says. "The elements are attention to core academics, qualified teachers, smaller classrooms, discipline and a sense of community and parental involvement. These are the elements that will enable any child in any situation to learn. To say that it's a single-sex school that's achieved such good results really begs the question."

Rowe says his research does indicate advantages from single-sex education, but "gender-class grouping" is not the critical factor, he insists. "Whether schools are single-sex or coed or have single-sex classes within coed settings matters far less than the quality of the teaching and learning provided," he says.

Do single-sex schools reinforce gender stereotypes?

A two-year pilot project in six California public school districts from 1998-2000 affords the best opportunity to date to study the effects of single-sex schools in U.S. public systems. But researchers who studied the effects on gender-related issues report mixed results.

Professors Amanda Datnow of the University of Toronto, Lea Hubbard of the University of California at San Diego and Elisabeth Woody of the University of California at Berkeley found that — as proponents predicted — boys and girls in single-gender settings engaged in more candid conversations about such issues as gender roles than boys and girls in coeducational schools.[9] They also found that eliminating distractions from the opposite sex helped academic learning, especially for girls.

On the other hand, the researchers also found that single-gender classes actually exacerbated teasing and disruptive behavior among boys and cattiness among girls. In addition, teachers perpetuated stereotypes about gender roles — depicting men, for example, as primary wage earners for families. Teachers also based disciplinary and instructional practices on gender stereotypes:

Boys received more discipline and were taught in individualistic settings, while girls were treated in a more nurturing manner and afforded opportunities for collaborative work.

"There is a tendency to teach to a particular notion of boys and a particular notion of girls," Datnow says. "There's really much more variation among boys or among girls as there is between boys and girls."

But advocates of single-sex education believe it helps reduce gender stereotyping. "You break down gender stereotypes by letting the sexes be separate," Sax says. "When you put boys and girls together, you intensify the gender roles. The boys do things that are thought of as typical for boys, and girls do things that are thought of as typical for girls."

"Girls are judged in their own right, not in relation to each other or in relation to the other gender," says Moulton, of the National Coalition of Girls' Schools. "It's a lot easier for a girl to be a girl in a single-gender setting."

Boys, too, find it easier to be themselves in a single-sex setting, Wadsworth says. "Freed from the need to impress girls, boys are more open," he says. "They allow themselves to be more vulnerable to making mistakes."

In her visits to same-sex schools, Salomone of St. John's University says she was struck by boys' willingness to engage in what would be considered "feminine activities," like choir or drama club. "At one school, I saw a whole classroom of boys playing the violin," she recalls.

Riordan says single-sex schools also reduce the incidence of sexual harassment. "A great deal of sexual harassment occurs on school grounds, even in classes," he says. "That does not occur in single-sex schools."

But Datnow and Hubbard reported what they called an unexpected type of harassment of students attending single-sex schools. Students from coeducational schools would tease them with homophobic comments, reflecting an assumption that enrollment in a single-sex school either meant someone was or might become gay or lesbian.

Opponents contend that single-sex schools are more likely to strengthen rather than weaken gender stereotyping. "The concern is the perpetuation of stereotypes in the name of protecting [boys and girls] by taking steps that indeed don't protect either sex but in fact perpetuate the stereotypes that hamstring their development in life,"

says Donna Lieberman, executive director of the New York Civil Liberties Union. "The school system should not be about reinforcing those."

For his part, Sadker of American University believes single-sex schools "can promote gender stereotypes or hinder them. Being single-sex of itself will do neither."

From her study of the California experiment, Datnow concludes that teachers will be the determining factor on whether single-sex schools increase or decrease gender stereotyping. "Teachers need relevant training and support to address student needs in a single-sex setting so they don't presume that all girls learn in a particular way or that boys are naturally rowdy and need kinetic activities," she says.

Datnow says the schools in the California experiment did not provide that kind of support. "Most of the schools did not have a strong ideological commitment to single-sex education," she says. "The administrators were particularly attracted by the generous grant offered by the state."

Do single-sex schools help or hurt the goal of gender equity?

Desperate to keep the city's black teenagers out of prison or the morgue, Detroit's school board decided to open three all-male academies in 1991. The new schools — initially designed to serve about 250 students from pre-school through fifth grade — were to offer an Afrocentric curriculum and a mentoring program aimed at improving students' academic performance, character and self-esteem.

Shortly before the academies were to open, however, two women with young daughters sued the school district in federal court, claiming that barring girls from the new schools would amount to sex discrimination in violation of Title IX and the equal-protection provisions of both the Michigan and U.S. constitutions. Judge George Woods agreed. The "important" purpose of helping the city's black youth, Woods said, "is insufficient to override the rights of females to equal opportunities."[10]

Opponents of single-sex education say separate schools for boys and girls necessarily violate students' rights to equal educational opportunities. "Single-sex public schools are contrary to the spirit of Title IX and — as a practical matter — impossible to police under the Equal Protection Clause," says Martha Davis, senior counsel of the National Organization for Women (NOW) Legal Defense and Education Fund. "The notion that you can have separate but equal is as false for women as it is for minorities."

"Focusing special attention on one sex over the other is a violation of the public trust," Davis adds. "We need to be addressing the ills that kids in an urban setting face regardless of their gender."

"In every legal challenge about the establishment of a boys school or a girls school, [it] has always been found that the boys school has been superior," says Leslie Annexstein, senior counsel with the National Women's Law Center in Washington. She notes that Pennsylvania courts ordered Philadelphia's all-boys Central High School to adopt an open admissions policy in 1984 after finding that the school's facilities were superior to those at a counterpart all-girls school.[11]

Advocates of single-sex schools believe the opponents are fighting battles from the past. "We're beyond that," Providence College's Riordan says. "That was a generation ago. Today, we're talking about schools that would be equal in resources, equal in prestige: We have laws in place to assure that. I don't think that in today's world there's a remote possibility that the school for boys or the school for girls would take on greater prestige or would have greater resources."

"There are pretty strong lobbies and awareness on both sides," says Moulton, of the National Coalition of Girls Schools. "By serving one population, I don't see you disserving another."

In its most recent decision on the issue, the U.S. Supreme Court ordered the state of Virginia to admit female students to the previously all-male Virginia Military Institute (VMI). In a 7-1 decision, the court held that the state's plan to provide a military program for women at another public university was insufficient.[12]

"VMI should serve as an object lesson of what not to do," Salomone says. But, she adds, "you can see the factual distinctions between VMI and the kind of second-generation [single-sex] programs that we see growing up around the country."

The Education Department, in its announcement that it was considering changes in Title IX, said it wants to provide "more flexibility" to permit single-sex classes and schools "while at the same time ensuring appropriate safeguards against discrimination." The final proposal, the department promises, "will ensure that educational opportunities are not limited to students based on sex, and that single-sex classes are not based on sex-role stereotypes."

Critics of single-sex schools are still concerned. "Is this the first step toward undoing Title IX?" Sadker asks. "Can you undo a civil rights protection like this without endangering that protection?"

"There's a perception that the gender problem has been solved," Datnow says. "If we're going to experiment, there needs to be some very specific language around gender equity and some monitoring. We can't simply devolve money to the local level and let them take it away. There needs to be some accountability."

BACKGROUND

'Tide of Coeducation'

Coeducation gradually emerged during the 19th century as the dominant practice in the United States, first in primary and secondary education and later at the college level. Historians David Tyack and Elisabeth Hansot say economics was a major impetus for what they call a "tide of coeducation."[13] Particularly with the advent of the one-room schoolhouse, it became cheaper and more efficient to educate boys and girls together than to operate separate schools for both sexes. Feminists of the day also viewed coeducation as a necessary step in women's emancipation, and some education policymakers believed it would benefit boys and girls alike.

The earliest schools and colleges in Colonial America were for boys only. Girls were educated in informal settings — at home or in so-called "dame schools," which evolved from mere child tending into a forerunner of the American primary school. Coeducation began making inroads early, however. The 19th-century education reformer Horace Mann observed that one of the first educational improvements in Colonial New England was to begin "smuggling" girls into schools for limited periods after the boys had left. By the American Revolution, some reformers were arguing that, just like boys, girls had a right to — and a need for — a good education.

Coeducation became "embedded" in public schools in the first half of the 19th century, Tyack and Hansot

Helping Young Women in Harlem

Lori-Anne Ramsay did not speak up much at the coeducational public high school she attended in New York City. "When I was in physics class, I expected all the boys to be smarter than me," Ramsay recalls.

In two years at The Young Women's Leadership School (TYWLS) in East Harlem, however, Ramsay has blossomed. She graduated in June with honors and in September will be off to Bates College in Maine to study economics.

Ramsay credits much of her success to TYWLS' all-girl environment. "It allows you to focus more," Ramsay says. "Having the opposite sex in the room is a distraction."

But Ramsay concedes there are downsides to a single-sex school. "The social aspects are not all that good," she says. "If you're not a person who goes out and makes friends, you definitely suffer."

Ramsay's classmates and her teachers generally echo her positive feelings toward the six-year-old experiment in public, single-sex education. A few, however, note some disadvantages or credit the school's success primarily to other factors. "It's the school itself — the teachers, the staff," says Oberlin-bound graduate Jasmine Cruz-Oquendo.

"Our school is unique not only because it is single-sex but also because we have small classes, very dedicated teachers and kids have to apply to be here," says Spanish teacher Roseanne Demammos. "Certainly, some of the students could have experienced the same success" at a coeducational school.

Principal Kathleen Ponze also acknowledges the school's small size — 370 students in grades 7-12 — necessarily limits its offerings: There are only two advanced-placement courses, for example. "It's extremely difficult to meet the needs of every kid," Ponze says. She also laments the limited social opportunities the school can provide.

Still, TYWLS tries to fill the gaps. The school partners with New York University for a drama club and with an all-boys Catholic school for socials. And juniors and seniors can take courses at nearby Hunter College. "We don't have any of the frills here," Ponze says. "We try to make the frills."

More worrisome has been the high staff turnover. Ponze is the school's third principal, and more than a dozen teachers left last year. "The school is very demanding of its faculty as well as its students," says Demammos. "It's not necessarily the right situation for everyone."

This year, however, staffing has stabilized. "We appear to have stopped the bleeding," Ponze says.

A visitor to the school — housed on five floors of a nondescript office building in southernmost East Harlem — sees little to suggest shortcomings, however. The school is clean, the walls decorated with student projects, the girls neatly uniformed in plaid skirts or navy trousers with white blouses under vests or blazers. Classrooms use tables instead of rows of desks, to encourage girls to study together, rather than competitively.

As with most of the nation's two-dozen or so single-sex public schools, the students are overwhelmingly from minorities — in TYWLS's case, primarily Latina and African-American. Of 34 seniors, 23 live at or below the poverty level. Twenty-two graduates will be the first in their families to attend college. But Columbia-bound valedictorian Maryam Zohny follows three older siblings to college.

---

write. Small towns and rural communities could not afford to go beyond single, one-room schoolhouses; larger cities also found separate schools impractical. Women's-rights advocates thought coeducation the most likely way to make girls' education more nearly equal to that of the boys.

A broader rationale emerged by the second half of the 19th century. In an important paper, William Harris, superintendent of St. Louis schools and later U.S. commissioner of education, argued in 1870 that

mixing the sexes in the classroom improved instruction and discipline for boys and girls by merging their different abilities and allowing pupils of each gender to serve as a "counter-check" on the other.[14]

Despite the advance of coeducation, upper-class families continued to send their sons and daughters to single-sex schools through the 19th century — and, less uniformly, through the 20th century.

Meanwhile, in the late 19th century some prominent academics began attacking coeducation. In his book *Sex*

TYWLS founder Ann Rubenstein Tisch got the idea for the school while covering education stories as an NBC correspondent. "I didn't think we were doing enough for inner-city kids," she says. "If it's OK for affluent boys and girls, and Catholic boys and girls, wouldn't it follow that it would work in another community?"

Tisch, who married into the family that controls the Loews Corp., set up a foundation to help support the school — to the tune of about $200,000 last year. New York's Board of Education pays for the building, teachers and books and supplies. Classes have about 20-22 students — a low teacher-student ratio that depends on several budgeting arrangements with the Board of Education.

Tisch's foundation helps buy curricular materials, gives some summer scholarships and pays for a full-time college counselor. That last investment pays off. For the second year in a row, all of the school's seniors gained admittance to four-year colleges, although one graduate is joining the Navy instead — for financial reasons.

The school is listed in *New York* magazine as one of the city's top public high schools, but the admissions policy is targeted to applicants performing at or below grade level. Applicants must tour the school with a family member. Once a student is admitted, she and her parents or guardians sign a contract promising to support the school's mission of rigorous academics, attendance and "thoughtful habits of mind" and to keep the lines of communication open between parents and the school.

For the coming year, the school has 550 applicants for 60 seventh-grade slots and 1,200 applicants for three openings in the ninth grade.

In contrast to the student body, two-thirds of the 26-member teaching staff is white. Ponze acknowledges the disparity but notes that she recently hired five persons of color, including an assistant principal.

TYWLS graduates gather around 2002 commencement speaker Alma Powell, wife of Secretary of State Colin Powell. All but one of the girls will attend college this fall.

Teachers cite a range of experiences indicating that single-sex education can benefit girls in and out of the classroom. "By not having [boys], they were able to compete with themselves," says science teacher Melissa Melchior. "There wasn't that level where guys would dominate."

"Socially, girls become less competitive with each other when there aren't any boys around," says math teacher Deb Carlson-Doom. "There's less sparring in general because there aren't boys."

The graduating students echo their teachers' observations. "We could be ourselves," says Karla Carballo. "We didn't have to pretend to be anyone else."

Many stress the close bonds of sisterhood with their classmates. "It was a lot of support," says Leslie Cortez. "It was very much a family."

"The girls are so united, so focused on [each other's] education," says Denise Fernandez. "It's not for everyone, but it was good for me."

in Education, Edward Clarke, a professor at the Harvard Medical School, argued in 1873 that academic competition with boys overloaded girls' brains and interfered with the development of their reproductive organs. With Darwinian theories much in vogue, Clarke's views attracted interest and support, but they had little effect on schools' practices.

Coeducation came under more sustained challenge in the 20th century — first, in the early 1900s, from male educators complaining of boys' lagging educational performance compared to girls, and, in recent decades, from feminist critics who accuse schools of shortchanging girls.

The so-called "boy problem" consisted simply of boys' doing less well than girls. For example, more boys repeated grades or dropped out of school than girls. Some educators blamed the "feminization" of schooling that supposedly resulted from the preponderance of female teachers. To solve the problem, some educators called simply for "differentiation" in instruction by gender, but others went further and called for segregating classes by sex. Some experiments were tried — to mixed reviews — but eventually fizzled out.

Since the early days, educators and advocates seeking to improve schooling for girls contended with a tension between women's roles in the home and family and their roles in the workplace and society. In the 1800s, schooling had been aimed at making girls "better wives and mothers," Tyack and Hansot write. But in the early-20th century, reformers established "scientific" home economics courses for girls to counter a perceived deterioration in family life.

With the emergence of a strengthened women's movement in the latter-20th century, the tension became more manifest. Feminists discovered what Tyack and Hansot call "the hidden injuries" of coeducation: perpetuation of male dominance and an "implicit hidden curriculum of sex stereotyping in coeducational public schools."

Gender Equity

The feminist critique of public education contributed to the passage of a federal law — Title IX of the Education Amendments of 1972 — aimed at guaranteeing gender equity in federally financed schools, colleges and universities. The effects of the law have been felt mainly in higher education — most visibly, perhaps, in athletics.[15] Women's groups marking the 30th anniversary of the law this year say it has prompted significant progress, but has fallen short of equalizing opportunities for boys and girls in K-12 education or for men and women in colleges and universities.

The National Organization for Women (NOW) included a demand for "equal and unsegregated education" in the women's bill of rights approved by the group at its second national conference in 1967. Five years later, though, Congress was preoccupied with racial busing issues when it worked on reauthorizing federal aid to education programs and gave little attention to what emerged as Title IX.

As enacted, the law forbade discrimination on the basis of sex in any "education program or activity" receiving federal financial assistance. (*See box, p. 152.*) However, the law specifically exempted admissions policies at public elementary and secondary schools and private undergraduate institutions.[16]

Writing the regulations to implement Title IX took three years. As issued in July 1975 by what was then the Department of Health, Education and Welfare, the regulations included several provisions sought by feminists to make public elementary and secondary coeducation more nearly identical for both sexes. School districts were generally barred from offering single-sex activities or programs, except for contact sports or sex education. Any other single-sex admissions policy, courses or services were legal only if the school district offered "comparable" courses, services or facilities to persons of the opposite sex.[17]

Two years later, the NOW Legal Defense Fund called enforcement of the regulations "indifferent, inept, ignorant of the law itself or bogged down in red tape."[18] The record improved under President Jimmy Carter — partly because of a court order to enforce the law — but enforcement again lagged in the 1980s under President Ronald Reagan. Women's-rights groups, however, began winning enactment of gender-equity laws at the state level. And school administrators, fearful of litigation, generally moved to comply with the law. In one highly visible area, girls' participation in high school sports increased fivefold in the 1970s — while still lagging far behind boys' programs in number and funding.[19]

The Supreme Court missed an opportunity to deal with the issue at the K-12 level in 1977 when the justices — divided 4-4 with one justice not participating — left standing a lower court's decision upholding Philadelphia's Central High School all-male admissions policy.[20] The justices also limited the impact of Title IX by ruling in 1984 that the penalty for violating the law would be to cut off federal funds only for the specific programs or departments guilty of discrimination, not the entire institution.[21]

In two other decisions, however, the high court made clear that single-sex admissions policies at public colleges and universities would be difficult to sustain. In 1982, the court struck down the exclusion of men from the Mississippi University for Women's School of Nursing. Then in a heavily publicized case in 1996, the court similarly struck down VMI's all-male policy. In her opinion for the court in the VMI case, Justice Ruth Bader Ginsburg said any form of sex discrimination in higher education could be upheld under the 14th Amendment's Equal Protection Clause only if a state presented an "exceedingly persuasive justification" for the policy.[22]

CHRONOLOGY

1800s-1960 *Coeducation becomes dominant practice in U.S. public schools by turn of century; many Catholic, private schools continue as single-sex.*

1960s-1970s *Civil-rights era produces new concerns about "gender equity" in education; many men's and women's colleges become coeducational.*

1967 National Organization for Women calls for "equal and unsegregated" education as part of the group's women's bill of rights.

1972 Congress passes Title IX, barring sex-based discrimination in any federally financed school, college or university; law permits single-sex admissions policies at elementary and secondary schools and private colleges and universities.

1975 Department of Health, Education and Welfare issues Title IX regulations, which generally bar single-sex classes or programs in K-12 except for contact sports, sex education, choir; women's-rights groups later complain of weak enforcement.

1977 Supreme Court, divided 4-4, upholds appeals court ruling allowing all-male policy at Philadelphia's Central High School.

1979 Women outnumber men in U.S. colleges and universities for first time except during wartime.

1980s *Title IX brings changes in K-12, higher education; court rulings tilt against single-sex schools.*

1982 Supreme Court strikes down all-female admissions policy at Mississippi University for Women's School of Nursing.

1984 Supreme Court limits enforcement of Title IX by ruling that penalty for violation does not require funds cut-off for entire college — only for affected program or department; Pennsylvania state court requires open admissions at all-male Central High School because of unequal funding of counterpart school for girls.

1990s *Interest in single-sex education increases.*

1991 Detroit drops plan for academies for African-American boys after federal court ruling; Milwaukee also opens to girls its planned school for minority boys after opposition is voiced.

1992 American Association of University Women issues report charging that public schools are "shortchanging" girls.

1995 American Association of University Women (AAUW) gives guarded endorsement to single-sex policies on short-term basis.

1996 Young Women's Leadership School opens in East Harlem; civil-rights groups file complaint with Department of Education, but no action is taken.

1997 AAUW adopts more critical stance toward single-sex policies.

1998 California provides grants to school districts for single-sex programs; six districts participate, with mixed results; most drop experiment when state ends grants in 2000.

2000s *Single-sex education gains support from Congress, Bush administration.*

2000 Australian researcher finds girls and boys do better in single-sex schools than in coeducational settings but says quality of teaching is more important; conservative author Barbara Hoff Sommers argues in *The War Against Boys* that public schools are shortchanging boys, not girls.

2001 Senate includes incentive grants for single-sex schools and classes in President Bush's education-reform package.

2002 Bush signs No Child Left Behind Act on Jan. 8, with funds for single-sex demonstration projects; Department of Education on May 8 starts process of revising Title IX regulations to make it easier for schools to adopt single-sex policies; at least four single-sex schools to open at start of new school year.

How Title IX Prevents Discrimination

Title IX of the Education Amendments of 1972 seeks to guarantee gender equity in federally financed schools, colleges and universities. The Bush administration would rewrite the regulations to make it easier for school districts to experiment with single-sex schools.[1]

"No person in the United States shall, on the basis of sex, be excluded from participation in, be denied the benefits of, or be subjected to discrimination under any education program or activity receiving Federal financial assistance."

Current Title IX Regulations:

Area Regulated	Impact of Law	What Title IX Regulations Say
Admissions	Discrimination prohibited, with exceptions	"No person, shall on the basis of sex, be denied admission, or be subjected to discrimination in admission, by any recipient." Single-sex institutions of higher education were grandfathered; non-vocational elementary and secondary schools were exempted.
Housing	Separation permitted	"Separate housing on the basis of sex," if "proportionate in quantity to the number of students of that sex applying for housing" and "comparable in quality and cost to the student."
Comparable facilities	Separation permitted	"Separate toilet, locker room and shower facilities on the basis of sex" if "comparable to such facilities provided for students of the other sex."
Access to course offerings	Separation permitted, in certain cases	"Grouping of students in physical education classes and activities by ability as assessed by objective standards of individual performance developed and applied without regard to sex."
		"Grouping of students by sex within physical education classes or activities during participation in wrestling, boxing, rugby, ice hockey, football, basketball and other sports, the purpose or major activity of which includes bodily contact."
		"Separate sessions for boys and girls" in "[p]ortions of classes in elementary and secondary schools which deal exclusively with human sexuality . . ."
		"Requirements based on vocal range or quality which may result in a chorus or choruses of one or predominantly one sex."
Athletics	Separation permitted	"Separate teams for members of each sex where selection for such teams is based upon competitive skill or the activity involved is a contact sport," provided that for non-contact sports students of both sexes must be allowed to try out for a team unless the school sponsors teams for both sexes.
		"Unequal aggregate expenditures for male and female teams allowed," but may be considered "in assessing equality of opportunity for members of each sex."

[1] 34 Code of Federal Regulations sections 106.21, 106.32-34, 106-41.

Through the mid-1990s, the Department of Education's Office of Civil Rights (OCR) — the unit charged with enforcing Title IX — reported that the relatively few complaints involving single-gender issues at the K-12 level had all been "resolved."[23] The office took no action against the Philadelphia High School for Girls and Baltimore's all-girl Western High School after receiving assurances that both schools were — nominally — open to boys as well.

In a similar vein, the office told school systems contemplating single-gender classes that unless the classes were open to students of both sexes they would be violating Title IX. And OCR officials told the Prince George's County, Md., school board to open all its mentoring programs to boys and girls after finding that the multimillion-dollar boys program was significantly bigger than the program for girls.

Single-Sex Revival

Single-sex education drew renewed interest through the 1990s from researchers, advocacy groups and policymakers. Some local initiatives were thwarted by legal challenges, but others survived opposition. By decade's end, at least 10 single-sex public schools were operating in the United States. Academic proponents of single-sex education accumulated evidence seeking to show its benefits, but some researchers and advocacy groups remained unconvinced. Meanwhile, congressional efforts to encourage single-sex experiments finally culminated in the provision in the president's education-reform bill to authorize incentive grants for school districts wishing to experiment with separate schools or classrooms for boys or girls.[24]

Detroit's effort to establish Afrocentric academies for young black males in 1991 ran up against concerted opposition from the national ACLU, the NAACP Legal Defense Fund and the NOW Legal Defense and Education Fund, and then a federal court suit. In his ruling blocking the plan, Judge Woods noted that the Detroit school board had acknowledged "an equally urgent" crisis facing female students. He also said the school board had failed to show that "the coeducational factor" was to blame for the school system's failures. The academies opened with a stated policy of accepting boys or girls. Opposition to a similar plan in Milwaukee forced officials there also to allow boys and girls to apply for the new school.

Tisch drew similar opposition from civil rights and women's organizations when she started The Young Women's Leadership School. A coalition that included NOW New York City, the New York Civil Liberties Union and the New York Civil Rights Coalition filed a complaint with OCR, charging that the planned school violated Title IX and state and local anti-discrimination laws. Anne Conners, president of New York City NOW, called the school "a Band-Aid approach to gender equity for girls." Six years later, OCR has not acted on the complaint. "It didn't stop us from doing what we wanted to and needed to do," Tisch says.

California tried a more ambitious experiment in single-gender schooling in the late 1990s, but the pilot program shrank for lack of political support. Legislation pushed by Republican Gov. Pete Wilson provided $500,000 apiece to school districts to operate equivalent single-gender academies at the middle and high school levels for boys and girls. Six school districts participated in the program from 1998-2000: Four operated as schools within a school, while two operated self-contained single-gender schools.

In their report on the program, Datnow and Hubbard found that the school districts were careful to provide equal resources for boys and girls, and that single-gender classes reduced distractions. But they also said the participating school districts appeared to be primarily interested in getting more money to address needs of at-risk students rather than using single-gender classes to improve learning or reduce gender stereotyping. In any event, the program proved to be "not sustainable," Datnow and Hubbard conclude. Wilson's Democratic successor, Gray Davis, ended state support for the project; only two of the single-sex programs are still operating.

As the 1990s ended, single-sex education was being vigorously debated both among experts and advocacy groups and on Capitol Hill. In 1995, the AAUW voiced "guarded enthusiasm" for single-sex classes on a short-term basis to compensate for past discrimination against girls.[25]

A 1997 AAUW symposium on single-sex education included speakers on both sides. Riordan of Providence College presented his research concluding that single-sex schools "work for boys and girls," in particular for girls and minority boys or girls. But in her review of research in the field, Valerie Lee, a professor of education at the University of Michigan, concluded that separating students by gender was "misguided." In publishing the proceedings,

Women's Colleges Refuse to Fade Away

When feminist educator Mary Lyon founded Mount Holyoke Female Seminary in western Massachusetts in 1837, American women had very few opportunities for higher education. There were a few other female "seminaries" in New England and the South, but only one college — Oberlin in Ohio — admitted women to study alongside men.[1]

By the late-20th century, however, U.S. higher education had become overwhelmingly coeducational — not only at public colleges and universities, most of which had been coeducational from their founding, but also at formerly all-male universities such as Harvard and Yale.

Women's place in higher education changed so much that Mount Holyoke's administrators, faculty, students and alumnae twice within the last three decades seriously considered following the trend toward coeducation. And both times — most recently in the mid-1990s — Mount Holyoke College, as it is now called, decided to remain exclusively for women.

"In the world, women still do not have equal opportunity," says Patricia Vandenberg, director of communications for the 2,000-student college. "There is a real sense that a women's college like Mount Holyoke that challenges women and expects them to achieve gets results that the world needs."

Mount Holyoke is one of a dwindling number of women's colleges in the United States, however. From a high of nearly 300 all-female institutions in the 1960s, the number of women's colleges today has dropped to around 70, according to the Washington-based Women's College Coalition. The sharp drop began in the late 1960s, according to coalition President Jadwiga Sebrechts. More than

half ceased operating as women's institutions within a five-year span at the turn of the decade.

About half of those former women's colleges — including such prominent schools as Vassar and Bennington — became coeducational. About half of the others merged with brother institutions, including many Catholic colleges. The remainder simply closed their doors.

The movement toward coeducation continued apace over the next two decades. Meanwhile, men's colleges became all but extinct. Today, only three remain: historically black Morehouse College in Atlanta with about 3,000 students; Hampden-Sydney College in Hampden-Sydney, Va. (1,000 students); and Wabash College in Crawfordsville, Ind. (860 students).

In public education, two Supreme Court decisions sharply limit the states' freedom to establish or maintain single-sex institutions. The two rulings — requiring admission of men to the Mississippi University for Women in 1982 and of women to all-male Virginia Military Institute in 1996 — both require states to show an "exceedingly persuasive justification" for treating men and women differently in public higher education.[2]

Today, only three public women's colleges remain. One of those — Douglass College of Rutgers University in New Jersey — is part of a coeducational university. The other two — Mississippi University for Women and Texas Woman's University — both admit men, but state in promotional materials that their mission is to further women's education.

Despite the declining number of women's colleges, enrollment is increasing. Over the past decade, the number of students has nearly doubled — from about 50,000 in

the AAUW adopted a largely critical tone, concluding that there was "no evidence that single-sex education in general 'works' or 'is better' than coeducation."[26]

Meanwhile in Washington, lawmakers were pushing proposals in Congress to encourage local school systems to experiment with single-sex programs. The Senate approved money for demonstration grants in 1994 as part of an omnibus education bill, but the provision was dropped from the final version. Sen. Kay Bailey Hutchison, R-Texas, introduced a bill in 1995 to give school districts

a waiver from Title IX for single-gender programs for disadvantaged pupils, but it died in committee. Through the rest of the decade, other proposals similarly failed to advance.

With a new Congress and a new administration, single-sex advocates picked up a visible and influential ally: former first lady Hillary Rodham Clinton, New York's newly elected junior senator. Clinton — a graduate of Wellesley College, one of the nation's most prestigious women's schools — teamed with Hutchison last

1990 to 98,000 today. Mount Holyoke has maintained its enrollment at around 2,000, but applications have increased by about 44 percent since the mid-'90s, according to Vandenberg.

Women's college advocates make parallel arguments to those being advanced for all-girl schools at the elementary and secondary levels: the need to give women a better opportunity to develop self-esteem and confidence and to present more women as role models in the curriculum and at the institution itself.

"It's much, much easier for men to be validated as learners in most educational settings," Sebrechts says. "For women, when they are in a women-centered setting, it is often the first time that they've been feeling that kind of validation."

"The environment is different," Vandenberg says. "We have almost 50 percent women faculty. Students' peers are other smart women."

For its part, the American Association of University Women — the major organization opposing expanded single-sex education at the K-12 level — does not oppose private women's colleges. "Women's colleges came up at a time when there was no other way," says Nancy Zirkin, the association's director of public policy. "It's a completely different set of circumstances."

Despite a high retention rate of around 80 percent, Vandenberg concedes that some women leave Mount Holyoke

Women's Colleges Decline, Enrollments Rise

Although the number of U.S. women's colleges has been declining for 40 years, enrollments nearly doubled over the past decade.

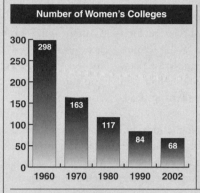

Number of Women's Colleges

1960	1970	1980	1990	2002
298	163	117	84	68

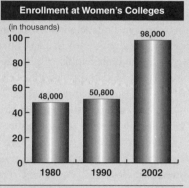

Enrollment at Women's Colleges
(in thousands)

1980	1990	2002
48,000	50,800	98,000

Source: Women's College Coalition

to go to coeducational schools. The women who stay can find plenty of men at the other members of a five-college consortium — Amherst, Hampshire, Smith and the University of Massachusetts-Amherst — located within a nine-mile radius.

Overall, students and alumnae continue to favor maintaining Holyoke as a women's college, Vandenberg says. "I don't see it changing in the near future," she concludes.

---

[1] For background, see Irene Harwarth, Mindi Maline and Elizabeth DeBra, "Women's Colleges in the United States: History, Issues, and Challenges," U.S. Dept. of Education, Office of Educational Research and Improvement (www.ed.gov/offices/OERI/PLLI/webreprt.html), June 1997; and Barbara M. Solomon, *In the Company of Educated Women: A History of Women and Higher Education in America* (1985).

[2] The cases are *Mississippi University for Women v. Hogan*, 458 U.S. 718 (1982), and *United States v. Virginia*, 518 U.S. 515 (1996).

year to insert funding for single-sex schools and classes into President Bush's education-reform bill as it moved through the Senate. "There should not be any obstacle to providing single-sex choice within the public school system," Clinton, a Democrat, said during Senate debate on June 7.

The amendment passed by voice vote and stayed in the final bill. As enacted, the law authorized up to $450 million for a variety of demonstration projects, including single-gender schools or classes, but Congress ended up

appropriating only $385 million. The law — which Bush signed on Jan. 8 — directed the secretary of Education to issue guidelines and criteria for grants within 120 days of enactment.

CURRENT SITUATION

Starting New Schools

Lynn Spampinato helped introduce single-sex classes five years ago at Maria Mitchell Elementary School in inner-city

Denver. She credits the decision with an academic turnaround that slashed by 50 percent the number of students at the school scoring in the lowest quarter on a nationwide achievement test.

Now, back in her native Pennsylvania, Spampinato hopes to introduce what she calls "gender-separate" education to help turn around a high-poverty, all-black middle school in Philadelphia. As regional director for a private company named to manage three failing schools in the troubled Philadelphia system, Spampinato plans literally to cut FitzSimons Middle School in half and divide the 660 students into separate "leadership academies" — one for boys and one for girls.

"We hope to take the social pressure off the kids and really raise the standards," she says. "We believe that in a gender-separate environment, we can do a lot in building self-esteem, developing character and creating a very safe, homey place for children to excel."

FitzSimons is one of at least four public schools across the country likely to open with single-sex classrooms for the first time when the new academic year starts later this summer. Others include Brighter Choice Charter School in Albany, N.Y.; William A. Lawson International Peace and Prosperity Preparatory Academy for Boys in Houston; and Southern Middle School in Louisville, Ky.

Other education activists are busily putting together plans for single-sex schools to open later. A conference of boys' schools late last month heard organizers making pitches for two new all-boy schools for minority neighborhoods in Brooklyn and Lower Manhattan.

Spampinato, who served as an administrator in the Philadelphia school system for two years before assuming her current position with Victory Schools, Inc., took her idea to the city's newly created School Reform Commission. The commission supplanted the former Board of Education after the state took over the city's public schools in December 2001. "They were very supportive if we had community support," Spampinato says.

So far, Spampinato says she has found "more support than dissent" from parents. "One of the things that parents are most concerned about is safety," she says. "They seem to like it [from] that perspective."

The *Philadelphia Inquirer*, however, found divided reaction among teachers and students.[27] Reporter Susan Snyder described teachers as "on the fence," with some questioning whether the plan would make any difference

in academic performance. Students' opinions were said to be divided along gender lines: "Girls liked the idea, but boys didn't."

Spampinato acknowledges that the changed attitude in Washington has helped her push the idea. "The secretary of Education is offering support," she says. "There will be new funding." A graduate herself of a Catholic girls' high school in Pittsburgh, Spampinato believes single-sex education should be available for low-income youngsters in the same way that it has been available in private or parochial schools for families who could afford it.

Organizers of the other new single-sex schools voice similar sentiments. "This is an option that is widely available for private schools, says Tom Carroll, chairman of Brighter Choice, scheduled to open with 90 kindergartners and first-graders divided by gender. "Wherever these schools are set up, people are fighting to get into them."[28]

In Louisville, Southern Middle School will separate the students for most classes, though boys and girls will be together for some activities — such as band and choir — and at lunch. Principal Anita Jones says the plan will reduce distractions for students. "They'll focus on education instead of on the opposite sex," she says. "This isn't a panacea . . . but we had to do something."[29]

Houston's new boys' academy — already being designated as WALIPP Prep — is expected to open in a predominantly black neighborhood. The school is aimed at giving black students strong male role models and mentors. "What I want to do is develop strong men, and I think that can be done by bringing strong men around these boys," says Audrey Lawson, whose husband is pastor of a local Baptist church.[30]

Revising Federal Rules?

Advocates of single-sex education are urging the Department of Education to impose few requirements for public school systems wanting to institute single-sex schools or classes. Opponents are urging the department to leave Title IX regulations completely unchanged. Alternatively, they say school systems should be required to justify any single-sex schools or classes and to be subject to prior approval and continuing oversight from federal officials.

The opposing positions emerge in comments filed before a July 8 deadline in response to a "notice of intent to regulate" issued by the department's Office of Civil

AT ISSUE

Should federal regulations make it easier for school districts to establish single-sex schools or classes?

YES   Cornelius Riordan
Professor of Sociology,
Providence College

Written for the *CQ Researcher,* July 2002

Since evaluation is a concurrent part of funding for all school reform efforts, a wealth of data exists on most reform programs. Scientific investigation of education programs has become the benchmark, as it should, for judging the promise of any reform. In fact, the reauthorization of the Elementary and Secondary School Act of 2001 has raised the level of research to a higher level, calling for more studies using rigorous, scientifically based, objective procedures to obtain valid knowledge.

Yet, research on single-sex schooling has never been conducted in a scientific manner in the public sector. Until now, the politicalization of the issue by opposition groups has closed down the scientific process on single-sex schools.

Despite the posturing by opponents and proponents, no one knows the full extent to which single-sex schools are more effective than coeducational schools, and for what types of students, and at what grade levels and for how long. There is simply not enough research on the issue to make such a determination, especially in the public sector. The relaxing of Title IX guidelines by the Department of Education will provide the necessary first step towards increasing the number of single-sex schools and classes so the research can be conducted.

What do we know from the high-quality empirical studies that have been done, primarily in the private sector? Single-sex schools help to improve student achievement. They work for girls and boys, whites and non-whites, but this effect is limited to students of low socioeconomic status and/or students who are disadvantaged historically.

The major factor that conditions the strength of single-sex effects is social class, and since class and race are inextricably linked, the effects are also conditioned by race, and sometimes by gender. Impoverished, desperate and powerless children in lower-tiered schools stand to gain the most from single-sex schools. There is no evidence in the United States showing that they would do better in coeducational schools.

Single-sex schools are no longer limited to providing an alternative educational avenue for some girls; today some boys also need this type of school organization in order to learn effectively.

Moreover, single-sex schools can help to bring about greater race and social-class equity that have now become the final frontiers in establishing true equality of educational opportunity for everyone.

NO   David Sadker
Professor of Education,
American University

Written for the *CQ Researcher,* July 2002

The proposed loosening of the rules on creating single-sex public schools is problematic for several reasons, but I will focus on three: the need for research, the potential misuse of such schools and the nation's history of gender-biased funding.

First, the effectiveness of single-sex schools is a big educational question mark. Some studies show that they are more effective for girls than boys, others that only lower-class students benefit and still others that such schools intensify gender stereotypes and homophobia. Critics point out that many of the academic successes of these schools may be due to smaller classes, engaged parents and well-trained teachers, not to the fact that they are single sex. No wonder there is confusion!

We need to craft a thoughtful, controlled and studied implementation of single-sex schooling to untangle this conflicting body of research. The administration's proposed loosening of the regulations sidesteps the many unanswered research questions, creating schools rather than examining them. I predict that some will fail and some will succeed, and we will miss many opportunities to learn why.

My second concern is some of these schools could do harm. While the girls' schools in Harlem and Chicago seem to be successes, the college-prep model is not the only one out there. Many supporters of single-sex schools describe the very different schools that they would create, ranging from schools built on each sex's unique "brain structure" to schools teaching that female submission is part of a "natural law." Their idea of a good girls' school is one focusing on child rearing and de-emphasizing careers in science, while boys would learn how to read by using war poetry. In the failed California experiment, single-sex schools were seen as a means to discipline boys. Without clear protections from unfair treatment, sex-role stereotypes may be intensified, and individual needs ignored.

My final point is a history lesson, reminding us why Title IX restricted single-sex schools in the first place. Three decades ago, Philadelphia, Boston and most major cities were proud of their single-sex schools. While the cities argued that the girls' and boys' schools were "comparable," the courts found the girls' schools underfunded and clearly inferior.

Without safeguards requiring "equitable" schools, we may once again create two sets of schools, separate and unequal. This gender gap in educational spending is a trend we should reverse, not promote, and Title IX is a law we should strengthen, not weaken.

Mount Holyoke College in western Massachusetts is among a dwindling number of U.S. women's colleges. Twice in recent years it considered following the trend toward coeducation — but decided to remain exclusively for women.

Rights (OCR) on May 8. The notice asked for comments on a series of questions to be considered in drafting rules designed "to provide more flexibility for educators to establish single-sex classes and schools at the elementary and secondary level."

The major participants in the debate appear to agree on only one of the major questions presented: participation in single-sex schools or classes should be voluntary, not mandatory, for students and families. But they disagree sharply on other questions.

Supporters says schools should not be required to "explain the benefits" of single-sex classes before instituting the practice. While saying that the benefits are well established, Sax, of the National Association for the Advancement of Single-Sex Public Education, warns that a future administration opposed to single-sex education could use such a requirement to block proposed programs.

Opponents, however, insist that existing law dictates that school districts justify any use of single-sex classes. "Both Title IX and the Constitution properly place the burden of justifying single-sex programs on the school district choosing to establish such programs," the National Women's Law Center says. The center says that school districts should be required to seek approval from OCR before implementation of any single-sex classes and that OCR "must monitor the implementation . . . to ensure continued compliance with the law."

Opponents are also calling for several other conditions for establishing single-sex schools or classes that supporters

warn could effectively prevent school districts from adopting such programs. Most significantly, they say single-sex schools or classes must be provided for both sexes rather than relying on a coeducational school or class to serve students who do not have a single-sex program available to them. And the opponents say that schools or classes for both sexes must be "equal," not just "comparable" — as the department's notice suggested.

"Equality, not comparability, must be the standard," the NOW Legal Defense Fund says, "and only a single-sex option could meet that standard."

Supporters, however, say school districts should be allowed to establish programs for students of one gender but not the other. "The needs of each sex are often different," Providence College's Riordan writes. "Thus, the emphasis of a school for boys should not be required to be comparable to the emphasis of a school for girls."

"Where a school district offers a single-sex school for girls, it should suffice to prove that it offers equal opportunities to boys in a coed school," says Salomone of the St. John's University School of Law. Pointing to the Supreme Court's decision in the VMI cases, she says the ruling does not require programs to be "exactly identical" for both sexes. A stricter standard, she says, "could hobble" single-sex initiatives.

The opposing sides have a measure of agreement on one minor question in the notice: "Are there any classes which should not be permitted to be single-sex?" Citing past and continuing gender discrimination in vocational training, the NOW Legal Defense Fund says there should be no "general green light" for single-sex vocational or technical classes.

Sax says he is "sympathetic" to the concern that single-sex classes in some subjects could "reinforce gender stereotypes." For that reason, he says, the rules might prohibit girls-only cosmetology classes or boys-only computer classes.

Groups opposing any change in the rules include two powerful education lobbies — the National Education Association and the National Congress of PTAs — as well as the American Civil Liberties Union. "Public schools have the obligation to ensure that both females and males can obtain an education in a coeducational setting free from sex discrimination," the ACLU says.

Supporters counter that single-sex programs will promote rather than retard the goal of equal educational opportunity. "Impoverished, desperate and powerless children in lower-tiered schools stand to gain the most from single-sex schools," Riordan writes.

Another comment period will be required once OCR officials draft a proposed rule — making it unlikely that a final rule will be adopted before fall, at the earliest.

OUTLOOK

A New Era?

Single-sex education seemed on the verge of virtual extinction in the United States a decade ago. Separate schools for boys and girls were widely thought to be illegal in public education and were becoming less and less popular among private or parochial schools as well as colleges and universities.

The cumulative effect of guardedly favorable research studies and reconsideration of boys' and girls' respective learning styles and behavior, however, has put single-sex education back on the map. With the Bush administration's support for revising the legal rules on single-sex education, advocates are predicting a sharp increase in the number of single-sex schools or classes at the elementary and secondary levels, while critics and skeptics are softening their previous opposition.

"I really think that we are on the brink of a new era," says Sax, of the National Association for the Advancement of Single-Sex Public Education. "In the next few years, we're going to see a tremendous increase in the number of single-sex schools."

Sax notes not only the new schools expected to open this year or next but also the recent disclosure that Moten Elementary School in southeast Washington, D.C., had quietly instituted single-sex classes without notifying the school system's central office. The move came to light only when officials noticed a sharp increase in students' test scores and asked for an explanation.[31] "I suspect that there are other schools out there that we don't know about," Sax says.

The AAUW's Zirkin emphasizes that even with the four new schools slated to open later this summer, the number of single-sex public schools remains tiny. "I don't call four a trend," she says. Along with other opponents or critics, however, Zirkin now calls for carefully constructed pilot projects to study the effectiveness of single-sex schools or classes — without any changes in the Title IX regulations covering sex discrimination at federally financed schools and colleges.

"The parameters have to be designed in such a way as to not disadvantage girls or boys, so that there isn't sex stereotyping of girls going on and so that there isn't any bias from the get-go," Zirkin says. "Then evaluate the pilot project and see where you are."

Academic skeptics are also muting their criticisms. "As a choice for some students, this is worth trying," the University of Toronto's Datnow says. American University's Sadker agrees on the need for more research but cautions against exaggerating the potential benefits of single-sex education or ignoring the potential costs to other public schools.

"It's fine to have limited single-sex schools that we can evaluate and judge in an objective way, not a politicized way, because we could learn from that," Sadker says. "I am against saying this is a solution to the problem: Let's pull off the most active girls and parents from the public school system and put them in a single-sex schools."

Long-time proponent Riordan of Providence College cautions advocates that even with support from the administration and Congress, advances in single-sex education will be slow in coming. "It takes an awful lot of effort to open a school even when there's no one against you," Riordan says. He says a realistic expectation is for the number of single-sex schools to double over the next three to five years.

"What we may see is an increase in coeducational schools of single-sex classes," says Wadsworth of the International Boys' School Coalition. "That could be done with changes that are less complex as long as it's viewed as legally viable."

Meanwhile, at Harlem's Young Women's Leadership School, Principal Ponze says she is baffled by the debate. "I don't understand why this should be a bone of contention," she says. "Why can't there be this choice for girls?"

Creating single-sex schools, Ponze concludes, "should be as easy as the demand in the community creates. If that's what the community wants, then the community should have the right to open single-sex schools or classrooms."

NOTES

1. The school's Web site is at www.tywls.org; information about the loosely affiliated Young Women's Leadership Charter School of Chicago can be found at www.ywcls.org.

2. Quoted in Katherine Roth, "Ahead of New Federal Guidelines, Education Secretary Visits Single-Sex Public School," The Associated Press, May 30, 2002.

3. For background, see Sarah Glazer, "Boys' Emotional Needs," *The CQ Researcher*, June 18, 1999, pp. 521-544; and Charles S. Clark, "Education and Gender," *The CQ Researcher*, June 3, 1994, pp. 481-504.

4. American Association of University Women Educational Foundation, *How Schools Shortchange Girls* (1992).

5. Christina Hoff Sommers, *The War Against Boys: How Misguided Feminism Is Harming Our Young Men* (2000).

6. See Patricia B. Campbell and Ellen Wahl, "What's Sex Got to Do With It? Simplistic Questions, Complex Answers," in *Separated by Sex: A Critical Look at Single-Sex Education for Girls* (1998), American Association of University Women Educational Foundation, p. 64.

7. Kenneth J. Rowe, "Gender Differences in Students' Experiences and Outcomes of Schooling? Exploring 'Real' Effects from Recent and Emerging Evidence-Based Research in Teacher and School Effectiveness," Oct. 31, 2000 (www.acer.edu.au). The April 17, 2000, press release, "Boys and Girls Perform Better at School in Single-Sex Environments," can also be found on the Web site.

8. Cornelius Riordan, *Girls and Boys in School: Together or Separate?* (1990), pp. 110-113.

9. Amanda Datnow, Lea Hubbard and Elisabeth Woody, "Is Single Gender Schooling Viable in the Public Sector? Lessons From California's Pilot Program," May 2001, http://www.oise.utoronto.ca/depts/tps/adatnow/research.html#single. For a shortened version, see Amanda Datnow and Lea Hubbard, "Are Single-Sex Schools Sustainable in the Public Sector?" in Datnow and Hubbard (eds.), *Gender in Policy and Practice: Perspectives on Single-Sex and Coeducational Schooling* (forthcoming, July/August 2002).

10. *Garrett v. Board of Education of School District of Detroit*, 775 F.Supp 1004 (E.D. Mich. 1991). For coverage, see Mark Walsh, "Detroit Admits Female Students," *Education Week*, Sept. 4, 1991.

11. The case is *Newberg v. School District of Philadelphia*, 478 A.2d 1352 (Pa. Super. Ct. 1984).

12. The case is *United States v. Virginia*, 518 U.S. 515 (1996). See Kenneth Jost, *The Supreme Court Yearbook, 1995-1996* (1996), pp. 38-42.

13. David Tyack and Elisabeth Hansot, *Learning Together: A History of Coeducation in American Schools* (1990), p. 11. Further background drawn from their account.

14. William T. Harris, "St. Louis School Report for 1870," summarized in Tyack and Hansot, *op. cit.*, pp. 101-103.

15. For background, see Jane Tanner, "Women in Sports," *The CQ Researcher*, May 11, 2001, pp. 401-424.

16. See U.S. Dept. of Education, "Guidelines on Current Title IX Requirements Related to Single-Sex Classes and Schools," *Federal Register*, May 3, 2002, www.ed.gov/offices/OCR/t9-guidelines-ss.html.

17. *Ibid.*

18. Project on Equal Education Rights, NOW Legal Defense and Education Fund, "Stalled at the Start: Government Action on Sex Bias in the Schools" (1977), pp. 33-39, cited in Tyack and Hansot, *op. cit.*, p. 256.

19. *Ibid.*, p. 264.

20. The case is *Vorcheimer v. School District of Philadelphia*, 532 F.2d 880 (3d. Cir. 1976), affirmed by an equally divided court, 430 U.S. 703 (1977).

21. The case is *Grove City College v. Bell*, 465 U.S. 555 (1984).

22. The cases are *Mississippi University for Women v. Hogan*, 458 U.S. 718 (1982) and *United States v. Virginia*, 518 U.S. 515 (1996).

23. See U.S. General Accounting Office, *Public Education: Issues Involving Single-Gender Schools and Programs*, May 1996, pp. 7-11.

24. Some background drawn from *ibid.*

25. American Association of University Women Educational Foundation, "Growing Smart: What's Working for Girls in Schools," 1995, pp. 2, 10-11.

26. American Association of University Women Educational Foundation, "Separated by Sex: A Critical Look at Single-Sex Education for Girls," 1998, pp. 2-3. Riordan's paper appears at pp. 53-62, Lee's at pp. 41-52.

27. See Susan Snyder, "A School Trial Will Separate the Sexes," *The Philadelphia Inquirer*, June 17, 2002, p. A1.

28. Quoted in Rick Karlin, "School Champions Single-Sex Classes," (Albany) *Times Union*, May 9, 2002, p. A1.

29. Quoted in Chris Kenning, "Southern Middle Will Separate Boys, Girls," *The* (Louisville) *Courier-Journal*, June 18, 2002.

30. Quoted in Melanie Markley, "Helping Boys Make the Grade," *Houston Chronicle*, May 2, 2002, p. A1.

31. See Justin Blum, "Scores Soar at D.C. School With Same-Sex Classes," *The Washington Post*, June 27, 2002, p. A1.

BIBLIOGRAPHY

Books

Datnow, Amanda, and Lea Hubbard, eds., *Gender in Policy and Practice: Perspectives on Single-Sex and Coeducational Schooling, Routledge*, 2002.
An anthology of 16 articles by experts representing a range of views on single-sex and coeducational schools. Datnow is an assistant professor of education at the University of Toronto; Hubbard is an assistant research scientist in sociology at the University of California-San Diego.

Faragher, John Mack, and Florence Howe, *Women and Higher Education in American History, W.W. Norton*, 1988.
Includes 10 essays on the history of women and higher education in America.

Riordan, Cornelius, *Girls and Boys in School: Together or Separate? Teachers College*, 1990.
Reviews the then-existing research on academic results of single-sex and coeducational schools. Includes 16-page list of references. Riordan is a professor of sociology at Providence College and an advocate of expanded single-sex education. His more recent review of the issue is included in the Datnow and Hubbard anthology.

Sadker, Myra, and David Sadker, *Failing at Fairness: How America's School Cheat Girls, Charles Scribners' Sons*, 1994.
Non-technical survey of issues that authors say keep females from achieving as well as males in school. David Sadker is a professor of education at American University; his wife was also a professor at American until her death in 1995.

Solomon, Barbara M., *In the Company of Educated Women: A History of Women and Higher Education in America, Yale University Press*, 1985.
Details the history of higher education for women from the evolution of "seminaries" for women into women's colleges in the 19th century through the expansion of coeducation and the decline in the number and student population of women's colleges in the late 20th century. Includes detailed notes, 28-page bibliography.

Sommers, Christina Hoff, *The War Against Boys: How Misguided Feminism Is Harming Our Young Men, Simon & Schuster*, 2000.
Sommers, a fellow at the American Enterprise Institute, criticizes claims that schools shortchange girls, arguing instead that boys are being shortchanged by school systems that "fail to address the problem of male underachievement."

Stabiner, Karen, *All Girls: Single-Sex Education and Why It Matters, Riverhead*, 2002.
Journalistic account of a pivotal year in the lives of two young women — one white and the other African-American — attending all-girls' schools, located on opposite coasts: an elite Los Angeles prep school and The Young Women's Leadership School in East Harlem, N.Y.

Tyack, David, and Elisabeth Hansot, *Learning Together: A History of Coeducation in American Schools, Yale University Press*, 1990.
Traces the history of coeducation in America from its gradual evolution through the 19th century through the critiques from gender-equity advocates in the 1970s and '80s. Includes detailed notes. Tyack is professor emeritus and Hansot professor emerita at Stanford University's School of Education.

Articles

Ransome, Whitney, and Meg Milne Moulton, "Why Girls Schools? The Difference in Girl-Centered Education," *Fordham Law Journal*, Vol. 29, No. 2 (December 2001), pp. 589-599.
Arguments for single-sex education for girls by the executive directors of the National Coalition of Girls' Schools.

Webb, Stephen H., "Defending All-Male Education: A New Cultural Moment for a Renewed Debate," *Fordham Law Journal*, **Vol. 29, No. 2 (December 2001), pp. 601-610.**
Defense of single-sex education for boys by an associate professor of religion and philosophy at Wabash College, in Crawfordsville, Ind.

Reports and Studies

American Association of University Women, How Schools Shortchange Girls: The AAUW Report, **1992.**
Critical report compiled by Wellesley College Center for Research on Women claimed girls are shortchanged by less attention in classrooms and fewer role models than boys. Includes detailed notes, appendixes.

American Association of University Women Educational Foundation, **"Separated by Sex: A Critical Look at Single-Sex Education for Girls,"** **1998.**
The 93-page report includes a somewhat critical summary and an overview of research followed by four papers by experts representing a range of views presented at an AAUW-sponsored symposium. Each paper includes detailed notes. For an earlier, less critical report, see American Association of University Women Educational Foundation, "Growing Smart: What's Working for Girls in Schools," 1995.

For More Information

American Association of University Women, 1111 16th St. NW, Washington, DC 20036; (202) 728-7700; http://www.aauw.org.

American Civil Liberties Union, 125 Broad St., New York, NY 10004; (212) 549-2500; www.aclu.org.

International Boys' Schools Coalition, P.O. Box 117, 7 Forehand Dr., Dennis, MA 02638; (508) 385-4563; www.boysschoolscoalition.org.

National Association for the Advancement of Single-Sex Public Education, P.O. Box 108, 19710 Fisher Ave., Poolesville, MD 20837; (301) 972-7600; www.singlesex-schools.org.

National Coalition of Girls' Schools, 57 Main St., Concord, MA 01742; (978) 287-4485; www.ncgs.org.

NOW Legal Defense and Education Fund, 395 Hudson St., New York, NY 10014; (212) 925-6635; www.nowldef.org.

8

Religion in Schools

Should the Courts Allow
More Spiritual Expression?

Patrick Marshall

Advocates of prayer before football games show their support last Sept. 1, at Santa Fe High School stadium in Texas. The vigil occurred at the first home game following a U.S. Supreme Court ruling last June banning student-led prayer over loud speakers at football games.

From *CQ Researcher*,
January 12, 2001.

To the delight of Christian activists, religion made a comeback in schools across the country last year:

- Volunteers visited elementary schools in Vest, Ky., to give Bible lessons.
- Gideons International distributed free Bibles at Hope Sullivan Elementary School in Southhaven, Miss.
- Indiana legislators approved a bill allowing schools to post the Ten Commandments.
- Etowah County High School in Alabama featured public prayers before football games.

"Number one, we think it's the right thing to do," said Etowah principal David Bowman. "And, number two, football is a contact sport where kids are apt to get hurt, and you need God on your side."[1]

According to some observers, religion's resurgence reflects a rise in spirituality among the students in public schools. "Spirituality is becoming more popular," says Dick Carpenter, education policy director at Focus on the Family, a Colorado-based Christian outreach group.

According to others, however, the resurgence is being coordinated by conservative Christian groups and seriously threatens the nation's public schools.

"They want to use schools as a place of witnessing and of getting legitimization for their perspective," says Fritz Detwiler, chairman of the Department of Religion/Philosophy at Adrian College

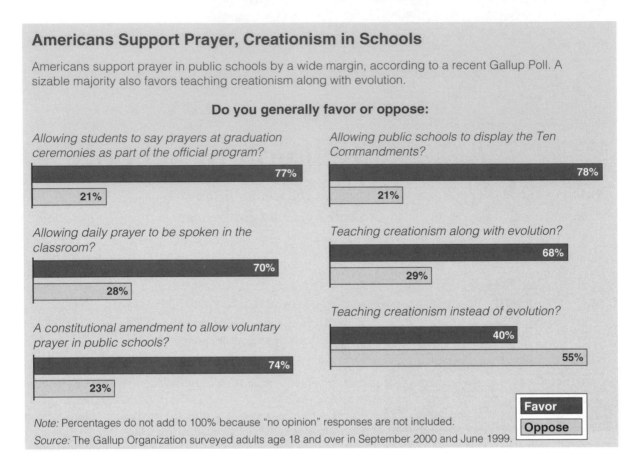

Americans Support Prayer, Creationism in Schools

Americans support prayer in public schools by a wide margin, according to a recent Gallup Poll. A sizable majority also favors teaching creationism along with evolution.

Do you generally favor or oppose:

Allowing students to say prayers at graduation ceremonies as part of the official program?

77%
21%

Allowing public schools to display the Ten Commandments?

78%
21%

Allowing daily prayer to be spoken in the classroom?

70%
28%

Teaching creationism along with evolution?

68%
29%

A constitutional amendment to allow voluntary prayer in public schools?

74%
23%

Teaching creationism instead of evolution?

40%
55%

Favor
Oppose

Note: Percentages do not add to 100% because "no opinion" responses are not included.

Source: The Gallup Organization surveyed adults age 18 and over in September 2000 and June 1999.

---

in Michigan and a consultant to educators on religious issues. Detwiler says he's convinced that at least some Christian groups want to "destroy the public schools if they can't Christianize them."

Civil liberties groups like the American Civil Liberties Union (ACLU) say that a number of Supreme Court rulings ban religion in schools, including *Abington Township v. Schempp*, which in 1963 banned any public school exercise that was exclusively religious.

Carpenter says that after *Schempp*, the pendulum swung dramatically away from religious expression in the schools. "For many years, there was little reference to religion at all," he says. But now, "the number of students who are saying, 'I want to go to school and pray around a [flag]pole or form a Bible club,' is on the increase, and not just in the Bible Belt. There are schools here in Colorado where students are saying they want some kind of religious expression in school."

"This is light years from where we were even in 1990," adds Doug Clark, director of field ministries at the National Network of Youth Ministries. "Christian students have been rising to the challenge of the culture, and they've been boldly living out their faith on their campuses in ways that shock many of us who have been involved in youth ministries. We estimate that 37,000 secondary schools have an organized, student-led Christian presence and have been adopted by local ministries trying to serve that campus."

But experts on both sides of the issue — Christian groups and civil libertarians alike — agree that school officials are often misinformed about just what sorts of religious observances are permissible on campus under federal law.

"We receive two or three complaints a week about religious activity in the public schools," says Steven Green, legal director of Americans United for Separation of Church and State. "A vast majority of the issues are resolved with an initial letter. Sometimes it's just that school officials don't know what the rules are."

And, paradoxically, in some cases perfectly legitimate religious expression may be stifled by school officials who don't understand that such behavior is allowed, he points out.

That's partly because Supreme Court rulings have left a significant amount of wiggle room. In fact, the behaviors proscribed by the Supreme Court are not illegal per se, but are not permissible in certain contexts. But those same behaviors might be allowed in a slightly different context, the court has implied, spawning a string of court tests.

The cases keep coming up because it's not easy to draw the line between accommodating religious expression in a public school and endorsing religion, explains Jay Sekulow, chief counsel at the American Center for Legal Justice, founded by televangelist Pat Robertson, the founder of the Christian Coalition. "I expect these cases will keep coming up for the next 50 years as well," he says.

Some civil liberties groups contend, however, that not all instances of impermissible religious expression in schools are due to innocent confusion.

Since the 1960s, a significant vocal minority — sometimes called the Religious Right — has opposed the court decisions banning religious activity in public schools, says Elliot Mincberg, general counsel at People for the American Way.

"They have attempted, and continue to attempt, to promote sectarian religion in the public schools in whatever way they can," he says. "They look for whatever loophole they can find in whatever the last court decision was. No public prayer in classrooms? Well, how about at graduation? Can't do that? What about at football games?"

Generally, those who push the hardest for more religious expression in public schools are fundamentalist or evangelical Christian organizations, and even opponents concede that their motives are sincere in most cases. "I don't think most of it is malicious," Green says. "They're well-meaning people who believe it's important to instill religious and moral values in children and that the primary place to do that is the public schools."

Two factors make the issue of religious expression touchier for fundamentalist Christians than for most other religious groups. First, many fundamentalists believe that the non-religious values taught in public schools are actually harmful to students, particularly Christian students.

"There's no way in the world a Christian child can go through the public schools and expect to come out a Christian," says Robert Simonds, president of Citizens for Excellence in Education, a division of the National Association of Christian Educators. "It used to happen, but it can't now, not even if you're a Christian parent and you give them every ounce of attention and you send them to Sunday school and to church. We're losing 80 percent of all church children who go to public schools."

Secondly, evangelizing is an essential part of life for Christian fundamentalists. "The whole purpose is to reach out to people and to bring them into a relationship with God," Clark says. "It's an outreach-oriented thing. I know it is politically correct to keep your faith to yourself, but that's not the nature of genuine Christian faith."

As school officials, parents and interest groups debate the role of religion in public schools, these are the questions being asked:

Are barriers to prayer in schools too rigid?

No specific law prohibits prayer in public schools. Limitations on school prayer result from a series of Supreme Court decisions, which hold that certain religious activities violate the constitutionally mandated separation of church and state when they take place in publicly funded schools.

After banning school prayer in 1962, the Supreme Court in 1985 struck down Alabama's efforts to require a moment of silence at the beginning of each school day, calling it an attempt "to return prayer to the public schools." In 1992, the court ruled a school could not invite a member of the clergy to pray at graduation. Last June, the court disallowed student-led prayers over public-address systems at school events in Santa Fe, Texas. And on Oct. 2, the justices set aside a ruling that let public school students in Jacksonville, Fla., choose a class member to give a prayer at graduation.

But while the Supreme Court has said what is not permitted, it has done little to clarify what religious behaviors are permitted in public schools. For direction, the U.S. Department of Education advises school officials to refer to its guidelines, "Religious Expression in Public Schools," first published in 1995 and revised in 1998.

The guidelines say nothing in the Constitution prohibits students from engaging in "purely private religious speech" during the school day. "Students may pray in a non-disruptive manner when not engaged in school activities or instruction, and subject to the rules that normally pertain in the applicable setting," the guidelines say.

"Specifically, students in informal settings, such as cafeterias and hallways, may pray and discuss their religious views with each other, subject to the same rules of order as apply to other student activities and speech," the guidelines continue. "Students may also speak to, and attempt to persuade, their peers about religious topics just as they do with regard to political topics. School officials, however, should intercede to stop student speech that constitutes harassment aimed at a student or a group of students."[2]

Two key questions determine whether a religious activity is permissible: Is the activity "sponsored" in any way by school officials? And does it disrupt, harass or otherwise impose upon others who do not wish to engage in the activity?

But some lawmakers, school officials and religious organizations argue that the current limitations on school prayer are too tight.

In 1998, the House passed a proposed constitutional amendment preventing the courts from prohibiting voluntary individual or group prayer in schools, but it did not receive the two-thirds majority needed for passage.

"An outbreak of godless education has threatened to [break] our schools," said cosponsor House Majority Whip Tom DeLay, R-Texas, when it was reintroduced in 1999. "Our kids are no longer taught what is right and what is wrong. God is no longer welcomed in our secular schools."[3]

Some students, parents and school officials who disagree with the current Department of Education guidelines or Supreme Court decisions simply ignore them. At many schools across the country, and especially in the South, football games and other school-sponsored activities continue to be preceded by prayers. The Beauregard Parish School Board in Louisiana,

for example, formally voted last November to allow "nonsectarian, no-proselytizing student-initiated voluntary prayer" at school events.[4]

"There are some communities that have never accepted the decisions made back in the 1960s," notes Mincberg of People for the American Way. "Some communities won't change until they're encouraged to by the increasing heterogeneity that we're all experiencing. It's only when they're confronted by someone who wants to stand up for their individual rights that something does happen."

Meanwhile, "moment-of-silence" laws continue to be debated despite the Supreme Court's 1985 ruling that a school-mandated moment of silence before the school day was unconstitutional. For instance, Virginia passed a law last year calling for a daily minute of silence in the schools during which students may "meditate, pray or engage in other silent activity."

"From its beginnings, [Virginia's] law has had state-sanctioned prayer written all over it," said Kent Willis, executive director of the ACLU of Virginia. Willis says that while a "true" minute-of-silence law that did not mention prayer and had no religious intent would be constitutional, it is clear that the Virginia law does not fit that description.[5]

But federal Judge Claude M. Hilton saw the legislation differently when he upheld it on Oct. 30. "[Virginia] students may think as they wish — and this thinking can be purely religious in nature or purely secular in nature," Hilton held. "All that is required is that they sit silently. Nothing and no one is favored under the act."[6]

Carpenter of Focus on the Family agrees. "Focus on the Family would never advocate a teacher standing up and saying, 'OK, class, I'm going to lead you in prayer.' However, if a legislature such as Virginia's says it is going to allow a minute of silent prayer, that does not equal a teacher leading prayer. We absolutely support that."

Others, however, say that moment-of-silence laws are only a first step for fundamentalist religious groups. To Adrian College's Detwiler, "Silent voluntary prayer isn't enough for the Christian Right." Instead, he insists, they want to use schools as a place of witnessing and hope that by getting the schools to authorize public prayer they will achieve legitimization.

"It's such a hot issue for the Christian Right," Detwiler adds. "It really doesn't matter what the Supreme Court has said. The court has basically said no to all of the different formulations the [Christian Right] has come up with. But the issue keeps coming up because — both symbolically and actually — [it's important] for the Christian Right to get prayer into the schools."

Clark agrees. While his organization, the National Network of Youth Ministries, does not lobby for changes in the law, it is clear that the current policies are too restrictive for most Christians, he says.

"I'm working within the system and helping youth workers and students find ways to express their faith, to grow in their faith and to share their faith with others," he says. "Others are certainly working to change laws to have more freedom for prayer."

Are Christian groups "sneaking" religion into schools?

Critics complain that religious groups use the Bible and other religious symbols and Bible classes to expand the presence of religion, specifically the Christian religion, in public schools.

The Supreme Court has said that public schools may teach students about the Bible, as long as it is presented "objectively as part of a secular program of education."[7] But People for the American Way says some schools are not following the court's lead.

"A number of school districts around the country have ignored the court's admonition," the group contends in a recent study. "They have taught the Bible ... from a religious perspective, generally from a particular sectarian perspective of Christianity. In such courses, the Bible is typically presented as factually true, and students are required to engage in exercises more appropriate for a Sunday school than a public school, including exercises that emphasize rote memorization rather than critical thinking or analysis skills."[8]

The group said it found numerous examples of inappropriate Bible classes in Florida. For example, course

---

Measuring Support for School Vouchers

Polls show varying support for government-funded vouchers to help parents pay for private or religious schools. Americans are evenly split on vouchers, according to an NBC News/Wall Street Journal poll. But an increasing majority supported vouchers according to CNN/Time polls in 1992 and 1999.

NBC News/Wall Street Journal, 1999

Which position do you side with more?

Government should provide taxpayer funded vouchers to help parents pay for private and religious schools. **47%**

Government funding should be limited to children who attend public schools. **47%**

CNN/Time 1992, 1999

How should the government support education?

	1992	1999
Spend only on public schools	64%	54%
Help parents send children to private and religious schools	23	34

Note: Percentages do not add to 100% because "no opinion" responses are not included.

---

materials from Tampa's Plant City High School call the Bible "the most reliable source for history we have," the report says.[9]

People for the American Way blames the National Council on Bible Curriculum in Public Schools for much of the inappropriate religious instruction. The council "may say it wants to introduce Bible classes in public schools to improve students' understanding of literature and history," another report says, "but the real intent of the organization is to promote a religious, primarily Christian doctrine."[10]

Council President Elizabeth Ridenour denies that her group is involved in proselytizing. "Of course they're going to claim that," she says. "They claim that any time anything with God in it comes into the public arena. But we're very careful to follow all the Supreme Court guidelines."

Ridenour also says that her group does not advocate teaching the Bible as historical truth. "That's just a lie. It's never taught as the truth. We say this is what the

The Impact of the 'Establishment Clause'

Restrictions imposed by the federal courts on religious expression in public schools are based on the so-called establishment clause of the First Amendment to the Constitution. It states, "Congress shall make no laws respecting an establishment of religion, or prohibiting the free exercise thereof."

In 1947, the U.S. Supreme Court said in *Everson v. Board of Education:* "The 'establishment of religion' clause...means at least this: Neither a state nor the Federal Government can set up a church. Neither can pass laws which aid one religion, aid all religions, or prefer one religion over another. Neither can force or influence a person to go to or to remain away from church against his will or force him to profess a belief or disbelief in any religion...No tax in any amount, large or small, can be levied to support any religious activities or institutions, whatever they may be called, or whatever form they may adopt to teach or practice religion. Neither a state nor the Federal Government can, openly or secretly, participate in the affairs of any religious organizations or groups and vice versa."

The next year, the high court reinforced the *Everson* ruling, holding in *McCollum v. Board of Education* that, "The First Amendment has erected a wall between Church and State which must be kept high and impregnable."

Advocates of a greater presence for religion in public schools argue, however, that the Supreme Court has gone too far in its proscriptions on religious expression. They say, in fact, that the Founders never intended to erect a wall of separation between church and state.

"We are told that for us to encourage religion would be unconstitutional, that it would violate the Constitution so wisely devised by our Founding Fathers," Rep. Joseph R. Pitts, R-Pa., told the House in 1999. "This is an argument not founded in history or precedent. It is an argument of recent origin. It does not have its roots in our Constitution but rather in the criticisms of numerous revisionists who wish the Constitution said something other than what it actually does. In fact, those who wrote the Constitution thought it was proper for the government to endorse and encourage religion."[1]

As evidence, Pitts and others cite the writings of a number of the Framers of the Constitution, including John Jay, co-author of the *Federalist Papers* and first chief justice of the Supreme Court. "It is the duty of all wise, free and virtuous governments to countenance and encourage virtue and religion," Jay wrote, according to Pitts. Pitts also quotes Henry Laurens, president of the Continental Congress in 1778 and '79, who wrote: "I had the honor of being one who framed the Constitution. In order effectually to

Bible says, just as if it were Shakespeare, and then the students form their own opinions. People for the American Way and others like them throw that in to try to cause controversy."

Civil libertarians also charge that posting the Ten Commandments in school buildings and teaching creationism are thinly disguised attempts to expand religious expression in public schools.

In June 1999, despite the Supreme Court's 1980 *Stone v. Graham* ruling that the Ten Commandments could not be displayed in classrooms, the House approved an amendment permitting states to enact laws requiring the posting of the commandments in schools and other public buildings.

While the amendment was never enacted into law, at least one state took action on its own. In February 2000, Indiana legislators approved a bill allowing schools to post the Ten Commandments. The Indiana law attempts to skirt the Supreme Court by requiring the Commandments to be part of an exhibit that also displays copies of other texts, such as the Constitution.

Indiana is not alone, according to a June 1999 Gallup Poll. It showed that 74 percent of adults support allowing schools to display the Ten Commandments.

Similarly, Christian groups are trying to "sneak" religion into the schools by teaching creationism, despite Supreme Court rulings barring the teaching of religion, says People for the American Way's Mincberg. "The folks who are challenging evolution lost that battle, so they said, 'Well, how about creationism?'" he says. "'No,' they're told. 'That's really religion.' OK, how about 'intelligent design?' No? 'How about a disclaimer about evolution?'"

accomplish these great constitutional ends, it is especially the duty of those who bear rule to promote and encourage respect for God and virtue."

In making his case for religion in schools, Pitts told his colleagues, "Since the very Founders who prohibited 'an establishment of religion' also said that it was the duty of government to encourage religion, it is clear that they did not equate encouraging religion as an unconstitutional establishment of religion. It is time for [Congress] to get back to upholding the actual wording of the Constitution, not some substitute wording that constitutional revisionists wish that it had said."

There appears to be little, if any, evidence in the historical record, however, that the Founding Fathers intended for government to "encourage" religion by any means other than through the public pronouncement of politicians. Indeed, the key documents that preceded the First Amendment and which served as talking points for the debates seem to point clearly to the need for a wall of separation.

For example, the Virginia Bill for Religious Liberty, drafted by Thomas Jefferson, held that "to compel a man to furnish contributions of money for the propagation of opinions which he disbelieves and abhors, is sinful and tyrannical."

James Madison, another key Founder, also seems to have been arguing for a wall between church and state in his 1785 essay "Memorial and Remonstrance." "Rulers who wished to subvert the public liberty, may have found an established Clergy convenient auxiliaries," Madison warned. "A just Government instituted to secure & perpetuate it needs them not. Such a Government will be best supported by protecting every Citizen in the enjoyment of his Religion with the same equal hand which protects his person and his property; by neither invading the equal rights of any Sect, nor suffering any Sect to invade those of another."

In fact, the Supreme Court, based its later interpretations in no small degree upon the views of Jefferson and Madison, according to historians. In *Everson*, for example, the court held that "Memorial and Remonstrance" demonstrates that "Madison opposed every form and degree of official relation between religion and civil authority. For him, religion was a wholly private matter beyond the scope of civil power either to restrain or to support."

Even the dissenting justices in *Everson* agreed that the Constitution calls for a wall of separation between church and state. "With Jefferson, Madison believed that to tolerate any fragment of establishment would ... perpetuate restraint upon that freedom," wrote Chief Justice John Rutledge in the dissenting opinion. "Hence he sought to tear out the institution not partially but root and branch, and to bar its return forever. In view of this history no further proof is needed that the Amendment forbids any appropriation, large or small, from public funds to aid or support any and all religious exercises."

---

[1] *Congressional Record*, Oct. 12, 1999, p. H9880.

Unlike the debate over school prayer, where critics believe religious activists are sincere, opponents claim fundamentalist Christian organizations have a hidden agenda when it comes to these other issues.

"I do believe there's a hidden agenda," says Green of Americans United for Separation of Church and State, citing his experiences at a national lawyers conference sponsored by Focus on the Family. Although most sessions were "up front," he says, others had "very much of an agenda focused on returning organized religious expression to the public schools."

He continues, "You won't hear that from their press releases. All they say is that they want to advance free speech. But there's a real need out there for religious expression in the public schools to have the imprimatur of the state or of officials behind it."

And while most religious organizations deny that they want to proselytize in the schools, some groups declare that their purpose is just that.

"Jesus said, 'Go into all the world and make disciples of all nations.' It's clear that if a person is responding to the words of Jesus, they say, 'Go'," explains Clark of the National Network of Field Ministries. "The New Testament talks about ... being a light set on a hill and not to put it under the basket. Those images don't teach us a privatized, culturally safe, politically correct kind of faith."

Should taxpayer-supported vouchers help parents send their children to private or religious schools?

Liberal groups are not the only ones that complain of hidden agendas. Some religious groups see themselves

CHRONOLOGY

1492-1790 *Most of the Colonies support established religions.*

1647 Massachusetts passes the Old Deluder Satan Act, which makes education compulsory in order to prevent Satan from deluding children.

1790-1830 *The new government calls for a separation between church and state.*

1791 Congress passes the Bill of Rights, including the First Amendment, which reads: "Congress shall make no laws respecting an establishment of religion, or prohibiting the free exercise thereof."

1830-1940 *American education undergoes a gradual process of secularization.*

1830 The movement begins for publicly funded "common schools," designed to be nonsectarian but not devoid of religion.

1833 Massachusetts removes its official support for the Congregationalist Church, becoming the last of the Colonies to abolish established religion.

1868 The 14th Amendment is passed making the protections in the Bill of Rights, including the religion clause of the First Amendment, binding upon the states as well as upon the federal government.

1940-Present *Although the Supreme Court clarifies the "establishment clause," religious activists gain a stronger voice.*

1940 The Supreme Court's *Cantwell v. Connecticut* decision upholds the power of the 14th Amendment to make the religion, or "establishment," clause binding on the states as well as the federal government.

1947 In *Everson v. Board of Education* the Supreme Court rules that states cannot pay for transporting children to private religious schools.

1948 In *McCollum v. Board of Education* the Supreme Court decides that religious teachers cannot come to public schools to teach religion.

1962 In *Engel v. Vitale* the Supreme Court holds that it is not constitutional for students to read aloud a prayer composed by school authorities.

1980 Ronald Reagan is elected president with the help of fundamentalist Christian organizations.

1985 In *Wallace v. Jaffree* the Supreme Court holds that schools cannot authorize a period of silence for voluntary prayer.

1992 In *Lee v. Weisman* the Supreme Court decides that it is not constitutional for schools to invite members of the clergy to offer prayers at middle and high school graduations.

1997 The Rev. Ray Moore launches Exodus 2000, a call for Christian parents to take their children out of public schools. Moore is later joined by Robert Simonds, leader of the California-based Citizens for Excellence in Education.

1998 The three top positions in the U.S. House of Representatives are filled by members who received perfect ratings from Pat Robertson's Christian Coalition.

1998 An amendment authorizing school prayer wins a majority vote in the House, but not the two-thirds majority required for a constitutional amendment.

2000 On June 19, in *Santa Fe Independent School District v. Doe*, the Supreme Court holds that students cannot use a school public address system to recite prayers at school-sponsored events. Voters in Michigan and California turn down voucher proposals. A federal court rules that Cleveland's voucher program is unconstitutional because it uses tax money to send students to religious schools. Students and adults throughout the South continue to pray aloud before football games.

as victims of a campaign by "secular humanists" and others whom they view as anti-religious or anti-Christian.

"The campaign to isolate children from their parents and to indoctrinate them with humanistic ideas is being waged primarily in the public schools," writes James Dobson, founder of Focus on the Family."[11]

The Christian Coalition's Robertson offers a similar view. "The teachers who are teaching your children are not necessarily nice, wonderful servants of the community. They are activists supporting… values [like] affirmative action, ERA, gun control, sex education, illegal teachers' strikes, nuclear freeze, federal funding for abortions [and] decriminalization of marijuana," Robertson said.[12]

Simonds of Citizens for Excellence in Education delivers an even more dramatic call to arms in "America's last great war" against what he calls the atheism of the secular humanists in the public school system. "This is a battle for the heart, mind and even the very soul of every man, woman and especially every child in America," he wrote. "The combatants are 'secular humanism' and 'Christianity.'… The Christian is the key to God's victory over Satan and the atheism of secular humanism. We can change our world in this generation! Our job is to evangelize, while time remains. Our schools are the battleground."[13]

The perceived threat represented by the values taught in the public school system has led some fundamentalist groups to abandon the public schools altogether. The Rev. Ray Moore, president of Frontline Ministries in Columbia, S.C., launched Exodus 2000 in 1997 "in response to the precipitous, widespread concern among American parents and businessmen, especially in the Christian community, that 'Somebody has got to do something now about the education crisis in America.'" His goal is to help American families pull their children out of the public school system.[14]

Two years ago, Simonds set a 12-year deadline for pulling the estimated 20 million church children now in the public schools out of the system. "We've gotten 3 million out in the past two and a half years, so there's only about 17 million left," he says. "We're talking about children who would be lost not only to the church but to God and to heaven."

But Simonds and his followers don't only want to take their children out of the public schools. They also

High school students in Shreveport, La. (top) and Garden City, Kan., take part in "See You at the Pole" prayer rallies last Sept. 20. The Supreme Court permits such meetings if they are voluntary and held before school starts.

want to take the public funds allotted to educate those children.

"If the public school will not meet the very basic needs of preserving [a] child's faith, then the parent has to pay for a private school education on top of being taxed for a public school education," Simonds says. "That's unacceptable. We're being double taxed with no voice." He and others are lobbying for voucher programs and other tax breaks for parents wanting to send their children to private schools, including religious schools.

"We advocate a system that empowers parents to choose the best opportunity for their kids, and that may be a combination of things, including tax credits and vouchers," he says.

Teaching of Creationism Still Supported

Among the advocates of religion in the public schools are creationists — those who reject evolution in favor of the biblical explanation for the creation of the world.[1]

Creationists won a major victory in August 1999, when the Kansas Board of Education removed the teaching of evolution from state science standards, making it possible for a student in Kansas to graduate from high school without having been taught about evolution. However, the board's membership changed in the last election, and some observers say the policy will be reversed.

In addition, bills introduced in the Georgia and Ohio legislatures in 2000 would have required teachers of evolution to present alternative theories, such as creationism. And state boards of education in Alabama and Oklahoma required biology textbooks to say that evolution is just one possible theory of the creation of life.

"Biblical creation should not be taught as the sole theory of the origin of mankind — that would be proselytizing," says Jay Sekulow, chief counsel at the American Center for Legal Justice, which helps fundamentalist religious groups in the courts. "But saying there are alternative views to the theory of evolution is academic freedom."

But People for the American Way, a nonpartisan organization that protects First Amendment rights, said in a recent report that Christian advocacy groups are using "increasingly sophisticated strategies" to "inject their ideas into public school science curricula."[2] The report notes that in 1987 the U.S. Supreme Court rejected arguments for so-called "balanced treatment" — in which creationist or "intelligent design" explanations of creation are presented alongside the theory of evolution.[3]

In *Edwards v. Aguillard*, the court ruled that such balanced treatment is unconstitutional in that it "advances a religious doctrine by requiring either the banishment of the theory of evolution from public school classrooms or the presentation of a religious viewpoint that rejects evolution in its entirety."

---

[1] See David Masci, "Evolution vs. Creationism," *The CQ Researcher*, Aug. 22, 1997, pp. 745-768.

[2] *Ibid*, p. 1.

[3] People for the American Way, "Sabotaging Science: Creationist Strategy in the '90s," November 1999, p. 7.

But opponents argue that such proposals, if enacted, would drain sorely needed resources from the public schools. "How big a threat are vouchers to public schools?" asks Mincberg. "We know that in Milwaukee alone tens of millions of dollars have been drained from the public schools at a particularly critical time." Milwaukee has one of the nation's few voucher systems.

The damage such a system can cause to the public schools, he says, depends upon how large the program is and how it is implemented. "You have the draining of resources from public schools that accept everyone to private schools that are selective about who they take," he points out.

But others warn that public funds may have strings attached that may also prove to be hidden threats for the private schools that accept the vouchers. "They want federal money, but they don't want the responsibility for obeying federal laws, such as not discriminating," says Wendy Kaminer, a public policy analyst at the Radcliffe Institute in Cambridge, Mass. "If you

accept government funding, you have to accept government oversight."

Carpenter agrees. "People who are leading these schools are wary, and they should be wary, that when they take money there are strings attached," he says. "There's no way to get around that."

BACKGROUND

Colonial Intolerance

The wall of separation between church and state in the United States was constructed relatively recently.

In most of the American Colonies, one needed to be a church member in good standing to hold public office. Indeed, some Colonies had compulsory schooling for children, which was pointedly religious in nature and intent. For example, the legislation mandating compulsory education in 1647 Massachusetts was called the "Old Deluder Satan Act." Ensuring that all children were properly instructed was essential, the act said, because "one of the chief projects of that old deluder Satan [is] to keep men from the knowledge of the Scriptures" through employing "false glosses of saint-seeming deceivers."[15]

The Colonies were not only religious in character but also sectarian and, in many cases, intolerantly so. "The Puritans came to America for religious liberty — their own, not anyone else's. Moved by a sense of divine mission and confident of the truth, they, like most believers of that day, were decidedly intolerant," writes Warren A. Nord, a professor of philosophy at the University of North Carolina at Chapel Hill.[16] On occasion, the Puritans cut off the ears of heretics; from 1649 to 1651 they hanged four Quakers.

Like most Colonial societies, the Puritans had a state-established religion. All members of the society were taxed for the church's support, and required to attend church. In fact, only four Colonies — Delaware, New Jersey, Rhode Island and Pennsylvania — did not have established religions.

Some analysts argue that the multiplicity of established religions made it clear to the Framers of the Constitution that if the country was to be a united political entity the federal government should not establish or favor one religion over another. That philosophy led to the religion clause of the First Amendment, also called the "establishment clause:" "Congress shall make no laws respecting an establishment of religion, or prohibiting the free exercise thereof."

But the proscription did not prevent individual states from continuing to support an established religion — at least not until 1940, when the Supreme Court held that the First Amendment was also binding on the states. However, the issue was moot long before 1940, since the last state with an established religion — Massachusetts — disestablished it in 1833.

'Common' Schools

It was more than coincidental that the 1830s was also when the movement for tax-supported "common schools" began. Ironically, at least part of the motivation for the first generation of public schools was religious. "Protestants united behind common schools because of the growing flood of immigration — particularly, in the case of Massachusetts, from Catholic Ireland," Nord writes. "The

Protestant hope was that nonsectarian schools would be acceptable to Catholics, who would be socialized into becoming good Americans. To this end, Protestants were willing to dispense with much doctrinal content."[17]

However, most Roman Catholics, perhaps persuaded by violent anti-Catholic riots in Boston, New York and Philadelphia, developed their own system of parochial schools. In some places — echoing current debates over vouchers — Catholics pressed for tax support of their schools, arguing that the Protestants' common schools received it.

No state gave aid to Catholic schools, but several prohibited the use of tax funds for sectarian schools. By 1900, most states prohibited public funds going to parochial schools, and some banned religious instruction in the public schools.

While Catholic parochial schools developed without public funding, the Protestant common school system continued to receive public funds. As late as the Civil War, school texts were highly religious in nature, accepting the Biblical accounts of the creation of the world as fact. But by the 1890s, common schools and the texts they employed were largely devoid of religion. (Notable exceptions included the ubiquitous *McGuffey's Readers*, which were filled with Bible stories and moral lessons, and were used well into the 1920s.)

As Nord observes, "Between the time of the American Revolution and the end of the 19th century, an education revolution took place; religion dropped by the wayside as America marched in the modern world. The mantle of high purpose in the schools was passed on to democracy and Americanism, the new faiths of the new nation."[18]

Court Decisions

Until the 1940s, the First Amendment was seen as binding only on the federal government, not on states and localities. But the Supreme Court's *Cantwell v. Connecticut* ruling in 1940 turned that around. The court held that First Amendment protections for religious expression extended to state and local laws. "With those words, the doors of the federal courts were opened to those who wished to challenge state laws concerning the rights of individuals, and Americans responded by filing cases involving a great variety of religious issues," writes Lynda Beck Fenwick, a trial attorney and historian.[19]

Major Supreme Court Decisions on Religion in Schools

■ **June 19, 2000** — *Santa Fe Independent School District v. Doe*. Until 1995, the student council chaplain at Texas' Santa Fe High School offered a prayer over the public address system before each varsity football game. The practice was challenged in District Court as a violation of the "Establishment," or freedom of religion, Clause of the First Amendment. While the case was pending, the school district adopted a new policy permitting but not requiring a prayer initiated and led by a student at all home games. The District Court ruled that only nonsectarian, non-proselytizing prayers would be permitted. But the Court of Appeals rejected the modified prayer policy. The Supreme Court affirmed the Appeals Court, ruling that prayers over a public address system at school-sponsored events violated the First Amendment.

■ **June 28, 2000** — *Mitchell v. Helms*. The court upheld a federal program that gives equipment and other aid to religious schools. The majority opinion, written by Justice Clarence Thomas, held that aid is constitutional if it is "allocated on the basis of neutral, secular criteria that neither favor nor disfavor religion, and is made available to both religious and secular beneficiaries on a non-discriminatory basis," even if the funds go to a religious institution.

■ **1997** — *Agostini v. Felton*. The court reversed its 1985 decision in *Aguilar v. Felton* (see below) and held that public school teachers could be sent to teach remedial classes in parochial schools.

■ **1992** — *Lee v. Weisman*. The court held that allowing members of the clergy to offer prayers at middle and high school graduations violated the Establishment Clause. Even though the prayers were nonsectarian, the court found that the policy forced students to "support or participate in religion." The court also determined that simply making attendance at the event voluntary did not remove the coercion because of both peer pressure and pressure from the school to participate.

■ **1985** — *Aguilar v. Felton*. The court held that New York state could not send public school teachers to parochial schools to teach remedial classes. The court specifically said that such teaching must occur in non-religious settings.

■ **1985** — *Wallace v. Jaffree*. The court struck down an amendment to an Alabama statute that would have authorized a period of silence for "voluntary prayer" in public schools. The court said the primary purpose of the amendment was religious, but it left open the question of whether a differently worded moment-of-silence law might be constitutional.

■ **1981** — *Karen B. v. Treen*. The court held as unconstitutional a Louisiana law requiring school boards to permit teachers to lead prayers and allowing students to voluntarily lead prayers. The court said the statute lacked any secular purpose and promoted religion, even though it did not promote a specific religion or sect.

■ **1980** — *Stone v. Graham*. The court said a Kentucky statute requiring the posting of the Ten Commandments in public schools violated the Establishment Clause since it had no secular purpose.

■ **1963** — *Abington School District v. Schempp*. The court struck down Pennsylvania and Baltimore statutes calling for Bible readings and/or the Lord's Prayer to be read over the intercom before school. Although students could be excused from participation, the court held that, "there must be a secular legislative purpose and a primary effect that neither advances nor inhibits religion" for the practice to be constitutional. The court said, however, that the Bible can be studied for "its literary and historic qualities...as part of a secular program of education."

■ **1962** — *Engel v. Vitale*. The court held that a 22-word non-denominational prayer prepared by public school authorities and prescribed for use in classrooms violated the Establishment Clause. The court determined that, "It is no part of the business of government to compose official prayers for any group of the American people to recite as a part of a religious program carried on by the government."

■ **1948** — *McCollum v. Board of Education*. The court ruled that religious teachers could not be allowed to come to public schools to teach religion.

■ **1947** — *Everson v. Board of Education of the Township of Ewing*. The court held that New Jersey could not reimburse parents for money expended by them to transport their children to private religious schools.

A parent in Champaign, Ill., brought one of the first major religion cases before the high court in 1948. Vashti McCollum complained that her taxes were being used to support religious instruction in public school classrooms, because religious teachers were allowed into the public schools to teach religion. Not only did they have captive audiences, she said, but they were using facilities provided by tax dollars.

"The First Amendment has erected a wall between Church and State which must be kept high and impregnable," the justices said in reversing lower court rulings upholding the school's policy.[20]

Over the next 50 years, the court averaged two cases per year addressing the religion clause, many involving public schools. The clear trend in each case has been to further limit the opportunities for religious expression within the public schools. (*See sidebar, p. 174.*)

Conservative Christians

The development of a political voice among fundamentalist Christian groups in the latter half of the 20th century further highlighted the religion-in-schools issue.

Conservative Christian voters came out in droves to help elect Ronald Reagan to the White House in 1980. As a result, a number of Christian leaders stepped into the national spotlight, notably Jerry Falwell, a minister and televangelist, and Christian Coalition founder Robertson. Thanks to their new voice within the Reagan administration, Christian activists began the 1980s with high hopes that they could reform America and return religion to its schools.

However, the religious revolution largely fizzled. Despite all the campaign rhetoric, the eight years of the Reagan administration offered little for conservative Christian groups. After a series of seeming "victories," Christian activists experienced more disappointments than successes over the next 20 years, both in the courts and in national politics. As a result, most groups turned their attention to the state and local levels.

Most analysts see this shift as being at least partly responsible for the 1994 Republican takeover of Congress. And the increased number of conservative Christians in Congress gave Christian organizations a greater voice in the Republican Party. As one measure of their new influence, members with perfect ratings from the Christian Coalition held all three top House leadership positions in 1998.

"By 1996, Christian Right power was sufficient to impose its agenda on the party's presidential platform even though the party's presidential candidate, Robert Dole, expressed discomfort with a number of platform planks," writes Adrian College's Detwiler. "Yet, although conservative Christian voters constituted the largest single voting block within the Republican Party, their power from 1994 to 1998 was not sufficient to move the party to advance their social agenda."[21]

CURRENT SITUATION

Limits on Prayer

Both the courts and Congress have shown little, if any, inclination over the past year to lower the barrier between church and state on school property.

Indeed, the most recent Supreme Court decisions demonstrate a clear willingness to retain the wall of separation. In June, the court ruled that the Santa Fe Independent School District in Texas acted improperly in allowing students to read Christian prayers over the public address system at home football games. The majority opinion held that, "The delivery of such a message — over the school's public address system, by a speaker representing the student body, under the supervision of school faculty, and pursuant to a school policy that explicitly and implicitly encourages public prayer — is not properly characterized as 'private' speech."[22]

The court further held that even if the student-led prayer and students' attendance at football games were "purely voluntary," the prayer policy would still be coercive, because the school cannot exact religious conformity from a student as the price of attending a football game.

In its October Jacksonville decision, the court further limited the opportunity for prayer in schools by setting aside a lower court decision that allowed voluntary student-led prayer at graduation ceremonies.[23] In this case, the school played no role at all except in providing the forum of the graduation ceremony.

Like the courts, the 106th Congress also was less than open to expanding religious expression in schools. The only significant legislation relating to religious expression in the schools were the proposals for a constitutional amendment allowing voluntary prayer.

The legislation, sponsored by Rep. Lindsey Graham, R-S.C., would have amended the constitution to say that, "Nothing in this Constitution shall be construed to prohibit voluntary individual or group prayer in public schools or other public institutions. No person shall be required by the United States or by any State to participate in prayer. Neither the United States nor any State shall compose the words of any prayer to be said in public schools."

Although an earlier version of the legislation didn't win the two-thirds majority required for a constitutional amendment, Christian groups hope the measure will be reintroduced this year. But its prospects for final passage are dim. Congressional insiders say the only reason the bill reached a vote was that committee members were confident it would not pass.

Those working to increase the profile of religion in the public schools found more to cheer about last year in state legislatures. In addition to Virginia's moment-of-silence law, three other states — Indiana, Kentucky and South Dakota — passed laws allowing the Ten Commandments to be displayed in schools and on other public property. Similar legislation was proposed in at least eight other states.

Critics say it is unlikely that such laws would withstand challenge. "If any of these states are foolish enough to enact these bills into law, I would consider it an invitation to a lawsuit — and you can write that in stone," said Barry Lynn, executive director of Americans United for Separation of Church and State.[24]

Meanwhile, some school administrators say the rules about religious expression in schools remain so fuzzy that the best way to handle the issue is to be sensitive to the needs of all students.

"When you start squelching religious expression too much, you're ignoring what is really a pretty heavy part of some people's culture," says Dave Humphrey, principal of Roosevelt High School in Seattle.

What's more, he says, "Very often there are some things you don't know about people's religions. We have some Muslim kids who need to pray during the school day, and we allow them to be released from class. Would we allow Christians to be released? That's not a required part of their religion, so I'd be talking with their parents and saying, 'No, we really don't want that to happen because we'd be losing academic time.' There are other times during the day they can pray."

Voucher Battles

Analysts and advocates on both sides of the religion-in-schools controversy agree that the hot issue is vouchers and other proposals for public funding of parochial and other private schools.

But recent indicators are not encouraging for voucher supporters. In the last elections, voters in two states defeated hotly contested voucher proposals.

Michigan voters turned down vouchers — for up to $3,300 per year — for students in poorly performing schools. The Roman Catholic Church and other Christian organizations supported the measure, both financially and from church pulpits.

In California, voters rejected a proposal to provide every student — even those already in private schools — with a $4,000 voucher that could be used to pay for tuition. The Catholic Church declined to support the proposal, reportedly because it didn't target low-income families.

Although both voucher proposals failed, even critics acknowledge that they attracted substantial support and represent a real threat to the public schools.

"When you talk about school choice, that makes sense to people," says Kaminer of the Radcliffe Institute. "When you say that poor people ought to have the same opportunity to send their kids to good schools that rich people have, that resonates with a lot of people.

"But when you think about how the system would actually work; about how selective private schools are; about how limited the space is; and about how expensive they are, the only way to provide a good enough education for the greatest number of students is through a publicly funded school system.

"It's not as if these vouchers are going to create a system of alternative schools that are going to accommodate all of the kids who want to get out of their supposedly failing public schools," Kaminer adds.

Some critics warn that some voucher supporters actively seek to undermine the public schools. "All of those strategies for vouchers and tax credits for private schooling are aimed at substantially weakening public education in order to advance the Christian Right's cultural agenda," Detwiler of Adrian College says.

Mincberg of People for the American Way agrees. "There are plenty of people who have their feet in both camps," he says. "The Christian Coalition is a good example. They are vigorous proponents of vouchers and other methods to essentially undermine, or close up, the public schools, but at the same time as long as the public schools exist they're going to do their best to promote their agenda there."

In the view of Sekulow of the American Center for Legal Justice, "There isn't anything wrong with a voucher system that provides a voucher for parents to use to send their child to any school, including a parochial school."

At the same time, he says, "Ninety percent of Christian students attend public schools in this country. Private schools are just not [available] for everybody. So while there are students in these schools, their rights need to be protected. No, we're not calling for a mass exodus out of the public schools. That's something for each set of parents to decide."

The problem for the religious groups that push for vouchers is that they don't want the regulation that generally comes with public funds. "I'm in favor of vouchers if the vouchers are written so that Christian schools are not subject to government control," says Simonds of Citizens for Excellence in Education.

That is not likely to happen, voucher critics say. "Take the money and run? I think they're being rather naive," says Green of Americans United for Separation of Church and State. "That's not been the history of public funding; there is going to be a demand for accountability."

Green predicts that calls for regulations and efforts to professionalize teachers will "end up turning the private schools into mirror images of the public schools."

In addition to Milwaukee, voucher programs exist in only a handful of places, where they are mostly only available to low-income students. A statewide program in Florida, initiated by Republican Gov. Jeb Bush, remains tangled in court challenges. Bush's brother, President-elect George W. Bush, advocated vouchers during his campaign.

Sekulow notes that the Supreme Court "keeps ducking the [voucher] issue," but he predicts it will find its way to the court in the near future. "The pressure is building," he says.

In fact, in a ruling that may hasten the process, the 6th U.S. Circuit Court of Appeals on Dec. 11, held the

Nathan Good prays during religious instruction conducted on a private site near his public school in Timberville, Va. Some schools allow students to take time off for religious observances.

voucher program launched in Cleveland in 1995 unconstitutional because it uses tax money to send students to religious schools.

"To approve this program would approve the actual diversion of government aid to religious institutions in endorsement of religious education, something 'in tension' with the precedents of the Supreme Court," the court said.[25]

OUTLOOK

Bush's Impact

Civil libertarians and conservative Christian organizations agree that the election of Bush as president and the ongoing push for voucher programs will have the greatest impact on religion in the public schools in the next few years.

Bush's public position on school prayer appears to toe the constitutional line. "I support voluntary, student-led prayer and am committed to the First Amendment principles of religious freedom, tolerance and diversity," Bush told reporters during the campaign. "Whether Mormon, Methodist or Muslim, students in America should be able to participate in their constitutional free exercise of religion.

AT ISSUE

Should Congress amend the Constitution to allow prayer in public schools?

YES
Rep. Ernest Istook, R-Okla.

From remarks in the House, June 4, 1998

[The] Supreme Court...has protected Nazi swastikas on public property [and] burning crosses. But in 1962, they said, even when it is voluntary, for children during the school day to pray together is against the Constitution.

...In 1980, they said, if the Ten Commandments are posted on the wall of a school, it is unconstitutional because students might read them and might obey them. Imagine, in an era when guns, knives and drugs are common in public schools, we are told the Ten Commandments are not welcome....

In 1985, the State of Alabama said we can have a moment of silence; and one of the many purposes to which you can apply this, if we choose, is silent prayer. The Supreme Court said, nope, that it is unconstitutional to permit silent prayer.

In 1992, they said, to have a minister, in this case it was a Jewish rabbi, to come and speak at a school graduation was unconstitutional because there might be some students there who would disagree with the prayer, and they would not want to be expected to be respectful with something with which they disagree. That is what the Supreme Court said....

It is senseless to say that everyone else must be censored and silenced because someone chooses to be intolerant. Prayer is not divisive. Prayer is unifying. What is divisive is for people to teach that we should not respect the prayer of another person or that we should not respect prayer in general. If you teach your children that, shame on you. But if we want people to be united, [we must] give them the chance to come together and express things positively.

The Pledge of Allegiance is the proper standard. The Supreme Court has ruled, in the late 1940s, no one can be compelled to say the Pledge of Allegiance. I agree. But they did not permit someone who did not want to say it to censor and stop the rest of the students in that classroom who did want to join together.

That is the proper standard for prayer in public schools. If we want to do it, it is permitted. If we do not want to, we do not have to. But we do not have the right to shut people up and censor them just because we choose to be thin-skinned and intolerant when someone else is trying to express their faith.

NO
The Rev. Barry W. Lynn
Executive Director, Americans United for Separation of Church and State

Written for *The CQ Researcher*, January 2001

School prayer amendments in Congress are kind of like the common cold: They're annoying, recurrent and hard to shake, but eventually they fade away and are quickly forgotten.

The plain fact is the country does not need a school prayer amendment. There is a myth that prayer has been banned from public schools. However, the truth is that the First Amendment already protects the right to pray in school. Any student in any public school in America may pray at any time in a voluntary manner.

What some school prayer advocates want is mandatory prayer in schools — an entirely different animal. Mandatory prayer has been struck down time and time again by the Supreme Court and lower courts. And for that we should be thankful. Majority rule in religion or coercive worship should send shivers down the spine of any right-thinking person. Prayer is a deeply personal experience, best left to individual students and their families. It is not the government's job to promote or encourage prayer or to allow mobs to impose it on anyone.

School officials and student majorities should never be allowed to bully other children into religious worship they may not believe in. The Bill of Rights provides for individual freedom of conscience, not a tyranny of the majority. Religious minorities in public schools should not have to endure school-promoted worship that often conflicts with what they are taught at home and at their house of worship.

In religiously diverse America, school-sponsored religion is not only a bad idea; it is increasingly unworkable. There is no generic, nonsectarian prayer all faiths can agree on. Prayer between individuals and their God is deeply private and does not exist in a "one-size-fits-all" format. In any given community, there are diverse religious communities with different traditions and many people who have chosen no spiritual path at all. No prayer will please everyone.

America's public schools are not Sunday schools. They must be neutral on religion to protect the rights of everyone. Students should not be pressured to pray, whether it's in the classroom, before an assembly or football game or anywhere else. The Supreme Court has repeatedly put a stop to that type of unwanted, un-American religious coercion. Congress should recognize the wisdom of those rulings and give up on school prayer amendments.

"We should not have teacher-led prayers in public schools," he continued, "and school officials should never favor one religion over another, or favor religion over no religion (or vice versa). I also believe that schools should not restrict students' religious liberties. The free exercise of faith is the fundamental right of every American, and that right doesn't stop at the schoolhouse door."[26]

Bush is on somewhat less firm ground, constitutionally speaking, in his support for voucher programs. "I believe in local control of schools; therefore, I think it's up to individual states to decide whether to enact vouchers," Bush said. "I believe federal dollars should no longer subsidize failure."

Bush has said his first legislative priority will be education reform, including his version of a voucher program, which will be introduced on his first day in office or very close to it. However, given the slim majority held by the Republicans in the House and the 50-50 split in the new Senate, Bush is anxious to offer a proposal with bipartisan support. And his voucher plan would probably be so divisive as to scuttle any hope for bipartisanship.

"Vouchers would complicate any opportunity to act quickly on reforms to improve public schools, on which there is general agreement," said Daniel Weiss, spokesman for California Rep. George Miller, who is expected to be named ranking Democrat on the House Education Committee.[27]

Moderate and liberal Democrats, backed by teachers' unions, civil rights groups and liberal social policy groups, strongly oppose vouchers, and their opposition has intensified since the two state voucher defeats in November.

Even some conservative Democrats oppose them. "Vouchers are dead in the water," said Rep. Charles W. Stenholm of Texas, a member of the so-called "Blue Dog" coalition of conservative House Democrats.[28]

Many Republicans are advising Bush to eventually drop the voucher provision in order to achieve bipartisan support for the rest of his education-reform plan, which calls for more testing and accountability while granting states more flexibility to achieve higher student performance. Such proposals are more attractive to some moderate-to-conservative Democrats.

As a result, Bush is expected to offer a nominal voucher plan, but it will be more of a symbolic gesture to satisfy conservatives, transition and congressional officials told

The Washington Post. The proposal likely will be sacrificed during negotiations aimed at achieving Bush's testing and state-funding goals, they said.[29]

Bush's voucher ideas, said Sen. John F. Kerry, D-Mass., "are ripe for bargaining away, and I'm confident they will be."

Florida International University President Modesto "Mitch" Maidique, who was appointed to Bush's transition education advisory team, agreed. "I think [vouchers] in most cases end up being a hypothetical, but I think the idea of measuring performance and having a system of incentives and disincentives is pretty fundamental stuff."[30]

But Bush administration spokesman Ari Fleischer on Jan. 2 denied the suggestion that the voucher proposal would be dropped. Vouchers "will be part of the agenda…and [Bush] is going to work hard to enact school choice into law," he said.[31]

In the end, Bush is most likely to influence school prayer and vouchers by making appointments to the Supreme Court.

"The next president could well shape the future of the Supreme Court," says Sekulow of the American Center for Legal Justice. "The court is right now divided on these issues, and two justices one way or the other could tip the scales in favor of voucher programs or against them." And, he notes, Bush's "judicial philosophy would allow for vouchers to go to religious schools."

Green of Americans United for Separation of Church and State says Bush is likely to be under significant pressure to deliver legislation as well. "Bush certainly doesn't have a mandate, and he's certainly going to have to shore up his constituency," Green says. "Pat Robertson's and Jerry Falwell's organizations were [campaigning for Bush] down in Florida for weeks. I don't know what they were doing, but they think that they're somehow important and need to be paid off. We have concerns that they will be paid off, if not with the Supreme Court then with legislation."

Despite Bush's election, Simonds of Citizens for Excellence in Education remains pessimistic about working within the political system. "I don't really have that much hope anymore," he says. "The Democratic Party has so infiltrated the courts, and the National Education Association is nothing but an extension of that party. I don't think people of faith have a chance anymore."

Simonds says he believes that the Bush presidency may put off the inevitable, but that "the [liberals] eventually will dominate. The forces of evil are really sharper in deviousness than the forces of good, and their forces will eventually dominate the nation."

NOTES

1. The Associated Press, Sept. 23, 2000.

2. U.S. Department of Education, "Religious Expression in the Public Schools," p. 998.

3. "School Prayer Amendment Pushed Again," *Houston Chronicle,* Sept. 16, 1999.

4. "School Board Challenges ACLU with Decision on School Prayer," The Associated Press, Nov. 11, 2000.

5. "Judge Upholds Minute of Silence Law," The Associated Press, Oct. 30, 2000.

6. "ACLU Challenges Virginia's Minute of Silence," *The Washington Post,"* June 23, 2000.

7. *Abington Township v. Schempp* (1963).

8. "The Good Book Taught Wrong: 'Bible History' Classes in Florida's Public Schools," People for the American Way Foundation, April 2000, p. 1.

9. *Ibid,* p. 8.

10. "Wolf in Sheep's Clothing: National Council on Bible Curriculum in Public Schools," People for the American Way Foundation, http://www.pfaw.org/caphill/liberty.shtml.

11. James C. Dobson and Gary L. Bauer, "Children at Risk: The Battle for the Hearts and Minds of Our Kids," *Word,* 1990, p. 37.

12. James Davison Hunter, *Culture Wars: The Struggle to Define America* (1991), p. 204.

13. Robert Simonds, "Communicating a Christian World View in the Classroom," National Association of Christian Educators, 1983, p. i.

14. http://www.exodus2000.org/overview.htm.

15. Christopher Lucas, *Our Western Education Heritage* (1972), p. 476.

16. Warren A. Nord, *Religion and American Education: Rethinking a National Dilemma* (1995), p. 99.

17. *Ibid,* p. 72.

18. *Ibid,* p. 63.

19. Lynda Beck Fenwick, *Should the Children Pray?: A historical, judicial, and political examination of public school prayer* (1989), p. 126.

20. *McCollum v. Board of Education* (1948).

21. Fritz Detwiler, *Standing on the Premises of God: The Christian Right's Fight to Redefine America's Public Schools* (1999), p. 101.

22. *Santa Fe Independent School District v. Doe* (2000).

23. *Adler v. Duval County Board of Education* (Oct. 2, 2000).

24. http://www.au.org/pr2300.htm.

25. The Associated Press, Dec. 11, 2000.

26. "Bush and Gore on the Issues: 20 Questions and Answers," The Associated Press, Oct. 23, 2000.

27. Quoted in Adam Entous, "USA: Bush team pledges to fight for school voucher plan," Reuters English News Service, Jan. 2, 2001.

28. Quoted in Jim VandeHei and Shailagh Murray, "Bush's Ability to Exploit Democrats' Rifts Could Be Key to Advancing His Agenda," *The Wall Street Journal,* Jan. 3, 2001.

29. Dana Milbank, "Bush Likely to Drop Vouchers; Education Policy to Focus on Testing, States' Flexibility," *The Washington Post,* Jan. 2, 2001.

30. Karla Schuster, "Bush Calls on 2 Florida Educators," *South Florida Sun-Sentinel,* Jan. 3, 2001.

31. Entous, *op. cit.*

BIBLIOGRAPHY

Books

Alley, Robert S., editor, *The Constitution & Religion: Leading Supreme Court Cases on Church and State*, Prometheus Books, 1999.
Alley has effectively excerpted 50 of the most important Supreme Court decisions affecting religious freedom and the separation of church and state. Don't look for commentary here, but the volume does offer quick access to the important parts of the decisions without having to wade through lengthy volumes.

Alley, Robert S., *Without a Prayer: Religious Expression in the Public Schools,* **Prometheus Books, 1996.**
The commentary that is missing in Alley's *The Constitution & Religion* is clearly in evidence here. Rich with anecdotal material and interviews with figures involved in landmark court cases, the book offers much insight and detail.

Detwiler, Fritz, *Standing on the Premises of God: The Christian Right's Fight to Redefine America's Public Schools,* **New York University Press, 1999.**
Detwiler, a philosophy professor at Adrian College in Michigan, is a consultant to educators and school districts on the activities of Christian activist groups. This book, which is thoroughly documented, is an objective look at the history and current status of strategies being employed by fundamentalist Christian groups to reintroduce prayer and other religious expression to the public schools.

Dobson, James C., and Gary L. Bauer, *Children at Risk: The Battle for the Hearts and Minds of Our Kids,* **Word, 1990.**
Dobson, founder of Focus on the Family, and Bauer, a former presidential candidate, define the battle between religious tradition and family values on the one side and secular humanism on the other side. According to the authors, the two systems cannot coexist.

Edwards, June, *Opposing Censorship in the Public Schools: Religion, Morality and Literature,* **Lawrence Erlbaum Associates, 1998.**
This interesting and short (150 pages) volume delineates many of the issues being debated by the advocates and critics of religious expression in the public schools. Edwards first describes the positions of religious activists — freely excerpting from speeches and writings — then addresses each issue in detail.

Fenwick, Lynda Beck, *Should the Children Pray?: A Historical, Judicial and Political Examination of Public School Prayer,* **Baylor University Press, 1989.**
Fenwick, an attorney and historian, focuses on the early history of the religion in schools issue. The discussion of Colonial America and the development of the First Amendment's clauses on religion are particularly helpful.

Hunter, James Davison, *Culture Wars: The Struggle to Define America,* **Basic Books, 1991.**
Hunter traces the history of religious battles in American history. He shows how, in recent years, the traditional conflict between God and Satan has evolved into one between traditionalists and secular humanists. Hunter clearly aligns himself with the former group.

Nord, Warren A., *Religion and American Education: Rethinking a National Dilemma,* **University of North Carolina Press, 1995.**
An excellent historical discussion of the role of religion in American public education is supplemented by a cogent summary of the current issues facing educators.

Articles

Simonds, Robert, "Communicating a Christian World View in the Classroom," National Association of Christian Educators, 1983.
Simonds, president of Citizens for Excellence in Education, a division of the National Association of Christian Educators, urges teachers to convey Christian values in the public schools and describes the challenges faced by people "of faith." More recently, Simonds has urged Christian parents to remove their children from the public schools.

Reports and Studies

People for the American Way, "Sabotaging Science: Creationist Strategy in the '90s," November 1999.
This brief, 20-page report summarizes the attempts by fundamentalist Christian groups to introduce creationist concepts into public school curricula. The report focuses primarily on the situation in Kansas, where the state board of education voted recently to remove the topic of evolution from state science standards.

People for the American Way, "The Good Book Taught Wrong: 'Bible History' Classes in Florida's Public Schools," April 2000.
This report growing out of an on-site study explains how courses supposedly about the Bible as literature are actually teaching the Bible as history.

U.S. Department of Education, "Religious Expression in the Public Schools," 1998.
Federal guidelines advise administrators, parents and students what sorts of religious expressions and activities are allowed under the First Amendment of the Constitution.

For More Information

American Center for Legal Justice, P.O. Box 64429, Virginia Beach, VA 23467; (800) 296-4529; www.aclj.org. Founded by Christian Coalition head Pat Robertson, ACLJ is dedicated to researching legal issues of importance to Christian groups and aiding those groups in court cases.

American Civil Liberties Union, 125 Broad St., New York, NY 10004; (212) 549-2500; www.aclu.org. The ACLU initiates test court cases and advocates legislation to guarantee constitutional rights and civil liberties.

Americans United for Separation of Church and State, 518 C St., N.E., Washington, DC 20002; (202) 466-3234; www.au.org. AUSCS supports research on issues related to the separation of religion and government and lobbies for legislation to maintain that separation.

Focus on the Family, Colorado Springs, CO 80995; (719) 531-5181; www.family.org. A Christian organization dedicated to enhancing the role of religion in family life and in education.

National Association of Christian Educators, Citizens for Excellence in Education, Box 3200, Costa Mesa, CA 92628; (949) 251-9335; www.nace-cee.org. A Christian organization that recently urged Christian students to leave the public school system.

National Network of Youth Ministries, 12335 World Trade Dr., Suite 16, San Diego, CA 92128; (858) 451-1111; http://youthworkers.net. Seeks to coordinate and expand youth ministries and religion in the schools.

People for the American Way, 2000 M St., N.W., Suite 400, Washington, DC 20036; (202) 467-4999; www.pfaw.org. An advocacy and lobbying group strongly in favor of strict separation of church and state.

9

Students Under Stress

Do Schools Assign Too Much Homework?

Marcia Clemmitt

To reduce stress on students, a number of high schools around the country are reducing homework and other sources of stress that can cause depression, anxiety and family strife. Over the past two decades, high school homework loads have not increased, while first-, second- and third-graders have been getting more.

Getty Images/David Young-Wolff

From *CQ Researcher*,
July 13, 2007.

When Nancy Kalish's daughter was in seventh grade, she suddenly began saying, "I hate school," recalls Kalish, a journalist in New York City. "She started saying it every single day."

Kalish soon discovered that what had been "a reasonable amount" of homework for Allison in grade school "had mushroomed into four hours a night" in middle school.

Soon, "our entire relationship revolved around homework," with "the first question when she came in the door each afternoon, 'How much homework do you have?' " says Kalish. The answer determined whether Allison would see friends, attend a concert or a grandparent's birthday party or stay home studying.

The resulting family tension and their daughter's newfound anger toward school turned Kalish and her husband — once "true believers" in the value of homework — into activists who sought a school policy limiting homework at Allison's school. With a coauthor, Kalish wrote the 2006 book *The Case Against Homework*.

Kalish is part of a new wave of parents, many in middle- and upper-income communities, protesting what they say is too much homework — particularly in elementary and middle school — causing stress, sleep deprivation, depression and family strife.

Over the last two decades, worries about global competition have prompted U.S. business leaders and lawmakers to increase pressure on schools to raise achievement. Most of that pressure has fallen on the youngest children, however, even though it's U.S. high-schoolers who score lowest on international achievement tests.

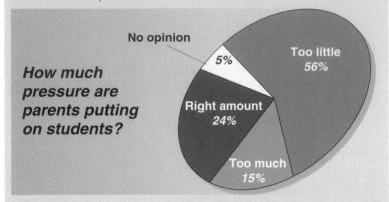

Should Students Be Pushed Harder?

More than half of U.S. adults say parents are not pushing their children hard enough in school. Only 15 percent think students are under too much pressure.

How much pressure are parents putting on students?

No opinion
5%

Too little
56%

Right amount
24%

Too much
15%

Source: Richard Wike and Juliana Menasce Horowitz, "Parental Pressure on Students: Not Enough in America; Too Much in Asia," Pew Research Center, Aug. 24, 2006

homework "is reinforcement" of what's studied in class, "but there's no evidence that it helps younger children," she says.

After a years-long struggle, the parents Bennett organized won a new homework policy that limited tests to two per week, declared Monday test-free and banned school projects over certain vacations.

A number of schools around the country are mulling similar moves.

In Massachusetts, for example, Needham High School Principal Paul Richards sought to limit stress after three student suicides in recent years. Richards urges teachers not to give homework over school vacations and to be more flexible about assignment deadlines. He also ended the tradition of publishing the school's academic honor roll in the local newspaper, which made him the butt of jokes and criticism from "Tonight" host comedian Jay Leno and conservative commentator Rush Limbaugh.

But Richards has stood firm, saying that critics don't understand the amount of stress his college-bound students feel, even as they try to act cool. For example, "there are perceptions that Boston College only takes two seniors from each high school," said Richards. "Students hear this and start ranking each other," adding more pressure to an already "product-oriented and competitive" culture that's "gone into overdrive."[1]

Education researchers who study student workloads say that such high-pressure situations may be more the exception than the rule, however.

"Most of what you hear" about excessive homework "is anecdotal," says Tom Loveless, director of the Brown Center on Education Policy at the Brookings Institution, a Washington think tank. "You have a group of kids who take tons of Advanced Placement (AP) classes and have lots of extracurricular activities" who experience a major school-related time crunch, he says. "But they're not numerous."

Overall, "all the data show that homework is not increasing," says Loveless. Currently 30 to 40 percent of

But high school homework loads haven't increased, while first-, second- and third-graders have been getting more homework, even though data show homework doesn't improve learning for young children. And with congressionally mandated standardized testing also aimed mainly at elementary school students, some schools also are pressuring kindergarten and preschool teachers to teach academic subjects to 4- and 5-year-olds, who often lack the physical and cognitive skills to handle them.

Meanwhile, under the 2002 No Child Left Behind law, teachers — especially in high-poverty schools — fear they'll be unable to bring their students to mandated achievement levels, which could lead to firings and school takeovers. That pressure on teachers may be seeping down to students in such schools, some researchers say.

Piles of homework dim children's love of learning — while depriving them of vital free time — without improving their school achievement, says Kalish's coauthor, Sara Bennett, a New York City lawyer.

"Polls say that kids no longer read for pleasure after age 8," mainly because of too much homework, "and I didn't like the future I was seeing for my children," says Bennett, who organized parents to fight homework at her children's schools. Many teachers argue that

U.S. students say that they have zero homework. Furthermore, a survey of college freshmen that's been repeated since the 1960s shows that high school homework reported by those students "is hitting all-time lows," about five hours per week — less than an hour per night, Loveless says.

Nevertheless, "I wouldn't want to trivialize the part of the population that's saying there's an overload," says Harris M. Cooper, director of Duke University's Program in Education. "It's unusual but not unheard of to find a teacher who's piling it on."

Especially in schools where many parents are professionals, some students voluntarily take on heavy homework burdens as they seek a competitive academic edge, says Cooper.

"There's lots of pressure to get into the best universities, and this has led some kids to take the most challenging courses they can," he says. "If you find a student with two AP courses and two honors courses, then each of those will be 45 minutes of homework a night" — three hours overall, more than the usually suggested maximum for high school of two hours a night, says Cooper. "Non-elite courses would only assign about 30 minutes a night each," he says.

Researchers agree that, to the extent homework burdens have increased in the past 20 years, it's the school backpacks of the youngest kids that have gained the most weight.

From 1997 to 2002, for example, the proportion of 6-to-8-year-old children being assigned homework on any given day rose from 34 percent to 64 percent.[2]

The increase has occurred even though reviews of research on homework by Cooper and others have turned up no evidence that homework actually improves achievement for children of that age.

"In my professional opinion, these trends suggest that the emphasis in the United States is kind of backwards,"

Students Do More Socializing Than Studying

A far higher percentage of high school students spend at least six hours per week on non-homework activities, such as socializing with friends, playing sports and surfing the Internet, rather than on homework or studying.

No. of Hours High School Students Spend on Various Activities in a Typical 7-Day Week

Activity	Number of Hours				
	0	1 or fewer	2-5	6-10	10+
Written homework	7%	36%	40%	12%	5%
Reading/studying for class	12%	43%	35%	7%	2%
Reading for self	16%	40%	30%	9%	5%
Participating in school-sponsored activities	32%	17%	21%	13%	17%
Practicing a sport or musical instrument	30%	12%	23%	16%	19%
Working for pay	34%	13%	18%	13%	21%
Volunteer work	48%	30%	16%	3%	2%
Exercising	8%	22%	36%	18%	15%
Watching TV/playing video games	6%	24%	39%	18%	13%
Surfing/chatting online	21%	27%	30%	14%	9%
Talking on the phone	8%	32%	32%	15%	13%
Socializing with friends outside of school	4%	10%	32%	27%	27%

* Percentages may not total 100 due to rounding.

Source: Ethan Yazzie-Mintz, "Voices of Students on Engagement: A Report on the 2006 High School Survey of Student Engagement," Center for Evaluation & Education Policy, Indiana University, Bloomington, 2006

says Gerald LeTendre, a professor of education at Pennsylvania State University.

Some school critics also say that new high-stakes testing mandated by some states and by the federal government over the past decade has increased pressure on teachers, whose anxiety often spills over onto students.

"We have a lot of discouraged teachers," especially in low-income schools, from standardized tests coupled with insufficient resources, says David C. Berliner, a professor of education at Arizona State University. "Schools of education aren't perfect," he acknowledges. "But it's bad when the students come back and say, 'This is not why I became a teacher.' They end up being drill sergeants."

Test pressure is increasing homework pressure in some schools, says Wendy A. Paterson, an associate professor of education at Buffalo State College, in New York. As "the curriculum becomes more loaded with requirements, such as expanded literacy classes" — extra reading-skills classes that have been added to improve test scores — "teachers get to the end of the day with material left, so they send it home" as homework, Paterson says. Such assignments, originally scheduled as in-class work, are usually "bad homework" — work that children should be doing with the teacher present and can't be expected to complete on their own — she says.

As parents and teachers debate the proper role of homework, testing and competition in American schools, here are some questions that are being asked:

Are students today under more academic pressure than in past generations?

With businesses and state and federal governments looking more to schools to produce savvier workers and entrepreneurs, some parents say today's kids face unprecedented school-related stress beginning as early as kindergarten. Critics of that view, however, point to data showing that many students, especially high-schoolers, may actually spend less time on schoolwork than in the past.

While some students probably are working harder these days, "about 90 percent aren't under much pressure," says Laurence Steinberg, a professor of psychology at Philadelphia's Temple University and author of one of the most extensive nationwide surveys ever done of U.S. teens. "A very high percentage of kids in our sample say they do as little as they can without getting into trouble," he says.

"Compared to high school kids in Japan or Korea, for example, our kids are coasting through a dream," says Steinberg. The difference shows up on international achievement tests. American elementary school students score well on tests, but by middle school U.S. scores begin to fall, and on the high school tests "we've fallen off the charts. If we were really making such great demands, this wouldn't be happening."

More information exists for today's children to absorb, but that isn't translating into excess academic pressure, said Lynn Spampinato, deputy superintendent of the Pittsburgh Public Schools. "There's more for children to learn today, more exposure to all kinds of information at younger ages." Nevertheless, "I'm not sure I believe we're pushing children to the edge. I'd say in many cases we're not challenging them enough."[3]

Education trends, such as a heavy focus on children's learning differences and "discovery" learning in which children follow their own interests, are making many classrooms less challenging, according to some analysts.

Learning "inevitably requires very substantial commitments of student time and effort," but contemporary trends require teachers "to produce learning in ways that are stimulating yet minimally obtrusive," with "only minimal levels of exertion" from students, said J. E. Stone, a professor of educational psychology at East Tennessee State University in Johnson City.[4]

Today's education mindset puts the whole burden on teachers to entice students to learn and to avoid boring or pushing them, a far cry from creating excessive stress, Stone says.

The American educational system puts ever more pressure on teachers but less on students, according to Paul A. Zoch, a longtime high school Latin teacher and classics scholar and the author of a recent book on school trends. Increasingly, "too many people in our society see the teachers as the ones who bear the responsibility for creating excellence," said Zoch. "When students fail to learn" today, parents and others "blame the teachers for not teaching in the correct way for each student."[5]

But others point to what they say are new, intense pressures on at least some children.

For example, as more families in the United States and around the world hope to send their children to top-tier colleges, students in those families and neighborhoods face more intense pressure to compete for limited spots.

"It's fair to say the pressure has increased on the top tier of kids applying to competitive colleges and universities," says Steinberg.

"It's gotten about 200 percent harder to get into Harvard than it was in the 1960s," says David P. Baker, an education professor at Pennsylvania State University.

In suburban areas where many parents are educated professionals, "we are seeing increasing anxiety and depression levels" and sleep deprivation, from students under pressure to be accepted at a handful of elite

Low-Income Kids Face Toughest Pressures

Creating a family atmosphere in the classroom helps

Stress is a universal affliction among students, but the impact of psychological stress and school pressure is particularly hard on low-income students, many analysts say.

New high-stakes testing required by the federal No Child Left Behind (NCLB) law, for example, puts more pressure on students in low-income areas, says Peter Sacks, the author of several books on standardized testing and the relationship between social class and education.

In suburban areas, where children typically enter school with the social, physical and cognitive skills needed to master academic requirements later on, test pressure doesn't constantly haunt the classroom, says Sacks. "Teaching and learning can be done for the sake of teaching and learning, not with [testing] proficiency targets always in mind."

In low-income schools, however, many kindergartners start out with well under half the skills and knowledge that school-ready children are expected to have, "so the ground they have to cover over time is so much greater," says Sacks.

"You want to talk about pressure? The entire school has a siege mentality because failure to meet the [NCLB] goals can lead to the firing of teachers" and takeover of the school, he says. "As a consequence, in many low-income schools teaching and learning is reduced to whatever is necessary to score on the test."

In the new age of high-stakes testing, "over and over again, I hear teachers say, 'We have no time if students have a question,' " says Sharon L. Nichols, an assistant professor of educational psychology at the University of Texas, San Antonio. Because schools with many low-income students have the most ground to make up, "this is disproportionately affecting poor and minority kids and further disenfranchising them," Nichols says.

High-stakes testing also can act as "a disincentive for recruiting" the neediest kids to good schools, since administrators may fear an influx of high-needs children will harm overall test scores, says Vielka MacFarlane, principal and founder of Celerity Nascent Charter School in Los Angeles. Nevertheless, her school "gives priority to kids who are several years behind" developmental and academic norms, she says.

She hopes to overcome testing hurdles by persuading state school auditors to "compare us to the specific schools our kids are coming from" and to "show progress through longitudinal assessment of our own kids," she says.

Even modest homework demands take a higher toll on poor students, according to John Buell, a former professor at the College of the Atlantic, in Bar Harbor, Maine, and the author of two books on homework. Students in poor families often have greater family responsibilities and lack basic supports for doing homework, such as a quiet, well-lit place to study, dictionaries and Internet access, he says.

In a study of high dropout rates among low-income, rural students in Maine, Buell and a colleague conducted extensive interviews, asking dropouts "if there was a point in their education when they knew they simply were not going to make it," he said. "Much to our surprise, every student had a story about homework."[1]

Indeed, among the lowest-income students, mostly black and Hispanic, "half don't even graduate" from high school in an era when graduation is expected of virtually everyone, says Laurence Steinberg, a professor of psychology at Philadelphia's Temple University and author of one of the largest sociological surveys ever done on U.S. teens. Impoverished children also have the highest rate of mental-health problems, another sign of stress in their lives, he says.

Building in supports to help students withstand such pressures is a mission of some schools that seek to raise academic achievement in city neighborhoods. To provide a supportive family atmosphere in the classroom, the New City Public Schools Charter School in Long Beach, Calif., teaches some lessons in mixed-age classrooms, says Co-Director Stephanie Lee. New City also aims to make its students bilingual in English and Spanish, so afternoons feature multi-age K-5 groups, with "the older kids serving as language models," says Lee. New City children also keep the same homeroom teacher for three years running, and teachers make frequent home visits.

"Many of our kids are coming in here feeling like failures," says MacFarlane. To boost students' faith that they can achieve, "every kid needs to feel success throughout the school day," she says. To do that, Celerity Nascent also "infuses the [extended] school day with martial arts, dance, painting and yoga," she says. "We're here on Saturdays and Sundays, too," says MacFarlane. "We have to kick the kids out."

---

[1] Quoted in "Author Does His Homework on Hot Topic," *Education World,* Feb. 10, 2006, www.education-world.com.

School Is Leading Cause of Stress

Nearly two-thirds of San Francisco Bay-area parents say the amount of schoolwork assigned to their children is a cause of stress. More than half the parents said pressure to excel also exerts stress.

Factors Contributing to Children's Stress, According to San Francisco Bay-Area Parents
(by amount of stress)

Source	Very much	Somewhat	Not very much	Not at all	Too young to say
Amount of schoolwork	23.8%	40.0%	15.0%	16.8%	4.1%
Pressure to excel in school	11.2%	42.6%	11.5%	29.5%	4.4%
Peer relationships	11.6%	35.5%	21.9%	28.6%	1.1%
Extracurricular activities	4.9%	28.1%	13.5%	52.0%	1.4%
Difficulties with family members	4.0%	18.3%	10.0%	65.9%	1.2%
Divorce or separation issues	8.5%	13.8%	5.0%	70.1%	1.1%
Family financial pressures	3.8%	12.2%	11.6%	69.3%	2.8%
Illness or death of loved one	4.5%	12.9%	8.6%	70.7%	2.3%

* Percentages may not total 100 due to rounding.

Source: "Child Stress, by Source: 2006" Kids Data, August 2006

colleges, says Denise Clark Pope, a lecturer at Stanford University's School of Education and author of a book on stressed-out students. In a recent survey of 10 schools in the San Francisco Bay area, Pope found schools reporting "higher percentages of kids with stress and anxiety and kids cheating."

In the Northeast, too, more affluent parents are "inappropriately pushing" kids beyond their capabilities to be "superkids," says Carl Arinoldo, a psychologist in Stony Brook, N.Y., who has written books on managing stress. The pressure reaches to the youngest children, says Arinoldo. "There are a number of preschools in Manhattan, for example, that are hammering away at academics," even though 3- and 4-year-olds "need to run around and play spontaneously" instead.

To the extent that increased school pressure exists, it's hitting younger children harder, many experts agree.

For example, the only place that school homework levels have been increasing "is the only place where it really doesn't make sense — elementary school," says Penn State's LeTendre.

From 1997 to 2002, the proportion of 6-to-8-year-old students assigned homework rose from 34 percent to 64 percent, according to professors from the University of Maryland and McGill University.[6]

"I have witnessed firsthand the changes in grade-level expectations," a parent from Roanoke, Va., wrote in an online chat. What were fifth-grade lessons three decades ago are third-grade lessons today, she said.[7]

Are schools assigning too much homework?

Several recent books have called for an end to homework, describing it as a growing burden on American children that threatens family life. Some analysts argue, however, that while a few teachers may go overboard, most students still bring home only modest amounts.

In surveys, about 10 percent of parents complain students get too much homework, 25 percent say not enough is assigned and the remainder — a strong majority — says the amounts are just about right, said Loveless of Brookings. "The issue has been overhyped," partly because "journalists run in the high-powered crowd whose children feel pressured to take four Advanced Placement courses," he says. There are students in that position, and some likely are overburdened, "but they're not numerous."[8]

In a 2006 Associated Press-AOL poll, 57 percent of parents said amounts of homework are "just right," and the rest split between "too little" and "too much," says Cooper of Duke. "Educators will never be able to please everyone, and they're doing well when three-out-of-five people are pretty happy with the current amounts."[9]

Given the level of distractions in modern life, it's likely that some families who complain about homework overestimate the amounts, says Loveless. "Compare a middle-class kid's bedroom today to one 30 years ago," he says. "It didn't have cell phones or instant messaging or downloading from the Internet. So when kids are supposedly in their rooms doing homework, how much time are they actually spending on homework?"

East Tennessee University's Stone argues that many adults are "too likely to ignore the key reality about learning: It's more than play."

"Learning takes work; it's a life-dislocating activity" that will inevitably lead to some parent-child struggle, Stone says. It's parents' job to require children to complete school chores, despite struggles, because the short-term pain brings long-term gain, he says. "Kids aren't aware of their long-term needs," so they protest, he says. "They don't realize they're going to run into a world where there are no excuses."

Homework loads are about the same as they've always been for most students, says Penn State's LeTendre. What has changed is the amount of "structured time" experienced by children today, a fact that "has been left out of policy discussions," he says. Unlike in the past, most "parents are no longer home to welcome the kids after school," in part because many children play sports or attend classes until nearly dinner time. The result is a changing perception about what constitutes "too much" homework, he says.

"Fifteen minutes of homework doesn't seem like a lot if you have nothing to do," but it can seem overwhelming if a child arrives home from another structured activity at 5:30 in the afternoon and has a 7:30 or 8 o'clock bedtime, LeTendre says.

But homework opponents say there's evidence that many children are assigned unreasonable amounts of work.

In the recent Associated Press-AOL poll, elementary school students reported an average of 78 minutes of homework each school night, and middle-schoolers

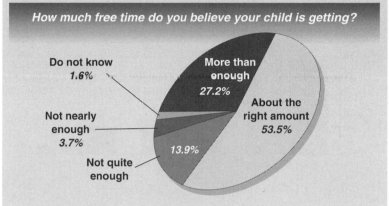

Parents Say Children Get Enough Free Time

More than three-quarters of San Francisco Bay-area parents say their children have the right amount or more than enough free time, despite homework and other activities. Affluent parents are typically concerned about their kids' lack of free time.

How much free time do you believe your child is getting?

Do not know 1.6%

More than enough 27.2%

About the right amount 53.5%

Not nearly enough 3.7%

13.9%

Not quite enough

* Percentages do not total 100 due to rounding.

Source: "Parent Ratings of Adequacy of Child's Free Time: 2006," Kids Data, August 2006

reported 99 minutes, says *The Case Against Homework* coauthor Bennett. That's a far bigger homework load than children would have if teachers were following the so-called 10-minutes-per-grade rule of thumb endorsed by groups like the National Education Association and the National Parent Teacher Association, Bennett points out.

In addition, "there is no evidence of any correlation between homework and achievement in elementary school," yet homework amounts for grade-school children have been rising, says Bennett, and possibly causing harm.

In researching her book, Bennett found that "homework can cause a lot of family conflict." Moreover, assigning homework to young children may be conditioning them to cheat later on, she says. Many parents "say their kids come home and need help in math" or help with a project, like a diorama or science project. "When the kids get a lot of parental help" in the early years, "they get dependent on it," Bennett says. "It confuses them about whether it's OK to get help with your work."

Researchers have found that about five math problems "are enough to tell whether a child understands the

Few Complain About Homework

A majority of parents and students think the right amount of homework is being assigned. Only one-fifth of students complain about too much work.

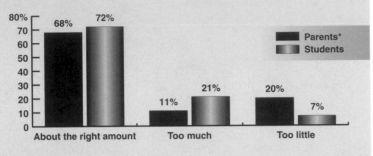

Overall, do you feel that you/your child is getting too much homework, too little or about the right amount?

* Percentages do not add to 100% due to rounding.

Source: "Reality Check 2006: A Report from Education Insights at Public Agenda," Public Agenda, 2006

concept and can move on or doesn't understand and needs help," yet many teachers assign 30 or more problems, says coauthor Kalish.

"Even the U.S. Department of Education" makes the five-problem recommendation, says Kalish. "If a child who didn't get the right idea in class slogs through 30 problems, she's just cementing the wrong method in her brain." Meanwhile, a child who did catch on, finds the 30 problems drudgery and ends up hating school, Kalish says.

Excessive homework has caused some low-income students to drop out of school, according to Etta Kralovec, an associate professor of education at the University of Arizona at Sierra Vista and author of the book *The End of Homework.* The more hectic family lives and greater responsibilities of many lower-income students, along with a lack of the Internet and other learning tools at home have led some to give up on school altogether, Kralovec said.[10] (*See sidebar, p. 187.*)

Despite popular belief, eighth-graders in some industrialized countries actually do less homework than U.S. children while scoring just as well or better on achievement tests, said Kralovec. (*See chart, p. 193.*) Many other countries depend on more in-class time and less homework than the United States, with better results, because

classrooms are a "sacred space" specially set aside for study, and teachers' help is available, she said.[11]

"It's not that homework is wrong," it's that too much current homework is of the fill-out-the-worksheet variety and keeps children from other valuable activities, like social interaction, says Arizona State's Berliner. "If homework has the effect of isolating the child from his family, then that's bad, generally," says Berliner. A better idea would be to ask children and parents to play some games together and talk about them or watch and discuss a television program, he says.

Experts on all sides of the issue agree that the current American practice of increasing homework for younger kids while allowing many high-schoolers to carry a relatively easy load makes little sense.

"All the data suggest that homework helps at the high school level, has mixed results in middle school and either makes no difference or even has negative consequences for elementary students," says LeTendre, yet current U.S. homework trends go exactly the other way.

Are high-stakes tests putting too much pressure on students?

About 20 years ago, some states began implementing so-called high-stakes tests — exams that students must pass to earn diplomas or move to the next grade. The 2002 No Child Left Behind law added another layer of tests, this time with high stakes for schools themselves. Under federal regulations set by NCLB, schools that don't produce required test scores could eventually have their entire staffs replaced or be taken over by the state or a private group.[12]

Some critics argue that the tests unduly increase pressure on students. Others, however, say there's no evidence that testing is creating rushed or anxious classrooms.

In a study of Arkansas fourth-graders, University of Arkansas Professor of Educational Statistics Sean

W. Mulvenon found "the vast majority of students do not exhibit stress and have positive attitudes towards standardized testing programs."[13]

While some students did express anxiety, the "overall student sentiment" was that the tests didn't raise anxiety or result in greater pressure from teachers or parents to perform, according to Mulvenon. Furthermore, students who did report more anxiety or pressure didn't do worse on the tests, Mulvenon reported.

In a study of Minnesota's high-stakes tests, University of Minnesota Assistant Professor of Evaluation Studies Stuart S. Yeh found that most principals and teachers believed that the state's program — which takes pains to make tests match the school curriculum — has improved the learning environment in many schools.

To prepare students for the tests, teachers now work as teams to "enrich the curriculum," a middle-school principal told Yeh. Contrary to what many experts fear, teachers aren't "teaching to the test" — by exclusively drilling students on questions similar to those on the exam or alerting them to test-taking tricks, said an elementary school principal. Instead, teachers concentrate on teaching academic "skills that enable kids to take the test without a high level of anxiety," the principal said.[14]

Minnesota's testing has also helped students with learning deficiencies, some teachers and principals told Yeh. Because of the tests, funding is now provided to bring in learning specialists. Under the testing regime, "we're seeing that help is made available to" more students who face learning difficulties, said a high school science teacher.[15]

Overall, "the upside" of the age of high-stakes testing "is that everybody takes school much more seriously now," says Steve Peha, an education consultant in Carrboro, N.C.

Under the new testing regimes, many teachers are "feeling an extraordinary amount of pressure, and that does affect the kids," says Peha. Nevertheless, "most of the pressure" teachers are feeling "is out of proportion to the reality," Peha argues. "Schools with low scores don't get shut down; some states do require passing tests, but most states have devised other ways for students to get diplomas, like attendance. Most of the pressure is really the fear of the unknown," because "we're really only 10 years into the accountability culture."

In at least some classrooms, teachers' testing anxiety clearly affects students, says Marshalita Peterson, an

Eighth-graders in Madison, W. Va., practice for an archery tournament in May 2006. Compared with students from other countries, Americans have less academic work but more extracurricular activities — lessons, team sports and after-school jobs — which may partly account for the feelings of pressure that some report.

AP Photo/Jeff Gentner

associate professor of education at historically black Spelman College in Atlanta. "There are some teachers who say, 'You have to do well on this test,' and in response students self-impose requirements" to achieve, Peterson says. "Some can't take the emotional strain of that, and it shows."

What gets lost for such students is not only "the pleasure of learning" but also the ability to apply their learning outside of the test, Peterson says. "If the class focus is, 'You have to do this because of the test,' " the goal of "mastery learning" — learning to transfer new skills to other places — often suffers, she says. "You end up only going through the motions."

Some testing pressure falls on the youngest children, preschoolers through second-graders, who aren't even old enough to be required to take the tests.

"If a school is getting pressure for students to perform on tests in third grade, then the third-grade teacher is looking to the second-grade teacher and the first-grade teacher" to help make that happen, says Peterson. Such pressure has an upside, when "a group of teachers ends up working more together."

But some schools take the collaboration too far, pushing teachers of younger children into teaching content that most of the children in their classes aren't ready to master, Peterson says.

International comparisons warn that too-early academic lessons actually may slow students down, says

CHRONOLOGY

1880s-1940s *Some educators and doctors argue against homework on health grounds. Boston, San Francisco and other cities ban or limit homework.*

1890 Less than 6 percent of American students attend high school.

1900 *Ladies' Home Journal* Editor Edward W. Bok calls homework "barbarous," publishes articles by doctors and parents who argue it harms children's health.

1930 Nearly 51 percent of American students attend high school, but academic courses begin to give way to classes that have no tests or homework, such as health.

1940 More than 73 percent of American teenagers attend high school.

1948 Only 8 percent of high school students do two hours or more of homework daily.

1950s-1960s *High school homework increases amid fears that the U.S. is becoming less economically competitive.*

1957 U.S. high schools increase homework in response to the Soviet Union's surprise launch of the first satellite, *Sputnik 1.* For most of the 1960s, about 20 percent of high-schoolers do two hours or more of homework daily, an all-time high.

1958 National Defense Education Act funds schools to beef up math, science and foreign-language courses.

1961 Sociologist James Coleman's book *The Adolescent Society* declares that a separate, influential, teenage culture has developed that values good looks over learning.

1970s *High school students' homework drops to pre-1950s levels.*

1970 Percentage of students taking demanding academic courses falls. . . . Harvard University accepts about a third of students who apply.

1980s *U.S. students' scores slip on international tests, prompting a rise in homework levels, especially for elementary- and middle-school students.*

1983 National commission initiated by President Ronald Reagan reports in "A Nation at Risk" that a "tide of mediocrity" is overwhelming American schools.

1990s *Parents and educators fight rising homework loads for children. Some states institute standardized tests as a high school graduation requirement.*

1997 Students 6 to 8 years old do twice as much homework as in 1981.

1999 TV host Oprah Winfrey highlights parents' complaints about an "onslaught of homework."

2000s *Congress inaugurates "high stakes" testing for schools, which can eventually face takeover or mass firings if they fail to meet federal goals.*

2002 Congress passes No Child Left Behind law (NCLB).

2006 The principal of Needham High School in Massachusetts limits homework and stops publishing the honor roll in the local newspaper. . . . College freshmen report some of the lowest levels of high school homework ever. . . . Associated Press poll finds 57 percent of parents say their children get the right amount of homework. . . . Schools in Greenville, S.C., limit homework.

2007 School districts in San Marcos, Calif., and Middletown, Ohio, try excluding homework from course grades. . . . Norwalk, Conn., considers limiting daily homework and banning weekend homework for grade-schoolers. . . . Several San Francisco Bay-area schools ban elementary-grade homework. . . . Harvard accepts about 10 percent of applicants.

2014 All U.S. students must demonstrate proficiency in math and reading by this date under NCLB.

Arizona State's Berliner. Finland and Sweden, for example, delay many formal lessons such as reading until first grade and later, and yet their students are "among the highest achievers" on international tests, he says.

BACKGROUND

Schooling Expands

Today's lawmakers and business leaders have upped the pressure on American schools, urging them to raise graduation rates to 100 percent. Meanwhile, a growing number of students, mostly from affluent families, compete ever more fiercely for a limited number of spots in top colleges.[16]

At the root of the pressure, according to Penn State's Baker, is a single, big idea that has come to dominate the thinking about education: Academic achievement "has become about the only way to invest in your kids' future."

In the past, numerous paths could be taken to successful adulthood, including joining a family business and learning a trade. But today, in the United States and, increasingly, worldwide, alternate opportunities "are gone," Baker says. As a result, "Longer and longer school careers are being seen everywhere. You're ending up with a schooled society, where school is the only game in town, so everybody has to play it." Even for students who don't fit the linguistic/mathematical mode of most academic schooling, "there are far fewer alternatives" than in the past. "That's what creates the pressure," he says.

It was only a hundred years ago that industrial nations came to believe that government should provide basic education to all, says Baker. Since then, the proportion of children attending school has grown rapidly. During the early 20th century, wealthier countries expanded their primary education, and in the 1930s and '40s secondary education took off. But "only in the mid-'60s was it assumed that everybody should finish high school," Baker says.

As early as 1930, about half of all American students attended high school. And by the late 1960s, only half of all students were graduating from high school, Baker says.

The change didn't happen just because modern jobs require more training, says Baker. Instead, it reflects "the success of a cultural idea — that we can make people better through education." That's evident in the fact that

Foreign Middle-Schoolers Do More Homework

The percentage of American elementary school students who spend four hours or more a day on homework is roughly the same as for the average student overseas. Among middle schoolers, however, the percentage of Americans is half that of the average foreign student.

Percentage of Students Who Spend Four or More Hours Daily on Homework
(in selected countries)

Elementary Students		Middle School Students	
Iran	18%	Lebanon	24%
Armenia	17	Armenia	23
Morocco	17	South Africa	22
Tunisia	16	Iran	18
Philippines	12	Russia	15
Italy	10	Italy	14
Hong Kong	9	Egypt	13
United States	**8**	Philippines	9
Australia	7	Israel	9
Taiwan	5	Singapore	8
Russia	5	**United States**	**5**
Singapore	5	Australia	3
England	4	Sweden	3
Netherlands	3	England	3
Japan	1	Japan	1
International average: 9%		**International average: 10%**	

Source: Gerald K. LeTendre and Motoko Akiba, "A Nation Spins its Wheels: The Role of Homework and National Homework Policies in National Student Achievement Levels in Math and Science," paper presented to the Comparative and International Education Society, February 2007

vocational training now takes a back seat to academic courses in most places, including the United States, says Baker. Governments around the world "have totally bought into" the idea that higher-order thinking skills and academic subjects, rather than vocational skills, should be the main content of education for virtually all students, he says.

Baker doesn't foresee any letup in the expansion of academic schooling. "Every time people predicted over the past 100 years that schooling wouldn't expand, they were totally wrong," he says. Today "graduate students and undergraduates want two degrees rather than one. A smart kid in law school wants a PhD in economics," too.

Different Visions

But while the world's children go to school in ever greater numbers, exactly how students learn best remains a matter of debate.

Among Americans, especially, some parents believe in allowing children to develop largely at their own pace, pressure-free, says Brookings's Loveless. These parents are likely to oppose both homework and testing, he says. Meanwhile, some cultures embrace a general belief "that children's main job is to master all the stuff that the culture thinks is important," leading parents there to value study highly, Loveless says.

Most American students are below the international average for time spent on academics, taking class time and homework time together, although many may be busier in some ways than students in other countries.

American teenagers "go to school less," with "a shorter school year . . . a shorter school day . . . and less homework," said Loveless. "When you look at how education is thought of as part of a teenager's life in Europe and Asia, it is totally different than the United States."[17]

By international comparisons, American students have less academic work but "more structured time" — in extracurricular lessons and clubs, team sports and after-school jobs — than in other countries, perhaps partly accounting for the stress that some feel, says Penn State's LeTendre.

"Over half of American seniors work part time at some point during the school year," said Loveless. Around the world this is . . . absolutely unheard of. In fact, it is a stigma in most of Europe and Asia if you work when you are a teenager; it means something bad. It means your parents don't care enough about education. Your family needs money," he said.[18]

When it comes to homework, international comparisons are tricky, partly because cultures have different notions about what actually counts as homework.

Some "high-achieving Asian nations report almost no homework," but that report may be deceiving, says Loveless. In China, for example, "a child may come home without a homework assignment, but nevertheless the kid will sit down at a table with mom and study all evening," he says. In countries like Korea and France, there's "a thriving market of after-school schools," but that work often isn't called "homework" when people are surveyed, he says. Whether there's formal homework or not, however, in most European and Asian countries "the kids are really focused on learning" as their main occupation, Loveless says.

Moreover, when it comes to assigned homework, international studies don't show a clear connection between homework and achievement.

For example, on international tests many countries with the highest scores, including Japan, the Czech Republic and Denmark, report very little assigned homework, says Penn State's Baker. Meanwhile, students in countries including Thailand, Greece and Iran get low average scores but attend schools that assign a lot of homework.[19]

Differing views of homework's purpose also make cultural comparisons difficult. For example, the United States is one of the few nations where teachers include homework scores as an element of course grades. Elsewhere, homework is often regarded as practice or preparation only. Eighty-two percent of American teachers give grades to homework, compared to 14 percent in Japan and 6 percent in Germany.[20]

Cold War Fears

In the United States, the pros and cons of homework are regularly debated. However, many researchers say that while attitudes have varied, the average American student has seldom been overburdened with take-home work.

Beginning in the final decades of the 19th century, education theorists, doctors and others launched a long campaign against what many thought was an overemphasis on at-home drill and memorization, especially in high schools.[21]

In 1901, for example, California legislators banned homework for children under age 15, who lawmakers declared would be better off playing outdoors. In 1941, an article in the *Encyclopedia of Education Research* declared that "the benefits of assigned homework are too small to counterbalance the disadvantages."

By the 1940s, homework opponents had largely won the day, and in 1948 only 8 percent of U.S. high school students reported doing more than two hours of homework daily.

Beginning around 1950, however, a new wave of critics complained that American schools had become anti-intellectual and soft.

In 1957, the Soviet Union's surprise launch of *Sputnik 1*, the world's first satellite, further roused the critics. Worried that schools weren't preparing students to best America's Cold War rivals, Congress in 1958 passed the National Defense Education Act, increasing federal aid for math, science, foreign language and technical education.

The new national focus on education ushered in an era of more homework, primarily in high schools. By 1960, more than 20 percent of high school students reported doing more than two hours of homework each day.

But the trend survived only for about a decade. By the early 1970s, high school homework levels were nearly back to the very low levels of the 1940s, with fewer than 10 percent of students reporting more than two hours daily. By the early 1980s, the proportion of high school students reporting more than two hours of daily homework edged up slightly, to just over 10 percent, where it has largely remained ever since.

Bulging Backpacks?

In the early 1980s, homework again became a national issue. In 1983, President Ronald Reagan's National Commission on Excellence in Education issued "A Nation at Risk," a report arguing the once mighty American education system was "being eroded by a rising tide of mediocrity."

Effort and discipline were prominent among the elements missing from the schools, the commission said. "Our society and its educational institutions seem to have lost sight of the basic purposes of schooling and of the high expectations and disciplined effort needed to attain them."[22]

AP Photo/John Raoux

Julia Austin teaches her middle school students in Orlando, Fla., not to use instant-messaging slang in their writing. Some educators say high-stakes testing mandated by the federal government and some states has increased pressure on teachers, who pass on their anxiety to students.

In response, schools began increasing homework, but mostly for younger children. Indeed, over the past 25 years, elementary and middle schools have increased homework loads, with the largest increases for the very youngest children — first- through third-graders.

Between 1981 and 1997, time diaries filled out by families showed that 6-to-8-year-olds' homework time more than doubled, from an average 52 minutes per week to 128 minutes.[23]

Meanwhile, in the same survey, average weekly homework time for 9-to-12-year-olds only rose from three hours and 22 minutes in 1981 to three hours and 41 minutes in 1997.[24]

High school students' homework burden has increased little overall. In a national survey in 1999, for example, 11th-graders reported only slightly more homework than eighth-graders.

Only 12 percent of 11th-graders reported two hours or more of daily study, compared to 8 percent of eighth-graders,

Tailoring Teaching to Fit the Brain

Neuroscience helps overcome students' cognitive difficulties

Learning research suggests that "the more homework is individually structured to the student, the better it may work," says Pennsylvania State University Professor of Education Gerald LeTendre. But time-pressed teachers often respond to demands for improved student achievement with one-size-fits-all assignments like worksheets. And "there is not a lot of evidence this is effective," says LeTendre.

Some education experts say that as the findings of neuroscience seep into schools of education, the tide may turn in favor of more individualized instruction. That prospect isn't as scary as some teachers think, says Mary Dean Barringer, CEO of the All Kinds of Minds Institute, in Chapel Hill, N.C., which educates parents and teachers on individualized approaches to teaching children, based on cognitive science.

"The main mistake teachers make is they think you need a different plan for every kid," says Barringer. "That's not it. The key is: Just don't go right down the middle" in your instruction, she says. Teachers can learn the particular cognitive challenges presented by different subject matter and point them out to students, along with some strategies that will help those with differently wired brains.

For example, many youngsters are more spatially than verbally oriented, says Michael Gurian, a family therapist in Colorado Springs who has written several books on learning.

One strategy that helps spatially oriented kids succeed at writing is having them tap into their spatial-thinking abilities before committing pen to paper, Gurian says. "Allow the kids to draw a storyboard of what they want to write; then, after an hour of drawing it have them start writing," he says. The visual kick-start makes their writing better organized and more detailed, he says.

Different lessons call for different learning skills, and students can be shown how to compensate if they're weaker in those areas, says Barringer.

For example, in a science course, "there are lots of sequences that students must keep track of," such as the individual steps of an experiment they're carrying out in class, she says. "You will have some kids whose minds aren't wired for temporal sequences," so it's important to point this out and suggest other ways they can approach the task, like visualizing a sequence as they read or hear about it, Barringer says.

Over the past three decades, neuroscience studies of conditions like Alzheimer's disease and dyslexia have shown a lot about the very different wiring of individual human minds, says Barringer. "There have been just amazing breakthroughs in brain research and learning," she says.

But while "much of the new science has emerged in the last decade, many teachers were trained 20 to 30 years ago" and aren't aware of the information, she says. Nevertheless, many observant teachers already have a repertoire of strategies that facilitate learning different kinds of material, although they don't often realize that they do, says Barringer.

The place for teachers and parents to start is by observing an individual child's behavior and schoolwork to see how the child's mind is wired. Too often, when a child has learning difficulties, the entire focus is on what is going wrong, says Barringer. Instead, "look first at what's going right," she recommends. "You get a very good profile from looking at the child's strengths," which enables teachers and parents to help the child compensate for deficiencies.

"Kids who have differences in learning have faced added pressure from being in schools where their minds were misunderstood, she says. But today there's a much greater possibility of finding a parent or an educator who has the knowledge to help. Kids in this decade have a better chance of finding someone."

---

although two hours of homework is often considered the gold standard for high school students and too much for middle-schoolers. Close to two-thirds of both eighth- and 11th-graders said that they had less than an hour of daily homework.[25]

Research shows little evidence that homework improves learning or school achievement for children in the early grades, says Arizona State's Berliner. "Through junior high,

the relationship between homework and achievement doesn't exist, while in high school there is a relationship," he says.

For older students, a moderate amount of homework — 60 to 90 minutes per night for middle-schoolers and 120 minutes for high-schoolers — has been shown to improve student achievement, says Cooper of Duke University. Students who do less as well as those who

How Cognitive Science Helps Teachers

Educators say research findings are not widely understood

Are our children overscheduled? Should preschool children be taught to read? When does academic challenge become academic pressure?

Cognitive science is beginning to answer such questions, but the findings don't always make it into the classroom.

Putting discoveries in cognitive science — the study of thought and learning processes — to work in education will happen, but the process is only beginning, says Bror Saxberg, chief learning officer at K¹² Inc., a Herndon, Va., firm that develops online-learning products. "When you look at how teachers are trained, there's still not much said about how minds work," he says.

Here are some of the research findings that analysts say should be more widely understood by schools and families:

- Many American children and teens are overscheduled and overstimulated, putting their health and ability to learn at risk. What look like activities that lead to children's success, such as sports teams and music lessons, are "overstimulation that actually can stress a growing child's brain," says Michael Gurian, a family therapist in Colorado Springs.

  Parents should remember that "boredom is crucial" for children to develop their own personalities and talent profiles, Gurian says. "You have to let your kids be bored for at least an hour a day" — with no TV or computer — to figure out what they enjoy doing. "If they're never bored, they'll never find out who they are."

  Sleep is also crucial for brain development and learning, and "about 40 percent of children don't get enough," Gurian says. Sleep deprivation is an unrecognized problem for many teenagers, too, says Denise Clark Pope, a lecturer at the Stanford University School of Education. "Not a lot of people know that adolescents need nine and a half hours."

- Studies show "that kids who attend preschool — traditional, non-academic preschool — do well in K-12," says

Gary Mangiofico, CEO of Los Angeles Universal Preschool, an independent public-benefit corporation promoting preschool.

"However, some have backward-mapped from that to argue that we should focus on preschool as an academic thing, to begin preparing children at age 4 for the high-stakes testing they will face later," Mangiofico says. But 4-year-olds' main developmental jobs include learning how to socialize, use their bodies in large-motor and fine-motor skills and get better control of their emotions — skills they must master before they can successfully tackle reading and writing, he says.

- Cognitive scientists say mastering a complex skill takes "10 years of deliberate practice," according to Saxberg. "It's the way Tiger Woods keeps rethinking his swing." After a period of slow, conscious practice, though, skills are mastered and move into "the huge infrastructure of subconscious modules in which expertise you've already developed is stored," he says. That's what has happened once we can write longhand and think through an essay at the same time, he explains.

  There's "no short cut" to going through an initial period of slow practice building any skill, says Saxberg. But the good news is that mastering a skill doesn't depend on innate talent but "whether you have the will, patience and interest to put in that practice," he says.

- Another lesson from cognitive science is that minds do best "when they're challenged, but not too challenged," says Saxberg. Teachers assigning homework must make sure that the work is doable and that kids have a way to prove that they've mastered the task; then they can stop practicing, Saxberg explains.

  "Some teachers think they're doing the right thing by assigning mounds of worksheets for practice," he says. But once children know how to do it, they begin to hate the work, and their performance drops off, Saxberg says. Assignments that are too difficult also prevent students from performing well, he says.

report doing more both achieve less, says Cooper, who published a study in 2006 synthesizing all existing research on homework amounts. (*See "At Issue," p. 199.*)

For elementary school students, no amount of homework raises academic achievement, Cooper says. Nevertheless, a rule of thumb for many educators is that

Heavy backpacks suggest these Boston students have plenty of homework. The National Education Association and the National Parent Teacher Association endorse the so-called 10-minutes-per-grade rule of thumb for homework.

10 minutes of daily homework per grade of school is appropriate, and that principle seems to be in line with children's developing attention spans and grasp of study skills, he says.

Even more important than how much homework is what kind, say many educators. Nevertheless, while schools of education acquaint teachers-in-training with theories of learning and lesson planning, none actually offers specific classes on assigning homework.

"I called 15 schools of education, and I've spoken to thousands of teachers, but I never came across a teacher yet who has taken a course" on homework, says *The Case Against Homework* coauthor Bennett.

Teachers don't always give enough thought to the ramifications of their assignments, but they should, said Bea McGarvey, an education consultant who formerly was executive director for education in the Portland, Maine, public schools.

She had traditionally asked her grade-school students to build dioramas depicting favorite scenes in the children's book *Make Way for Ducklings*, McGarvey recounted. But as she considered the issue of homework more

closely, she decided that the assignment didn't make sense.

Did students need to complete a three- to five-day project that in the end would demonstrate only a literal understanding of the story? No, McGarvey decided. Writing a short description of a favorite scene would demonstrate exactly the same amount of learning without wasting hours with scissors and glue, she concluded.[26]

The question of how much and what homework to assign will be crucial as long as schools look for the best ways to help students learn.

But the current battle — mostly led by parents who decry homework's threat to family time — reflects "larger cultural wars" over the place of work in Americans' lives generally, said John Buell, an education scholar and columnist for the *Bangor* [Maine] *Daily News* and the author of two books on homework.[27]

As commutes lengthen and more adults have a 24/7 connection to their jobs through cell phones and laptops, "Americans increasingly have a . . . love-hate relationship with work," considering it "one of the central meanings of life" but resenting the time it takes from other things, said Buell. "Although the debate over homework involves genuine pedagogical issues, one cannot fully understand . . . the heat surrounding it without . . . attention to this cultural civil war over whether work is to retain its all-encompassing place in our culture."[28]

CURRENT SITUATION

Reevaluating Homework

A spate of recent books and news reports questioning the value of homework has prompted many schools to reevaluate their policies. Meanwhile, data are just beginning to emerge about how the new era of high-stakes testing under NCLB is affecting students and teachers.

Dialogue among parents, teachers, and school administrators often leads to lighter loads of more carefully developed assignments, says anti-homework author Kalish. The dialogue can be a bit hard to launch, she says. Parents tend to consider homework such a time-honored tradition "that there's no hope of change," she says. At the same time, "the school administration often thinks parents want more homework."

Do American students get too much homework?

YES
Nancy Kalish
Coauthor, The Case Against Homework:
How Homework Is Hurting Our
Children and What We Can Do About It

Written for *CQ Researcher*, July 2007

When most of us were growing up, our homework was manageable. We were able to complete it without constant supervision, then run out to play (and burn some calories), have dinner with our families and go to bed at a reasonable hour. But today many young children are giving up all those things to spend hour after sedentary hour at their desks.

According to a 2006 Associated Press-America Online poll, elementary school students average 78 minutes of homework per night while middle school students average 99 minutes. That might not sound like much. But it means children are routinely spending 50 percent more time on their homework than the 10 minutes total per grade level per night recommended by the National Education Association, the National PTA and Duke University's Harris M. Cooper (essay at right). And when researching our book, my coauthor and I had no trouble finding many children who put in much more time, including first-graders working more than an hour each night.

Those time limits were established for a reason: When schools push beyond them, many children, including teens, are developmentally unable to cope. They react by misbehaving, becoming anxious, burning out and eventually coming to hate school — not exactly the way we want our young people to feel about learning. The stated goals of homework — to foster responsibility and reinforce learning — are often overshadowed by the crushing load.

For all this sacrifice, you'd assume there's a great payoff. But there isn't. Cooper's own review of the homework research found little correlation between homework and achievement in elementary school and only a moderate correlation in middle school. Even in high school, Cooper says more than two hours of homework can diminish its effectiveness and become counterproductive. Ironically, there's plenty of research showing that exercise, play and the family dinner — all things children are giving up — are more highly correlated with cognitive development and achievement than is homework.

So where does this leave us? I don't believe homework should be abolished — just brought back into balance. It's true that homework overload doesn't affect every child. But even if only 10 percent of America's 54 million schoolchildren are suffering (and I believe it's much more), it's still a serious problem for those 5.4 million. All children need time for active play, time to spend with their families and time to be, well, children. No American child deserves any less.

NO
Harris M. Cooper
*Professor of Psychology
and Neuroscience, Duke University*

Written for *CQ Researcher*, July 2007

An Associated Press poll in 2006 found that about 57 percent of parents felt their child was assigned about the right amount of homework. Another 23 percent thought it was too little, 19 percent thought it was too much.

Educators should be thrilled. Pleasing a majority of parents and having equal numbers shouting "too much!" and "too little!" is about as good as they can hope for.

My colleagues and I have conducted a combined analysis of dozens of homework studies to examine whether homework is beneficial and what amount is appropriate.

The question is best answered by comparing students who are assigned homework with students assigned no homework but who are similar in other ways. Such studies suggest that homework can improve scores on class tests. Students assigned homework in second grade did better on math, third- and fourth-graders did better on English skills and vocabulary, fifth-graders on social studies, ninth- through 12th-graders on American history and 12th-graders on Shakespeare.

Less authoritative are 12 studies that link the amount of homework to achievement but control for other factors that might influence this connection. Such studies, often based on national samples of students, also find a positive link between time on homework and achievement.

Yet other studies correlate homework and achievement with no attempt to control for student differences. In 35 such studies, about 77 percent find the link between homework and achievement is positive. Most interesting, though, these results suggest little or no relationship between homework and achievement for elementary school students.

Why might this be so? Younger children have less-developed study habits and are less able to tune out distractions. Studies also suggest that young students who are struggling in school take more time to complete assignments.

So, how much homework should students do? A parent guide from the National PTA and the National Education Association states, "Most educators agree that for children in grades K-2, homework is more effective when it does not exceed 10-20 minutes each day; older children, in grades 3-6, can handle 30-60 minutes a day; in junior and senior high, the amount of homework will vary by subject." These recommendations are consistent with the conclusions reached by our analysis.

My feeling is that policies should prescribe amounts of homework consistent with the research evidence, but also give schools and teachers some flexibility. In general, teachers should avoid either extreme.

"The most important step is not abolishing homework but thinking through what will work to help our kids become lifelong learners," which probably means limiting assignments to the most thoughtful and important ones, says Kalish.

Efforts to make such changes are occurring in private and public schools around the country. In 2006, for example, Greenville, S.C., public schools limited daily homework and how heavily homework could count in a student's final grade.[29]

Last spring, Norwalk, Conn., began considering a new policy to limit homework: Homework would not be assigned as a punishment; kindergartners and first- and second-graders would have a maximum of 10 minutes of homework daily; and no elementary students would have homework over the weekend, although they would be expected to read on their own each day.[30]

Middletown, Ohio, is considering a ban on grading homework. The policy would establish a more "level playing field" among students by putting "the emphasis of homework on practicing for assessments such as tests, projects and quizzes" and avoiding the possibility of some students ending up with higher course grades based on homework for which they got substantial help from their parents.[31]

Some parents and teachers have loudly opposed the plan, however. Older students won't study at all if they don't get an immediate payback for it in the form of grades for completion of homework, said a high school teacher.[32]

The private Hopkins School in New Haven, Conn., is also reconsidering its homework policies to ensure that only homework that really increases learning is assigned. "If five problems help students understand a concept, then don't assign 15," said Assistant Head of School John Roberts.[33]

Testing the Tests

Schools that fail to meet NCLB goals could eventually face compulsory reorganization, mass firings and state or private takeover.

With NCLB testing only a few years old, its effects on students are still largely unknown. Some information is emerging, however, about how the tests are changing things in classrooms.

"Teachers aren't all opposed to NCLB, but we saw a big problem with teacher morale" in a new large-scale study of teachers' and administrators' responses to high-stakes testing in California, Georgia and Pennsylvania, says Laura S. Hamilton, a senior behavioral scientist at the RAND Corporation, a Palo Alto, Calif., research organization. "Majorities of teachers were telling us that NCLB was badly affecting teacher morale," but majorities "also said it was having a good effect on coordination in the schools."

Teachers are particularly bugged by NCLB's measurement standard for schools — called Average Yearly Progress, or AYP — because it "doesn't reflect what they're really doing," Hamilton says. The AYP compares, for example, achievement by this year's fourth-grade class to last year's, and many teachers and education analysts point out that the two classes may not be comparable.

In addition, many teachers don't feel confident that current tests actually match their states' learning standards or curricula, and virtually all believe NCLB's ultimate goal — having 100 percent of students test at "proficient" levels by 2014 — is unrealistic, says Hamilton. For some, that dissatisfaction could lead to "dumbed-down" classrooms where teachers focus on test-taking strategies rather than important content, she says. "When people perceive goals as impossible to attain, they'll tend to take shortcuts," such as "teaching to the test," she says.

Many schools, especially in low-income areas, "can't possibly meet next year's goals," let alone the 2014 goal, says Hamilton.[34] That may create a feeling of defeat, even in teachers who believe they've made real progress, she says. "The teachers say, 'I've moved these kids up significantly, but it doesn't show up in the results.'"

The RAND study finds that "teachers are spending a fair amount of time with practice tests, test-taking strategies and problems that mirror what will be on the tests," says Hamilton. In addition, "a lot of states now have benchmarking tests," which don't carry any stakes but help teachers see how well students are doing and enable them to readjust their teaching accordingly — "four to six times a year," Hamilton says. "All these things together have classrooms very focused on tests."

In addition, today's test questions, state learning standards and textbooks "don't always fit with one another," says Hamilton.

That's a problem, because it means that tests — not decisions about what content students should master — "are driving what we teach," says Sharon L. Nichols, an assistant professor of educational psychology at the University of Texas, San Antonio.

"The more you specifically practice a skill in a single situation" — such as for a standardized test — "the less transferable your learning is," Nichols says. For example, "when teachers teach formulaic writing because they know that kind of written answer will succeed on a certain test," they are not actually preparing students to write in the real world, she explains.

High-stakes tests "are also dictating the pace and the timing of what's taught," sometimes in ways that make a hash of the curriculum, says Nichols. For example, middle school teachers she surveyed complained about tests that include Civil War information the state curriculum dictates should be taught in the weeks after the test. "So they have to roar through it" to cover it in time for the exam.

Too much focus on tests can damage students' motivation, Nichols says. Many who fear they won't pass give up too easily, while others who are confident of passing lose interest in school because the tests "don't challenge them and the test has become the only thing that matters in the classroom."

Meanwhile, beyond homework and standardized testing, an era of ultra-competitiveness has overtaken students in many affluent neighborhoods, says Stanford's Pope.

The belief among many parents and teachers that only superkids who graduate from Harvard are truly successful takes a devastating toll on some students, Pope maintains. Nevertheless, she says there's a growing awareness among psychologists, college admissions officers and school administrators that current ideas about success are skewed.

Some colleges now focus less on test scores and more on effort and other factors in admissions decisions, says Pope. "That gives me some hope" that criteria for success are beginning to broaden and that pressure may ease for teenagers, Pope says.

Pope and some of her Stanford colleagues are launching a campaign to alert families and schools to the dangers of what she calls overcompetitiveness, which she says is perpetuated by myths and ignorance.

For example, while many suburban parents focus on a handful of the best-known colleges for their children, "in fact there are about 200 different schools" whose graduates attain the same levels of career achievement,

According to a survey of college freshmen that has been repeated since the 1960s, amounts of high school homework are hitting all-time lows — about five hours per week. Today between 30-40 percent of U.S. students say they typically have no homework.

Pope says. "Two hundred vs. 10. That's a much healthier message to send."

OUTLOOK

Learning to Teach

One thing is certain for the future: The pressure on schools to provide more academics to more students is here to stay.

Education systems around the world are inexorably moving to require more years of strictly academic education for more students than ever before, says Baker of Penn State. The "slow death of vocationalism" that sees virtually all students pursuing a math-and-literacy-heavy curriculum through high school is occurring globally and in the United States, he says.

Exactly what that implies for homework and testing, however, is unclear. Much is still unknown about how particular homework practices and testing policies affect students and about how to teach academic subjects successfully to everyone.

For her part, anti-homework activist Bennett sees the tide turning against homework, especially for younger children.

"I've noticed that many people take it as a given now that homework and achievement don't go together," Bennett says. Ten years ago, when she first became alarmed about homework's ill effects on her own family, Bennett says most other parents in her children's schools simply assumed that more homework translated to greater academic success.

Today, more people question that assumption, and the questioning is beginning to pay off in revised homework policies as well as more scrutiny of other school traditions that reinforce overcompetitive attitudes, Bennett says. She expects that trend to continue.

"A school in Menlo Park [Calif.] just got rid of homework, and one in Ohio recently dropped grades altogether," Bennett says. "In a school in Alberta, Canada, the principal asked the teachers to read up on homework over the summer, and when school started in the fall they changed their policies," greatly limiting the homework assigned, Bennett says.

Many education researchers say the demands of educating all students to a high academic standard will require understanding much more about how students learn. Some also say Americans may have to make a tough shift to a more academics-friendly society to see real results.

"If you believe in very high academic achievement, you can't be satisfied" with the current U.S. showing on international tests, says Brookings' Loveless. To improve U.S. standings, increased study time on academic subjects would be required, as well as increased attention to academics and learning by families and the society at large, he says. But "even though everybody wants the nation's schools to be better, there's not a huge push" for that kind of cultural change.

Furthermore, just requiring kids to spend more time studying, in school or out, won't help all that much, Loveless says. Research shows that "you can add an hour to the school day" and "get a small gain in achievement but not nearly as much as you'd expect," he says. "The missing element is — productivity," says Loveless. Extra hours must be spent addressing individual children's specific academic deficiencies to pay off, he says.

In coming years, cognitive science will help in that direction, says Bror Saxberg, chief learning officer at K^{12}, a Herndon, Va., firm that develops online learning products.

The current need is to find out how people learn and then figure out what interventions can help learners past identifiable stumbling blocks, says Saxberg. Research to tackle those questions is just beginning, he says. "As we go forward and develop more sophistication about what goes wrong" when people get stuck in learning a skill, "we'll be able to provide teachers with a better set of tools" to diagnose individual problems and remedy them.

NOTES

1. For background, see Lauren K. Meade, "Honor Roll Story Makes Media Splash," *The Boston Globe*, Dec. 17, 2006 and Lauren K. Meade, "An Urgent Message for Stressed-Out Students: Relax," *The Boston Globe*, Feb. 1, 2007.

2. Sandra L. Hofferth and John F. Sandberg, "How American Children Spent Their Time," *Journal of Marriage and Family*, May 2001, p. 295.

3. Quoted in Sally Kalson, "Back to School: From Reading to Algebra, Everything in School Is Starting Earlier," *Pittsburgh Post-Gazette*, Aug. 27, 2006, p. A12.

4. J. E. Stone, "Developmentalism: An Obscure but Pervasive Restriction on Educational Improvement," *Education Policy Analysis Archives*, April 21, 1996, http://epaa.asu.edu/epaa/v4n8.html.

5. Quoted in Michael F. Shaughnessy, "An Interview With Paul Zoch: Doomed to Fail," *EducationNews .org*, March 21, 2007, www.ednews.org.

6. Hofferth and Sandberg, *op. cit.*

7. Quoted in Peg Tyre, "Talk Transcript: The New First Grade," *Newsweek* and MSNBC.com, Sept. 6, 2006, www.msnbc.com.

8. For background, see Marcia Clemmitt, "AP and IB Programs," *CQ Researcher*, March 3, 2006, pp. 193-216.

9. For more data from the poll, see "Attitudes of Parents and Teachers About Homework," *eSchoolNews Online*, Feb. 14, 2006, www.eschoolnews.com/news/showstory.cfm?ArticleID=6111.

10. Quoted in "Forum Brief: The End of Homework," American Youth Policy Forum, Nov. 20, 2000, www.apyf.org.

11. *Ibid.*

12. For background, see Barbara Mantel, "No Child Left Behind," *CQ Researcher*, May 27, 2005, pp. 469-492; Kenneth Jost, "Testing in Schools," *CQ Researcher*, April 20, 2001, pp. 321-344; Kathy Koch, "National Education Standards," *CQ Researcher*, May 14, 1999, pp. 401-424.

13. Sean W. Mulvenon, "Impact of Accountability and School Testing on Students: Is There Evidence of Anxiety?" paper presented at the annual meeting of the Mid-South Educational Research Association, Nov. 13-16, 2001, http://eric.ed.gov/ERICWebPortal/custom/portlets/recordDetails/detailmini.jsp?_nfpb=true&_&ERICExtSearch_SearchValue_0=ED460155&ERICExtSearch_SearchType_0=eric_accno&accno=ED460155.

14. Quoted in Stuart S. Yeh, "Limiting the Unintended Consequences of High-Stakes Testing," *Education Policy Analysis Archives*, Oct. 28, 2005, http://epaa.asu.edu/epaa/v13n43/.

15. Quoted in *ibid.*

16. For background, see David Baker and Gerald LeTendre, *National Differences, Global Similarities: World Culture and the Future of Schooling* (2005).

17. Transcript, "The 2006 Brown Center Report on American Education: How Well Are Our Students Learning?" Brookings Institution, Oct. 18, 2005.

18. *Ibid.*

19. "Too Much Homework Can Be Counterproductive," *Physorg.com*, www.physorg/printnews.php?newsid=4333.

20. Chick Moorman and Thomas Haller, "Synthesis of Research Findings on Homework," Jane Bluestein Instructional Support Services, Inc., www.janebluestein.com.

21. For background, see Brian P. Gill and Steven L. Schlossman, "A Sin Against Childhood: Progressive Education and the Crusade to Abolish Homework, 1897-1941," *American Journal of Education*, November 1996, p. 27; Brian P. Gill and Steven L. Schlossman, "The Lost Cause of Homework Reform," *American Journal of Education*, November 2000, p. 27; Brian P. Gill and Steven L. Schlossman, "A Nation at Rest: The American Way of Homework," *Educational Evaluation and Policy Analysis*, fall 2003, p. 319.

22. National Commission on Excellence in Education, *A Nation at Risk: The Imperative for Educational Reform*, April 1983, www.ed.gov/pubs/NatAtRisk/title.html.

23. Gill and Schlossman, "A Nation at Rest: The American Way of Homework," *op. cit.*

24. *Ibid.*

25. *Ibid.*

26. Quoted in Kathy Checkley, "When Homework Works," *Classroom Leadership*, September 2003, Association for Supervision and Curriculum Development, www.ascd.org.

27. Quoted in "Author Does His Homework on Hot Topic," *Education World*, Feb. 10, 2006, www.education-world.com.

28. *Ibid.*

29. Nancy Keates, "Schools Turn Down the Heat on Homework," *The Wall Street Journal*, Jan. 19, 2007, p. W1.

30. "Norwalk, Connecticut, Board of Education Considers Homework Policy Change," stophomework blog, May 22, 2007, http://stophomework.com/category/in-the-news/.

31. Megan Gildow, "Research Gives No Guidance on Policy," *Middletown Journal*, June 10, 2007, middletownjournal.com.

32. Quoted in *ibid.*

33. Quoted in Keates, *op. cit.*

34. For background, see Marcia Clemmitt, "Fixing Urban Schools," *CQ Researcher*, April 27, 2007, pp. 361-384.

BIBLIOGRAPHY

Books

Baker, David, and Gerald LeTendre, *National Differences, Global Similarities: World Culture and the Future of Schooling*, Stanford University Press, 2005.
Professors of education at Pennsylvania State University compare education trends gleaned from a four-year investigation of K-12 education in 47 countries, including homework, student achievement in math and science, private tutoring, teacher workloads and curriculum development.

Bennett, Sara, and Nancy Kalish, *The Case Against Homework: How Homework Is Hurting Our Children and What We Can Do About It*, Crown, 2006.
Two organizers of parental campaigns to change homework policies at their children's schools explain why they believe homework is harmful and what steps families can take to get schools to adopt better homework strategies.

Buell, John, *Closing the Book on Homework: Enhancing Public Education and Freeing Family Time*, Temple University Press, 2003.
A political economist and former professor at the College of the Atlantic in Bangor, Maine, argues that unstructured play is more important for children's learning than homework and that anti-homework activism is part of a larger cultural debate on the place of work in society.

Cooper, Harris M., *The Battle Over Homework: Common Ground for Administrators, Teachers, and Parents*, Corwin Press, 2001.
A Duke University professor of psychology and neuroscience examines academic research on homework and explains how it could be put into practice by teachers.

Cutler, William W., *Parents and Schools: The 150-Year Struggle for Control in American Education*, University of Chicago Press, 2000.
A professor of history at Temple University traces 150 years of ongoing struggle between parents and schools over who should control children's lives in and out of the classroom.

Kohn, Alfie, *The Homework Myth*, Da Capo Lifelong Books, 2006.
An education writer and critic argues that homework is detrimental to family life and discusses a century of research questioning homework's value as an educational tool.

Levine, Mel, *A Mind at a Time*, Simon & Schuster, 2002.
A professor of pediatrics at the University of North Carolina Medical School explains how differing brain structures cause children to struggle with different learning tasks and outlines strategies to help.

Pope, Denise Clark, *Doing School: How We Are Creating a Generation of Stressed-Out, Materialistic, and Miseducated Students*, Yale University Press, 2nd edition, 2003.
A lecturer at the Stanford University School of Education argues that American society's overcompetitive view of education harms students.

Zoch, Paul A., *Doomed to Fail: The Built-In Defects of American Education*, Ivan R. Dee, 2004.
A longtime teacher of high school Latin argues that current education trends put the onus for success on teachers and ask for far too little effort from students.

Articles

Kalson, Sally, "Back to School: From Reading to Algebra, Everything in School Is Starting Earlier," *Pittsburgh Post-Gazette*, Aug. 27, 2006.
Kindergartners are filling out the worksheets that first-graders used to do, and tutoring companies sell academic programs for preschoolers. Nevertheless, experts are divided on whether academic acceleration is too much too soon.

Keates, Nancy, "Schools Turn Down the Heat on Homework," *The Wall Street Journal*, Jan. 19, 2007, p. W1.
Public and private schools in some affluent neighborhoods are changing their homework policies, cutting down on the amounts of homework assigned and asking teachers to ensure that each assignment is worth students' time.

Reports and Studies

Gill, Brian P., and Steven L. Schlossman, *A Nation at Rest: The American Way of Homework*, Educational Evaluation and Policy Analysis, fall 2003, p. 319.
An education researcher at the RAND think tank and a Carnegie Mellon University history professor analyze

survey data and conclude American high school students in the 1960s had substantially more homework than subsequent students.

Hamilton, Laura S., *et al., Standards-Based Accountability Under No Child Left Behind: Experiences of Teachers and Administrators in Three States, RAND Education,* 2007, www.rand.org.
Analysts from a nonprofit research organization survey school teachers and administrators about pressure and other consequences of high-stakes standardized tests.

Loveless, Tom, *The 2006 Brown Center Report on American Education, Brookings Institution Press,* 2006.
The latest edition of this annual analysis examines current student-achievement scores and how student attitudes like confidence and enjoyment of classes affect learning.

For More Information

Alfie Kohn, www.alfiekohn.org/index.html. The Web site of an education writer and critic posts articles and research questioning the value of homework and testing and what Kohn says is the overcompetitive nature of U.S. education.

All Kinds of Minds, 24-32 Union Square East, 6th Floor, Suite A, New York, NY 10003; (888) 956-4637; www.allkindsofminds.org. A nonprofit institute that educates teachers and parents about neurodevelopmental differences that create different learning challenges for students.

AVID, AVID Center, 5120 Shoreham Place, Suite 120, San Diego, CA 92122; (858) 623-2843; www.avidcenter.org. A nonprofit group that establishes in-school support programs to help students who might otherwise not attend college.

Center for Public Education, 1680 Duke St., Alexandria, VA 22314; (703) 838-6722; www.centerforpubliceducation.org. Supported by the National School Boards Foundation, the center provides information on homework and other education issues.

Education Next, Hoover Institution, Stanford University; www.educationnext.org. An online quarterly journal on education reform produced by a conservative think tank.

FairTest (National Center for Open and Fair Testing), 342 Broadway, Cambridge, MA 02139; (617) 864-4810; www.fairtest.org. Campaigns against what it calls the abuses and flaws of standardized testing.

National Education Association, 1201 16th St., N.W., Washington, DC 20036-3290; (202) 833-4000; www.nea.org/index.html. The nation's largest teachers' union posts education articles and studies on its Web site.

Parenting Bookmark, www.parentingbookmark.com/index.html. Posts articles by psychologists and education experts on topics such as children's stress and choosing a preschool.

The Preteen Alliance, 400 Hamilton Ave., Suite 340, Palo Alto, CA 94301; (650) 497-8365; http://forum.lpfch.org/index.html?r=Bz7sao1d1OQ. A Web site sponsored by the Lucile Packard Foundation for Children's Health that posts articles and hosts discussions about adolescent issues, including school-related stress.

Stop Homework, www.stophomework.com. A parent's blog containing essays and links to news articles about homework and stress in schools.

10

Gender and Learning

Are There Innate Differences Between the Sexes?

Sarah Glazer

Harvard students and other supporters protest on Feb. 22, 2005, against remarks by Harvard President Lawrence Summers suggesting more men than women are scientists and engineers because of differences in "intrinsic aptitude." While many scientists criticized Summers, his supporters say he courageously raised a legitimate question for scientific inquiry. On May 16, Summers pledged $50 million to aid and recruit female faculty.

From *CQ Researcher*,
May 20, 2005.

arvard President Larry Summers recently confronted one of academia's most controversial questions: Why do so few women hold tenured faculty positions in science and engineering?

But his attempt at an answer reignited a long-simmering debate among researchers about how well women perform in math and science compared with men.

In speaking to a group of economists in January, Summers said the imbalance might be due mainly to "issues of intrinsic aptitude."[1]

Summers's suggestion that women are biologically inferior in math infuriated many female scientists. Some asserted that the other two factors he mentioned were far more important in keeping women out of science: sex discrimination and the way girls are taught to view math as male territory.

Women's-rights groups fault male hiring committees' bias against women and the lack of family-friendly policies for keeping the growing number of women with science degrees from attaining comparable numbers of faculty positions. For instance, while women now earn 31 percent of chemistry PhDs and 27 percent of math doctorates they hold only 12 percent of chemistry faculty positions and 8 percent of math positions at the nation's research institutions.[2] Harvard, for instance, has no females on its senior math faculty.

A "steel ceiling" keeps women's participation trapped at less than 20 percent of engineering, computer science and physics careers, where these social barriers are particularly steep, women's

207

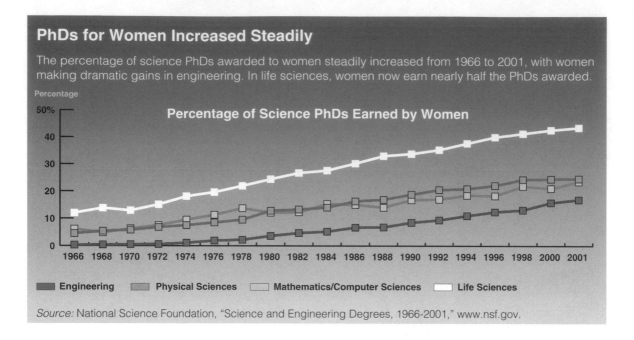

PhDs for Women Increased Steadily

The percentage of science PhDs awarded to women steadily increased from 1966 to 2001, with women making dramatic gains in engineering. In life sciences, women now earn nearly half the PhDs awarded.

Percentage of Science PhDs Earned by Women

Legend: Engineering | Physical Sciences | Mathematics/Computer Sciences | Life Sciences

Source: National Science Foundation, "Science and Engineering Degrees, 1966-2001," www.nsf.gov.

activists contend. But skeptics say gut female preferences, rooted in evolutionary biology, are more influential in steering women away from those fields.

"I'm not saying there aren't any biological, innate differences," says Sue Rosser, a biologist and dean at the Georgia Institute of Technology. "I'm saying there are also these overwhelming social differences, and those are the things you can do something about."

But Linda Chavez, president of the Center for Equal Opportunity, an anti-affirmative action think tank, insists boys simply are hard-wired for math and girls aren't. Summers was "just articulating what most researchers in this area believe," she said, "that biology plays a bigger role in explaining these differences than socialization does."[3]

Researchers have been vigorously debating how big a gender gap there really is in math aptitude. In fact, they find that a gap shows up mainly among the top scorers on high-stakes math exams like the SAT. On most other standardized elementary and high school tests, the difference between boys' and girls' average scores has diminished to a negligible level in recent years. And there's no consensus as to how much biology contributes to the difference.

Yet there are intriguing differences in how boys and girls learn, and those differences may be hard-wired, says Leonard Sax, a family physician in Poolesville, Md., and author of the 2005 book *Why Gender Matters.* "Boys enjoy plugging numbers into equations; girls are much more interested in knowing why," he says. One study found girls get turned off by physics classes that teach rote formulas; they're more engaged when teachers explore the explanations for physical laws.[4]

Some differences are well established. Girls do better on tests of content learned in class and score much higher on reading and writing tests than boys. Boys score higher on standardized tests with math and science problems not directly tied to their school curriculum. On tests of spatial awareness, boys do better on tests that involve navigation through space. Girls are better at remembering objects and landmarks.[5]

Studies also show differences in brain structure and hormonal levels that appear to influence spatial reasoning. But the implications of these differences for real-world math and science achievement remain unclear. "There is evidence that male and female brains differ anatomically in subtle ways, but no one knows how (or even if) these anatomical differences relate to cognitive performance," the journal *Nature Neuroscience* declared.[6]

For example, college men and women of equal math ability use different parts of the brain when taking the

Math SAT, according to a brain imaging study by Richard J. Haier, a psychologist at the University of California, Irvine.[7] "There are lots and lots of studies that show differences in the brain between men and women. What those differences mean — [that] gets a little controversial," Haier says.[8]

In 1992, a report on math and science education galvanized national attention. "How Schools Shortchange Girls" said girls took fewer advanced math and science classes than boys and received less attention from teachers in class, leading to poorer performance in those subjects.[9]

By the time the American Association of University Women (AAUW) released the report, however, the much-publicized gender gap already was closing. Indeed, gender differences on standardized math tests in elementary and high school have been small since 1990, according to the Department of Education.[10] Moreover, the 1970s gap in average math scores on standardized tests that favored 17-year-old boys had disappeared by 1999, and the science gap also had declined.[11]

In fact, girls now receive better math and science grades than boys — right up through college.[12] Today they constitute more than half the biology majors, almost half the math majors and half of medical school enrollments. Girls take more high school classes than boys in chemistry, biology and most types of math. Although more boys take advanced classes in physics and advanced calculus, the differences appear to be shrinking rapidly. (*See graph, p. 213.*)

Some experts contend that the dramatic speed with which girls have closed the average-score gap in math is proof that the original deficiency was caused by socialization. "If there had been some math gene, things wouldn't have changed quite as fast," says Susan Bailey McGee, executive director of the Wellesley Centers for Women at

Few Women PhDs Hold Faculty Positions

The pool of potential female candidates for faculty positions is plentiful, but faculty search committees and chairs say they receive few applications from women PhDs. Recent female PhDs say they do not perceive the academic environment as desirable and so they do not apply for faculty positions. For example, while women have earned 31 percent of the chemistry doctorates awarded in recent years at the top 50 U.S. research institutions, they held only 12 percent of the chemistry faculty positions. Similarly, 27 percent had math PhDs, but only 8.3 percent of math faculties were women.

Percentage of Female PhDs and Female Faculty

Discipline	PhDs (1993-2002)	All Faculty Ranks
Chemistry (2003)	31.3%	12.1%
Math	27.2	8.3
Computer Science	20.5	10.6
Astronomy (2004)	20.6	12.6
Physics	13.3	6.6
Chemical Engineering	22.3	10.5
Civil Engineering	18.7	9.8
Electrical Engineering	11.5	6.5
Mechanical Engineering	10.4	6.7
Economics	29.3	11.5
Political Science	36.6	23.5
Sociology	58.9	35.8
Psychology	66.1	33.5
Biological Sciences	44.7	20.2

Source: Nelson, Donna, "A National Analysis of Diversity in Science and Engineering Faculties at Research Universities," Jan. 6, 2005.

Wellesley College and principal author of the AAUW report.

Still, relatively few women enter the fields of physics or computer science. Some believe a "steel ceiling" has kept women below 20 percent of engineers in recent years. "There's a lot of stereotyping that goes on about what's appropriate for girls and boys," as evidenced by the far lower number of girls taking courses in those subjects, McGee says. When predominantly male university departments are making hiring and promotion decisions in those fields, she contends, "it's an unconscious bias to favor someone most like themselves."

It is unclear how big a role anti-female bias plays, but a recent study of the nation's top 50 research universities

Harvard Pledges $50 Million to Aid Women

Harvard President Lawrence Summers's announcement on May 16 committing Harvard to spending $50 million for recruiting women faculty and improving the campus climate for women capped four months of apologies.

Indeed, when Summers warned women students in April about the sex bias they're likely to face in science, he seemed the polar opposite of the man who in January had questioned girls' "intrinsic aptitude" in math.

At a Harvard conference on women in science organized by female science majors, he said professors should be aware of how influential they can be in discouraging female students. (Women at Harvard drop plans to major in science at a far higher rate than males.) To show he shared their pain, Summers described how he was made to feel inadequate in college physics: After giving the wrong answer to a problem, the instructor stared at him "with a certain stunned belief that I could be so stupid."[1]

So-One Hwang, a senior linguistics major, was one of several female students who think Summers's remarks rang true. "I feel embarrassed to admit I didn't pursue physics or math because I didn't want to deal with the sociological factors," she says. She cited anxiety about attaining success in the male-dominated sciences and male classmates who exclude females from study groups or treat them with disdain.

Undergraduates aren't the only women who feel this way, according to a task force that recommended numerous changes to retain women in science. "In some departments, women graduate and postdoctoral fellows report hearing disrespectful criticisms of their abilities from male colleagues and a lack of a supportive environment," the report said.

On May 16, the science task force and another on women faculty — both appointed by Summers in the wake of the controversy over his remarks — made several recommendations, including gender-bias training for graduate students who teach science to undergraduates, increased financial support for faculty child care and an automatic tenure extension during maternity or parental leave. Summers said he would institute some of the recommendations immediately, including hiring a senior vice provost for diversity charged with intensifying the search for women faculty.

Many of the task force recommendations are aimed at countering factors frequently cited as driving women from science: the lack of mentoring, informal job networking and female social support. According to Mariangela Lisanti, president of the undergraduate group Women in Science at Harvard-Radcliffe, her group asked for an on-campus summer dorm so women working in labs could live and eat with fellow researchers, a central place to find information about research internships and informal study centers where students could ask successful undergraduates questions about homework in difficult introductory science courses. These changes also will be implemented immediately, Summers said.

Summers "saw how what we said could be behind why women are leaving science," says Lisanti, a senior majoring in physics.

On Summers's watch, offers of tenure-track jobs to women have fallen precipitously to 4 out of 32 tenure offers last year in the Faculty of Arts and Sciences. Earlier found that in most science disciplines "qualified female candidates exist, but they are not being hired" as faculty.[13] Last year, the Government Accountability Office (GAO) complained that federal agencies handing out billions of dollars in science grants were not doing enough to ensure universities receiving the grants are not discriminating against women.[14]

At the heart of the current controversy is a serious societal implication — that the failure of an institution like Harvard to tenure even one woman mathematician can be blamed on the lack of top-flight women mathematicians, which in turn can be blamed on too-few top female minds in math. As evidence of intrinsic aptitude differences, Summers pointed out that more boys than girls receive top scores on standardized math tests. For example, last year boys outnumbered girls 2-to-1 among 12th-graders scoring 750-800 on the Math SAT, according to The College Board. Harvard scientists-to-be are drawn from those making scores at least that high, if not higher, and the ratio of men to women increases as the score rises, some argue.

"When we're talking about the pipeline for MIT and Harvard, we're talking about the exceptional high school graduate — not the average high school graduate," says task forces' recommendations aimed at retaining women have been implemented only "spottily," according to Harvard professor of natural sciences Barbara J. Grosz, chair of the Task Force on Women in Science and Engineering. Grosz chaired a task force in 1991 and again in the late '90s. Only some departments followed their recommendations for senior faculty mentors for junior women faculty, she says.

As for the most recent report, Grosz says, "There's a higher probability these recommendations will be put into effect and sustained over the long term because we built in mechanisms for monitoring, data collection and reporting that weren't present in the previous panel's recommendation in 1991."

For example, she says, information on recruiting and hiring will have to be reported to the new senior vice provost, and mentoring plans will become a required part of junior faculty reviews. Grosz says her task force wanted to "plug the leak" at each stage where women are known to leave science — from the first two years of college, when students get discouraged by difficult courses, to postdoctoral years when women often feel isolated in labs. Several measures are focused on helping women in childbearing years to keep their careers on track, such as a fund to pay for child care so junior faculty can travel to conferences, "which is where you get known," Grosz says.

Some skeptics say the $5 million a year over 10 years pledged by Summers is just a drop in the bucket considering Harvard's operating budget of about $2.5 billion a year. Grosz acknowledges some recommendations like subsidized child care will cost much more. "Five million dollars per year will not cover everything," she says, "but it's a significant contribution from Harvard's center — right upfront — that says they're behind this."

Getty Images/Jodi Hilton

Harvard President Lawrence Summers drew intense criticism as well as support for questioning girls' "intrinsic aptitude" in math.

Some advocates hope the current pressure to implement change will have national implications. As Harvard goes, so goes the world, many faculty believe.

As for Summers's apparent turnaround, Lisanti says, "The proof is going to be in the action."

---

[1] Marcella Bombardieri, "Summers Displays New Understanding of Women's Careers," *The Boston Globe*, April 8, 2005.

Linda Gottfredson, a professor of education at the University of Delaware, who sides with those arguing that biology is playing a strong role in weighting the pool of top scientists toward males.

But some experts say — and at least one judge has agreed — that girls may not do as well as boys on the Math SAT because it is biased in favor of boys. (*See story, p. 218.*) In any case, very high standardized math scores are actually poor predictors of who goes on to science majors or careers, particularly for girls, according to the sociologists whose data Summers cited. Twelfth-graders who continue in science actually come from the top

quarter, where women are better represented, rather than the top 5 percent, where boys outnumber girls 2-to-1, according to Kimberlee Shauman, a sociologist at the University of California, Davis, who calls Summers's use of her data on gender differences "naive."[15]

"What it takes to be a successful scientist is much more than math achievement," she says. "We need people who are creative, who have good communication skills, are good managers. Some of these skills — like communication — are more likely to be found among women."

Boys Maintain Slight Edge in Math Scores

Boys' scores on the mathematics portion of the national assessment test — given in grades 4, 8 and 12 — have been slightly higher than girls' scores during the past decade. However, scores for both males and females increased.

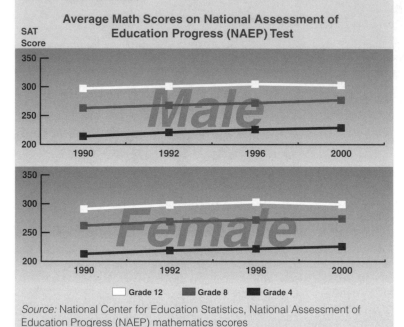

Average Math Scores on National Assessment of Education Progress (NAEP) Test

Grade 12 | Grade 8 | Grade 4

Source: National Center for Education Statistics, National Assessment of Education Progress (NAEP) mathematics scores

Gottfredson argues that the large numbers of women who recently have been going into "life sciences" like biology and medicine — rather than "hard sciences" like physics and engineering — demonstrate that biological, evolutionary differences rather than discrimination are keeping women out. "Women have moved up in massive numbers, but they've picked their fields," she says. "And some of the reason for the choice is basically different wiring of men and women in terms of their gut preferences." Studies frequently find, for example, that girls are more interested in people and living organisms; boys more interested in things and mechanics.

But, Shauman objects, "It's a huge leap to say that is based on a biological difference. There's no gene or complex of genes or hormone levels linked to this desire to work with people vs. things."

Others suggest the demands of motherhood may explain why many promising female PhDs leave science. Junior faculty must produce sufficient publications to

make tenure in their 30s, the prime child-bearing years. Married women with children under 6 are half as likely to enter a tenure-track position as married men with a child the same age, according to a University of California study.[16] Many universities are experimenting with family-friendly policies like tenure extensions to ease the burden on young faculty mothers.

On May 16, Harvard's embattled president pledged to spend at least $50 million to carry out task force recommendations aimed at improving the climate for women in science at Harvard as well as recruiting and retaining more women faculty.

And on May 18, *The New York Times* reported a recent study of the University of California — the nation's largest public university system — shows women's participation in some faculty departments has even decreased.[17]

As the debate over gender and learning continues, here are some of the issues being debated in academia, government and the press:

Is there really a gender gap in math and science?

In 1992, following the AAUW's headline-making report, states passed a flurry of laws designed to counter the perceived bias against females in the classroom, and a flood of books and articles lamented how girls' self-esteem was being crushed.[18]

But by 1992, in fact, girls had already closed the gap on most measures. Two years earlier, more female high school graduates than boys had taken first- and second-year algebra and geometry, according to a Department of Education report. Also in 1990, more female high school students than males had taken biology and chemistry. By 1994, physics was the only science course with higher male enrollment. Citing these statistics, Diane Ravitch, a professor of education at New York University and former Education Department official in the first George Bush administration, said in 1998 that the AAUW had ginned up a "phony crisis."[19]

The AAUW authors now concede their report was based on outdated statistics. "The data we had access to was late 1980s data," explains lead author McGee. In her defense, the report noted the math gap was shrinking — a finding generally overlooked in the bad-news-for-girls press coverage. But she adds, "The real issue was how girls felt about pursuing those subjects and whether they felt it was something to pursue as a career."

The AAUW report also had argued that adolescent girls suffered from low self-esteem and received less attention from teachers than boys, which further discouraged them from pursuing math and science. That conclusion and the negative implications that AAUW drew were disputed by Ravitch (who suggested teachers were reprimanding boys when they called on them) and by American Enterprise Institute scholar Christina Hoff Sommers, who questioned the validity of the data in her 2000 book *The War Against Boys.* Psychologist Judith Kleinfeld also pointed out that boys did far worse on standardized tests of reading and writing and got lower grades in school — trends that remain true today.[20]

Indeed, today a growing number of researchers contend boys are the ones who are shortchanged — judging by the larger proportion of boys in special-education classes and the declining proportion attending college. Women now make up 56 percent of students enrolled in college; By 2012, the Department of Education projects they will account for about 60 percent of bachelor's degrees.[21]

"Maybe we should be worried about boys having a much higher rate of dropout," says Diane Halpern, a professor of psychology at Claremont McKenna College in Claremont, Calif. "Girls are learning math and science in school very well," she says, based on their grades and tests on content learned in school.

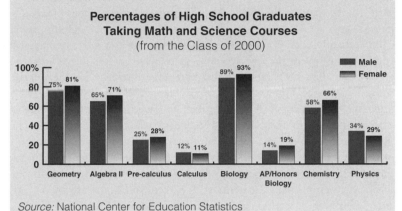

More Girls Take Advanced Math and Science

Higher percentages of females took advanced math and science courses than males among students who graduated from high school in 2000. However, higher percentages of males enrolled in calculus and physics.

Percentages of High School Graduates Taking Math and Science Courses
(from the Class of 2000)

Male / Female

Geometry: 75% / 81%
Algebra II: 65% / 71%
Pre-calculus: 25% / 28%
Calculus: 12% / 11%
Biology: 89% / 93%
AP/Honors Biology: 14% / 19%
Chemistry: 58% / 66%
Physics: 34% / 29%

Source: National Center for Education Statistics

Boys, meanwhile, score better, on average, on math tests on content they have not learned, she notes, including the SAT.

"Who's winning," Halpern says, "depends on what side [of the gender fence] you're standing on."

Today girls receive better grades than boys in math and science through high school, have closed the gap on average scores on most standardized math tests and take more advanced high school classes than boys in almost every category except physics and high-level calculus. In college they constitute nearly half the math majors and more than half the biology majors.

"In terms of course-taking and achievement, the gap is pretty well gone," agrees Patricia B. Campbell, a coauthor of the AAUW report, who recently revisited the gender-gap statistics. She found few gender differences in the math courses girls and boys take in high school until they reach Advanced Placement (AP) courses; about the same number of boys and girls are taking four or more years of high school math.[22]

Girls make up the majority of those taking AP exams and — stunningly — 57 percent of those taking the first-level calculus exam. "You have to get to the second level of calculus [known as BC] before you find any meaningful sex difference, and then it's a small percent of the population," notes Campbell. (Girls accounted for

39 percent of those taking the BC test.) In science, boys still make up the majority of students taking AP chemistry and higher-level physics.

Although Campbell concedes that "in the last 20 years there has been a tremendous decline in the gap," she worries that the decline "hasn't had the impact we would have expected" in all scientific and technical fields.

Specifically, Campbell cites computer science and engineering, where she says women's gains have stagnated. Less than 20 percent of girls take AP exams in computer science, and a low percentage take any computer science classes. Girls are less likely to have career aspirations in computer science and engineering. Among those taking the ACT (the college admissions equivalent of the SAT taken more commonly in the Midwest) or the SAT in 2001, only 2 percent of girls were planning to major in either field. By contrast, 9 percent of boys cited computer science, and 11 percent chose engineering as their majors of choice.[23]

At the college level, the disparity is most striking in engineering, physics and computer science, where women earned less than 20 percent of the bachelor's degrees, a gender gap that has changed little since 1989.[24] Considering girls' equally strong math and science preparation in high school, Campbell suggests, "Our perceptions [of what girls can do] don't seem to have kept pace with reality."

But vocational expert Gottfredson questions whether girls' relative lack of interest in those fields is really a problem. She says female clustering around the biological sciences represents females' natural inclination toward people and living organisms in contrast to boys' interests in mechanical things. Even within engineering, she notes, women have gravitated into sub-fields like biomedical engineering rather than mechanical or electrical engineering. "Why do we need equal proportions of men and women in every profession?" she has asked.[25]

Still, with women now accounting for half of all college majors in science and technology, the percentage of those pursuing advanced degrees and moving into academic jobs remains low. Only 19.5 percent of science and engineering faculty at four-year colleges and universities are women, with only 10 percent making full professor, according to the National Science Foundation.[26]

Even in a field like biology, where women have outnumbered men earning PhDs for several years, women make up only 30 percent (white males still make up more than half) of the assistant professors — the first rung on the academic employment ladder.[27] In almost every scientific field, women's participation decreases as they progress from PhD to graduate assistant to assistant professor to tenured associate and then full professor.

Summers's explanation for this trend focused on gender differences in high-stakes standardized test scores, as has most of the debate about gender differences.

While the average math and science score-gap on the closely monitored National Assessment of Educational Progress (NAEP) has either disappeared or dropped to a few points favoring males, females still score on average 36 points lower than males on high-stakes tests like the Math SAT and lower on the quantitative part of the Graduate Record Exam, a graduate school admissions test.[28]

Generally, more boys than girls receive top scores on such tests. For example, in 2004 about twice as many boys as girls scored at least 750 on the Math SAT — a test some claim is biased in favor of boys. (*See sidebar, p. 218.*)

Most girls and boys overlap somewhere around the average when it comes to math test scores. However, boys are more variable — more boys than girls are seriously disabled in math, and more are in the top 5 percent of scorers, a fact Summers highlighted. As the University of California's Haier explains, "The average boy can't do high-level math." Statistically, by the same logic, neither can the average girl.

Are there "innate differences" between males and females in math and science aptitude?

The fact that more boys than girls make top scores on standardized math tests is often invoked as evidence that boys possess an innate superiority in high-level math. In his book *The Blank Slate*, Harvard psychologist Steven Pinker argues that biological and evolutionary forces play a crucial role in male-female cognitive differences.

Like many such adherents, he cites a study that found precocious seventh-grade boys who scored at least 700 on the Math SAT for admission to an enrichment program outnumbered similar girls 13-to-1.[29] Does this huge gap suggest there will always be fewer brilliant female mathematicians? According to Pinker, the answer appears to be yes. Men "consistently" perform better on this and other tests of mathematical reasoning, he has argued[30] with the higher numbers of men at top scores "confirming an expectation from evolutionary psychology."[31]

But other researchers see environment as a greater influence on girls and question the immutability of the score differences. They note that the widely cited 13-to-1 ratio dates from 1983 and comes from a select sample of gifted children who volunteered to take the test in response to a talent search. In recent years, the boy-girl ratio in this talent search sample has fallen to about 3-to-1, according to psychologist Julian Stanley, founder of the Center for Talented Youth at Johns Hopkins University, in Baltimore. Stanley attributes the decline to girls' earlier and better math preparation in school.

This shrinking gap among exceptionally talented youngsters, along with the shrinking gender gap on other standardized tests, suggests these scores "are very malleable. It's conceivable we can change the ratio of women in that high end of distribution" to be equal to boys, says sociologist Shauman, who is dubious of a biological explanation. Boys' higher representation at the top end, she says, "could be caused by differences in how boys and girls are treated and socialized."

Well-recognized gender differences could help explain why girls perform more poorly on timed multiple-choice tests like the Math SAT. Compared to men, "Women are less likely to be cavalier; they're more methodical and check their answers, and they run out of time," says Ann Gallagher, an educational psychologist at the Law School Admission Council, which creates the Law School Admission Test. "On the SAT, a number of the questions need to be solved in a way girls are not taught to do it in the classroom; they need to think of an unconventional route. Girls may be hesitant because they're trying to do it the correct way."

Shauman believes girls may be socialized in ways that make them perform more poorly on high-stakes math tests but better on tests of material they learned in class. "We expect girls to behave well, do well in class, to follow directions," she says.

By contrast, "Men tend to be more likely to take leaps, to take risks," says James Kaufman, a psychologist at California State University, San Bernadino, and coeditor

with Gallagher of *Gender Differences in Mathematics*, published this year. While that approach may help men guess right on multiple-choice tests like the Math SAT, "in the classroom that doesn't necessarily help, and it doesn't necessarily help in real life, because these risks are just as likely to be wrong," he says. (Kaufman's explanation could help explain why girls who get the same grades in college math classes as boys often scored many points lower than their male peers on the Math SAT.)

Experts on both sides of the divide agree gender differences are real, even if they disagree about how much is socially learned and how much is biologically based. Girls do better on writing and on algebra problems, probably because algebraic equations are similar to sentences, and girls excel in language processing.[32] Boys are better at mathematical word problems; girls are better at mathematical calculation.

Boys and girls also differ on spatial skills, and experts are divided over how innate or important these differences are. A recent study of the Graduate Record Exam, for instance, found men did better on math problems where a spatially based solution was an advantage.[33]

Boys are better at geographic navigation and envisioning a three-dimensional object rotating in space; girls are better at remembering the location of objects and landmarks. When boys and girls are taken to an unfamiliar college campus and asked to draw a map of where they've been, "Boys get the position right: This building was x degrees northwest," according to David C. Geary, a psychologist at the University of Missouri in Columbia, Mo. "Girls get the landmarks, but the geometric position is not as accurate."

Sex hormones have been shown in several studies to affect the ability to envision an object rotating in space. Females who take male hormones to prepare for a sex-change operation improve on tests of 3-D rotation and get worse on tests of verbal fluency, at which women typically excel. During their menstrual cycle, women do better on 3-D rotation when levels of the female hormone estrogen are low; they do better on verbal fluency when estrogen levels are high.[34]

If differences between boys and girls stemmed mostly from socialization, Pinker argues in his book, "It would seem odd that the hormones that make us male and female in the first place also modulate the characteristically male and female mental traits."[35]

New research by Harvard anthropologist Carole Hooven, however, suggests the male hormone testosterone is tied not to better spatial ability but to greater confidence, which leads to better decisions on spatial tests. That finding, Hooven says, is "consistent with a huge amount of data on humans and non-human animals about what testosterone does — males have to be more aggressive for mating."

If differences in spatial abilities were innate, one might expect them to show up early in children's lives. But Harvard psychologist Elizabeth Spelke says that in 30 years of study on infants' and toddlers' cognitive and navigation skills, she has found no sex differences on any task. "If there were a genetic basis behind the fact that Harvard's math department has no women on its senior faculty, one place to look for that is early in development. And when we look there we see no differences whatsoever," she says.

Since many of these skill differences appear after adolescence, she suggests they're socially derived.

But Pinker disagrees. "Pubic hair, lowered voice and breasts don't show up until adolescence, but that does not mean they are products of socialization," he says, adding, "Spelke's research tests extremely basic cognitive abilities, such as the concept of number and space. The abilities in question here are far more esoteric and refined — we're talking about abilities that differentiate an MIT math professor from everyone else — and those could be sex differentiated even if basic concepts are not."

In any case, Gallagher and Kaufman point out in their book, there is no evidence that spatial skills "are actually necessary or important in solving complex mathematical problems of the type students encounter in college-level or graduate-level mathematics." Moreover, they note, the one skill the SAT does test — "speediness" in answering a question every two minutes — may be less prized by true mathematicians than persistence in solving a problem over days or weeks.[36]

Other researchers suggest there might be a middle ground in which biology and environment interact. For instance, says Beth Casey, a professor of applied developmental and educational psychology at Boston College, an attraction to experiences involving spatial and mechanical skills may be genetic, and, "because boys are attracted to them they do them more often and get better at them." The contention that interest in objects is inborn in males is, however, controversial and disputed by Spelke. (*See sidebar, p. 221.*)

Even a recent finding by Haier that men are more likely to use a part of the brain associated with visual-spatial processing when taking an IQ test — a region that was unusually large in Albert Einstein's brain — "doesn't speak to whether or not that's innate," Haier says.[37] "We know from one study that learning juggling seems to increase gray matter in some of the motor areas; there's a sense that environmental influences interact with genetic influences to produce biological differences. But how much of the math difference is due to biological and other differences — you can't put a number on that yet."

Is enough being done to encourage women in science and math?

Since the publication of AAUW claims that schools were shortchanging girls, schools across the country have introduced "girl-friendly" approaches to math and science designed to combat bias against girls, aided by millions of dollars in federal funding.

"We found if we taught science differently with a hands-on, inquiry-based approach, it sustains girls' interest in science," particularly in middle school, when girls tend to turn away from science, says Ruta Sevo, who directs the National Science Foundation's research program on gender in science and engineering. The foundation has spent $8-$10 million a year since 1993 to study successful teaching approaches for girls and share the findings with schools.

"Girls like to work in cooperative teams; [previously,] a lot of science was taught in a competitive mode," Sevo says. Programs like these, along with a more encouraging national climate, have helped shrink the gender gap in math and science achievement, supporters claim.

But Sommers, at the American Enterprise Institute, a conservative think tank, says the government wasted millions of dollars to study a "manufactured crisis." Federally funded programs to counter bias against girls have stigmatized boys, who are doing far more poorly in school, she contends. "A boy today, through no fault of his own, finds himself implicated in the social crime of 'shortchanging' girls," she writes in *The War Against Boys*. "Yet the allegedly silenced and neglected girl sitting next to him is likely to be the better student."[38]

CHRONOLOGY

1900s *Number of girls taking science falls as home economics, male science teachers gain ascendancy and colleges open doors to women.*

1900 Commissioner of Education recommends teaching girls housekeeping skills, not trigonometry.

1903 Marie Curie, first woman to win Nobel Prize, shares prize for physics with her husband.

1905 Girls score higher on first IQ test designed by Alfred Binet; he removes questions favoring girls.

1950s *Number of girls taking science continues to plummet.*

1955 Only 2 percent of high school girls take physics.

1957 Russians launch *Sputnik* satellite, focusing renewed attention on U.S. science education.

1960s-1980s *Women's movement spurs legal fight for equal education; research finds brain differences in men and women.*

1964 Canadian psychologist Herbert Lansdell reports anatomical differences between men's and women's brains.

1972 Congress passes Education Amendments, including Title IX prohibition on sex discrimination.

1989 In New York, federal judge finds SAT biased against girls, rules the state cannot use SAT scores to award scholarships.

1990s *Reports that schools shortchange girls in math and science spur federal programs to help girls. Critics say boys are in more trouble.*

1992 American Association of University Women (AAUW) releases report "How Schools Shortchange Girls," saying girls lag behind boys in math and science.

1994 Congress passes Gender Equity in Education Act to counter bias against girls in school.

1998 Department of Education report shows high school girls take as many math and science courses as boys in most subjects, a gap that was closing in 1992.

1999 Two teenage boys go on shooting rampage at Columbine High School in Littleton, Colo., shifting national concern to boys' poorer performance in school.

2000s *Congressional and university panels blame low hiring rate of female scientists on discrimination and family-unfriendly policies; debate rages over whether there are innate aptitude differences between the sexes.*

2002 Sen. Ron Wyden, D-Ore., chairs hearings urging stronger enforcement of Title IX to counter discrimination in university hiring of women scientists.

2003 Women make up 20 percent of all U.S. scientists, compared to less than 3 percent in 1960. But most are concentrated in life sciences.

2004 GAO report finds women lagging in rank, salary and numbers on university science faculties; urges stronger enforcement of Title IX.

Jan. 14, 2005 Harvard President Lawrence Summers suggests gender differences in "intrinsic aptitude" partly explain low number of women scientists.

February 2005 Ten university presidents recommend part-time tenure positions to counter flight of women from family-unfriendly universities.

March 2005 More than 6,000 women scientists urge Sen. Wyden to investigate low numbers of women in science academia.

May 2005 Harvard President Summers pledges to spend $50 million to implement task force recommendations aimed at improving the climate for women in science at Harvard as well as recruiting and retaining more women faculty. . . . A report on the University of California system finds a decline in the proportion of women faculty hired.

Is the Math SAT Biased Against Girls?

Since the development of the first IQ test in 1905, test-makers have struggled with gender bias but have usually resolved the issues in favor of boys, according to some experts.

In the early days of IQ testing, girls scored better than boys, a finding that was thought to undermine the test. So French psychologist Alfred Binet, the developer of the first IQ test, threw out the items most favorable to girls, and the gender difference disappeared.[1]

More recently, on the Math SAT, test-makers removed a girl-friendly class of questions — those asking whether there were sufficient data to answer a given problem. Likewise, when girls were found to score higher on the verbal section, boy-friendly problems on sports, politics and business were added, resulting in an increase in male test scores.

But today — even though girls score on average about 36 points lower than boys on the Math SAT, "no similar attempt has been made to 'balance' the Math SAT," an editorial in *Nature Neuroscience* recently charged.[2]

Such a history of anti-female bias in testing "should cast doubt" on the SAT as "some gold standard of mathematical ability," contends Susan F. Chipman, an educational psychologist at the Office of Naval Research.[3]

Indeed, FairTest, a nonprofit group in Cambridge, Mass., claims the Math SAT is biased against girls due to its reliance on multiple choice, speed and guessing. In 1989, the group won a favorable federal court decision from the Southern District of New York, barring the use of SAT scores to award New York state Regents' scholarships.[4]

FairTest also filed a complaint in 1989 with the Education Department's Office of Civil Rights, charging that the Preliminary SAT (PSAT) — which is given to 10th- and 11th-graders — discriminates against girls. The PSAT is the primary factor determining eligibility for National Merit Scholarships. In response, The College Board, which creates both the PSAT and the SAT, added a multiple-choice writing test to the PSAT, which helped bridge the gap between male and female performance on the test by 40 percent, according to FairTest.

However, the Math SAT "remains biased against girls," says Robert Schaeffer, public education director for FairTest. "The sole scientific claim made for the SAT is its capacity to predict first-year college grades. But despite their lower scores, women continue to earn higher grades in identical math classes than their male counterparts."

Some experts theorize that perhaps girls' average Math SAT scores are lower than boys' because more girls than boys apply to college — and thus take the test — including more girls with lower math preparation or ability.

Other studies suggest that girls perform more poorly on high-stress tests when reminded — by filling out questionnaires asking their sex — of the stereotype that girls are bad at math or by hearing examiners' statements about boys' superior performance.[5]

---

[1] See Robert Pool, *Eve's Rib* (1994), p. 23.

[2] "Editorial: Separating Science from Stereotype," *Nature Neuroscience*, March 2005, p. 253.

[3] Ann M. Gallagher and James C. Kaufman, *Gender Differences in Mathematics* (2005), p. 16.

[4] "Gender Bias in College Admissions Tests," at www.fairtest.org. The case was *Sharif v. New York State Education Department.*

[5] Gallagher and Kaufman, *op. cit.*, p. 199.

Some programs, for instance, have gone to ludicrous extremes to eliminate competition, she contends. One K-3 anti-harassment curriculum she cites, called "Quit It!" recommends that teachers replace tag with a new, less aggressive game, "Circle of Friends," where nobody is ever "out."[39]

While much of the concern about prejudice against grade-school girls has dissipated, women's groups say there is still a major problem in universities. For example, while women received close to 45 percent of the doctoral degrees in biology between 1993 and 2002, they accounted for only about 30 percent of the entry-level assistant professors in 2002.[40] The low number of women hired in science posts is not due to an "innate lack of ability but to discriminatory barriers," according to Jocelyn Samuels, vice president of education and employment at the National Women's Law Center.

She blames not only individual instances of bias against qualified women on hiring committees but also "a chilling environment where the atmosphere and culture sends the message, 'Women don't belong.' " Specifically, she contends that female graduate students and faculty tend to receive less lab space, less mentoring by senior faculty and fewer invitations to participate in large research grants. She points to a 1999 study at the Massachusetts Institute of Technology (MIT), which found that women received lower salaries than their male peers and were excluded from leadership positions.[41]

In a Jan. 27 letter, the center and 21 other women's groups called on Summers and other university officials to "aggressively pursue and ensure full compliance" with Title IX of the Education Amendments of 1972, prohibiting sex discrimination in education, and Title VII of the 1964 Civil Rights Act, which bars employment discrimination on the basis of sex. Meanwhile, the GAO last year said federal agencies that make science grants should do more to ensure that universities receiving grants are complying with Title IX.[42] Women's groups also have cited the low percentages of full-time women faculty in engineering (10 percent), mathematics (26 percent) and physical sciences (16 percent) and a drop in the numbers of women receiving undergraduate degrees in computer sciences (from 37 percent in 1984 to 28 percent in 2001) as evidence of discrimination and a climate unfriendly to women.[43]

But some experts say women's low numbers in those fields represent their differing interests from men, not discrimination. "Women worldwide are more interested in nurturing, and men are more interested in things. It makes perfect evolutionary sense," vocational expert Gottfredson says. That divide explains why women get a small proportion of the PhDs in physics and engineering (things) but account for 71 percent of doctorates in clinical psychology (people), according to Gottfredson. "It's putting unrealistic pressure on everyone to expect 50-50 in everything," she says. "It just doesn't fit what women themselves say they want" in surveys.

Gottfredson's "people vs. things" dichotomy is "just the kind of stereotype Title IX and Title VII were enacted to eliminate," Samuels retorts. Women's interest in something "cannot be measured in the absence of opportunity," she says. "You're really measuring lack of exposure." She points to the explosive growth of women entering medicine and law once the doors of professional schools opened to them and the quadrupling of women in

Three professors led the task forces that recommended sweeping changes to improve the climate for women students and faculty at Harvard: from left, Radcliffe Institute Dean Drew Gilpin Faust, Professor of the History of Science and of African and African-American Studies Evelynn Hammonds, and Barbara J. Grosz, Higgins Professor of Natural Sciences and Dean of Science at the Radcliffe Institute.

college sports following the enforcement of Title IX. "Their genes haven't changed," she says.

Motherhood also has an impact on why more women don't progress up the academic ladder, several studies have concluded. At nearly every stage of the academic track, married women — especially those with children — "leak out of the academic pipeline at a disproportionately high rate," researchers at the University of California-Berkeley found. Since the average age for granting tenure to a PhD is 33, junior women faculty are expected to increase their publication rate during the very years when childbearing and child-raising duties are heaviest.[44]

Responding to these trends, 10 university presidents recently recommended that universities offer a family-friendly policy considered highly innovative for academia — part-time tenured faculty positions. U.S. higher education "cannot afford to lose any of its potential intellectual work force," particularly in science and technology, they said in a report highlighting the loss of women from science.[45]

But some skeptics of family-friendly policies question whether women who drop out of the tenure track or cut back on work hours to care for their children do so unwillingly. "A lot of it is choice," says Wayne State University Professor of Law Kingsley Browne. "A lot of studies show that women think they need to be taking care of children because their husbands don't do a good enough job."

Women scientists also earn less than men. In fact, full-time female life scientists earn $72,000 a year — 23 percent less than the $94,000 earned by their male counterparts.[46]

But it's only fair that women who work fewer hours face the economic consequences of lower salaries and less status, Browne argues in his 2002 book *Biology at Work: Rethinking Sexual Equality.*

Increasingly, economists are starting to agree that the leakage of women from the pipeline has something to do with the fact that women's child-raising responsibilities coincide with the years when most universities decide tenure. "We're still working from a model that worked well when men had stay-at-home wives," says Harvard researcher Cathy Trower, who is conducting a nation-wide study of junior faculty. Most promotion and tenure standards were formulated in 1940 by an all-male con-ference of the American Association of University Professors, she notes.

Most of the top 50 research universities and many smaller colleges already offer an option known as "stop-ping the tenure clock" so faculty who take a leave during a child-related break will not be penalized for slowing down publication. But several studies have found that women are often reluctant to take advantage of these policies for fear that it will cast doubt on their profes-sional commitment and productivity when they come up for tenure.[47]

"It's not just a matter of putting programs and poli-cies in place. You've got to create a culture where it's OK to take advantage of them," says Gloria Thomas, associ-ate project coordinator at the American Council on Education, which issued a report this year recommend-ing part-time tenure positions and other family-friendly policies.

BACKGROUND

Women in Science

"The question is not why there haven't been more women in science; the question is rather why we have not heard more about them," Naomi Oreskes, a historian of science at the University of California-San Diego, has observed.[48]

For example, Ada Byron — the Countess of Lovelace (1815-1852) and the daughter of the British Romantic poet Lord Byron — is often identified as the founder of scientific computing. Her mother, Lady Byron, had her tutored in mathematics to shield her from the loose morals and passions inspired by poetry. Ada wrote some of the first computer programs — or computing tables — for Charles Babbage, a mathematics professor at Cambridge University and inventor of the elaborate calculating machine known as the Difference Engine.[49]

Marie Curie (1867-1934), who with her husband Pierre discovered radium, is of course known for having received two Nobel Prizes. In 1903 she and Pierre received the Nobel Prize for physics for their study into spontane-ous radiation. In 1911, she received a second Nobel, this time in chemistry for her work in radioactivity. But other female Nobel Prize winners have been less well known: Two received prizes in chemistry, two in physics and seven in physiology and medicine, most recently Linda B. Buck, of the Fred Hutchinson Cancer Research Center in Seattle, in 2004 for discovering the body's odor receptors and the organization of olfactory systems.

As the biographies of Ada Byron and Marie Curie suggest, math and science were not always considered men's work. In many early-19th century U.S. schools, more girls than boys studied science, and girls routinely outperformed boys on math and physics through much of the 1800s. Upper- and middle-class boys concentrated on learning the classics — Latin and Greek — because they were a status symbol and required for entering col-lege. Since most colleges at the time barred women, girls focused on science. Physics, astronomy, chemistry and botany were seen as morally and spiritually uplifting subjects for upper- and middle-class girls.[50]

With the rise of coeducational schools later in the century, it became clear many boys were failing in their studies, while far more girls were excelling. Some educators blamed the feminizing influence of women teachers and textbooks that taught science through stories about anthropomorphized plants and animals. At the end of the 19th century, these views triggered a backlash against female science teachers and marked the beginning of a gradual decline in the proportion of women entering science education.

Why Girls Like Dolls

In a famous experiment, more than 100 day-old babies were shown a smiling female student and then a dangling mobile of similar size. Female babies looked longer at the face; boys looked longer at the mobile.[1]

The experiment by Cambridge University psychologist Simon Baron-Cohen has generated much controversy between believers and skeptics of innate differences. Baron-Cohen says it proves "beyond reasonable doubt" that sex differences in social interest are "in part biological in origin" and supports his theory that girls tend to be "empathizers" (better at social relations) while boys are "systemizers" (better at math, science and mechanical tinkering).[2]

But Harvard psychologist Elizabeth Spelke questions whether the smiling student might have biased the experiment by acting more expressively with the girls than with the boys, and whether the babies' parents may have behaved differently according to the infants' sex. Hundreds of experiments by her and other researchers have found no differences in the ways infants perceive objects, she argues.

Maryland physician Leonard Sax has yet another explanation: The babies' actions may reflect sex differences in the anatomy of the eye rather than in the anatomy of the brain. Studies have shown that the male retina has mostly cells that compile information about movement and direction while the female retina has smaller cells that compile information about texture and color. That explains why young girls are more likely to crayon in colors while boys prefer to draw in black and white, according to Sax.

That may also explain why girls are more attracted to the more complex texture of a human face and to dolls while boys are attracted to a dangling mobile and a moving toy truck, he suggests.[3]

[1] Simon Baron-Cohen, *The Essential Difference: The Truth about the Male and Female Brain* (2003), pp. 54-56.

[2] Quoted in Leonard Sax, *Why Gender Matters* (2005), p. 19. Jennifer Connellan, Simon Baron-Cohen, *et al.*, "Sex Differences in Human Neonatal Social Perception," *Infant Behavior and Development*, 2000, pp. 113-18.

[3] Sax, *ibid*, pp. 18-22.

After the Civil War, college doors were opened to women, who took up the study of Latin in growing numbers. But by 1900, so-called progressive educators were advocating making schooling more "practical," recommending, for instance, that high school girls be taught home economics, which drew girls away from enrolling in science and mathematics classes. Girls would be far better prepared "for a full, happy life," said a 1900 report issued by the Commissioner of Education, by taking a course in "dressmaking or cookery and arithmetic" instead of studying "trigonometry and art."[51]

Partly as a result, fewer young women entered institutions of higher education with the necessary background to major in a scientific field.

Growing Sexism

At the turn of the 20th century, women were particularly interested in the nature-study movement, which peaked in 1900-1910 and provided opportunities for women as science teachers, amateur collectors and museum and laboratory assistants. Much of the attack against women teachers, which gathered force after 1910, was aimed at the nature-study movement, which with its spiritual overtones was criticized for being too sentimental and feminizing to appeal to boys.

During the first decades of the 20th century, male science teachers began to dominate the newly formed professional associations. Textbooks and curriculum increasingly emphasized the physical sciences with the goal of encouraging more boys to take up science as a vocation. The National Research Council, which dispensed Rockefeller and Carnegie foundation grants for scientific projects, played a role by supporting men but rejecting women for funding. Although women represented 13 percent of the doctorates in the sciences, they received only 5 percent of the fellowships between 1920 and 1938.

The launch of the Soviet satellite *Sputnik* in 1957 aroused alarm that American science education was lagging behind its Cold War rival's. The federal government supported curriculum initiatives to train gifted students in science, but when asked to identify those who might be potential scientists, "contemporaries almost always identified boys," writes Kim Tolley, director of the master of education program at Notre Dame de Namur University, in Belmont, Calif.[52]

Physicists' central role in developing nuclear bombs may also have steered many girls away from physics. In the 1950s, high school students described the scientist as a "mad, godless 'brain' or a sort of sorcerer's apprentice," according to anthropologist Margaret Mead. By 1955, the proportion of girls taking high school physics had fallen to less than 2 percent, down from 23 percent in 1890.[53]

'Weak-minded' Women

Throughout much of the 19th and early 20th centuries, numerous theories claimed women were biologically incapable of engaging in reason, science and medicine. German physician Paul Julius Mobius's bestseller, *Regarding the Physiological Weak-Mindedness of Women,* argued that the smaller size of women's skulls explained their weaker intellect. While that theory appears to have validity for men, we know today that women with high IQs do not have larger brains than women with low IQs.[54]

However, scientists have continued to find differences in men's and women's brains. In men, greater gray matter is correlated with higher IQ; for women more white matter is related to intellectual functioning. In his most recent imaging study, psychologist Haier found women and men of equal intelligence used different parts of the brain while taking an IQ test. "We concluded that there seem to be two different brain architectures — one for men, one for women — both leading to equivalent performance on tests of intelligence," he says.

The modern era of research in gender differences began in 1964, when Canadian psychologist Herbert Lansdell reported the existence of anatomical differences in the organization of female and male brains. Over the next two decades, a series of studies demonstrated that while the left hemisphere of the brain is clearly specialized for language functions in men, such asymmetrical organization is less noticeable in women. Women tend to use more parts of their brain to accomplish specific intellectual tasks, which may explain why they often have better recoveries from stroke, using healthy parts of the brain to compensate for injured regions.[55]

Maryland physician Sax says one of the most important findings of recent brain research is that different regions of the brain mature in different sequences for boys and

girls. Some of the regions involved in mechanical, visual and spatial reasoning appear to mature four to eight years earlier in boys. Parts of the brain that handle language and fine motor skills like handwriting mature several years earlier in girls.[56]

"The fact that girls may not excel in geometry at 12 doesn't mean they won't have the brain of a Euclid or Einstein," Sax says. Boys' inferior language skills in the early grades "doesn't mean among boys we won't have a Faulkner or a Hemingway," he adds.

Gender-Equity Fight

The women's movement, which gained momentum in the 1960s, focused attention on careers that had previously been barred to women. Title IX of the Educational Amendments of 1972, barring gender discrimination in education, provided a legal basis for women to fight in court for gender equity. In 1983 in *Newburg v. Board of Education,* a Pennsylvania state court ruled that Girls High School in Philadelphia had inferior course offerings in math and science, compared to the all-boys Central High. The court ordered Central to admit girls.

Rising concern about the neglect of girls in the classroom beginning in the 1980s sparked new efforts to interest girls in math and science. In the early 1990s, research by Harvard psychologist Carol Gilligan (now at New York University) described adolescence as a time when girls experience an erosion of self-esteem.[57]

Gilligan's work was bolstered in the 1980s by the observations of David and Myron Sadker, who reported that boys dominated classroom discussions and were more likely to get attention from teachers, which helped boys' superior achievement.[58]

National attention focused on the issue in 1992 when an AAUW study reported that girls were lagging seriously behind boys in math and science, particularly in taking advanced courses in those subjects. The report leaned heavily on research by the Sadkers reporting that teachers gave more classroom attention to elementary and middle-school boys, who called out answers more often than girls. By contrast, when girls called out they were usually corrected with comments like, "Please raise your hand if you want to speak," the Sadkers reported.[59]

These conclusions were harshly criticized by the American Enterprise Institute's Sommers, who said the Sadkers were never able to supply the original data for

Did Evolution Make Males Better at Math?

Evolution is often offered as an explanation for differences in boys' and girls' math abilities, usually put forward by those who believe that boys have an innate, biological advantage. Although the theories may sound logical, they are just theories. "They're certainly not quoting any archeologist who's ever dug a site," says Shirley Gorenstein, professor emeritus of anthropology at Rensselaer Polytechnic Institute. "We have only a vague idea" what life was like for the hunter-gatherer societies of 10,000 years ago, according to Gorenstein. And as psychologist Diane F. Halpern at Claremont McKenna College has noted, "almost any result can be explained post hoc" by an evolutionary theory.[1]

Here are three commonly offered evolutionary explanations:

- Men have better navigational skills and can better visualize an object rotating through space because early man needed these skills to hunt and find his way home. "If you're hunting or going on a raiding party, you don't know exactly where you're going before you start the trip. Men almost certainly engaged in activities that involved more moving around and that would lead to a better ability to represent 3-D space," says David C. Geary, a University of Missouri psychologist.

   Counterargument: The spatial skills used to solve math and physics problems are "conceptually closer" to those typically used by females in traditional societies, such as weaving, Halpern argues.[2] According to Gorenstein, we don't even know for sure that men rather than women were the original hunters.

- Men are more interested in mechanical things than women because in early societies men made tools. The areas of the brain associated with spatial abilities "seem engaged when people are thinking about or using tools," says Geary, arguing it might explain males' superior ability in some forms of spatial reasoning.

   Counterargument: "We don't know who the tool makers were," Gorenstein says. If Stone Age men dragged rocks back to home camps from the quarry, women could have made the tools at home, she says.

- Men are more variable in ability than women are (there are both more brilliant male minds and more subnormal male minds) because a male can have more offspring than a female. To achieve better reproductive success, Harvard psychologist Steven Pinker argues, men are more likely to be polygamous, seeking quantity in offspring, while women

seek quality. In a recent *New Republic* article, Pinker stated "an exceptional son who might sire several-dozen grandchildren can more than make up for his dull, childless brothers."[3]

Counterargument: The problem with Pinker's philandering caveman, writes *New York Times* science reporter Natalie Angier, is that biologically "each episode of fleeting sex has a remarkably small probability of yielding a baby."[4] The bed-hopper might not have survived very long because each new effort at wooing a fertile female "would have pushed him smack up against a thicket of other suitors' spear tips."[5]

It's not clear why more men than women score at both the upper and lower ends on achievement tests, says Kimberlee Shauman, a sociologist at the University of California-Davis, nor that the greater number of top-scoring men is immutable.

"When people refer to the past to sustain a current argument, they either need archaeological data as direct evidence or they can imagine the past," Gorenstein says.

Imagining is just what the new school of evolutionary psychologists is doing when they promote ideas like these, Angier complains. But evolutionary psychology has found a popular audience, as evidenced by Pinker's best-selling book *The Blank Slate*, which argues that many feminists have gone too far in elevating nurture over nature.[6]

Angier contends that evolutionary psychologists often have little evidence to support their view of nature. In her book *Woman: An Intimate Geography*, Angier denounces evolutionary psychology as a form of "neo-Darwinism that has trampled across the campus of public opinion . . . feeling no humbleness for want of evidence or for the many exceptions to their book of rules."[7]

---

[1] Diane F. Halpern, "A Cognitive-Process Taxonomy for Sex Differences in Cognitive Abilities," *Current Directions in Psychological Science* (2004), pp. 138-9.

[2] *Ibid.*

[3] Steven Pinker, "The Science of Difference," *The New Republic Online*, post date Feb. 7, 2005.

[4] Natalie Angier, *Woman: An Intimate Geography* (1999), p. 368.

[5] *Ibid.*, p. 385.

[6] Steven Pinker, *The Blank Slate: The Modern Denial of Human Nature* (2002).

[7] Angier, *op. cit.*, p. 378.

Are gender differences in math and science innate?

YES — Steven Pinker
Professor of Psychology, Harvard University

From a debate at Harvard, April 22, 2005, posted online at www.edge.org

There is much hard evidence for innate sex differences, evidence that cannot be explained away by socialization and bias.

There are large differences between males and females in levels of sex hormones, and there are receptors for those hormones all over the brain. There are many small differences in men's and women's brains, including the overall size of the brain (even correcting for body size), the density of cortical neurons, the degree of cortical asymmetry and several others.

Sex differences seem to emerge even in the first week of life. Girls respond more to sounds of distress and make more eye contact than boys. Newborn boys [are] more interested in looking at a physical object than a face, whereas newborn girls are more interested in looking at a face than an object.

[L]ater in development there are vast and robust differences between boys and girls, seen all over the world, in all types of cultures, pre- and post-waves of feminism. Boys far more often than girls engage in rough-and-tumble play, which involves aggression, physical activity and competition. Girls spend a lot more time in cooperative play [and playing at] parenting.

Evidence disproves that these behaviors are just the products of socialization. In a famous 1970s incident called the John/Joan case, one member of a pair of identical twin boys lost his penis in a botched circumcision. Following advice from the leading gender expert of the time, the parents agreed to have the boy castrated, given female-specific hormones and brought up as a girl. All this was hidden from him throughout his childhood.

[I]t turned out that from the youngest age he exhibited boy-typical patterns of aggression and rough-and-tumble play, rejected girl-typical activities and showed a greater interest in things than in people. At age 14, his father finally told him the truth. He underwent surgery, married a woman, adopted two children and got a job in a slaughterhouse.

There seems to be a widespread assumption that if a sex difference conforms to a stereotype, the difference must have been caused by . . . differential expectations for boys and for girls. But, in fact, stereotypes might reflect differences rather than cause them. For example, there is a stereotype that basketball players are taller than jockeys. But that does not mean that basketball players grow tall, and jockeys shrink [just] because we expect them to have certain heights!

NO — Elizabeth Spelke
Professor of Psychology, Co-Director, Mind, Brain and Behavior Initiative, Harvard University

From a debate at Harvard, April 22, 2005, posted online at www.edge.org

From the moment of birth, there are unintentional but pervasive and important differences in the ways males and females are perceived and evaluated.

Studies . . . have found that parents of boys describe their babies as stronger, heartier and bigger than parents of girls, although medical records revealed the boys and girls were indistinguishable in weight, strength and coordination.

When parents of sixth-grade students were asked how talented their child was in mathematics, [boys'] parents were more likely to say their sons had talent than parents of daughters. Objective measures — including math grades, performance on standardized tests, teachers' evaluations and children's expressed interest in math — revealed no differences between the girls and boys.

So there's clearly a mismatch between what parents perceive in their kids and what objective measures reveal. If knowledge of a child's gender affects adults' perception of that child, then male and female children are going to elicit different reactions from the world and different patterns of encouragement.

These biased perceptions may deter some female students from even attempting a career in science or mathematics. . . . There's also likely to be a snowball effect. All of us have an easier time imagining ourselves in careers where there are other people like us. In a situation where there are few female scientists and mathematicians, young girls will be less likely to see math and science as a possible life.

Moreover, because of social forces it is currently impossible to evaluate whether biological differences factor into propelling more men than women into careers in mathematics and science.

As long as discrimination and biased perceptions affect people so pervasively, we'll never know if the argument holds any weight. The only way we can find out is to allow all of the evidence that men and women have equal cognitive capacity to permeate through society. Allow people to evaluate children in relation to their actual capacities, rather than one's sense of what their capacities ought to be, given their gender. Then we can see, as those boys and girls grow up, whether different inner voices pull them in different directions.

I don't know what the findings of that experiment will be. But I do hope that some future generation of children gets to find out.

their finding that boys called out answers eight times more often than girls. "Whatever the accurate number may be, no one has even shown that permitting a student to call out answers in the classroom confers any kind of academic advantage," she wrote in *The War Against Boys*. Boys were probably less attentive than girls as evidenced by their generally poorer academic performance, she suggested, which might be why teachers called on them more.[60]

In 1998, former Education Department official Ravitch blamed the AAUW, as well as a gullible press, for diverting attention from the much larger gaps among African-Americans and Hispanics. She told *The New York Times* that the AAUW report had come out as "girls had just overtaken boys in almost every area."[61]

Indeed, sex differences in high school math course participation had disappeared or even shifted to favor females. Even the differences in those taking calculus was small — 11.2 percent of males and 10.6 percent of females; AP calculus was taken by 7.3 percent of males and 6.4 percent of females.[62] Women earned close to half of all science and engineering bachelor's degrees that year. Beginning in the late 1990s, they were more likely than men to enter graduate school after obtaining a science bachelor's degree.[63]

Some of these changes had even predated the AAUW report. Between 1960 and 1972, the percentage of girls taking four years of high school math had more than doubled.[64] American women have received more college degrees than American men every year since 1982, a gap that continues to widen every year.[65]

In 1994, Congress passed the Gender Equity in Education Act, which defined girls as an "under-served population" on the same level as other discriminated-against minorities. The AAUW helped write provisions requiring teacher training in gender equity and mandating gender-equitable teaching methods in high-poverty schools. The federal government awarded millions of dollars to researchers to study the plight of girls and to educators to counter the bias against them. According to Sommers, this helped to foster a cottage industry of gender-bias experts, whom schools felt pressured to hire to avoid being charged with discrimination.

In the late 1990s, a spate of books about the plight of boys shifted attention to their far worse average performance in reading, their higher numbers in remedial education and the fact that they were a shrinking minority

of those entering college. The mass murders committed by two adolescent boys at the Columbine High School in Littleton, Colo. in 1999 suddenly put boys in the spotlight as the troubled sex.[66]

CURRENT SITUATION

Discrimination or Choice?

The recent debate over the remarks by Harvard's Summers has sparked renewed attention to an area some would say has been studied to death. Earlier this month, women's science groups gathered over 6,000 signatures on a letter to Sens. Ron Wyden, D-Ore., and George Allen, R-Va., urging Congress to conduct a broad-ranging inquiry investigating "persistent under-representation" of women in science and engineering and to study how federal laws could address inequities.[67]

"People are really tired of waiting for there to be a change. They'd like attention to be paid to this consistently," says Carol Muller, one of the organizers of the signature drive and founder and CEO of Mentornet, an organization that pairs budding scientists with professional mentors.

Repeatedly, congressional committees and commissions have bewailed the low number of women in science careers, but action has been slow to follow, Muller says. For example, in 2000 the congressional Commission on the Advancement of Women and Minorities in Science, Engineering and Technology Development recommended national education standards to encourage better preparation in math and science of girls and minorities and more aggressive efforts by employers to hire women and minorities in science and technology.[68] There was no follow-up, Muller contends.

Wyden chaired hearings in 2002 questioning the low representation of women in many university science departments and calling for stronger enforcement of Title IX prohibitions on sex discrimination. The hearings led Congress to pass legislation that year mandating a National Academy of Sciences report on women's careers in science. That report, expected by the end of 2005, will investigate gender differences in hiring, promotion and such benefits as lab space at 89 research universities.

In a report last year, also mandated by the legislation, the GAO found that most federal science agencies responsible for distributing billions of dollars in research grants to universities have not set up procedures to ensure that the schools are complying with Title IX. While the proportion of women faculty in the sciences has increased in the past three decades, the report said, "they still lag behind men faculty in terms of salary and rank." It also cited studies suggesting that discrimination "may still affect women's choices and professional progress."[69]

In response to the GAO report, federal agencies including the National Science Foundation (NSF), the Department of Education, the Department of Energy and NASA have formed an interagency committee to jump-start Title IX enforcement. The NSF will be looking to see whether discrimination complaints have been filed, whether grievance procedures are in place at the schools and how many women are employed in math and science departments, according to Ronald Branch, director of NSF's Office of Equal Opportunity Programs.

The GAO also found that relatively few sex-discrimination complaints have been filed by women scientists against universities, suggesting little overt discrimination in the view of some critics of affirmative action. But women's advocacy groups say women either don't know about their legal rights or are afraid to file a complaint. "There's a real fear of retaliation out there," says Samuels of the National Women's Law Center. "That's why federal enforcement is so critical."

Just by threatening to withhold research grants from universities that don't comply with Title IX, federal agencies could have a huge impact on women's participation, says Harvard researcher Trower. "You need the big stick," she says. "You need to withhold money from people until they do what they say they're going to do."

More Women Scientists

Women's participation in the sciences has grown dramatically in the last four decades. In 1960, women made up less than 3 percent of all scientists; by 2003 they composed 20 percent of scientists, according to the GAO. In 1960 they constituted less than 1 percent of engineers and 26 percent of mathematicians. By 2003, they made up 14 percent of engineers and a third of mathematicians.[70]

But women's representation in academic departments has not kept pace with their growth in science bachelor's and doctoral degrees. For example, female students now account for 47 percent of bachelor's degrees in chemistry but only 12 percent of chemistry faculty. They account for 48 percent of bachelor's degrees in math but only 8 percent of faculty.[71]

Harvard economist Claudia Goldin calls this trend puzzling considering that "the pipeline is now fuller at the start" with women getting degrees in science. "It is the leakage along the way to the top that is the new matter for concern."[72]

One factor may be the low turnover in academic departments, where full professors can retain tenure well into their 70s.

Some argue that discrimination still plays a big part in the way academic departments search for new faculty. "It's still the case at the majority of campuses that males constitute the majority of search committees," says Elizabeth Ivey, president of the Association for Women in Science. "They've got to learn you have to call more than just your male buddies."

The problem is exacerbated by the fact that women often lack female mentors and role models in science departments. Women's greater child-care responsibilities often mean they don't have the time to network informally like their male peers.

Protestations from faculty that they're unable to find qualified women often hide unconscious bias, critics say. Rhea Steinpreis, a neuroscientist at the University of Wisconsin-Milwaukee, tested this contention by sending the identical résumé to 238 randomly selected psychology professors. Fewer than half said they would hire the applicant when the name "Karen Miller" appeared at the top; two-thirds endorsed the applicant when the name "Brian Miller" headed the résumé.[73]

OUTLOOK

Crisis Ahead?

Pressure to bring more women into science may intensify along with growing national concerns about a potential shortage of homegrown scientists, engineers and technicians. Shirley Ann Jackson, president of Rensselaer Polytechnic Institute, in Troy, N.Y., has called the country's failure to meet its need for technically skilled workers a "crisis" that "could jeopardize the nation's pre-eminence" in the world.[74]

As the American Council on Education noted in a recent report, the United States can no longer rely so heavily on foreign students, many of whom used to assume faculty or research careers. Immigration restrictions imposed since 9/11 have recently stemmed this tide, and burgeoning economic powers like India and China are establishing their own universities to retain native-born scientists.[75]

A study by Harvard researchers now getting under way will rate universities based on their family-friendly policies. Survey researcher Trower hopes junior women faculty will request the ratings when they're seeking jobs, placing competitive pressure on universities to institute such policies in order to attract the best and the brightest. "We're trying to bring market forces to bear on [colleges and universities], because all the task forces and recommendations are not changing the workplace," she says.

But some educational experts say the focus on shrinking gender differences in science seems misplaced, considering that the most disturbing educational lag in achievement is found among minority boys, not girls.

"Only one-third of Latinos and less than half of African-Americans are graduating from high school; that's very serious news," says Halpern, noting African-American boys perform more poorly than African-American girls on almost every measure.

In addition, many areas of research on gender differences are still in their infancy. Only recently have scientists been able to look inside the brain with the new technology of functional magnetic resonance imaging to see what parts of the brain light up when men and women perform intellectual tasks. The significance of these exciting new pictures in explaining gender differences in learning could take many years to tease out.

Other schools of thought are highly speculative and controversial, such as evolutionary explanations attributing women's growing numbers in the biological sciences to their traditional nurturing roles or boys' superior spatial skills to their territorial wanderings as early hunter-gatherers.

Meanwhile, research from the environmental camp concluding that negative gender stereotypes hurt girls' performance on high-stakes math tests has been dismissed as flimsy by experts in the biological camp.

Historically, differing pictures of science have been marshaled by advocates depending on how much stock they put in innate differences, how they picture feminine "nature" and whether they think women's participation

in science can increase dramatically. That fight is likely to continue.

NOTES

1. Summers phrased his comment this way: "So, my best guess, to provoke you, is . . . there are issues of intrinsic aptitude . . . and that those considerations are reinforced by what are in fact lesser factors involving socialization and discrimination." For his complete remarks, see "Full Transcript: President Summers' Remarks at the National Bureau of Economic Research, Jan. 14, 2005," *The Harvard Crimson*, Feb. 18, 2005 at www.thecrimson.com. His comment that there were "innate differences" came in a later interview: See Marcella Bombardieri, "Summers' Remarks on Women Draw Fire," *The Boston Globe*, Jan. 17, 2005, p. A1.

2. Donna J. Nelson, "A National Analysis of Diversity in Science and Engineering Faculties at Research Universities," Jan. 6, 2005.

3. Linda Chavez, "Harvard Prez's Admission: Men and Women are Different," *Jewish World Review*, Jan. 19, 2005, at www.jewishworldreview.com.

4. Anat Zohar, *et al.*, "Her Physics, His Physics: Gender Issues in Israeli Advanced Placement Physics Classes," *International Journal of Science Education*, Vol. 25, No. 2, 2003, pp. 245-268.

5. Diane F. Halpern, "A Cognitive Process Taxonomy for Sex Differences in Cognitive Abilities," *Current Directions in Psychological Science*, Vol. 13, No. 4, 2004, pp. 135-139.

6. Editorial, "Separating Science from Stereotype," *Nature Neuroscience*, March 2005, p. 253.

7. Richard J. Haier and Camilla Persson Benbow, "Sex Differences and Lateralization in Temporal Lobe Glucose Metabolism During Mathematical Reasoning," *Developmental Neuropsychology*, 11(4), 1995, pp. 505-414.

8. A recent study showed men and women use different parts of the brain while taking an IQ test. Richard J. Haier, *et al.*, "The Neuroanatomy of General Intelligence: Sex Matters," *NeuroImage*, Jan. 16, 2005 (online), pp. 320-327.

9. American Association of University Women, "How Schools Shortchange Girls," 1992 at www.aauw.org.

10. Department of Education, press release, "Study Shows Educational Achievement Gender Gap Shrinking," Nov. 19, 2004.

11. Jay R. Campbell, *et al.*, "NAEP 1999 Trends in Academic Progress: Three Decades of Student Performance," August 2000, Department of Education.

12. Halpern, *op. cit.*

13. Nelson, *op. cit.*

14. Government Accountability Office, "Gender Issues: Women's Participation in the Sciences Has Increased, but Agencies Need to Do More to Ensure Compliance with Title IX," July 2004.

15. These score statistics are from Yu Xie and Kimberlee Shauman, *Women in Science* (2003). Excerpts at www-personal.umich.edu/~yuxie. Also see presentation at National Bureau of Economic Research, Jan. 14-15, 2005, at http://nber15.nber.org/~sewp/events/2005.01.14/Agenda-1-14-05-WEB.htm.

16. American Council on Education, "An Agenda for Excellence," February 2005, p. 4. For background, see Sarah Glazer, "Mother's Movement," *The CQ Researcher*, April 4, 2003, pp. 297-320.

17. Tamar Lewin, "University of California System Said to Lag in Hiring Women," *The New York Times*, May 18, 2005, p. A14.

18. The report can be found at www.aauw.org.

19. Diane Ravitch, "Girls are Beneficiaries of Gender Gap," *The Wall Street Journal*, Dec. 17, 1998.

20. See Sarah Glazer, "Boys' Emotional Needs," *The CQ Researcher*, June 18, 1999, pp. 521-544, see p. 529.

21. National Center for Education Statistics, "Projections of Education Statistics to 2012," at http://nces.ed.gov/pubs2002/proj2012/ch_2.asp.

22. Beatriz Chu Clewell and Patricia B. Campbell, "Taking Stock: Where We've been, Where We Are, Where We're Going," *Journal of Women and Minorities in Science and Engineering*, Vol. 8, issues 3 & 4, 2002, pp. 255-284, p. 259.

23. *Ibid.*, p. 260.

24. *Ibid.*, p. 263.

25. New York Academy of Sciences, "Women in Science: Are They Being Held Back?' panel discussion held April 14, 2005, Cooper Union, New York City.

26. Georgia Institute of Technology, press release, "Breaking Down Gender Barriers: New Book Looks at Roadblocks Impeding Women Scientists and Engineers," Feb. 16, 2004.

27. Nelson, *op. cit.*, p. 3.

28. Department of Education, press release, *op. cit.*

29. Steven Pinker, *The Blank Slate* (2002), p. 344. For original data see Camilla Persson Benbow, *et al.*, "Sex Differences in Mathematical Reasoning Ability at Age 13," *Psychological Science*, November 2000, pp. 474-480.

30. See www.edge.org.

31. Pinker, *op. cit.*, p. 344.

32. Halpern, *op. cit.*, p. 136.

33. *Ibid.*, p. 138.

34. Pinker, *op. cit.*, p. 348.

35. *Ibid.*, p. 350.

36. Ann M. Gallagher and James C. Kaufman, *Gender Differences in Mathematics* (2005), p. 318.

37. Haier, *et al.*, *op. cit.*

38. Christina Hoff Sommers, *The War Against Boys* (2000), p. 43.

39. *Ibid.*, p. 52.

40. Nelson, *op. cit.* This study was of the top 50 research universities.

41. "A Study on the Status of Women Faculty in Science at MIT," MIT Faculty Newsletter, March 1999, at http://web.mit.edu/fnl/women/women.html.

42. For background on Title IX, see Jane Tanner, "Women in Sports," *The CQ Researcher*, May 11, 2001, pp. 401-424.

43. Letter to Lawrence Summers at www.nwlc.org/pdf/1-27-05LarrySummersSignOnLetter.pdf. For percentages of women faculty in math, engineering and physics, see American Council on Education, "An Agenda for Excellence: Creating Flexibility in Tenure-Track Faculty Careers," February 2005, p. 2.

44. American Council on Education, *ibid.*

45. *Ibid.*, p. iv. The panel is composed of presidents of Tufts University, University of North Carolina, Syracuse

University, University of Michigan, University of California-Riverside, Vanderbilt University, State University of New York at Albany, Ohio State University, University System of Maryland and Pennsylvania State University.

46. Natalie Angier, "Pay Gap Remains for Women in Life Sciences," *The New York Times*, Oct. 16, 2001, p. A3.

47. American Council on Education, *op. cit.*

48. Quoted in "The San Diego Supercomputer Center Presents Women in Science," at www.sdsc.edu/sciencewomen/index.html.

49. *Ibid.*

50. Kim Tolley, *The Science Education of American Girls* (2003), see pp.182-3, 184.

51. *Ibid.*, p. 171.

52. *Ibid.*, p. 215.

53. *Ibid.*, pp. 215-216.

54. Leonard Sax, *Why Gender Matters* (2005) pp. 31-32.

55. *Ibid.*, pp. 11-12.

56. Amanda Ripley, "Who Says a Woman Can't Be Einstein?" *Time*, March 7, 2005, p. 50.

57. Carol Gilligan, *In a Different Voice* (1982) and *Making Connections* (1990).

58. The Sadkers' research was outlined in their book *Failing at Fairness* (1994).

59. Glazer, *op. cit.*, June 18, 1999, p. 531.

60. Sommers, *op. cit.*, p. 23.

61. *Ibid.*, p. 22.

62. Gallagher and Kaufman, *op. cit.*, p. 5.

63. Clewell and Campbell, *op. cit.*, p. 262.

64. Gallagher and Kaufman, *op. cit.*, p. 4.

65. Halpern, *op. cit.*, p. 135.

66. See Glazer, June 18, 1999, *op. cit.*

67. For text of letter see www.mentornet.net/wyden-allen.

68. *Land of Plenty* (2000). Summary of report is at www.spie.org/web/oer/september/sep00/landofplenty.html.

69. GAO, *op. cit.*

70. *Ibid.*

71. Nelson, *op. cit.*, p. 2.

72. Claudia Goldin and Lawrence F. Katz, "Summers is Right," *The Boston Globe*, Jan. 23, 2005.

73. Rhea Steinpreis, "The Impact of Gender on the Review of Curriculum Vitae of Job Applicants and Tenure Candidates: A National Empirical Study of Sex Role," October 1999, pp. 509-528.

74. American Council on Education, *op. cit.*, p. 18.

75. *Ibid.*, p. 18.

BIBLIOGRAPHY

Books

Angier, Natalie, *Woman: An Intimate Geography*, Anchor Books, 1999.
This readable book by a *New York Times* science reporter disputes several cardinal premises of evolutionary psychology, including the contention that men's and women's core preferences were determined thousands of years ago.

Baron-Cohen, Simon, *The Essential Difference: The Truth about the Male and Female Brain*, Basic Books, 2003.
A Cambridge professor of psychology and psychiatry argues that most boys are born "systemizers" and therefore better at math, while most girls are born "empathizers" and therefore better at human relations.

Browne, Kingsley R., *Biology at Work: Rethinking Sexual Equality*, Rutgers University Press, 2002.
A Wayne State University law professor argues that females' biologically based inclinations, rather than discrimination, explain the gender gap in pay and women's low representation in male-dominated fields.

Gallagher, Ann M., and James C. Kaufman, eds., *Gender Differences in Mathematics: An Integrative Psychological Approach*, Cambridge University Press, 2005.
Scholarly articles summarize research in gender differences.

Pinker, Steven, *The Blank Slate: The Modern Denial of Human Nature*, Penguin Books, 2002.
A Harvard psychologist contends there is a biological and evolutionary basis for boys' cognitive advantages — a conclusion widely believed to have influenced Harvard President Lawrence Summers's controversial Jan. 14 remarks.

Rhoads, Steven E., *Taking Sex Differences Seriously,* *Encounter Books,* **2004.**
A professor of politics at the University of Virginia criticizes public policies that he says ignore biological sex differences, including Title IX.

Sax, Leonard, *Why Gender Matters: What Parents and Teachers Need to Know about the Emerging Science of Sex Differences,* *Doubleday,* **2005.**
Physician Sax draws on research in gender-based brain differences to argue that girls and boys have such different ways of learning they should be educated separately.

Sommers, Christina Hoff, *The War Against Boys: How Misguided Feminism is Harming our Young Men,* *Touchstone,* **2000.**
A scholar at the conservative American Enterprise Institute argues it is boys, not girls, who are doing poorly in school.

Tolley, Kim, *The Science Education of American Girls: A Historical Perspective,* *RoutledgeFalmer,* **2003.**
This fascinating history by an education professor at Notre Dame de Namur University finds that, contrary to today's stereotypes, 19th-century girls took more science courses than boys.

Articles

Angier, Natalie, and Kenneth Chang, "Gray Matter and the Sexes," *The New York Times,* **Jan. 24, 2005, p. A1.**
Researchers dispute Harvard President Summers's comments, saying that neurological and hormonal differences do not necessarily equate to differences in real-life performance.

Monastery, Rich, "Women and Science: The Debate Goes On," *The Chronicle of Higher Education,* **March 4, 2005.**
Experts respond to the question, "Are Boys Born Better at Math?"

Ripley, Amanda, "Who Says a Woman Can't Be Einstein?" *Time,* **March 7, 2005, p. 50.**
The author summarizes current research about sex differences.

Reports

American Council on Education, **"An Agenda for Excellence: Creating Flexibility in Tenure-Track Faculty Careers," 2005.**
A panel of 10 university presidents recommends offering part-time tenure jobs and other family-friendly policies to retain junior faculty, especially women.

Government Accountability Office, **"Gender Issues: Women's Participation in the Sciences Has Increased, but Agencies Need to Do More to Ensure Compliance with Title IX," July 2004.**
Most of the federal science agencies have not instituted procedures to make sure universities are enforcing Title IX.

Harvard Task Forces, **"Report of the Task Force on Women and Faculty;" "Report of the Task Force on Women in Science and Engineering," May 2005. Available at www.news.harvard.edu/gazette/daily/2005/05/16-wtaskforce_release.html.**
Two task forces appointed by Harvard President Summers recommend steps to improve the hiring and retention of women at Harvard, including mentoring, gender-bias training and child-care scholarships.

Nelson, Donna J., "A National Analysis of Diversity in Science and Engineering Faculties at Research Universities," Jan. 6, 2005.
The number of women science faculty at the top 50 research universities falls far short of the numbers getting PhDs in science and math, a widely cited report finds.

For More Information

Association for Women in Science, 1200 New York Ave., N.W., Washington, DC 20005; (202) 326-8940; www .awis.org. Promotes women in scientific fields.

Committee on Women in Science and Engineering, National Academy of Sciences; www7.nationalacademies .org/cwse/About_CWSE.html. Aims to increase women's participation in the sciences.

Edge; www.edge.org. This site posts an April 22, 2005, debate on gender differences between Harvard psychologists Steven Pinker and Elizabeth Spelke and other online debates.

FairTest, 342 Broadway, Cambridge, MA 02139; (617) 864-4810; www.fairtest.org. This gadfly organization considers the SAT biased against girls.

Implicit Association Test; https://implicit.harvard.edu/ implicit/demo/. Offers a much-discussed 10-minute online test, which reveals unconscious assumptions about gender and science. The test, developed by Harvard psychologist Mahzarin Banaji, has been cited as proof of widespread gender bias against women in science.

National Center for Education Statistics, 1990 K St., N.W., Washington, DC 20006; (202) 502-7300; http:// nces.ed.gov. The federal database for national education statistics.

National Science Foundation, 4201 Wilson Blvd., Arlington, VA 22230; (703) 292-5111; www.nsf.gov. Links to recent studies funded by the NSF's Research on Gender in Science and Engineering program, at www.nsf.gov/ funding/pgm_summ.jsp?pims_id=5475.

New York Academy of Sciences Women Investigators Network; www.nyas.org/channels/index.asp?channelID=53. Posts numerous conferences on women in science.

UC Faculty Family Friendly Edge, http://ucfamilyedge. berkeley.edu/ucfamilyfriendlyedge.html. Maintained by University of California researchers, contains numerous studies about academia's work/family conflicts.

11

AP and IB Programs

Can They Raise U.S. High-School Achievement?

Marcia Clemmitt

George Mason High School

George Mason High School, in Falls Church, Va., is among more than 450 U.S. schools that offer International Baccalaureate diplomas. Research shows that challenging coursework improves student achievement, but little data specifically show the effects of IB and AP programs. Rigorous academic programs are far more likely to be offered to affluent rather than disadvantaged students, though increasing numbers of minority students are taking AP courses.

From *CQ Researcher*,
March 3, 2006.

In Pflugerville, Texas, outside Austin, high-school senior Joshua Garza gets a $5 gift card every time he attends an after-class review session for his Advanced Placement (AP) calculus class. If he passes the standardized exam in May, he'll receive $100, and possible college credit.* And his calculus teacher will get an extra $100 for each student who passes.[1]

Garza has taken five AP classes in high school, but so far he has tried only one exam, which he didn't pass. But he's not in it for the money or even the college credit; he wanted the challenge. "AP classes prepare me for more rigorous classes in college," he said. They teach "discipline and time management, which are skills I need."[2]

An anonymous donor provided a $1 million grant for Pflugerville's AP incentives, but many other communities get help as well in drumming up interest in advanced high-school programs like AP and the International Baccalaureate (IB), which is typically offered to 11th and 12th graders.**

In fact, encouraging greater enrollment in such programs is one of the hottest new trends in secondary education. Over the past

---

* Grading is on a 1-5 scale, with 1 equivalent to an F, 3 equal to a C and 5 equal to an A. Many universities give college credit for high-school AP courses if the student scores at least a 3 on an AP final exam.

** Internationally accepted IB diplomas are awarded to students who pass written and oral exams and submit a lengthy research paper after completing an intense, two-year, comprehensive curriculum.

High-School Graduation Requirements Lag

Only 10 states had high-school graduation requirements that matched the course requirements for admission to public universities in their states. Twenty-eight states had no alignment.

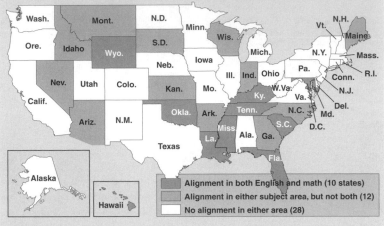

Alignment Between Requirements for High-School Graduation and College Admission*

Alignment in both English and math (10 states)
Alignment in either subject area, but not both (12)
No alignment in either area (28)

* Based on the number of courses required by high schools and state colleges/universities

Source: American Association of State Colleges and Universities, February 2005

from less than 400 three years ago — a 20 percent increase. (A total of 610 American schools offer some part of the IB program, which includes a K-10 curriculum.)[5]

But fundamental questions remain: Will getting students to take AP and IB classes rescue public schools from mediocrity, as many educators and public officials hope? Or will bright kids from affluent families be the main beneficiaries?

Since 1992, the federal Advanced Placement Incentive Program has provided federal grants for AP programs, particularly to encourage lower-income students to participate. In his recently released annual budget proposal, President Bush calls for training 70,000 new teachers of AP and IB math and science courses.

Such efforts are needed, say AP and IB enthusiasts, because high schools are a weak link in the U.S. education system. For example, on the 2003 Trends in International Mathematics and Science Survey (TIMSS), U.S. fourth-graders did better on the math test than fourth-graders in countries ranging from Australia and Norway to the Slovak Republic and Sweden. But by age 15 the tables had turned, with students in those countries outscoring U.S. students on the math portion of the 2003 Program for International Student Assessment (PISA).[6]

American high schools have fallen behind in preparing students for college and work, according to a survey of 1,487 recent, public high-school graduates, 400 employers and 300 college faculty members. Among the graduates, 39 percent of those in college and 39 percent of those in the work force said there were significant gaps in their high-school preparation. And 46 percent of the workers said they lacked preparation for jobs they hoped to get in the future.[7]

Among the employers, 41 percent were dissatisfied with the ability of graduates to understand complicated materials. Overall, only 18 percent of the professors thought most of their students were "extremely" or "very

four summers, for example, a group of businesses in Greensboro, N.C., helped the Guilford County School District award four cars, 20 laptop computers and nearly two-dozen $1,500 scholarships to AP students. Last year's winner of a new car — Laura St. Cyr, a freshman at North Carolina's Elon University — was eligible because she passed five or more AP tests.[3]

Arkansas, Florida, South Carolina and Florida are among the states that have recently begun paying students to take AP exams.[4] A 2004 Arkansas law requires all high schools to offer either the IB diploma or AP courses in four major subject areas by 2008. A 2005 Minnesota law authorizes full or partial state payment of exam fees for all public and private students, and a 2005 Texas law requires universities and colleges to offer credit for IB and AP.

The efforts appear to be paying off: In the last five years the number of students taking AP exams swelled from about 400,000 to more than 600,000. And while only 479 U.S. schools offer IB diplomas, that figure is up well" prepared for college, but the percentage dropped to 7 percent at two-year colleges. Overall, professors said half of the high-school graduates aren't prepared to do college-level math or college-level writing.[8]

Advocates argue that AP and IB programs can improve learning for low-achieving as well as above-average students. "Many communities have found that adding AP really turns a school around," according to education reporter Jay Mathews, originator of the Challenge Index. Published by *Newsweek*, it ranks school quality based on the proportion of students who take AP and IB tests.[9] Moreover, he adds, AP and IB courses "give average students a chance to experience the trauma of heavy college reading lists and difficult college examinations."[10]

Even students who only scored a 2 on their AP exam "come back from college and tell me they did really well in freshman English because they'd been so well prepared," said Michael Watkins, guidance director at W. T. White High School in Dallas.[11]

Preliminary research at DePaul University shows that IB programs may prepare disadvantaged students well for college, says Brian Spittle, the school's assistant vice president for enrollment management. After tracking the progress of 44 Chicago IB graduates enrolled at DePaul, the university found that 97 percent went on to enroll as sophomores after completing the freshman year, compared to 85 percent of freshmen overall. The IB students also had a slightly higher college GPA — 3.1 compared to 3.0 for all freshmen — and took a heavier courseload: 15 hours per quarter, on average, compared to the 13-hour average.

Those results are especially striking given the socioeconomic background of the IB students, says Spittle. Of the IB group, 79 percent are eligible for federal Pell grants for low-income students, compared to 24 percent of DePaul freshmen. Twenty-seven percent of the IB students — but only 7 percent of DePaul freshmen overall — are African-American, and 39 percent are Hispanic, compared to 13 percent overall. Sixty-six percent of the IB students are first-generation collegians, compared to 33 percent of all DePaul freshmen.[12]

But many researchers warn against viewing AP and IB as a panacea for what ails U.S. education. "I don't know what you're smoking" if you see AP "as a massive

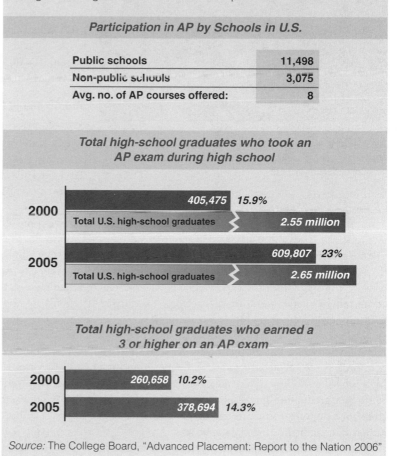

Number of AP Exam Takers Rose

Twenty-three percent of the U.S. high-school students who graduated in 2005 took an AP exam at some point in high school, compared with 10 percent in 2000. The percentage that received a score of 3 or better (equal to a "C" on a scale of 1-5) rose from 10.2 percent of all high-school graduates in 2000 to 14.3 percent in 2005.

Participation in AP by Schools in U.S.

Public schools	11,498
Non-public schools	3,075
Avg. no. of AP courses offered:	8

Total high-school graduates who took an AP exam during high school

2000 — 405,475 — 15.9%
Total U.S. high-school graduates — 2.55 million

2005 — 609,807 — 23%
Total U.S. high-school graduates — 2.65 million

Total high-school graduates who earned a 3 or higher on an AP exam

2000 — 260,658 — 10.2%
2005 — 378,694 — 14.3%

Source: The College Board, "Advanced Placement: Report to the Nation 2006"

President Bush greets AP students at the School of Science and Engineering at Yvonne A. Ewell Townview Magnet Center in Dallas. Bush's new budget proposal calls for training 70,000 AP and IB math and science teachers.

solution," says Michael Kirst, an education professor at Stanford University. AP was intended to provide college-level classes for advanced students likely to attend selective colleges, he points out. Rather than more AP courses, he says, most students need more college-preparatory work to ready them for the expectations of the two-year community colleges and four-year regional universities that most high-school graduates attend, he says.

Meanwhile, unchallenging courses and lack of college readiness remain a big problem, says Kirst, who heads Stanford's Bridge Project to improve the transition from high school to college. "We have not increased significantly our graduation rate" from four-year colleges, and "tons" of new college students end up in remedial courses rather than credit-bearing classes, he says.

But simply injecting more challenging coursework in the upper grades will leave far too many high-school students behind, says Samuel Stringfield, co-director of the Nystrand Center of Excellence in Education at the University of Louisville. Particularly hard-hit will be low-income and minority students, who need more — and earlier — help to succeed, Stringfield says.

Furthermore, many educators point out, the most devastating high-school achievement gaps involve drop-outs and students who barely achieve literacy — often from the most disadvantaged neighborhoods. Offering more challenging courses to high-school students may

increase college attendance rates for "borderline kids," says Stringfield, but it won't affect the dropout rate "for kids in trouble."

What clearly makes the most difference in raising high-school achievement is attending a rigorous middle school, Stringfield argues. "So, is AP the answer?" he asks. "No, it's better middle-school programs," coupled with external supports like tutoring. "If you want to see [AP] fail and become last year's fad, try it by itself."

As educators and lawmakers struggle to create high schools for the 21st century, here are some of the questions they are considering:

Are AP and IB programs effective?

When judged on whether they achieve the goals for which they were designed, both AP and IB programs generally get good marks. AP courses provide college-level curricula, and graduates who score high enough on the final exam usually receive college credit for their AP work. Likewise, IB graduates end up with a diploma that satisfies pre-college requirements at selective universities around the world.

Some educators question, however, whether IB, and particularly AP, courses succeed in improving high schools across the board, which is the reason many high schools are now using them. For example, AP's presumably college-level work has become a standard substitute for other college-preparatory courses in many schools. But critics worry that the switch may shortchange rank-and-file students on the college preparation they really need. IB programs get less criticism on these grounds because they are designed as college-prep — not college-level — courses, although some colleges offer credit for completing the IB diploma.

AP courses, however, are presumably advanced enough to gain credit at selective colleges. Yet most high-school college-prep courses lag far behind the skill levels needed to succeed at even the local community college, says Stanford's Kirst. Before schools replace their college-prep courses with AP, they should figure out what level of college prep is needed for regional universities and local community colleges and then design their college-prep courses to meet those needs, Kirst says. (*See map, p. 234.*)

Robert Sternberg, a Tufts University psychologist who studies learning, agrees. Adopting AP just because it's there — before figuring out what schools want to accomplish — is a cart-before-the-horse approach, he says.

But Aaron Pallas, a professor of the sociology of education at Columbia University Teachers' College, praises AP and IB courses for being tied to curricula developed by subject-matter experts rather than by individual teachers. Thus, the programs are more likely to serve broad, significant educational goals, he says, and the standards and syllabi are public so educators can see if the courses "reflect the competencies we want students to master."

Moreover, standard AP and IB exams, which are devised and graded by people outside of a student's school, change the dynamic in classrooms for the better, says John Bishop, an associate professor of human resource studies at Cornell University.[13] In other classes, students typically tell the teacher, " 'Hey, let's have an enjoyable class. We can't really do all this work you're assigning,' " says Bishop. And in many cases "teachers cave in."

However, when demanding external tests loom on the horizon, suddenly, teachers, parents and students are "all on one team, trying to prove that they can live up to the standard," he says. The shift is especially pronounced in low-income neighborhoods, he says, where schools want to show that their ability to achieve should not be underestimated.

Such external assessments are also usually better than individual teachers' exams, says Bishop, noting that high school exams devised by teachers are "pretty awful," mainly testing memorization and seldom calling on students to integrate information and ideas. But a National Research Council report had the same complaint about AP and IB math and science courses, pointing out many AP and IB syllabi push teachers to cover so many topics that shallow memorization too often replaces deep understanding.[14]

In addition, said Lawrence Weschler, director of the New York Institute of the Humanities, judging from his daughter's AP experience in European history and English, some AP courses may encourage too much cramming for the test. "The kids got very involved in the causes of World War I and wanted to talk about it, but the teacher said they couldn't because they had to move on and cover all the material for the test." And in AP English, he complained, her poetry unit assignment was to do little more than devise two multiple-choice questions about a poem that might be used on the test.[15]

But the IB program, insists Carol Solomon, who heads both the AP and IB programs at Richard Montgomery High School, in Rockville, Md., encourages students to take a full range of pre-college courses. It's "an integrated program that does not just say to students, 'Take advanced college work,' " she says.

Also on the positive side, the National Research Council said the AP and IB programs challenge students and represent the higher expectations that high schools should promote. In particular, the IB curriculum's required two-year Theory of Knowledge seminar fosters "metacognition" — the practice of monitoring one's own learning, the panel pointed out. Research shows that strong metacognitive skills "are characteristics of experts in any field, as well as of school-age learners," the report said.[16]

The Theory of Knowledge course "helps students become critical thinkers and readers, which should prepare them for anything college throws at them," says Robert Snee, principal of George Mason High School in Falls Church, Va., which has had an IB program since the early 1980s. "We like to think of it as a total package that prepares students better for college than anything else," he says.

AP may be another matter, however, say some researchers. "I'm increasingly convinced that AP is doing a great job at its original role" — allowing a few advanced kids who are already bored with high-school-level work to earn college credit — says Kristin Klopfenstein, an assistant professor of economics at Texas Christian University, in Fort Worth. But AP courses are now widely viewed as standard college-prep courses. "And I am not at all convinced that AP is doing a good job of preparing kids for the rigors of college.

"It's important that we remember that AP courses are college level," she continues. They "throw you in the deep end" rather than preparing you to swim there.

Louisville's Stringfield says that while anything that increases the opportunity to learn is "at least vaguely going in the right direction," some schools adopt AP to make them look good, without actually changing what and how they teach or figuring out what best suits students' needs. "Some schools just put a fancier name on the same old, same old," he says.

U.S. High-School Graduation Rate Lags

At least 90 percent of the high-school students in six nations graduated in 2005 compared with only 73 percent in the United States.

Country	Graduation Rate
1. Germany	97%
2. Greece	96
3. Norway	92
4. Ireland	91
5. Japan	91
6. Switzerland	90
7. Czech Republic	88
8. Hungary	87
9. Denmark	86
10. Poland	86
11. Finland	84
12. France	81
12. Italy	81
14. Iceland	79
15. Sweden	76
16. United States	73
17. Luxembourg	71
18. Spain	67
19. Slovak Republic	56
20. Turkey	41

Source: Organization for Economic Cooperation and Development, 2005

Should AP and IB be more broadly available?

Most educators say all students who want to earn early college credit should have the chance to do so. But critics are concerned that broadening AP access both dilutes the program and encourages schools to neglect their responsibility to make the rest of the curriculum as challenging as possible for all students.

But AP is not necessarily out of reach for most college-bound students, says Cornell's Bishop. "People have the impression that it's beyond the pale" to propose an AP standard for college-bound students generally, he says. But AP exam requirements are similar to regular graduation requirements in most industrialized countries, including France, Canada and the Netherlands, he says, proving that AP-level courses should not be viewed as "only achievable by the most intelligent students."

AP may seem out of reach to many Americans in part because U.S. middle and high schools lag so far behind world standards, says Bishop. "We lose a lot of ground in the period between the end of eighth grade and the end of high school." But in a globally competitive world, "if you want to have a population of young Americans who compare with Europe and East Asia, then you need as many students as possible" taking courses like AP, Bishop says.

Critics complain, however, that schools around the country seem to be focusing more on getting the maximum number of students into AP courses than on improving teaching overall — a trend that hurts AP as well as non-AP students. "In my four sections of AP English, about 40 percent of the 96 students do not have the motivation and/or the ability to do the work and are making it difficult for me to push the other half to their limits," said Patrick Welsh, a veteran English teacher at T. C. Williams High School in Alexandria, Va., and occasional newspaper columnist on education. "If we had a traditional college-prep course for those who are having difficulty, they would learn much more than they are learning now sitting in my AP course."[17]

"The basic mission of schools" is "to take their students and stretch them as far as possible," he said. "The number of kids taking AP tests is but one tiny measure of whether a school fulfills that mission."[18]

Today, many students try to take as many AP courses as possible, starting as early as possible. The trend has been driven by college admissions policies that favor students with AP courses on their transcripts and high schools that weight AP courses much more heavily when they compute grade-point averages. (*See sidebar, p. 248.*)

Philosophy Professor William Casement, founder of the Great Books program at Minnesota's University of St. Thomas, fears the trend undermines the original mission of AP programs — offering college-level work to advanced students. "Originally, AP was for high-school seniors," wrote Casement. "Today 11th-, 10th- and ninth-graders comprise between 40 and 50 percent of AP students."

As a result, he notes, many students skip non-AP courses and go straight to AP. "Readiness for college study requires intellectual growth and a maturation process," Casement contends. "How many 15- and 16-year-olds are truly ready?"

Some researchers argue that even "gifted" students often don't mesh well with AP and IB courses. A study led by Professor Carolyn Callahan of the University of Virginia's Curry School of Education found that many AP and IB classes use a one-size-fits-all teaching strategy best suited for memorization whizzes who learn well in lecture classes.

Based on surveys and site visits to 15 schools in four states, Callahan and her colleagues concluded that most IB and AP classes are "dominated by lectures, rapid-fire discussions and heavy reliance on motivated students taking initiative." Students who take the classes "accept and expect 'one-size-fits-all' learning," and "appear to believe these instructional approaches are the most efficient methods for covering a large amount of content in a short period of time," said Callahan's group.[19]

After an expanded survey of 22 high schools in nine states, Callahan again concluded that current AP and IB courses do not accommodate the varied learning styles even of many gifted students. "The rigidity of the programs" discourages teachers from accommodating a broad ranger of learners, the researchers said. "Unique students meet with resistance and cognitive dissonance" from teachers and fellow students.

To accommodate a broader range of AP and IB learners, they said teachers must "recognize that 'modifying' does not equal 'dumbing down.'" But such problems are solvable, say other educators, and opening the highest level of education to a broad swath of high-schoolers is worth the extra effort.[20]

In Washington state's Bellevue School District, pushing AP enrollment has driven up academic achievement schoolwide, says Superintendent Michael Riley. "The mission of the Bellevue School District is to give every student the kind of education traditionally reserved for America's elite class, [which] will allow the student to graduate from college, not just be admitted to college," Riley wrote. "Nationwide only about 25 percent of our high-school students receive this kind of education." An elite, college-prep curriculum would include four years of English, four years of math, three years of lab science, three years of social studies, at least two years of a world language and one or more AP or IB courses.[21]

Research shows that a challenging high-school curriculum is the best predictor of whether a student will graduate from college, says Riley. But, unlike Europe, the United States does not make AP or IB programs available universally but doles them out to the kids who "qualify," or to those "savvy enough to request it," he adds. "In our district, we believe all students can be AP or IB students" if they receive good teaching, strong elementary- and middle-school preparation and adequate supports like tutoring.[22]

Riley says Bellevue's results speak for themselves: In last year's 1,000-member senior class, 84 percent completed at least one AP or IB course, and 44 percent completed four or more. Even more impressive, 68 percent of seniors from low-income neighborhoods and 82 percent of those taking English as a second language took at least one AP or IB course.[23]

More Disadvantaged Students Taking AP

More than four times as many Latino students and three times as many blacks took AP courses in 2005 compared with a decade ago. But relatively few minority students participate in AP programs compared with the overall number of minorities in schools.

No. of students

AP Participation by Disadvantaged Students at U.S. Public Schools

Year	African-American Students	Latino Students	Native American Students
1995	19,797	32,195	2,098
2000	31,764	65,358	3,106
2005	62,179	134,811	5,058

Source: "The College Board's AP Report to the Nation"

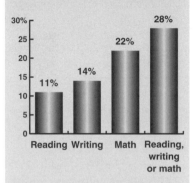

Many Students Need Remedial Courses

More than a quarter of the first-year college students in two-year and four-year institutions need remediation in reading, writing or mathematics.

First-Year College Students Requiring Remedial Courses

Reading: 11%
Writing: 14%
Math: 22%
Reading, writing or math: 28%

Source: "The Expectations Gap: A 50-State Review of High School Graduation Requirements," Achieve, Inc., 2004.

Can advanced high-school courses close the achievement gap?

Proponents of expanding AP and IB accessibility say it will raise achievement for all students, reducing the achievement gap between advantaged and disadvantaged students. But others say the worst gaps begin in elementary and middle school, and that adding advanced-level high-school courses won't answer those students' needs.

American middle-school and high-school students overall show mediocre achievement in international comparisons, but "huge gaps . . . continue to leave the children of low-income, African-American and Latino families" far behind even their lagging American peers, said Kati Haycock, director of the nonprofit Education Trust. Citing statistics that she calls "potentially devastating" for both the students and the country, Haycock noted that while one-fifth to one-quarter of white and Asian students leave high school without learning "basic"

math skills, one-half to two-thirds of Latino and African-Americans "suffer the same fate."[24]

Large dropout rates among African-American and Hispanic students continue to plague the U.S. education system. Each year 1.3 million students drop out before graduation — producing a U.S. graduation rate far lower than in Europe. In addition, studies show that dropouts earn less, on average, than those with high-school diplomas, and their job prospects are significantly curtailed, says Bob Wise, a former West Virginia governor who heads the nonprofit Alliance for Excellent Education.

Cornell's Bishop says pulling up a school's achievement by increasing enrollment in advanced classes works better than trying to push from below using minimum-competency tests, which penalizes high failure rates.

Minimum competency seeks to set a minimum standard, achieve it and keep raising the bar, Bishop explains. But the method backfires if the initial standard is too high, he says, risking increased dropouts among those who fail the tests.

"Some schools try to set up [minimum competency] tests so that you get huge failure rates," hoping that teachers and students will rise to the stiff challenge, Bishop says. But then teachers end up "teaching to the test," which does not lead to excellence because test questions aim at the low end of what students should achieve.

On the other hand, encouraging more students to try AP and IB tests pulls the whole school's achievement up gradually, Bishop argues, as teachers aim their instruction at the higher standard, and a growing number of students learn that they can achieve more.

Richard Montgomery's Solomon agrees. Her school's muscular AP and IB programs have made the school "a place where committed teachers come and stay," she says. IB students are selected competitively — about 800 apply each year for 100 slots — but since IB teachers must also teach non-IB courses, she points out, instructional "best practices" promulgated by the International Baccalaureate Organization reach all students. "Once you start building that critical mass," the belief "that school is a place for learning . . . affects almost every child."

"You won't find a school that's had IB for three years or more that will say the program didn't affect the whole school," echoes Snee of George Mason, where IB teachers also teach non-IB. The program "raises the bar for students generally." Only about 10 percent of George Mason's students come from disadvantaged households, but Snee says he "absolutely" would initiate IB if he headed a school in a low-income area.

In the past decade, South Side High School, in Rockville Centre, Long Island, has attacked the achievement gap by pushing students into ever-more challenging classes, with a focus on IB, says Principal Carol Burris.

"Higher achievement follows from a more rigorous curriculum," writes Burris. And since African-American and Hispanic students are consistently overrepresented in lower-track classes, "a highly proficient student from a low socioeconomic background has only a 50-50 chance" of being placed in a higher track with more challenging classes, she writes.[25]

"We are very careful" to maintain a [balanced] student mix in each course section, Burris points out. As a result, all students' performance on the New York state Regents' exams has improved, and there has been a "dramatic" narrowing of the achievement gap, according to Burris.[26]

In 2000, 88 percent of the school's white and Asian students but only 32 percent of the African-American and Hispanic graduates earned Regents diplomas, which are awarded for passing at least eight end-of-course exams covering major subject areas. By 2003, 82 percent of African-American and Hispanic seniors and 97 percent of whites and Asians earned diplomas.[27]

When South Side began detracking, it also dropped AP classes in favor of IB, which Burris calls the "new frontier" for raising schoolwide achievement. More and more students began choosing IB, and Burris now envisions a future when the upper grades are IB-only. About half the students aim for the full IB diploma, and as enrollments have risen IB scores have not declined.

But even at a suburban, middle-class school like South Side, with about one-fifth African-American and Hispanic students and 13 percent of students from disadvantaged homes, considerable extra effort is needed to help students manage challenging work.[28] Teachers give extra-help periods daily, and "every other day we have support classes," Burris says.

But, she contends, if the school wanted to switch to IB-only in the upper grades, teachers will have to work harder at differentiating instruction to suit different learners. "We talk about cooperative learning, multiple intelligences, tiering assignments with readings at different reading levels on the same topic," she explains. "That's hard stuff. It's going to take us some years to really get that right."

To succeed, teachers must have an "instinctual understanding that the playing field is not level for all children," says Burris. Luckily, she says, her faculty tend to be "reformers at heart."

Other supports are also needed, such as tutoring and giving students information about college standards and life. That's the philosophy of AVID — Advancement Via Individual Achievement — a California-based nonprofit that establishes school-based programs around the country. "Rigor without support is a recipe for failure," says AVID Communications Director Adam Behar.

The group helps establish advanced courses in schools where most students come from non-college-going families, and achievement expectations are low. "We start with the position that all students — with very few exceptions — are capable of taking a rigorous courseload," says Behar. "One way to do that" is to enroll in challenging courses like IB and AP, "but they need support — and that's often the missing piece."

But AVID doesn't claim its programs can directly raise achievement for the lowest-performing or most disadvantaged students. We succeed with the "average, invisible" student who may have low expectations for success. "We're really good at turning 1.8-to-2.5 GPAs into 3-to-3.5 GPAs," says Behar. Nevertheless, he notes, AVID schools experience "a kind of ripple effect" when going to college suddenly becomes "kind of cool."

However, other researchers say that with education money tight, it is shortsighted to focus too much on AP and IB if it siphons resources from earlier interventions or lower-achieving students. Pushing AP and IB too hard puts the cart before the horse because many students lack the necessary preparation, says Eric Hanushek, a senior fellow at the Hoover Institution, a conservative think tank based at Stanford University. The most important first step may be to improve the quality of instruction, particularly in the early grades.

"AP is expensive to institute," agrees Texas Christian University's Klopfenstein. "You take teachers away and give them a small class. I would much rather see the money spent on early intervention."

Even though the biggest achievement gap exists among minority and low-income students, resources for those students remain scarcest in many states, according to a new report by the Education Trust. In 27 of 49 states, the highest-poverty school districts spent $907 less per student in 2005 than the richest districts.[29] Nationwide, districts that enrolled the most students of color spent $614 less per student than districts with the least minority students. "The result is that children who have less in their personal lives end up with less in . . . their lives spent as students preparing to be educated citizens," says the Trust. The spending gaps have been "effectively unchanged over the six years" the group has tracked education funding.

Fewer resources mean fewer academically challenging courses for low-income and minority students, according to a new report by Clifford Adelman, a senior research analyst at the U.S. Department of Education who in 1999 discovered a strong link between challenging high-school curricula and college graduation rates. The "academic intensity" of a student's high-school curriculum still counts more than anything else "in providing momentum toward completing a bachelor's degree," he writes in an updated version of his original analysis, "Answers in the Toolbox." But low-income and minority students have much less chance to encounter high-level academic courses, he writes.[30]

BACKGROUND

It's Not Academic

Low interest in challenging academics has long been a feature of American high schools, according to some historians.[31] "Since at least the 1930s, the function of high schools for many, many students has been primarily custodial," says Jeffrey Mirel, a professor of educational studies and history at the University of Michigan.

High-school enrollment has risen dramatically over the past century or so, swelling from 6 percent of the nation's 14- to 17-year-olds in 1890 to 92.2 percent by 1970. During much of the 20th century, economic conditions made it desirable to keep as many teens as possible in school and out of the job market, which Mirel says helped to lower academic standards.[32]

Since the late 19th century, the nation has "been fighting about whether our high schools should be college prep for the masses or . . . a 'cafeteria-style curriculum' " in which time-in-seat is the primary criterion for a diploma, even if the time is mostly spent in non-academic classes like home economics and physical education, Mirel writes.

The country came close to creating a national curriculum in 1893, when a committee of college presidents and other luminaries headed by Harvard University President Charles Eliot issued the "Report of the Committee of Ten on Secondary School Studies."[33]

This influential document recommended a traditional array of studies in Greek and Latin, math, chemistry, natural history, government and economics. It argued that studying Greek and Latin "trains the mind" and that geography "enhances the powers of observation and reasoning."

The classics approach of the Committee of Ten was largely superseded by a 1918 report, "The Cardinal Principles of Secondary Education," prepared not by university chiefs but by education specialists, public officials and high-school principals. Greatly influenced by the progressive, utilitarian philosophy of educator John Dewey, it emphasized "health, command of fundamental processes, worthy home membership, vocation, citizenship, worthy use of leisure and ethical character."

The same emphasis on psychology and real-world applications was also apparent in *The Curriculum*, a groundbreaking book also published in 1918 by University of Chicago education Professor Franklin Bobbitt. It argued that human life "consists in the performance of specific activities. Education that prepares for life is one that prepares definitely and adequately for these specific activities."

It was this philosophy, as interpreted variously by local school districts — many of them dealing with newly diverse populations brought about by immigration — that would hold sway in the United States for much of the 20th century.

By 1920 the advocates of a cafeteria-style high school had won, with most schools offering curricula with low-academic rigor, according to Mirel. They also had begun tracking students.

By 1920, most big-city high schools were offering four high-school tracks: college prep, commercial (primarily

CHRONOLOGY

1950s-1970s *Public high schools increasingly offer a cafeteria-style curriculum, with many non-academic options and less college-prep emphasis. States establish "minimum-competency" tests for high-school students. The Advanced Placement (AP) program is launched for gifted students, while the International Baccalaureate (IB) program is developed to provide an international university-entrance diploma.*

1951 United Nations Educational, Scientific and Cultural Organization founds the International Schools' Association (ISA) to develop curricula and teaching methods to advance international understanding.

1956 The first AP tests are given.

1963 ISA receives a grant to develop a common curriculum and exam program that would meet the admissions requirements of any university in the world.

1970 The first IB diploma exams are given. Twenty schools worldwide have IB programs.

1980s-1990s *U.S. middle-school and high-school students fall behind international students. As efforts to establish national curricular standards lag, states begin establishing new graduation requirements and standards. AP and IB enrollments increase.*

1983 "A Nation at Risk" report calls for a more challenging high-school curriculum.

1992 Congress establishes Advanced Placement Fee Payment Program to subsidize exam fees for low-income students.

1995 The first Trends in International Mathematics and Science Study (TIMSS) is released. Successive TIMSS reports through 2003 show that U.S. students score well as fourth-graders, fall to average by middle school and are among the lowest performers by the end of high school. . . . States nationwide begin drafting statewide academic standards.

1998 Congress renames AP fee-subsidy program the Advanced Placement Incentive Program, adding grants for states to train teachers to offer AP in low-income schools. . . .

Newsweek publishes first "Challenge Index" listing the 100 U.S. high schools with the highest number of AP and IB tests taken compared to the number of seniors in the school.

1999 "Answers in the Toolbox" study by Education Department analyst Clifford Adelman shows that taking difficult high-school courses, such as trigonometry or calculus, is the surest indicator that a student will graduate from college. . . . American Civil Liberties Union files a class-action lawsuit charging that California provides unequal access to AP courses for minority students.

2000s *No Child Left Behind (NCLB) law expands federal influence on education, but high schools still are exempt from most requirements. Federal government and states strengthen incentives to broaden access to AP and IB. States look to align high-school graduation standards with college admission requirements.*

2002 President Bush signs NCLB law requiring high schools to employ only "highly qualified" teachers and to administer state achievement tests to all students at least once during grades 10 to 12.

2005 Congress rejects Bush's bid to extend nationally required annual testing through high school. . . . Minnesota requires state colleges to give college credit to high-scoring AP and IB students; Colorado adds AP and IB measures to high-school accreditation standards; Tennessee urges governor to fund statewide AP expansion; 13 states form the American Diploma Project Network and pledge to align high-school standards with skills and knowledge needed for college.

2006 Congress raises hackles in some states when it passes budget bill allowing the secretary of Education to certify certain high-school curricula "rigorous" enough for their low-income graduates to be eligible for new Academic Competitiveness Grants. Bill authors explain that they are not authorizing the federal government to set high-school curriculum standards. . . . College Board launches audit program to ensure that AP courses meet quality standards.

'Bored' Students Sparked AP Program

Advanced Placement (AP) courses were launched in the early 1950s by educators worried that bright but bored students might drop out of high school, depleting the nation's pool of academic talent.

The Ford Foundation-sponsored pilot program featured 12 secondary schools and 12 colleges offering college credit based on high-school students' test scores in any of 11 academic areas.[1]

The exams were "open to any able high-school student, wherever he may be and whether he achieved his knowledge through his own efforts, through tutorial assistance, or by taking special courses." In the 1955-56 school year, the nonprofit College Board took over management of AP testing. In 1956, 1,229 students from 110 high schools took 2,199 exams; the group attended 138 different colleges that September, although nearly half enrolled at five elite schools — Harvard, Yale, Princeton, Cornell and the Massachusetts Institute of Technology.[2]

In the 1960s, The College Board began offering summer training workshops to AP teachers at universities. By 2005 students could take AP tests in 34 subject areas.

The number of students taking AP exams has risen quickly in recent years. In the graduating class of 2005, around 610,000 of the nation's 2.7 million high-school seniors — or 23 percent — had taken at least one AP exam. That's up from 15.9 percent — 405,000 — of seniors in the class of 2000. Altogether, 2005 graduates took more than 1.5 million individual AP exams.[3] The most popular exams in 2005 were U.S. history (207,817 test takers), English literature and composition (203,697), English language and composition (162,357), AB calculus — the easier of two calculus options (141,732), U.S. government and politics (103,224) and biology (88,223), according to The College Board.

Individual colleges determine how much, if any, credit is offered, based on a range of possible scores from 1 to 5. A score of 3 generally is considered equivalent to a C in an introductory college-level course. Scores of 3, 4, or 5 typically earn credit, although only less selective colleges offer credit for 3s.

In recent years, a few highly selective colleges have severely limited the credit they offer for AP courses. Harvard, for example, generally requires a 5 for credit and doesn't offer any credit for some tests, such as the U.S. government and politics exam.

In 2005, 14.3 percent of graduates scored 3 or higher on at least one exam, compared with 10.2 percent in 2000.[4]

In response to concerns that AP's growing popularity has led schools to simply relabel courses with the AP name, The College Board in early 2006 launched an audit system. Beginning with the 2007-08 school year, AP designations will be officially granted only to courses that have passed the audit, which includes an evaluation of the course syllabi, method of instruction and other factors.

Rise of the International Baccalaureate Program

The International Baccalaureate program has its roots in the "international education" movement that began in the early 1950s. That's when the United Nations Educational, Scientific and Cultural Organization (UNESCO) established the International Schools' Association (ISA) to find practical curricula and teaching methods that would "enhance international understanding."[5]

In 1963, ISA received a grant to develop a common curriculum and exam program that could meet admission requirements for any university in the world, mainly to serve students such as diplomats' children who lived abroad with their families.[6]

While AP courses were created to help individual students meet their educational goals, true to its UNESCO roots, the IB program has broader aims.

Three main principles underlie IB education, according to the International Baccalaureate Organization (IBO), in Geneva, Switzerland:

- providing a broad general education that includes the basic knowledge and thinking skills secondary students will need to pursue university studies;
- giving students a "balanced," well-rounded curriculum while allowing some individual choice in what to study; and
- developing international understanding and citizenship as a means to "a more peaceful, productive future."[7]

Because IB navigates the divide between many national education systems, "it was developed as a deliberate compromise between the specialization required in some national systems and the breadth preferred in others," says the IBO.[8]

IB courses such as math and literature may be taken individually, and students who take the courses may also take IB assessment tests. Graded on a 1 to 7 scale, IB exams are taken at the end of each two-year course and include both oral and written portions. As with AP, some colleges offer credit for the exams; scores of 5, 6, or 7 usually are required for college credit. Students who take the entire IB diploma curriculum and pass the associated exams earn an IB diploma accepted at universities worldwide and also earn college credit at some colleges.

The full IB diploma program includes two-year courses in a student's native literature and language; a second language, either modern like Spanish or classical like Latin or Greek; social studies such as history or economics, with a global focus; math and computer science; the arts and a laboratory-science course that includes opportunities for students to develop and pursue their own research questions.

In IB lingo, those courses form a "hexagon" that is centered on three other key pieces of the IB curriculum. In a two-year required Theory of Knowledge (TOK) course, students examine philosophical questions related to knowledge and learning. TOK exams consist of 1,200-to-1,600-word essays marked by an international team of exam assessors, as in other IB courses. In recent exams, students could choose from lists of questions like these: Can a machine know? Can we know something that has not yet been proven true? "All ethical statements are relative"; by examining the justifications for — and implications of — making this claim, decide whether or not you agree with it.

Rounding out the curriculum is an "extended essay," an "independent, self-directed piece of research, culminating in a 4,000-word paper," plus a requirement for a specified number of hours spent in outside activities, including sports, arts groups and social-service projects.[9]

Like the AP program, IB also offers teacher-training seminars and suggests syllabi.

Currently, 1,740 schools in 122 countries offer IB, which includes a K-10 curriculum as well as the diploma course; 620 of those schools are in the United States. The diploma program is offered by 1,355 schools in 121 countries, including 479 in the United States.[10]

George Masan High School

IB students ponder a lab experiment at George Mason High School, in Falls Church, Va.

[1] *They Went to College Early*, The Fund for the Advancement of Education, 1957.

[2] *Ibid.*

[3] *Advanced Placement: Report to the Nation 2006*, The College Board, p. 79, apcentral.collegeboard.com.

[4] *Ibid.*

[5] G. Renaud, of UNESCO, 1974, quoted in G. Harold Poelzer and John F. Feldhusen, "The International Baccalaureate: A Program for Gifted Secondary Students," *Roeper Review*, March 1997, p. 168.

[6] *Ibid.*

[7] "A Basis for Practice: The Diploma Program," International Baccalaureate Organization, www.ibo.org.

[8] *Ibid.*

[9] *Ibid.*

[10] IB World School Statistics, www.ibo.org.

History and English Are Most Popular

U.S. history and English literature and language were the most-popular AP exams among students in the class of 2005. Many educators worry about the relatively low interest in advanced math and science tests. The least-popular AP exam was in French literature (793 students).

The 10 Most-Popular AP Exams Among the Class of 2005

(Exam)	(No. of students)
1. U.S. History	(207,817)
2. English Literature and Composition	(203,697)
3. English Language and Composition	(162,357)
4. Calculus AB (the less-challenging level)	(141,732)
5. U.S. Government and Politics	(103,224)
6. Biology	(88,223)
7. Spanish Language	(71,517)
8. Psychology	(68,847)
9. Statistics	(61,018)
10. European History	(58,474)

Source: "The College Board's AP Report to the Nation 2006"

preparation for secretarial work), vocational (industrial arts and home economics) and general, which merely offered a high-school diploma without specific preparation for educational or vocational endeavors. Most students still enrolled in academic classes like foreign languages and science, but that changed as the 20th century wore on.

Two factors led ever-growing proportions of students into low-challenge curricula. First, waves of new immigration and industrialization resulted in burgeoning enrollments, and some education leaders believed that the new high-school students were less intelligent than previous generations. Secondly, a series of economic crises — starting with the Great Depression and ending with the return to the work force of World War II veterans — made it good economic sense to keep students out of the labor market as long as possible.

To keep students from dropping out, schools allowed them to take easier classes. For example, from 1928 to 1943, health and physical education (PE) courses increased from 4.9 to 11.5 percent of total course-taking nationwide. "These courses were entertaining, relevant to young people's lives outside of school, required little or no homework, and . . . were amenable to high student/teacher ratios," writes Mirel. Over the next half-century, health and PE

were the fastest-growing courses: By 1973 they were second only to English classes in the percentage of students taking the courses nationwide.[34]

As a result, high school became a "hothouse for youth culture," from the raw energy of the hot-rod cruising 1950s to the rock 'n' roll counterculture of the 1960s, explains Mirel. Teachers increasingly resorted to an unspoken bargain with students that led to further abandonment of rigorous academics: "I'm not going to demand too much of you if you don't give me a hard time."[35]

Starting Small

While academically undemanding high schools were popular with many Americans, as early as the 1950s some policymakers began to worry about a gap between public high-school preparation and college requirements, and about a potential talent drain as some bright students grew bored with school.

The concern led to the establishment in 1951 of a Ford Foundation pilot program — the School and College Study of Admission with Advanced Standing — which eventually became today's Advanced Placement program. (*See sidebar, p. 244.*)

"Many able students, marking time in an unchallenging high-school environment, lose interest in education and do not go on to college," said a 1957 history of the program from the foundation's Fund for the Advancement of Education.[36]

By the 1955-56 school year, the program had grown from a pilot involving a few schools and colleges to a full-fledged national program. In 1956, 1,229 students from 110 high schools took 2,199 exams and attended 138 different colleges that September. Nearly half enrolled at five elite schools — Harvard, Yale, Princeton, Cornell and the Massachusetts Institute of Technology.[37]

Over the decades, the proportion of high schools participating in AP grew to about 60 percent. About 10 times as many students participate in AP today as in 1980, and the number of subjects for which there are AP exams has grown from 11 to 34.[38]

In the 1960s, international educators — led by the International Schools Association established by the U.N. Educational, Scientific and Cultural Organization (UNESCO) — sought to solve another education dilemma: how to create a common curriculum and diploma that universities around the world would recognize, mostly to serve students living abroad, such as the children of diplomats and international businessmen. (*See sidebar, p. 244.*)[39]

To earn an IB diploma, students must complete a two-year comprehensive curriculum that includes science, math, the student's native language and a second language, history and the arts as well as the Theory of Knowledge course. They must also complete a 4,000-word essay based on self-directed research and participate in creative and service projects in the community.

After opening at a handful of international schools around the world in 1970, IB diploma programs today exist at 1,348 schools in 121 countries, including 479 schools in the United States.

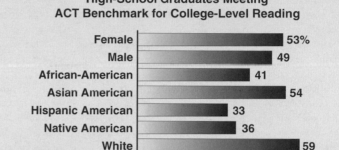

Many Graduates Are Deficient in Reading

Only 51 percent of U.S. high-school graduates are ready for college-level reading, according to the 2005 ACT test. White students, females and graduates from affluent families are the most prepared; African-Americans and Latinos are among the least prepared.

High-School Graduates Meeting ACT Benchmark for College-Level Reading

	Percentage
Female	53%
Male	49
African-American	41
Asian American	54
Hispanic American	33
Native American	36
White	59
Family Income < $30,000	33
Income $30,000-$100,000	54
Income >$100,000	70
All students	51

Source: "Reading Between the Lines: What the ACT Reveals About College Readiness in Reading," ACT, Inc., March 2006. Findings are based on 1.2 million high-school students who took the ACT; 27% were from the East, 40% from the Midwest, 14% from the Southwest and 19% from the West.

Reform Movement

During the 1980s and '90s, as standardized test scores declined — particularly on international comparative tests — and businessmen complained that American graduates were unprepared for the work force, U.S. presidents from both parties called for a common core curriculum nationwide and mandatory testing to ensure that students were learning the material.

But resistance both from the right and the left led Congress repeatedly to reject mandatory nationwide standards or testing. Conservatives generally objected to the idea of the federal government interfering in curriculum development, which has historically been done by the nation's 15,000 local school districts. And liberals feared that without a massive injection of additional funding, imposing mandatory testing and achievement standards on disadvantaged inner-city schools would ensure their failure.

In the end, each of the 50 states drafted its own statewide academic standards — a situation many called untenable, since they varied widely in rigor and content.[40]

By the late 1990s, states were trying to strengthen their statewide standards, and many even adopted mandatory testing — called high-stakes tests — as a prerequisite for graduation. But often the tests were not properly aligned with the new, statewide curricula, causing high failure rates. Low test scores in some states triggered heated parental rebellion against the mandatory testing.[41]

Then in 2001, newly elected President George W. Bush jumped into the fray, proposing his No Child Left Behind law (NCLB). Adopted on Jan. 8, 2002 — a year after his inauguration — it authorized around $135 billion in extra federal funding for education over five years in exchange for mandatory math and reading testing in grades 3 through 8. The tests were to be developed by the states and aligned with statewide academic standards.[42]

Does AP Predict College Success?

Taking challenging classes — not necessarily Advanced Placement courses — is the best predictor of a student's eventual success in college, according to several recent studies. They take issue with the greater emphasis some high schools and colleges place on AP courses than on other tough classes.

"The original goal of AP was to have upper-middle-class kids who were bored take courses at the college level," and the program does a "great job" for those students, says Kristin Klopfenstein, an assistant professor of economics at Texas Christian University, in Fort Worth. "Now, however, AP has taken on a second job" — acting as the marker by which college admissions officers pinpoint the most highly qualified applicants.

In addition, many high schools "weight AP courses much, much heavier" when computing student grade-point averages (GPAs), says Klopfenstein. That practice gives AP students an additional leg up on college admissions, especially in states like Florida, Texas and California, where high GPAs earn public high-school students automatic admission to some universities.

But those practices don't jibe with what research is finding, says Klopfenstein. In a study of 28,000 Texas high-school graduates who attended four-year public universities, "AP doesn't provide additional predictive power" to pinpoint the students who will succeed in college, she says. In fact, she says, students who take challenging courses in general, like trigonometry or precalculus, are most likely to succeed on campus. AP is "not a necessary component" of such a curriculum, Klopfenstein says. Earlier research that suggested taking AP courses specifically predicted college success "didn't control for the rest of the curriculum experience," she says.

While research on the question is scant, some studies seem to buttress Klopfenstein's argument. For example, a 2004 study by education researchers from the University of California-Berkeley found that while scoring high on AP exams "is strongly related to college performance," the "number of AP and honors courses taken in high school bears little or no relationship to students' later performance in college," after controlling for other academic and socioeconomic factors.[1]

Based on a sample of 81,445 University of California freshmen between 1998 and 2001, Berkeley education researchers concluded that "many students who take AP courses do not complete the associated AP exams, and merely taking AP or other honors-level courses in high school is not a valid indicator of the likelihood that students will perform well in college. . . . AP coursework, by itself, contributes almost nothing to the prediction of college performance," However, "AP examination scores are among the very best predictors," according to the UC data.[2]

Meanwhile, substantial research backs up the idea that the most successful college students are those who took the

States Back AP, IB

In passing NCLB, Congress and President Bush gave the federal government an unprecedented, dominant role in education policy for the nation. But it kept one tradition intact: The new federal requirements mostly applied to elementary schools, leaving most policy-setting for high schools to states and localities.

However, NCLB does "basically outlaw" a common high-school practice that interferes with offering challenging coursework: assigning teachers to subjects in which they don't have a college major or minor, says Richard Ingersoll, a professor at the University of Pennsylvania's Graduate School of Education. Beginning this school year, NCLB requires high schools to have "highly qualified" teachers in each class. School principals frequently run afoul of that requirement as they try to juggle faculty to cover a complex schedule, he says.

But, Ingersoll points out, it is usually lower-track classes — which disproportionately enroll low-income and minority students — that are most likely to have misassigned teachers. "The equity people go bonkers at that," he says, but it is unclear whether and how NCLB can enforce the ban on misassignment.

In addition, over the past several years, federal policy-makers have continued to encourage high schools to strengthen their academic course content, mostly because U.S. students lag behind on international comparative tests. As a result, federal grants have helped many states develop incentive programs to increase AP and IB highest number of solid academic courses, in all curriculum areas, throughout high school.

"No matter how one divides the universe of students, the curriculum measure," predicts "a higher percent of those earning bachelor's degrees" than any other factor in students' pre-college background, such as standardized test scores or GPAs, says U.S. Department of Education senior analyst Clifford Adelman. "The academic intensity and quality of one's high-school curriculum" is a "dominant determinant" of whether a student earns a college degree, according to his study, which followed a national sample of students from high school to age 30, he says.[3]

Furthermore, the impact of a high-quality high-school curriculum is a "much greater" predictor of college success for African-American and Latino students than for white students, Adelman says.[4]

Adelman's study included AP courses as one factor among several in his measure of challenging curricula, so it does not address the AP question directly. However, he does identify one curriculum area as "a key marker in precollegiate momentum." The "tipping point" for math courses that point to college success is "now firmly above Algebra II," Adelman says.[5]

College admissions officers use the AP program to pinpoint the most highly qualified students, says Assistant Professor Kristin Klopfenstein, of Texas Christian University.

Courtesy of Texas Christian University

[1] Saul Geiser and Veronica Santelices, "The Role of Advanced Placement and Honors Courses in College Admissions," Research and Occasional Paper Series, Center for Studies in Higher Education, University of California, Berkeley, 2004.

[2] *Ibid.*

[3] Clifford Adelman, "Answers in the Toolbox: Academic Intensity, Attendance Patterns, an d Bachelor's Degree Attainment," U.S. Department of Education, 1999.

[4] *Ibid.*

[5] Clifford Adelman, *The Toolbox Revisited*, U.S. Department of Education, 2006.

participation and have partially paid AP and IB fees for low-income students.

Many state legislators have concluded that all local school districts should increase participation in AP and, to a lesser extent, IB courses. But offering students equitable access to educational opportunity has been a long-term struggle for states, since public schools are financed mainly through local property taxes. Because of that approach, poor areas get less money per student than rich areas — something that no other industrialized country does.[43]

Perhaps nowhere has the struggle for educational equity been more apparent than in efforts to make AP courses accessible to students from all economic backgrounds. In 1999, for example, the American Civil Liberties Union (ACLU) filed a class-action suit against the state of California on behalf of a group of minority students, who the ACLU said had no access to AP courses. In response, some California legislators have proposed requiring every high school in the state to offer six AP courses, and the ACLU has worked with educators to devise a solution. To date, the case has no judicial resolution.

CURRENT SITUATION

States Resist

In 2006, the struggle to make U.S. high schools more academically challenging continues, even as state representatives fight off federal attempts to standardize high-school learning.

Should schools encourage most high-school students to take AP and IB courses?

YES John Bishop
Associate Professor of Human Resource Studies, Cornell University

Written for the *CQ Researcher,* March 2006

I encourage students to take rigorous, externally examined courses like Advanced Placement (AP) and the International Baccalaureate (IB) because they will learn more and benefit more from what they learn. Let's look at the evidence. Students from countries that require everyone to take AP-style exams — such as Australia, Denmark and France — score more than a grade-level equivalent ahead of students from equally advanced nations that don't require such exams.

Similarly, students from Canadian and German provinces with AP-style exams outperform students from provinces that lack such exams. Finally, Americans taking externally examined AP/IB classes learn considerably more during the year than equally able students taking other classes.

Why? First, the teachers are better prepared. Nations and provinces with external exam systems expect even middle-school teachers to have majored in the subjects they teach. Outside of AP/IB, however, most history, chemistry and physics classes in America are taught by teachers who did not major or minor in the subject during college. Second, externally set and graded exams protect AP teachers from pressures to reduce the difficulty and amount of work they assign and instead push them to demand more of their students and themselves. The teacher becomes the coach of a team where every member's effort and success is valued.

Most important, AP students have willingly taken on the challenge of higher standards. They are not competing against each other, so they no longer feel they must hide their interest for fear of being considered a "suck up." Class discussions are more animated because everyone has read and thought about last night's assignment. Learning is more fun.

There are, of course, exceptions to these generalizations. But please do not avoid AP because it's "too hard" or "only for the gifted." Lots of students with 500 SATs take AP and get college credit. In Europe and Asia, calculus starts in high school. Why should we be different?

Ignore the adults who tell you AP is unnecessary because they succeeded without AP. You face a much more competitive world. Real wage rates of young adults without a bachelor's degree are significantly below their level in 1970. Even maintaining the standard of living of your parents will require you to develop skills that substantially exceed those your parents brought to the labor market a generation ago.

Don't wait for college. Seek out challenges now, and you will develop habits of mind that will serve you for the rest of your life.

NO Kirk A. Johnson
Senior Policy Analyst, The Heritage Foundation

From "Expanding Opportunity for Low-Income High-School Students: Pell Grants vs. Advanced Placement Classes," March 2004

There are two basic ways that bright high-school students can perform college-level work. First, they may enroll in Advanced Placement (AP) or International Baccalaureate (IB) classes. The second way is simply to take one or more classes at a community college or state university. Virtually all states have a program that allows high-school students to take such classes.

Federal programs have clearly favored the establishment of AP courses. The No Child Left Behind legislation authorized Advanced Placement Incentive Program Grants, which provided roughly $24 million annually to state and local education agencies to fund AP and pre-AP programs in low-income communities.

But high-school-based AP classes may not be the most efficient and cost-effective means to expand access to higher education for low-income students. Generally speaking, AP classes are far more expensive to operate than regular high-school classes. Taking into account differences in the average class size and teacher's pay, the cost of the typical AP class is more than twice that of the average, non-AP high-school class.

Another drawback is that these courses may duplicate classes that are currently being offered in institutions of higher education. Classes similar to those in AP programs can be found at virtually all of the nearly 2,100 community colleges and state universities across America.

For the most part, these institutions already have the infrastructure to offer these types of classes, and they exist in close proximity to high-school students — especially those in low-income urban areas. In short, expanding AP programs would tend to duplicate the kinds of classes that are already available at a broad range of colleges and universities.

As an alternative to the AP system, Pell grants could be offered to bright, low-income high-school students as a fiscally responsible way to expand their access to college-level classes. Using the $24 million the federal government currently spends on the Advanced Placement Incentive Program every year, more than 18,500 low-income students could be given $1,200 Pell grants, enabling them to take a class in both the fall and spring semesters.

Such a program would have the ancillary benefit of allowing students to choose from a wider variety of classes than might be offered in a limited, school-based AP program. Under a Pell grant program, for example, low-income students who might be particularly gifted in computers could take computer science courses at a local junior college — an option they would not enjoy in most AP programs.

For the past few years, President Bush's budget proposals for education have raised the hackles both of members of Congress and state lawmakers. First, Bush's budgets for implementing NCLB were below authorization by about $7 billion in fiscal 2003 and $9 billion below in fiscal 2004, for example.[44] This year's presidential budget for fiscal 2007, released in January, also curtails NCLB funding.

In addition, last year Bush proposed extending NCLB's mandatory yearly reading and math testing to grades nine through 11.

By 2005, however, states were complaining bitterly that the federal 2006 budget severely underfunded existing NCLB requirements, and they were in no mood to accept more. "The well has been poisoned," said California Rep. George Miller, the top-ranking Democrat on the House Education and the Workforce Committee. "Given the history of this administration in not funding [NCLB], no member of Congress is going to put their chips on this plan."[45]

Even moderate Republican Rep. Michael Castle of Delaware, chairman of the House Education Subcommittee, who supports Bush's testing proposal, declared it "dead on arrival" because so many conservative Republicans opposed it.

States would welcome help from the federal government to increase high-school rigor, but it must be the right kind of help, says former West Virginia Gov. Wise, now president of the nonprofit Alliance for Excellent Education coalition. "Rigor demands resources. Dollars are important," he says. "You have to be willing to get good teachers and supply extra help."

Also on Wise's wish list are federal incentives for states to form "P-16" or "P-20" councils to begin coordinating state instructional programs from preschool through graduate school.

Meanwhile, in another budget bill enacted last month, Congress ran afoul of both state-control advocates and some college leaders when it authorized new Academic Competitiveness Grants. Based on a Bush proposal, the grants would assist low-income students to study math, science, engineering and high-demand foreign languages.[46]

Critics decry the law's stipulation that students can only receive the money if they've completed a high-school curriculum deemed "rigorous" by the secretary of

A course in basic writing at the University of Connecticut, in Storrs, helps students polish sub-par skills. More than 25 percent of first-year college students need remedial courses in writing, reading or math.

Education. That gives the Education Department too much say over high-school policymaking, critics say.

But the measure's authors quickly shot off a letter to Education Secretary Margaret Spellings insisting that prior federal education law "prohibits the secretary from establishing any curriculum in any school, public or private."[47]

While states have cautioned federal lawmakers to lie low, state governments have launched their own initiatives to increase the rigor of high-school curricula, both through AP and IB and other means, such as centering diploma requirements on skills and knowledge that state colleges and universities say students require to succeed on campus.

In 2005 legislative action, for example, Illinois created a public-awareness program to inform parents of the importance of AP courses; Minnesota required its state colleges and universities to award college credit to students scoring a 3 or higher on an AP exam or a 4 or higher on IB exams; and Colorado revised its high-school accreditation standards to include the percentage of students enrolled in AP and IB courses.[48]

In addition, 13 governors and the nonprofit group Achieve formed the American Diploma Project (ADP) Network, which has pledged to work with employers and colleges to align their high-school graduation requirements with students' post-graduation needs. Currently 22 states are ADP members.

OUTLOOK

Challenge for All?

Many educators believe that after years of talk without action, a change is sure to come to U.S. high schools. But much more research and more and better data from schools are needed before educators will know exactly what works for high schools, say education analysts. Otherwise, says the University of Louisville's Stringfield, too many education proposals become "politicized" rather than based on knowledge.

Finding out what works will take more meaningful data, agrees David Conley, director of the Center for Education Policy Research at the University of Oregon. For example, to find out which curricula work best, "what goes on in classes — not just course titles — needs to be studied."

Meanwhile, efforts to bridge the high-school-college gap are in their infancy and will increase, researchers say. "The whole high-school-college connection is just getting going," says Conley. Unfortunately, the high-school standards movement of the 1990s "was misguided" and will need to be thoroughly overhauled, he says, because states established graduation standards without first figuring out what students need to succeed in postsecondary education and training.

Conley sees high schools and colleges working together much more closely in the future. For example, "Can you imagine submitting a paper" in a high-school class "and having them say, 'You're ready for college in sentence construction and punctuation but not in organization?'" Such helpful assessments eventually will become the norm, he predicts.

AP and IB programs are good models because they base student assessment on meaningful curricula and train teachers, says Kirst of Stanford. However, "we need to take these models and adapt them" to the academic standards set for most U.S. high-schoolers, as Colorado, Illinois and Maine are doing. "We're groping at it, and I think we'll see more in five or 10 years."

When it comes to expanding top students' access to the most challenging courses, like AP, online education is the wave of the future, says Hanushek of the Hoover Institution. "If you have a high school of 50 kids, you can't offer German IV very easily," he says. "But distance education is starting to work." Especially in the West, "some states are beginning to use it effectively."

Many researchers say the United States is on the brink of undertaking major high-school reform, after discussing it without action for more than 20 years. "The country is currently at the will-building stage," says former Gov. Wise. Economic changes will galvanize that will eventually, he says. "The folks laid off at Ford plants will realize that, though they got their good jobs with a high-school degree, when Ford retools and starts hiring again, their sons and daughters won't get a job the same way."

AP and IB will play a large role in that process, says Cornell's Bishop. "Essentially, we're in a slow transition from a low-standard system to one that's much more like the European system," he says.

When it comes to AP and IB, "everybody can't do them right now. But we're moving in the direction that more and more can take them and succeed," he continues. "It's a slow movement." But as pressure builds for students to take challenging courses, schools will be forced to hire better teachers and increase other learning supports. "It'll take us 10, 15 or 20 years."

The problems of low achievement and dropouts "are solvable," says Michigan's Mirel. And while better-trained teachers are part of a solution, it will take more than just ensuring that teachers study more subject-matter courses. Ensuring that all math teachers have at least college math minors, for example, won't do the trick, he says. Many people who know subject matter have trouble communicating it effectively to others, let alone to students of widely varying abilities and learning styles, he notes. To do the job right, schools of education must "give teachers better ways to teach."

The bottom line, says Mirel, is that to sustain the U.S. economy and maintain democracy by producing an informed public, the education system must tackle "the great challenge of the 21st century:" learning how to teach challenging courses to kids of all levels of ability.

NOTES

1. Whitney L. Becker, "AP Classes Gaining in Popularity, But Passing Rates Lag," *Austin American-Statesman*, Feb. 1, 2006.
2. *Ibid.*
3. Tamar Lewin, "The Two Faces of AP," *New York Times Education Life Supplement*, Jan. 8, 2006.

4. "Tons of Test Takers," *Inside Higher Ed*, Feb. 8, 2006, www.insidehighered.com.

5. IB Statistics, www.ibo.org/school/statistics/. The International Baccalaureate Organization expanded its programs to include middle school in 1994 and elementary school in 1997. As with IB for 11th- and 12th-graders, schools must be certified by IBO to offer the comprehensive curricula, which focus on interdisciplinary learning, development of thinking and learning skills, communication and research skills and global and environmental understanding.

6. "Comparing NAEP, TIMSS, and PISA in Mathematics and Science," National Center for Education Statistics, U.S. Department of Education, http://nces.ed.gov/timss/pdf/naep_pisa_comp.pdf.

7. "Rising to the Challenge: Are High School Graduates Prepared for College and Work?" survey by Peter D. Hart Research Associates/Public Opinion Strategies, February 2005, conducted for Achieve, a group of governors and business leaders pushing for more rigorous high-school curricula.

8. *Ibid.*

9. Jay Mathews, "The 100 Best High Schools In America," *Newsweek*, June 2, 2003, p. 48.

10. Jay Mathews, "Inside the Challenge Index: Rating High Schools," *Washingtonpost.com,* May 27, 2003. For additional recent coverage, see Jay Mathews, "As AP Expands, Studies Disagree on Its Value," *The Washington Post*, Feb. 28, 2006, p. A8.

11. Lewin, *op. cit.*

12. For background, see Ann R. Martin, "International Baccalaureate Programs Making Impact on City Schools," *Chicago Tribune Special Section: Education Today*, Jan. 15, 2006.

13. For background, see "Testing in Schools," Kenneth Jost, *CQ Researcher*, April 20, 2001, pp. 321-344.

14. *Ibid.*

15. *Ibid.*

16. *Learning and Understanding: Improving Advanced Study of Mathematics and Science in U.S. High Schools* (2002), National Research Council Committee on Programs for Advanced Study. The Theory of Knowledge philosophy seminar examines complex questions about the nature of knowledge and its relationship to truth, belief and perception.

17. *Ibid.*

18. Quoted in Jay Mathews, "Is AP Good for Everybody? It's Debatable," *The Washington Post*, April 10, 2005, p. B3.

19. Carolyn M. Callahan, Ellen P. Hench, Catherine M. Brighton, "Advanced Placement and International Baccalaureate Programs," presentation to the National Association for Gifted Children, November 2002.

20. *Ibid.*

21. Michael N. Riley, "A District Where Everyone's on the Advanced Track," School Administrator, American Association of School Administrators, Jan. 1, 2005.

22. *Ibid.*

23. *Ibid.*

24. Kati Haycock, "Still at Risk," *Thinking K-15, Education Trust,* Summer 2002.

25. Carol Corbett Burris and Kevin G. Welner, "Closing the Achievement Gap by Detracking," *Phi Delta Kappan*, April 2005, p. 594.

26. *Ibid.*, p. 596.

27. *Ibid.*, p. 597.

28. *Ibid.*, p. 596.

29. *The Funding Gap 2005*, The Education Trust, 2006.

30. Clifford Adelman, *The Toolbox Revisited: Paths to Degree Completion From High School Through College*, U.S. Department of Education, February 2006.

31. For background, see Jeffrey Mirel and David Angus, *The Failed Promise of the American High School, 1890-1995* (1999).

32. Unless otherwise noted, this historical background is taken from Jeffrey Mirel, "The Traditional High School," *Education Next*, Hoover Institution, Winter 2006, www.educationnext.org.

33. Unless otherwise noted, information below is from Charles S. Clark, "Education Standards," *CQ Researcher*, March 11, 1994, pp. 217-240.

34. *Ibid.*

35. *Ibid.*

36. "They Went to College Early, Evaluation Report Number 2," The Fund for the Advancement of Education, 1957.

37. *Ibid.*

38. www.apcentral.collegeboard.com.

39. For background, see G. Harold Poelzer and John F. Feldhusen, "The International Baccalaureate: A Program for Gifted Secondary Students," *Roeper Review*, March 1997, p. 168.

40. For background, see Clark, *op. cit.*, and Kathy Koch, "National Education Standards," *CQ Researcher*, May 14, 1999, pp. 401-424.

41. For background, see Jost, *op. cit.*

42. For background, see Barbara Mantel, "No Child Left Behind," *CQ Researcher*, May 27, 2005, pp. 469-492.

43. For background, see Kathy Koch, "Reforming School Funding," *CQ Researcher*, Dec. 10, 1999, pp. 1041-1064.

44. Vincent L. Ferrandino and Gerald N. Tirozzi, "Getting Ahead of No Child Left Behind," *Education Week*, Nov. 20, 2002 (fiscal 2003); Howard Dean, "No Child Left Behind Should Be More Than a Slogan," *Seattle Times*, Jan. 8, 2004 (fiscal 2004).

45. Gil Klein, "Bush's High School Reform Plan Bombs," Media General News Service, Jan. 17, 2005.

46. "The Gift Colleges Don't Want," *Inside Higher Ed*, Jan. 24, 2006, www.insidehighered.com.

47. Rep. John Boehner and Rep. Michael Enzi, letter to U.S. Education Secretary Margaret Spellings, Feb. 1, 2006, http://edworkforce.house.gov.

48. *Recent State Policies/Activities: High School — Advanced Placement*, Education Commission of the States, www.ecs.org.

BIBLIOGRAPHY

Books

Angus, David L., and Jeffrey E. Mirel, *The Failed Promise of the American High School, 1890-1995,* **Teachers College Press, 1999.**
Two University of Michigan professors of education history put the long battle over curriculum choices into historical context and discuss the ramifications of giving students a range of curriculum choices.

Conant, James Bryant, *The American High School Today: A First Report to Interested Citizens, McGraw Hill,* **1959.**
A former Harvard University president offers his much-discussed recommendations for improving high schools.

Kirst, Michael W., and Andrea Venezia, (eds.), *From High School to College; Improving Opportunities for Success in Postsecondary Education, Jossey Bass Publishers,* **2004.**
The directors of Stanford University's Bridge Project present case studies of efforts to align high-school standards and graduation requirements with the skills and knowledge required by postsecondary institutions.

Mathews, Jay, and Ian Hill, *Supertest: How the International Baccalaureate Can Strengthen Our Schools, Open Court,* **2005.**
An education reporter (Mathews) and the director general of the IB program recount both the international history of IB and its use at a U.S. high school.

Articles

Lewin, Tamar, "The Two Faces of AP," *The New York Times Education Life Supplement,* **Jan. 8, 2006.**
Lewin describes current debates over the value of AP courses and exams for college preparation, based on interviews with students, high-school teachers and college admission officers with wide-ranging views on AP's importance.

Mathews, Jay, "Inside the Challenge Index — Rating High Schools," *The Washington Post,* **May 27, 2003.**
Mathews, a *Washington Post* reporter who devised the Challenge-Index high-school quality ranking system explains why he believes that the number of students in a high school who take Advanced Placement and International Baccalaureate exams is a good measure of school quality.

Mollison, Andrew, "Surviving a Midlife Crisis," *Education Next, The Hoover Institution,* **Winter 2006, www.educationnext.org.**
A veteran education writer recounts the history of the AP program and outlines the current research controversies over AP's relationship to success in college.

Reports and Studies

"Advanced Placement Report to the Nation, 2006," *The College Board*, **February 2006.**
The organization that operates the AP program reports on 2005 test results and participation rates.

"Measuring Up 2004: The National Report Card on Higher Education," *National Center on Public Policy and Higher Education*, **September 2004.**
The nonprofit think tank examines state-by-state trends in college preparation as well as college graduation rates and the affordability of secondary education. It finds college preparation has been improving in many states.

"A Nation at Risk," *The National Commission on Excellence in Education*, **April 1983, www.ed.gov/ pubs/NatAtRisk/index.html.**
A panel of education experts convened by President Ronald Reagan issues a harsh assessment of what American high-school students learn and calls for tougher graduation requirements in academic subjects.

"On Course for Success: A Close Look at Selected High School Courses that Prepare Students for College and Work," *ACT, Inc., and The Education Trust*, **2005.**

Analysts describe in detail curricula, course syllabi and teaching practices from high schools whose graduates have a record of college success.

"Ready or Not: Creating a High School Diploma That Counts," *The American Diploma Project*, **2004.**
Education think tanks describe specific high-school curricula and class syllabi that employers as well as college and university instructors say would better prepare high-school students.

Adelman, Clifford, "The Toolbox Revisited," *U.S. Department of Education*, **February 2006.**
A senior government education analyst finds that a challenging high-school courseload is the strongest predictor of whether a student will graduate from college.

Venezia, Andrea, Michael W. Kirst and Anthony L. Antonio, "Betraying the College Dream: How Disconnected K-12 and Postsecondary Education Systems Undermine Student Aspirations," *Stanford University Bridge Project*, **2003.**
Stanford University professors of education argue that public school systems are too disconnected from local colleges and universities and that the disconnect allows school curricula to lag behind college requirements.

For More Information

Achieve, Inc., 1775 Eye St., N.W., Suite 410, Washington, DC 20006; (202) 419-1540; www.achieve .org. An independent, bipartisan group formed by state governors and business leaders to promote higher academic standards.

Alliance for Excellent Education, 1201 Connecticut Ave., N.W., Suite 901, Washington, DC 20036; (202) 828-0828; www.all4ed.org. A nonprofit research and advocacy group that pushes for development of national and state policies to help at-risk high-school students attain college and workplace readiness.

AVID, AVID Center, 5120 Shoreham Place, Suite 120, San Diego, CA 92122; (858) 623-2843; www.avidcenter .org. A nonprofit group that establishes in-school support programs to help low-achieving students tackle a college-prep curriculum.

The Bridge Project, Stanford Institute for Higher Education Research, Stanford University School of Education, 485 Lasuen Mall, Stanford, CA 94305-3096; (650) 725-1235; www.stanford.edu/group/bridgeproject/. A research group that studies efforts to link colleges with public-school systems to improve students' college readiness.

The College Board, 45 Columbus Ave., New York, NY 10023; (212) 713-8000; http://apcentral.collegeboard .com/. A nonprofit membership organization of colleges and universities that produces and manages the Advanced Placement program.

Education Next, Hoover Institution, Stanford University; www.educationnext.org/. The online quarterly journal on education reform is published by the conservative think tank.

The Education Trust, 1250 H St., N.W., Suite 700, Washington, DC 20005; (202) 293-1217; www2.edtrust .org/edtrust. An independent nonprofit research and advocacy group that focuses on closing the achievement gap in learning and college preparation for low-income and minority students.

International Baccalaureate Organization, Route des Morillons 15, Grand-Saconnex, Geneva CH-1218, Switzerland; www.ibo.org. The nonprofit education foundation that supports international education and develops, manages and conducts student assessments for the IB program and its participating schools.

National Center for Accelerated Schools PLUS, University of Connecticut, Neag School of Education, 2131 Hillside Road Unit 3224, Storrs, CT 06269-3224; (860) 486-6330; www.acceleratedschools.net. A national collaborative of universities and schools that brings curricula and learning strategies developed for gifted and talented students to all students in 1,500 affiliated schools, mostly in low-income communities.

National Center for Education Statistics, 1990 K St., N.W., Washington, DC 20006; (202) 502-7300; http://nces.ed.gov/. The U.S. Department of Education office that provides data on student attendance and achievement and international comparisons.

Teaching Math and Science

12

Are Students Being Prepared for the Technological Age?

Joan Hennessy

Scott Hammond checks a math problem in his sixth-grade class in Hartland, Vt. Despite performance gains, American students continue to perform below students from many other countries. The National Commission on Mathematics and Science Teaching for the 21st Century has called for dramatic improvements in math and science teaching. Scott's teacher participated in the statewide Vermont Math Initiative.

From *CQ Researcher*,
September 6, 2002.

W hen Maria Santos was a fledgling high-school math teacher in San Francisco, the simplistic courses she taught constantly frustrated her.

"They had classes called fundamental math, general math, business math — any kind of math that wasn't college-preparatory math," she recalls. "But I knew that high-school kids needed college-preparatory math."

Years later, as assistant superintendent in charge of curriculum, Santos made sure students got those higher-level math and science courses.

Nationwide, like-minded school officials also have been reinforcing their curricula, responding to the steady drumbeat of criticism from businessmen, parents, legislators and educators. Professors have warned that American high-school graduates are unprepared not only for college-level math and science but also for work in today's technologically advanced world. As a result, many more students today are taking higher-level math and science courses than they did 20 years ago.

For instance, by 1998, 75 percent of all graduates had taken geometry, up from only 47 percent in 1982, according to the National Center for Education Statistics (NCES). And 60.4 percent of the class of 1998 had studied chemistry, compared to only 32 percent of 1982 graduates.[1]

Perhaps as a result, by the 2001-2002 school year average mathematics scores for all students on the college-entrance Scholastic Assessment Test (SAT) had risen to 516, the highest level in 32 years. It was 501 a decade ago.[2]

Top Teachers' Strategies

Math and science teachers who received a Presidential Award were significantly more likely than their peers nationally to spend more class time on such reform-oriented strategies as having students do hands-on activities and work cooperatively in small groups. They were less likely to spend time lecturing and having students complete worksheet problems or take tests or quizzes.

Percentage of Classes in Which Activity Occurs

| | Science | | | | Mathematics | | | |
| | Grades K-6 | | Grades 7-12 | | Grades K-6 | | Grades 7-12 | |
Activity	P.A.*	Nat.*	P.A.*	Nat.*	P.A.*	Nat.*	P.A.*	Nat.*
Discussion	85	90	75	77	95	89	93	92
Students doing hands-on manipulative activities	79	60	66	49	80	67	38	23
Students working in small groups	78	53	66	51	77	51	72	52
Lecture	27	60	45	65	40	66	69	85
Students reading about science/mathematics	21	40	13	27	21	19	18	18
Students completing textbook/worksheet problems	16	45	30	51	45	77	58	78
Students using calculators	10	1	35	24	37	14	80	73
Students using computers	8	6	19	9	15	8	9	3
Students using other technologies	15	6	16	10	9	3	3	2
Test or quiz	5	9	8	10	10	12	16	16

* P.A. = Presidential Awardees; Nat. = Non-awardees, nationally

Note: The Presidential Awards for Excellence in Science and Mathematics Teaching program, sponsored by the National Science Foundation, was established by the White House in 1983. Presidential Awardees as a group have much more experience than the national teaching force.

Source: Iris R. Weiss, et al., "The Presidential Award for Excellence in Mathematics and Science Teaching: Results from the 2000 National Survey of Science and Mathematics Education," December 2001.

Those scores — on a 200-800 scale — reflect the fact that more college-bound seniors are taking advanced mathematics course work, says Gaston Caperton, president of The College Board, the national nonprofit that created the SAT. Of last June's college-bound seniors, 45 percent had taken pre-calculus, up from 33 percent a decade ago, he said.

Despite the gains, however, U.S. students continue to perform inconsistently on math and science tests. For instance:

- The National Assessment of Educational Progress (NAEP) — often called the nation's report card — shows an upward trend in mathematics scores. Fourth-, eighth- and 12th-graders had higher average math scores in 2000 than a decade earlier, but

seniors' scores declined from 1996-2000. And only a quarter of fourth- and eighth-graders and a mere 17 percent of 12th-graders were performing at or above the "proficient" level in math.[3]

- Fourth-grade students scored above the international average in math and science on the 1995 Third International Mathematics and Science Study (TIMSS), and eighth-graders scored above the international average in science.* However, eighth-graders

---

* The TIMSS is the most extensive investigation of mathematics and science education ever conducted, with about 42 countries participating. The survey is sponsored by the International Association for the Evaluation of Educational Achievement (IEA). In the United States, it is funded by the National Science Foundation (NSF) and the Department of Education.

More Students Taking Math and Science

The percentages of high-school graduates taking science and math courses increased — and in some cases doubled — from the early 1980s to the late 1990s. In 1998, the percentages were higher for white students than for minority students in all courses.

Courses	1982	1987	1990	1994	1998	1998 White	1998 Black	Hispanic
Mathematics								
Algebra	55.2	58.8	63.7	65.8	62.8	63.5	62.3	61.4
Geometry	47.1	58.6	63.2	70.0	75.1	77.7	72.5	62.3
Algebra II	39.9	49.0	52.8	61.1	61.7	64.6	55.6	48.3
Trigonometry	8.1	11.5	9.6	11.7	8.9	10.0	4.8	5.6
Analysis/Pre-Calculus	6.2	12.8	13.3	17.3	23.1	25.0	13.8	15.3
Calculus	5.0	6.1	6.5	9.3	11.0	12.1	6.6	6.2
Science						White	Black	Hispanic
Biology	77.4	86.0	91.0	93.2	92.7	93.7	92.8	86.5
AP/IB Biology	10.0	9.4	10.1	11.9	16.2	16.7	15.4	12.6
Chemistry	32.1	44.2	48.9	55.8	60.4	63.2	54.3	46.1
AP/IB Chemistry	3.0	3.5	3.5	3.9	4.7	4.8	3.5	4.0
Physics	15.0	20.0	21.6	24.5	28.8	30.7	21.4	18.9
AP/IB Physics	1.2	1.8	2.0	2.7	3.0	3.0	2.1	2.1

Note: AP = advanced placement; IB = international baccalaureate

Sources: National Center for Education Statistics, Digest of Education Statistics 2000, 2001

fell below the average in mathematics, and seniors scored among the lowest in both subjects. When the TIMSS was repeated in 1999 for eighth-graders, U.S. students exceeded the international average in math and science, but they performed lower than students in 14 other nations in both subjects.

"I don't think very many people who have spent time with the statistics or who have thought about the labor market or about what it takes to be successful in careers today would argue that there is not a problem," says Judith Ramaley, assistant director of education at the National Science Foundation (NSF). Rather, she says, the discussion centers around two questions: "What is the nature of the problem and what do we do about it?"

Some say that the advanced mathematics courses being introduced in public schools present simplistic, watered-down curricula, and that mathematics tests aren't very difficult. Jerome Dancis, an associate professor of mathematics at the University of Maryland, College Park, complains that a statewide algebra test given in Maryland does not truly test students in algebra but in what he calls "pretend" algebra.

Meanwhile, The College Board recently announced plans to ask more challenging questions on both the verbal and math portions of the SAT exam. By March 2005, for example, students will be tested on their knowledge of Algebra II.

Even as educators agree that students need more math and science, they disagree — often vociferously — about how the two subjects should be taught. Noted academicians who have compared U.S. math curricula to those of students from countries that score higher on the TIMSS say U.S. math curricula are a "mile wide and an inch deep" — covering many topics superficially, but never guiding students to mastery.

"Our textbooks are much larger and heavier than those of all other TIMSS countries," wrote TIMSS project researchers. "Fourth-grade schoolchildren in the United States use mathematics and science textbooks that contain an average of 540 and 397 pages, respectively. Compare this to the international average length of mathematics and science textbooks intended for children of this age of 170 and 125 pages, respectively."[4]

Critics also complain about the way math and science are taught in U.S. schools. In a TIMSS video analysis of mathematics classes in Germany, the United States and Japan, researchers found that Japanese lessons follow a unique pattern.

"Whereas in German and U.S. lessons instruction comes first, followed by application, in Japanese lessons the order of activity is generally reversed," the report said. "Problem-solving comes first, followed by a time in which students reflect on the problem, share the solution methods they have generated, and jointly work to develop explicit understandings of the underlying mathematical concepts. Whereas students in the U.S. and German classrooms must follow the teacher as he or she leads them through the solution of example problems, the Japanese student has a different job: to invent his or her own solutions, then reflect on those solutions in an attempt to increase understanding."

In addition, U.S. classrooms are frequently interrupted, lessons contain more topics than Japanese lessons and Japanese teachers are more likely to provide explicit links or connections between different parts of the same lesson.[5]

To improve math competency, many school districts have overhauled their math curricula in recent years, but college professors claim that the reforms have not given incoming freshmen the skills needed to do higher-level math. Parents call it "fuzzy" math because they say students often can't do basic math computations.

Meanwhile, U.S. science curricula lack the rigor present in other countries, academicians say, and the sequence in which high-school students study science does not allow them to build on their understanding.

However, the process of reforming science curricula has run into political and religious resistance in some areas of the South and Midwest, where the teaching of evolution remains controversial. In the most recent turn, some school boards are debating whether to teach "intelligent design" with evolution (*see p. 275*).

Moreover, longstanding questions persist about the ability and training of math and science teachers. Education advocates and academicians say teachers need more professional development — not in classroom management, but in the math and science content.

Ramaley and others say students' inability to excel in math and science today could have punishing economic ramifications tomorrow. The fastest-growing jobs through the year 2010 will involve computers and technology, according to the U.S. Department of Labor.[6] And the NSF estimates that employment in science and engineering occupations will increase three times faster than all other occupations during the current decade.[7]

But students don't necessarily envision themselves as mathematicians, engineers and scientists. Only 5 percent of those taking the 2001 SAT test said they were planning to major in biological sciences; 7 percent said they would major in computer or information sciences; 9 percent planned to major in engineering and just 1 percent indicated they would major in math.[8]

Americans' aversion to math and science is clear: In 1999, non-citizens held 27 percent of U.S. doctorates in science and engineering.[9]

Eventually, if industries can't hire the workers they need on American soil, they will move elsewhere, says Gerald Wheeler, executive director of the National Science Teachers Association. In fact, many already are. Hundreds of thousands of foreign technology workers flooded into the United States in the 1990s after the high-tech industry convinced Congress to increase the number of special, temporary visas granted each year for technology workers from overseas. In addition, businesses began outsourcing much of their technology work to lower-paid employees overseas.[10]

Educators also point out that citizens today need a solid knowledge of basic science in order to understand key political issues — ranging from global warming to nuclear energy, cloning and genomics.

"What should people think about stem-cell research?" asks Susan Sclafani, an adviser to Education Secretary

Rod Paige. "If people don't have any basic understanding, it's hard to make informed decisions."

Americans are too quick to accept the adage that some students "just don't get" math and science, Wheeler says. "You might say you were bad at math and science," Wheeler says. "[But] you would never say you were ignorant of Shakespeare."

Apparently, lots of U.S. adults "don't get it" when it comes to science. A recent NSF survey found that only 45 percent of respondents could define DNA (the molecular basis of heredity), only 22 percent knew what a molecule was and only half knew that early humans did not live during the age of the dinosaurs.

Mathematicians also suffer from image problems among students. "We're seen as the nerds with the pocket protectors," says Johnny Lott, president of the National Council of Teachers of Mathematics (NCTM). "We must change the perception of math and math teachers."[11]

Meanwhile, educators and policy-makers are grappling with their role in the math and science equation. The new No Child Left Behind Act requires school systems to develop educational standards for various subjects and to test how well students are meeting those standards. Schools and teachers will then be held accountable for the results of those tests.

Maria Santos, who started her career in a math classroom, is now vice president for programs at Achieve Inc., a nonprofit educational organization that helps states examine and develop academic standards.

Santos says states are very interested in developing more rigorous standards, because of the TIMSS results. "That's how things get on the radar," she says. "I think that's created a level of attention from the states as well as from everybody in the community."

As state policymakers, educators and parents try to push U.S. students to greater science and math achievement, here are some key questions they are debating:

Are U.S. students proficient in math and science?

The Center for Workforce Preparation, an affiliate of the U.S. Chamber of Commerce, surveyed more than 1,500 employers this year and found that among the job applicants they see, 40 percent have "poor or no employment skills" and 30 percent have the wrong skills. Nearly a quarter of the employers said they can't get enough applicants to meet their needs.[12]

Meanwhile, many universities offer remedial courses for freshmen who arrive on campus unprepared. In 1995, for instance, nearly all two-year schools, more than three-quarters of the four-year public institutions and half of all private colleges offered remedial math courses. Among freshmen in 1995, 24 percent enrolled in remedial mathematics.[13]

The University of Maryland's Dancis recalls giving a take-home pre-calculus test to a freshman calculus class at the start of the semester to determine how much they knew. "They were in the honors program, so right away, they're special," Dancis says. "So you know something's wrong when one-third of them basically flunk."

Critics of the U.S. education system also frequently cite somewhat lackluster results from the NAEP tests. Average fourth- and eighth-graders' science scores did not change from 1996 to 2000, and seniors' average scores dropped three points.[14]

But more optimistic educators cite the fact that fourth- and eighth-graders' math scores have trended upward over the past decade.

"It appears that the NAEP is the best across-the-board reading we get right now," says Lott of the NCTM, and math scores "have been holding their own or rising slightly over time."

But Lott worries about overemphasizing test scores. "My bigger concern is that we make far too much of these test results," he cautions. "We shouldn't ignore them. But I'm not sure they should be the driving force."

Nonetheless, over time, an increasing percentage of fourth- and eighth-graders are performing at or above the basic and proficient levels in the NAEP math tests. "We want them [all] to be proficient," says Peggy Carr, associate commissioner for assessment at the National Center for Education Statistics (NCES). "There's still lots of improvement to be made, by anyone's interpretation."

But the NAEP is not a simple test, she also points out. "This is a challenging assessment."

But she cannot explain seniors' declining math and science scores. "The picture isn't quite as good or convincing for 12th grade," Carr says. "We're not as sure what is going on."

Those concerned about student achievement in math and science also cite disappointing results from the

AP Photo/Jason Turner, The Journal

Travis Jennings gets a glimpse of surveying during the Jefferson County Science Olympiad at the National Conservation Training Center in Shepherdstown, W.Va., in May. Elementary students learned about water quality, soil science and other subjects. The National Research Council recommends hands-on, inquiry-based approaches to teaching science.

TIMSS. Although U.S. students performed well in the lower grades, they showed declining abilities in the higher grades.

American fourth-graders scored above the international average in math and close to the top in science. Eighth-graders performed below average in math and slightly above average in science. Seniors were at the bottom of the scale in both subjects.[15]

"The longer American students stayed in school and studied these disciplines, the less favorably they compare with students in other countries," said former Sen. John Glenn, D-Ohio, who led the National Commission on Mathematics and Science Teaching for the 21st Century.[16]

When the TIMSS was repeated in 1999 for eighth-graders, U.S. students performed in the middle-of-the-pack, with pupils in such countries as Singapore, Hungary and other countries outdoing the Americans in both subjects.[17]

However, some educators say that a closer look at the results confirms what they have long believed: that some school districts excel at teaching students math and science, while others — often in rural or inner-city districts — are failing miserably.

"Some of our schools are doing fine," wrote David Berliner, an Arizona State University professor of education

psychology. TIMSS scores mask the performance of students from "terrific public schools," he said, and hide the scores of those in "shamefully inadequate schools."[18]

Kurt M. Landgraf, president and CEO of the Educational Testing Service, which administers the SAT, contends that international achievement comparisons are unfair. "Not every country shares our bedrock commitment to educating its entire population through high school," Landgraf wrote.[19] Most other countries' only serve superior students in their secondary-education systems while lower-achieving students are channeled into vocational training.

Others point out that, overall, more U.S. students are taking advanced-level math and science courses today than in previous years. In 1982, for example, 14.9 percent of high school graduates had completed chemistry or physics. But by 1998, 30 percent had completed one of the two courses, according to the Department of Education.[20]

However, some educators question whether students of all racial and socioeconomic backgrounds have equal access to higher-level courses. For instance, an analysis of TIMSS data on eighth-graders found that demography is destiny when it comes to math opportunities. "[S]chools with a larger percentage of minority enrollment or a smaller enrollment (a smaller class) for a grade were less likely to offer the more-challenging opportunities," the report said.[21]

In fact, in rural and inner-city settings only about 60 percent of students attended schools offering algebra or other more challenging classes, while in suburban and mid-sized city settings, more than 80 percent of students had such opportunities.[22]

"We tend to invent systems that allow elite kids to go on further," says William Schmidt, executive director of the TIMSS National Research Center at Michigan State University. "The other kids are left doing elementary arithmetic."

Partly due to such class systems, high-school students taking college-prep math and science are disproportionately white. In 1998, for example, 64.6 percent of white high-school graduates had completed algebra II compared with only 55.6 percent of their African-American counterparts and 48.3 percent of Hispanic students. Similarly, 12 percent of white students completed calculus that year but only 6.6 percent of black students and 6.2 percent of Hispanics.[23]

Not surprisingly, then, minority students generally score lower than whites on the math portion of the SATs. In 2001-2002, white students averaged 533 on the mathematics section, compared to 427 for African-Americans. Mexican-Americans, Puerto Ricans, other Hispanics, American Indians and Alaskan Natives all scored higher than blacks. Asian students beat all groups, with an average of 569.

Today's black-white achievement gap is larger than it was in 1992, when African-American students scored 419 compared to 515 for whites.

However, 35 percent of test takers this year were minority students, according to The College Board — an all-time high. Education Secretary Paige said last year that while he is pleased that more minority students are taking the SATs than ever before, the achievement gap "cannot and must not be ignored."[24]

But the good news is that blacks are improving slightly faster than others: Their average SAT math scores rose 16 points from 1986-1987 to 2001-2002, while average math scores for all students rose 15 points during the same period.[25]

A gender gap also persists in SAT math scores as well, although it is narrowing slowly. Males score about 34 points higher than women on the math test, compared to 37 points 10 years ago.

Are U.S. math and science curricula adequate?

Many educators say improving math and science curricula will raise American students' test scores. However, curricula reform in the United States is complicated by the fact that it is strictly a local affair.

U.S. Slipped in International Rankings

U.S. fourth-graders matched the average performance of foreign students in math in 1995, but four years later, when they were eighth-graders, their ranking had dropped significantly below the international average.*

Rankings in Mathematics

Fourth Grade, 1995		Eighth Grade, 1999	
Country	**Points Above/ Below Avg.**	**Country**	**Points Above/ Below Avg.**
Singapore	73	Singapore	80
South Korea	63	South Korea	63
Japan	50	Hong Kong	58
Hong Kong	40	Japan	55
Netherlands	32	Netherlands	16
Czech Republic	23	Hungary	8
Slovenia	8	Canada	7
Hungary	4	Slovenia	6
United States	**0**	Australia	1
Australia	0	Czech Republic	-4
Italy	-7	Latvia	-19
Canada	-12	**United States**	**-22**
Latvia	-18	England	-28
England	-33	New Zealand	-33
Cyprus	-42	Italy	-39
New Zealand	-48	Cyprus	-48
Iran	-130	Iran	-102

Significantly above international average
At or about international average
Significantly below international average

The 17 nations were among those participating in the Third International Math and Science Survey.

Source: National Center for Education Statistics, "Pursuing Excellence: Comparison of International Eight-Grade Mathematics and Science Achievement from a U.S. Perspective, 1995 and 1999," 2000

Unlike most European countries, which adopt nationwide curricula taught in every school, America's 15,000 school districts historically have developed their own individual curricula. During the late 1980s and early '90s — at the urging of then-President George Bush and later President Bill Clinton — efforts to develop national academic standards and tests for all subjects, including math and science, were scuttled after they aroused intense political opposition from both the right and the left.[26]

Eventually, officials abandoned the idea of developing national standards in favor of individual statewide academic standards, which were adopted by most states during the 1990s for the four core subjects — math, science, social studies and English.[27]

Although school districts still develop their own curricula, they must follow the parameters of their statewide academic standards, because most states now test students to see whether they are learning material that coincides with the statewide standards. Moreover, the new No Child Left Behind Act eventually will require students to be tested yearly against statewide standards.

Thus, reforming U.S. math and science curricula requires changing how thousands of individual school districts teach math and science.

Currently, arithmetic is taught as a set of content and skills that are revisited in U.S. classrooms year after year, according to the TIMSS center's Schmidt and Gilbert A. Valverde, an assistant professor of educational administration and policy at the State University of New York, Albany. "Even in grade eight, when most high-achieving TIMSS countries concentrate their curriculum on algebra and geometry, arithmetic is a major part of schooling in this country," they wrote.[28]

In fact, despite the monumental effort to revamp state curricula, textbook manufacturers may, in the end, exert a greater influence over U.S. math and science education than the standards. Rather than creating a different text for each school district, textbook publishers try to satisfy the curriculum needs of as many districts as possible in a single text that can be adopted nationwide.

"That's why our books are 700 pages long and have an incredible collection of topics," Schmidt says. In other countries, he says, a national ministry usually articulates national standards and sets the curriculum. As a result, math texts in some high-performing countries, like Singapore, are slim paperbacks.

But in America, a teacher who tries to get through the entire 700 pages in a year can only cover each concept superficially, Schmidt says.

Schmidt and Valverde found that most teachers surveyed indeed try to cover all the material in their textbooks. "Rarely can this dubious goal be accomplished," they wrote. "The result is that U.S. teachers cover more topics per grade than is common in most TIMSS countries . . . squandering the resources that teachers and children bring to bear" in learning.[29]

Issuing nationally marketed texts that suit all curricula not only makes textbooks overlong but also gives what some say is undue influence over the nation's education curricula to a handful of conservative "watchdog" groups in Texas and California — the nation's two largest textbook markets. Interest groups in both states review prospective texts line by line.

In Texas, conservative monitoring groups have in the past lobbied against science texts for their treatment of the Endangered Species Act and global warming. The groups say they are concerned about inaccuracies and bias from what they call the liberal academicians who write textbooks. Their complaints about the teaching of evolution are longstanding.

Now, warns Samantha Smoot, executive director of the Texas Freedom Network, which monitors conservative watchdog groups, publishers have begun self-censoring their texts, "so that a book can get past the army of would-be censors in Texas."

Some educators say U.S. students spend too much time practicing mathematical computations and not enough time using reasoning to solve math problems. The debate over reasoning vs. computation — often heatedly joined by parents — evolved during the 1990s into a nasty national argument. It focused on efforts to reform math education using a concept called "constructivism," in which students are encouraged to understand equations by constructing their own solutions, rather than using rote computation.

But parents and math professors, claiming students were no longer gaining a solid foundation in computation, ridiculed the new approach as "fuzzy math." In 1999, educators complained to then-Secretary of Education Richard Riley — in a full-page open letter in *The Washington Post* — that a Department of Education panel had rated as "exemplary" and "promising" a reform-math curriculum.

But some professors defend the reforms. The new methods evolved in a response to a string of reports raising alarms about the quality of the nation's old-style math and science education, which emphasized rote computation.

"Numerous scientific studies have shown that traditional methods of teaching mathematics not only are ineffective but also seriously stunt the growth of students' mathematical reasoning and problem-solving skills," wrote Michael T. Battista, a professor of mathematical education at Kent State University. "For most [U.S.] students, school mathematics is an endless sequence of memorizing and forgetting facts and procedures that make little sense to them." As a result, although the same topics "are taught and re-taught year after year, the students do not learn them."[30]

However, the new approaches may not be better for some students, says Andy Isaacs, a second-edition author of the math text *Everyday Mathematics*. "Some [parents] want a traditional, Catholic-school approach," he says. "I don't think there's one best curriculum for all situations."

Today, a growing group of educators sees the need to emphasize both approaches, says Ramaley of the NSF.

For example, the NCTM attempted to take a balanced view with its *Principles and Standards for School Mathematics*, published in 2000, which recommended a mix of both approaches.

Although most curricula reform has involved mathematics, some also say science curricula need tweaking. Some educators even disagree with the sequence in which American students typically learn the sciences: first biology, then chemistry, with physics taught in the third year.

Leon Lederman, winner of the Nobel Prize in physics, resident scholar at the Illinois Mathematics and Science Academy and professor of science at Illinois Institute of Technology, blames the current sequence for U.S. students' poor performance on international science tests.

The practice of teaching biology first dates back to the 19th century, Lederman says. But there have been a great many advances in the sciences since then, especially in biology, which now involves discussion of DNA.

Lederman says schools should teach physics first, followed by chemistry and then biology. "Physics underlies all of modern chemistry," he says, and biology should follow chemistry, since it is molecularly based.

Are U.S. math and science teachers well trained?

Two years ago, the National Commission on Mathematics and Science Teaching for the 21st Century issued a report calling for improvements in the nation's math and science teaching force.

The most direct route "to improving math and science learning for all students in this country is to improve the quality of teaching," the report said.[31] To achieve that goal, the panel recommended that the United States:

- Establish an ongoing system to improve the quality of mathematics and science teaching in grades K-12.
- Increase significantly the number of mathematics and science teachers and improve the quality of their preparation.
- Improve the working environment and make the teaching profession more attractive for K-12 mathematics and science teachers.[32]

But the commission was not alone in calling for more qualified teachers. The University of Maryland's Dancis says his children's teachers sometimes marked correct answers wrong on their math work. He contends that teachers need math fluency to teach it properly.

A 1996 report showed that students perform better when they are taught math by teachers who majored in mathematics.[33] Moreover, 1996 and 2000 studies found that teachers who received Presidential Awards for Excellence in Science and Mathematics Teaching are more likely than their peers to have taken extensive coursework in math and science.

However, in the United States, many math and science teachers did not major or minor in the subjects they are teaching. According to a 2002 Department of Education report, 69 percent of middle-school students were taught math by teachers who did not major in math in college and were not certified to teach it. And about 64 percent of middle-school students learned biology or life sciences from teachers who had not majored in those subjects.[34]

So-called out-of-field teaching is only slightly less acute in high schools. The report found that about a third of the high-school math students and 45 percent of the biology/life sciences students were taught by out-of-field teachers. But the situation is improving somewhat: For example, in physics during the 1987-88 school year, 81.6 percent of students were taught by a teacher with no major and certification in that field. Now, the percentage is 66.5.[35]

CHRONOLOGY

1900-1940s *Leaders of education's "Progressive Movement" advocate eliminating algebra and geometry as irrelevant for most students.*

1920 The Commission on the Reorganization of Secondary Education, headed by Progressive Movement leader William Heard Kilpatrick, recommends teaching high-school mathematics to a select few.

1923 Refuting Kilpatrick, a Mathematical Association of America report underscores the importance of algebra "to every educated person."

1925 High-school biology teacher John Scopes is charged with violating a Tennessee law forbidding teaching evolution theory. His conviction is eventually overturned, but the law remains on the books until 1967.

1949 Life Adjustment Movement among educators argues that most students need only enough math training for daily living — not algebra, geometry or trigonometry.

1950s-1960s *Space Age begins amid the Cold War, spurring renewed interest in science education; controversial New Math movement is born.*

1957 *Sputnik* is launched, marking the beginning of the Space Age and focusing national attention on the poor quality of American math and science education.

May 1961 Soviet cosmonaut orbits the Earth, prompting President John F. Kennedy to vow that the United States will put a man on the moon within 10 years.

1965 Congress balks at a nationwide testing program in core subjects after education groups say it would mean federal control of local schools.

July 20, 1969 Two U.S. astronauts land on the moon and return to Earth, fulfilling Kennedy's vision.

1970s-1980s *Microchip revolution lays the foundation for the coming Computer Age. Educators and*

industry leaders continue to call for more rigorous math and science curricula; a back-to-basics movement takes root in math education.

1983 "A Nation at Risk" report complains that U.S. students spend less time learning math and science than their international counterparts.

1989 The National Council of Teachers of Mathematics (NCTM) issues its first math curriculum standards, which de-emphasize rote computations. In September, President George Bush convenes governors in an education summit in Charlottesville, Va.

1990s *Controversial national standards — including those for math and science — are developed with federal funds, but Congress refuses to impose them nationwide. States develop their own standards. Growing demand for high-tech workers spurs bitter industry complaints that not enough Americans are majoring in math and science.*

1995 U.S. students' lackluster performance on the Third International Mathematics and Science Study (TIMSS) spurs studies on how U.S. math and science curricula differ from those in high-scoring countries.

1999 The TIMSS is repeated for eighth-graders. U.S. students perform in the middle of the pack in math and science.

2000s *George W. Bush is elected president, vowing to impose testing to make sure students are learning up to state standards.*

2000 A blue-ribbon panel calls for improved teacher preparation and working conditions. The NCTM issues updated math standards emphasizing both calculations and problem solving.

2001 Congress passes No Child Left Behind Act; states must set standards for each grade in core subjects.

2002 Some grades will be tested in math for the first time this year and in science by 2007-2008.

The shortage of certified math and science teachers worsened during the economic boom in the 1990s, when high-tech companies lured new math and science graduates away from teaching with higher-paying technology jobs. And, even though new-teacher salaries were rising faster than veteran teachers' salaries, schools couldn't compete with the high-tech industry wages.

In 2000-2001, for instance, new graduates were offered average wages of $42,712 for non-teaching jobs compared with less than $29,000 for the average rookie teacher, according to the American Federation of Teachers.[36] However, since the economic downturn that began in 2000 — which hit the high-tech industry particularly hard — schools report that some laid-off tech employees have applied to school districts for teaching positions.

The shortage of certified math and science teachers is even worse in high-poverty schools, according to the Education Department — and the situation is expected to worsen as large numbers of Baby-Boom teachers begin retiring.[37]

NCTM President Lott points out that although some would-be teachers choose higher-paying careers, "That doesn't mean the ones we have aren't doing a good job. America has some fantastic teachers who are working really hard at what they're doing. The concern is that as teachers are retiring, we aren't producing enough teachers to replace them. That's where you start getting teachers who maybe aren't as qualified."

In fact, the ongoing shortage may have led some school districts to lower their hiring standards for teachers, according to an Education Department report. On a popular teacher-licensure test used by 29 states, only one state set its passing score near the national average in reading, the report said, while 15 set their respective passing scores below the 25th percentile. On math and writing tests, only one state set its passing score above the national average.

"Not surprisingly, more than 90 percent of teachers pass these tests," the report said.[38]

However, some educators say that just because teachers are certified in a particular subject doesn't guarantee that they will be good classroom teachers. They point to studies in 1996 and 2000 that showed a correlation between award-winning teachers and the way they conduct their classes.

For example, a study comparing the teaching styles of teachers who received Presidential Awards and other teachers found that award-winning teachers tended to involve students in class activities more than their peers. (*See table, p. 258.*)[39]

But TIMSS center Director Schmidt says the teaching strategy used is not as important as the curriculum. "One of the things that really distinguishes math classes is not so much the pedagogical style of the teacher," he says, "but the rigor and demanding nature of the mathematics being taught."

BACKGROUND

Wake-up Call

Discussions of math and science reform inevitably mention *Sputnik*. The first satellite launched into orbit around the Earth gave the Russians the early lead in the race to explore outer space. The seminal 1957 event shattered America's self-image as the world's technology leader and spurred a national debate over the need to reform U.S. math and science curricula.

Actually, the discussion about how much math and science students should know began long before then. In a famous 1799 letter about the need for math, Thomas Jefferson opined: "Trigonometry, so far as this, is more valuable to every man. There is scarcely a day in which he will not resort to it for some of the purposes of common life. The science of calculation also is indispensable as far as the extraction of the square & cube roots; algebra as far as the quadratic equation & the use of logarithms are often of value in ordinary cases: but all beyond these is but a luxury."[40]

Nearly a century later, in 1893, Harvard University President Charles Eliot and the so-called Committee of 10 prescribed the courses — including math and science — that every properly educated man should study. The educators' efforts laid the groundwork for the way school subjects would be taught for the next century.

In some regions, there was deep-seated mistrust of science education, particularly the teaching of evolution — the theory that man descended from apes. Controversy over evolution boiled over at the 1925 trial of John Thomas Scopes, a Dayton, Tenn., biology teacher. He was charged with teaching evolution after the Tennessee legislature had declared such instruction illegal.

Scopes's conviction (he was fined $100) was overturned a year later on a technicality. But four decades elapsed before Tennessee, in 1967, repealed the ban on the teaching of evolution.

In the mid-1940s, the National Council of Teachers of Mathematics created the Commission on Postwar Plans to recommend math curricula reforms to help establish the United States as a world leader and continue the technological advances that helped the Allies win World War II. Although the commission documented problems with the nation's high-school math curricula, its reports had little lasting effect.[41]

Then, in the 1950s, *Sputnik* underscored the importance of math and science education. "[O]n Oct. 4, 1957, the Soviet Union shocked America by launching the first Earth satellite, a 184-pound ball of steel and wire called *Sputnik*," wrote former Sen. Glenn. "The United States had announced that it planned to put a satellite in orbit in 1958. To be beaten to the punch dealt a devastating blow to Americans' self-image of technological superiority."[42]

The 'New Math'

Sputnik loosened Congress's purse strings. The National Defense Education Act of 1958 increased federal support for math and science education, including materials aimed at improving education as well as student loans.[43] Math curricula reforms developed in the 1960s — which came to be known as the "New Math" movement — were aimed at pushing American children into advanced thinking by introducing them to concepts such as set theory, a branch of mathematical logic. Teachers attended NSF-funded summer institutes to learn the innovative programs.

Befuddled parents, however, found they could no longer help their children with their math homework and reacted coolly to the reforms.[44]

But starting in 1972, a steady decline in SAT math scores produced more consternation among parents, educators, legislators and businessmen. In 1973, Morris Kline — a New York University math professor and an outspoken critic of the New Math — published the controversial book *Why Johnny Can't Add*. The concerns sparked the emergence of a back-to-basics movement in mathematics instruction during the 1970s.

SAT mathematics scores gradually improved starting in 1982, but the onset of the technology age prompted many educators and business leaders to question whether enough students were taking advanced math courses.

Meanwhile, on the science front, a flood of discoveries was further complicating science education. In 1962, for instance, James Dewey Watson, a biochemist, and F.H.C. Crick, a molecular biologist, received the Nobel Prize after they proposed the double-helix structure of DNA.[45]

The discoveries prompted major changes in science, says the University of Maryland's Dancis. "It was mathematized and quantified," he says. For instance, biology — which once was mostly descriptive — now incorporates more chemistry and physics.

'A Nation at Risk'

In 1965 Congress for the first time considered a proposal to institute a nationwide testing program to ensure that students were learning and achieving. After bitter debate, it was killed due to opposition by those fearing federal control of schools and a national curriculum. Later, presidents George Bush and Bill Clinton would propose similar tests and national curricula for math and science, as well as for English and social studies. Both proposals also would be shot down by Congress.

In 1983, a blue-ribbon panel issued a landmark report, "A Nation at Risk," which sent shock waves through Congress, state legislatures and the education community. Published by the National Commission on Excellence in Education, the devastating assessment of the state of American public education alerted the public to the need to overhaul the U.S. education system.

The report noted that middle-school students in particular were falling behind in math and science. "In many other industrialized nations, courses in mathematics (other than arithmetic or general mathematics), biology, chemistry, physics and geography start in grade six and are required of all students," the report said. "The time spent on these subjects, based on class hours, is about three times that spent by even the most science-oriented U.S. students, i.e., those who select four years of science and mathematics in secondary school."[46]

Throughout the 1980s, various groups — motivated by different agendas — took on math and science literacy issues. For example, civil rights leader Robert

Singapore Math Boosts Inner-City Scores

Outside Felicity Ross's class at Robert Poole Middle School in Baltimore, the hallway buzzes with the chatter and constant motion of several hundred youngsters switching classes.

But inside, about 20 purposeful sixth-graders are already settled into their seats. They are part of a unique experiment in math education. The textbook they use comes from Singapore, the tiny Asian nation that made headlines a few years ago by sentencing a young vandalizer to be lashed with a cane.

Ross's class is part of the Ingenuity Project, sponsored by The Abell Foundation of Baltimore, to strengthen math, science and technology education for selected students in five city schools. The program chose Singapore's curriculum because its students consistently score at the top on international math exams.

And some of Singapore's success appears to be rubbing off on Ingenuity Project students. At Poole, roughly half the students in the program are on free and reduced lunch.

At the beginning of the 2000-2001 school year, sixth-graders in the project scored in the 86th percentile on a standardized test. At the end of the year, they scored in the 96th percentile.

Singapore math is rigorous. "The word problems are very challenging," says Karol Costa, executive director of the project. "So many schools are using reform approaches, but they are not successfully teaching arithmetic in elementary school."

"A lot of the [non-Ingenuity] students can't even multiply," Ross says. "That's ridiculous in sixth grade. Gosh, you give them a fraction and they're scared silly. So I think there is a real crisis going on."

That's why the Ingenuity Project chose to look at Singapore's curriculum. "We said, 'Hey, we can't import their values on education; we can't make the parents all feel the same way that all the parents do in Singapore about education. But let's look at the textbooks. That's one thing we can control,'" Ross recalls.

There is no time to spare in her classroom. Students quickly reach into their backpacks and pull out the slim paperbacks. "The main difference between Singapore textbooks and traditional American textbooks is that [Singapore texts] go much more in-depth in each subject, as opposed to covering lots and lots of subjects," Ross says.

Students must learn and truly understand a few select concepts. For instance, sixth-graders routinely study volume.

The traditional American textbook will explain that length, times width, times height equals the volume, she says. "Maybe they'll get imaginative — really go crazy — and give you volume and length and width, and they'll ask students to find the height. But really, that's as far as they'll go," she says.

But the Singapore text will also discuss water displacement, she explains. "If we put cubes into the tank and the water level rises this much, what's going on?" she asks. "And the kids have to really understand."

Singapore math isn't the only advantage for students in the Ingenuity Project. Ross holds after-school coaching sessions with students. She also sends them homework during the summer, which they must complete and return by mail.

Additionally, when the school made the switch to Singapore math about four years ago, Ingenuity Project teachers received special training. During the first year, as they grappled with the transition, Ross and a cadre of other teachers attended Saturday classes with a consultant.

"I was fairly new at that point, so I was much more malleable and open to new ideas," she remembers. "There are some teachers who have been teaching 20 years a completely different way, and they are like, 'Why is this method better?'"

To be sure, there are criticisms of Singapore math. "Every word problem has some man giving some woman money," Ross says. To compensate for the sexism, she writes her own word problems, in which the women involved might be playing soccer or chess.

On a recent morning, Ross snapped on an overhead projector and a complicated word problem appeared on a screen. A girl with a tiny voice read aloud: "Meihua spent one-third of her money on a book. She spent three-fourths of the remainder on a pen. If the pen cost $6 more than the book, how much money did she spend altogether?"

Step by step, students tackled the problem. They drew a box representing all of the girl's money and divided it into thirds. One-third represented the money the girl spent on the book. Then they started working on the calculations.

"When I talk about problem solving, I don't mean the students solve a couple of problems per week," Ross says. "They work on long, extended problems. This is very grounded in mathematics. They also have to be able to do the basics."

P. Moses founded the Algebra Project, arguing that learning algebra is a civil right that minority students too often have been denied.

"The political process has opened," Moses wrote in his recent book, *Radical Equations, Math Literacy and Civil Rights*. "There are no formal barriers to voting — for example — but economic access, taking advantage of new technologies and economic opportunity, demands as much effort as political struggle required in the 1960s."[47]

Among its activities, the Algebra Project has developed algebra curricular materials aimed at African-Americans and other minorities; trained teachers; and recruited youths to tutor younger peers in math.

Setting Standards

Some mathematics curricula were once again overhauled in the late 1980s and early '90s, spurred on by a 1989 education summit of state governors convened by then-President Bush in Charlottesville, Va. — chaired by then-Arkansas Gov. Clinton. The governors laid groundwork for six national education goals, which subsequently formed the basis of both Bush's and Clinton's education-reform proposals. One stated that by 2000, U.S. students would be best in the world in science and math.[48]

The NCTM in 1989 released its national academic standards for mathematics, which emphasized "finding and justifying solutions to problems, in addition to performing calculations." They were designed to encourage teaching math "in ways that help students make sense of important concepts through representing, communication, reasoning about and making connections among mathematical ideas."[49]

Critics called the standards "fuzzy" math. One of the loudest debates came from California, where academicians and parents said students were not learning basic math.

In a criticism of the new curricula, mathematics Professor David Klein of California State University wrote: "The mathematics books and curricula that parents of school children resisted . . . typically failed to develop fundamental arithmetic and algebra skills. Elementary school programs encouraged students to invent their own arithmetic algorithms, while discouraging the use of the superior standard algorithms for addition, subtraction, multiplication and division."[50]

In 1991 Bush made his controversial proposal for nationwide academic standards for core subjects and nationwide testing. The measure was opposed by both the right and the left — victim of the U.S. tradition that educational curriculum is strictly a local issue.

The federal government's role in setting math and science standards turned into another, hotly contested political matter after Clinton was elected President and took up Bush's standards-and-assessments mantle. His 1993 Goals 2000 package gave money to states to develop "voluntary" national content and performance standards and tests to go with them.

The plan drew bipartisan flak. The left feared that the tests would be used to penalize poor students who had not been provided the same educational opportunities — such as advanced math and science classes — as children in the suburbs. They wanted educational improvements first and tests later.

The right saw the proposal as a federal power grab, and latched onto it as a campaign issue in the historic 1994 midterm elections that ushered in the Republican takeover of Congress. "Conservatives hated Clinton and tried to demonize Goals 2000 and national testing to energize people to vote," said John F. Jennings, director of the Center on Education Policy and author of a history of the legislative battles over nationwide standards and tests.[51]

In 1997 Clinton again proposed a voluntary national program testing fourth-graders in reading and eighth-graders in math. Once again, Congress blocked the measure despite support from the business community.

During the rest of the 1990s, business leaders turned their attention to the governors and the individual state legislatures. By 1999, 40 states had developed and adopted their own statewide academic standards, facing opposition from both the right and the left at each step in the process. In addition, many states instituted new exams demanded by state lawmakers.

The lawmakers began to insist that teachers and schools be held accountable for improving learning. But, in the rush to impose mandatory "accountability" testing, also called "high-stakes" tests, the exams often were not properly coordinated with the new classroom curricula, prompting howls of outrage from parents and legislators when large numbers of students failed the new tests. Some states went back to the drawing board to revise both their standards and their tests.

Adding Science to the 3 R's

Parents have long fretted that Johnny can't read or Mary can't cipher, but there has been no such hue and cry that they don't know atoms from molecules.

Now science-education advocates are working to build public interest in the importance of "reading, writing, arithmetic *and* science."

Project 2061 — an education-reform initiative of the American Association for the Advancement of Science (AAAS) — will use part of a new $5.9 million National Science Foundation (NSF) grant to build public support for scientific literacy. Named after the next year that Halley's Comet appears, Project 2061 will develop both a public outreach campaign and new tools for teachers, curriculum developers, textbook authors and publishers.[1]

"So far, educators and scientists have largely talked to each other about needed reforms," said Project Director George D. Nelson. "To have a lasting impact on our schools, we need to convince parents, community leaders and state and local policymakers of the importance of science literacy, and to enlist their help . . . to achieve it."[2]

Educators say science literacy is necessary for voters to understand such hot-button national policy issues as cloning, stem-cell research and global warming. Yet, student performance on national and international science tests has been lackluster, and U.S. science curricula are too broad and superficial, educators say.

Since the mid-1990s, states have developed their own academic standards for science, based on 1996 recommendations by the National Research Council. The voluntary guidelines encourage school districts to cut back the amount of material covered in favor of targeting fewer topics in more depth. For instance, the content guidelines suggest that students:

- In grades K-4 should learn to distinguish the difference between natural objects and those manufactured by humans;
- In grades five through eight should learn about reproduction and heredity, populations and ecosystems;
- In grades nine-12 should understand the structure of atoms and chemical reactions.

The standards also stressed the need for effective learning techniques. Science should be taught "the way children learn about the world," says Shirley Malcom, director of education at the AAAS. "Science curricula ought to have hands-on, inquiry-based approaches — not the encyclopedia treatment."

As Leon Lederman, a Nobel laureate in physics and an advocate of improved science education, points out, science is "rich in play, rich in the process of how you find out things."

However, a 2001 study funded by the NSF found that the states' new science standards have not changed what happens inside the classroom. "We saw little change since the introduction of the standards in how [science] is being taught," said P. Sean Smith, a senior researcher at Horizon Research Inc., the Chapel Hill, N.C., firm that conducted the NSF study.[3]

The disconnect between the state standards and what's actually taught may disappear, however, now that Congress has ordered states to test students in grades three through eight annually. In fact, the new No Child Left Behind Act requires every state to develop and adopt science standards by the 2005-2006 school year. Unlike the states' existing standards, which sometimes only specified what was to be learned at two or three grade levels, the new law calls for science standards for every level.

Once new standards are written, students and schools will be held accountable — through standardized tests administered beginning in the 2007-2008 school year — for learning the material outlined in the standards. Within 12 years after that, all students must meet a state-defined "proficient" level in science.

---

[1] "2061 Today," American Association for the Advancement of Science, winter 2002.

[2] "AAAS's Project 2061 to Build Public Support for Science Literacy in Four-Year Outreach Campaign," AAAS press release, Oct. 1, 2001.

[3] Quoted in "Science Standards Have Yet to Seep Into Class, Panel Says," *Education Week*, May 22, 2002.

Efforts at math reform continued to be dogged by criticism even as late as 1999, when an open letter appeared in *The Washington Post* bitterly complaining that an Education Department expert panel had endorsed 10 math curricula as "exemplary" or "promising." The professors who signed the letter — including several Nobel laureates — complained that the panel did not include "active research mathematicians," and that even before the endorsements were announced, mathematicians and scientists from leading universities had "pointed out serious mathematical shortcomings in them."[52]

Meanwhile, the NCTM has consistently defended its standards, pointing out that student proficiency in math on the NAEP had increased between 1990 and 1996, and that SAT math scores had increased between 1990 and 2002. Nonetheless, in April 2000, the council revised its 1989 standards, emphasizing the need for accuracy and mastery of basic skills.

CURRENT SITUATION

Congress OKs Testing

One of the first priorities of newly elected President Bush was to pass education reform. In 2001 he was able to garner broad bipartisan support and convince Congress to pass the No Child Left Behind Act. It requires all students to be tested to ensure that they are learning the material included in their statewide curricula. But because it did not try to impose a single nationwide curriculum or test, Bush's plan did not run into the same opposition encountered by his father and Clinton.

The law mandates that students in grades three through eight should be tested annually in math and reading by the 2005-2006 school year. Some grades will begin testing this year. Student achievement in science will be tested beginning in 2007-2008.

Before students can be tested, the law requires that states revise their existing standards — developed in the 1990s — if those standards were not written for specific grade levels. "States have standards actually, [and] some of them are quite rigorous," says Santos of Achieve. "Others probably need some attention."

But many of the state standards specify what students need to know in several grades, such as what children should learn in kindergarten through second grade. Under the new law, those standards will have to delineate what students learn in each grade.

States are scrambling this year to rewrite their standards, "so that they are clear to teachers," Santos says.

But debate continues about whether the tests and individual state standards — the quality of which vary widely — will produce meaningful education reform or improve the teaching of math and science. Many still feel nationwide standards are still needed.

"National standards are [still] very, very important," says Heritage Foundation education specialist Nina Shokraii Rees, as long as the federal government does not set them. "We ought to be able to measure our kids against a high national bar. Right now, when you move from Texas to Alabama, or even from San Antonio to Houston, you don't take the same tests or study the same curriculum."[53]

Improving Teachers

Beyond the academic debates about what to teach in math and science is the real world of Mary Jane Centola, chairwoman of the math department at Gar-Field Senior High School, outside Washington, D.C.

With 2,800 students and a mix of nationalities, Gar-Field is one of the biggest schools in Virginia. "Some of these children have been passed along," says Centola. "They're coming out of middle school not prepared for high school. With some students, we're having to do sixth-grade math review."

But recruiting qualified math teachers is an even bigger challenge. Among other things, potential recruits — like their counterparts nationwide — cannot afford housing in Northern Virginia's hot real estate market.

Sen. Glenn's commission recommended improved working environments for teachers — including better pay to make it competitive with industry.[54]

But raising teachers' salaries is always controversial among public-school critics, who point out that private-school teachers often produce better academic results on lower salaries. Teachers' unions counter that private schools aren't required to accept inadequately prepared inner-city children, those with special needs and those learning English.

In June, Education Secretary Paige asked universities to revamp their teacher-preparation courses, de-emphasizing

> Sen. Glenn's commission recommended improved working environments for teachers — including better pay.

Should all students be required to take algebra?

YES

Dorothy S. Strong
Former Regional Coordinator, National Science Foundation's Urban Systemic Initiative

Nell B. Cobb
Associate Professor, DePaul University

From *Mathematics Education Dialogues*, April 2000, National Council of Teachers of Mathematics

Any discussion of the appropriate role and importance of algebra . . . eventually boils down to answering four questions: If not algebra, then what? If not all children, then whom? If not at all schools, then in which ones? If not now, then when? [A]nswers to these questions are fundamentally related to issues of equity, expectations and effectiveness.

Algebra . . . has always been a civil right for a select few. [T]he struggle for equality for minorities is directly linked to mathematics and scientific literacy. . . . [T]he successful completion of algebra will ensure that all students are prepared for college-level mathematics or for careers in [math-related] fields. . . . [A]ll students [should] successfully complete pre-algebra by seventh grade, a full year of algebra by eighth grade and four years of high school mathematics. . . .

[S]tudents, parents, teachers and administrators — indeed, all members of society — must believe and expect that all children can and must learn algebra. . . . Only when this commitment happens will all students learn algebra and thereby break the illiteracy cycle in mathematics and science that has reached epidemic proportions in some schools. . . .

[In addition,] the study and use of algebra must begin at the start of every student's formal schooling and continue throughout each student's academic experience.

Teacher preparation and . . . professional development [also] raise equity and expectation issues. To minimize the impact of students' mathematical deficiencies and to enable disadvantaged students to compete on the same level playing field as advantaged students, teachers must be prepared to remediate students' deficiencies while helping them learn new concepts and procedures. To accomplish this challenging task, technological support is critically important.

Also, we have found that teachers should be prepared to teach by following an approach that consolidates selected principles of both standards-based and traditional mathematics instruction. This approach to instruction, called BiMathematics, is similar to bilingual instruction, in that it produces students proficient in two mathematics languages — [one] skills-based and [the other] standards-based.

All children, at all schools, can have algebra competence now.

NO

Nel Noddings
Professor Emeritus of Child Education, Stanford University

From *Mathematics Education Dialogues*, April 2000, National Council of Teachers of Mathematics

Many secondary schools require all students to pass courses — and sometimes, standardized tests — in algebra. [Some say this approach] focuses on equality of opportunity; [others say] algebra is widely needed in the work world. Both arguments are questionable. My objections here are directed at . . . requiring traditional algebra courses, not at teaching specific topics selected wisely from algebra.

The argument [about] equality says . . . all children should have the educational opportunities once reserved for a few. It's hard to oppose such a generous gesture, but . . . the requirement begs fundamental educational questions: Why is academic mathematics a requirement for college entrance? Why [can't] American students, [like] students in many other [countries], choose a humanities track for college preparation? Second, can we claim to be offering an opportunity through coercion? [W]ith the advent of high-stakes testing, many students who could have earned a high-school diploma will fail to get one.

In our zeal to give everyone a chance at college, we are tolerating — perhaps even encouraging — courses that bear little resemblance to "real" algebra, [and] youngsters . . . find that they are utterly unprepared for college-level work. This borders on fraud and scarcely represents "equal opportunity."

In most parts of the United States, treatment of non-college-bound students is shameful. [W]e force everyone into courses suitable only for some future career. . . . Instead of showing truly democratic respect for all honest work and for the students who will . . . do this work, we treat everyone as college-bound. Students who take jobs without going to college do so by default because they are considered "not good enough" for college.

But maybe . . . the requirement [that all students take algebra] has a genuine educational rationale. I doubt it. Although some relatively new occupations surely use lots of mathematics, many older ones use less than they did 50 years ago. . . . Arguments for the non-occupational uses of mathematics — citizenship, personal finance and so on — are similarly flawed. They might [support] overhauling the mathematics curriculum, but [not] requiring traditional courses in algebra. . . .

Students should be able to choose either college or non-college curricula proudly and with confidence that their choices will yield a genuine valued education.

teaching-method requirements and putting more weight into requiring that aspiring teachers know subject content.

Education Department adviser Sclafani points out that the new law provides $2.8 billion in state block grants to improve the math and science teaching work force. "We did it as block grants so locals can figure out what to do," she says. "But clearly, teacher quality is the key ingredient in student learning. Measure after measure shows us that."

But some advocates for math and science teachers worry that the block grants will not help recruit math and science teachers, because community and school leaders are free to spend the money however they choose. Instead of spending it on improving math and science teacher salaries, says Wheeler, of the National Science Teachers Association, communities may "put resources into whatever [subject] is being tested [at the time]."

What Works?

Parents are often skeptical about some of the educational strategies and practices used at their local schools.

For example, Dancis at the University of Maryland complains that students are allowed to use graphing calculators on a statewide algebra test. "They're using hand calculators instead of [gaining] conceptual understanding," he says.

In fact, studies about calculator use have been inconclusive. In one, using calculators has been correlated with poor student-test performance.[55] But others show calculators do not hurt basic skills.

Teachers themselves disagree over students using calculators. For example, winners of the Presidential Award for Excellence in Science and Mathematics Teaching are more likely than their counterparts to have permitted calculators in the classroom.

The study of Presidential Awardees found that outstanding teachers used many classroom strategies that differed from the average teacher. (*See table, p. 258.*)

Ramaley of the NSF points out that states and local school systems decide which classroom strategies to adopt. But local school officials don't always know whether a particular approach or curriculum will actually improve test scores. Sclafani, of the Education Department, concedes that the government needs to finance as much solid research

on how best to teach science and math as it has for teaching reading.

"We can create the research agenda in science and mathematics that will enable us to say, definitely — as we can now in reading — that if you include [certain] components in your program, the children will learn," she says.

In August, the Department of Education announced it had awarded a five-year, $18.5 million contract for development of a national What Works Clearinghouse, which will summarize evidence on the effectiveness of different programs.

Plus, Harvard researchers — using a $3 million NSF grant — are studying which methods of teaching high-school science best prepare students for college. The study will focus on how 24,000 college students at 40 schools perform in freshman science courses.[56]

Revisiting the Standards

Although there is wide agreement that local school districts should be able to choose their own curricula, some educators believe that having different sets of academic standards for every state is just too unwieldy.

"We need coherence," says TIMSS Director Schmidt. "We won't succeed until we get national agreement." Schmidt recommends that states collectively work together to develop common standards.

Achieve, the nonprofit that evolved from the 1996 National Education Summit of governors and corporate leaders, is trying to help states set standards that compare to what students must do in top-scoring countries.

"Achieve works with a consortium of states that really want to look at themselves, and benchmark themselves against international standards," Santos says.

For instance, she says, "Math textbooks from Japan engage the students with topics in more depth and at a more rigorous level in the middle grades than our books. So that's one key objective — to provide the opportunity for all students to learn by rigorous world-class standards. And that means everybody."

Achieve currently is reviewing standards for 14 states, ensuring that their tests are aligned with the curricula being taught in the classroom. "We also review their standards and compare them to internationally benchmarked standards," Santos says.

Evolution Debate

Evolution is still a controversial subject in some parts of America. In fact, a 2002 NSF study found that, "For the first time, a majority (53 percent) of respondents answered 'true' to the statement 'Human beings, as we know them today, developed from earlier species of animals.' "

The Supreme Court has twice ruled on the issue. In 1968 it ruled that states cannot ban the teaching of evolution and in 1987 it said states may not require the teaching of creationism along with evolution.[57]

In 1995, the Alabama Board of Education required publishers to include a disclaimer for science textbooks stating that evolution is only one possible theory of life's origins. Then in 1996, legislatures in Ohio, Georgia and Tennessee considered anti-evolution measures, but none became law.

The latest trend began in 1999, when Kansas's Board of Education voted to exclude evolution from its statewide academic science curriculum. Voters later ousted board members who supported the measure, and in 2001 a new board restored evolution to the standards.

Currently, school boards in a handful of Southern and Midwestern states are debating whether students should be taught evolution, creationism, or a new concept, called "intelligent design" — a variation on creationism — which teaches that the universe is too complex to be explained except as the product of an "intelligent designer" or creator. While critics have characterized teaching creationism and intelligent design as religion masquerading as science, the practice has public support in some parts of the country.

In August, the Cobb County School District, outside Atlanta, tentatively approved a requirement that teachers give equal weight to evolution and creationism. And in reviewing its curriculum guidelines this year, the Ohio Board of Education became embroiled in a controversy over whether to require the teaching of intelligent design along with evolution.

"Ohio will become an international laughingstock, the butt of late-night jokes, and possibly become involved in a costly lawsuit that will keep Ohio in the spotlight as a scientific and intellectual backwater for years to come," Ohio University physiology Professor Steven A. Edinger wrote to the state's governor recently. "Biotechnology firms will be the first 'science-dependent' industries to shun or flee Ohio if we start teaching non sense in the science classroom."[58]

But advocates of creationism or intelligent design note that a Gallup Poll last year showed that 45 percent of Americans believe in creationism. Only 12 percent said they believed in an evolutionary process in which God had no part.

OUTLOOK

Funding Questioned

The Glenn Commission's 2000 report, "Before It's Too Late," warned bluntly that too many math and science classes were being taught by unqualified and underqualified teachers: "Newer, technologically oriented industries are having trouble finding enough qualified workers from among those teachers' students. Worse, creativity atrophies, and innovation suffers."[59]

The NSF budget for fiscal 2003 seeks $200 million for its Math and Science Partnership program, which engages college and university professors in efforts to improve public-school math and science instruction.

Physics professor and Nobel laureate Lederman says teachers need more in-service training. But he also agrees with TIMSS Director Schmidt that they need more knowledge of math and science content.

The Department of Education's Sclafani agrees. "We've got to surround our teachers with knowledgeable experts, so they feel like they're not in this by themselves," she says. "And in mathematics, very often it means bringing in mathematicians to teach some mathematics to the teachers."

For fiscal 2003, the administration proposes spending $2.85 billion on state grants to improve teacher quality. The program consolidates funding from previous professional-development and class-size reduction programs.

But the way the government is already spending its money has upset some advocates of science and math education. James M. Rubillo, executive director of the National Council of Teachers of Mathematics, told the House Appropriations Education Subcommittee in May that his group was disappointed that the Math and Science Partnership Program — authorized at $450 million — only received appropriations of $12.5 million in fiscal 2002.

And teachers, for their part, face mounting scrutiny. "I know I'm accountable," says Gar-Field math

Chairwoman Centola. But students and parents should also be accountable, she says.

Whenever educators talk about future math and science requirements, they invariably use words like "demanding" and "rigorous" to describe the math courses that future high schools will offer to students.

Schmidt likes the fact that people are talking about the content of math and science courses. He has reservations, though. Unless school systems ratchet up the requirements in math or science, in another decade, he warns, "People will be having the same conversation."

NOTES

1. "Science and Engineering Indicators 2002," Vol. 1, National Science Foundation, Chapter 1, p. 23.

2. Figures released Aug. 27, 2002, at a National Press Club press conference with College Board President Gaston Caperton.

3. "The Nation's Report Card," National Center for Education Statistics, http://nces.ed.gov/nations reportcard/pubs/main2000/2001517asp.

4. Gilbert A. Valverde and William H. Schmidt, "Refocusing U.S. Math and Science Education," *Issues in Science and Technology*, winter 1997, http://www.nap.edu/issues/14.2/schmid.htm.

5. James W. Stigler, *et al.*, "The TIMSS Videotape Classroom Study: Methods and Findings from an Exploratory Research Project on Eighth-Grade Mathematics Instruction in Germany, Japan and the United States," TIMSS Research Center, p. VI.

6. Bureau of Labor Statistics, Occupational Employment Projections to 2010, http://stats.bls.gov/emp/emptab3.htm. For background, see Jane Tanner, "Future Job Market," *The CQ Researcher*, Jan. 11, 2002, pp. 1-24.

7. National Science Foundation, *op. cit.*, Chapter 3, p. 27.

8. "2001 Profile of College-Bound Seniors — College Plans," The College Board.

9. National Science Foundation, *op. cit.*, Chapter 3, p. 29.

10. For background, see Kathy Koch, "High-Tech Labor Shortage," *The CQ Researcher*, April 24, 1998, pp. 361-384, and David Masci, "Debate Over Immigration," *The CQ Researcher*, July 14, 2000, pp. 569-592.

11. National Science Foundation, *op. cit.*, Chapter 7, pp. 10, 28.

12. "Keeping Competitive: Hiring, Training and Retaining Qualified Workers in 2002," Center for Workforce Preparation, U.S. Chamber of Commerce.

13. National Science Foundation, *op. cit.*, Chapter 1, p. 49.

14. "The Nation's Report Card," National Center for Education Statistics, http://nces.ed.gov/nations reportcard/science/.

15. TIMMS results available at http://nces.ed.gov/timss/timss95/more.asp.

16. Quoted from a statement prepared for the Senate Committee on Health, Education, Labor and Pensions, June 19, 2002.

17. National Center for Education Statistics, http://nces.ed.gov/timss/timss-r/highlights.asp.

18. David Berliner, "Our Schools vs. Theirs," *The Washington Post*, Jan. 28, 2001.

19. Kurt M. Landgraf, "Education Reform: Reasons for Positive Thinking," Educational Testing Service, http://www.ets.org/aboutets/issues3.html.

20. "Trends in Advanced Science and Mathematics Coursetaking," *The Condition of Education 2002*; National Center for Education Statistics, http://nces.ed.gov/programs/coe/2002/pdf/26_2002.pdf.

21. Leland S. Cogan, *et al.*, "Who Takes What Math in Which Track? Using TIMSS to Characterize U.S. Students' Eighth-Grade Mathematics Learning Opportunities," *Educational Evaluation and Policy Analysis*, winter 2001, pp. 323-341.

22. *Ibid.*

23. National Science Foundation, *op. cit.*, Chapter 1, p. 23.

24. Paige's Aug. 28, 2001, remarks can be found at, www.ed.gov/PressReleases/08-2001/08282001a.html.

25. Scores available at http://nces.ed.gov/pubs2002/digest2001/tables/dt134.asp.

26. For background, see Kathy Koch, "National Education Standards," *The CQ Researcher*, May 14,

1999, pp. 401-424, and Charles S. Clark, "Education Standards," *The CQ Researcher*, March 11, 1994, pp. 217-240.

27. Iowa's curricula are based on the Iowa Test of Basic Skills, so that state does not have official statewide standards.

28. Valverde and Schmidt, *op. cit.*

29. *Ibid.*

30. Michael T. Battista, "The Mathematical Miseducation of America's Youth," *The Phi Delta Kappan*, February 1999, www.pdkintl.org/kappan/kbat9902.htm.

31. "Before It's Too Late," National Commission on Mathematics and Science Teaching for the 21st Century, Sept. 27, 2000, pp. 24-37.

32. *Ibid.*, p. 7.

33. D. D. Goldhaber and D. J. Brewer, "Evaluating the Effect of Teacher Degree on Educational Performance," *Developments in School Finance*, 1996, http://nces.ed.gov/pubs97/97535l.html.

34. "Prevalence of Out of Field Teaching, 1987-88, 1999-2000," National Center for Educational Statistics, 2002, p. 21.

35. *Ibid.*

36. "Survey and Analysis of Teacher Salary Trends 2001," American Federation of Teachers, AFL-CIO, p. 1.

37. For background, see Brian Hansen, "Teacher Shortages," *The CQ Researcher*, Aug. 24, 2001, pp. 633-656.

38. "Meeting the Highly Qualified Teachers Challenge," U.S. Department of Education, June 2002, p. viii.

39. Iris R. Weiss, *et al.*, "The Presidential Award for Excellence in Mathematics and Science Teaching; Results from the 2000 National Survey of Science and Mathematics Education," Horizon Research, December 2001.

40. Thomas Jefferson, "Writings," *The Library of America* (1984), p. 1064.

41. Terese A. Herrera and Douglas T. Owens, "The 'New, New Math'? Two Reform Movements in Mathematics Education," *Theory Into Practice*, spring 2001, pp. 84-92.

42. John Glenn, with Nick Taylor, *John Glenn, A Memoir* (1999), p. 175.

43. For a summary of federal involvement in education, including the National Defense Education Act, see this page from the Brookings Institution's "Government's 50 Greatest Endeavors," http://www.brook.edu/dybdocroot/gs/cps/50ge/endeavors/postsecondary.htm.

44. Herrera and Owens, *op. cit.*

45. For more on Watson and Crick, see: http://www.nobel.se/medicine/laureates/1962/index.html.

46. "A Nation At Risk," http://www.ed.gov/pubs/NatAtRisk/findings.html.

47. Robert P. Moses and Charles E. Cobb, Jr., *Radical Equations, Math Literacy and Civil Rights* (2001), p. 6.

48. For background, see Koch, "National Education Standards," *op. cit.*

49. "Setting the Record Straight about Changes in Mathematics Education," National Council of Teachers of Mathematics, www.nctm.org.

50. David Klein, "A Brief History of American K-12 Mathematics Education," www.mathematicallycorrect.com.

51. Quoted in Koch, "National Education Standards," *op. cit.*, p. 413.

52. Advertisement, *The Washington Post*, Nov. 18, 1999, p. A5.

53. Quoted in Koch, *op. cit.*, p. 403.

54. "Before It's Too Late," *op. cit.*

55. National Science Foundation, *op. cit.*, p. 45.

56. See www.news.harvard.edu/gazette/2001/11.08/12-grant.html.

57. For background, see David Masci, "Evolution vs. Creationism," *The CQ Researcher*, August 22, 1997, pp. 745-768.

58. Quoted in Catherine Candisky, "Life: By Chance or Design?" *The Columbus Dispatch*, Feb. 10, 2002.

59. "Before It's Too Late," *op. cit.*, pp. 5-6.

BIBLIOGRAPHY

Books

Moses, Robert P., and Charles E. Cobb Jr., *Radical Equations, Math Literacy and Civil Rights*, Beacon Press, 2001.
This compelling book tells the story of how Moses, a noted civil rights activist, organized black voters in Mississippi during the 1960s. Moses founded the Algebra Project, which focuses on math education for minority students.

Schmidt, William H., *et al.*, *Why Schools Matter: A Cross-National Comparison of Curriculum and Learning*, Jossey-Bass, 2001.
Education professors and researchers analyze data from the Third International Mathematics and Science Study (TIMSS), in which students from more than 40 countries were tested in math and science. The book focuses on the relationship between curriculum in various countries and achievement.

Articles

Battista, Michael T., "The Mathematical Miseducation of America's Youth," *Phi Delta Kappan*, February 1999, www.pdkintl.org/kappan/kbat9902.htm.
A math professor at Kent State University argues that attacks on mathematics-reform efforts are misplaced and obscure genuine issues in education.

Cogan, Leland S., *et al.*, "Who Takes What Math in Which Track? Using the TIMSS to Characterize U.S. Students' Eighth-Grade Mathematics Learning Opportunities," *Education Evaluation and Policy Analysis*, winter 2001, Vol. 23, No. 4, pp. 323-341.
The authors use data from TIMSS to compare students' learning opportunities in various school settings.

Stutz, Terrence, "Define 'fact': Texas squabbles over textbooks ignite and spread," *Dallas Morning News*, Dec. 2, 2001.
Texas is well known for its epic battles over school textbooks. This article outlines the differences between conservative groups questioning the accuracy of school textbooks, and opponents contending that content is being censored.

Reports and Studies

American Association for the Advancement of Science, Science For All Americans, www.project2061.org/tools/sfaa/default.htm.
The association set out to answer a big question: What should future generations know about science and technology? This report offers guidelines for scientific literacy. Another association report, "Benchmarks for Science Literacy," outlines what students should know by various grade levels.

Goldhaber, Dan D., and Dominic J. Brewer, *Teacher Licensing and Student Achievement: Found in Better Teachers, Better Schools, Thomas B. Fordham Foundation*, 1999, www.edexcellence.net/better/goldhab.pdf.
The report examines the correlation between the education of teachers and student achievement.

Herrera, Terese A., and Douglas T. Owens, "The 'New New Math'?: Two Reform Movements in Mathematics Education," in *Theory into Practice*, spring 2001, pp. 84-92.
The authors discuss the genesis of two math-reform movements — "new math" and "new new math."

National Commission for Excellence in Education, A Nation At Risk, 1983, www.ed.gov/pubs/NatAtRisk/index.html.
While this report is not limited to math and science education, it provides thought-provoking perspective about the current debate. Two decades ago, educators reported that other industrialized nations started courses in mathematics (other than arithmetic or general math) and science earlier than the U.S.

National Commission on Mathematics and Science Teaching for the 21st Century, Before It's Too Late, 2000, www.ed.gov/inits/Math/glenn/toolate-execsum.html. The full report is linked.
The commission assesses students' math and science preparation as inadequate. The report centers on improving preparation and conditions for science and math teachers.

National Council of Teachers of Mathematics, Principles and Standards for School Mathematics, 2000, www.nctm.org.

The council's Web site includes grade-level recommendations for students as well as overarching education-philosophy ideas.

National Science Board, National Science Foundation, Science and Engineering Indicators 2002, 2002.
This reference includes chapters on math and science education, the science and engineering work force and public attitudes and public understanding. In addition to statistics, it includes perspectives on issues from educational research.

Wu, H, *The Mathematics Education Reform: Why You Should Be Concerned and What You Can Do*, 1997, http://math.berkeley.edu/~wu.
A University of California at Berkeley mathematics professor takes issue with reform efforts and the material covered in the new curricula.

For More Information

American Association for the Advancement of Science, 1200 New York Ave., N.W., Washington, DC 20005; (202) 326-6400; www.aaas.org. Publisher of *Science*, the AAAS seeks to advance science and innovation.

National Council of Teachers of Mathematics, 1906 Association Dr., Reston, VA 20191-1502; (703) 620-9840; www.nctm.org. Serves as forum and information clearinghouse on issues related to mathematics education.

National Science Foundation, 4201 Wilson Blvd., #1025, Arlington, VA 22230; (703) 292-5111; www.nsf.gov. Provides grants for research in mathematical sciences.

National Science Teachers Association, 1840 Wilson Blvd., Arlington, VA 22201-3000; (703) 243-7100; www.nsta.org. Seeks to improve science education; provides a forum for exchange of information.

U.S. TIMSS National Research Center, Michigan State University, College of Education, 455 Erickson Hall, East Lansing, MI 48824-1034; (517) 353-7755. Its Web site http://ustimss.msu.edu/ contains information on the Third International Mathematics and Science Study.

Reading Crisis?

Do Today's Youth Read Less Than Past Generations?

Marcia Clemmitt

Teens and 20-somethings are reading on their own much less than in the past and have the lowest reading scores ever, according to a recent report. Some literacy experts call the trend a crisis, but others note that young Americans like Lewis Grove, 19, of Heath, Ohio, are using new forms of literacy today as they blog, write fan fiction, instant-message and read on the Internet.

From *CQ Researcher*,
February 22, 2008.

A re today's youths really reading alarmingly less than previous generations?

Last November, a controversial National Endowment for the Arts (NEA) report revealed that all Americans, and especially teens and 20-somethings, read on their own much less than in the past. For example, 60 percent of 18-to-24-year-olds in 1982 said they read literature like novels outside school, but in 2002 only 43 percent did.[1]

But some reading experts are dubious, among them Bronwyn T. Williams, an associate professor of English at the University of Louisville who studies young people's relationship to literacy and media.

Literacy — reading and writing — is moving swiftly from paper to the Internet, especially for young people, Williams says. But while the NEA survey attempted to include online reading, "I'm not sure the report had the methodology" to capture that reading, he says. In fact, "I would say that, compared to 10 years ago and even 20 years ago, young people actually are doing a lot more with text, a lot more making meaning of text." As examples, he points to the proliferation of blogs and other online genres such as fan fiction.

Research data could be a bit off base because the meaning of literacy is changing so fast that young adults may not identify themselves as readers and writers even when they read and write daily, Williams suggests. As an example, he describes a college student who instant-messages (IMs) her friends nonstop and has written two 5,000-word fan fiction stories. Nevertheless, "she says she isn't a writer," Williams says.

Reading for Fun Declines With Age

More than half of American 9-year-olds read almost every day for fun, but by age 17 the percentage drops to less than a quarter.

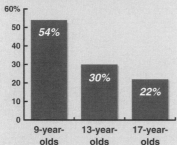

Percentage of Children Who Read Almost Daily for Fun, 2004

Sources: "To Read or Not to Read: A Question of National Consequence," National Endowment for the Arts, November 2007; U.S. Department of Education, National Center for Education Statistics

No matter where analysts come down on the validity of the NEA's conclusions, just about everyone agrees that the hallmark of literacy today is change.

"Fifty years ago, you could find a major novelist on the cover of *Time*," something that's hard to imagine happening today, says Sunil Iyengar, NEA's director of research and analysis. "Reading is currently not promoted as much in the mainstream culture."

The dawn of the television age half a century ago began a cultural shift that saw electronic media gaining ground on print. The NEA didn't begin surveying Americans' reading habits until 1982, but that year "was the high mark" in NEA data for time spent reading in all demographic groups, Iyengar says.

Today, however, the Internet may be not so much supplanting reading and writing as changing the way we read and write, literacy analysts say.

While fewer people may be reading traditional texts like novels or magazines, "the number of people posting original material online is large" and represents a new form of literacy, says University of Wisconsin Professor of English Deborah Brandt. "The idea that reading will now develop in the context of writing is a new chapter in the history of literacy," she says. "We've been under the impression that people learn to write by reading — that you write to share what you're reading" — but now writing is beginning to rival reading in time spent on that activity.

Whether or not one agrees with the NEA's conclusion about a precipitous dropoff in reading, the shift to the new media has worrisome aspects. The proliferation of electronic media that swallow students' time could prevent some of them from developing valuable thinking skills fostered by fluent reading, according to some reading experts.

"Even avid readers don't necessarily have the time" to read today, says Kylene Beers, president-elect of the National Council of Teachers of English. She recalls one middle-schooler who dubbed himself a "dormant reader" because his schedule doesn't leave time for the reading he enjoys. But as with flower bulbs buried in a winter garden awaiting spring, "dormant things can too easily become dead," and "dormant readers" can easily become non-readers, Beers says.

"Among the questions I find most interesting and perhaps troubling is how speed of taking in information" — a highly valued and frequently exercised online skill — "could replace the slowing down to reflect" that's a hallmark of reading traditional text, says Williams. "When students talk about having multiple screens open, I think, 'Well, you can do that, but then you're not really slowing down and reflecting' " on what's been read, he says.

Some research supports the concern that online reading encourages quick, surface skimming over sustained concentration, to the potential detriment of learning.

In a study commissioned by the British Library, researchers from University College London found that readers of academic journals and similar material in online "virtual libraries" do hardly any sustained reading. Sixty percent of readers of online academic journals "view no more than three pages," and a solid majority look briefly at a journal one time only and don't return to the site again. The average reader spends four minutes looking at an e-book and eight minutes on an e-journal, the researchers said.[2]

"There are signs that new forms of 'reading' are emerging as users 'power browse' . . . through titles, contents pages and abstracts," said the University College analysts. "It almost seems as if they go online to avoid reading in the traditional sense."[3]

Despite traditional readers' qualms, this "new reading" is only a continuation of the long history of shifting definitions of literacy, which changes every time a new technology — like the pen or the printing press — is invented, says Williams.

"There's always anxiety with a new medium," he notes. "Socrates was against writing; newspapers were accused of destroying the command of language."

The skills and practices that online-information seekers develop are indeed revolutionary compared to traditional literacy, and they will dominate the lives of the next generation, according to Marc Prensky, a creator of education-oriented video games in New York City. "Digital technology fits only awkwardly into the old 'tell-test' paradigm of education," he explained.

"In that paradigm, you keep your best ideas to yourself, rather than sharing. You don't go looking up information during a test, because it's 'cheating.' You don't take other people's work and use it in new ways because it's 'plagiarism,' " he added. "You can't use your cell phone as a lifeline (like you can do on TV to win a million bucks) because it's taking 'unfair advantage.' " So-called digital natives will do all of those things and more, Prensky said.[4]

Most troubling to many is the possibility that today's struggling students will be left further behind as online literacy joins traditional reading as a vital skill.

The test-score gap for traditional reading is widening between top students and struggling students, many of whom are low-income, says Katherine

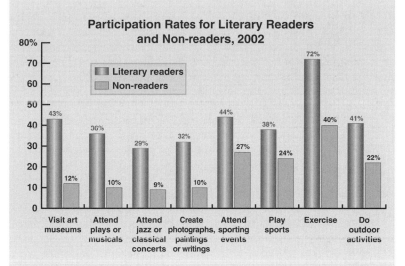

More Readers Participate in Outside Activities

Literary readers participate much more than non-readers in cultural, sports and civic activities. Nearly three-quarters of readers exercise, for example, compared to only 40 percent of non-readers.

Participation Rates for Literary Readers and Non-readers, 2002

- Literary readers
- Non-readers

Activity	Literary readers	Non-readers
Visit art museums	43%	12%
Attend plays or musicals	36%	10%
Attend jazz or classical concerts	29%	9%
Create photographs, paintings or writings	32%	10%
Attend sporting events	44%	27%
Play sports	38%	24%
Exercise	72%	40%
Do outdoor activities	41%	22%

Source: "To Read or Not to Read: A Question of National Consequence," National Endowment for the Arts, November 2007

Wiesendanger, a professor of education at Longwood University in Farmville, Va. That's a "quite frightening" scenario because "we have this underclass of low achievers perpetuating themselves," she says. "More resources need to go to the poorer schools. We need to get into the junior highs and put in strong reading programs for the children who are falling behind at that level, because children don't catch up on their own."

As the online world grows dominant, "it's a huge challenge, because we've never been in a position where every month or every year there are new reading and writing skills" that one must acquire to cope with new technologies, such as understanding how to use search engines effectively, said Donald Leu, a professor of literacy and technology at the University of Connecticut's Neag School of Education in Storrs.[5]

In addition, low-income schools and students are at a disadvantage online, said Leu. The very students "who require the most support and who have the least access to the Internet at home" are the least likely to learn online-reading strategies in class because their schools

Understanding of Dyslexia Is Emerging

Sufferers make connections more slowly.

"We have misunderstood many aspects of dyslexia in the past," says Maryanne Wolf, director of the Tufts University Center for Reading and Language Research in Medford, Mass. But today, thanks to brain imaging and other research, she says, scientists now have a better grasp of where some brains run into trouble with learning to read.

"We human beings were never born to read," said Wolf. "Each new reader comes to reading with a 'fresh' brain — one that is programmed to speak, see and think, but not to read. Reading requires the brain to rearrange its original parts to learn something new."[1]

Building the new connections to become a reading brain — the task that children's brains must perform as they move through kindergarten and grade school — means linking up the brain's speech areas with visual and conceptual areas to connect written marks on paper with words and their meanings. This turns out to be easier for some kinds of brains than others.

Dyslexics have "differently organized" brains, says Wolf. "There's more than one kind of dyslexic," but "by and large in much classic dyslexia the brain's right hemisphere is trying to take over the job of the left for written language." The dyslexic brain can make the connections required for decoding text, "but more slowly" than other brains.*

For example, research shows that one of the best predictors of reading problems turns out to be how fast children can identify pictures of letters or colors. "Readers with dyslexia can name colors perfectly well, but they cannot name them rapidly," Wolf wrote in her new book, *Proust and the Squid: The Story and Science of the Reading Brain.* It takes more time for these brains to connect visual and linguistic processes in order to respond to a picture with a name. Those brains also read more slowly, because the same connecting processes underlie both activities.[2]

Children whose brains are just milliseconds slower at making connections will struggle to become fluent readers, said Wolf. That's because "the whole development of reading is directed toward the ability to decode so rapidly that the brain has time to think about incoming information," she said.[3]

The adjective "slow" should never be misunderstood to mean that dyslexic brains lack intelligence, including verbal intelligence, says Wolf. Some of the most creative people have a history of dyslexia. But when it comes to specific tasks like decoding print, "the dyslexic brain is doing everything

---

* The right and left half of a human brain tend to specialize in different processes, with the left hemisphere more involved in language functions like processing the smallest speech sounds — phonemes — while the right hemisphere handles more spatial and pattern-recognition skills.

have fewer resources and must spend more time prepping struggling students for state achievement tests, he said.[6]

As teachers, librarians and parents question the place of traditional reading in the 21st century, here are some questions being asked:

Do young people read less than in the past?

Recent surveys show all Americans reading less, but the drop-off among teens and 20-somethings is steepest. But not all reading experts are convinced by these findings. Some argue that as more reading takes place online and on the job, traditional surveys may not pick up the reading done by the digital generation.

The NEA's November report, based on multiple surveys by NEA and others, showed teens and young adults — once the most frequent pleasure readers — now reading the least. While 18- to 24-year-olds were the most frequent readers in older surveys, "now, 20 years later, they're the least likely" to pick up a book, says NEA's Iyengar. "So something's going on."

The November report, "To Read or Not to Read," cites 2006 Department of Labor statistics showing that 15-to-24-year-olds spend an average of seven minutes per day outside of school reading. By comparison, 35-to-44-year-olds average 12 minutes of daily reading and 55-to-64-year-olds 30 minutes.[7]

slightly delayed," leaving too little time to both decode words and comprehend meaning while reading, she says.

Future research will help to clarify the organizational differences in dyslexic brains and why so many people think "outside the box" and "see patterns" others may miss, she says.

Visiting a famous radiologist for an ultrasound examination, a pregnant Wolf asked technicians what made the radiologist so successful. "It was her unerring ability to find unrecognized patterns within seconds," the staff replied. Later, Wolf learned that the doctor had a family history of dyslexia.[4]

Over the past decade, "we've made leaps" in understanding what makes dyslexic brains tick and how to help children with dyslexia improve their reading, says Wolf. For example, a program designed by Wolf and her colleagues — called RAVE-O — involves teaching children just a few carefully chosen "core words" per class — interesting words that have multiple meanings and that also contain the same combined vowel and consonant combination, such as "jam" and "ram." As the children practice spotting the repeated letter pattern "am" and its associated sound in the initial core words and in other similar-pattern words, they increase their skill at identifying chunks of letters that will help them decode more complicated words later on.[5]

"We're a light-year from where we were in the 1970s and 1980s. We're really good at the lower decoding levels" — for example, picking up children's difficulties knowing which sounds go with which letters — "and these were the biggest bottlenecks" even in the 1980s and 1990s, she says.

Nevertheless, "we still have miles to go" to the ultimate goals — fully understanding the brain functions that make up the more complex tasks, such as fluency and comprehension, and "tailoring interventions to individual children," Wolf says.

AFP/Getty Images/Stan Honda

Creative people and entrepreneurs are often dyslexic, like Virgin Atlantic founder Sir Richard Branson.

---

[1] Maryanne Wolf, "Reading Worrier," PowellsBooks.BLOG, Oct. 12, 2007, www.powells.com/blog?p=2459.

[2] Maryanne Wolf, *Proust and the Squid* (2007), p. 178.

[3] *Ibid.*, p. 179.

[4] *Ibid.*, p. 200.

[5] Maryanne Wolf, Lynne Miller and Katherine Donnelly, "Retrieval, Automaticity, Vocabulary Elaboration, and Orthography," *Journal of Learning Disabilities*, July/Aug. 2000, p. 375, http://newfirstsearch.oclc.org/images/WSPT/wsppdf1/HTML/02284/QL6OX/PSA.HTM.

In a 2007 American Library Association/Harris Interactive survey, teenagers proved much less likely to visit or use the online services of a public library than younger children. Seven percent of 11-to-15-year-olds and 6 percent of 16-to-20-year-olds said they'd used public-library services the previous year, compared to 16 percent of 6-to-10-year-olds.[8]

Young adults report doing less reading and participating less in the arts and civic activities, but they use electronic media — like television, video games and the Internet — more than in the past, NEA's Iyengar says. (*See graph, p. 286.*) Teens and young adults report having "the most free time, outside of retirees," but "they're still spending less on reading," he adds.

Beers at the English teachers' association says she was disheartened by the NEA findings, but not surprised. "Kids graduating from high school say, 'In second and third grade I liked to read, but by high school I didn't,'" Beers says. She suspects that school turns reading from "an aesthetic experience" — wherein readers immerse themselves in text to vicariously participate in others' lives — into a simple task of extracting information to answer test questions.

"I would call the years 2000 to 2006 testing-frenzy years, with the mind-set of, 'If we test it, they will learn it,'" Beers says. But the "national focus on test, test, test" has been shown to negatively affect the ability to read critically, and now possibly the desire to read.

Spending on Reading Declined

The percentage of total household spending on reading material dropped by nearly half between 1995 and 2005, while the percentage spent on TV and audio equipment rose from a third of family entertainment spending to 37 percent. The trend reflects the loss of reading time among American consumers and the rise of screen time.

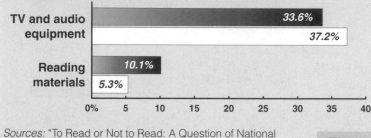

Average Annual Spending on Reading Materials vs. TV/Audio Equipment, 1995 and 2005
(as a share of household entertainment spending)

TV and audio equipment: 33.6% / 37.2%
Reading materials: 10.1% / 5.3%

Sources: "To Read or Not to Read: A Question of National Consequence," National Endowment for the Arts, November 2007; U.S. Department of Labor, Bureau of Labor Statistics

■ 1995
□ 2005

However, some reading experts question whether current research really captures all the reading young people do as text moves from printed newspapers and books to online sources.

"We have always thought of reading in the form of books or a newspaper or magazine," says Stan Steiner, a professor of children's and young-adult literature at Boise State University in Idaho. "I look at my own kids, and I see that a lot of their assignments are connected to doing stuff online," for example. Much of the online reading — some related to school, some not — may be missed in current data, Steiner suggests.

Teenagers say, " 'I hate reading,' but then they spend two hours reading Facebook or blogs," says Paula Brehm-Heeger, president of the American Library Association's Young Adult Library Services Association. Studies may miss some of who's reading and how much because survey definitions haven't changed to match today's reading habits, says Brehm-Heeger.

"Many libraries are expanding their teen areas," and "librarians will tell you that it's happening because we have so many teens here after school," says Brehm-Heeger, a librarian at the Public Library of Cincinnati-Hamilton County, Ohio, where a new teen area with books and

two-dozen computers is opening this year. "In 1995, only 11 percent of libraries employed at least one full-time employee to work with young adults, but by 2007 nearly 52 percent of libraries did.

"If it wasn't producing results," she continues, "we wouldn't see it."

Is there a literacy crisis?

Stagnant or falling reading scores for teenagers, coupled with television and video-game time that crowds out reading, are triggering concerns among literacy experts because more than ever today's job market and participatory democracy both demand literate, reflective citizens. But other analysts say literacy may be merely shifting to new forms, making it premature to declare a crisis.

The consequences of a decline in reading are serious, according to NEA Chairman Dana Gioia, a poet. "The story the data tell is simple, consistent and alarming," he said. While elementary-school children are gaining in reading, "all progress appears to halt as children enter their teenage years," and fewer teens and adults read often. "Most alarming, both reading ability and the habit of regular reading have greatly declined among college graduates," developments that could have "demonstrable social, cultural and civic implications." (*See graph, p. 297.*)[9]

For example, he noted, as young people lose the reading habit, their reading-ability test scores have dropped off. After rising for about two decades, 17-year-olds' average reading scores on the National Assessment of Education Progress (NAEP) have dropped to 1971 levels. And between 1992 and 2005, the percentage of 12th-graders reading at or above a "proficient" level dropped from 40 percent to 35 percent, according to the Department of Education. Over that period, average scores for all students dropped, except for those scoring at the 90th-percentile and above; their scores held steady.

As literacy levels stagnate, workplace demands for literacy are growing, says Laura Westberg, director of research and special projects at the National Center for Family Literacy in Louisville, Ky. She cites a Verizon executive who says many résumés that would have led to a quick hire in the past now don't even get to the interview stage because the applicant appears unable to meet rising job demands for capable reading and writing.

In a world where economic competition is international, young American adults are falling behind, according to the Alliance for Excellent Education, a Washington advocacy group. Reading scores of U.S. "high-school students have not improved over the last thirty years," while in international comparisons, "U.S. 11th-graders have placed very close to the bottom — behind students from the Philippines, Indonesia, Brazil and other developing nations," said the alliance.[10]

Personal lives also increasingly depend on reading skill, say some literacy experts. The ability to read, comprehend and follow medical instructions can be a matter of life or death, according to health policy researchers. In a 2007 study, older adults with lower reading and comprehension skills had higher death rates. Poor reading comprehension of health and medical material "is associated with . . . worse self-management skills for patients with hypertension, diabetes mellitus, asthma and heart failure," as well as lower rates of vaccination and cancer screening, said researchers from the Northwestern University School of Medicine.

The growing gap between able readers and struggling readers also may be dangerous for democracy, some reading experts say.

Newspaper reading continues to plummet, and many Americans aren't picking up news elsewhere, leading to a potentially uninformed voting public, according to NEA's November report. The circulation of major U.S. newspapers fell 2-3 percent each year from 2005 and 2007, the NEA observed, and by 2004 only 21 percent

of college-age Americans read a daily newspaper — down from 46 percent in 1972.

Furthermore, "young people's lukewarm stance to newspapers extends to news from other media," according to NEA's report. While one-fifth of teens and young adults say they read some news every day on the Internet, only 32 percent of the teenagers and 46 percent of the young adults who see Internet news say they actively sought it out; the rest stumbled across it by accident.

Those declining reading habits — and growing gaps between able, habitual readers and others — could spell trouble for participatory democracy, "which is based on having an across-the-board literate society," says Beers of the English teachers' association.

The decline in traditional reading is also "taking its toll in the civic sphere," said NEA's Gioia. Traditional newspaper reading, for instance, involves a certain amount of serendipity: turning the pages a reader stumbles across articles about intriguing but completely unfamiliar subjects that the reader would never find by using only the "search" button on an online newspaper page to

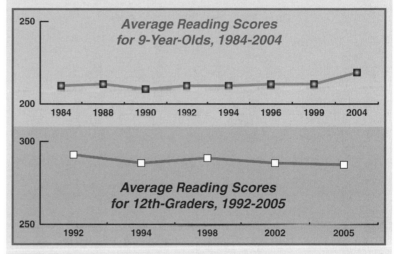

Reading Scores Drop for 12th-Graders

The average reading score for 9-year-olds rose eight points from 1984 to 2004 (top) while scores for 12th-graders have decreased by six points since 1992 (bottom). Reading experts consider the changes significant.

Average Reading Scores for 9-Year-Olds, 1984-2004

1984 · 1988 · 1990 · 1992 · 1994 · 1996 · 1999 · 2004

Average Reading Scores for 12th-Graders, 1992-2005

1992 · 1994 · 1998 · 2002 · 2005

Sources: "To Read or Not to Read: A Question of National Consequence," National Endowment for the Arts, November 2007; U.S. Department of Education, National Center for Education Statistics

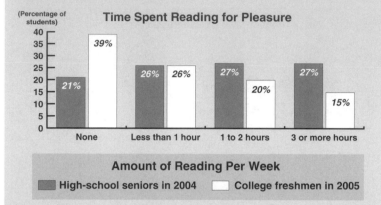

College Freshmen Read Less

College freshmen spend significantly less time reading for pleasure than high-school seniors. Nearly 40 percent of college freshmen spent no time reading for pleasure in 2005, almost twice the percentage of high-school seniors the year before.

Time Spent Reading for Pleasure

(Percentage of students)

Amount of Reading Per Week

■ High-school seniors in 2004   □ College freshmen in 2005

Source: "To Read or Not to Read: A Question of National Consequence," National Endowment for the Arts, November 2007

find one's favorite subject. Reading books and newspapers helps us "imagine and understand lives quite different from our own" and imparts the "civic and historical knowledge" needed for full participation in a democracy, Gioia said. The National Conference of State Legislatures concluded in a 2003 study of political and civics awareness among 15-to-26-year-olds that as traditional reading wanes, "Young people do not understand the ideals of citizenship . . . and their appreciation and support of American democracy is limited."[11]

But other observers counter that literacy may mainly be changing rather than dropping off, and that demographic trends may account for some apparent decreases.

There's a tendency to overhype literacy problems, says the University of Wisconsin's Brandt. "How could we have the technologies we do if people's literacy skills are so pathetic?" she asks. "Our skills are getting reshaped" in ways that make it harder for traditional literacy surveys to tally them, she says.

According to Nancy Kaplan, executive director of the University of Baltimore's School of Information Arts and Technologies, the concern expressed in the NEA report about teens' reading scores reflects the report's tendency

to overhype the situation. While teens' scores have dropped over the short term, America's 17-year-olds actually read just as well as they did in 1971, she said. The 2004 average score for 17-year-olds "is exactly the same as the average score for that age group in 1971. . . . In short, there is no downward trend in reading proficiency over the whole period for which we have data," Kaplan said.[12]

NEA's key argument — that a decline in the habit of reading is taking its toll on Americans' reading ability — isn't necessarily buttressed by data, said Kaplan. Having English as a second language decreases adults' proficiency on English literacy tests, and the foreign-born adult population has grown in recent decades, from 7.9 percent of the total population in 1990 to 11.1 percent in 2000, so declining English-language reading scores may simply reflect this change, she said.

While book and magazine reading may drop off, literacy can still flourish as Americans read and write online, says Brandt. Online reading is overlooked because it isn't part of the list of texts traditionally judged by scholars as the most important in the culture, she says. "Reading is down, but writing is up. There's an explosion of amateur literature going onto the Web," a phenomenon overlooked by those who declare a literacy crisis, she says.

Moreover, most workers face and meet significant literacy requirements on the job, some reading analysts say. Today's workplace "takes up a lot of mental energy," says Brandt. "When most people worked in factories, we used our hands and backs on the job and were hungry for intellectual excitement" after work. "But when we're in front of screens reading and writing all day, our literacy is being largely redeployed into our work."

Will harm be done if new technologies crowd out traditional reading?

As the reading of traditional text wanes and technologies such as TV, video games and the Internet take more of our time, some literacy experts worry that young people will miss out on important skills and experiences fostered by traditional reading. But technology analysts counter that 21st-century technologies will make many traditional literacy skills outmoded and foster different abilities suited for a new era.

"Because the brain doesn't have a program for reading, it can organize itself in a great many ways" to do the task, so children who learn to read mostly online will have differently organized brains from those who've learned from books, explains Maryanne Wolf, director of the Tufts University Center for Reading and Language Research in Medford, Mass.

A key reward of becoming a fluent, traditional reader is being able to "bring our own life to the text," Wolf says. That's something that must be learned by building fluency through sustained attention. Online, by contrast, "there are lots of sidebars" plus hyperlinks to audio, video and text, says Wolf. "I worry that the new format will reward moving on quickly to the next thing rather than holding onto a thought," building depth of concentration, Wolf says.

Because of the constant availability of many media, such as television and text-messaging, "kids are multitasking more — reading while they're doing other things — and that has its disadvantages," says Longwood University's Wiesendanger. "You can do three things at once if they're all very easy. But it takes away from being able to concentrate on one thing and, in the case of books, it takes away from the ability to be absorbed in a book," she says.

By becoming absorbed in a book, one is able to have many experiences vicariously, Wiesendanger says. "The person is changed," she explains. "You make connections between the text and yourself, between the text and the world you know."

Television and online material heavily feature visual content, often as a replacement for what would be written text in a traditional magazine. But if written text were to be replaced by video images, as some futurists say will happen, it would dramatically change the way people think, says the University of Louisville's Williams. "Images give you surface, print gives you interiors," he says. "An image on the film doesn't give you the interior life of a character."

From constant interaction with shifting television images, fast-trigger video games and the like, the brains of "digital natives" are attracted and attuned to speed, a characteristic that may endanger the traditional cognitive habit of reflection, said educational-game expert Prensky. Reflection may enable our brains to generalize as we create "mental models" from our experiences — the process of "learning from experience," said Prensky. But "in our twitch-speed world, there is less and less time and opportunity for reflection," a potentially worrying development, he said.[13]

Reading narratives — stories — could be a casualty of a switch from pleasure reading of traditional text to online activities, says Boise State University's Steiner. A continued sharp decline in pleasure reading of narrative would be "devastating" because pleasure reading builds "higher-order thinking skills and use of the imagination," he says.

In addition, electronic technologies like television use a much smaller vocabulary than text, potentially limiting vocabulary growth after the third grade, said Keith Stanovich, research chair of applied cognitive science at the University of Toronto.[14]

Searching for information online may not have the same power as traditional reading to build a lifelong reading habit, says Beers at the English teachers' association. Instead, those who've enjoyed "getting caught up in a book" are most likely to become lifetime habitual readers, she says.

But analysts say online life fosters its own set of competencies. Twenty-first century literacy is "more about synthesis than analysis," the key mode of 20th-century literacy, says Beers. Online literacy is also non-linear, she says, because it requires readers to be more critical and do more synthesizing. Students must decide on their own how to navigate Web pages and "use their own assessment of what information is missing to decide whether to follow a hyperlink or not," for example. "The role of the reader is much more front and center," she adds.

Unlike traditional reading, online literacy does not involve a shared set of texts or a common experience, says Laura Sterponi, assistant professor of language and literacy at the University of California, Berkeley. "If a class of students all begin on the same [Web] page, they may all read different texts," as they follow links to other pages. "This is very engaging and empowering for readers."

Just as the proliferation of books elevated reading as an activity in the past, the Internet now elevates the importance of writing, says the University of Wisconsin's Brandt. "In the past we've ascribed a lot of values to reading — reflectiveness, sensitivity to others' points of view — but people I've interviewed are now getting these things from writing," she says.

Online writers in the workplace understand that their words matter, whether they're writing an e-mail or writing a meeting agenda, says Brandt. And kids writing in chat rooms are teaching each other thinking and communication skills, she says, such as what constitutes evidence and what behavior is civil and not civil. "Questions like these are being negotiated every evening," she says.

Because so much online material is text, the computer has actually intensified alphabetic literacy while integrating it with the visual, says Brandt. "They reinforce each other," she says. "For example, we know from studies of TV that up to a certain level of use it tends to support traditional literacy."

Communication is a basic skill, said Prensky, with reading and writing "merely the best methods of the moment" — methods that must be taught until better ways emerge. But in the future — once all books are recorded, the Internet reads itself aloud and everyone has a text scanner in his cell phone that can read any printed text aloud — "Should we still spend all those years teaching our kids phonics?[15]

"Modern technology fits perfectly with the kids' 21st-century paradigm," he continued. "Find information you think is worthwhile anywhere you can. Share it as early and often as possible. . . . Within 30 years, which is well within the working lifetimes of today's kids and the careers of today's starting teachers, the power of technology will have increased by a factor of a billion.

"How long do you think it will be before the growing power of technology dooms the old educational paradigm in our schools?"

BACKGROUND

Breaking the Code

Twenty-first century understanding of the brain sheds light on why reading is hard, why it's especially hard for some kinds of brains and how best to teach it.[16]

Unlike speech, for which human brains are genetically programmed, reading doesn't have its own special genetic programming that gets passed down from generation to generation. And because reading hasn't been around long enough — on an evolutionary time scale — for brains to have evolved with reading circuitry, reading isn't yet encoded into the brain's wiring, according to Terrence Deacon, professor of biological anthropology and linguistics at the University of California, Berkeley. Human ancestors began developing the capacity for speech hundreds of thousands of years ago, while the earliest writing was not invented until perhaps 10,000 years ago, a mere blip on the scale of human evolutionary time.

So while the average brain — born with a built-in speech center — takes to oral language like a duck to water, each brain must struggle on its own to adapt its wiring to comprehend and produce written words.

Crucial to understanding how brains learn to read is the notion of the brain's "plasticity."[17] While scientists once believed that brain networks were cemented into place fairly early in life, they now know that the brain can continue to reorganize itself throughout life to do new tasks or to do old tasks in new ways, such as learning to read the Braille alphabet if one loses his sight.

But the plastic brain doesn't develop "like building something from a plan," said Deacon. Instead, a network to accomplish a new task like reading is "cooked up on the fly as brains develop," in a kind of engineering patchwork.[18] For instance, the earliest Western written symbols appeared between 6,000 and 8,000 years ago, when marks scratched onto a piece of clay, for example, constituted a kind of accounting system that could be "read" to find out how many sheep or goats a farmer had sold.

Simple as it was, this early "writing" demanded that each would-be reader's brain develop new connections and capacities, said Wolf of Tufts University. "To 'read' a symbol demanded two sets of novel connections," she explained. "Among the long-established brain circuits for vision, language and conceptualization, new connections developed and new . . . pathways" between the eye and certain areas of the brain devoted to visual processing "became assigned to the tiny" symbolic marks.[19]

Gradually, written languages like Sumerian cuneiform and Egyptian hieroglyphics vastly expanded the number and complexity of their symbols — which were initially more pictographic — visually similar to the objects they

CHRONOLOGY

1950s-1970s *Availability of paperbacks spurs book-buying boom, but television viewing increases. Interest grows in helping low-income children own books.*

1955 Reading expert Rudolf Flesch publishes *Why Johnny Can't Read*, his controversial book arguing that phonics is the best way to teach reading.

1960 Sales of paperbacks to adults are up nearly 800 percent from 1950. . . . Circulation of "serious" magazines like *Atlantic, Harper's* and *Fortune* is up 250 percent over 1940.

1966 Former teacher Margaret McNamara founds Reading is Fundamental in Washington, D.C., to distribute free books to low-income children.

1971 "The Electric Company" PBS TV series features songs and comedy skits using phonics to teach reading.

1975 Congress creates Inexpensive Book Distribution Program to provide matching grants for local Reading is Fundamental centers.

1977 Library of Congress founds Center for the Book to promote reading.

1979 Library of Congress and CBS television launch "Read More About It" TV spots, directing viewers to books with more information about program topics. Actor Richard Thomas presents the first spot, following the made-for-TV movie "All Quiet on the Western Front," about World War I.

1980s-1990s *Teen reading scores rise, then begin falling in the mid-1990s. Leisure reading declines.*

1982 National Endowment for the Arts conducts survey of literary reading.

1983 Hosted by "Roots" star LeVar Burton, the PBS children's program "Reading Rainbow" begins promoting reading to children.

1984 Florida establishes nation's first state Center for the Book.

1989 National Center for Family Literacy is founded in Louisville, Ky. . . . Congress enacts Even Start law to help low-income parents.

1992 A "Read More About It" TV spot following the Super Bowl reaches 70 million viewers.

1999 Great Britain appoints humor writer Quentin Blake as its first Children's Laureate to promote reading by young people. . . . Library of Congress ends "Read More About It" after CBS participation dwindles to two TV spots per year.

2000s *Reading scores rise for grade-schoolers after enactment of No Child Left Behind law but drop for teenagers. . . . More reading migrates online.*

2002 Congress enacts Reading First program to increase use of scientifically based reading instruction and improve elementary-school reading performance. . . . Leisure reading by 18-to-24-year-olds is down 12 percentage points from 1992.

2004 Twenty-six percent of 15- to 18-year-olds read for pleasure 30 minutes or more a day. . . . Fifty-eight percent of middle- and high-school students listen to music, watch TV or browse the Web while reading. . . . Google Scholar is launched. The freely accessible Web search tool offers full-text scholarly articles and books, although many publishers restrict Google's access.

2006 Government auditors accuse Reading First administrators of unfairly steering states to buy school materials only from companies to which the administrators had ties.

2007 National Endowment for the Arts study finds American youths are reading less, and not as proficiently. . . . Congress cuts Reading First funding by two-thirds. . . . *American Born Chinese*, a graphic novel, wins the American Library Association's prize for young-adult literature. . . . The gap in reading scores between U.S. low-income and high-income teenagers is greater than in other nations. . . . Online bookseller Amazon.com launches its e-book device, Kindle.

2008 British Library study finds that online researchers mainly skim instead of read and are unskilled at using search tools. . . . Children's humor-book author Jon Scieszka is appointed first National Ambassador for Young People's Literature. . . . President George W. Bush proposes elimination of the Inexpensive Book Distribution Program.

Turning Non-Readers Into Readers

Parents should talk about books with their kids.

Young people retain an interest in reading both on the page and online — if they find material that really interests them, insist many literacy experts.

"If you go into a class of students for a book talk and choose good books, there is still interest, and you still see the books checked out," says Paula Brehm-Heeger, president of the American Library Association's Young Adult Library Services Association. "I don't think there's any intrinsic rejection" of books.

Furthermore, "people are still very willing to pick up even the classics" if their attention is captured, says Mary Mokris, leader of materials development for Kumon North America, an international math and reading tutoring company in Teaneck, N.J. Kumon uses book excerpts as part of students' reading practice, "and we get a lot of letters saying, 'You have a small excerpt in your worksheet, and I'd like to read the rest of it,' " she says.

So, how can teachers spread the reading bug? Reading experts have some ideas, such as:

- Make sure the parents of struggling kids enjoy the pleasures and benefits of reading themselves, says Sharon Darling, founder of the National Center for Family Literacy (NCFL) in Louisville, Ky. Illiteracy is passed down through families, so "when parents with low literacy see their children having trouble in school, they figure, 'This is just the way it is for our family,' " she explains.

  "Every child wants to be like their mother or father," so the cycle of illiteracy continues, Darling says. "But with just a little bit of help, the parents get turned on, and as soon as they do, as soon as they feel they're not stupid, they automatically want to help their children," she says.

- Show parents how to help their kids learn to read, says Laura Westberg, NCFL director of research and special projects. For example, she says, explain to parents that "listening to children and talking with them about books has a much stronger effect on improving school reading outcomes than just reading to them out loud." Stan Steiner, a professor of children's and young-adult literature at Boise State University, encourages teachers to send home lists of books that kids enjoy.

- Use non-traditional, less "linear" texts, which attract boys into the action, according to William G. Brozo, professor of literacy at George Mason University in Fairfax, Va., and co-author of a study on engaging young people in reading. In the United States, Ireland and the United Kingdom, "boys were more motivated to read and achieved higher scores with non-continuous text," or text with varying type sizes, numerous sidebars and color photos, the study found.[1]

  Luckily, there are many "non-continuous" books on subjects with high kid appeal like dinosaurs and sports, says Steiner. The *Eyewitness* nonfiction series launched in 1988 by London-based Dorling Kindersley — now DK — changed the look of nonfiction, "and that has been the dominant look of nonfiction ever since," he says.[2]

  On the fiction side, graphic novels have the highest check-out rates in local libraries, says Steiner. "They've just exploded over the past five years," although not all librarians have bought in, he says. "They think of

represented. As they became more abstract and linguistically demanding, these expanding writing systems asked even more of the brain. "Considerably more pathways in the visual and visual-association regions would be necessary in order to decode what would eventually become hundreds" of characters, explained Wolf.[20]

Bigger and more complex changes were to come. As Sumerians added new words to their written language, they began using the "rebus principle" — allowing a symbol to stand for an object and for the related sound as well. Pressing written symbols into that double duty required still "more elaborate cerebral circuitry," as readers were called upon to develop links among brain areas that hadn't cooperated before, such as areas dedicated to processing sights, sounds and concepts, according to Wolf.[21]

Becoming a reader meant years of painstaking practice, as each individual built brain networks to efficiently link them as comic books, and there was a myth that comics were substandard in vocabulary," but that isn't always true and is even less true of graphic novels, Steiner says. In 2007, Gene Luen Yang's *American Born Chinese* became the first graphic novel to win the American Library Association's Michael L. Printz Award for Young Adult Literature.[3]

- Encourage reading as a social activity, suggests Laura Sterponi, an assistant professor of language and literacy at the University of California, Berkeley. Throughout history "reading was an experience of sociability," with people meeting to share and entertain each other with books, she says. Children often enjoy — and learn from — "clandestine sharing" of books, says Sterponi. She studied second- and third-grade classrooms and found that young friends chose similar books for "silent reading" time and then seated themselves in out-of-the-way corners to discuss the texts among themselves, out of teachers' earshot. Such book talk motivates children to keep reading and "enhances reading comprehension, because reading implies taking different perspectives," she says.

So called self-proclaimed readers among 6-to-19-year-olds "all have somebody to talk to about what they read," says Steiner. "Mothers are first on the list, then friends," he says. "When we read a good book, what's the first thing we want to do? Share it with people."

- Keep school libraries open year-round, he continues. Studies show that halting a young person's reading during summer months seriously slows his academic progress. Although 65 to 70 percent of kids get their books from the school library, those libraries traditionally shut down in the summer. "We cut off their supply for three months," he complains.

Youngsters toast skewered bananas dipped in chocolate fondue at the Albany County Public Library in Laramie, Wyo. Libraries around the country are starting such programs to attract young adults to libraries.

School districts and parent groups should work together "to get the libraries open for, say, a couple of mornings a week," he suggests. "Parents who may not be comfortable with their kids biking across town to the public library are comfortable with them going to their schools."

[1] William G. Brozo, Gerry Shiel and Keith Topping, "Engagement in Reading: Lessons Learned From Three PISA Countries," *Journal of Adolescent & Adult Literacy*, International Reading Association, December 2007/January 2008, pp. 304-315.

[2] "About DK," DK Canada, http://cn.dk.com/static/cs/cn/11/nf/about/history.html.

[3] Matt Berman, *American Born Chinese*, Common Sense Media, www.commonsensemedia.org/book-reviews/American-Born-Chinese.html.

visual characters to individual sounds from spoken language as well as to concepts and objects. "It is little wonder that . . . practice [writing] tablets depict miserable students . . . with their teacher, followed by the oft-repeated line, 'And then he caned me,' " said Wolf.[22]

Finally, more than 2,500 years after the earliest Western written languages emerged, the Greeks invented what many scholars consider the first true alphabet of the kind most languages use today — a set of written letters that,

among them, represent all the basic sound units in the language, called phonemes.

That phonemic alphabets eventually dominated is no surprise and reflects how strongly spoken language is encoded in the brain, says Deacon. Even Egyptian hieroglyphics and the Chinese pictorial alphabet eventually shifted toward symbolizing sounds and things, he says. A written language that symbolizes sound suits the human brain's biases, since brains have large areas hard-wired for

Learning Online Literacy

The definition of literacy is changing — again.

The key skills that make a person "literate" have changed throughout history and may be undergoing major change today, as the life of the mind moves online.[1]

"The definition of reading in society is always undergoing change and is always contentious," says University of Wisconsin Professor of English Deborah Brandt.

Before the Greeks developed their written alphabet about 2,500 years ago, knowledge was passed down from generation to generation in the form of memorized, recited narratives, like Homer's epic poem, "The Odyssey."

The invention of the alphabet threatened the powerful elite, who could control access to vital cultural knowledge when communication was all oral, said Leonard Shlain, a San Francisco surgeon and author of *The Alphabet Versus the Goddess*, a book about language and brain evolution. "Once you have an alphabet, no one can keep it from the masses," he explained.[2]

The philosopher Socrates opposed the new, written language, as did the elites, because he feared books would destroy the Greeks' prodigious memorization ability and keep future learners from making knowledge their own. Instead of learning texts "by heart," they would consign to the written page the task of holding onto cultural knowledge.

Ironically, Socrates' greatest student, Plato, used the very written language his teacher distrusted to record Socrates' dialogues for posterity. And by the time Plato had students of his own, including the philosopher Aristotle, reading and writing had become the main methods of learning and communicating.

Since then, the skills required to be considered a "literate" person have changed often. In the United States, for example, people were considered literate if they could sign their names. Later, good penmanship and memorization — both outmoded today — became important marks of literacy, says Kylene Beers, president-elect of the National Council of Teachers of English.

"Reading at the beginning of this nation principally took place in a religious context, with a few religious books — the Bible, maybe a tract or a concordance," says Brandt. "It was very intensive reading for a specific purpose." Even when more people began reading books, and the religious focus decreased, "people still had just a few books that they read over and over again.

"Only in the early-20th century did we start reading new books all the time," Brandt continues. "At that time there was a big increase in the educational level. Agriculture was collapsing, and the number of people in school spiked, so there was a lot of surplus literacy around that sparked consumer reading."

Today, literacy is undergoing another big change, due to electronic technologies like television, video games and, especially, the Internet. Most online texts feature sidebars,

speech and can therefore handle multiple, complex, sound-based systems better than picture-to-symbol correspondences, he says.

Reading Truce?

Although phonemic alphabets suit our brains best, that doesn't make learning to read easy. Just as when our ancient ancestors invented the first written languages, each human brain must still slowly develop the networks that facilitate connecting written letters, sounds and the objects and ideas they stand for.

As a result, children just learning to read experience a confusing relationship between their automatic, unconscious oral-language facilities and written language — "this external, very ambiguous code that has a very rough correspondence" to spoken language, said David Boulton, a developer of education technology and creator of *Children of the Code*, a Web-based documentary on the science of reading.

The so-called reading wars have long pitted advocates of carefully teaching children about phonemes — phonics — and other language elements against so-called whole-language enthusiasts — those who argue that children learn best by being immersed in interesting texts and encouraged to recognize whole words at one time, rather than phonemic building blocks.[23]

pictures, audio, video and hyperlinks that, with a few clicks, take a reader far away from the original author. Online texts also let readers add written comments or e-mail the text to others.

But unlike traditional books and magazines, which are produced and pre-selected by editors, publishers, bookstore owners and librarians, online texts are written by a myriad of professional and amateur authors, whose credibility readers must evaluate on their own. Thus, while basic reading-comprehension skills are the same on the Internet as in traditional reading, locating information and critically evaluating material requires new skills.

"There are new strategies required to do these things online," says Donald Leu, a professor of literacy and technology at the University of Connecticut's Neag School of Education, in Storrs. Finding out who created a Web site in order to evaluate the information there is much tougher than finding out the author of a book or magazine article, he says.

For example, if one types "Martin Luther King" into a search engine like Google, one of the first sites to be listed is martinlutherking.org. Before accepting information from the site at face value, "a skilled information seeker will ask, 'Who created this?' " says Leu. But the martinlutherking.org site, like many others, makes that information hard to find, stating only at the very bottom of the home page that the site is "hosted by Stormfront," which further research reveals is a white-supremacist group.

"Few students would figure that out," says Leu. For the kids he works with — in mostly low-income city

A youngster learns to use a computer reading program at the John F. Kennedy Community Center in Henderson, Ky.

schools — "reliability is determined by the amount of information on the screen," not by who created the page, he says.

The brave, new online world requires that everyone — young and old — learn new literacy skills, Leu says. For example, surveys show that many adults put significant faith in health-information Web sites, "but nobody thinks about who created these sites and whether they're trustworthy or not," he says.

---

[1] For background, see Steven Roger Fischer, *A History of Reading* (2003).

[2] "What the Alphabet Engenders: An Interview with Leonard Shlain," *Children of the Code*, a Web-based documentary on reading, www.childrenofthecode.org.

Today, although some education experts continue to bicker about how best to teach reading — and serious questions remain about how best to teach some complexities, such as English letter combinations like "ea" that can map to four or more different vocal sounds — cognitive science seems to have settled the main question: Teaching children to read requires teaching details of the phonemic code, but the motivation that's sparked by interesting material is also crucial to creating habitual readers.

"You can learn to talk relatively well without . . . really needing to break the sounds down in your mind," said Paula Tallal, a professor of neuroscience at Rutgers

University. "It's only when you hit reading that you must become aware that words are made up of smaller units."[24]

For that reason, systematic teaching of language elements like letter sounds is necessary, said Tallal. One good test, she contends: whether a child can pronounce nonsense words they've never seen before. "If you give children a list of real words . . . many children who nonetheless have a significant reading problem can pass that test" because "they can pronounce the individual words; they can memorize the word patterns from the visual display," said Tallal. "But they haven't really cracked the code. They haven't really learned that each of the letters has a sound that goes with it, and those sounds can change in different contexts."[25]

Getting to that point requires very "systematic teaching" of the alphabet followed by facts about the various sounds each letter can represent, said Marilyn Jager Adams, chief scientist at Waltham, Mass.-based Soliloquy Learning, which develops speech-recognition software for reading education. "You want to convince the kids . . . that there's a system here" that they can understand and master."[26]

Each English letter can be pronounced several different ways, and in many cases the right pronunciation depends on what other letters are in the word, such as the silent "e" that changes how other vowels are pronounced. That means teachers must "reinforce the message that, 'Look, there's a logic to this system. You can understand it. That's your job. I'm going to illustrate through examples how it works . . . and then you're going to take it from there,'" said Adams. "You're asking them constantly . . . to generalize. . . . Okay, so we just did cat . . . hat, bat and rat. Now what do you think this word is? M-a-t. What could that be?' "

Learning to read is "so much work," said Adams. "There are so many pieces that have to go together."

Furthermore, says Wolf, the ultimate goal is fluent comprehension — reading that is so fast and automatic that the brain can think about what it's read, adding layers of meaning as the reading is occurring. "As we know a word well, we no longer need to analyze it in a labor-intensive way," said Wolf. Once the decoding becomes automatic, a young brain learns to integrate more background and experiential knowledge. "The brain becomes fast enough to think and feel differently," she said, to meld the reader's thoughts with an author's, which is one of the key benefits of reading.[27]

Getting to that point requires not just learning skills but being motivated enough to practice to make them automatic, say many reading experts. "Engagement . . . is imperative," said Wolf. "You need an engaged teacher and an engaged learner," because motivation, or engagement, can make or break learning.[28]

Lack of motivation is at least part of the reason why the skills of American 17-year-olds are dropping off while 9-year-olds are improving their reading skills, say some literacy experts. "Somewhere around the intermediate grades and middle-school years, motivation to read and

learn and actual reading achievement tend to decline," says William Brozo, a professor of literacy at George Mason University in Fairfax, Va. "It's no coincidence that at this time in most school curricula youth are asked to make the transition from reading mostly narrative texts to negotiating informational prose found in textbooks," Brozo says. "With testing pressures and curricular mandates, there is less and less time for reading for fun. This is deadly for many kids, who once may have enjoyed reading but now find it a difficult requirement with high-stakes implications."

"We also have to provide some time and space for kids to read, especially books that they choose for themselves, and I don't see that happening in school, particularly for the young-adult audience," says Boise State's Steiner.

In elementary schools, however, "I see us shifting back to a balance," Steiner says, teaching the phonemic element while including books keyed to kids' interests.

CURRENT SITUATION

Boys, Teens Lag

As new media proliferate, the habit of traditional reading is dropping off, as are the reading-ability scores for young adults.

Over the two decades from 1984 to 2004, pleasure reading by teenagers dropped significantly. The percentage of 13-year-olds who said they read for pleasure "almost every day" dropped from 35 percent to 30 percent while the percentage who "hardly ever" read for fun rose from 8 percent to 13 percent, according to the NEA's 2007 report. And while 31 percent of 17-year-olds said they read on their own almost daily in 1984, only 22 percent did so in 2004. Meanwhile, the percentage of 17-year-olds who "hardly ever" read for pleasure rose from 9 percent to 19 percent.[29]

"Television still saps the most leisure time — two-and-a-half hours a day," on average, says the NEA's Iyengar, while 15- to 24-year-olds spend only about 7 to 9 minutes a day on non-school reading.

And while researchers can't say for certain that regular reading improves reading ability, numerous studies "show abundantly" that those who read for pleasure are better readers and better students, he says. For example, having a large number of books at home correlates strongly with high academic achievement for young people, independent of families' economic status, he says. The children of graduate-school-educated parents with few books fare less well, academically, than poorer, less-well-educated parents with many books, he says

Recent data on reading achievement provide a mixed picture, with younger children doing better but teenagers — especially boys — doing worse, says Longwood University's Wiesendanger. About 70 percent of fourth-graders are reading at basic level or above, and the trend is upward, she says, but 12th-grade scores have declined below what they were in 1992 and just slightly better than in 1971.

Perhaps more troubling, the 12th-grade decline comes almost entirely among students in the lower three-quarters of ability, signaling a growing literacy gap, Wiesendanger says. Average scores for students in the 90th percentile and up haven't changed since 1992, and scores for students between the 75th and 90th percentile have dropped slightly. But scores for students in the bottom two quartiles "have gotten steadily worse over the past several years and are below 1992 levels," she says.

"There is an increasing gap in ability between children who can read and the children who are struggling," Wiesendanger says.[30]

Meanwhile, a gender gap in reading scores between boys and girls, "while not extremely wide, continues to widen," she says. For example, 12th-grade boys' reading ability scores in 2005 averaged 13 points lower than girls' on the 500-point NAEP national reading test, but had been only 10 points behind in 1992.[31] Comparable male-female gaps exist in most countries, she says.

On a 2006 international comparison, U.S. students did as well as or better than students in 34 out of 44 nations and have been largely holding their own, says Wiesendanger. Nevertheless, a few countries that used to be below the United States are now "way above us" in reading scores, she says. Those include Russia, India, Hong Kong and Singapore — which by and large have made dramatic economic gains.

Economic imbalance in the United States may be holding U.S. students back, says Wiesendanger. "Some of the poor schools, both inner-city and rural, are as bad as what you would see in a Third World country," she says.

Since Congress passed the 2002 No Child Left Behind Act, federal funding for reading instruction has averaged

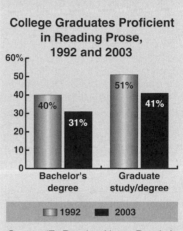

College Graduates' Proficiency Drops

Only 31 percent of college graduates were proficient in reading prose in 2003, a 23 percent decline since 1992. Among students in graduate programs or holding advanced degrees, the drop in proficiency was 20 percent.

College Graduates Proficient in Reading Prose, 1992 and 2003

Bachelor's degree: 40% (1992), 31% (2003)
Graduate study/degree: 51% (1992), 41% (2003)

1992 2003

Source: "To Read or Not to Read: A Question of National Consequence," National Endowment for the Arts, November 2007

$1 billion annually, earmarked for the Reading First program — a pet project of the Bush administration. In the past few years, however, federal audits found that some government officials had conflicts of interest related to private companies that supply Reading First materials and may have unduly influenced states' decisions about what programs and tests to buy.

Last fall, the new Democratic majority in Congress slashed the program's fiscal 2008 budget to $393 million.[32]

Online Literacy

The United States lags other nations in teaching online literacy skills and in offering widespread access to true high-speed Internet, says the University of Connecticut's Leu. "I can't begin to tell you how hard it is going to be for us" if this trend continues, he says.

Will reading remain a vital skill in the 21st century?

YES   Dana Gioia
Chairman, National Endowment for the Arts

NO   Marc Prensky
*CEO of Games2train,
a game-based learning company*

From "To Read or Not to Read," National
Endowment for the Arts, November 2007

From the Web site MarcPrensky.com

Although there has been measurable progress in recent years in reading ability at the elementary-school level, all progress appears to halt as children enter their teenage years. There is a general decline in reading among teenage and adult Americans.

Most alarming, both reading ability and the habit of regular reading have greatly declined among college graduates. These negative trends have more than literary importance. The declines have demonstrable social, economic, cultural and civic implications.

As Americans, especially younger Americans, read less, they read less well. Because they read less well, they have lower levels of academic achievement. With lower levels of reading and writing ability, people do less well in the job market. Poor reading skills correlate heavily with lack of employment, lower wages and fewer opportunities for advancement. Deficient readers are less likely to become active in civic and cultural life, most notably in volunteerism and voting.

The habit of daily reading, for instance, overwhelmingly correlates with better reading skills and higher academic achievement. On the other hand, poor reading skills correlate with lower levels of financial and job success. Whether or not people read, and indeed how much and how often they read, affects their lives in crucial ways.

Regular reading not only boosts the likelihood of an individual's academic and economic success . . . but also seems to awaken a person's social and civic sense. Reading correlates with almost every measurement of positive personal and social behavior surveyed. It is reassuring, though hardly amazing, that readers attend more concerts and theater than non-readers, but it is surprising that they exercise more and play more sports — no matter what their educational level. The cold statistics confirm something that most readers know but have mostly been reluctant to declare as fact — books change lives for the better.

The data confirm — without any serious qualification — the central importance of reading for a prosperous, free society. They demonstrate that reading is an irreplaceable activity in developing productive and active adults as well as healthy communities. Whatever the benefits of newer electronic media, they provide no measurable substitute for . . . frequent reading.

If America continues to lose the habit of regular reading, the nation will suffer substantial economic, social and civil setbacks.

Reacting to my discussing the need to delete things from the curriculum in order to make room for topics about the future, teachers almost invariably ask some version of the following: "But what if the technology breaks down? What will our kids do then?"

Teachers who ask these questions and voice these opinions often get applause from their colleagues, making them think they are right in holding these attitudes. But these questions make me realize that we have a real problem.

It's a problem because what the teachers are really saying is this: "We don't trust the technology of today, or the future. We don't trust the world in which you kids are going to live. We believe the way we did it in our time was the 'real' way, the only reliable way, and that's what we want to teach you kids — the basics."

Unfortunately, thinking that many of the things we have students learn and memorize — from the multiplication tables to the long-division algorithm, to making change, to the state capitals — are "the basics" is confusing the "best method" of the moment with what is important to know. The reason we memorized so many of these things in the past was only because there was no handy/speedy way to look them up. But the "best methods" to the basics change over time.

For example, telling time is a "basic." At one time the best method we had was the sundial. Now we all just strap a machine to our wrist.

Communication, too, is a basic skill, with reading and writing merely the best methods of the moment. Now, reading and writing are both very useful methods, which, to be clear, I think we need to teach until better ways emerge for getting the same information. But once all books are recorded, the Web reads itself [aloud] and every child and adult has a text scanner in his or her cell phone that can read any printed text aloud, should we still spend all those years teaching our kids phonics?

Those teachers who want to give their kids a backup education can't understand or accept that the world of their students is diverging incredibly quickly from their own. They don't understand that their well-intentioned instinct to "protect" their kids prevents them from learning what they need to know to succeed in the 21st century.

Currently no states assess students for online literacy, although a few are putting state tests online. "They think they've solved the problem, but they're only putting traditional paragraph reading on the Internet," Leu says. Almost no funds have been dedicated to research online literacy, he complains, even though it's critical to determine what critical skills are needed to be an effective reader and researcher on the Internet and what institutional strategies are needed to teach those skills.

Finland gives every teacher five weeks of paid professional-development time to create lesson plans incorporating Internet literacy, and some Australian states include writing e-mail in literacy tests for first-graders. Countries like South Korea and Ireland are surging ahead as computer innovators and Internet users, and many nations have made universal high-speed-Internet access a priority, Leu says. For example, Japan has Internet speeds 16 times faster than the U.S. average, and it costs consumers only $22 a month.

In 2009, the world's major international comparison of student achievement — the Program for International Student Assessment (PISA) — will include online reading comprehension for the first time, with questions developed by the Australian Research Council, says Leu. But U.S. students won't participate in the test, and the U.S. Department of Education has declined to include online literacy in its own NAEP tests.

Cuts in Reading Programs

Family literacy programs, which help low-income, low-literacy parents improve their own literacy skills while also helping their children learn reading, are burgeoning worldwide and in the United States, but they aren't always an easy sell with the government or with educators, says Sharon Darling, founder of the National Center for Family Literacy (NCFL) in Louisville, Ky.

"I do think we're making progress on reading [such as in education initiatives like the No Child Left Behind law], but I also think we're missing the boat in a lot of areas," she says. "Good quality child care increases reading achievement," for instance, but only 50 percent as much as having families with the skills and ability to support children's learning.

Darling would like to see continued support for the federal Even Start program. Launched in 1989 to coordinate local early-childhood programs with adult literacy

Key Club member Kasey Rogers reads to a youngster in Paris, Texas. Experts say discussing books with children encourages them to read more and helps them build reading skills.

and parenting-skills initiatives, Even Start's annual budget rose from about $15 million to more than $250 million by 2001.[33] But the Bush administration has argued that Even Start is ineffective and should be eliminated. Congress has slashed the program's 2008 fiscal year funding to $63 million.[34]

Darling thinks policymakers have been too quick to give up on Even Start, because coordinating early-childhood and adult-education programs — which ordinarily don't even speak each other's language — is uphill work. "Involving parents is messy" for schools, she says, and adult educators "don't know much about early-childhood learning."

Furthermore, "working with families never gives the kind of instant results" that government program evaluators want, Darling says. "Many people have messy lives; they have to drop out and drop back in." But NCFL programs are so popular, she says, "they break down the doors to get in."

Another federal family-reading initiative, the Reading Is Fundamental/Inexpensive Book Distribution program — which supplies about 16 million children's books annually to low-income families — has been slated for elimination in President Bush's fiscal 2009 budget, released in February.[35]

Over the past two decades, reading-promotion programs have gradually sprung up in the states as well as in countries around the world, as reading advocates try to reignite a love of book reading, says John Y. Cole, director of the Library of Congress' Center for the Book since its founding in 1977.

The center has spurred — but not funded — creation of a nationwide network of state book centers to develop local reading-promotion projects. Florida launched the first center in 1984, but it took until 2003 to sign up the last state, Cole says. Today, however, "there is greatly increased interest in reading promotion, perhaps because of anxiety" about reading's future, he says.

A key strategy has been restoring the social aspect of book reading by getting people across a city or even a state to read the same book and talk about it together. After the center in Washington state launched the first "One Book" program in 1998, similar projects have been started around the country and internationally.[36]

"We have also inspired Russia and South Africa" to open their own centers for the book, even though "the idea didn't really take off there until after democracy came," says Cole.

This year the center is launching the first National Ambassador for Young People's Literature. The first appointee, Jon Scieszka — author of children's humor books including the fractured fairy tale *The True Story of the Three Little Pigs* — will receive a $50,000 stipend for his two-year tenure. "A big part of my platform will be to reach reluctant readers," including reassuring parents that often-despised forms like graphic novels or comic books are a good way to get kids hooked, he said.

"I was so honored that they chose me," Scieszka continued. "My first response was . . . 'Do you know who you're asking? I'm the guy who wrote *The Stinky Cheese Man.*' "[37]

OUTLOOK

Future of Reading

As technology advances, few doubt that book and periodical reading will continue to decline. It isn't clear what else the shift portends, although some fear it will mean a less-informed and reflective public. But for many educators, a top worry is that low-income Americans, already falling behind their peers in traditional literacy, will be further disadvantaged by policies that undermine their ability to learn the new literacy skills demanded by 21st-century media.

Under current conditions, "our kids are not going to be prepared" for the 21st-century technological world of work, says the University of Connecticut's Leu, and "other nations are going to clobber us."

With the No Child Left Behind law's primary focus on raising standardized test scores to minimum levels, the nation's poorest school districts are under the greatest pressure to stick solely to material assessed by the tests, none of which include online literacies, says Leu. "That means these kids aren't getting any online skills at all at school" and are falling behind in the new literacies as well as the old, especially since low-income children are less likely to have computers at home, Leu says.[38]

American educators already are alarmed by the large achievement gap between low-income students and their richer peers, but "if anyone gets around to measuring [online literacy], the gap there will make the other gaps look minuscule," Leu says.

With the Internet becoming the dominant site for reading and writing, especially among young people, some scholars predict that eventually only a small "reading class" will ever read novels, book-length nonfiction texts or serious magazines.

Sociological research demonstrates that there's long been a distinction between "reading as a matter-of-fact practice of just about everyone" and the reading of serious literature "as an esteemed, cultivated . . . practice of an educated elite," wrote three Northwestern University sociologists. "The gap between the two literacies seems likely to widen." Still an open question, however, is whether a larger gap between very literate people and others will lead to more social "stratification and inequality."[39]

To many analysts, the ideal is for future students to become fluent in today's literacies and tomorrow's. "I'm concerned about 'new literacy' advocates who themselves possess expansive levels of traditional print literacy suggesting that youth do not need to be literate in the same way," says George Mason's Brozo.

But it's not clear there are enough hours in the day for both. "If we're serious about maintaining different kinds of literacy, we need to reorganize society" to make room for them, says the University of Wisconsin's Brandt. That will be difficult in a world that moves ever faster, "where college students don't just go to class but take internships and double majors," she says.

"The education system might at least look at allowing more time for older kids to read," says Longwood University's Wiesendanger. "But to get to a world where teenagers have time for sustained reading 30 minutes a day? I'm not sure it's possible in our culture."

NOTES

1. "To Read or Not to Read: A Question of National Consequence," Research Report #47, National Endowment for the Arts, November 2007, www.nea.gov/research/ToRead.pdf.

2. "Information Behavior of the Researcher of the Future," University College London/British Library, Jan. 11, 2008, www.ucl.ac.uk/slais/research/ciber/downloads.

3. *Ibid.*

4. Marc Prensky, "Changing Paradigms," MarcPrensky.com, 2007, www.marcprensky.com, originally published in *Educational Technology*, July-August 2007.

5. Quoted in Zach Miners and Angela Pascopella, "The New Literacies," *District Administration*, October 2007, www.districtadministration.com.

6. *Ibid.*

7. "To Read or Not to Read," *op. cit.* For further information see the Pew Internet study, Dec. 30, 2007, www.pewinternet.org/PPF/r/231/report_display.asp.

8. "Youth and Library Use Study," American Library Association and Harris Interactive, Inc., June 2007, www.ala.org/ala/yalsa/HarrisYouthPoll.pdf.

9. "To Read or Not to Read," *op. cit.*, p. 5.

10. Michael L. Kamil, "Adolescents and Literacy: Reading for the 21st Century," Alliance for Excellent Education, November 2003, www.all4ed.org/files/archive/publications/AdolescentsAndLiteracy.pdf.

11. Dana Gioia, "Why Literature Matters," *The Boston Globe*, April 10, 2005, www.boston.com.

12. Nancy Kaplan, "Reading Responsibly," if: book blog, The Institute for the Future of the Book, Nov. 20, 2007, www.futureofthebook.org/blog/archives/2007/11/reading_responsibly_nancy_kaplan.html.

13. Marc Prensky, *Do They Really Think Differently?* (2001), www.marcprensky.com, originally published in *On the Horizon*, NCB University Press, December 2001.

14. "Keith Stanovich: Cognitive Science: The Conceptual Components of Reading and What Reading Does for the Mind," *Children of the Code* interview, www.childrenofthecode.org/interviews/stanovich.htm.

15. Marc Prensky, "Backup Education," Marc Prensky.com, 2008, www.marcprensky.com, originally published in *Educational Technology*, January-February 2008.

16. For background, see Maryanne Wolf, *Proust and The Squid: The Story and Science of the Reading Brain* (2007).

17. For background, see "Brain Plasticity, Language Processing, and Reading," *Brain Briefings*, Society for Neuroscience, July 2000, www.sfn.org/index.cfm?pagename=brainBriefings_brainPlasticityLanguageProcessing AndReading.

18. "Terrence Deacon: The Co-evolution of Language and the Brain," *Children of the Code* interview, www.childrenofthecode.org/interview/deacon.htm.

19. Wolf, *op. cit.*, p. 28.

20. *Ibid.*, p. 34.

21. *Ibid.*, p. 35.

22. *Ibid.*, p. 37.

23. For background, see Charles S. Clark, "Learning to Read," *CQ Researcher*, May 19, 1995, pp. 441-464; Kenneth Anderson, "The Reading Wars: Understanding the Debate Over How Best To Teach Children To Read," National Right to Read Foundation, 2000, www.nrrf.org/article_anderson6-18-00.htm; "Hot Topics: Reading Wars Reignite," Early Childhood Educators' and Family Web Corner, http://users.stargate.net/~cokids/hot_topics_reading_wars.htm; Nicholas Lemann, "History of the Reading Wars," *The Atlantic*, November 1997, p. 128, www.pbs.org/weta/twoschools/thechallenge/history.

24. "Paula Tallal: Neuroscience, Phonology and Reading: The Oral to Written Language Continuum," *Children of the Code* interview, www.childrenofthecode.org.

25. *Ibid.*

26. "Marilyn Jager Adams: Thinking and Learning About Beginning-to-Read," *Children of the Code* interview, www.childrenofthecode.org.

27. Wolf, *op. cit.*, p. 142.

28. "Maryanne Wolf: Rapid Naming, Double-Deficits, and Dyslexia," *Children of the Code* interview, www.childrenofthecode.org/interviews/Wolf.htm.

29. "To Read or Not to Read," *op. cit.*, p. 29.

30. For background, see Marcia Clemmitt, "Fixing Urban Schools," *CQ Researcher*, April 27, 2007, p. 361-384.

31. "To Read or Not to Read," *op. cit.*

32. Kathleen Kennedy Manzo, "Massive Funding Cuts to 'Reading First' Generate Worries for Struggling Schools," *Education Week*, Jan. 16, 2008.

33. Gail McCallion, "Even Start: Funding Controversy," Congressional Research Service, Jan. 17, 2006, www.ed.psu.edu/goodlinginstitute/pdf/CRS_even_start_funding_controversy.pdf.

34. "NCL Update," National Coalition for Literacy, November 2007, www.national-coalition-literacy.org/NovemberUpdatefromNCLPolicyDirector/NCLUpdateNovember2007FINAL.pdf.

35. Carol H. Rasco, "President Bush Eliminates Funding for Reading Is Fundamental's Historic Book Distribution Program," press statement, www.rif.org.

36. For background, see " 'One Book' Reading Promotion Projects," Library of Congress, www.loc.gov/loc/cfbook/one-book.html.

37. Walter Minkel, "The Big Cheese: Jon Scieszka, National Ambassador for Young People's Literature," *School Library Journal*, Feb. 1, 2008, www.schoollibraryjournal.com.

38. For background, see Kathy Koch, "The Digital Divide," *CQ Researcher*, Jan. 28, 2000, pp. 41-64.

39. Wendy Griswold, Terry McDonnell and Nathan Wright, "Reading and the Reading Class in the 21st Century," *Annual Review of Sociology*, 2005, pp. 127-141.

BIBLIOGRAPHY

Books

Brandt, Deborah, *Literacy in American Lives*, Cambridge University Press, 2001.
A University of Wisconsin professor of English describes the shifting meanings and importance of literacy for average Americans over the course of the 20th century.

Fischer, Steven Roger, *A History of Reading*, Reaktion Books, 2003.
A New Zealand-based linguistics scholar traces the history of reading in societies around the world, from the earliest written symbols to e-mail.

Wolf, Maryanne, *Proust and the Squid*, Harper, 2007.
A Tufts University associate professor of child development explains the neuroscience behind reading and dyslexia and reading's effects on brain development.

Articles

Crain, Caleb, "Twilight of the Books," *The New Yorker*, Dec. 24, 2007, p. 134.
If visual media like the Internet and television continue gaining dominance, and reading becomes the esoteric hobby of an educated few, the skills of deep concentration and conceptual thinking may be lost.

Goodnow, Cecelia, "Teens Buying Books at Fastest Rate in Decades," *Seattle Post-Intelligencer*, March 7, 2007, p. 7, http://seattlepi.nwsource.com/books/306531_teenlit08.html.
Despite publicized declines in teen reading, publishers are actively courting young-adult readers with new titles.

Kittner, Gina, "Graphic Novels Enliven Literature for Students," *Wisconsin State Journal*, Jan. 11. 2008, p. A1.
Graphic novels' popularity grows beyond teens and young adults to librarians and teachers, as schools look for ways to entice reluctant readers.

Manzo, Kathleen Kennedy, "Dark Themes in Books Get Students Reading," *Education Week*, March 30, 2007, p. 1.

In a quest to tempt reluctant readers, more teachers are dumping classic novels from their syllabi in favor of young-adult books on edgy themes, but some educators question whether class time is wasted on books that teens don't need help to read.

Miners, Zach, and Angela Pascopella, "The New Literacies," *District Administration,* **October 2007, www.districtadministration.com/viewarticlepf.aspx? articleid=1292.**
Successful use of online information requires learning new skills to find and evaluate it, but American schools lag other nations in teaching technological literacy.

Reports and Studies

"Information Behavior of the Researcher of the Future," *University College London/British Library,* **January 2008, www.bl.uk/news/pdf/googlegen.pdf.**
Researchers find that online readers and researchers have not learned systematic online research skills, spend most of their time skimming material rather than reading deeply and prefer visual information and text excerpts rather than full text.

"To Read or Not to Read," *National Endowment for the Arts,* **November 2007, www.nea.gov/research/ ToRead.pdf.**
The independent federal agency that supports the arts synthesizes current data on Americans' reading habits and reading ability and concludes that a continuing steep decline in pleasure reading correlates to lower literacy scores for teens and adults and decreased participation in civic and arts activities.

Baer, Justin D., Andrea L. Cook and Stephane Baldi, "The Literacy of America's College Students," *American Institutes of Research/Pew Charitable Trusts,* **January 2006, www.air.org/news/documents/ The%20Literacy%20of%20Americas%20 College%20Students_final%20report.pdf.**
The report finds that no literacy gap exists between students in four-year private and four-year public institutions; the male-female literacy gap is much smaller among college students than in the general population; and the literacy gap between white and minority college students is the same as in the population overall.

Griswold, Wendy, Terry McDonnell and Nathan Wright, "Reading and the Reading Class in the 21st Century," *Annual Review of Sociology,* **2005, pp. 127-141.**
Sociologists from Northwestern University synthesize current research from around the world about who reads, who doesn't, who worries about a decline in literacy, and why.

Kamil, Michael L., "Adolescents and Literacy: Reading for the 21st Century," *Alliance for Excellent Education,* **November 2003, www.all4ed.org/files/ AdolescentsAndLiteracy.pdf.**
A Stanford University professor of education synthesizes research about how to train teenagers for traditional and online literacy.

Moats, Louisa, "Whole-Language High Jinks: How to Tell When 'Scientifically-Based Reading Instruction' Isn't," *Thomas B. Fordham Institute,* **2007, www.edexcellence.net/doc/Moats2007.pdf.**
The report explains that successful reading programs must give students detailed instruction in how speech sounds translate into written letters and that much current reading instruction includes too few such lessons.

For More Information

Center for the Book, Library of Congress, 101 Independence Ave., S.E., Washington, DC 20540-4920; (202) 707-5221; www.loc.gov/loc/cfbook. Public/private partnership promotes reading, literacy and libraries.

Children of the Code, www.childrenofthecode.org. Web-based documentary on the science of reading includes extensive interviews with literacy experts and scientists.

Guys Read, www.guysread.com. Web site of children's author and National Ambassador for Young Adult Literature Jon Scieszka has book lists for reluctant male readers.

International Reading Association, 800 Barksdale Rd., P.O. Box 8139, Newark, DE 19714-8139; (800) 336-7323; www.reading.org. Organization for literacy and reading professionals provides advocacy and research on teaching reading.

Marc Prensky.com, PO Box 325, Gracie Station, New York, NY 10028; (917) 826-6965; www.marcprensky.com/contact/default.asp. Web site of education-game designer includes information and commentary on how technology is reshaping literacy.

National Center for Family Literacy, 325 West Main St., Suite 300, Louisville, KY 40202-4237; (502) 584-1133; www.famlit.org. Develops programs to increase literacy among parents and teach parents how to help children learn reading.

National Council of Teachers of English, 1111 W. Kenyon Rd., Urbana, IL 61801-1096; (217) 328-3870; www.ncte.org. Provides information about traditional and online literacy and reading.

National Endowment for the Arts, 1100 Pennsylvania Ave., N.W., Washington, DC 20506; (202) 682-5400; www.nea.gov. The federal grant-making agency for the arts conducts extensive research on Americans' reading habits and sponsors the reading-promotion program The Big Read.

New Literacies Research Team, University of Connecticut, Neag School of Education, 019 Gentry, 249 Glenbrook Rd., Storrs, CT 06269; (860) 486-0202; www.newliteracies.uconn.edu/blog.html. Researches Internet literacy and how to teach it.

Reading Is Fundamental, 1825 Connecticut Ave., N.W., Suite 400, Washington, DC 20009; (202) 536-3400; www.rif.org. National group enlists local volunteers to distribute books to low-income families.

Reading Rockets, WETA Public Television, 2775 S. Quincy St., Arlington, VA 22206; (703) 998-2001; www.reading-rockets.org. Public television- and Internet-based information program on teaching and encouraging children to read.

Young Adult Library Services Association, American Library Association, 50 East Huron St., Chicago, IL 60611; (800) 545-2433; www.ala.org/ala/yalsa/yalsa.cfm. Provides research and information about young people's evolving library and information needs and sponsors author awards for young-adult literature.

14

Video Games

Do They Have Educational Value?

Sarah Glazer

Detroit Lions running back Kevin Jones goes airborne for extra yardage in the 2007 edition of the popular video game "Madden NFL." Some scholars claim video and computer games help literacy, but others say they don't assist with reading literature or understanding the humanities. Experts also remain divided about whether addiction to games is widespread and whether some games produce violent behavior.

Electronic Arts

From *CQ Researcher*,
November 10, 2006.

O n a hot summer afternoon, eight teenagers gathered in the darkened basement of the Bronx Central Library to play the top-selling football video game "Madden NFL." The Madden tournament in the Bronx, complete with prizes, is part of a growing effort at libraries across the country to lure a client who rarely darkens the door of a public library — the adolescent boy.

"If it wasn't for the gaming stuff dragging me in that first time, I would have gone maybe once in the past two years," says Ian Melcher, 17, a gamer in Ann Arbor, Mich., who had just checked out two calculus books. "I realized the library was pretty cool and had other things I was interested in."

To persuade skeptical libraries to put video games on the shelf next to books, young librarians who grew up on games are drawing support from a surprising source — academic researchers. They claim that playing video games is practically a requirement of literacy in our digital age.

To many parents and baby boomers, playing video games looks like mindless activity. Yet the knowledge built into "Madden," for example, employs a playbook the size of an encyclopedia. To win, players must have a sophisticated understanding of strategy and make split-second decisions about which play to choose.

"Games stress taking your knowledge and applying it. That's pretty crucial in the modern world," says University of Wisconsin Professor of Reading James Gee, author of the 2003 book *What Video Games Have to Teach Us about Learning and Literacy.*

Sports and Multiplayer Games Most Popular

The 10 highest-selling video games are either about major-league sports, auto racing or "Star Wars," which largely appeal to boys; most are rated suitable for the entire family. Among computer games, four of the top 10 are "Sims" games, which also appeal to girls, and several are warfare games. Multiplayer games like "World of Warcraft" — which has 6 million players — are heavily female.

Top 10 Video Games, 2005		
Rank	**Title**	**Rating***
1.	Madden NFL 06 (PlayStation version)	E
2.	Gran Turismo 4	E
3.	Madden NFL 06 (Xbox version)	E
4.	NCAA Football 06	E
5.	Star Wars: Battlefront II	T
6.	MVP Baseball 2005	E
7.	Star Wars Episode III: Sith	T
8.	NBA Live 06	E
9.	Lego Star Wars	E
10.	Star Wars: Battlefront II	T

Top 10 Computer Games, 2005		
Rank	**Title**	**Rating***
1.	World of Warcraft	T
2.	The Sims 2: University Expansion Pack	T
3.	The Sims 2	T
4.	Guild Wars	T
5.	Roller Coaster Tycoon 3	E
6.	Battlefield 2	T
7.	The Sims 2 Nightlife Expansion Pack	T
8.	MS Age of Empires III	T
9.	The Sims Deluxe	T
10.	Call of Duty 2	T

* T = Teens (suitable for ages 13 and older)

E = Everyone (suitable for ages 6 and older)

Source: Entertainment Software Assn., "2006 Sales, Demographic and Usage Data"

"World of Warcraft" — played online simultaneously with thousands of players — lead some teens to engage in esoteric, online conversations about strategy and to create their own literary spin-offs or so-called fanfiction.

"Many video games require players to master skills in demand by today's employers," concluded a report released in October by the Federation of American Scientists, citing complex decision-making and team building. The organization urged the federal government to invest in research and development of educational games for K-12 students and for adult work-force training.[1]

Science writer Steven Johnson, who popularized the pro-game argument in his 2005 book *Everything Bad is Good for You*, argues that when a child enters the world of a computer game, he is "learning the scientific method" as he tries out multiple hypotheses.[2] For instance, today's youngsters don't first sit down and read a rule book, the way baby boomers did. They start pushing buttons to see what happens.

That willingness to learn from failure uniquely prepared members of the dot-com generation, giving them an advantage as entrepreneurs and creative thinkers in the new economy, argue business experts John C. Beck and Mitchell Wade in their 2004 book *Got Game*. "A kid in the classroom has to worry about looking like an idiot. In a game, they're raising their hand all the time, and true learning comes from failing," concurs Dmitri Williams, assistant professor of speech communication at the University of Illinois at Urbana-Champaign. "When you strip away all the explosions, blood, magic coins, princesses and castles, video games are problem-solving tasks — puzzles. There's some irony

Indeed, the argument that video and computer games are superior to school in helping children learn is gaining currency in academic circles. Claimed benefits include improved problem-solving, mastery of scientific investigation and the ability to apply information learned to real-life situations. Some of the more complex games, especially multiplayer games like in the fact that kids are bored at school but rush home to solve these games where they learn math and history."

As evidence that kids are willing to master language and concepts usually considered over their head, Johnson describes an hour spent teaching his nephew to play the urban planning-style game "SimCity." While Johnson was trying to figure out how to save a dying industrial neighborhood, the 7-year-old piped up, "I think we need to lower industrial tax rates."[3]

"SimCity" creator Will Wright says the youngster probably didn't understand tax rates any more than baby boomers understood mortgages when they played "Monopoly" as kids. But he thinks games teach something else. "The ability to reverse-engineer in your head a model of some arbitrarily complex thing is an incredibly valuable skill that you can apply to almost anything in this world," he says, whether that's doing your taxes, programming a new cell phone or predicting the effect of global warming.

Despite the worries of baby-boomer parents, there's no evidence that video gaming is replacing reading among teens. According to a Kaiser Family Foundation survey, reading for pleasure has remained steady in the past five years even as video-gaming time has risen.[4]

But what about teens who seem to spend most of their leisure time on games? Heavy gamers — more than an hour a day — actually spend more time reading for pleasure (55 minutes daily) than teens who play no video games at all (41 minutes), according to the Kaiser survey. And Kaiser found only 13 percent of adolescents were heavy gamers.

Nevertheless, the persistent anecdotes about teens and adults who skip meals, classes and even work to indulge in hours of video-gaming has led some to worry the games are addictive. Clinics have even sprung up claiming to treat "Internet addiction disorder."

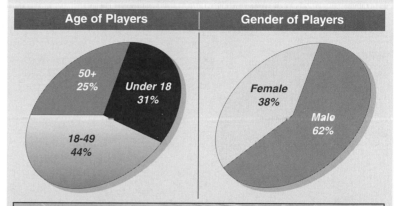

Most Gamers Are Males

Sixty-two percent of video-game players are males between 18 and 49, and fully one-quarter are at least 50.

Age of Players	Gender of Players
50+ 25% · Under 18 31% · 18-49 44%	Female 38% · Male 62%

Gamers at a Glance
- The average gamer is 33 years old.
- Women over 17 represent a larger portion of the game-playing population (30 percent) than boys under 18 (23 percent).
- Sixty-nine percent of U.S. heads of households play computer/video games.
- The average age of the most frequent game purchaser is 40.
- Adult gamers have been playing for an average of 12 years.
- Among the most frequent gamers, adult males average 10 years of playing, females, eight years.

Source: Entertainment Software Association

CQ Press/Joe King-Shaw

But many psychologists remain skeptical. "There's hardly anyone I would class as a genuine video-game addict," says Professor of Gambling Studies Mark Griffiths of Nottingham Trent University in Nottingham, England. Few players, he says, meet a strict definition of addiction, which includes withdrawal symptoms and a preoccupation so single-minded that every other aspect of life is neglected.

Experts are also divided over whether graphic violence in games like "Grand Theft Auto" has any lasting negative effects on players' behavior, despite a few cases in which a teen's murderous frenzy has been blamed on games by the victim's parents. Recent studies indicate that the younger a player is, the more likely he is to be negatively affected by video violence and the longer lasting the effect. (*See sidebar, p. 316.*)

Concerns about both addiction and violence have led to efforts to curb online role-playing games like "World

High-school students in Laramie, Wyo., play "Restaurant Empire," a video game that teaches them about the restaurant industry, in March 2006. Researchers are increasingly urging educators to incorporate games' best learning features into school programs.

of Warcraft" and "Lineage II." Last year, the Chinese government imposed penalties on gamers who spend more than three hours playing a game by reducing the abilities of their characters. All the biggest online game operators said they would adopt the new system. The measures were designed to combat addiction in a country where more than 20 million Chinese play games regularly, mainly in net cafes. In one case, a player killed a fellow player who had stolen his virtual sword. (The penalties were later rescinded after widespread protests.)

Aside from worries about addiction and violence, not all scholars are equally enthusiastic about the learning value of video games on the market. In most games, the content is "garbage," according to Harvard Graduate School of Education Professor Christopher Dede, "in the sense that it deals with imaginary situations that are not close to the

knowledge and skills people need for the 21st century. To claim that learning magic spells is good preparation for the knowledge-based workplace is just plain silly."

Dede is among those interested in adapting one of the most popular offshoots of gaming — virtual worlds — to educational aims. Player create characters (or avatars) who enter a virtual world. Hundreds of thousands of teenagers now participate in virtual worlds like There.com and Second Life, where they can create a character, buy clothes and real estate and meet other players' avatars. (*See sidebar, p. 320.*)

In "River City," created by Dede's team at Harvard, players try to figure out the cause of a mysterious epidemic in a 19th-century town. Researchers found that middle-schoolers using "River City" improved their biological knowledge and science skills more than peers taught more traditionally.[5]

Another sign of university interest: Colleges now offer courses in "Second Life." Starting this fall, teens entering There.com will be able to take classes in areas like copyright law taught by university professors.

But some advocates worry that all this high-level learning will be limited to middle-class kids, who have access to fancier, faster hardware and to educated parents who can guide their choice of games — creating a new equity gap on top of the existing reading gap between income groups.

While 83 percent of young people ages 8-18 have a video console at home, they may not be using them the same way.[6] A recent study of Philadelphia libraries with computers found that middle-class 12- to 13-year-olds typically used computers to increase their knowledge, by looking up — for example — Christopher Columbus on the encyclopedia site Encarta. But those from low-income neighborhoods were more likely to play "Magic School Bus," a game for 9-year-olds.[7]

The difference can be traced to the lack of guidance from a parent or other adult, which is as crucial for good games as for good books, says the University of Wisconsin's Gee. "Giving a kid a book [or game] is okay, but with no adult to mentor the child and talk about the material it isn't very helpful," he says.

As video games increasingly become a fact of life in the lives of children and adults, here are some of the questions being debated by parents, academics, the gaming industry and players themselves:

Does playing video games improve literacy?

For the past year, nearly two-dozen 8-to-13-year-olds from low-income neighborhoods in Madison, Wis., have gathered after school to play the best-selling game "Civilization," under the watchful eyes of University of Wisconsin researchers. Players rule a society from 4,000 B.C. to the present, building cities, trading, gathering natural resources and waging war. A single game requires about 20 hours to play; achieving high-level mastery requires 100 hours or more.

The children encounter words like "monarchy" and "monotheism" for the first time — but more important, they have to figure out how those and other factors, like natural resources, help a civilization survive or fail, says Kurt Squire, an assistant professor of educational communications and technology, who is directing the study.

"We found when they're expert gamers, they can tell you the differences between civilizations, what technologies they would need, what resources they'd need," he says. To Squire, the game's lifelike simulation is a powerful twist on the progressive-education adage, learning by doing.

Students remember only 10 percent of what they read and 20 percent of what they hear but almost 90 percent if they do the job themselves, even if only as a simulation, according to research cited by the Federation of American Scientists.[8] The University of Wisconsin's Gee even claims that the mind works like a video game in that "effective thinking is more like running a simulation" than forming abstract generalizations.[9]

An academic camp led by Gee argues video games foster a more sophisticated kind of literacy than the simple decoding of words. Video games foster creative thinking — producing "gaming literacies" in the words of Katie Salen, a designer at Parsons The New School for Design in New York City. Gamers not only follow the rules "but push against them, testing the limits of the system in often unique and powerful ways," she says.[10]

Digital literacy also means learning to take information from multiple sources, including Web sites and other players, rather than from one authoritative source like a teacher or textbook.

But Harvard's Dede says that while games may be powerful learning tools, their content leaves much to be desired, and so far no research backs up the claim that games teach kids to think like scientists. To produce those results, he argues the engaging qualities of games must be married to scientific content.

Dede developed "River City" to teach basic science skills, such as forming a hypothesis. After 7,000 middle-school students tested the game-like simulation, they improved their scientific-inquiry skills and increased their knowledge of biology at twice the rate of peers using traditional hands-on labs.[11]

But hard data like Dede's are scant, and most studies have been done with only small numbers of children. The Federation of American Scientists, while enthusiastic about games' learning potential, noted that while kids "seem to do better," the research suffers from a lack of concrete measures of learning.[12]

"We don't have anywhere near sufficient evidence about whether playing computer games helps literacy," says Justine Cassell, professor of communication studies and computer science at Northwestern University. On the other hand, she adds, "There's no evidence that computers hurt literacy."

A computer game Cassell has developed for toddlers with a clown-like character can — much like an imaginary friend — help them develop sophisticated language

Gamers Are Not Isolated, Obsessed

Contrary to the stereotype, gamers are not socially isolated people glued to their PlayStations, Xboxes or computers. Players say they spend more than three times as much time each week (20.4 hours) exercising, playing sports, volunteering, attending cultural activities or reading than they spend playing games (6.8 hours).

Percent of gamers who say they:

Exercise or play sports at least 20 hours a month	79%
Volunteer at least 5.4 hours per month	45%
Regularly read books or daily newspapers	93%
Attend concerts, museums, theater	62%
Play games with others in person at least 1 hr/wk	51%
Play games with others online at least 1 hr/wk	25%

Source: Peter D. Hart Research Associates, 2004

'Sims' Inventor Exploring New Frontiers in Creativity

The creator of the most popular PC game of all time is lanky, bespectacled and surprisingly bookish. Will Wright is already famous for creating "The Sims," akin to playing house, which has sold close to 60 million copies.[1] He's also famous for designing one of the most creative games, "SimCity," an urban-planning game so sophisticated it was later used to train city planners.

But the game world is most excited about the new game — "Spore" — that Wright is developing to be released next year by Entertainment Arts. It started out as a game about extra-terrestrial life. But in preparation, Wright says, he read 100 books, including many about biology, which led him to a fascination with evolution, the current game's theme.

In "Spore," players create characters who progress from a one-celled organism to an entire race of creatures using principles of evolution. Will your creature be an herbivore or a carnivore? Will you give it two limbs or 5? And will it survive with the claws you've picked out? (If not, go back and pick something different.) Once you've created a creature, you'll move on to creating tribes, communities and planets. Wright estimates it would take 70 years to visit every planet in "Spore."

But the most revolutionary part of "Spore," may be players' ability to access other gamers' creations for their own play. Once players' creations are uploaded onto Spore's server, they can even request their friends' creations.

As a child, Wright was drawn to taking things apart, which got him interested in robots and ultimately computers, he said in an interview at his studio in Emeryville, Calif. Yet Wright, 46, considers himself part of the generation that grew up reading manuals. By contrast, today's kids press buttons in a game to see what happens — a practice he says leads to more creativity. It also gives kids an early experience with testing models in a simulated environment, an important skill as science and other fields increasingly revolve around simulation, he believes.

Wright challenges the basic notion that it's more educational to read a book than to play a game. "You can step back and see that our natural mode of interacting with the world is not to sit back passively, observe it as a movie or book would present it, but to interact with it and actually have effects on the system and study the effects," he says. Play was probably the first educational activity, he suggests, which permitted us to parse out patterns in the world around us.

"I think you can do that to a limited degree with storytelling but not nearly as deeply as with an interactive

earlier because they must explain what's happening to an absent person. (For example, toddlers get more precise on the phone, saying, "John went to the store" instead of "He went there.") Teens, she says, have a similar experience when blogging because they learn to write like journalists for an unseen audience.

The more than 4 million players of "Lineage" compete against one another for castles in a virtual kingdom of wizards, elves and knights. These "castle sieges" engage players in complex arguments online about strategy, according to University of Wisconsin researcher Constance Steinkuehler.[13]

Steinkuehler found players' online posts typically written at a 12th-grade reading level or above and often involve scientific reasoning. "I've watched kids who, in an effort to 'cheat' the game, gather data, build simple mathematical models and argue about those models," which, she adds, educators say "is extremely difficult to get high-schoolers to do."

Parents often despair because their teen is "not sitting on a couch reading a storybook, which is what we think literacy is," says Gee. But "the kids' version of literacy is better for a modern-world understanding of technical language," Gee maintains.

In the best games, players must master a specialized game vocabulary, consulting Web pages for hints on winning that probably use syntax far more complex than their reading in school, Gee argues. "I believe firmly the experience," Wright says. "Yeah, *Harry Potter* is a great universe and all that, but you can't take the stuff you know about Harry Potter's universe and apply it anywhere else."

Players are starting to use his games increasingly for self-expression, not just entertainment, Wright observes, which could help explain their enduring popularity. A feature added to "The Sims" that allows players to write stories in the game and save them on a Web page resulted in several-hundred-thousand short stories, novels and biographical accounts that players "were pouring their heart and soul into," says Wright. Fans "form a very tight community around these games," he observes, as they browse one another's stories, download content and create new elements. A moviemaking feature in "Sims2" led to tens of thousands of movies being created by players.

"Spore" will give players unprecedented room for creation. In "The Sims," players can manipulate the face, but it's still a two-legged creature, Wright points out. "This is designing content in a different way that allows the player to have all the freedom," he says. But when this visitor played a preview of the game, it was apparent even the most imaginative designers set limits, suggesting that creativity inside a game isn't the same as creativity outside — a major concern of some educators.

First there's the aesthetic style — cute creatures familiar to young watchers of Pixar movies and reminiscent to older viewers of Flintstone dinosaurs. What if one wanted to create something more frightening?

Will Wright, creator of "The Sims," loved to take things apart as a child.

"Within 'Spore' we offer a series of editors that serve as creative toolkits for making everything from creatures and vehicles to plants and buildings," says Executive Producer Lucy Bradshaw. "What these look like is up to the player. So, I might do something cute and cuddly and sort of Teddy Bear-ish, or I might make a really frightening creature with spindly spider legs and an angry-looking beak that looks like it came out of a horror film. It's all about my personal aesthetic. We want Moms to enjoy this just as much as their 15-year-old sons!"

---

[1] "How to Create a Game About Creating a Universe," *Computer Gaming World*, June 2006, p. 70.

key to school success is handling technical language," he says.

To see how complex the language can get, Gee suggests looking at a Web site offering hints on playing "Yu-Gi-Oh" (both a video and card game). A typically impenetrable sentence reads, "The effect of 8-Claws Scorpion is a Trigger Effect that is applied if the condition is correct on activation." Seven-year-olds are reading sentences like this, even though its complexity won't be matched in the classroom until middle or high school, Gee says.

But can games produce the kind of literacy we most value? The technical material highlighted by enthusiasts is closer to technical manuals than novels and "more likely to appeal to techies than to dreamers, humanists and conversationalists" and to boys rather than girls, worries Harvard Professor of Cognition and Learning Howard Gardner. Immersing oneself in long novels like *Madame Bovary*, in poetry or in a philosophical text involves a skill many game enthusiasts disparage — linear thinking over many pages. That's "an entirely different mental faculty than is exploited when one surfs the Web from one link to another," Gardner argues.

Moreover, even a good video game can't compete with a great teacher, asserts former teacher Joan Almon, coordinator of the Alliance for Childhood in College Park, Md. "It bothers me that people are using these as the great way of learning. They're a modest alternative to very bad teaching," she says.

In its recent report, however, the Federation of American Scientists urges teachers to change from their "tell and test" method — which encourages passive learning — to incorporating the highly interactive, challenge-reward environment of video games. Game developers have incorporated the best learning features recognized by cognitive science, the report says, including:

- tons of practice;
- continual monitoring and feedback on the player's progress;
- encouragement to seek out information on the game strategy from other gamers, friends and Web sites; and,
- bridging the gap from what's learned to real situations.[14]

Some enthusiasts point out that the Internet is already allowing teenagers to become online creators on a huge scale via blogs, music and mini-films known as *machinima* — often inspired by games. Players have posted several-hundred-thousand stories ranging from 10-page plots to small novels as part of the best-selling computer game of all time, "The Sims," where players create their own family and play virtual house.

Some of that interaction could even raise the level of public discourse. In a study of an international Internet community of 3,000 teens, Northwestern's Cassell found, "the boys came to talk like the girls in a way that would make many of us happy," such as incorporating language that synthesized the ideas of others, and younger teens adopted the language of older teens.

Thanks to the Internet, teens are "no longer just media consumers" but are producing content, which is good for literacy, says Cassell. "We know that media creation — in whatever medium — is good for children's imagination and good for their ability to create a text for someone else."

Are video games addictive?

Jeffrey Stark, a high-school student from Ontario, Canada, claimed his compulsive playing of the sword-and-sorcery game "EverQuest" ruined his life. He went for a week without bathing or eating a proper meal and stopped going to school for a semester.[15]

Similarly, a 30-year-old registered nurse who plays "EverQuest" with her husband said, "We spend hours — hours! — every single day playing this damn game. My fingers wake me, aching, in the middle of the night. I have headaches from the countless hours I spend staring at the screen. I hate this game, but I can't stop playing. Quitting smoking was never this hard."[16]

About 40 percent of players of multiplayer online games like "EverQuest" say they consider themselves "addicted."[17] Some players call the game "Evercrack." "EverQuest" is an early version of a so-called massively multiplayer online role-playing game (MMORPG), where players create a character who enters a fantasy world and interacts with other players. Online sites like EverQuest Widows, the Yahoo group WOW Widows for spouses of the more than 6 million players of the online "World of Warcraft," and gamewidow.com attest to the despair of gaming spouses and significant others.[18]

In South Korea, the epicenter of online gaming, game addiction reportedly claimed 10 lives in 2005, mainly by cutting off circulation when sitting for hours at the screen. In April, the South Korean government launched a game-addiction hotline, and hundreds of hospitals and private clinics treat the addiction, said to afflict an estimated 2.4 percent of Koreans ages 9-39.[19]

Europe's first clinic for video-game addicts opened in the Netherlands in 2005, and several psychologists treat Internet addicts in the United States. Since starting the Computer Addiction Services program at McLean Hospital — a noted psychiatric facility in Belmont, Mass. — in 1995, Harvard psychologist Maressa Hecht Orzack has treated many gamers who she said were neglecting their jobs, schoolwork and families. "They have withdrawal symptoms. They can't wait to get back on [the game] again," she said, adding that the games "are made to be addictive."[20]

But some prominent addiction experts say even those who play games excessively rarely meet all the characteristics of addiction — such as developing physical withdrawal symptoms like sweating (true for gambling), needing to play more and more to get the same kick and being preoccupied to the point it is destructive to one's livelihood and family. Even though some psychologists talk about "Internet addiction disorder," the American Psychiatric Association has not recognized it in its official handbook, the *Diagnostic and Statistical Manual of Mental Disorders*.

Psychologist and gambling studies professor Griffiths, at Nottingham Trent University, found in a study that one-in-20 British children reported playing more than 30 hours a week. But Griffiths says very few of those children — or the population generally — meet all of the criteria for addiction. "It's quite clear when a parent rings me and says, 'My little Johnny is addicted,' it's hard to fulfill more than one or two of the criteria," he says. "Their real concern is the vast amount of time they're playing. The real question is: To what extent is it having a negative effect on their life?"

For a 38-year-old man with three children and a good job, playing 14 hours daily will negatively affect his livelihood and family. But for an unemployed 23-year-old with no partner or children, the same amount of time "has nothing but positive effects" if it brings him into a social network and raises self-esteem, says Griffiths.

Even if they're not technically addicted, users of multiplayer online role-playing games who play on average 20 hours a week tend to describe their game play as "obligation, tedium and more like a second job than entertainment," according to Stanford University researcher Nick Yee.[21]

For example, if a player wants to engage in pharmaceutical manufacturing, one of many possible career choices in "Star War Galaxies," it takes about three to six weeks of normal game play to acquire the abilities to be competitive. Most such games — which get harder as the player becomes more skilled — use designs based on behavioral conditioning, according to Yee, which conditions players to work harder and faster as they improve, creating a kind of digital treadmill of which players are often unaware.[22]

The work required to advance a character's abilities is so time-consuming that companies like TopGameSeller, based in Shanghai, China, offer services to bring one's character up to a more advanced level. Bringing a character in "World of Warcraft" to a higher level can cost up to $1,488. "We assign two or three expert players to your character to do the leveling," the company promises on its Web site (www.topseller.com), which largely involves "simply killing monsters over and over."

Even Griffiths notes that magazines often rate games on their "addictiveness" as a positive attribute. "It's quite clear that the reward systems in video gaming are similar to gambling," he says. "I don't pick up a video game unless I know I have six hours to burn. If I start now, I'll still be playing at 10 p.m. As soon as you've beaten the high score, you want to beat it again."

Many parents worry that video games are displacing other activities like socializing, creative play and reading. But recent surveys show that teen reading has not declined, even as video-gaming hours have risen. And researchers like Yee find that online gaming takes on a social cast, as players communicate over typed chat.

In any case, game enthusiasts and critics alike say parents must set limits, as with any activity.

Do video games prepare young people for the future job market?

"You play 'World of Warcraft'? You're hired!" Someday those words may be spoken by employers — if they're not already — two technology experts wrote in *Wired*, praising multiplayer games for teaching important workplace skills.[23]

In "Warcraft," players band together in guilds to share knowledge and manpower in a "quest," such as slaying monsters. To run a large guild, a master must be able to recruit new members, create apprenticeship programs, orchestrate group strategy and settle disputes. One young engineer at Yahoo! used to worry about whether he could do his job. "Now I think of it like a quest," he said. "By being willing to improvise, I can usually find the people and resources I need to accomplish the task."[24]

Indeed, becoming a guild master "amounts to a total-immersion course in leadership," argue John Seely Brown, former director of Xerox's Palo Alto Research Center, and Douglas Thomas, an associate professor of communication at the University of Southern California's Annenberg School for Communications.[25]

Business experts Beck and Wade came to similar conclusions after surveying 2,100 young professionals, mainly in business. In their book *Got Game*, they claim those with extensive gaming experience were better team members, put a high value on competence and had more potential to be superior executives. Perhaps most important, they argue, gamers understand that repeated failure is the road to success. They found that 81 percent of those under age 34 had been frequent or moderate gamers.[26]

In their most provocative assertion, Beck and Wade claim the dot-com phenomenon was "structured exactly like a video game" in that it called for entrepreneurial skills and a fearlessness toward failure in a generation that grew up gaming. Among the rules learned from gaming were:

- If you get there first, you win;
- Trial and error is the best and fastest way to learn;
- After failure, hit the reset button; don't shrink away.[27]

As Stanford researcher Yee has discovered, many players view playing multiplayer online games as work. Players in "Star War Galaxies" who pick pharmaceutical manufacturing as a career must decide how to price and brand their products, how much to spend on advertising and whether to start a price war with competitors or form a cartel with them. Once players acquire the skills to be competitive in the market, their business operations require a daily time commitment.[28]

Yet today's schools, obsessed with reading and writing, are preparing children for jobs that soon will be outsourced oversees, claims David Williamson Shaffer, associate professor of learning science at the University of Wisconsin-Madison. "The only good jobs left will be for people who can do innovative and creative work," he writes, arguing that video games that teach professional-level language can accomplish that task better than traditional schooling.[29]

A Federation of American Scientists report recently endorsed that view, urging government, industry and educators to take advantage of video-game features to "help students and workers attain globally competitive skills."[30] It said video games could increase the speed at which expertise is acquired, improve players' ability to apply learning and improve decision-making — all important for the coming "conceptual economy."

Already gamers are running political campaigns, negotiating treaties and building environmentally sensitive communities, the report notes.[31] Ashley Richardson was a middle-schooler when she ran for president of Alphaville, the largest city in the popular multiplayer game, "The Sims Online." She debated her opponent on National Public Radio in her campaign to control a government with more than 100 volunteer workers, which made policies affecting thousands of people.[32]

By contrast, students who pass typical school tests often can't apply their knowledge to real-life problems,

according to research cited by Shaffer. Students who can write Newton's laws of motion down on a piece of paper still can't use them to answer a simple problem like, "If you flip a coin into the air, how many forces are acting on it at the top of its trajectory?"[33]

Shaffer has designed games that teach middle- and high-school students to think like professionals in solving real-life problems. Students who play urban-planning or science games developed by Shaffer soon develop more sophisticated, professional-level language in those areas, he reports. For example in one game, students help the Chicago Transportation Authority choose what type of seats to put on new buses. "Before playing the game, a player was likely to say, 'I'd choose this seat because it looks comfortable,' " says Shaffer. "Afterwards, the same player says, 'I'd choose this one because you get more seats on the bus, it's less expensive and has a higher safety rating.' These were exactly the criteria the bus company was looking at."

Indeed, simulation games have long proven to be effective in training people for a variety of skills, including performing surgery. More than 6 million people have registered to play "America's Army," a game released by the military in 2002 to teach military skills; 3 million completed the basic combat-training course and 3 million completed the three-lecture medic course.[34] And some soldiers in Iraq say playing video games gave them the skills they needed for real battles.[35]

Simulations might be a powerful technique, but they are not the same as real life, observes Harvard's Gardner. "I am happy to have medical students or airplane pilots in training learn as much as they can from simulations — but I also want them to have some real, high-stakes experience," he says. And these are two areas where simulation makes sense, he notes. "I don't think it makes sense for many professions, ranging from poet to priest."

The biggest success stories involve skills associated with science, technology or engineering. "I want my children — indeed all young people — to learn how to think like a historian, a philosopher, an economist, a literary critic," says Gardner. "I want to stimulate their imaginations to create their own worlds, not just that conjured up by the makers of 'World of Warcraft.' "

Some critics worry that the game-playing 20-something generation never gained some of the socialization skills and creativity needed in the workplace. The Alliance for Childhood's Almon doubts that chatting

C H R O N O L O G Y

1950s-1960s *Pinball becomes popular among young adults. Early video games are included on computers used by computer students.*

1958 Government physicist William A. Higinbotham invents first computer game — electronic Ping Pong.

1961 MIT student Steve Russell creates the rocket-ship game "Spacewar!" Loaded into computers used in tech courses, it exposes computer-science students to the first video game.

1970s *First commercial video games are marketed to families and young singles in arcades.*

1972 Magnavox introduces Odyssey, first home video-game console.

1976 Computer game "Adventure" first allows players to control characters' behavior.

1977 Atari introduces first video home console with plug-in cartridges.

1980s *Video-game popularity spikes with Atari in early 1980s; Atari goes bust and industry collapses; Nintendo revives industry at end of decade.*

1980 "Pac-Man" is introduced.

1982 Atari sells almost 8 million units. . . . Surgeon general says games create taste for violence.

1984 Warner sells Atari as sales wane.

1985 Popular games "Tetris," "Where in the World is Carmen Sandiego?" and "Super Mario Bros" are introduced.

1989 Nintendo introduces Game Boy; "SimCity," popular urban-planning computer game, is released.

1990s *"First-person shooter" games introduce realistic violence; as sales spike, juvenile violence declines. Multiplayer online games, complex PC games are introduced.*

1991 "Civilization," a history game that takes hours to play, is introduced.

1992 "Wolfenstein 3D" is introduced — the first first-person shooter game.

1993 Introduction of "Doom," with more blood and gore.

1994 Sony PlayStation is introduced.

1997 "Grand Theft Auto," a gang-member survival game, is introduced.

1999 "EverQuest," early online multiplayer game, is introduced.

2000s *Concern about excessive game violence and potential for game addiction leads to calls for curbs; number of female gamers rises.*

2000 "The Sims," a game about relationships popular with girls, is introduced; becomes best-selling computer game of all time.

2002 Microsoft launches Xbox Live, the first online multiplayer console network. . . . U.S. Army launches "America's Army" to recruit and train soldiers.

Nov. 9, 2004 "Halo2," sci-fi game, creates biggest-growing media day in history.

2004 The parents of British teenager Steven Pakeerah, murdered by a friend in England, blame his killer's obsession with violent games.

2005 Chinese government penalizes gamers who play for more than three hours. . . . American Psychological Association calls on companies to reduce violence in video games for children and teens. . . . Sen. Hillary Rodham Clinton, D-N.Y., introduces bill to ban rentals, sales of Mature or Adult Only games to minors.

October, 2006 MacArthur Foundation announces grant of $50 million over five years to research how people learn from video games, other digital media. . . . Federation of American Scientists recommends federal research on educational potential of video games.

Do Video Games Make Kids More Violent?

After 14-year-old Stefan Pakeerah was savagely murdered in England by a friend, his parents claimed the murderer had been obsessed by the violent computer game "Manhunt," which awards points for savage killings. Warren Leblanc, 17, who pleaded guilty in 2005 to the murder, had beaten Stefan with a hammer and stabbed him repeatedly after luring him to a local park, the press reported.

Stefan's parents blamed the game and asked retailers to stop selling it. "It's a video instruction on how to murder somebody; it just shows how you kill people and what weapons you use," Patrick Pakeerah said last year, after several major British retailers agreed to stop selling the game.[1]

There is substantial debate among psychologists over whether violent behavior can be blamed on video games, since game players are often exposed to violence from other sources, such as TV or their own lives. Although few long-term studies have been done to see if the effects are long-lasting, many U.S. psychologists are alarmed. Last year, the American Psychological Association adopted a resolution recommending that all violence be reduced in video games marketed to children and youth. The policy decision came after an expert committee reviewed research indicating that exposure to video-game violence increases youths' aggressive thoughts and behavior and angry feelings.[2]

In violent scenes, the committee noted, perpetrators go unpunished 73 percent of the time — teaching children that violence is an effective way to resolve conflict. Some studies also suggest that the active participation peculiar to video games may influence learning more than the kind of passive observation involved in watching TV, the panel pointed out.

"Playing video games involves practice, repetition and being rewarded for numerous acts of violence, which may intensify the learning," said Elizabeth Carll, a New York psychologist who co-chaired the committee. "This may also result in more realistic experiences, which may potentially increase aggressive behavior."[3]

Mark Griffiths, a psychologist at Nottingham Trent University in Nottingham, England, agrees. "I've concluded the younger the person, the more likely there is to be an effect," he says. "If children watch or play video games, right afterwards they will mimic what they see on the screen."

But Griffiths is more skeptical about the lasting effects of video-game violence, especially in older teens and adults. "Video games may have a contributory effect, but overall the evidence is quite slim," he says. "I think there's a predisposition of people who play violent video games to violence anyway. Youthful offenders play more violent video games [than average]. My guess is these people already have problems to start with and seek out that kind of game — not that they become more violent as a result of playing those games."

Another leading researcher at the other end of the spectrum, Iowa State University psychologist Craig Anderson, finds some effects persist in young children. In a recent study of third-, fourth- and fifth-graders, he found that those who played more video games than their peers early in the school year became more verbally and physically aggressive over the course of the year. He describes exposure to violent video games as a "risk factor" — one of many — that could contribute to this behavior.[4]

online in a multiplayer game can substitute for face-to-face interaction.

"We've been told by one software company that they have to spend so much time teaching the young 20s how to work with others because they've grown up in isolation," she says. The way children traditionally developed those problem-solving skills was by creating their own play situations with one another, which were "extremely complex, nuanced and filled with social learning, problem-solving and creativity," she says. But children don't do that much independent play anymore, she observes.

Some enthusiasts counter that video games can turn gamers into little scientists who have to figure out the rules on their own. Simulation games like "The Sims" help in mastering sciences that utilize computer-based simulation, including biology and cognitive science, suggests the University of Wisconsin's Gee.[36]

But Harvard's Dede is skeptical. "Do kids learn some things about taking a confusing situation and puzzling about it? Sure. But we wouldn't need schooling if learning was as simple as just putting people into experience and letting them figure it out," he says. "That's just as

Seven states limit or ban the sale of violent video games to minors. But most such laws have been overturned after legal challenges by the game industry, usually as unconstitutional infringements on free speech. None of the laws is currently being implemented, according to the Child-Responsible Media Campaign, which advocates restrictions.[5]

Sen. Hillary Rodham Clinton, D-N.Y., introduced a bill in Congress last year that would make it illegal to rent or sell a video game with Mature or Adult Only ratings to minors. Clinton, who said she was disturbed by the sexually explicit content of "Grand Theft Auto," as well as the violence, cited findings that boys as young as 9 often could buy Mature-rated games.[6] But Clinton's bill also could run into constitutional problems, say even those who advocate restrictions.[7]

"Grand Theft Auto: Vice City," which debuted in 2002, drew criticism for its violence. Players can steal vehicles, engage in drive-by shootings and robberies and buy weapons ranging from submachine guns to hand grenades. Members of gangs also engage in shoot-outs.

Courts have been skeptical of a link between video games and violence. For example, a district court in Michigan blocked implementation of a state ban on sales of violent video games to minors. The decision reflected concern that Anderson's studies had "not provided any evidence that the relationship between violent games and aggressive behavior exists. It could just as easily be said that the interactive element in video games acts as an outlet for minors to vent their violent or aggressive behavior, thereby dimming the chance they would actually perform such acts in reality," the court declared.[8]

Yet game-industry spokesmen also point out that juvenile-crime statistics dropped sharply as the violence in video games crested and have not spiked since. (The breakthrough in realistic video-game violence can be traced to the 1992 release of "Wolfenstein 3D," the first major "first-person shooter" game, where the player saw the game world through the eyes of the character and enemies fell and bled on the floor.)

"Just as violent video games were pouring into American homes on the crest of the personal-computer wave, juvenile violence began to plummet," according to University of Pennsylvania criminologist Lawrence Sherman. "Juvenile murder charges dropped by about two-thirds from 1993 to the end of the decade and show no signs of going back up. If video games are so deadly, why has their widespread use been followed by reductions in murder?"[9]

[1] BBC News, "Manhunt Game Withdrawn by Stores," Feb. 18, 2005; http://news.bbc.co.uk. See also "Grand Theft Auto Sparks Another Lawsuit," *GameSpot*, retrieved Aug. 18, 2006.

[2] American Psychological Association press release, "APA Calls for Reduction of Violence in Interactive Media Used by Children and Adolescents," Aug. 17, 2005; www.apa.org/releases.

[3] Quoted in *Ibid.*

[4] Douglas A. Gentile and Craig A. Anderson, "Violent Video Games: The Effects on Youth, and Public Policy Implications," in N. Dowd, *et al.*, *Handbook of Children, Culture and Violence* (2006), p. 231 (from page proofs.)

[5] Washington, Illinois, Michigan, California, Minnesota, Oklahoma and Louisiana have passed laws restricting the sale of violent games to minors. See www.medialegislation.org. Also see Gentile and Anderson, *op. cit.*, p. 240. In the past five years, U.S. courts have ruled at least eight times that computer games and video games are protected speech under the First Amendment, according to the Entertainment Software Association; on Oct. 11, 2006, a U.S. district judge in Oklahoma issued a preliminary injunction halting implementation of Oklahoma's law, calling the act's language unconstitutionally vague.

[6] News release, "Sens. Clinton, Lieberman and Bayh Introduce Legislation to Protect Children from Inappropriate Video Games"; http://clinton.senate.gov.

[7] The Child-Responsible Media Campaign; www.medialegislation.org.

[8] Entertainment Software Association, "Essential Facts about Video Games and Court Rulings;" www.theesa.com.

[9] Quoted in John C. Beck and Mitchell Wade, *Got Game* (2004), pp. 53-54.

true for gaming experiences as for real-world experiences." The key is to adapt the methods developed for entertainment to educational games so they can be "a powerful vehicle for education."

BACKGROUND

Pinball Precursor

Pinball was the mechanical precursor of video games, say some historians, rousing many of the same fears that video games do today. In the 1930s, New York Mayor Fiorello La Guardia smashed pinball machines with a sledgehammer and banned them — a ban that was only lifted in the 1970s.[37]

In 1958, William A. Higinbotham, a physicist at Brookhaven National Laboratory on Long Island, invented a game of electronic Ping-Pong. Although the game was dismantled the next year — its components were needed for other projects — it was remembered by a future editor of *Creative Computing* magazine, David Ahl, who had seen the game during a high school visit. He dubbed Higinbotham the grandfather of video games.[38]

Software engineer Tammy Yap designs video games at Midway Home Entertainment in San Diego. Some experts blame girls' lower interest in video games on the scarcity of sympathetic female characters and game designers.

However, Massachusetts Institute of Technology (MIT) student Steve Russell is generally considered the inventor of video games. In 1961, he created a rocket-ship game called "Spacewar!," which could be played on one of MIT's computers. The manufacturer of the computer, Digital Equipment Corp., began shipping its computers pre-loaded with the game, exposing computer-science students across the country to "Spacewar."[39]

In 1972, Magnavox introduced "Odyssey," the first home video-game console, which Magnavox marketed as a family game. Until the early 1980s manufacturers also marketed arcade games to single adults as having sex appeal.

Slow adoption of video games through the 1970s culminated in the 1977 introduction of Atari — the first video-game console to use plug-in cartridges rather than built-in games. Atari became one of the most successful introductions in history, selling about 3 million consoles a year. Atari was considered wildly popular in the early 1980s until its manufacturer collapsed.[40]

Nintendo revived the industry in the late 1980s, and since then a wide variety of consoles and games have been introduced, including Sony's PlayStation and Microsoft's Xbox. A variety of other games have been designed for personal computers. As computer animation permitted film-like dramas with original scripts and music, computer games became increasingly sophisticated, bearing little resemblance to the black and white blips of Higinbotham's original game.

The late 1980s were a crucial turning point in the social history of video games, according to Williams, at the University of Illinois. Games began moving from bars, nightclubs and arcades to homes as prices dropped, houses expanded and Americans had more disposable income. Driven by Nintendo's marketing, games became the province of children for the next 10 years.[41]

Video games also ushered in a new generation of young people "comfortable and techno-literate enough to accept personal computers, electronic bulletin boards, desktop publishing, compact disks and the Web," he writes, and pushed the development of microprocessors, broadband networks and display technologies.[42]

Today half of all Americans 8-18 have a video-game player in their bedrooms.[43] They also have less contact with people they know (within the family) but more contact with unknown people from a variety of backgrounds, particularly with the rise of multiplayer games, Williams points out. That gives a 12-year-old boy access to the knowledge of a 40-year-old lawyer playing the same game (and vice versa) but also rouses fears about whom children are meeting online.[44]

Besides worrying that children might meet potential predators online, adults also were concerned about the violent content of video games. In 1982, Surgeon General C. Everett Koop claimed that video games were hazardous, creating aberrant behavior and increasing a taste for violence. Nearly 25 years later, researchers still have not found definitive proof of long-lasting negative effects from video violence, or of the predicted increase in withdrawal and social isolation, according to Williams. But these worries survive.

Meanwhile, video games long ago became more than child's play. Today, the average age of video gamers is 33, a quarter of gamers are over 50 and only 31 percent are under 18, according to the Entertainment Software Association.[45]

Equity Gap?

With video-game consoles in 83 percent of the homes of the under-18 crowd, one would expect the benefits of gaming to be pervasive.[46] But surveys suggest that low-income children aren't getting the same access to technology as their middle-class peers — a video-gaming "equity gap" that resembles the so-called digital divide between those with and without Internet access. Although

87 percent of teens use the Internet, those who don't are generally from lower-income households with limited access to high-tech hardware and are disproportionately African-American.[47]

That could mean they lack access to some of the more complex games played on computers and online. Convinced of games' educational potential, Global Kids, a nonprofit that provides education on international issues to urban youth, has obtained a Microsoft grant to teach disadvantaged New York City teens to design and play games.

"Some of these kids don't know how to move a cursor into a Web browser," says Global Kids' Online Leadership Director Barry Joseph. Paradoxically, most attend schools with plenty of computer equipment — courtesy of Clinton-era funding. But many of the students are not connected to the Internet because teachers are often unfamiliar with the technology, Joseph says.

"Middle-class homes have multiple gaming consoles, broadband and adults familiar enough with systems to encourage young people" to play games with learning potential, Joseph says. By contrast, lower-income kids may only have access to a computer at the school library, where daily time is limited to 10 minutes, mandatory filters block the ability to blog and computers have no capacity to store kids' creations, notes MIT's Director of Comparative Media Studies Henry Jenkins.

However, surveys about access may not tell the real story about who's benefiting from technology. "Some folks are using the technology in new ways; others are less digitally savvy and are just playing Gameboy. That may be the real divide in who has positive effects," says Connie Yowell, director of educational grant-making at the MacArthur Foundation, which is helping Global Kids and other groups study how young people are using technology.

Gender Gap Narrows

Boys between 8 and 18 spend more than twice as much time playing video games as girls, according to a recent Kaiser Family Foundation survey.[48] Some have blamed girls' lower interest on the scarcity of sympathetic female characters and game designers.

"Games were built by boys for boys," Northwestern's Cassell found in 1997 when she co-edited *From Barbie to Mortal Kombat*, a book of scholarly essays on the gender slant of video games.[49]

But Cassell and other experts say the gender gap has been narrowing. Today, women over 18 represent 30 percent of U.S. gamers — a greater proportion than do boys 17 and under (23 percent).[50] "Boys may be playing more traditional video games," Cassell says, "but girls are playing more 'Sims,' " which is akin to playing house.

And virtual worlds are much more popular among females. Females make up the majority of the 400,000 subscribers to There.com, a virtual world where participants can create a character to interact with others, according to Michael K. Wilson, CEO of Makena Technologies, the company behind the site. Socializing and shopping seem to be two major draws for teenage girls, he says.

"It's very clear to us that teens are very interested in shopping. There.com is the holy grail of shopping sites. You can try on a dress [or your avatar can] and ask friends how you look in it," says Wilson. There.com has also experimented with Nike and Levi Strauss & Co. to turn that click on a product into a real-world purchase.

In Second Life, another virtual world, companies like Reebok and Amazon.com have set up shops to sell real-world versions of their products as well as virtual ones.[51]

Another magnet drawing women has been the rise in so-called casual games — which may take as little as 10 minutes to play, such as Solitaire, mahjong and some short action games. In the past few years, thousands of such games have sprung up on the Internet and game consoles.

The typical casual game players are women in their 40s, one of the fastest-growing sectors of the industry, according to the International Game Developers Association. From almost nothing in 2002, casual games grew to a $600 million business by 2004, and by 2008 industry experts expect to see $2 billion in U.S. sales alone.[52]

Female gamers spend an average of two hours more per week playing video games than a year ago, for an average of 7.4 hours a week, according to the Entertainment Software Association. While male gamers still spent more daily time than females on video games in 2003, the gap had narrowed from 18 minutes to six minutes by 2004.[53]

Males still comprise the majority of those who play online, but the games played most often online — puzzle board and trivia games — are among those most favored by females.[54]

Entering the New Virtual World of Education

Students enrolled in "Law in the Court of Public Opinion" at the Harvard Extension School in fall 2006 log onto their computers every Thursday evening and send animated versions of themselves into a virtual classroom. There, a so-called avatar — another animated persona — representing Law Professor Charlie Ness (looking about 20 years younger) teaches the course in real time, using Ness's real voice. An avatar representing Ness's daughter Rebecca, a computer expert, occasionally flies down from the ceiling to help teach the course.

Harvard is one of several universities that have begun entering game-like virtual worlds to reach a wider audience. The audience is large and growing at a rate of 10-20 percent a month by some estimates.[1]

Ness teaches his course in the virtual world of Second Life, which boasts more than 1 million inhabitants.[2] Participants enter the Second Life fantasy world to meet people and buy and sell virtual real estate, clothes and other goods. (Linden Labs, the company behind Second Life, makes most of its money leasing virtual land to tenants.) In spring 2006, the 20 courses offered in Second Life included "Theatre and Culture," from Case Western Reserve University, and Stanford University's "Critical Studies in New Media."

Second Life's virtual library offers monthly book discussions, talks by authors (as avatars, of course) and a reference service. It was created because of college students' tendency to use online resources instead of brick-and-mortar libraries, according to Lori Bell, director of innovation at the Alliance Library System in East Peoria, Ill., which helped create the virtual library. As for being in virtual worlds, she observes, "The library needs to be there or we're going to start losing people."

So far, 2,000-3,000 people a day visit the library, according to Bell. "We get a lot of people coming because it's a safe place." Elsewhere in Second Life, she notes, "There's a lot of sex, gambling and adult places. The library is somewhere you don't have to buy anything, you don't have people hitting on you, and people are friendly."

Much like the real world, people enter a virtual universe for a variety of reasons, and education is not necessarily at the top of the list. Lauren Gelman, associate director of the Stanford Law School's Center for Internet and Society, says when she first entered the popular virtual world of There.com — with 400,000 subscribers between ages 13 and 26 — "the first thing that happened is I got propositioned." With islands populated by avatars in bikinis, she says, "It's a very Club Med kind of environment."

This fall, Gelman became dean of a virtual university in There.com — the State of Play Academy — which will offer courses by experts in technology-related areas of law such as copyright, patents and trade secrets.[3] Eventually, the academy might even offer a degree-like certificate, Gelman says.

Students who come to these classes are expected to bring a better grasp of technology than the law professor, permitting a two-way transfer of information. "Sometimes I'll be the teacher and sometimes the student," says Gelman, who teaches a course on technology and law at Stanford.

The power of virtual worlds to project situations in 3-D means students can "experience" what they're learning. To train health-care professionals in how to deal with bioterrorism and natural disasters, for example, Idaho State University provides simulations in Second Life of earthquakes and fires, injured victims and how to treat them.[4] Recently, the library invited residents to heckle Tudor King Henry VIII of England and ask his wife Ann Boleyn what it felt like to be beheaded. Two librarians acted out the roles as avatars in full 16th-century dress.

This summer, teens in Second Life participated in a virtual summer camp aimed at building awareness of global issues like sex trafficking, sponsored by Global Kids, a New York-based group that teaches urban youth about leadership and global citizenry.[5] "We take real-world issues and do something about it in a way you could never do in real life," says Barry Joseph, online leadership director at Global Kids. "In Second Life, you can click on someone's 'Save Darfur' green wrist band and get information about what's going on right now in Darfur."

The argument that kids learn better in the video universe has been a major influence on pioneers like Gelman. "If we know there's educational value in that kids think differently when they navigate these worlds, could we put it to better use to teach them substantive stuff while they're sitting in front of 'World of Warcraft' for 10 hours on a Saturday?" asks Gelman. "It could be at the cusp of something completely revolutionary in education — or it might not work."

---

[1] Richard Siklos, "A Virtual World But Real Money," *The New York Times*, Oct. 19, 2006. According to the Second Life Web site, $7.4 million changed hands in September.

[2] http://secondlife.com. Regular users — those who logged on in the last 30 days — totaled 427,838 in mid-October 2006.

[3] http://stateofplayacademy.com/

[4] http://www.isu.edu/irh/IBAPP/second_life.shtml.

[5] www.globalkids.org.

Do video games significantly enhance literacy?

YES James Paul Gee
*Tashia Morgridge Professor of Reading,
University of Wisconsin
Author,* What Video Games Have to Teach Us
about Learning and Literacy

Written for *CQ Researcher*, November 2006

Popular culture today often involves quite complex language, and that matters because the biggest predictor of children's school success is the size of their early vocabularies and their abilities to deal with complex language.

Consider, for example, a typical description of a "Pokemon" ("pocket monsters" found in video games, cards, books, movies and television shows): "Bulbasaur are a combination of Grass-type and Poison-type Pokémon. Because they are Grass-type Pokémon, Bulbasaur have plant-like characteristics." Or consider this from a Web site for "Yu-Gi-Oh" (another card, game, book, movie phenomenon): "The effect of '8-Claws Scorpion' is a Trigger Effect that is applied if the condition is correct on activation." Lots of low-frequency words here; complex syntax, as well. Children as young as 6 and 7 play "Pokemon" and "Yu-Gi-Oh." To play they have to read — and read complex language.

The biggest barrier to school success is the child's ability to deal with complex "academic" language, the sort of language in textbooks. Such language starts to kick in about fourth grade and ever increases thereafter in school. Children who learn to decode, but can't read to learn in the content areas later on, are victims of the well-known "fourth-grade slump." Worse yet, research shows that even children who can pass tests in the content areas often can't apply their knowledge to real problem-solving.

Without lots of practice, humans are poor at learning from words out of their contexts of application. Good video games put young people in worlds composed of problems to be solved. They almost always give verbal information "just in time" — when players need and can use it — and "on demand," when the player asks for it. They show how language applies to the world it is about.

Research suggests that people really know what words mean only when they can hook them to the sorts of actions, images or dialogues to which they apply. That is why a game manual or strategy guide makes much more sense after someone has played a game for awhile than before. So, too, science textbooks, cut off from the images and actions science is about, are like a technical game manual without any game.

But, a warning: Good video games — good commercial ones like "Civilization 4" and good "serious games" made around academic content — will not work by themselves. Mentors are needed to encourage strategic thinking about the game and the complex language connected to them.

NO Howard Gardner
*Hobbs Professor of
Cognition and Education,
Harvard Graduate School of Education*

Written for *CQ Researcher*, November 2006

It's difficult to argue with many of Gee's points, and the jury is still out on others. Yet I'd point to several biases in the cited examples. I) They are oriented toward competition (despite the fact that some also entail cooperation); 2) The literacy highlighted is that used in technical manuals; 3) These games, and the epistemology underlying them, are more likely to appeal to boys rather than to girls, and to "techies" rather than dreamers, humanists and conversationalists; 4) They foreground simulation, a very powerful technique, but it's not the same as real life.

I am happy to have medical students or future airplane pilots train on simulations — but they also require real, high-stake experience. Patients have feelings; simulacra and robots don't. And note that these are two areas where simulation makes sense. In many other professions, from poets to priests, they don't.

Which leads to the most important point. Literacy is far more than expertise in technical manuals or even in understanding science and technology, important as they are. It entails the capacity to immerse oneself and, ultimately, to love long, imaginative pieces of fiction, such as *Madame Bovary* or *One Hundred Years of Solitude*; poring over difficult philosophical texts and returning time and again to key passages (Kant, Wittgenstein); and spending time and exercising emotional imagination with challenging poets (Gerard Manley Hopkins, Jorie Graham).

Literacy involves linear thinking over many pages — an entirely different mental faculty than is exploited when one surfs the Web from one link to another, often randomly encountered one. I want all young persons to learn how to think like a historian, a philosopher, an economist, a literary critic (four very different "frames of mind"). I want to stimulate their imaginations to create their own worlds, not just that conjured up by the makers of "World of Warcraft."

In sum, the treasures and skills entailed in the video games of today are impressive, but they still represent only a very partial sampling of the kinds of minds that young people have and the kinds that can and should be cultivated. Some can be cultivated in front of a screen. But too much time there is not healthy on any criterion — and any slice of life — no matter how engrossing — is only partial at best. So two cheers for Jim Gee — but two cheers as well for Mark Hopkins* on one end of a log, and an eager questioner and listener on the other.

* A 19th-century president of Williams College.

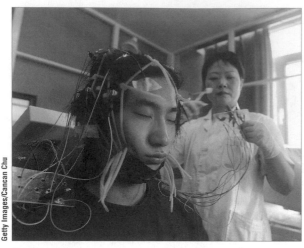

A young man receives an electroencephalogram at a clinic for video-game "addicts" in Beijing in July 2005. Such clinics have opened in several countries, but many psychologists question whether game playing can lead to true addiction.

Nevertheless, many young girls don't think they're good at games, Cassell says, because they buy the traditional definition that "real" video games involve action or sports. In the late 1990s, many experts feared the gender gap in game playing would further widen the gender gap in access to technology and science generally. But that may be changing as girls become a major presence in games and virtual worlds that emphasize interaction and creativity over competition.

And some researchers, like Harvard's Dede, find girls are just as interested in a game involving science if it minimizes the things that bore them — like scoring points and violence — and stresses personal interaction instead. For instance, girls trying to discover the cause of a mysterious epidemic in the "River City" simulation game approach the problem differently from boys. "Girls on balance try to establish a relationship with the residents of this virtual town," through the characters they create, and use those relationships to solve the mystery, Dede says.

"Typically, research shows girls aren't interested in science," notes "River City" Project Director Jody Clarke, particularly in middle school, the age the Harvard team is observing. But "we're finding girls are interested in open-ended exploration and engaging with teams, so they're doing science differently," she says. Similarly, multiplayer online games that are drawing female players are designed around open-ended exploration that allows team-like player networks to develop, she says.

"I ask girls whether they're good at computers and they say 'No' even though they are," says Northwestern's Cassell, noting their growing presence in games and blogging. "The traditional definition of a game excludes the kinds of things girls like. It's not true that girls don't like games."

CURRENT SITUATION

Big Business

Today, about half of all Americans play computer and video games, according to the Entertainment Software Association (ESA), and Americans spend more money on video games each year than they do going to the movies.[55] Americans also spend more time playing video games than watching rented videos.[56]

In the past 10 years, U.S. video-game sales have almost tripled to $7 billion last year — after peaking at $7.4 billion in 2004 — representing nearly 230 million computer and video games.[57]

In fact, the largest-grossing one-day media sale ever occurred on Nov. 9, 2004, when stores sold $125 million worth of "Halo 2" games — the eagerly awaited sequel to the hit Xbox game "Halo", in which individual players defend Earth against alien invaders.[58]

Today, the personal computer is the most popular game machine, contrary to earlier industry predictions that game consoles would dominate. Until recently, Microsoft hadn't marketed games as a core part of its computer. But now it plans to make games easier to install and will emphasize that in its marketing.

Hundreds of millions of people around the world use computers that run the Windows operating system, and about half of them play games, according to Microsoft surveys. The driving force, most analysts say, are subscription-based online multiplayer games played on computers. Games like "World of Warcraft" are expected to take in more than $2 billion worldwide.[59]

Teens have been a big contributor to this growth, with 81 percent of teens — 17 million people — using the Internet to play games online, according to the Pew Internet & American Life Project. That's a 52 percent jump since 2000.[60]

Social Networking

With 81 percent of all teens playing online video games — up from 66 percent in 2000 — online games have become a widespread form of social networking, according to Amanda Lenhart, senior research specialist at the Pew Internet & American Life Project.[61]

"As with all things on the Internet, it's possible to meet all sorts of people," says Lenhart. "I've heard from a law-enforcement officer about a person who was preyed upon by somebody they met in a game. But the vast majority of people I've talked to have not mentioned any trouble with that sort of thing."

Virtual worlds help teens with two crucial developmental issues — developing an identity and interacting with peers, says Northwestern's Cassell. "That's why they're so popular. They're all about trying on different identities and manifestations," she says.

Although multiplayer games and virtual worlds are clearly places for social networking, they have not become the target of legislation, as have other networking spaces like Myspace.com.[62] Rep. Fred Upton, R-Mich., and others in Congress have proposed restricting children's access to social-networking Web sites. Due to such efforts, as well as entertainment-industry threats to tighten copyright restrictions on kids' variations of games or movies, MIT's Jenkins fears that authorities will "shut down [digital media] before we understand them."[63]

Meanwhile, age, ethnic and social stratifications are breaking down as youngsters play online with older people from cultures around the world. "This is social broadening, which can be scary" to society, says the University of Illinois's Williams. While mixing is positive for diversity, the bonds are different than with a face-to-face friend. "An online friend can console you but can't drive you to the hospital," he points out.

Libraries Log On

One Friday night each month, nearly 100 Michigan teenagers gather at the Ann Arbor District Library to compete in the Nintendo racing game "Mario Kart." "It's just like story-time, only noisier and smellier," says the library's technology manager, Eli Neiburger.

Libraries increasingly are offering such gaming events, and younger librarians are trying to persuade colleagues that video games are a legitimate part of libraries' mission. A new Young Adult Library Services Association task force is examining whether to recommend video games for teens alongside its annual list of recommended books.

When kids ask, "What can I read?" librarians should give the answer a gaming spin, advises task force member Beth Gallaway, a trainer/consultant for youth services at the Metrowest Massachusetts Regional Library System in Waltham. "No matter what kind of game kids are playing, they come in genres just like the books we're so familiar with — science fiction, fantasy — and you can pull out these elements from the game," she says.

"There seems to be a lot of interest right now," says Christopher Couzes, director of institutional marketing at Baker and Taylor in Charlotte, N.C., which sells books and other media to libraries. But so far, only about 200 libraries have purchased video games from his firm.

According to the University of Wisconsin's Squire, nearly every student he's met who has played a content-rich game like "Civilization" has checked out a library book on a related topic. But those mind-teaser games are not the games libraries are purchasing. "Libraries want to bring in titles that are popular and that circulate," says Couzes, such as sports games and the popular "Mario Brothers."

Saying Less?

Although no one knows for sure whether the rising use of video gaming is affecting national literacy and problem-solving abilities, the percentage of U.S. college graduates with proficient English literacy has declined — from 40 percent in 1992 to 31 percent in 2003.[64]

Citing that decline, longtime technology critic Jeremy Rifkin, founder of the Foundation on Economic Trends, blames the increasing use of video games and other electronic media like TV and text messaging. "The human vocabulary is plummeting all over the world, making it more difficult to express ourselves," he says. "It appears that we are all communicating more, but saying less."[65]

However, science writer Johnson observes IQ scores in most developed countries have increased over the past century. He also notes the rate of increase has accelerated in the past 30 years and attributes the rise to the increasing cognitive labor in our mental diet. Compared to the simple children's games of a century ago, today's 10-year-old must master "probing and telescoping through immense virtual worlds," switching from instant-messaging to e-mail and troubleshooting new technologies, Johnson writes. The fact that the U.S. lags behind other countries in educational assessments just shows that students are getting their IQ advantage outside of school, he argues.[66]

A Federation of American Scientists report recently called on the federal government to research the education and work-force-training potential of video games. The report followed a yearlong evaluation and conference sponsored by the National Science Foundation, which is funding projects to develop educational science games, including multiplayer online games.[67]

While video games could improve learning and motivation, the scientists' report said most commercial games probably will not accomplish those goals, and more educational games should be developed. More research is needed to understand exactly which features of games are important for learning, it said.

High costs and an uncertain market make production of purely educational games too risky for private industry to develop, the federation report said. While some classrooms already use games like "Civilization" for history, "SimCity" for urban planning and "Roller Coaster Tycoon" for physics, schools are unwilling to abandon textbooks and traditional teaching for games whose effectiveness is unknown. The scientists urged educators to develop educational materials around content-rich games like "Civilization" and develop tests to find out what students learn in games.

OUTLOOK

Testing the Hypothesis

As video games become more sophisticated and broaden their audience, some cultural observers say it's time to look beyond fears of lurking pedophiles and rotting brains and conduct research to find out what's genuinely good and bad about games.

In October the MacArthur Foundation announced it was committing $50 million to understanding how video games and other digital media affect learning by young people.[68] The foundation is giving grants to game enthusiasts like Wisconsin's Gee and Global Kids' Joseph, as well as to skeptics like Harvard's Gardner.

Unlike school, games are producing "kid-driven learning," says Yowell, noting the foundation will fund innovations based on "what we learn from the kids." MacArthur's hypothesis is that digital media *do* affect how children

learn. "That has huge implications for parents, teachers and policymakers, and we need to understand that," Yowell says.

Edward Castronova, an associate professor of telecommunications at Indiana University, will use his $240,000 grant to build an online game around Shakespeare's plays, then study how kids' alter-egos dressed in 17th-century costumes learn the bard's words and change their social behavior while living in a very different society.[69]

Some of the enthusiasts' biggest claims will be tested with MacArthur-funded research. Do kids experience failure differently in games? Are they problem-solving differently? What's the effect of giving kids immediate feedback in a game? How do you test what they've learned in a game?

MacArthur grantees will also be asking some of the critics' questions, such as: What's being lost with all the time spent playing? Are players socially isolated? Are they daydreaming less? "We're agnostic," says Yowell.

At least one grant, to Gardner, will examine how kids make ethical decisions about what they share publicly about themselves and their creations. In virtual worlds and multiplayer games, "If I get to pretend to be someone else, what does that mean about how I make ethical decisions?" Yowell asks.

Increasingly, much of our national political debate comes down to disagreements over whether a model is accurate: Will the Earth really suffer from global warming? Did the Iraq war reduce terrorism or stimulate more of it? Since games are all about testing models, they could provide a test-bed for citizenship. Increasingly, they're also about collecting information from many sources — not just rote memorization from a central source.

The big question, enthusiasts say, is whether educators will adapt those techniques to make school as engaging and complex as the best video games. But can games move beyond blood and monsters to become socially positive? Global Kids thinks so and has developed a game about poverty set in Haiti. In a family's struggle to survive, the player has to choose between sending the children to school (and going into debt) or sending them out to work and reaping short-term additional income.[70]

Yet will these kinds of games fly with children who've grown up on the thrills of "Grand Theft Auto"? It's hard to predict, especially as games become ever more realistic and enthralling in this fast-changing industry.

One of the more futuristic visions foresees virtual characters who can respond emotionally to players. "Laura," a computerized exercise trainer developed at MIT, provides empathetic verbal and facial feedback. To technology critic Rifkin, it's hard to know whether to see such attempts as "sadly pathological . . . or whether to be truly frightened."[71]

Ultimately, says MIT's Jenkins, video games are not simply an add-on to mainstream education but a "basic paradigm shift" in how kids learn — one that's here to stay. Parents will have to be actively involved in the digital world to understand it and offer guidance, he says — whether it's questioning the ethics in Second Life or steering kids to the fanfiction sites where they can learn to become better writers.

His advice to parents: Sit down and play a game with your kids.[72]

NOTES

1. Federation of American Scientists (FAS), "Summit on Educational Games 2006," October 2006; www.fas.org.

2. Steven Johnson, *Everything Bad is Good For You* (2006), p. 45.

3. *Ibid.*, p. 31

4. Kaiser Family Foundation, "Generation M," 2005; www.kff.org. The survey was among children ages 8-18.

5. C. Galas and D.J. Ketelhut, "River City," *Leading with Technology*, 2006, pp. 31-32; http://muve.gse.harvard.edu/rivercityproject/research-publications.htm.

6. Kaiser Family Foundation, *op. cit.*

7. Susan B. Newman and Donna Celano, "The Knowledge Gap," *Reading Research Quarterly*, April/May/June 2006, pp. 176-201; www.reading.org/publications/journals/rrq.

8. FAS, *op. cit.*

9. James Paul Gee, "Reading, Specialist Language Development, and Video Games," unpublished paper, p. 36.

10. MacArthur Open Forum, "Dialogue 2: Gaming Literacies"; http://community.macfound.org.

11. Galas and Ketelhut, *op. cit.*

12. Federation of American Scientists, *op. cit.*, p. 43.

13. Constance A. Steinkuehler, "Massively Multiplayer Online Video Gaming as Participation in A Discourse," *Mind, Culture and Activity*, 2006, 13 (1), pp. 38-52.

14. FAS, *op. cit.*

15. Julia Scheeres, "The Quest to End Game Addiction," *Wired News*, Dec. 5, 2001; www.wired.com.

16. Nick Yee, "The Labor of Fun: How Video Games Blur the Boundaries of Work and Play," *Games and Culture*, January 2006, pp. 68-71. This and other articles/surveys by Yee are at www.nickyee.com/daedalus.

17. www.nickyee.com/daedalus.

18. http://games.groups.yahoo.com/group/WOW_widow/; Scheeres, *op. cit.*

19. Anthony Faiola, "Experts Fear Epidemic of Gaming Addiction," *The Miami Herald*, June 4, 2005, p. A25.

20. Gregory M. Lamb, "Are Multiplayer Games More Compelling, More Addictive?," *The Christian Science Monitor*, Oct. 13, 2005, p. 13.

21. Yee, *op. cit.*, p. 68.

22. *Ibid.*

23. John Seely Brown and Douglas Thomas, "You Play World of Warcraft? You're Hired," *Wired*, April 2006, p. 120.

24. *Ibid.*

25. *Ibid.*

26. John C. Beck and Mitchell Wade, *Got Game* (2004), p. 10.

27. *Ibid.*, p. 42.

28. Yee, *op. cit.*, p. 69.

29. David Williamson Shaffer, *How Computer Games Help Children Learn* (2006).

30. Federation of American Scientists, press release, "Study Recommends Fix to Digital Disconnect in U.S. Education and Workforce Training," Oct. 17, 2006; www.fas.org.

31. Federation of American Scientists, "Summit on Educational Games 2006," *op. cit.*, p. 14.

32. Henry Jenkins, *et al.*, "Confronting the Challenges of Participatory Culture," John D. and

Catharine T. MacArthur Foundation, 2006, p. 5; www.digitallearning.macfound.org.

33. *Ibid.*

34. Federation of American Scientists, "Summit on Educational Games 2006," *op. cit.*, p. 12.

35. Jose Antonio Vargas, "Virtual Reality Prepares Soldiers for Real War," *The Washington Post*, Feb. 16, 2006, p. A1.

36. James Gee, *What video games have to teach us about learning and literacy* (2003), p. 48.

37. Chris Suellentrop, "Playing With Our Minds," *Wilson Quarterly*, summer 2006, pp. 14-21.

38. *Ibid.*

39. *Ibid.*

40. Beck and Wade, *op. cit.*, p. 8.

41. Dmitri Williams, in P. Vorderer and J. Bryant, eds., *Playing Computer Games* (2006) in press; https://netfiles.uiuc.edu/dcwill/www/.

42. *Ibid.*, p. 6.

43. Kaiser Family Foundation, press release, "Media Multi-Tasking Changing the Amount and Nature of Young People's Media Use," March 9, 2005.

44. For background see Brian Hansen, "Cyber-Predators," *CQ Researcher*, March 1, 2002, pp. 169-192.

45. Entertainment Software Association; www.theesa.com. See "Facts and Research."

46. Kaiser Family Foundation, "Generation M: Media in the Lives of 8-18 Year Olds: Executive Summary," March 2005; www.kff.org.

47. Pew Internet & American Life Project, "Teens and Technology: Youth are Leading the Transition to a Fully Wired and Mobile Nation," July 27, 2005; www.pewinternet.org. For background see Kathy Koch, "Digital Divide," *CQ Researcher*, Jan. 28, 2000, pp. 41-64.

48. Kaiser Family Foundation, *op. cit.*, March 9, 2005, p. 17. Boys spend an average of 1 hour 12 minutes a day compared to girls' 25 minutes.

49. Justine Cassell and Henry Jenkins, eds., *From Barbie to Mortal Kombat: Gender and Computer Games* (1998).

50. Entertainment Software Association, "Facts and Research"; www.theesa.com.

51. Richard Siklos, "A Virtual World But Real Money," *The New York Times*, Oct. 19, 2006.

52. International Game Developers Association, "2006 Casual Games White Paper"; www.igda.org/casual.

53. *Ibid.*

54. *Ibid.*

55. Suellentrop, *op. cit.*, pp. 16-17.

56. Beck and Wade, *op. cit.*, p. 3.

57. The NPD Group, Point-of-Sale Information.

58. Kurt Squire, "From Content to Context," presentation made at Serious Games Summit, Feb. 24, 2004, p. 2.

59. Seth Schiesel, "The PC Embraces Its Gaming Abilities," *The New York Times*, July 18, 2006, Arts Section, pp. 1, 4.

60. Pew Internet & American Life Project, *op. cit.*

61. *Ibid.*

62. For background see Marcia Clemmitt, "Cyber Socializing," *CQ Researcher*, July 28, 2006, pp. 625-648.

63. MacArthur Foundation Webcast of briefing, "Building the Field of Digital Media Learning," Oct. 19, 2006; www.macfound.org.

64. National Center for Education Statistics, "A First Look at the Literacy of America's Adults in the 21st Century," Dec. 15, 2005; http://nces.ed.gov.

65. Jeremy Rifkin, "Virtual Companionship: Our Lonely Existence," *International Herald Tribune*, Oct. 12, 2006, p. 8.

66. Steven Johnson, *Everything Bad is Good for You* (2006), pp. 142-144.

67. Federation of American Scientists, "Summit on Educational Games 2006," *op. cit.*

68. MacArthur Foundation press release, "MacArthur Investing $50 Million in Digital Learning," Oct. 19, 2006; www.macfound.org.

69. Daniel Terdiman, "Shakespeare Coming to a Virtual World," *The New York Times*, Oct. 19, 2006.

70. "Ayiti — the Cost of Life"; thecostoflife.org and www.holymeatballs.org.

71. Rifkin, *op. cit.*

72. MacArthur Foundation Webcast, *op. cit.*

BIBLIOGRAPHY

Books

Beck, John C. and Mitchell Wade, *Got Game: How the Gamer Generation is Reshaping Business Forever*, *Harvard Business School Press*, 2004.
Two business experts argue video games provide the kind of leadership, entrepreneurship and team-building skills needed for today's workplace.

Gee, James Paul, *What Video Games Have to Teach Us About Learning and Literacy*, *Palgrave Macmillan*, 2003.
An education professor at the University of Wisconsin-Madison argues that video games provide an intricate learning experience in a modern world where print literacy is not enough.

Johnson, Steven, *Everything Bad is Good for You*, *Riverhead Books*, 2006.
Science writer argues that gamers are learning the scientific method when they try to figure out the "physics" of a game.

Prensky, Marc, *Don't Bother Me Mom-I'm Learning!* *Paragon House*, 2006.
In this enthusiastic book, the founder of an e-learning company urges parents (whom he calls "digital immigrants") to start engaging with digital natives — kids who've grown up with games as a positive learning experience.

Articles

Brown, John Seely and Thomas Douglas, "You Play World of Warcraft? You're Hired!" *Wired*, April 2006, p. 120.
Skills learned in multiplayer games like "World of Warcraft" are training young people for workplace leadership roles.

Rauch, Jonathan, "Sex, Lies, and Videogames," *The Atlantic Monthly*, November 2006.
The future of video-game technology includes interactive dramas and Spore, a game coming out next year, that will give players new scope in designing new worlds.

Rifkin, Jeremy, "Virtual Companionship," *International Herald Tribune*, Oct. 12, 2006, p. 8.
Technology critic worries that the nation is becoming less literate as video games proliferate, and expresses disgust at futuristic interactive computer characters.

Shaffer, David Williamson, *et al.*, "Video Games and the Future of Learning," *Phi Delta Kappan*, October 2005, pp. 105-111.
University of Wisconsin educational researchers argue that video games offer "learning by doing" on a grand scale and that schools need to catch up.

Siklos, Richard, "A Virtual World But Real Money," *The New York Times*, Oct. 19, 2006.
The popularity and economies of virtual worlds like Second Life are growing rapidly.

Suellentrop, Chris, "Playing with Our Minds," *Wilson Quarterly*, summer 2006, pp. 14-21.
A *New York Times* columnist suggests games do not permit innovation because they force players to play within the system.

Tompkins, Aimee, "The Psychological Effects of Violent Media on Children," Dec. 14, 2003, *AllPsych Journal*, http://allpsych.com.
So far, research on the effect of violent video games and other media on children only shows evidence of short-term effects.

Wright, Will, "Dream Machines," *Wired*, April 2006, pp. 111-112.
The creator of "The Sims," the best-selling PC game of all time, argues that gamers are learning in a "totally new way" and "treat the world as a place for creation." As guest editor, he invited other authors to write about the future and impact of video games for this special issue.

Reports

Federation of American Scientists, Summit on Educational Games: Harnessing the Power of Video Games for Learning, 2006; www.fas.org.
After a yearlong study, the federation recommended that the federal government fund research into the most effective educational features of video games and help develop new educational games.

Jenkins, Henry, *et al.*, *Confronting the Challenges of Participatory Culture*, 2006, *MacArthur Foundation*; www.digitallearning.macfound.org.
MIT's Jenkins and other technology experts argue that involvement in digital media has given young people

new skills and new scope for creativity, and they urge schools to do more to foster "media literacies."

***Kaiser Family Foundation*, "Generation M: Media in the Lives of 8-18 Year-olds," 2005; www.kff.org.** More than 80 percent of adolescents have a video console player at home, and the amount of time spent playing video games has increased in the past five years.

***Pew Internet & American Life Project*, *Teens and Technology*, July 27, 2005; www.pewinternet.org.** The vast majority of U.S. teens use the Internet and 81 percent of those play games online.

For More Information

Daedalus Project; www.nickyee.com/daedalus. The research findings of Stanford researcher Nick Yee, who has surveyed more than 35,000 players of online multiplayer games.

Federation of American Scientists, 1717 K St., N.W., Suite 209, Washington, DC 20036; (202) 546-3300; www.fas.org. Scientists' organization that has called on the federal government to use video games to strengthen education.

Games, Learning and Society, University of Wisconsin, Teacher Education Bldg., 225 North Mills St., Madison, WI 53706; (608) 263-4600; http://website.education.wisc.edu/gls/research.htm. Studies the learning potential of video games.

Global Kids, Inc., 561 Broadway, New York, NY 10012; (212) 226-0130; www.globalkids.org. Educates urban youth on international issues and is teaching disadvantaged teens to design and play games.

Kaiser Family Foundation, 2400 Sand Hill Rd., Menlo Park, CA 94025; (650) 854-9400; www.kff.org. Conducts surveys on media use by youth and teens.

MacArthur Foundation, 140 S. Dearborn St., Chicago, IL 60603; (312) 726-8000; www.macfound.org. Provides grants for research on the learning potential of video games and other digital media.

Pew Internet & American Life Project, 1615 L St., N.W., Suite 700, Washington, DC 20036; (202) 419-4500; www.pewinternet.org. Surveys youth media use.

15

Teacher Shortages

Should States Ease Certification Standards?

Brian Hansen

Millions of veteran teachers are expected to retire in the next few years, exacerbating the nation's already-serious teacher shortage. Growing school enrollments and the nationwide trend toward smaller classes are adding to the problem.

Corbis Images

From *CQ Researcher*,
August 24, 2001.

For Laverne Moss, North Carolina's teacher shortage was the ticket to a whole new life. It was January 1999, and Moss, then 36, had just finished a three-year hitch in the U.S. Army, where she served as a patient administrator at the 28th Combat Support Hospital at Fort Bragg, N.C.

While in the service, Moss had earned a bachelor's degree in business administration, but she had never taken any education classes. Moreover, Moss had no experience working around kids, aside from a pre-Army stint managing a convenience store.

Nonetheless, Moss was a hot commodity at Rochelle Middle School in Kinston, 70 miles southeast of Raleigh, the capital. The school desperately needed a mathematics teacher, and Moss not only had a math background but was willing to come to Rochelle for a starting salary under $26,000.

"The principal begged me to work for her," recalls Moss, who had learned about the job through the Department of Defense's Troops to Teachers program.[1] "They were really happy when I showed up for my first day, because they had had such a shortage problem."

Serious shortages plague many of the nation's public school systems, and they are expected to get worse. According to the Department of Education, U.S. schools will need 2.2 million new teachers over the next 10 years, or about 200,000 teachers per year.[2] That's double the number of teachers now graduating annually. In addition to graduates of college and university teacher-preparation programs, the new crop of teachers will include former teachers

Most School Districts Have Teacher Shortages

Nearly two-thirds of U.S. school districts have shortages of teachers in particular subjects, administrators say. More than a quarter of the urban districts have widespread shortages, and two-thirds of the suburban systems have shortages in particular areas.

Is your district facing a widespread shortage of teachers or shortages only in particular subject areas?

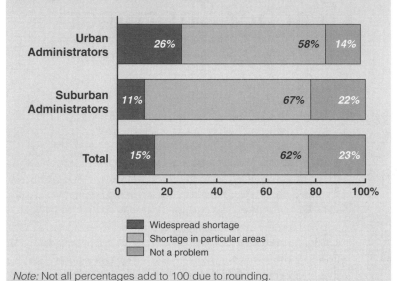

Note: Not all percentages add to 100 due to rounding.

Source: Public Agenda, April 2000

Robert F. Chase, president of the 2.6-million-member National Education Association (NEA), the nation's largest teachers' union. "Of the people who began teaching in urban areas this year, 50 percent will have left the profession five years from now. That's an enormous turnover."

Not all areas of the country have shortages. In fact, some states and localities enjoy an overabundance of qualified teachers. California, for example, has approximately 1.3 million credentialed teachers and only 280,000 teaching positions.[6] Nationwide, many areas have too many English, social studies and physical-education teachers, experts say.

However, severe teacher shortages are now commonplace at inner-city and rural schools, says William J. Hussar, an economist at the Department of Education. Even California has a serious shortage of teachers in inner-city schools, because many certified teachers are not willing to work in those areas. And most

re-entering the classroom after taking time off and graduates of alternative-certification programs, which can put non-teachers in front of a class after as little as four weeks' training. And for good or for ill, many of the new teachers will be "career-changers" like Moss.

Swelling school enrollments cause a large percentage of the nation's teacher shortages, along with the widespread retirements of veteran teachers and the nationwide movement to reduce class sizes.[3] The shortages persist despite the efforts of the nation's schools of education, which have churned out more than 100,000 teachers every year for the last 10 years.[4] Unlike in years past, however, many of the graduates — citing low pay, lack of institutional support and other reasons — are not entering the profession.[5] Others start teaching but abandon the classroom after just a few years.

"The shortage would be much less severe if we were only able to retain the people who begin teaching," says

schools struggle to find teachers in hard-to-staff subjects, such as mathematics, science, special education and foreign languages, Hussar adds.

"The shortages are real," he says.

But education experts and policy-makers bitterly disagree over how best to address the shortages. Some say that many of the proposed remedies could affect teacher quality — a hot-button issue for local school officials and national education experts alike.

Each state largely determines its own standards for certifying public school teachers. Some states attack their shortages by lowering, revising or even eliminating their teacher-qualification standards. For example, of the 39 states that require teachers to pass a basic-skills test before being certified, legislative loopholes in 36 of the states allow at least some failing candidates to enter the classroom with a temporary or provisional license.[7]

Indeed, more than one-fourth of all American teachers now begin work without having fully met state licensing standards, according to the National Commission on Teaching and America's Future, a New York-based group of education professionals dedicated to improving the quality of teaching nationwide. Moreover, as many as one-third of all teachers teach "out of field," or in areas where they have little or no training, notes commission Executive Director Linda Darling-Hammond, a professor of education at Stanford University. "That's not good for kids or for the teaching profession as a whole," she says.

Teacher quality certainly can be compromised through ill-advised schemes designed to combat teacher shortages, acknowledges Michael Poliakoff, president of the National Council on Teacher Quality, a Washington, D.C.-based group that assists states and districts in raising teacher quality.

But teacher quality does not necessarily improve as a result of state licensure or certification, no matter how rigorous the process, Poliakoff argues. On the contrary, states that attempt to bolster teacher quality by imposing more requirements on prospective teachers often dissuade qualified prospects from entering the profession, he says. For example, requiring math majors to take courses in pedagogy, or the art of teaching, before they can be certified has discouraged many highly qualified people from pursuing teaching, Poliakoff says.

"Certification does not equal qualification for teaching," Poliakoff says. "It's time we stopped putting roadblocks and obstacles in the path of highly qualified people who want to enter the teaching profession."

Critics like Poliakoff felt somewhat vindicated in 1998, when Massachusetts instituted a new teacher-certification exam and an astonishing 59 percent of seniors and recent graduates failed. Students from some of the state's best-known teacher colleges had some of the highest failure rates, and chagrined school officials vowed to revamp their curriculums.

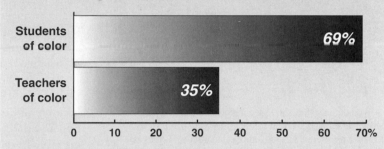

More Teacher Diversity Sought

More than two-thirds of the K-12 students in the nation's 57 largest urban systems are minorities, compared with only 35 percent of the teachers. Many educators say more minority teachers are needed to provide role models for students of color.

Minority Students and Teachers in the Largest Urban School Districts, 1999

Students of color: **69%**

Teachers of color: **35%**

Sources: Council of the Great City Schools, Department of Education, Recruiting New Teachers, Inc.

"These scores were a real gut check for us," said a Northeastern University spokeswoman, Janet Hookailo, after the scores were released. "We have put all our teacher-education classes under administration review."[8]

To attract newcomers during the current shortage, many school districts employ innovative programs to recruit and train new teachers and accelerate their entry into the profession.[9] Some of the programs, known as alternative-certification initiatives, put novices in classrooms after only four to six weeks of training — a vast departure from the four- or five-year preparatory programs required by most education schools.

Typically, the alternative programs place teachers in inner-city and other chronic-shortage areas. For example, Teach For America (TFA) provides an intensive five-week teacher-training program for young college graduates who did not study education. TFA corps members, as they are called, usually teach for two years in urban and rural schools in the neediest areas, such as South Central Los Angeles, the Mississippi Delta and Washington, D.C. (*See sidebar, p. 340.*)

First Lady Laura Bush, a former teacher, strongly supports the Troops to Teachers program, which has helped Moss and more than 16,000 other former service members into second careers as teachers.

Corbis Images

To overcome teacher shortages, many states permit "fast-track" certification programs that can put college graduates into classrooms after as little as four weeks' training. Critics fear that alternative-certification initiatives are lowering teacher-quality standards.

"My husband [President Bush] thought I was kidding when I told him I was going to call in the military" to address the teacher-shortage problem, Mrs. Bush told a Troops to Teachers rally at the San Diego Naval Station in March. "But he supports me 100 percent, and he supports you 100 percent. Troops to Teachers is designed especially for you, as you move from the battleships to the blackboards as America's newest teachers."[10]

But critics fear that Troops to Teachers and other, similar efforts to counter teacher shortages will compromise teacher-quality standards. A better way to attract new teachers, they say, is to revamp the public education system and give teachers the professional recognition and financial compensation they deserve. Raising teachers' pay and giving them more of a voice in policy matters will bolster the nation's teacher corps without lowering standards, the critics say.

As school districts around the country scramble for teachers this fall, here are some of the major questions being debated:

Should "fast-track" or alternative-certification programs be used to reduce teacher shortages?

"Fast-track" programs provide would-be teachers at all life stages with a rapid and relatively easy process for entering the teaching profession. Fast-tracking differs greatly from the traditional teacher-preparation route, which certifies young students as ready to enter the teaching profession after completing a state-approved teacher-education program at a four-year college or university.[11]

But in recent years, a combination of low teacher pay, lucrative employment opportunities outside of teaching and other factors has prompted many graduates of traditional teacher-education programs to not even try teaching, or to abandon the profession after only a few years. In response, many states and school districts turned to alternative teacher-preparation programs targeted at people who did not study education in college.[12]

Because graduates of fast-track programs haven't had time to take the pedagogy classes required by most state licensing authorities, they don't receive state certification prior to entering the classroom. Those who stay in teaching usually take the required education classes and become certified at a later date — but many do not. In states with severe teacher shortages, uncertified teachers with fast-track training often teach for years with "emergency" or "provisional" licenses.[13]

Despite the limited professional training they offer, fast-track programs are popular with critics of longer, more traditional teacher-education programs. Such programs, the critics say, train teachers in abstract pedagogical theories rather than in tangible, content-based subject matter. By contrast, they say, talented college graduates who get fast-track training often make better classroom teachers than teachers with years of pedagogical study at traditional schools of education.

Talented non-teaching professionals who want to go into education, however, often rule out teaching careers if fast-track programs are not available. "It's not reasonable to expect these people to give up their salaried jobs and go back to school so that they can get qualified to teach," says C. Emily Feistritzer, president of the National Center for Education Information, a nonpartisan research organization in Washington.

But proponents of traditional teacher education say "fast track" undercuts teacher quality standards and, therefore, is detrimental to students.

"We don't let scientists practice medicine like doctors just because they understand the chemistry," says Jean Miller, director of the Interstate New Teacher Assessment and Support Consortium, a Washington, D.C., group that works to advance the professionalism of teachers.

Moreover, allowing people to teach after only a few weeks of training is tantamount to treating kids like guinea pigs, Miller and other critics maintain.

Calling the guinea pig charge "utterly irresponsible," Poliakoff, of the National Council on Teacher Quality, argues there is no guarantee that teachers produced by education schools will be any more effective than those prepared by fast-track programs.

"A lot of people who go through the traditional programs turn out to be disasters in the classroom," he says.

Fast-track programs, Poliakoff says, are especially effective in bringing highly qualified teachers into hard-to-staff urban schools.

"Many alternatively certified teachers grew up in cities themselves, so they have particular knowledge, experience and empathy that they bring into their classrooms," Poliakoff says. "Alternative-certification programs are one of the best ways to obtain a more balanced and diverse teaching force for our urban schools."

David Haselkorn, president of Recruiting New Teachers, a Belmont, Mass., group dedicated to improving teacher training and recruitment, acknowledges that some alternative-certification programs maintain high teacher-quality standards. And fast-track programs, he says, can attract a diverse range of people to the teaching profession. But that diversity, he argues, does not guarantee success in the classroom.

"Too often, we put our most novice teachers in our hardest-to-staff schools and our most challenging classrooms, where we leave them to sink or swim," Haselkorn says. "Alternative-certification programs can ultimately end up shortchanging not only the recruits who are brought into the teaching profession in that manner but also the kids who wind up being the guinea pigs of the individuals who really struggle in their first years of teaching."

The notion that student achievement suffers under fast-track teachers has been widely promoted by

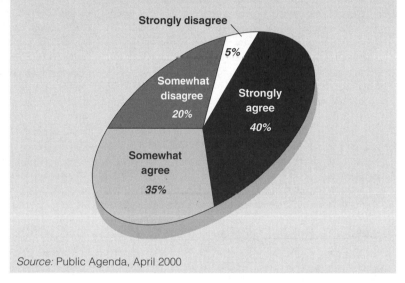

Most New Teachers Feel 'Seriously Underpaid'

Three-quarters of new public school teachers say they are "seriously underpaid" compared with a quarter who say they aren't.

"I am seriously underpaid." Do you agree strongly or somewhat with that statement? Asked of public school teachers with five years' experience or less.

Strongly disagree — 5%
Somewhat disagree — 20%
Strongly agree — 40%
Somewhat agree — 35%

Source: Public Agenda, April 2000

Darling-Hammond, of the National Commission on Teaching and America's Future.

"Students of teachers with little or no preparation for teaching learn less than students who have fully prepared teachers," says Darling-Hammond, a professor of education at Stanford University.

Students taught by alternatively certified teachers tested six points lower on the language-arts portion of the Iowa Test of Basic Skills than did students taught by traditionally prepared teachers, Darling-Hammond notes.[14] Studies also have found that fast-track teachers often experience difficulties in curriculum development, teaching methods, classroom management and student motivation, she says.[15]

But fast-track program proponents reject the argument that students learn less from teachers who entered the profession via non-traditional preparation programs. A study released last year found that students taught by teachers with probationary or emergency credentials performed just as well on some national standardized exams as

Innovative Incentives Hook New Teachers

With teacher shortages looming across the nation, many states and school districts have begun offering hefty bonuses and other innovative incentives — like "combat pay" and mortgage assistance — to lure teachers into their leaderless classrooms.

Sweetening the pot to attract new teachers is nothing new. For decades, states have offered scholarships and student-loan-forgiveness programs to get young people to teach in public schools, especially if they specialize in math, science or a foreign language and are willing to teach for a certain number of years in urban or rural schools. At least 27 states currently offer such programs to high school students and recent college graduates, according to a survey conducted by *Education Week*.[1] While 19 of the programs require participants to teach special subjects, like math or science, only 10 require or encourage recipients to teach in rural or urban schools.

Virginia Roach, deputy executive director of the National Association of State Boards of Education, is troubled at how few of the programs are designed to place teachers in inner-city and other troubled schools. "One of the biggest issues are blanket state policies that aren't refined enough to meet the real needs of the state," Roach said. "They just basically pump out more teachers."[2]

To make sure they are attracting new teachers to the districts where they are most needed, some states and school districts are offering large, one-time bonuses, and others are even recruiting teachers from overseas.

The signing bonuses are similar in principle — if not in size — to those commonly given to professional athletes. They are often coupled with fast-track teacher-preparation programs, which give young liberal arts graduates, as well as older "career-changers," a streamlined pathway to teaching. Massachusetts operates one of the most successful bonus programs. A few years ago, the state began offering $20,000 bonuses in exchange for promising to teach in the state for four years. Last year, more than 800 people from 36 states and two foreign countries applied for 165 slots in the state's intensive, seven-week teacher-preparation course. Many participants said the bonuses — which are paid out over the four years — helped them to survive financially during the summer between quitting their old jobs and starting to teach.

But for others, the accelerated pathway into teaching provided an even bigger payoff. "The traditional path would have been to go back to school, and I don't know if I could have made that kind of two-year commitment," said Diane Fowler, 51, who already holds a master's degree in history. "So to be able to complete this program in seven weeks is a big plus."[3]

However, some critics object to paying hefty bonuses to so-called crash-coursers, who typically lack four-year undergraduate degrees in education. "It's unfair to those people

students who had been taught by fully certified teachers, fast-track supporters note.[16] The study also found that students taught by teachers who majored in mathematics significantly outperformed students taught by former education majors who later went on to teach math. The authors of the study, Dan Goldhaber of the Washington, D.C.-based Urban Institute and Dominic Brewer of the RAND Corporation, in Santa Monica, Calif., conclude that the result should "cast doubt on assertions that standard certification should be required of all teachers."

Would raising teacher pay or overhauling the teacher-compensation system solve the teacher-shortage problem?

Low pay and the manner in which teacher salaries are set often get blamed for teacher shortages. Some experts say that simply boosting salaries could eliminate the problem. Others call for higher pay for teachers in hard-to-staff schools or subject areas, such as mathematics and special education. Still others advocate replacing the widely used uniform salary schedules with merit-pay systems, which link higher salaries with demonstrated teaching competence or better student performance.

The nation's two largest teachers' unions — the NEA and the American Federation of Teachers (AFT) — both have long advocated wage hikes for all teachers. According to the AFT's annual salary survey, the average K-12 teacher earned $41,820 in 1999-2000.[17] The average for first-year teachers was $27,989, but beginning salaries varied substantially by state, with neophytes in North Dakota earning an average of $20,422.

who . . . have busted their backs for 20 years," said Joseph Gauvain, president of a local teachers' union in Lynn, Mass.[4]

Other school districts go to global lengths to snare teachers. In the past two years, recruiters from Maryland have traveled to India while those from several California districts have tried the Philippines and other distant nations. In New York City, Schools Chancellor Harold Levy has proposed hiring as many as 800 foreign teachers this fall, and is even providing immigration lawyers to help facilitate their visa applications. "We have to recruit in every conceivable place where we might find certified, qualified teachers," Levy said.[5]

But not all education experts support recruiting teachers from abroad. Houston teachers' union President Gayle Fallon objects to her school district's recruiting in Moscow. "All these games to attract people are nothing more than a Band-Aid," said Fallon, who blames low pay — not a general lack of qualified people — for problems in recruiting and retaining good teachers.[6]

Instead of upping salaries, some states and school districts offer financial incentives to help with home buying. A program in Connecticut provides low-interest mortgages and down-payment assistance to teachers who work in needy communities and "high-priority" subject areas, such as math and science. Similarly, a California program offers $7,500 housing loans to teachers in low-performing schools. And in Mississippi, teachers can get up to $6,000 for down payments and closing costs on houses in areas hardest hit by teacher shortages.[7]

Meanwhile, federal programs that enabled teachers and police officers to purchase federally subsidized houses at half their listed prices were suspended for 120 days in late March, after allegations that several dozen police officers had abused the programs' occupancy rules. The Officer Next Door and Teacher Next Door programs, which were restarted late this summer, are designed to revitalize down-at-the-heels urban neighborhoods.[8]

Still, most housing incentives only mask the much bigger problem of low teacher salaries, maintains David Haselkorn, president of Recruiting New Teachers, a Belmont, Mass.-based teacher-advocacy group.

"The issue is not so much the cost of housing," Haselkorn said, "but the teacher salaries relative to the local labor markets."[9]

---

[1] Lynn Olson, "Sweetening the Pot," *Education Week*, Jan. 13, 2000.

[2] *Ibid.*

[3] Quoted in Jeff Archer, "Mass. 'Bonus Babies' Get Crash Course," *Education Week*, Sept. 6, 2000.

[4] Quoted in "Teacher Recruitment: Pulling Out All the Stops," *American Teacher*, March 2001.

[5] Quoted in Jessica Kowal, "Levy Seeks to Hire Foreign Teachers," *New York Newsday*, May 9, 2001.

[6] *American Teacher, op. cit.*

[7] See Michelle Galley, "For Sale: Affordable Housing for Teachers," *Education Week*," March 7, 2001.

[8] Department of Housing and Urban Development press release, Aug. 1, 2001.

[9] Galley, *op. cit.*

"The teacher shortage plaguing school districts nationwide will not abate unless salaries improve," AFT President Sandra Feldman says.

But Public Agenda frames the pay issue somewhat differently. In a report released last year, "A Sense of Calling: Who Teaches and Why," the New York-based public policy organization found that low pay is a major reason young college graduates don't become teachers. However, 86 percent of the teachers surveyed said they would choose better-behaved students and more supportive parents over a significantly higher salary. (*See graph, p. 342.*) Similarly, 82 percent of teachers would prefer more supportive administrators to more money. And 74 percent of teachers would choose to work at a school with an educational mission similar to their own, as opposed to one that paid them a significantly higher salary.[10]

"This study shows that policy-makers would absolutely be missing the mark if they think that higher salaries are the magic bullet that will keep new teachers in the classroom," says Public Agenda President Deborah Wadsworth. "Higher salaries, by themselves, are not going to head off the teacher shortages that have been widely predicted."

Education experts also disagree about paying teachers more for working in hard-to-staff inner-city or rural schools, or for teaching certain subjects, such as mathematics and special education. Economics professors Michael Podgursky at the University of Missouri-Columbia and Dale Ballou at the University of Massachusetts-Amherst note the irony that many schools have trouble recruiting teachers in fields that command high salaries outside of education, such as mathematics

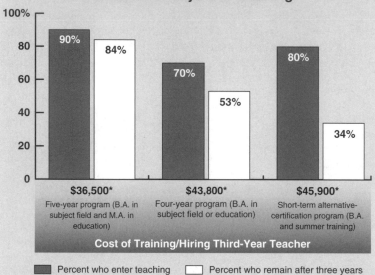

Teachers With Most Training Stay Longest

Far more students who took five-year teacher-training programs actually went into teaching and stayed in teaching than students who took shorter programs. In addition, teachers with the most training were cheapest to replace after three years.

Average Retention Rates for Different Pathways Into Teaching

	Five-year program (B.A. in subject field and M.A. in education) $36,500*	Four-year program (B.A. in subject field or education) $43,800*	Short-term alternative-certification program (B.A. and summer training) $45,900*
Percent who enter teaching	90%	70%	80%
Percent who remain after three years	84%	53%	34%

Cost of Training/Hiring Third-Year Teacher

■ Percent who enter teaching   □ Percent who remain after three years

* Includes cost of teacher preparation, recruitment, induction and replacement.

Source: National Center for Education Statistics

"The salaries paid to teachers are pretty competitive when you're competing for liberal arts graduates," Ballou says. "But the sciences are way behind. It therefore stands to reason that schools would be able to attract more applicants to teach these types of subjects if they paid more."

That's a troubling proposal for the NEA's Chase. He rejects the notion that public education should be reformed through the application of marketplace solutions, as the Bush administration and many conservative think tanks advocate.

"Allowing salaries to be determined by marketplace values could very well result in another set of problems," Chase says. "I don't know how we can use the promise of higher pay to attract people to chronic-shortage areas without negatively impacting on the morale of other teachers."

Likewise, Chase opposes merit pay, which pegs compensation to teaching competency, often based on students' performance on standardized tests and similar benchmarks. Merit-pay plans differ greatly from the traditional compensation model, in which teachers are paid according to their years of experience and the educational credits or degrees they have accumulated. Merit-pay plans, Chase says, do not recognize the complex challenges teachers confront in the classroom, or the difficulties they face trying to implement new, higher, state-based standards. "The issue is teacher quality," he says. "We are looking for an opportunity for our members to explore creative [salary] approaches that recognize excellence and attract and keep high-quality teachers. Arbitrary, top-down merit-pay systems do not" recognize excellence.

Some experts believe that merit pay would lessen teacher shortages by making teaching more attractive to talented college graduates and mid-career professionals, as well as encourage outstanding teachers to remain in their classrooms.

and science. During the technology boom of the 1990s, graduates with math or science expertise were heavily recruited for higher-paying jobs in the computer technology field.

Because the traditional teacher-compensation system is not designed to respond to "market realities," schools cannot address their shortages by raising pay in such "hot" specialty areas, Podgursky and Ballou explain. Consequently, schools are often forced to hire unqualified candidates to teach mathematics, science and other shortage-plagued courses, the researchers note. Moreover, without pay incentives, veteran teachers at inner-city schools often use their seniority to transfer to more desirable schools, leaving the neediest children to be taught by the youngest and most inexperienced teachers, they point out.

"The standard pay model contributes to the teacher shortage problem because people can't make more money if they excel," says Krista Kafer, a policy analyst at the Heritage Foundation, a conservative think tank. "With merit pay, high quality teachers can make more money."

But other policy experts see serious flaws in merit pay. Compensation based on teacher evaluations, they argue, can be little more than popularity contests. Nor is it fair to link teacher compensation to student performance, they contend, because student achievement is determined in large part by socioeconomic background and other factors beyond teachers' control. Barbara E. Kerr, vice president of the 295,000-member California Teachers Association, says that merit-pay schemes make teachers reluctant to work at schools with difficult-to-reach children.

"Who will want to teach the poor students?" Kerr says. "What about the students who don't speak English as well? Everyone wants teachers to receive higher wages, but merit pay just won't work."

BACKGROUND

Early Reforms

Teacher shortages were not a problem in the United States before 1830, when the nation's free public school system was established. Wealthy families typically sent their children to private tutors or elite academies, while the children of less affluent families attended poorly maintained "public" schools.

But because school attendance was not mandatory, the demand for quality teachers was almost non-existent at early public schools. Absenteeism ran rampant, and school terms rarely lasted more than a few weeks.

The public schools received little support from local or state taxes, so they were generally in a perpetual state of disrepair. Likewise, the teachers were often young, inexperienced and untrained. Churches operated many schools, and people hired to teach in them were selected on the basis of moral character, not knowledge of a particular subject or training in education. Many teachers had only rudimentary skills in reading, writing and arithmetic. Not surprisingly, teaching generally was viewed as a second-class occupation.

Increasing teachers' wages is one of the best ways to retain older teachers, the two largest teachers' unions say. The average U.S. teacher earns $41,820, according to the American Federation of Teachers. The average for first-year teachers is $27,989.

By the mid-19th century, the nation's makeshift public-education system had become inadequate as the widespread use of indentured servitude collapsed under the weight of a host of social reforms and an expanding national economy. The newly progressive society required a better and more uniform public school system to prepare young people for the jobs associated with the burgeoning economic transformation.

Prompted by education reformers such as Horace Mann, Henry Barnard and Catherine Beecher, cities and states began to establish free, non-sectarian schools for all religious denominations and social classes. Known as "common schools," the precursors of contemporary public schools were designed to give young people the skills and knowledge necessary to be productive members of the fledgling democratic society.

Some reformers also thought the early public schools would curb juvenile delinquency, especially in impoverished urban areas. Toward that end, states began to enact compulsory school attendance laws in the latter half of the 19th century. In 1852, Massachusetts ordered children between ages 8 and 14 to attend school for at least three months each year. By 1918, all the states had compulsory school attendance laws.

First Shortages

The advent of common schools and compulsory attendance prompted the nation's first widespread teacher

CHRONOLOGY

1800s *The demand for more and better teachers grows as the nation strives to establish a free public school system.*

1839 At the urging of education reformer Horace Mann, the first teacher-training institute — dubbed a "normal" school — is established in Massachusetts.

1852 Massachusetts passes the nation's first compulsory school-attendance law, creating an immediate need for more teachers.

1910s-1950s *Teacher training shifts from normal schools to liberal arts colleges and universities, many of which lower their academic standards to accommodate growing numbers of students.*

1910s At the urging of educators, the licensing of new teachers shifts from local officials to state bureaucracies.

1918 Compulsory school-attendance laws are on the books in all states.

1946 The union-backed National Commission on Teacher Education and Professional Standards is formed to work for higher teacher-quality standards, which are being compromised in some locations struggling with teacher-shortage problems.

1954 U.S. Supreme Court rules in *Brown v. Board of Education* that schools can no longer be racially segregated.

1960s-1980s *Teachers struggle for professional recognition as concerns about education quality prompt reforms.*

1965 Congress passes the Elementary and Secondary Education Act (ESEA), which strengthens programs for educationally deprived children in low-income areas. The act also provides incentives for the professional development of teachers, administrators and other school staff at schools plagued by teacher shortages.

1970s California, Minnesota and Oregon become the first of a dozen states to create autonomous boards to control standards for teachers.

1983 U.S. Department of Education publishes "A Nation at Risk," which holds teachers largely responsible for the "rising tide of mediocrity" in American schools.

1984 New Jersey permits an abbreviated "alternative" route for certifying teachers, in part to offset teacher shortages.

1990s-Present *Innovative programs are launched to combat serious teacher shortages.*

1990 Teach For America, founded by Princeton University student Wendy Kopp, places about 500 recent college graduates in teaching jobs in the nation's neediest public schools. By 2000, the program will recruit more than 5,000 new teachers.

1994 Federal government launches Troops to Teachers to help retiring members of the armed forces to find jobs as public school teachers.

1998 President Bill Clinton launches federal effort to help school districts hire 100,000 fully qualified teachers. Massachusetts offers $20,000 "signing bonuses" to entice college graduates in other careers to take jobs as teachers.

1999 Forty-one states and the District of Columbia have some type of "alternative" teacher-licensing program in place.

2000 A coalition of education-policy groups concludes that the largest school districts will experience "severe" teacher shortages in mathematics, science and other subjects for at least the next five years.

2001 President Bush submits to Congress his plan to reauthorize the Elementary and Secondary Education Act. Versions of the bill passed by the House and Senate both contain provisions to attract and retain highly qualified teachers but do not provide funding for former President Clinton's program to hire 100,000 new teachers.

shortages.[19] Mann played a key role in addressing the need for more and better-trained teachers by spearheading the establishment of the first state-sponsored teacher-training institution. Built in Lexington, Mass., in 1839, it was dubbed a "normal" school because it provided prospective teachers with systematic "norms" designed to ensure high levels of teaching expertise.

States built normal schools at a rapid pace in the second half of the 19th century, as the nation's new common schools scrambled to find sufficient numbers of teachers. By the turn of the century, there were 127 state normal schools and slightly more private normal schools. Nonetheless, they weren't able to turn out enough teachers for the nation's new common schools, especially in rural areas.

"During the whole 19th century, there was a chronic shortage of teachers," noted David F. Labaree, a professor of education at Michigan State University.[20]

In the first few decades of the 20th century, four-year liberal arts colleges and universities largely took over the task of preparing teachers, establishing "departments of education" for teacher training.[21]

Meanwhile, at the urging of professional educators, state bureaucracies began to wield greater control over the licensing, or "certification," of education school graduates. This represented a major departure from previous licensing practices, which had vested local officials with the authority to decide who was qualified to teach in their schools.

The move made the process of certifying teachers far less responsive to localized market needs, and according to some education experts it is the main cause of teacher shortages today.

But many education professionals welcomed the centralization of the licensure process and the new university-based education departments, which they believed would bolster the legitimacy of the oft-maligned teaching profession.

Lowering Standards

Still, teacher shortages continued to plague the nation's fledgling public school system during the first decades of the 20th century. University-based "teachers' colleges" of the period grappled with a situation they face even today: Many young students enrolled not to become teachers but because they wanted college degrees to bolster their chances of finding decent employment in other professions.

Some state legislatures reacted to the resultant teacher shortages by lowering admission and graduation standards at their state teachers' colleges. Lowering standards, many lawmakers believed, could legitimately and innocuously bolster the overall supply of teachers.

Then as now, professional educators led by the NEA tried to block all attempts to lower standards for teacher-preparation programs. In 1946, the teachers' union formed the National Commission on Teacher Education and Professional Standards (TEPS) to spearhead the push for higher teacher-quality standards. In the 1950s the battle was joined by several other organizations, including the National Council for Accreditation of Teacher Education (NCATE), a coalition of policy-makers and professional educators that bestows its imprimatur on worthy teacher-preparation programs. Programs that pass NCATE muster typically require extensive coursework in pedagogy, the study of teaching. Until the early 1980s, pedagogy-based teacher-preparation programs — which can take up to five years at some institutions — were the primary gateway to the teaching profession.

New Jersey broke with that tradition in 1984, when lawmakers enacted legislation that established an "alternative" route for certifying teachers.[22] The move was prompted, in part, by a teacher shortage. Under the state's new program, college graduates without an education background could begin teaching after completing a short training course administered by the hiring school district. The new teachers later could become fully certified teachers by completing a 200-hour training program in "essential professional knowledge and skills," which was administered on nights and weekends. Texas launched a similar program the following year in Houston, based on teacher-shortage projections.

Today, 41 states and the District of Columbia have alternative-certification programs. As of 1999, the programs had licensed more than 125,000 teachers, according to the National Center for Education Information. Many of the programs are designed to place new teachers in hard-to-staff schools and subject areas.

"These alternative routes are effective in getting more people of color into teaching, and in placing teachers in classrooms where the demand for teachers is greatest," says Feistritzer, the group's president.

How Caring, Young Teachers . . .

A dozen years ago, a 21-year-old Princeton University senior named Wendy Kopp founded Teach For America to train young teachers for hard-to-staff schools. Since then, TFA has sent more than 7,000 recent college graduates who did not study education into the nation's neediest urban and rural areas. Corps members take an intensive, five-week teacher-training program before beginning their two-year teaching commitments. Here are some of their stories:

• **Maurice Rabb** taught kindergarten in Los Angeles after majoring in Chinese at Georgetown University. When he started, 16 of his 20 students were not academically ready for school. So Maurice set about helping his students catch up.

He built a powerful culture within his classroom; when children would distract their peers, the other kindergartners would ask, "Does that help us read and write?" When he realized he needed more teaching time, he organized reading workshops for the students' parents to explain how to read to children in a way that promotes comprehension.

By year's end, all of Maurice's students were fully prepared academically for first grade.

• **Nicole Sherrin** taught seventh and eighth grade math in Phoenix after graduating in psychology from Boston College. All of her students were from low-income families and 50 percent were labeled Limited English Proficient. Nicole built positive peer pressure by organizing her students in groups and rewarding them when all their members achieved. She got to know her students and their families outside of school to build their trust and investment. And she brought in speakers from the community to talk about college and the importance of school. Two-thirds of Nicole's students performed in the top category on the district's achievement test, with only 2 percent at the lowest level.

• **Paola Ramirez** graduated in art history from the University of Notre Dame, then went back home to teach in an elementary school special-education class. "As a person who grew up in East Los Angeles, I feel that one of my greatest accomplishments was being able to communicate to my students and their parents that with a lot of hard work they too would be able to go to college. I helped six children exit the Special Education department and move into General

Marika Paez teaches at the John A. Reisenbach Charter School in New York City. Some 7,000 young college graduates have joined Teach For America since its start in 1988.

Education, and I also helped one of my students get identified for 'gifted' programs.

"One of my greatest accomplishments was helping my students understand their different learning styles, which helped them gain patience, pride, and success. They looked forward to coming to their reading, writing or math class because they knew the many years of failing and frustration were now over."

• **Liz Marcell** taught pre-K special education in the Rio Grande Valley after graduating in Italian from Smith College. When Liz took over, her class was not much more than day care, with no real academic expectations for the children. Liz knew little about her students' disabilities, but she dove in and learned everything she could — from the Internet, from special-education resource staff and from her students' parents. She developed a long-term plan and a structured routine for teaching, enlisting parents' help and even learning Spanish to better communicate with them.

Liz's 13 students included three who were considered mentally retarded, two with cerebral palsy, two with Down's Syndrome and one who had witnessed severe abuse and was non-verbal. By the end of the first year, all of the students had made significant progress, and six entered first grade on a regular education track.

• **Camika Royal** taught seventh-grade language arts in Baltimore after majoring in English literature and political

. . . Create Classroom Miracles

science at North Carolina Central University. Camika's students' reading ability ranged from below second-grade to 12th-grade level. Camika created a culture of respect, and organized her classroom in a way that would challenge all her students. In her first year, the school district instructional supervisor said she was perhaps the best teacher he had ever observed. While 50 percent of the students in Camika's school typically pass the state writing exam, 70 percent of her students did.

• **Brent Maddin** taught high school science in southern Louisiana after graduating from Arizona State University. Brent did whatever it takes to help his students meet high academic expectations, including holding three-hour Thursday night study sessions at the local McDonald's. "As I reflect back on my two-year commitment," he says, "I think of the Saturday practices that transported the Academic Decathlon team to a third-place state finish; I think of the Thursday nights at McDonald's; I think of the pride my students shared when they raised their state science exam scores 20 percent; I think of Jeohn and the look on his face when we opened his acceptance to Yale after spending the entire winter break working through 12 drafts of his application; and I think about how often I was struck by the feeling that I was really the student learning from all those around me."

• **Greg Wong** graduated from Western Washington University in human services and was assigned to tiny Helena, Ark. Despite initial misgivings over not working in an urban, low-income community, Greg went off to the TFA summer training institute, where he learned the teaching strategies he used so effectively in his classes.

"I instill a sense of urgency in my kids," Greg says. "I insist that they believe everything we do matters, that we have to learn it right now. And I try to connect with kids. I respect them, and they respect themselves and me."

Greg used his leadership to secure a grant to bring computers to every classroom at his school. "They're good computers," he boasts. "Pentium II's." He also assumed the leadership of his school's quiz-bowl team. Greg again made his students view it with a sense of urgency. He bought team T-shirts, insisted they call him coach, and instituted rigorous expectations for discipline and sportsmanship. Last year, they finished the regular

Reed Dyer is in his fourth year with Teach For America. Corps members initially commit to two years but often continue teaching longer.

season undefeated and finished in the top 10 at the state tournament, the only team finishing that high with a roster of exclusively or even mostly African-American players.

Greg says teaching in the deep South has helped him better understand poverty.

"The rhetoric of poverty is never totally accurate," he says. "My kids are seen as poor, black, oppressed, as just victims. Before, I bought into that rhetoric of victimization. As I work with them, I tell them what others think about them. They have to be personally responsible for combating that impression, for overcoming their challenges. I have to enable them to exercise personal responsibility, but to do so in a cooperative way."

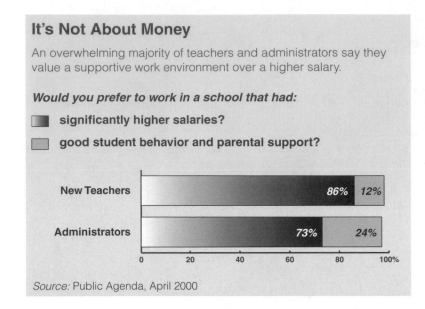

It's Not About Money

An overwhelming majority of teachers and administrators say they value a supportive work environment over a higher salary.

Would you prefer to work in a school that had:

■ **significantly higher salaries?**

■ **good student behavior and parental support?**

New Teachers: 86% 12%
Administrators: 73% 24%

Source: Public Agenda, April 2000

Still, the proliferation of alternative-certification programs troubles many education professionals, even if they do relieve some of the teacher shortages. Programs that give short shrift to pedagogy, these experts say, weaken the entire teaching profession, which in turn will lead to poorer student performance and more teacher shortages in the long run.

"Americans wouldn't dream of entrusting our homes or our health to an unlicensed professional — or one with fly-by-night training," said the NEA's Chase. "Yet again and again, we entrust the education of our children to teachers without adequate licensure. Such a lack of quality control would be criminally negligent in any other profession."[23]

CURRENT SITUATION

Revamping ESEA

Teacher shortages have been a hot topic in Washington in recent months, as Congress has debated President Bush's plan for overhauling the 1965 Elementary and Secondary Education Act (ESEA). Bush's plan, dubbed "No Child Left Behind," would prompt the most sweeping changes in public education in 35 years. Both the House and Senate had passed modified versions of the plan by mid-June; a conference committee is expected to reconcile the two measures into a single bill for Bush's signature sometime this fall.

The two versions of the president's plan share several common elements. For example, both bills call on states to administer standardized reading and mathematics tests to K-12 students. States that fail to do so, under both measures, would not be eligible to receive federal education funds. Likewise, both bills would provide federal monies to bolster student performance at "failing" schools. And both would provide penalties for schools that fail to improve.

While both bills authorize funds for teacher recruitment and training programs, neither measure funds the initiatives at the levels that had been sought by Democrats and favored by many professional educators. On May 15, on a party-line vote, Senate Republicans killed a teacher-hiring amendment offered by Sen. Patty Murray, D-Wash. It would have earmarked $2.4 billion in the coming school year to hire tens of thousands of new teachers at impoverished and understaffed urban and rural schools. By fiscal 2005, the federal assistance for hiring teachers would have totaled $7.1 billion.

Murray's amendment would have reauthorized former President Bill Clinton's 1998 program to help needy school districts hire 100,000 new teachers. Nearly 40,000 new teachers were hired under the Clinton program, which aimed to reduce class sizes at the most overcrowded and understaffed schools. Smaller classes help school districts recruit and retain high-quality teachers, Murray noted, lambasting her Republican colleagues for voting against the measure.

"Senate Republicans told parents, students and teachers that smaller classes are not a national priority," Murray said after her initiative was defeated. "[This] vote was a test of whether this Congress is serious about giving schools the tools they need to improve. On today's partisan vote, Congress failed that test."[24]

Senate Republicans were quick to reject Murray's analysis, noting that the Bush education plan would provide $3 billion that states could spend on either class reduction or teacher-quality initiatives. The president's plan lets local educators determine how the funds are spent, said Sen. Bill Frist, R-Tenn.

"Who best decides how to . . . boost student achievement?" Frist asked. "Is it Washington, D.C., the federal government? Or is it parents, local communities, local schools?"[25]

Murray wasn't the only lawmaker who tried this year to incorporate Clinton's teacher-hiring scheme into Bush's education plan. In March, Rep. David Wu, D-Ore., introduced a measure that would have set aside $2 billion next year for states to recruit, hire and train new elementary school teachers. The bill, which is intended to reduce class size, has more than 100 co-sponsors. However, Wu spokeswoman Holly Armstrong predicts that the bill will remain bottled up in the Republican-controlled Subcommittee on Education Reform, where it has languished since late May.

"The bill puts forth a solid idea, but it has the unfortunate stigma of being associated with Bill Clinton, so it's something that the Republicans don't want to move," Armstrong says. That's a cop-out for the Heritage Foundation's Kafer. According to her, teacher-hiring proposals like Wu's are simply not grounded in reality.

"We've already seen some significant reductions in class size since 1970 . . . but we haven't seen corresponding changes in [student achievement] scores," Kafer says. "Class size doesn't make a difference — changes come by getting highly qualified teachers into classrooms."

States' Efforts

Indeed, recruiting and keeping high-quality teachers is now a top local and state priority. Low pay has long been viewed by experts as the prime deterrent to attracting more quality teachers, so many states and school districts are considering a wide variety of financial incentives to skilled educators. Some states have instituted financial rewards for high school-level performance, or for teachers who acquire and demonstrate particular knowledge and skills. In addition, several states and districts are implementing new teacher-pay schedules that revolve around assessments of teacher knowledge and skill, such as earning "national" certification through the National Board for Professional Teaching Standards.

Other states are implementing more rigorous tests of subject-matter knowledge for prospective teachers, who are typically required to pass tests of basic skills,

Council of Great City Schools

Minority teachers provide important role models in schools with high minority enrollments, such as Houston's Will Rogers Elementary School (above). Two-thirds of the K-12 students in the nation's biggest urban systems are minorities compared with only 35 percent of the teachers.

subject-matter knowledge and pedagogy in order to be "licensed" by a state. Critics have long complained that the tests are too easy and the passing thresholds too low. The Massachusetts Board of Education addressed the issue last fall, when it approved new teacher-certification regulations aimed at boosting the subject-matter knowledge of prospective teachers. Chairman James Peyser called the new regulations "long overdue."[26]

But a report released in March by the National Research Council found that most licensure tests provide an "inadequate basis" for determining who would make a good classroom teacher.[27] "When screening teacher candidates, greater attention should be paid to factors that more directly relate to student learning," says David Z. Robinson, who chaired the committee that wrote the report. Robinson, a retired executive vice president of the Carnegie Corporation of New York, says that "A variety of assessments should be used, including evaluations of candidates' teaching performance and . . . their ability to work effectively with a diverse student population."

Faced with an "extreme" shortage of teachers, School Superintendent T.C. Wallace, left, of Mount Clements, Mich., prospects last May at a job fair at Jackson State University, Jackson, Miss. He discusses job opportunities with Cedric Johnson, a coach and instructor at Terry High School in Terry, Miss.

Meanwhile, state departments of education are currently poring through reams of data collected from their teacher-preparation programs. Under a measure passed by Congress in 1998, all states must compile "report cards" on the programs, ranking them on criteria such as enrollment levels, faculty-to-student ratios and licensure pass rates. The legislation was passed after years of complaints that teacher-training programs were unwilling to make the changes necessary to prepare greater numbers of highly competent teachers. The report cards, which are intended to improve the accountability of teacher-training programs, will be submitted to the Education Department next year.

Some critics, though, maintain that the report cards won't provide meaningful information to Congress, the public or to the teacher-preparation programs themselves. They're also troubled over the law's requirement that preparation programs be "ranked" according their purported quality. Such a ranking scheme could be grossly distorted by the news media or local education officials, critics charge.

"If the intent is to demand greater accountability or to punish colleges of education, I think [the federal government] could have found a better way to do it," says Feistritzer, of the National Center for Education Information. "The report is going to be relatively meaningless."

OUTLOOK

Bush's Plan

Some experts fear that the teaching profession is poised to become less appealing — and thus more prone to personnel shortages — because of the testing-based education plan that President Bush is expected to sign into law this fall, once a compromise bill is hashed out by House-Senate conferees. The plan requires public schools to test all students in grades 3 through 8 in reading and mathematics every year. Backers say the tests will bolster student achievement and give parents and public officials a way to assess the performance of teachers and school districts.

Many veteran teachers, though, say that mandated testing hampers their teaching effectiveness.

"What happens is it becomes very clear that you have to teach to the test," said Eva Morris, who teaches pre-algebra at South Park Middle School in Corpus Christi, Texas. "There's not enough time for enrichment. And there's also not enough time for review, because there's so much to cover."[28]

Currently, every state except Iowa requires that students be tested in math and reading sometime between grades 3 and 8. In most states, students are tested on only three or fewer occasions during that period. Only 15 states, Texas among them, currently test students every year, as the Bush plan would require.[29]

Many teachers share Morris's feelings about government-mandated testing. According to a recent survey, nearly seven in 10 public school teachers complained that their approach to instruction was shaped "too much" or "somewhat too much" by state tests. Moreover, about two-thirds of these teachers said that state-mandated tests forced them to ignore important material because it would not be covered on the tests. And that could portend problems for the teaching profession once the Bush education plan is implemented, says Haselkorn of Recruiting New Teachers.

"We've certainly seen an increase in news reports and anecdotal reports of teachers who are leaving the profession . . . because they feel that testing requirements constrain the curriculum and constrain their teaching," he says. "I think [requirements] will have a negative effect if they force teachers to teach less creatively and less fully than they otherwise would."

Should school districts use uncertified teachers in chronic-shortage areas?

YES
Michael B. Poliakoff
President, National Council on Teacher Quality and former Pennsylvania Deputy Secretary for Postsecondary and Higher Education

Written for *The CQ Researcher*, July 2001

School districts should be empowered to hire good teachers with or without certification, not only in chronic-shortage areas but wherever they are needed. Uncertified teachers are among the best teachers we have in many different settings. Affluent parents may pay $15,000 per year to send their children to private schools where virtually none of the teachers are certified. Many successful public charter schools have the advantage of hiring teachers on the basis of qualification, rather than a teaching credential. And there are superb teachers at community colleges who do not have certification but often have experience with multiple learning styles and students from disadvantaged backgrounds.

It is a mistake to believe that traditional teacher preparation and certification offer quality assurance. The National Center for Education Statistics (NCES) report "Condition of Education 2001" tells us that education majors, principally in the elementary track, tend to have the worst SAT or ACT scores among college majors. An earlier NCES report tells of rampant grade inflation in education-school courses. A recent study of education schools shows that they often do a brisk business retraining the teachers after their schools complain of their poor performance.

Among those education schools accredited by the prestigious National Council on Accreditation of Teacher Education (NCATE) are a number with appalling failure rates on state licensure exams. And on top of all that, a recent Public Agenda survey showed that 62 percent of the new teachers believed their preparation program only did a "fair" or "poor" job getting them ready for the pressures of teaching.

Alternative-certification programs have had great success in attracting fine teachers to public schools by offering them streamlined entry paths. Some 25 percent of New Jersey's teachers now enter the classroom each year through alternative routes. They generally have higher licensure-examination scores, stronger minority representation and less first-year attrition than their peers from conventional training programs.

For emergency hires — and other hires, as well — we should build on this model: screen candidates to ensure they have a college degree; perform a criminal background check; provide an intensive orientation program; require them to pass the appropriate licensure exams to continue in their positions and support new hires with experienced mentor teachers.

Our children deserve the chance to have terrific teachers; it's time to let public schools look beyond the education schools, to look beyond certification for true qualification.

NO
Barnett Berry
Director for Policy and State Partnerships, National Commission on Teaching and America's Future

Written for *The CQ Researcher*, July 2001

It is not necessary to lower standards to attract more teachers. The simple fact is that the current staffing crisis has been caused mainly by the inability of schools and districts to retain qualified and veteran teachers. In light of mounting evidence connecting teacher quality to student achievement, the question to ask is, "What should school districts do to attract and keep qualified teachers?"

Richard Ingersoll of the University of Pennsylvania found that the demand for new teachers is not primarily due to expanding student enrollments but rather to qualified teachers migrating from their jobs. Ingersoll concluded that the most effective way to decrease the demand for teachers is to decrease turnover, by giving teachers better salaries, more support from administrators and a greater voice in decision-making.

The National Commission on Teaching and America's Future works with a group of partner states to develop compensation systems that reward teachers' skills. To help fill positions in high-need areas, we advocate incentives that include student-loan forgiveness, portability of teacher credentials and pensions and scholarships for teachers who pledge to work in shortage areas.

Many states are filling the teacher gap by recruiting through alternative-certification programs, but their quality varies widely. There are high-quality alternative programs for mid-career entrants, usually about nine to 15 months, which combine rigorous coursework about teaching and learning with extended clinical training. At the other end of the spectrum are "crash-course" programs, which typically give post-baccalaureate candidates four to 12 weeks of teacher training, leaving them largely unprepared for the challenges they will face. Nationally, over 60 percent who enter teaching this way are gone by their third year. And underqualified teachers are disproportionately to be found in schools characterized by low academic performance and high poverty.

Research has shown that well-prepared certified teachers are more likely to be effective with students and more likely to stay at their jobs. Further, such teachers have the knowledge and skills necessary to ensure that all students can meet high academic standards. This includes an understanding of how to teach students from diverse backgrounds; an ability to assess why students are learning (or not); how to connect content to what children know, and how to motivate them.

There are solutions to the teacher shortage. A collapse of standards that would entrust the neediest student populations to the least qualified, and least likely to stay in teaching, is not among them.

Troops to Teachers

Retired Navy officer Ben Whetstone now teaches science at a middle school in Pensacola, Fla. The Department of Defense's Troops to Teachers program helps reduce teacher shortages by encouraging service members to start second careers as teachers.

Kafer, at the Heritage Foundation, acknowledges that state-mandated tests certainly can be a "burden" to effective teaching if they're poorly crafted or overused. But she says good tests are "important diagnostic tools" that can help teachers assess the quality of their instruction.

"Teachers who flat-out say that they don't like tests and don't want to use them are not the teachers I would want for my child," Kafer says.

Meanwhile, as a congressional conference committee drafts a final version of the Bush education plan, debate continues to simmer over the policies and programs implemented to stave off further teacher shortages.

Secretary of Education Roderick R. Paige dove headfirst into the debate in June, telling a conference organized by the Council for Basic Education, a group promoting high academic standards, that alternative-certification programs could "remedy the teacher shortage quickly."[30] Many in the audience of educators did not embrace Paige's prescription, fearing that the nation's burgeoning reliance on alternative certification will hurt the teaching profession in the long run.

Still, Paige's brief comments spoke volumes about how the Bush administration may address teacher shortages, according to council President Christopher T. Cross. "He went farther than most in the administration in saying that alternative certification is the answer," Cross said.[31]

NOTES

1. Moss found her job through the Department of Defense's Troops to Teachers program, located on the Internet at http://voled.doded.mil/dantes/ttt.

2. For a comprehensive review of the teacher supply-and-demand situation in the United States, see the National Center for Education Statistics, "Projections of Education Statistics to 2010," November 2000.

3. *Ibid.*, p. 83.

4. Testimony by C. Emily Feistritzer, president, National Center for Education Information, presented to House Subcommittee on Labor, Health and Human Services, Education and Related Agencies, May 22, 2001.

5. Public Agenda, *A Sense of Calling: Who Teaches and Why*, 2000.

6. According to research conducted by Linda Darling-Hammond, as cited in "The Challenge to Our Schools," *Educational Leadership*, May 2001.

7. *Education Week*, "Who Should Teach?" Jan. 13, 2000.

8. Ellen O'Brien, "Colleges vow to retool after failures on teacher tests," *The Boston Globe*, July 24, 1998.

9. For a comprehensive look at these programs, see, for example, C. Emily Feistritzer and David T. Chester, *Alternative Teacher Certification: A State-by-State Analysis*, 2000.

10. Scott Sutherland, "First Lady Asks Troops to Become Teachers," American Forces Press Service, March 28, 2001.

11. The terminology used to describe the various types of teaching certifications and licenses can be very confusing. States and school districts use more than 50 titles to describe the documents they issue to teachers under their jurisdiction.

12. Feistritzer and Chester, *op. cit.*, pp. 3-4.

13. *Education Week*, *op. cit.*, pp. 12-18.

14. See D. Gomez and P. Grobe, *Three Years of Alternative Certification in Dallas: Where Are We?* 1990.

15. See Linda Darling-Hammond, "The Challenge to Our Schools," *Educational Leadership*, May 2001.

16. Dan D. Goldhaber and Dominic J. Brewer, "Teacher Licensing and Student Achievement," 2000.

17. The AFT salary survey is available at www.aft.org.

18. The report is available on the Web at http://www.publicagenda.org/specials/teachers/teachers.htm.

19. For background, see David F. Labaree, "The Trouble With Ed Schools," *Educational Foundations*, summer 1996, p. 32.

20. Quoted in Thomas J. Billitteri, "Teacher Education," *The CQ Researcher*, Oct. 17, 1997, p. 925.

21. For background, see David L. Angus and Jeffrey Mirel, "Professionalism and the Public Good: A Brief History of Teacher Certification," January 2001.

22. Feistritzer and Chester, *op. cit.*, p. 6.

23. Quoted in Lynn Olson, "Finding and Keeping Competent Teachers," *Education Week*, Jan. 13, 2000, p. 14.

24. Statement, May 15, 2001.

25. Quoted in Nick Anderson, "Party-Line Vote Kills Teacher Hiring Plan," *Los Angeles Times*, May 16, 2001.

26. Quoted in Scott S. Greenberger, "Ed Board Alters Teaching Standards," *The Boston Globe*, Nov. 29, 2000.

27. *Testing Teacher Candidates: The Role of Licensure Tests in Improving Teacher Quality*, National Research Council, March 27, 2001.

28. Quoted in Lynn Olson, "Overboard on Testing?" *Education Week*, Jan. 11, 2001.

29. For background, see Kenneth Jost, "Testing in Schools," *The CQ Researcher*, April 20, 2001, pp. 321-344.

30. Quoted in Julie Blair, "Remedy for Shortages," *Education Week*, June 20, 2001, p. 31.

31. *Ibid.*

BIBLIOGRAPHY

Books

Feistritzer, C. Emily, and David T., *Alternative Teacher Certification: A State-by-State Analysis 2000,* **National Center for Education Information, 2000.**
The authors, the center's president and editor, respectively, provide detailed data on the scores of alternative teacher-preparation programs being used across the country and argue that they are effective in combating teacher shortages.

Kopp, Wendy, *One Day, All Children*, **Public Affairs, 2001**
Kopp tells the story of the Teach For America program, which she founded in 1988 as a 21-year-old student at Princeton University. The program has trained more than 7,000 young college graduates to serve as teachers in the nation's neediest public schools.

Articles

Darling-Hammond, Linda, "The Challenge to Our Schools," *Educational Leadership,* **May 2001.**
Darling-Hammond, executive director of the National Commission on Teaching and America's Future and a professor of education at Stanford University, proposes a number of policy options for alleviating teacher shortages. She opposes "abbreviated" teacher-preparation programs, arguing that they do not produce a stable, high-quality teaching force for schools with the greatest needs.

Goodnough, Abby, "A Novice's Hard Lesson: Bringing Order to a Class," *The New York Times,* **Sept. 28, 2000.**
Chronicles the experiences of Donna Moffet, who at age 45 gave up a comfortable job as a legal secretary to teach at a troubled school in Brooklyn.

Ingersoll, Richard M., "The Problem of Underqualified Teachers in American Secondary Schools," *Educational Researcher,* **March 1999**
Ingersoll explores why so many public school teachers are assigned to subjects for which they have little training.

Odden, Allan, "Rewarding Expertise," *Education Matters,* **Spring 2001.**
Odden blames the teacher-supply problem in part on the "single-salary schedule," which bases a teacher's salary on the number of years worked and the number of education credits and degrees obtained. A better system, Odden argues, would pay teachers more for better performance.

Philadelphia, Desa, "Rookie Teacher, Age 50," *Time,* **April 1, 2001.**
Describes how schools are recruiting middle-aged people from fields other than education to work as teachers.

Sack, Kevin, "Facing a Teacher Shortage, American Schools Look Overseas," *The New York Times*, **May 19, 2001**

Examines how schools are hiring foreign nationals to offset teacher shortages.

Reports and Studies

Darling-Hammond, Linda, "Solving the Dilemmas of Teacher Supply, Demand and Standards: How We Can Ensure a Competent, Caring and Qualified Teacher for Every Child," *National Commission on Teaching and America's Future*, **August 2000.**

Describes strategies that schools can use to obtain highly qualified teachers, such as linking higher salaries with stringent standards, providing mentors to new teachers and expanding teacher-education programs in high-need fields.

Farkas, Steve, Jean Johnson and Tony Foleno, "A Sense of Calling: Who Teaches and Why," *Public Agenda*, **2000.**

The authors analyze the nation's teacher shortage by focusing on three groups: new teachers, young college graduates who decided not to teach and the school principals and administrators who hire and supervise teachers.

Ingersoll, Richard M., "Teacher Turnover, Teacher Shortages and the Organization of Schools," *Center for the Study of Teaching and Policy*, **January 2001.**

Ingersoll concludes that the teacher-shortage problem is largely due to factors rooted in the "organizational characteristics" of the nation's schools, such as low pay, inadequate support, student discipline problems and limited decision-making powers.

The Urban Teacher Collaborative, "The Urban Teacher Challenge," January 2000.

Explores how the nation's largest urban school districts are coping with severe teacher shortages in critical subject areas and also highlights the urgent need for more minority teachers in urban districts, where minorities make up approximately 69 percent of total student enrollment but only 36 percent of the teaching force.

U.S. Department of Education, "Projections of Education Statistics to 2010," August 2000.

Gives the federal government's projections of public school enrollments, graduates, classroom teachers and expenditures through 2010.

For More Information

American Federation of Teachers, 555 New Jersey Ave., N.W., Washington, DC 20001; (202) 879-4400; www .aft.org. The AFT represents many of the nation's teachers.

National Center for Education Information, 4401 Connecticut Ave., N.W., Suite 212, Washington, DC 20008; (202) 362-3444; www.ncei.com. A nonpartisan research organization that specializes in survey research and data analysis. NCEI is the leading source of information about alternative teacher-preparation programs.

National Commission on Teaching and America's Future, Teachers College, Columbia University, 525 West 120th St., Box 117, New York, NY 10027; (212) 678-4153; www.nctaf.org. A nonpartisan group dedicated to improving the quality of teaching nationwide. NCTAF strives to advance the professionalism of teachers and opposes "fast-track" initiatives that allow school districts to hire non-certified teachers.

National Council for Accreditation of Teacher Education, 2010 Massachusetts Ave., N.W., Suite 500, Washington, DC 20036; (202) 466-7496; www.ncate.org. The professional accrediting organization for U.S. schools and colleges. It is comprised of more than 30 organizations representing teachers, teacher educators, policy-makers, and the public.

National Council on Teacher Quality, P.O. Box 725, Falls Church, VA 22040; (703) 734-6760; www.nctq.org. An offshoot of the Manhattan Institute for Public Policy Research, which supports school vouchers, charter schools and other market-based initiatives to reform the nation's education system. NCTQ serves as a clearinghouse for information on teaching and assists states and school districts in crafting innovative initiatives, such as alternative-certification and merit-pay programs.

National Education Association, 1201 16th St., N.W., Washington, DC 20036; (202) 833-4000; www.nea.org. The 2.7 million-member NEA is the nation's largest teachers' union.

Teach For America, 315 W. 36th St., 6th Floor, New York, NY 10018; (800) 832-1230; www.teachforamerica.org. Prepares recent college graduates to teach in the nation's neediest schools through an intensive five-week training program.

U.S. Department of Education, 400 Maryland Ave., S.W., Washington, DC 20202; (800) 872-5327; www .ed.gov. Administers most federal assistance to the nation's 88,000 public elementary and secondary schools and coordinates federal programs to combat teacher shortages in certain geographic locations and subject areas.

16

Discipline in Schools

Are Zero-Tolerance Policies Fair?

Thomas J. Billitteri

Students hold a vigil for peace following two apparently racially motivated brawls involving Latino and African-American students at Thomas Jefferson High School in Los Angeles in April 2005. Although non-fatal crimes against students steadily declined in the U.S. since 1992, 86 percent of public schools say they still have at least one serious incident per year.

From *CQ Researcher*,
February 15, 2008.

M ilwaukee school Superintendent William Andrekopoulos is concerned.

Students are being suspended by the thousands, many for minor infractions such as disrupting class, he says. Among the city's more than 9,000 ninth-graders, nearly 40 percent are suspended at least once a year, typically for one to three days. Many are sent home multiple times.

"The suspension data is terrible," Andrekopoulos says. "This is a grave concern."[1]

School systems around the country are beginning to look hard at their discipline practices — particularly how they affect suspension and expulsion rates, not to mention learning and morale. They are especially scrutinizing so-called zero-tolerance polices, which rely heavily on suspension or expulsion to deal with misconduct, often regardless of the severity of the infraction.[2]

Civil-rights and child-advocacy groups say such codes have led to too many cases of harsh punishment for relatively minor violations, sometimes sending youngsters out onto the street where they get into much worse trouble.

The fact that black students are disproportionately targeted by such policies raises serious concerns among policymakers, educators and parents. According to an analysis of federal 2004-05 school-year data conducted by the *Chicago Tribune*, African-American students in the average New Jersey public school were nearly 60 times as likely as whites to be expelled for serious infractions.[3]

Critics also worry that get-tough policies can undermine common sense in dealing with problem students, leading to unfair or

351

Violent Crimes Against Students on the Decline

Fourteen homicides were reported among students ages 5 to 18 in the 2005-06 academic year, 20 less than in 1992-93 (top graph). Homicides dropped significantly following the 1999 shooting at Columbine High School in Littleton, Colo. Similarly, rates of nonfatal crimes against students decreased to about one-third of 1992-93 levels (bottom).

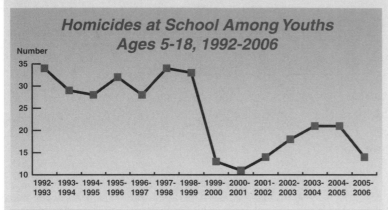

Homicides at School Among Youths Ages 5-18, 1992-2006

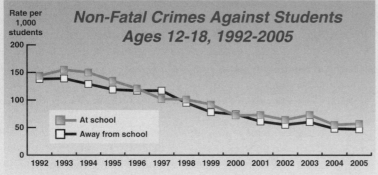

Non-Fatal Crimes Against Students Ages 12-18, 1992-2005

Source: "Indicators of School Crime and Safety, 2007"; National Council for Educational Statistics, Bureau of Justice Statistics

In February, a female student at Louisiana Technical College in Baton Rouge shot and killed two other women in a classroom before killing herself.[6] And rowdy or bullying behavior undermines learning and drags down teacher morale in classrooms around the country. (*See chart, p. 353.*)

Yet critics say that while zero-tolerance policies are appropriate when students endanger themselves or others, punishment for lesser offenses — such as "disrespect" — can be highly subjective and ultimately counterproductive.

Jane Sundius, director of the education and youth development program at the Open Society Institute-Baltimore, a nonprofit group working to reduce suspension in the city's schools, acknowledges the "justifiable fear" that teachers and administrators may feel over school violence. "Children do dangerous things," she says. But schools must be able to differentiate between violent actions that merit suspension or expulsion and non-violent behavior that may require a different approach, she says.

"School is where we need to teach kids to act appropriately," she says. "Punishing [acts of disrespect or minor disruption] doesn't help them manage that. And the nature of adolescence is to rebel. It's the job of parents and also the school to guide them in how to do that appropriately."

even irrational decisions. In California last June, for instance, a principal ordered "graduating" fifth-graders to cut off the plastic rifle tips from tiny toy soldiers they used to adorn their mortarboards. The principal's rationale: The toy guns violated the school's zero-tolerance firearms policy. After parents raised a ruckus, school officials apologized.[4]

Of course, schoolteachers and officials know only too well that schools are not immune from horrendous crimes. In Chicago this year, for example, a student was accused of stabbing a teacher, blinding her in one eye.[5]

Kathleen Buzad, assistant director of the Educational Issues Department at the American Federation of Teachers (AFT), says the group endorses zero tolerance for illegal drugs, weapons and "extreme acts of violence." A well-implemented zero-tolerance policy, she says, can reduce discrimination and favoritism, she says. For instance, "The captain of the football team wouldn't get off, as opposed to another kid who's not liked by teachers."

Bullying More Common Among Younger Students

Nearly 37 percent of sixth-graders reported being bullied in 2005, more than all higher grades. Name calling and insults were the most common form of bullying. Overall, more females than males reported being bullied and higher percentages of whites than blacks or Hispanics.

Percentage of Students Ages 12-18 Who Reported Being Bullied, 2005

Student or school characteristic	Total	Made fun of, called names or insulted	Subject of rumors	Threatened with harm	Pushed, shoved, tripped, spat on	Tried to make do things did not want to do	Excluded from activities on purpose
Total	28.1	18.7	14.7	4.8	9.0	3.5	4.6
Sex							
Male	27.1	18.5	11.0	5.2	10.9	3.9	4.1
Female	29.2	19.0	18.5	4.4	7.1	3.1	5.2
Race/ethnicity							
White	30.0	20.1	15.8	5.1	9.7	3.6	5.3
Black	28.5	18.5	14.2	4.9	8.9	4.7	4.5
Hispanic	22.3	14.7	12.4	4.6	7.6	2.6	3.0
Other	24.6	16.3	11.6	2.1	6.8	2.1	2.5
Grade							
6th	36.6	26.3	16.4	6.4	15.1	4.4	7.4
7th	35.0	25.2	18.9	6.3	15.4	4.7	7.1
8th	30.4	20.4	14.3	4.3	11.3	3.8	5.4
9th	28.1	18.9	13.8	5.3	8.2	3.2	3.8
10th	24.9	15.5	13.6	4.9	6.8	3.6	3.6
11th	23.0	14.7	13.4	3.2	4.2	2.8	3.3
12th	19.9	11.3	12.5	3.5	2.9	1.8	2.2

Source: "Indicators of School Crime and Safety, 2007", National Council for Educational Statistics, Bureau of Justice Statistics

But, she adds, "Zero tolerance is not a silver bullet for the problem of school violence and order." Along with a clear, effective and "rigorously enforced" discipline policy, she says, schools need a "comprehensive approach" that includes behavior-modification tools for students, efforts to enlist parent and community help to improve school climates, better teacher training and academically sound alternative programs for students removed from class.

Building one-on-one relationships with students is most crucial of all, adds Bill Bond, a safe-schools specialist at the National Association of Secondary School Principals. "Developing true safety in schools depends on students trusting the adults," he says.

"Sure, there's got to be some zero tolerance," Bond says. "You cannot allow guns in school. Weapons, knives,

absolutely." But, he adds, "if you leave no discretion for your professionals to make any judgments, then why are you hiring professional principals? Even in law enforcement, we allow police officers and district attorneys some discretion in which charges they file."

Bond is no novice at dealing with school violence. Ten years ago he was the principal of a school in Paducah, Ky., when a 14-year-old male student brought five guns to school and opened fire, killing three girls and wounding five other students.[7] Good education policy, he says, means concentrating on the school environment and climate and surveying students, teachers and parents about what they perceive is going on in the school and where the problem areas are.

In various ways, some administrators and policy advocates are trying to move schools away from cookie cutter discipline codes and make room for a more discretionary approach. In Baltimore, for example, the Open Society Institute is spearheading a $1.5 million effort to reduce suspensions and expulsions in city schools. It includes counseling and mental-health services, programs to teach children how to resolve conflicts, and services to help teachers, administrators and parents reduce violence and other misconduct and improve academic performance.

Open Society also is helping school officials rework the discipline code. In 2006-2007, nearly 10,000 Baltimore students — representing 12.5 percent of total enrollment — were subject to out-of-school suspensions, primarily for insubordination, disruption and disrespect.[8]

Baltimore schools CEO Andres Alonso has discouraged principals from suspending students for cutting class, insubordination and other non-violent misbehavior. "I never want to suggest to a principal, 'Don't suspend,' " he said. "What I want to suggest is, 'Use your common sense.' I do believe a child being in school is the only way to intervene. . . . You cannot suspend a system into good outcomes."[9]

Nationwide, nearly 7,200 schools in 44 states now participate in a process known as School-wide Positive Behavior Support, which combines efforts to teach and reinforce good behavior, social skills and academic standards, discourage inappropriate behavior and coach teachers and staff in how to make the process effective and efficient. An important component is careful data collection, so schools can identify problems and chart the effectiveness of intervention strategies.[10]

Schools adopting the program have seen a 20-60 percent reduction in the number of disciplinary referrals to the principal's office, says Robert Horner, a professor of special education at the University of Oregon who helped develop the program under a federal grant from the Office of Special Education. "If you want to change behavior, you must define the behavior you want, actively teach that and build a formal system where [the student] is rewarded for doing things the right way and not rewarded for doing things the wrong way," he says.

The movement to review discipline policies is occurring against a backdrop of mixed data on school crime. Student killings, while tragic, remain rare. School-associated student homicide rates fell significantly between 1992 and 2006. From 1999 to 2006, for instance, student homicides totaled 116, or an average of 16.5 per year, according to a new study by the Centers for Disease Control and Prevention.[11]

"Schools remain safe places for students," said co-author Jeff Hall.[12]

Non-fatal crimes against students also declined steadily from 1992 to 2005, according to the latest federal statistics, released in December.[13] Still, 86 percent of public schools reported at least one violent crime, theft or other serious crime during the 2005-2006 school year, according to the data.[14]

Whether serious or not, student misconduct can take a toll on teachers, who find themselves on the front lines in fighting the disruptions. In a survey of 2,000 unionized West Virginia school employees — including teachers, bus drivers and instructional aides — half said they felt intimidated by a classroom bully last year. Among teachers, more than a third said they lost 20 percent of instructional time weekly to disruptive behavior.[15]

"The discipline issue has gotten much worse, as the survey shows," said Judy Hale, president of the AFT-West Virginia. "It's a common occurrence for teachers to be cursed. And the children who are there to learn are being shortchanged. It is a small number of students who constantly disrupt, so it's time we took a good hard look at this again."[16]

And in a 2004 national study, more than a third of middle- and high-school teachers said they had seriously considered quitting the profession, or knew a colleague who had left, because student discipline and behavior had become intolerable.[17]

When teachers do quit, the price tag is high. The National Commission on Teaching and America's Future estimated the cost of public-school teacher turnover at more than $7 billion a year.[18]

As schools continue to grapple with student-discipline problems, here are some of the questions they are asking:

Have zero-tolerance policies made schools safer?

Many zero-tolerance policies were strengthened in the wake of school shootings in the 1990s, and the strict, no-nonsense approach found favor in conservative law-and-order circles.

Domoine D. Rutledge, general counsel for the East Baton Rouge Parish School System in Louisiana, says zero-tolerance policies have helped to create a culture within school districts and schools that "certain things will not be tolerated, period."

But whether or not that policy works depends on "how fairly it's enforced and how consistently it's enforced" and whether the student is afforded appropriate due process, he says.

"Given the incidences of violence — unspeakable violence — that we've seen on some of our school campuses," he continues, "schools districts have had to really balance the interest of the whole school, the student body, teachers and faculty . . . as well as the rights of individual bad actors. The ability to strike that balance, and to do it fairly, more than likely influences the effectiveness of the zero-tolerance policies."

The East Baton Rouge system has a zero-tolerance policy for fighting, which states that law-enforcement authorities will be called in for any fight involving students 14 or older.[19] But Rutledge describes the policy as more flexible than that. For example, he says, if two students 14 or older are caught fighting, a school resource officer is called in who can offer counseling, call the students' parents, arrest the students or issue a misdemeanor summons. But if more than two students are involved, he says, they are recommended for expulsion.

In addition, in recent years the district has implemented a "positive behavior intervention program" that he says has reduced the number of expulsions.

Kay S. Hymowitz, a contributing editor for a magazine published by the conservative Manhattan Institute, noted in 2001 that the arrest of a pair of New Jersey 8-year-olds for pointing paper guns at classmates was just the kind of episode that leads people to question zero-tolerance policies. But she also listed far more serious incidents involving juveniles.

"It's not so easy to distinguish the prankster from the wild-eyed adolescent with a [lethal] plan when lives are at stake," she wrote. In the end, "Zero tolerance may be more symptom than cure for the uneasy disciplinary climate of our schools. Certainly it's no final answer to out-of-control 5-year-olds or revenge-crazed teenagers. But as the threats continue and the bombs and guns appear, it's all we've got."[20]

While that view still prevails today in many school systems, critics of the get-tough approach see no evidence that zero-tolerance policies have made schools

safer. On the contrary, after reviewing a decade of research on such policies, the American Psychological Association concluded in 2006 that such codes "can actually increase bad behavior and also lead to higher dropout rates."

"[S]chools are not any safer or more effective in disciplining children than before these zero-tolerance policies were implemented," the association said.[21]

Ruth Zweifler, founder of the Student Advocacy Center of Michigan, agrees. The zero-tolerance approach "breeds a poisonous environment," she says. "On various levels, children who have concerns either about something they have done or about other kids will hesitate to go to an adult because the response is punishment rather than help. It reinforces for staff that these kids are dangerous. It just doesn't build a healthy, trusting, learning community."

In defense of "sensible" zero-tolerance codes, Charles Patrick Ewing, a professor of law and psychology at the State University of New York at Buffalo, wrote that critics cite a handful of cases in which zero tolerance led to absurd results, such as young children being suspended for having nail clippers. "If this is what is meant by zero tolerance, the critics are right," he acknowledged.

"But what about the more common applications?" he continued, such as when a student brings a loaded gun to school, shows it to a classmate and then turns it over to a teacher, or a high-school student punches another in the face. "Under most zero-tolerance policies, each of these students would be suspended from school."[22]

Sensible applications of zero-tolerance policies are warranted in all schools for several reasons, he concluded, including — first and foremost — the need to at least temporarily separate a dangerous or potentially dangerous student from the rest of the school population. Beyond immediate safety concerns, he added, applying zero tolerance "serves as a deterrent . . . by sending a clear message that acts that physically harm or endanger others will not be permitted at school under any circumstances."

But have such policies really made schools more secure? Russell J. Skiba, a professor of counseling and educational psychology at Indiana University who has studied discipline codes and school violence extensively, insists, "There really is no evidence that zero-tolerance policies have made schools any safer."

AP Photo/The Citizens' Voice/Kristen Mullen

A K-9 dog helps inspect open lockers at Wyoming Area High School in Exeter, Pa., in May 2007 after school officials received a note threatening violence at the school. After the school reopened, entering students had to pass through a metal detector.

If such policies were effective, he says, one would expect to find certain traits in schools that employ them: lower rates of problem behavior, a favorable view among students and teachers of the school's governance and higher student performance on state tests.

But research has not shown such outcomes in schools with zero-tolerance codes, Skiba says. In fact, schools that rely heavily on suspension and expulsion to deal with misconduct appear to have more student behavior problems, a poorer school climate and lower student achievement, he says.

No school should tolerate violence, weapons and other serious threats to physical safety, Skiba says. But, he adds, research indicates that a system of "graduated discipline" is more effective when dealing with other kinds of student misconduct than using a sweeping zero-tolerance approach.

Studies have found that between a third and half of suspended students are repeat offenders, indicating that an overreliance on suspension and expulsion is ineffective at deterring misconduct, Skiba noted in a review of zero-tolerance policies. "In one study, students who were suspended at the sixth-grade level were more likely to be referred to the office or suspended in eighth grade, leading the researchers to conclude that 'for some students, suspension functions more as a reinforcer than a punisher.'"[23]

Inconsistent application is one of zero-tolerance policies' flaws, Skiba said. For instance, one study found that the probability of middle-school students being suspended if they were referred to the principal's office ranges from 11 to 86 percent, depending on how discipline policies were applied by individual schools and administrators, Skiba says.

Like Skiba, Horner at the University of Oregon says there is no empirical evidence that zero-tolerance policies have made schools safer. Rather, he says, research shows that discipline codes that rely heavily on punishment can inadvertently reward problem behavior. Students penalized by adults often are admired by their peers, he notes. And a suspension or expulsion also can relieve misbehaving students of what they might loathe the most: Students who are "unhappy being in class aren't unhappy being sent to the office or removed from class."

"Negative consequences alone have not been found to produce broad improvement in the social behavior of children in schools," Horner concludes. Teaching and acknowledging appropriate behavior also is necessary, he says.

Many educators also worry that relying too heavily on suspensions or expulsions puts young people — even those accused of non-violent misconduct — in alternative programs where they can fall behind academically or find themselves out on the street where they often get into more serious trouble. "Students whose education is disrupted for a period of time may have difficulty catching up and may eventually drop out of school," noted a report on disciplinary offenses in Tennessee, where 13 percent of zero-tolerance offenders were expelled in 2004-2005 without placement in an alternative school.[24]

Daniel Losen, senior education law and policy associate at the Civil Rights Project at the University of California, Los Angeles, has studied student suspensions extensively. He says it is the "abuse" and "overuse of suspensions" that trouble him. "I'm not against suspending kids as a principle," he says, "but when you're suspending a third of the kids, you've got a problem."

Most students are suspended under zero-tolerance policies for non-violent, non-criminal behavior, Losen notes. "One of the biggest increases [in suspension rates] is for truancy," he says. And such suspensions "abrogate the school's responsibility," he adds. "They don't have to go out and collect the kids" and get them back into class.

Suspensions increase not only the risk that students will get into worse trouble but also the chances that students will drop out of school, Losen also says. "Being suspended once increases the risk of dropping out by three times." Middle-school suspension rates are often higher than those for high school because many middle-school students simply drop out after being suspended and never move up to higher grades, Losen says.

"The answer to school violence is not to transform schools into totalitarian police states and lock up every naughty child," wrote Trent England, a legal policy analyst, and Steve Muscatello, a researcher, at the conservative Heritage Foundation's Center for Legal and Judicial Studies.[25]

"Zero-tolerance policies rob the rule of law of its moral authority by focusing on punishment rather than justice," they continued. Writing six years after the Columbine shootings, they said, "the time has come to break the cycle of hijacking the memories of violent school tragedies to defend zero-tolerance injustice."

Is racism responsible for high suspension rates among minorities?

No discipline-related issue is more fraught with controversy than the disproportionate effect that punitive policies have on black students.

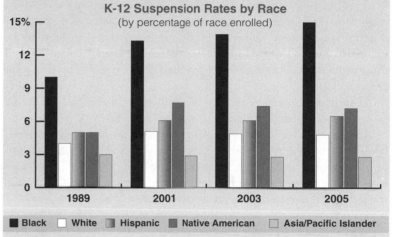

Racial Gap Widens for Suspensions

Suspension rates for black students rose to 15 percent since the 1988-1989 school year. Blacks are now three times as likely to be suspended as whites and more than twice as likely as Hispanics. Civil-rights and child-advocacy groups worry that zero-tolerance policies result in too many cases of harsh punishment for relatively minor violations, and that minorities are unfairly targeted.

K-12 Suspension Rates by Race
(by percentage of race enrolled)

■ Black □ White ▨ Hispanic ▨ Native American □ Asia/Pacific Islander

Note: Data from the 2004-05 school year are the most recent available.

Sources: Office of Civil Rights, U.S. Department of Education, 2008; Daniel Losen, UCLA

In South Carolina's Charleston County School District, 83 percent of the 5,837 middle- and high school students suspended at least once in 2006 were black.[26] In Minnesota, blacks are suspended six times as often as whites, and in 21 states the proportion of black suspensions is more than double their percentage of total enrollment, according to the *Chicago Tribune*.[27]

Indeed, the *Tribune*'s analysis of U.S. Department of Education public-school data for 2004-2005 found that in every state except Idaho, "black students are being suspended in numbers greater than would be expected from their proportion of the student population. . . . [O]n average across the nation, black students are suspended and expelled at nearly three times the rate of white students." Yet, the *Tribune* added, "black students are no more likely to misbehave than other students from the same social and economic environments, research has found."[28]

Moreover, "No other ethnic group is disciplined at such a high rate," the newspaper found. "Hispanic students are suspended and expelled in almost direct proportion to their populations, while white and Asian students are disciplined far less."

And Yale University researcher Walter S. Gilliam found that the disproportionate expulsion rates aren't just a phenomenon in elementary and high schools. A study published in 2005 found that African-Americans attending state-funded pre-kindergarten were roughly twice as likely to be expelled as Latino and Caucasian children — and more than five times as likely as Asian-American youngsters.[29] Surprisingly, he also found that pre-kindergarten students in general were more than three times more likely to be expelled than children in grades K-12.

As stark as the racial disparity in school-discipline cases may be, explaining it is no easy matter.

Researchers have found no evidence that poverty or family instability explains the phenomenon, says Skiba of Indiana University. While poverty and family problems can contribute to a student's misconduct, he says, research shows that minorities are disciplined more than whites even after accounting for those factors.

Moreover, he says, in any given school district there is no evidence that blacks are more prone to misbehave than whites are. "If anything, you find in any district study that African-Americans are more likely to be treated more harshly for the same offense" than other students, he says.

In fact — even though zero-tolerance policies were designed to level the discipline playing field and eliminate favoritism — research shows that discipline often is meted out subjectively. For instance, in 2002 Skiba and three colleagues concluded that blacks tend to get in trouble for less-serious reasons than whites. Whites were significantly more likely to be referred to the principal's office for smoking, leaving without permission, vandalism and using obscene language, while blacks were more likely to be sent for disrespect, excessive noise, threats and loitering.[30]

Some researchers attribute part of the reason for racial disparity in discipline to cultural differences between minority students and white teachers. The *Tribune* found some of the highest rates of racial disparity in states with the lowest minority populations, where, it said, "the disconnect between white teachers and black students is potentially the greatest."

"White teachers feel more threatened by boys of color," Isela Gutierrez, a juvenile-justice expert at the Texas Criminal Justice Coalition, told the newspaper. "They are viewed as disruptive. What might be their more assertive way of asking a question is viewed as popping off at the mouth."

But cultural differences cannot explain all the disparity, the *Tribune* concluded. Even in mostly black urban schools, African-American students are disciplined out of proportion to their enrollment.

Horner of the University of Oregon says better data collection on the nature, number and disposition of student discipline cases, along with other data on school climates, would shed important light on why the disparity is occurring and help schools eliminate it.

"When we give people in schools regular information — their own data — that's incredibly powerful," he says. "It changes the problem-solving they're engaged in."

For now, though, "we don't have the answer" to explain why minorities are disciplined more harshly than whites, Horner says. "It could be that kids are just behaving with higher rates of problem behavior. It could be they are just behaving consistent with what they think is a perfectly appropriate way to deal with adults that is learned at home and on the street. It could be simply that racism is involved. It could be that [discipline] systems are so archaically organized that they don't work very well.

"You could come up with a lot of what-ifs," he concluded, "and the truth is it's probably all of the above."

Youth advocates express grave concern that many minority students hit with out-of-school suspensions or expulsions will wind up adrift out on the street, get into deeper trouble and end up in jail — a phenomenon often called the "prison track" or "school-to-prison pipeline."

"Such phrases depict a journey through school that becomes increasingly punitive and isolating for its travelers," two scholars wrote.

"Many will be taught by unqualified teachers, tested on material they never reviewed, held back in grade, placed in restrictive special-education programs, repeatedly suspended and banished to alternative outplacements before dropping out or getting pushed out of school altogether. Without a safety net, the likelihood that these same youths will wind up arrested and incarcerated increases sharply."[31]

The *Tribune* noted that black youths represent 16 percent of adolescents in the United States but 38 percent of those incarcerated in youth prisons.

Should students have more legal rights in discipline cases?

Whenever students are disciplined, no matter their ethnic background or family circumstances, the issue of due-process protection always is in the background. In some respects, the Supreme Court has addressed that issue, most notably in the 1975 case *Goss v. Lopez*, which held that students facing out-of-school suspension of 10 days or less are entitled to certain due-process rights, including oral or written notice of the charges and some type of hearing in which they could present their version of the incident in question.[32]

But some argue that *Goss* failed to do enough to shield students from faulty disciplinary policies. For example, the court did not require that administrators in such cases allow students to cross-examine witnesses or present their own, nor did it grant the right to have a lawyer present.

"Providing students with an undeniable right to access legal counsel would . . . establish a checks-and-balances system," one scholarly article argued last year. "[L]egal counsel would be better suited than the average middle- or high-school student, or parent in some cases, to pinpoint due-process violations when they occur."[33]

Others contend, though, that students accused of wrongdoing already have sufficient legal safeguards. "The public schools do afford sufficient due process, particularly in expulsions or high-stakes hearings," says Julie Underwood, dean of the School of Education at the University of Wisconsin-Madison and an expert on school law.

But some experts worry that school authorities don't always have a good understanding of the law. "Students have plenty of due-process protections," says Robert S. McCord, an associate professor of educational leadership at the University of Nevada, Las Vegas, who trains school administrators. That being said, he's still "a little uncomfortable how those due-process protections are executed in the schools.

"In other words," he continues, "are the people who are responsible — teachers, principals, superintendents, school boards — all as equally informed and sensitive to

due-process protections? Sometimes their knowledge and their actions are a little spotty in that regard."

School officials may be "well-intended," McCord says, "but there is a certain sophistication in conducting due-process hearings and making sure rights are protected." If administrators have varying degrees of preparation, "you end up in long litigation." Schooling arguably has become equivalent to a property right, he notes, so "if we're going to remove students or threaten to remove them, you have to ratchet up the care that must be taken." Having lawyers who specialize in education law not only can help protect students but also allow administrators to be assertive when they need to be, McCord says. He notes that courts sometimes interpret laws in the criminal setting differently from in the school setting.

In a lengthy scholarly article last year, McCord and his colleagues noted that determining "a true threat" in the school environment is a "slippery slope" that can be "perilous" for those who act without careful investigation of the facts before taking action.[34]

Perhaps the slipperiest of slopes involve free-speech rights. Last year's Supreme Court decision in *Morse v. Frederick* did little to quell confusion in that area. The justices upheld a principal's right to punish a student who displayed a "Bong Hits 4 Jesus" banner across the street from school during a parade. School officials can censor and punish student speech that can be seen as advocating or celebrating illegal drug use, the justices ruled.[35]

In another case an appeals court relied on the *Morse* decision to further limit student speech. In that case, a high-school sophomore had kept a journal in which he discussed creating a pseudo-Nazi group to commit a variety of violent acts. His claim to a school administrator that the diary was a work of fiction fell on deaf ears. The administrator determined the writings posed a "terroristic threat" to the school, suspended the student for three days and reported the diary to police, who arrested him. The county attorney's office declined to prosecute.[36]

The appeals court ruled that "administrators must be permitted to react quickly and decisively to address a threat of physical violence against their students without worrying that they will have to face years of litigation second-guessing their judgment as to whether the threat posed a real risk of substantial disturbance."

Some analysts fear the ruling could open the door to zero tolerance of a wide array of speech, including clearly fictional speech about violence against students and even speech that advocates alcohol or tobacco use.[37]

BACKGROUND

Rise of Zero Tolerance

Although worries about school disorder and racial disparity in discipline have intensified in recent years, they are not new. During the Vietnam War era, many administrators viewed student activism as a scourge.

"To ignore student activism . . . is to invite total chaos in a school," a Delaware high-school principal declared. Said another, "To be a principal in times like these is not for the faint-hearted."[38]

Even then, youth advocates worried that minorities, especially African-Americans, were being punished, suspended or expelled at higher rates than whites. In 1975 the Children's Defense Fund, a liberal child-advocacy policy group in Washington, concluded from a study of federal data that suspension rates among black students were two to three times those of whites.[39]

In the ensuing years, several school-discipline issues came to a head, propelled in large part by growing drug use in both the population at large and among students. In fact, the zero-tolerance philosophy grew out of 1980s-era federal anti-drug policy. The first time the term was used may have been in 1983 to describe a U.S. Navy crackdown on drug abusers within their ranks.

In 1986, the term was used in connection with a federal program in San Diego aimed at impounding ships carrying any amount of drugs.[40] Then in 1988, as a crack epidemic was devastating inner cities nationwide, Attorney General Edwin Meese III used the San Diego program as a model for a nationwide "zero-tolerance" policy ordering U.S. Customs Service officials to impound vehicles or property of anyone entering the country with any amount of drugs and to charge them in federal court.[41]

Within months the Coast Guard had seized more than 1,000 boats, cars and motorcycles, sometimes after finding trace amounts of marijuana or other drugs in the vessels. A citizen backlash ensued, triggering angry testimony before Congress, and by May of that year Customs officials had agreed to confiscate vessels only when there was clear evidence they were being used for drug trafficking.[42]

But by that time zero tolerance had already caught on in schools. In 1986, Education Secretary William J. Bennett had urged Congress to withhold federal education money from schools that didn't adopt zero-tolerance expulsion policies for students using or selling drugs at school. Bennett didn't succeed, but by late 1989 school districts in California, New York and Kentucky had created zero-tolerance policies for drugs and gang activity.[43]

In 1994 zero tolerance received a massive boost with enactment of the Gun-Free Schools Act, which required school districts receiving federal money to expel for at least a year any student caught carrying a gun on school grounds. The law was enacted amid a get-tough-on-crime trend that swept the country in the 1990s, resulting in minimum-sentence laws, three-strikes-and-you're-out penal codes for habitual offenders and burgeoning prison populations.[44]

Soon, states were broadening the no-gun mandate, requiring school districts to bar anyone carrying anything that could be used as a weapon. Critics began complaining that such rules were being applied indiscriminately to innocuous items such as nail clippers and to all manner of misconduct — even minor infractions like smoking, violating dress codes and skipping class.

While the Gun Free Schools Act gave administrators authority to modify their expulsion decisions on a case-by-case basis, critics say many began applying zero-tolerance codes in narrow ways, treating every case — minor or major — the same. "They felt there was a need to be draconian," arguing that " 'we're trying to keep our schools safe — we're under siege,' " says Ronnie Casella, an education professor at Central Connecticut State University who has written extensively on school discipline.

"Also," he says, "there was a feeling that when you do look at [discipline violations] on a case-by-case basis, you're open to charges of racism," with students, parents and civil-rights groups asking why the rules were applied inconsistently. "So this whole idea that everybody gets the same kind of punishment was almost a way of dealing with past biased discipline policies."

Casella also cites a push in the 1990s to fill a growing number of alternative schools, boot camps and other facilities built to accommodate young ruffians. "Once you develop those institutions, it becomes a self-fulfilling

CHRONOLOGY

1960s *Vietnam-era protests spark concern over student conduct; juveniles gain due-process rights.*

1967 Supreme Court rules in *In re Gault* that juveniles accused of misconduct deserve many of the rights given to adult criminal defendants. . . . Students for a Democratic Society, a leftist organization started on college campuses, circulates information on how to "take over" a high school.

1969 Supreme Court rules in *Tinker v. Des Moines Independent Community School District* that school officials violated students' First Amendment rights by suspending them for wearing armbands to protest the Vietnam War.

1970s *Protections broadened for students; schools pour more resources into security programs as school crime rises.*

1975 Congress passes Education for All Handicapped Children Act. . . . Supreme Court rules in *Goss v. Lopez* that suspended students are entitled to a hearing. . . . Children's Defense Fund reports disproportionate rates of suspensions for black students.

1980s *Federal push for no-tolerance policies for illegal drug use and other crimes begins filtering down to schools.*

1986 Education Secretary William J. Bennett unsuccessfully urges Congress to withhold money from schools rejecting zero-tolerance expulsion for students using or selling drugs at school.

1989 School districts in California, New York and Kentucky have zero-tolerance policies for drugs and gang activity.

1990s *Gun violence in schools spurs tough new laws.*

1990 "Gun-free school zones" law makes it a felony to bring firearms near a school. . . . Individuals With Disabilities Education Act (IDEA) passes.

1994 California and a dozen other states pass "three-strikes-and-you're-out" laws. . . . Omnibus Crime Bill includes mandatory drug sentences; Gun-Free Schools Act requires expulsion for not less than a year for students caught with a firearm.

1995 Supreme Court strikes down Gun-Free School Zones Act, upholds random drug tests for school athletes.

1998 More than 30 students and teachers are killed in a spate of school shootings across the country.

1999 Two heavily armed students at Columbine High School in Colorado kill 12 students and a teacher and wound 23 before committing suicide. Schools nationwide tighten security and discipline codes.

2000-Present *More student violence occurs; courts and the federal government continue involvement in student-conduct issues.*

2002 President George W. Bush signs No Child Left Behind Act mandating that states identify "persistently dangerous" schools.

2004 IDEA is reauthorized, providing greater leeway for school districts to discipline students.

2006 Gunman kills five girls and then himself at a one-room Amish schoolhouse in Pennsylvania.

2007 In the deadliest shooting rampage in U.S. history, Seung-Hui Cho, a student at Virginia Tech University, kills 32 students and teachers, then commits suicide. . . . Supreme Court rules in *Morse v. Frederick* that school officials can punish student speech that can be interpreted as advocating illegal drug use. . . . Delaware State University student is charged in the shooting of two students, one of whom dies.

2008 Families of Virginia Tech victims call for tighter gun control, but Virginia lawmakers defeat a bid to close a loophole on gun-show sales. . . . President Bush urges reauthorization of No Child Left Behind bill, which remains stalled in Congress. . . . Rep. Linda Sanchez, D-Calif., introduces legislation to require schools to include anti-bullying policies in their conduct codes. . . . Two students at Louisiana Technical College are shot and killed by a student, who then commits suicide.

Effective Schools Build Relationships With Students

Fights and discipline problems decline as trust develops.

Extreme school-discipline policies typically grab the headlines, yet it is often the quiet efforts with troubled students that are most effective at creating order in schools.

At Greenfield Middle School in central Indiana, principal James A. Bever says, "We emphasize relationships over rules."

That's also a theme at Garrison Middle School in inner-city Baltimore, where the Meet Me Halfway Village Center, started by a community volunteer in 2004, offers counseling, tutoring, conflict resolution and other support.

The relationship theme echoes, too, at racially diverse West Potomac High in Alexandria, Va., where principal Rima Vesilind emphasizes the importance of communication among students, teachers, parents and administrators.

"If kids are treated respectfully," she says, "they know we're trying to support them, and they most often come around."

Support, communication and respect are big words, too, at Greenfield Middle School. Despite its suburban setting, a fourth of the students come from low-income families, and Bever deals with the same kind of challenges — from drugs and fights to everyday classroom disruptions — that urban schools do.

"With 500 early adolescents, coming from every conceivable background, we're going to have situations that come up," Bever says. All the more reason, he says, to build ties with each student.

"It is important for our students to feel a great sense of belonging, for them to know they each are individually important to us, that we know who they are. If a student engages in a behavioral indiscretion, we don't come in and literally start throwing the book at them. We look at the issues underlying the behavior, address it, and if it's appropriate, there are consequences."

Even when the misconduct calls for suspension or expulsion, Bever says, the process is a collaborative one among the school, the student and the student's parents. "Our goal is that there's a handshake and a mutual understanding."

Bever says that in the two years before he took over in 1999, more than 300 students a month were being removed from class for disciplinary reasons, and some violence had occurred, including the serious beating of a student. A redistricting plan had raised tensions (some complained that the best students were shifted to another school), and Indiana had placed Greenfield Middle on academic probation.[1]

Upon his arrival, Bever took a tough approach to discipline, enlisting the help of local police and hiring uniformed

Greenfield Middle School/Sandra Hall

Principal James A. Bever often talks with sixth-graders during their first year at Greenfield Middle School. "These newly formed relationships then grow throughout their remaining two years in the school," he says.

guards for after-school events. But once safety was restored, he began working with teachers, students and other administrators to adopt the method used today.

Bever, who was named the Indiana Middle School principal of the year in 2004 by the Metlife/National Association of Secondary School Principals, reviles one-size-fits-all zero-tolerance policies. While they may make it easier for schools to protect themselves in court, they also relieve administrators from the duty to exercise discretion and leadership in dealing with school challenges, he says.

At Baltimore's Garrison Middle School, where nearly 85 percent of the students come from poor, single-parent families, Meet Me Halfway provides academic mentoring, conflict resolution and behavioral help. The nonprofit program, housed in the school's basement, was formed in 2004 by Bernard Fayall, a neighborhood resident who first volunteered at the school as a hallway monitor.[2]

Rita Fayall, Bernard's wife and Meet Me Halfway's program coordinator and chief fundraiser, says her husband started volunteering at the school after he was laid off from his shipyard welding job. He quickly found that students opened up to him, and soon he was working with kids who were misbehaving, being bullied or struggling in class.

Mrs. Fayall, who attended Garrison as a youngster, says Meet Me Halfway has a $350,000 annual budget, supported by the Open Society Institute-Baltimore, Goldsmith Family Foundation and other grant makers. The program receives in-kind help, including rent, janitorial help and teaching and health aides, from the school system and other city agencies, she says.

Meet Me Halfway has a wide variety of components. Students may drop in before or after school or on their lunch hour for a listening ear, classroom mentoring or perhaps to take advantage of a fitness program. Sometimes students who have been suspended come in for the support they need to get back on track. Teachers may send students to the program during the day for counseling. Or Meet Me Halfway staff may offer tutoring in a regular classroom.

Programs include a community food bank, job-skills training in printing and even a hair salon and barber shop staffed by volunteers who offer students free styling or haircuts — which build self-esteem, Mrs. Fayall says. A licensed counselor is on staff, and skills training in carpentry and technology are coming soon, she says. Dances and other recreational activities also take place.

And the doors are always open to parents, Mrs. Fayall says.

During the summer, in fact, the Fayalls invite parents to come in to discuss their children's goals and ways to improve communication. Letters go out over the name of the Garrison Middle School principal, she says. Mr. and Mrs. Fayall, along with other volunteers, have conducted hundreds of such interviews, she says.

"We find out what the parents' goals are for the child, what the students' goals are, what the family needs," she says. The information is put into a database, and appropriate resources are found to help the families. The aim, she says, is to form a "positive relationship" among students, parents and the school.

Meet Me Halfway also helps to support a separate Garrison program, the Rising Scholars Academy, which offers alternative learning for students having trouble in the regular classroom setting.

Mrs. Fayall credits her husband's conflict-resolution skills for much of Meet Me Halfway's progress, saying he has a gift for working one-on-one with feuding students and building trusting relationships with them. "He can turn that thing around in 30 minutes," she says of the typical squabble between students.

In a single month back in 2005, he worked on resolving 61 conflicts between students, she says, adding: "In September 2007 he did nine, so the kids are learning to do it themselves. Now they come down here [to Meet Me Halfway] before they fight."

Meet Me Halfway Village Center

Bernard Fayall, founder of the Meet Me Halfway Village Center at Baltimore's Garrison Middle School, helped students build a "racecar" from a bathtub. The after-school program offers counseling, tutoring, conflict resolution and other support.

Relationship-building is also important at ethnically diverse West Potomac High, where roughly a third of the nearly 2,000 students come from low-income families. The "primary approach" at West Potomac "is trying very hard to make sure this is a safe and secure [place] and that everybody feels part of a family," says principal Vesilind.

"We definitely have zero tolerance for some things," she says. "Weapons or weapon-like things, drugs — there's no wiggle room on those."

But Vesilind stresses that West Potomac is a "place for learning." To make that so, she says, she and her staff try hard to build relationships with students, offer one-on-one help, provide regular feedback and pay attention when students are struggling.

"There's no kid who wants not to be successful, but sometimes they can't figure out how to do it," she says.

The key, Vesilind says, is communication. "If you have kids who are being pulled gradually into a gang, you talk to those kids all the time and make sure they know you don't want them to do that. I've had kids who were walking the line [of joining a gang] who say, 'I decided to make myself be a better student because I didn't want to disappoint you.'"

The approach has paid off, Vesilind says. "This is my fourth year" as principal. "The year before I came, there were 170 fights." Now, she says, that number is "way down. It's more like 10."

[1] M. Karega Rausch and Russell Skiba, "Doing Discipline Differently: The Greenfield Middle School Story," Center for Evaluation and Education Policy, July 9, 2004, www.indiana.edu/~ceep.

[2] "Description of Project Garrison's Meet Me 1/2 Way Initiative at Garrison Middle School," Open Society Institute-Baltimore.

Taylor Hess, an honor student and varsity swimmer at L.D. Bell High School in Fort Worth, Texas, was suspended for a year after a school guard saw a non-serrated bread knife lying in his pickup truck, which he had just used to haul household goods to Goodwill. School systems around the country are scrutinizing so-called zero-tolerance polices, which rely heavily on suspension or expulsion to deal with misconduct regardless of the infraction.

prophecy. There was a push to fill these outplacements, and now they're a part of the school system."

In the 2000s, according to some critics of zero tolerance, administrators have used stiff disciplinary penalties to winnow out low-achievers because schools are under intense pressure to get their students to pass standards-based achievement tests mandated by the Bush administration's No Child Left Behind law. Facing sanctions for poor student performance, administrators have less and less patience with students who create disruptions that jeopardize classroom learning, or drag down test scores.

Meanwhile, other federal laws have played a role in shaping disciplinary procedures. Among the most controversial: the Individuals with Disabilities Education Act (IDEA), first passed in 1975, which guaranteed a public-school education to all disabled youngsters. Disciplinary provisions in the act have been highly contentious. Among the law's provisions is one that makes it difficult to impose long-term suspensions or expulsions if their misconduct stems from their disability, although if they commit a crime or are a danger to themselves or others they can be removed immediately.

"Schools have often argued that the discipline provisions for children with disabilities should be the same as those for children without disabilities and that the provisions of IDEA created too much of a paperwork burden," the Congressional Research Service noted.[45]

Children's advocates, on the other hand, say the law aimed in part to prevent schools "from unilaterally denying services to children with disabilities when they misbehaved, that due-process procedures are necessary to prevent this denial of education and that children with disabilities should not be punished for behavior that was caused by their disability."[46]

Violence and Bullying

In the late 1990s, a spate of school shootings helped strengthen administrators' resolve to keep schools safe. In October 1997 a student in Pearl, Miss., murdered his mother, then opened fire on classmates, killing two students and wounding seven. Two months later came the Paducah shootings. In 1998 two middle-school students in Jonesboro, Ark., killed four students and a teacher and wounded nine others.

After several more school shootings came the devastating Columbine massacre of 1999, in which 12 students and a teacher were shot and killed, and 23 were wounded, by two heavily armed students who then killed themselves. Columbine was a watershed event that stunned the country and triggered nationwide soul-searching about its cause.

It also helped strengthen support for no-tolerance discipline policies. "There was pressure on school districts to look like they were doing something about this rampage of violence that was taking over in the 1990s," Casella says, "and a lot of the pressure was coming from parents."

But the shootings also opened discussion on the psychology of troubled students, leading some critics to argue that school administrators and policymakers were focusing too much on truancy and drugs and not enough on the problem of bullying as a catalyst for violent student behavior. Several post-Columbine studies into the causes of the shootings found that most teenage school shooters had felt bullied or persecuted.

By 2005, 17 states had passed anti-bullying statutes, according to the Education Commission of the States.[47]

Recently, a National Association of Attorneys General task force pointed to the significance of bullying in episodes of school violence and noted the growth of "cyber bullying" in schools. "The growth in the use of technology and social-networking sites by younger Americans has fueled a fear among professionals that cyber bullying will become the means most often utilized to harass, threaten or otherwise cause distress," said the task force.[48]

A Pew Research Center study last year found that one in three teenagers who use the Internet said they had been targets of annoying and potentially menacing online activities, including receiving threatening messages and having rumors about them spread online.[49]

Bond, the safe-schools specialist at the National Association of Secondary School Principals, says that rather than relying on indiscriminate zero-tolerance policies to stop bullying, administrators must do a better job of staying on top of what is happening in their schools. That requires training teachers in classroom management, collecting and analyzing data on student conduct and listening carefully to student concerns, he says.

"Kids at my school . . . were being humiliated and ridiculed by words," Bond says of his days as a principal in Paducah, "and words cut people all the way to the heart and do more damage than being hit upside the head. If we just focus on [physical violence] and ignore the emotional damage, it just doesn't work."

Zero-tolerance policies are appropriate for serious offenses such as weapons, Bond says, but with issues like bullying, using the threat of suspension or expulsion can backfire. "You can't have zero tolerance for bullying because the definition in itself doesn't apply — what's going to be bullying and what's not? If a kid says something to another kid out of emotion, you use that and suspend a kid? That's not improving education.

"When you're dealing with 50 million kids and you try to make rules that apply to all 50 million circumstances with words like 'zero tolerance,' you're going to have a problem," he concludes.

Teacher Education

With teachers on the front lines of forming relationships with students and maintaining order, their ability to manage the classroom is crucial. And studies suggest that ability is sorely lacking, in part because of poor teacher training.

A four-year study conducted by Arthur Levine, former president of Teachers College at Columbia University, concluded that many students graduate from teacher-education programs lacking the skills and knowledge needed to be effective teachers.

"Only about one-third of principals said that their teachers are very or moderately well-prepared to maintain order in the classroom or to address the needs of students with disabilities," the study concluded.[50]

On the other hand, teachers who are well-trained in dealing with student misconduct can face an uphill battle when tough discipline is warranted. Buzad of the American Federation of Teachers says teachers often are afraid of reprisals from aggressive students or litigious parents. And, she adds, they may not be adequately backed up by the school administration.

"Some places are doing this well [and have] high standards," she says, but "teachers are facing more and more accountability and less and less power around decision making." In many cases, "there's no power to have a kid removed from class where it would be beneficial for the kid as well as the kids in the class."

CURRENT SITUATION

'Scarlet Letter'

As schools continue to struggle to maintain order and safety, all eyes are watching whether Congress will overhaul the controversial No Child Left Behind law. Reauthorization of the measure, a signature of the Bush administration, has stalled on Capitol Hill amid bitter debates over how to change the law or even whether to keep it at all.

Among the law's most controversial provisions is a requirement that states identify "persistently dangerous schools" using criteria set by each state. Schools designated as dangerous must give students the option of transferring to a safe school within their district.

The provision has drawn a barrage of criticism from administrators, education theorists, policymakers and pundits. Critics argue that state benchmarks for identifying dangerous schools are grossly inconsistent and that in many states the number of dangerous incidents is vastly underreported.

According to preliminary Department of Education data for the 2007-2008 school year, only 48 out of roughly 94,000 schools are classified as "persistently dangerous." For the previous school year, the total was only 46, with none in such big states as Illinois, Florida or California. A Department of Education Inspector General report last year pointed out that a Los Angeles high school with 289 cases of battery, two assaults with a deadly weapon, a robbery and two sex offenses in one school year did not meet California's definition of a persistently dangerous school.[51]

Lawmakers Balk at Closing Gun-Show Loophole

Plea by Virginia Tech families is ignored.

After Eric Harris and Dylan Klebold carried assault weapons into Colorado's Columbine High School in 1999 and killed 12 students and a teacher, states and school districts moved quickly to strengthen school security and disciplinary codes on firearms and bullying.

Such events "really have impacted the way we think about student safety," says Julie Underwood, dean of the School of Education at the University of Wisconsin, Madison.

But getting lawmakers to act on gun-control measures in the aftermath of school violence has been an uphill battle. In Virginia, for instance, legislators balked even after last spring's massacre at Virginia Tech, where mentally ill student Seung-Hui Cho shot 32 students and teachers before taking his own life. With support from victims' families, Democratic Gov. Tim Kaine had asked the state's General Assembly to require criminal background checks on anyone buying a gun from an unlicensed dealer at a gun show. Although Cho had bought guns from licensed dealers and passed background checks, a state panel noted he could have avoided such checks by exploiting the so-called gun-show loophole.

However, even the emotional appeals of the Virginia Tech families failed to persuade the Virginia Assembly. The Republican majority in the House of Delegates' Militia, Police and Public Safety Committee voted along party lines in January 2008 to kill a measure designed to close the loophole. A similar bill failed in the state Senate, which is controlled by Democrats.

Less than a week later, Democratic Sens. Frank R. Lautenberg of New Jersey and Jack Reed of Rhode Island introduced federal legislation to close the gun-show loophole nationwide, flanked by Virginia Tech families.

"We saw what happened at Virginia Tech and Columbine High School when dangerous people have easy access to guns," said Lori Haas, whose daughter Emily was wounded by Cho. "Congress should do all that it can to prevent other American families from suffering the ordeal of gun violence like the Virginia Tech families have had to suffer."[1]

Such family involvement in the legislative process is important, says Paul Helmke, president of the Brady Campaign to Prevent Gun Violence. "It puts a human face on the issue, and it's something that [elected officials] have to listen to." But in fact, officials don't always listen. Not only did Virginia lawmakers turn aside family appeals, but much the same thing happened after the Colorado rampage.

In the wake of that school-shooting spree, families — along with business and civic leaders — pressed state lawmakers to close the Colorado gun-show loophole that Harris and Klebold had exploited to obtain weapons. But the effort faltered. The loophole was finally closed after voters approved a subsequent ballot initiative.

Whether Lautenberg and Reed's bill will make headway is an open question. It could find favor in the Democrat-controlled Congress. On the other hand, conservatives and pro-gun forces are likely to oppose it as an infringement on Second Amendment rights.

"It's simply a drive to make it impossible to have guns without being regulated by the government," said Larry Pratt, executive director of Gun Owners of America. "From what the government itself has found, shows are seldom where guns get into the hands of criminals. Gun shows are a freedom, and they're trying to take away another freedom."[2]

Lautenberg introduced the first bill to close the gun-show loophole in 1999. In the aftermath of the Columbine shootings, the Senate passed the measure, with Vice President Al Gore casting the tie-breaking vote. The legislation, opposed by the gun lobby, died in a House-Senate conference. The gun lobby then vigorously fought Gore's 2000 bid for the presidency, and some pundits say their opposition helped to doom Gore. Since then many Democrats have backed away from gun control.

Lautenberg and Reed's new legislation would require background checks for every gun purchased at a gun show. "It defies common sense that a loophole in federal law lets unlicensed dealers sell firearms at gun shows without running a background check on the buyer," Lautenberg said. "Without this change in the law, felons, fugitives and severely mentally ill people will continue to be able to buy guns — no questions asked."[3]

---

[1] Quoted in "Brady Campaign Urges Support For Bill To Close Gun Show Loophole," press release, Brady Campaign, Jan. 30, 2008, www.bradycampaign.org/media/release.php?release=961.

[2] Quoted in Ben DuBose, "Senators try to widen scope of firearm background checks; Two Democrats seek to close a loophole regarding sales at gun shows. A similar effort in Virginia failed," *Los Angeles Times*, Feb. 1, 2008, p. A11.

[3] Press release, office of Sen. Frank R. Lautenberg, "Sens. Lautenberg, Reed Join Law Enforcement Officials and VA Tech Victims in Call to Close Gun Show Loophole," Jan. 30, 2008.

Should school districts be able to search student lockers without probable cause?

YES — Dr. Richard J. Caster

Executive Director, National Association of School Resource Officers

Written for *CQ Researcher*, February 2008

Schools exist for a single purpose: to educate the youth within their walls. If this statement is false, then the buildings should be sold to Wal-Mart so at least they could be put to more productive use.

In his 1943 paper *A Theory of Human Motivation*, psychologist Abraham Maslow proposed his ground-breaking Hierarchy of Needs pyramid. Maslow argued that certain needs must be met to reach the "self-actualization" level, which allows individuals to achieve problem solving, morality and creativity. The first rung on the pyramid is "physiological needs" — breathing, food, water and sleep. The next rung is "safety" — body security, possessions and health.

Our young people must be assured that the schools they walk into are providing the best level of safety that is humanly possible. If students fear they may be subject to physical attacks, put in substandard buildings incapable of withstanding Mother Nature's hazards or forced to deal with a staff that cannot cope with daily threats to students' safety, then self-actualization — i.e. learning — will never occur.

Fortunately for the millions of youth attending our nation's schools, local, state and federal courts have given school officials the authority and responsibility to provide a safe learning environment. The hallmark of this authority lies in the ability of schools to search lockers if school officials or safety personnel have a "reasonable suspicion" the locker contains drugs, weapons or other contraband.

Let's make one point very clear: The locker is owned by the school district. It is loaned to the student for use under the condition that all board of education policies and codes of conduct be followed. There is no expectation of privacy beyond the requirement that school personnel have a reasonable suspicion before making a search.

Drugs, weapons and contraband of any type can be stored in a student locker. The fact that students know lockers can and will be searched for items that can do harm is a major deterrent to bringing these items to school and presents a tremendous feeling of safety to the vast majority of students, who expect and demand that school officials assure a safe and secure environment for learning.

NO — Catherine Yonsoo Kim

Staff Attorney, Racial Justice Program, American Civil Liberties Union

Written for *CQ Researcher*, February 2008

Unrestricted searches of student lockers are part of the larger school-to-prison pipeline problem — the alarming trend of punishing, criminalizing and incarcerating youth, instead of educating them. In the name of school security, school officials conduct locker searches, bag searches, even strip searches — all without probable cause. They handcuff children as young as 5 for throwing temper tantrums. They have students arrested for "disorderly conduct" or "disturbance of school" when they misbehave. They have armed police officers patrolling school hallways with little to no training on how to interact with youth.

These policies have been initiated even though school violence has actually dropped in recent years, and even though there is no evidence suggesting that these practices are effective in creating safer schools.

In a South Dakota public school, officials found reasonable suspicion to search a Native American student's locker and referred him to law enforcement upon finding a printout of rap lyrics, a sign of gang activity, according to the school administration.

In one California public school, Hispanic students — and only Hispanic students — were photographed in connection with the school's efforts to crack down on gang activity, even though there was no allegation that any of the children photographed were affiliated with a gang.

School officials in a South Carolina district invited armed police officers to conduct SWAT-like searches, complete with canines and pointed guns, of 150 mostly black students in a majority-white school on the suspicion that one student — who was absent that day — was dealing marijuana.

The lack of adequate safeguards to place a check on such "security" measures invites these types of abuse as well as racial profiling. As a result, students across the country report that their schools increasingly resemble prisons.

Of course school officials, just like law enforcement, should be permitted to search lockers when there is probable cause to suspect a crime. But at the same time, school officials must be held accountable against exercising their discretion to alienate and criminalize the very children who need their protection the most.

Dangerous Incidents Seem Underreported

Only 46 of the nation's 94,000 public schools were classified as "persistently dangerous" during the 2006-2007 school year, according to data provided by the individual schools. Under the No Child Left Behind law, schools designated as persistently dangerous must allow students to transfer to a safe school within their district. Critics say state-set benchmarks for identifying dangerous schools are grossly inconsistent and that schools underreport dangerous incidents to avoid negative publicity and the "persistently dangerous" label.

Schools Identified as "Persistently Dangerous" (2006-2007)

State/Territory	No. of Schools
Maryland	6
New Jersey	4
New York	17
Oregon	1
Pennsylvania	9
Puerto Rico	4
South Dakota	1
Texas	4
TOTAL	**46**

Source: U.S. Dept of Education

One reason for the inconsistent reporting is that some states use a broader time horizon than others. A 2004 analysis by the Education Commission of the States found that more than half the states considered incidents that occurred during a three-year period, and more than a fourth used a two-year window.[52]

"There's very little oversight" of the persistently dangerous provision of the law, says Buzad of the American Federation of Teachers. "If there's a fight in the main hall of the high school, whether those kids receive suspension or detention or the state requires the principal to report that as a violent incident, it varies from state to state and district to district."

Kenneth S. Trump, president and CEO of National School Safety and Security Services, a consulting company in Ohio, told the House Committee on Education and Labor last April that the "persistently dangerous school" label "is considered to be the 'Scarlet Letter' of education today." As a result, "states have created definitions of 'persistently dangerous' that are so unreachable that they

could not be met by most school districts even if they wanted the label."[53]

The concern about the label's inconsistency was reinforced last year by an advisory panel appointed by Education Secretary Margaret Spellings to evaluate the controversial provision and other school-safety issues. Reporting standards "vary from state to state, and some schools may not even be reporting," stated the panel, which included school administrators, education researchers and federal officials. "As a result, schools that are accurately reporting incidents are being penalized for doing it."[54]

Some principals may keep dangerous incidents under wraps, critics say, possibly to keep from drawing negative attention to their schools or because they simply can't accurately categorize an episode. "What's an assault and what's not an assault?" asks Bond of the National Association of Secondary School Principals. "That's really a decision to be made by district attorneys and police officers, and [their] interpretation of that varies greatly. If you have a first-grader hit another kid on the shoulder, is that an assault or not?"

Critics also say that the "persistently dangerous" provision does nothing to make schools safer. "If you call a school persistently dangerous, it has no hope of becoming less dangerous or even surviving with language like that," says Bond, who participated in the advisory committee. Congress, he says, should "look at what really helps a school be safe and orderly and not what makes a school dangerous."

Spellings's advisory panel recommended, among other things, that the persistently dangerous terminology be changed and that the focus shift toward "providing help for potentially unsafe schools." It also suggested using school-climate surveys to determine whether schools are becoming safer.[55]

In a controversial "discussion draft" last fall, the House Education Committee proposed shifting the existing "persistently dangerous" section of the law to a new "challenge schools" grant that would define such schools as those found "not to have a safe climate for academic achievement."[56]

Whether and how Congress might overhaul the No Child Left Behind law remains an open question. But one thing is clear: Both supporters and detractors of the law believe much more needs to be done to make schools safe.

SAVE Act

U.S. Rep. Carolyn McCarthy, D-N.Y., is among those working to improve school safety. She ran for Congress after her husband was shot and killed along with five others on the Long Island Railroad in 1993. Last year she introduced the Safe Schools Against Violence in Education (SAVE) Act, which, among other things, calls for more accurate reporting of school-violence incidents. The bill would replace the "persistently dangerous" term with "safe climate for academic achievement."

McCarthy's measure has won support from school-safety experts like Trump. "One of the 'dirty, little secrets' in our nation's education community is that there is no comprehensive, mandatory, federal school-crime reporting and tracking of actual school-crime incidents for K–12 schools," Trump said in his testimony before the House Education and Labor panel. "Federal school-crime and violence data by and large consists of a hodgepodge collection of just over a half-dozen academic surveys and research studies."

Trump pointed out that the Gun-Free Schools Act only requires schools to report the number of students expelled for gun offenses that occur on campus. It does not require schools to report non-students arrested on campus with firearms or expelled students who return to campus with a firearm.

The SAVE Act would not only close such loopholes, he said, but also require states to use FBI "incident-based" data, a move that "would provide the first meaningful effort to shift the conversation on school safety in this country from one based on perception and opinion surveys to actual incident-based data on real crimes . . . at our nation's schools."

Other proposals addressing the school-discipline problem include an anti-bullying measure introduced by Rep. Linda Sanchez, D-Calif., which would require schools to include anti-bullying policies in their conduct codes.[57] A broad coalition of education, civil-rights, law-enforcement and youth-advocate groups is pushing for anti-bullying legislation, including Sanchez', under an umbrella organization called the National Safe Schools Partnership.

State Proposals

States are focusing on student discipline along with the federal government. In 2007 alone, at least 11 states passed laws related to school safety and discipline, according to the Education Commission of the States.[58] In some cases, states stiffened penalties for misconduct, while in others they have eased up on the rules, reflecting concern that certain disciplinary approaches may be counterproductive.

States passing legislation on school discipline last year included:

- North Carolina, which mandated that parents receive notice of a student's expulsion or suspension.[59]
- Louisiana, which lengthened expulsion periods for students caught with a firearm on school property, school buses or at school-sponsored events.[60]
- Kansas, which required school boards to adopt anti-bullying policies that include staff and student training.[61]
- Rhode Island, which required that disciplinary actions for students who possess or use alcohol, drugs or weapons be decided on a case-by-case basis.[62]

"There were a number of children who were unfairly being disciplined," says state Rep. Anastasia P. Williams, the Providence Democrat who co-sponsored the legislation in Rhode Island. "There was case after case, and it was like, enough already." In 2004 a Rhode Island sixth-grader was arrested and suspended for six days for bringing a kitchen knife to school to peel an orange, and in 1995 a kindergartner had been suspended for 10 days for bringing a butter knife to cut cookies.[63]

"There are other ways we can approach the situation," says Williams.

OUTLOOK

Zero Tolerance?

With the never-ending array of situations presented by student misconduct — from guns and assaults to dress-code violations — state lawmakers and local school districts will continue to face the question of whether to tighten up on certain laws and loosen others.

Daniel P. Mears, an associate professor at Florida State University's College of Criminology and Criminal Justice, points out that when it comes to the juvenile-justice system and student misconduct, there are "classic gray areas" that make many situations difficult to weigh. "It's great when you're dealing with extremes," he says, "but it's the gray areas that are hard."

In the coming months, differing views will emerge on the local, state and federal levels. Although President Bush urged renewal of the No Child Left Behind measure in his State of the Union address, many remain skeptical of its chances.[64] While some Capitol Hill observers believe a revised measure could be acted upon this spring, others think nothing is likely to happen at least until a new president takes office in 2009.

On the local and state levels, zero-tolerance policies remain the approach of choice among many school authorities, but concerns about soaring suspension and expulsion rates — especially for relatively minor offenses — are likely to put pressure on school districts to find new methods for retaining order and safety.

"My sense is that we really are much more evenly divided" on zero-tolerance policies, says Skiba of Indiana University. "When I started looking at zero tolerance in 1997, I was kind of a voice crying in the wilderness. By 2000 some were expressing doubts. Now, my sense is that school systems around the country are pretty evenly divided on the use of zero tolerance versus other approaches."

Of course, another shooting spree at a school can propel that momentum in the opposite direction.

"As a society, we careen wildly from extreme to extreme," notes Jamin B. Raskin, an American University law professor who writes on juvenile-justice issues. When student misconduct involves weapons, he says, "the solution is to take away all student rights." On the other hand, if a school goes too far with its get-tough policies, "people remember the Bill of Rights and due-process protection."

Adds Raskin: "People have a hard time maintaining contrary principles in their minds."

NOTES

1. Quoted in Alan J. Borsuk, "Suspension rate deemed too high," *Milwaukee Journal Sentinel*, Jan. 6, 2008, www.jsonline.com, and Milwaukee Public Schools data.

2. For background, see Kathy Koch, "Zero Tolerance," *CQ Researcher*, March 10, 2000, pp. 185-208.

3. Howard Witt, "School discipline harder on blacks," *Chicago Tribune*, Sept. 25, 2007, p. 1.

4. Paul Clinton, "RPV principal in flap over guns leaves job," *Daily Breeze*, Sept. 21, 2007.

5. Clifford Ward, "New charges for stabbing suspect," *Chicago Tribune*, Jan. 26, 2008, p. 15.

6. "Police: Female student kills 2 others, self at Louisiana college," CNN, Feb. 8, 2008.

7. For background, see Kathy Koch, "School Violence," *CQ Researcher*, Oct. 9, 1998, pp. 881-904.

8. "Suspension Fact Sheet: Maryland and Baltimore City, 2006-2007," Open Society Institute-Baltimore, www.soros.org/initiatives/baltimore/articles_publications/articles/suspensionfact_20080124.

9. Quoted in Sara Neufeld, "City Schools Suspend Fewer; Decline Comes After Action by Alonso," *Baltimore Sun*, Nov. 28, 2007, www.baltimoresun.com/news/local/baltimore_city/bal-md.ci.suspensions28nov28,0,7872813.story.

10. For more information, see www.pbis.org.

11. J. Hall, *et al.*, "School Associated Student Homicides, United States, 1992-2006," Centers for Disease Control and Prevention, 2008. The study counted killings occurring at elementary, middle or high schools, on school-sponsored trips or while students were traveling to or from school.

12. Quoted in The Associated Press, "Report Finds School Slayings Lower Than in Previous Decade," accessed at www.edweek.org, Jan. 17, 2008.

13. Rachel Dinkes, Emily Forrest Cataldi and Wendy Lin-Kelly, "Indicators of School Crime and Safety: 2007," U.S. Department of Education and U.S. Department of Justice, December 2007.

14. *Ibid.*

15. The Associated Press, "Survey: Teachers often feel threatened by bullies," www.herald-dispatch.com, Jan. 16, 2008. The survey was conducted by the American Federation of Teachers–West Virginia and the West Virginia School Service Personnel.

16. Quoted in *ibid.*

17. "Teaching Interrupted: Do Discipline Policies in Today's Public Schools Foster the Common Good?" Public Agenda, with support from Common Good, May 2004.

18. "Policy Brief: The High Cost of Teacher Turnover," National Commission on Teaching and America's Future, June 2007, p. 1.

19. For the zero-tolerance policy, see www.ebrschools.org/explore.cfm/schoolinfo/zerotolerancepolicy.

20. Kay S. Hymowitz, "Zero Tolerance" Is Schools' First Line of Defense," *Newsday*, April 18, 2001, www.manhattan-institute.org.

21. "Zero Tolerance Policies Are Not As Effective As Thought In Reducing Violence and Promoting Learning In School, Says APA Task Force," press release, American Psychological Association, Aug. 9, 2006, www.apa.org/releases/zerotolerance.html.

22. Joan First and Charles Patrick Ewing, "The Pros and Cons of Zero Tolerance," *Harvard Education Letter*, January/February 2000.

23. Russell Skiba, "Zero Tolerance: The Assumptions and the Facts," *Education Policy Briefs*, Center for Evaluation and Education Policy, Vol. 2, No. 1, summer 2004, http://ceep.indiana.edu/projects/PDF/PB_V2N1_Zero_Tolerance.pdf.

24. "Zero Tolerance: An Update, 2006," Offices of Research and Education Accountability, Tennessee Comptroller of the Treasury, July 2006.

25. Trent England and Steve Muscatello, "Six Years After Columbine? Time for Common Sense Again," The Heritage Foundation, April 20, 2005.

26. Mindy B. Hagen, "Expulsions show racial disparity," *The* [Charleston, S.C.] *Post and Courier*, Oct. 24, 2007.

27. Witt, *op. cit.*

28. *Ibid.*

29. "Pre-K Students Expelled at More than Three Times the Rate of K-12 Students," news release, Yale University, May 17, 2005. In a new study, released this year, Gilliam found that preschool classes with longer days, more youngsters per teacher and teachers who report high stress levels have higher expulsion rates than other classes. See Arielle Levin Becker, "Cutting Pre-K Expulsions," *Hartford Courant*, Jan. 11, 2008.

30. Russell J. Skiba, *et al.*, Indiana Education Policy Center, and Reece Peterson, University of Nebraska, Lincoln, "The Color of Discipline," Indiana Education Policy Center, Policy Research Report #SRS1, June 2000.

31. Johanna Wald and Daniel J. Losen, "Defining and redirecting a school-to-prison pipeline," in Johanna Wald and Daniel J. Losen, *New Directions for Youth Development* (2003), p. 11.

32. The case is 419 U.S. 565 (1975), — U.S. — (2007).

33. Simone Marie Freeman, "Upholding Students' Due Process Rights: Why Students Are in Need of Better Representation at, and Alternatives to, School Suspension Hearings," *Family Court Review*, Vol. 45, No. 4, October 2007.

34. Robert McCord, James Hager, T. C. Mattocks, "Zero Tolerance: Balancing an Uncertain Expulsion Policy," Feb. 27, 2007, p. 12, http://cnx.org/content/m14361/latest/.

35. Linda Greenhouse, "In Steps Big and Small, Supreme Court Moved Right," *The New York Times*, July 1, 2007. For background see "Student Journalists Fight Campus Censorship," in Kenneth Jost, "Free-Press Disputes," *CQ Researcher*, April 8, 2005, pp. 293-316, and Susan Philips, "Student Journalism," *CQ Researcher*, June 5, 1998, pp. 481-504.

36. *Ponce v. Socorro Independent School District* (5th Circuit, 2007).

37. See, for example, Douglas Lee, "5th Circuit extends limits on student speech," First Amendment Center online, Nov. 27, 2007, www.firstamendmentcenter.org.

38. H. B. Shaffer, "Discipline in Public Schools," *Editorial Research Reports*, Aug. 27, 1969, available at

CQ Researcher Plus Archive, http://library.cqpress.com.

39. Johanna Wald and Michal Kurlaender, "Connected in Seattle? An exploratory study of student perceptions of discipline and attachments to teachers," in Wald and Losen, *op. cit.*, p. 35. The study referred to is Children's Defense Fund, "School suspensions — Are they helping children?" 1975.

40. Skiba, "Zero Tolerance, Zero Evidence," *op. cit.*, p. 2.

41. *Ibid.*

42. "Ship Seizure Policy Is Revised," *The New York Times*, May 25, 1988.

43. *Ibid.*

44. For background, see Kenneth Jost, "Three-Strikes Laws," *CQ Researcher*, May 10, 2002, pp. 417-432, and "Sentencing Debates," *CQ Researcher*, Nov. 5, 2004, pp. 925-948.

45. Richard N. Apling and Nancy Lee Jones, "Individuals with Disabilities Education Act (IDEA): Analysis of Changes Made by P.L. 108-446," Congressional Research Service, Jan. 5, 2005. For background, see Kathy Koch, "Special Education," *CQ Researcher*, Nov. 10, 2000, pp. 905-928.

46. Apling and Jones, *op. cit.*

47. Jennifer Dounay, "State Anti-bullying Statutes," Education Commission of the States, www.ecs.org, April 2005.

48. "Report and Recommendations," National Association of Attorneys General Task Force on School and Campus Safety, September 2007.

49. Amanda Lenhart, "Mean Teens Online: Forget Sticks and Stones, They've Got Mail," Pew Research Center, June 27, 2007.

50. Arthur Levine, "Educating School Teachers," Education Schools Project, 2006, www.edschools.org/pdf/Educating_Teachers_Report.pdf.

51. "An OIG Perspective on the Unsafe School Choice Option," U.S. Department of Education, August 2007, p. 7.

52. Gloria Zradicka, "Persistently Dangerous School Criteria," Education Commission of the States, September 2004.

53. Statement of Kenneth S. Trump, Committee on Education and Labor, U.S. House of Representatives, April 23, 2007.

54. "Enhancing Achievement and Proficiency Through Safe and Drug-Free Schools," U.S. Department of Education, August 2007, pp. 25-26.

55. *Ibid.*, p. 4.

56. David Hoff, "The latest news on the reauthorization of the No Child Left Behind Act," *Education Week*, http://blogs.edweek.org, Sept. 12, 2007.

57. "Rep. Linda Sanchez Introduces Safe School Improvement Act," press release, July 23, 2007. The bill is H.R. 3132.

58. "Recent State Policies/Activities: Safety/Student Discipline — Expulsion, Suspension," Education Commission of the States, www.ecs.org.

59. North Carolina H.B. 1739.

60. Louisiana Act 385.

61. Kansas S.B. 68.

62. Rhode Island H.B. 5352.

63. Jennifer D. Jordan, "Schools' zero-tolerance rules could get second look," *Providence Journal*, June 21, 2007, p. 9A.

64. Libby George, "Despite Bush's Plea, Skepticism Remains on Changes for 'No Child' Reauthorization," *CQ Today*, Jan. 28, 2008.

BIBLIOGRAPHY

Books

Ahranjani, Maryam, Andrew G. Ferguson and Jamin B. Raskin, *Youth Justice in America*, CQ Press, 2005.
This book combines material from criminal-law cases with expert commentary on crime, justice and youth rights. Ahranjani is associate director of the Program on Law and Government and Raskin is a professor of constitutional law at American University. Ferguson is a public defender in Washington.

Brown, Dan, *The Great Expectations School: A Rookie Year in the New Blackboard Jungle*, Arcade Publishing, 2007.

A graduate student at Teachers College at Columbia University describes his year as a beginning teacher at a Bronx elementary school, an experience that tested his mettle and revealed shortcomings in the nation's educational system.

Wald, Johanna, and Daniel J. Losen, eds., *New Directions for Youth Development, Jossey-Bass,* fall 2003.
Experts in education, civil rights and psychology explore how school-discipline policies can set youths on a so-called "prison track" and identify programs that can help schools retain order while reaching out to students in need of guidance.

Articles

Freeman, Simone Marie, "Upholding Students' Due Process Rights: Why Students Are in Need of Better Representation At, and Alternatives To, School Suspension Hearings," *Family Court Review,* Vol. 45, No. 4, October 2007.
The author argues that providing students with legal advocates at suspension hearings will help students make better decisions and advocates mediation as an alternative to suspension and suspension hearings.

Marshall, Tom, and Jonathan Abel, "When Students Are Suspects, Lines Blur," *St. Petersburg Times,* Jan. 20, 2008.
Florida police "frequently skirt state and federal laws" when questioning children at school."

Witt, Howard, "School Discipline Harder on Blacks," *Chicago Tribune,* Sept. 25, 2007.
Witt analyzed federal data and concluded that "[f]ifty years after federal troops escorted nine black students through the doors of an all-white high school in Little Rock, Ark. . . . America's public schools remain as unequal as they have ever been when measured in terms of disciplinary sanctions such as suspensions and expulsions."

Reports and Studies

"Report and Recommendations," *National Association of Attorneys General Task Force on School and Campus Safety,* September 2007, www.atg.wa.gov/uploaded-Files/Another/Protecting_Youth/School_Safety/FINAL%20REPORT%20090407.pdf.
Produced in the aftermath of the Virginia Tech shootings, the report recommends that schools and colleges report disturbing student behavior to trained individuals who can take action when appropriate.

"Teaching Interrupted: Do Discipline Policies in Today's Public Schools Foster the Common Good?" *Public Agenda,* May 2004, www.publicagenda.org/research/research_reports_details.cfm?list=3.
Too many students are losing the opportunity to learn, and too many teachers are leaving the profession, because of the bad behavior of a few troublemakers, concludes this study based on a national survey of middle- and high-school teachers and parents.

Dinkes, Rachel, et al., "Indicators of School Crime and Safety: 2007," *National Center for Education Statistics, U.S. Department of Education, and Bureau of Justice Statistics, U.S. Department of Justice,* December 2007, http://nces.ed.gov/programs/crimeindicators/crimeindicators2007/.
"There is some evidence that school safety has improved," according to this massive statistical report, which adds that "violence, theft, drugs and weapons continue to pose problems in schools."

Mukherjee, Elora, "Criminalizing the Classroom: The Over-Policing of New York City Schools," *New York Civil Liberties Union and American Civil Liberties Union Racial Justice Program,* March 2007, www.nyclu.org/files/criminalizing_the_classroom_report.pdf.
Since the NYPD took control of school safety in 1998, the "massive deployment of inadequately trained police personnel" has created an environment that is "often hostile and dysfunctional," the report concludes.

Skiba, Russell J., "Zero Tolerance, Zero Evidence," *Indiana Education Policy Center,* August 2000, www.indiana.edu/~safeschl/ztze.pdf.
A national expert on school-discipline policies concludes there is little evidence that the strategies typically associated with zero tolerance contribute to improved student behavior or overall school safety,

Skiba, Russell J., et al., "The Color of Discipline," *Indiana Education Policy Center,* June 2000, www.indiana.edu/~safeschl/cod.pdf.
African-Americans are disproportionately represented in office referrals, suspensions and expulsions, according to the authors.

For More Information

American Federation of Teachers, 555 New Jersey Ave., N.W., Washington, DC 20001; (202) 879-4400; www.aft .org. Nationwide union representing classroom teachers and other personnel.

Applied Research Center, 32 Broadway, Suite 1801, New York, NY 10004; (212) 513-7925; www.arc.org. Promotes racial justice through research, advocacy and journalism on education, poverty and other issues.

Center for Evaluation and Education Policy, 509 East Third St., Bloomington, IN 47401-3654; (800) 511-6575; http://ceep.indiana.edu. Conducts research on education policy, including student-discipline practices.

Education Commission of the States, 700 Broadway, #1200, Denver, CO 80203-3460; (303) 299-3600; www .ecs.org. Maintains extensive online resources on education policy.

National Association of Secondary School Principals, 1904 Association Dr., Reston, VA 20191-1537; (800) 253-7746; www.nassp.org. Promotes the interests of middle- and high-school administrators.

National Center for Education Statistics, 1990 K St., N.W., Washington, DC 20006; (202) 502-7300; http:// nces.ed.gov. Collects and analyzes data on education.

National Education Association, 1201 16th St., N.W., Washington, DC 20036-3290; (202) 833-4000; www.nea .org. Nationwide union representing classroom teachers and other personnel.

National School Boards Association, 1680 Duke St., Alexandria, VA 22314; (703) 838-6722; www.nsba.org. Federation of state school-board associations.

Open Society Institute-Baltimore, 201 North Charles St., Suite 1300, Baltimore, MD 21201; (410) 234-1091; www.soros.org/initiatives/baltimore. Part of the international foundation started by philanthropist George Soros; addresses drug addiction, youth, and the social and economic costs of incarceration.

17 Zero Tolerance

Is Mandatory Punishment in Schools Unfair?

Kathy Koch

A classmate shot and killed 6-year-old Kayla Rolland last month at school in Mount Morris Township, Mich.

Reuters/Rebecca Cook

O n a school bus last fall in rural Mississippi, five high school students passed the time on the long ride home by tossing peanuts at each other.

But the fun ended when the driver got hit. She pulled over, called the police and had the boys arrested for assault, punishable by five years in prison. The criminal charges were soon dropped, but the teenagers were suspended and lost their bus privileges. Unable to make the 30-mile trip to school, all five dropped out.

The recent shooting death of a 6-year-old Michigan girl by another 6-year-old underscores the fear of violence that has invaded America's schools. But the strict, one-strike-and-you're-out policies being imposed to nip school violence and misbehavior in the bud sometimes go too far, critics say. Other examples from the public school crime blotter:

- A 6-year-old boy in York, Pa., was suspended for carrying a pair of nail clippers to school.
- A second-grader in Columbus, Ohio, was suspended for drawing a paper gun, cutting it out and pointing it at classmates.
- A 9-year-old Ohio boy was suspended after writing, "You will die an honorable death" as a fortune-cookie prediction for a class assignment.
- A 12-year-old Florida boy was handcuffed and jailed after he stomped in a puddle, splashing classmates.
- A 13-year-old boy in Manassas, Va., who accepted a Certs breath mint from a classmate was suspended and required to attend drug-awareness classes.
- Jewish youths in several schools were suspended for wearing the Star of David, sometimes used as a symbol of gang membership.

From *CQ Researcher*, March 10, 2000.

375

Most Schools Adopt Zero Tolerance

School systems began adopting zero-tolerance policies after Congress passed the 1994 Gun-Free Schools Act, which required one-year expulsions for bringing a firearm or bomb to school. More than 90 percent of U.S. public schools had zero tolerance for firearms or other weapons in 1997.

U.S. public schools with zero-tolerance policies, 1996-97

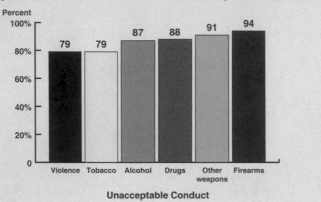

Source: U.S. Department of Education, "Principal-School Disciplinarian Survey on School Violence," 1997.

Zero-tolerance policies punish all offenses severely, no matter how minor. School systems began adopting the tough codes after Congress passed the 1994 Gun-Free Schools Act, which required one-year expulsions for any child bringing a firearm or bomb to school.

But zero-tolerance rules in many states also cover fighting, drug or alcohol use and gang activity, as well as relatively minor offenses like possessing over-the-counter medications, disrespect of authority, sexual harassment, threats and vandalism. More than 90 percent of U.S. public schools had zero-tolerance policies for firearms or other weapons in 1997, and more than 85 percent had the policies for drugs and alcohol.

After the massacre last April at Columbine High School in Littleton, Colo., nervous legislators and school boards further tightened their zero-tolerance policies, creating what some critics call a national intolerance for childish behavior. In some jurisdictions, carrying cough drops, wearing black lipstick or dying your hair blue are expellable offenses. Even writing a paper about murder or suicide can land a student in trouble.

"Things got a lot worse post-Columbine," says John Whitehead, president of the conservative Rutherford Institute, a Charlottesville, Va., group dedicated to protecting civil liberties.

In the current atmosphere, merely displaying the image of a weapon is unacceptable, as Samantha Jones, of Nevis, Minn., learned. The 17-year-old Army recruit was forbidden from using her favorite photo of herself — sitting atop a howitzer at the local VFW post — for her yearbook picture.

"A real vortex has been created that sucks in otherwise good kids who make a single mistake," Whitehead says.

"Some call it zero-zero tolerance," says Paul Kingery, director of the Hamilton Fish Institute on School and Community Violence at The George Washington University.

He discovered that while the number of students expelled for firearms has decreased since 1994, expulsions and suspensions for non-gun offenses have skyrocketed.[1] In Chicago, for instance, expulsions jumped eightfold after zero-tolerance policies were adopted in 1995 for weapons, alcohol and drugs.

Meanwhile, because minor infractions are punished so severely, administrators are ratcheting up punishments for more serious offenses. Two-year and permanent expulsions are on the rise. In Pennsylvania, long-term expulsions jumped nearly 960 percent from 1996 to 1997, Kingery writes.[2]

To accommodate all the expulsions, the number of alternative schools in the United States jumped from 2,604 in 1994, when most zero-tolerance rules were enacted, to 3,380 in 1997, according to the U.S. Education Department.

Only nine states require expelled students to attend an alternative school. Research shows that expelled students who don't attend alternative classes are less likely to re-enter school and more likely to get mixed up in gang activity and drugs and otherwise run afoul of the law.

Critics say the biggest problem with zero-tolerance policies is their lack of flexibility, which prohibits officials from taking a child's age or past history into account.

"The absolute punishment applies whether you're carrying a nail clipper or a bazooka, Tylenol or illegal drugs," says Nadine Strossen, president of the American Civil Liberties Union (ACLU).

Strossen says school zero-tolerance policies grew out of drug-war laws that abolished discretion and curtailed civil liberties, such as mandatory minimum sentences, three-strikes-and-you're-out laws, civil-asset forfeiture and stop-and-frisk tactics.

"Judges were seen as too lenient," says Eugene Volokh, a professor of law at the University of California at Los Angeles, "and many people perceived that some school administrations tolerated things that shouldn't have been tolerated."

But critics say the zero-tolerance laws that resulted are either too vague or all-encompassing. One such law, an Alabama judge said recently, was unreasonable because it meant that "a sharpened pencil, chemistry supplies and a tennis racket could all be used as weapons."[3]

Expulsions Hit Black Students Hardest

In some large school districts, black students are three to five times more likely to be expelled than white students, according to a recent survey. Moreover, the percentage of blacks expelled far exceeds blacks' enrollment.

Public school expulsions, by race, 1998-99

SCHOOL LOCATION	PERCENTAGE BLACK	PERCENTAGE WHITE
Austin, Texas		
Enrollment	18%	37%
Expulsion Rate	36%	18%
Boston		
Enrollment	55%	13%
Expulsion Rate	70%	9%
Columbia, S.C.		
Enrollment	78%	20%
Expulsion Rate	90%	9%
Los Angeles		
Enrollment	14%	11%
Expulsion Rate	30%	8%
Miami-Dade County, Fla.		
Enrollment	33%	12%
Expulsion Rate	48%	8%
Providence, R.I.		
Enrollment	23%	21%
Expulsion Rate	39%	13%
San Francisco		
Enrollment	18%	14%
Expulsion Rate	56%	11%

Source: The Applied Research Center, 1999

School administrators defend strict policies, arguing that they're needed because it's difficult to distinguish what is and isn't a weapon or gang-related paraphernalia. They say that students have been caught carrying hairbrushes with blades in the handles, or necklaces with large metal crosses made of knife blades. And gang symbols can range from a Star of David to a rolled-up pants leg.

William Modzeleski, director of the Education Department's Safe and Drug-Free Schools Program, says local zero-tolerance policies go far beyond the federal gun-free schools legislation. "The federal law is very narrowly defined," he says. "It says a child should be expelled for bringing a firearm or bomb to school. Not drug-abusing behavior, not nail clippers, not nail files, not water pistols, not pellet guns."

The federal law also allows local administrators to waive or reduce the one-year expulsion if there are extenuating circumstances. In fact, about one-third of the students expelled for firearms serve less than a year's suspension, he says.

Modzeleski says some schools also may be misinterpreting an Education Department publication on recognizing troubled kids. It recommended that children exhibiting certain behaviors, like writing about death, be referred to a professional counselor. Yet some schools suspend such students.

School officials in Kansas suspended senior honors student Sarah Boman, 17, for displaying artwork at school that included a poem written from a madman's perspective. School officials considered it a threat and said Boman can return to school only if she had psychological testing.

"We have to send a message that we're serious about no guns and drugs," says Michael Resnick, associate executive director for advocacy and issues management at the National School Boards Association (NSBA). "We can't be fuzzy around the edges about that message."

Educators say they cannot relax their guard because life-threatening incidents continue to plague U.S. schools. Last fall, authorities shut down a Cleveland high school after uncovering a bomb plot. On Dec. 6, a 13-year-old honor student in Oklahoma took a semi-automatic handgun from his backpack and fired 15 rounds at classmates, injuring five. And on Feb. 29, there was the shooting in Michigan of first-grader Kayla Rolland.

While a handful of silly cases make headlines, most zero-tolerance cases involve real weapons, says Vincent Ferrandino, executive director of the National Association of Elementary School Principals (NAESP).

He rejects suggestions that the policies reflect administrators' fear of liability suits if violence should erupt in their schools. "These policies are meant to protect the kids," he says.

But Peter Blauvelt, president of the National Alliance for Safe Schools (NASS), says, "There are a lot of administrators who are comfortable having no discretion, especially when they have to discipline the mayor's child. It's much easier to say they must treat all kids the same because of zero-tolerance laws."

Allowing "flexibility" also allows more racial and ethnic discrimination, Ferrandino contends. But students' advocates say that zero tolerance disproportionately targets minorities, the poor and the disabled.

That was the charge made last fall by the Rev. Jesse Jackson, who led marches in Decatur, Ill., to protest the expulsions of six African-American teenagers for starting a brawl at a football game. White boys, Jackson said, never would have been expelled for two years for a fight that involved no weapons and no injuries.

Similarly, says Judith A. Browne, senior attorney for the Advancement Project, a civil rights group in Washington, D.C., the five Mississippi peanut throwers were treated harshly because they were black and the bus driver white.

Critics say zero-tolerance policies teach children to be intolerant and don't prepare them for making difficult judgments later in life. "School boards somehow expect children to value differences in each other when adults seem unable to differentiate between the behavior of 6-year-olds and 16-year-olds, between an aspirin and cocaine, and between a friendly, first-grade hug and a sexual attack," writes Bethany Baxter, an educational consultant.[4]

As parents, educators and policy-makers debate the pros and cons of zero-tolerance policies, here are some of the questions they are asking:

Are zero-tolerance policies effective?

Proponents credit zero-tolerance policies with recent declines in crime and school weapons cases, even though they acknowledge there are little data to support that claim.

"All we have is anecdotal experience and the broad acceptance among administrators that zero-tolerance policies have been very helpful," says Ronald Stephens, executive director of the National School Safety Center, in Westlake, Calif.

"There is no good, quantitative research to show whether zero-tolerance policies are effective or ineffective," Modzeleski says. "But many educators and law enforcement officials will tell you that because of zero tolerance, we have less violence in schools than we had five years ago."

Federal statistics confirm that the number of crimes in schools per 1,000 students decreased from 155 in

1993 to 102 in 1997. There also were declines in the number of students carrying weapons to school and the number of student fights.

In Baltimore, school officials credit the aggressive zero-tolerance law adopted last spring with a 67 percent drop in arrests and a 31 percent decline in school crime in the first two months of the 1999-2000 school year. [5] And after Texas adopted zero tolerance for drugs and weapons, the percentage of teachers reporting that assaults on students was a "significant problem" dropped from 53 percent in 1993 to 31 percent in 1998. [6]

Moreover, says Stephens, the dramatic increase in the number of alternative schools around the country reflects the fact that zero-tolerance policies have "taken the troublemakers out of the schools and allowed the teachers to get back to the mission of teaching."

But critics argue that if zero tolerance were responsible for either falling street crime or the decline in school weapons-possession, proponents would have statistics showing that crime or weapons possession dropped faster in schools and communities with zero-tolerance policies than in those without them.

"They don't have those statistics," says Jason Zeidenberg, a policy analyst at the Justice Policy Institute.

"It may just be that violent crime and drug use are down everywhere, so they are down in the schools as well," NASS' Blauvelt says.

Despite the lack of compelling statistics, 85 percent of principals, 79 percent of teachers and 82 percent of students credit zero-tolerance policies with keeping drugs out of schools, according to a 1998 Columbia University survey. [7]

However, a 1998 federal government survey of more than 1,000 school principals indicated that there were only minor improvements in school discipline and drug problems from 1990 to 1996. [8] The percentage of principals reporting "serious problems" with fighting, alcohol use and weapons possession dropped somewhat. But an increase was posted among principals who said tobacco and drug use, drug sales and verbal and physical abuse of teachers were "moderate or serious" problems.

"The bottom line is that the rate of school violence has remained fairly level since the early 1990s," wrote researchers Russell Skiba and Reece Peterson. [9]

The policies are highly effective at sending an unequivocal message to kids, says Gerald Tirozzi, executive director of the National Association of Secondary School Principals. "I can't prove that zero-tolerance policies alone were responsible [for the declines in violence], but with the violence going down, I'd like to think that message is sinking in."

But Skiba, an associate professor of counseling and educational psychology at Indiana University, says the right message may not be getting through, or may be reaching the wrong people. Several studies show that 35 to 45 percent of suspensions are for repeat offenders, he points out. "So we end up punishing honor students to send a message to bad kids. But the data indicate that the bad kids aren't getting the message."

While no studies show conclusively that get-tough tactics work, Skiba says there are good data showing the effectiveness of comprehensive violence-prevention programs focusing on conflict resolution, peer mediation, mentoring and bullying prevention.

Yet zero-tolerance policies are the quickest and cheapest way to put a program in place, Skiba says, "and it makes good rhetoric. We certainly need to set boundaries and limits. But let's not kid ourselves by thinking that we are going to solve school safety problems simply by drawing a line in the sand. Zero-tolerance policies by themselves will not ensure that our schools are safe."

But even proponents agree that the toughest policies won't totally eradicate violence, says John Mitchell, deputy director of education issues at the American Federation of Teachers (AFT). "If a kid is so driven that killing becomes the major thing in their lives, schools can't protect against that just with a zero-tolerance policy," he says. "Other things have to be put into place."

Modzeleski points out that zero-tolerance policies are only effective if they are developed with input from the parents and students and are relevant to the culture of the community and the age of the students. "What you do in Des Moines might be different from what you do in Dubuque," he says. "What is appropriate for a 17-year-old is not necessarily appropriate for a 7-year-old."

Effective programs also include early intervention, violence and gang prevention and programs to promote racial and ethnic tolerance. Efforts to get kids connected to their schools and communities through after-school opportunities, smaller schools, smaller classes and better-prepared teachers are also helpful, he says.

"If the policies are carefully worded, extremely narrowly focused and used in conjunction with a comprehensive violence-prevention program, they can be effective," says Gerald Newberry, executive director of the Health Information Network at the National Education Association (NEA). "And they must be communicated in a way that encourages cooperation, rather than rebellion."

But zero-tolerance measures that turn schools into military or penal institutions "foster anxiety, fear and insecurity — precisely the opposite of their intended effect," the ACLU's Strossen says.

Critics are particularly concerned about zero-tolerance programs run by 14 states that expel students without providing alternative educational opportunities.

"If a child is already ostracized and alienated, the most irrational response is suspension or expulsion," Strossen says. "You want to bring them back into the fold."

Are zero-tolerance policies constitutional?

Strossen maintains that students' rights to privacy, free speech and due process are being abridged by zero-tolerance rules. "Kids have been thrown out of school for completely innocuous things like wearing certain T-shirts, creating works of art or wearing the Star of David," she says.

The Supreme Court has ruled that children have a property interest in public education, and thus the government cannot deprive them of their education without due process, she says. The court ruled in the landmark *Tinker v. Des Moines* case in 1969 that neither students nor teachers shed their constitutional rights at the schoolhouse door, she adds.

"Yet, consistently, we see a whole host of actions being taken that violate civil liberties," Strossen says, "including everything from prosecuting parents when their children are truant, to throwing kids out of school for minor infractions, to censorial discipline for innocuous statements made on students' own Web sites."

Many lawsuits challenging zero-tolerance rules charge that students' rights to free speech were violated. In the wake of schoolyard murders by boys who first wrote about death or made verbal threats or dressed a certain way, teachers are quick to report — and schools

prone to expel — a student for what he or she wore, drew or said.

Other challenges to zero-tolerance rules allege that schools failed to follow due-process procedures, Strossen says. Students must be given notice of the charge against them, she says, and allowed to respond to the charge before being penalized.

"But a lot of zero-tolerance policies are being automatically implemented without even giving the student an opportunity to respond," she says. Often the student doesn't even have the right to have a parent or lawyer present.

The Rutherford Institute's Whitehead says the constitutionality of a zero-tolerance code depends on the case and how the code is written. "Some of the policies I've looked at are vague and a bit overbroad, which I think goes to their constitutionality," he says.

Nonetheless, zero-tolerance policies have generally received favorable treatment from the current Supreme Court, which "almost always rules in favor of state laws, police actions and school actions," Whitehead says. "Starting with President [Ronald] Reagan's appointments, the court has shifted to the right," he says. "That has had a big impact on these cases."

For instance, in *Veronia School District v. Acton,* the court said in 1995 that student athletes have a reduced expectation of privacy and thus could be randomly tested for drugs without probable cause. "In another time, with a different court, you may get a different interpretation," Whitehead says.[10]

Charles B. Vergon, an attorney and professor of educational leadership at Youngstown State University, in Ohio, analyzed about 60 lawsuits brought on behalf of students expelled or suspended for weapons or firearms possession since 1990. In three-quarters of the cases, the schools' right to ensure safety on their premises was upheld, even though in some cases "a reasonable person could have taken a very different posture," Vergon says.

"School districts continue to enjoy substantial deference from the courts in governing the conduct of students at school and coming and going from school, particularly if it enhances the safety of students," he says.

NSBA staff attorney Julie Lewis says zero-tolerance policies are usually upheld as constitutional unless they are too vague or overbroad, or the school district violates due-process rules, infringes upon students' free-speech rights or enforces the policies inconsistently.

"Most courts have been flexible in enforcing due process if they see that there was some procedure followed or notice provided," Lewis says. If a principal discusses the accusation with the student, many courts say the student received due process.

Ironically, Lewis says, some school districts are "broadening and broadening and broadening" their zero-tolerance policies, hoping to discourage civil-rights and equal-protection lawsuits. But instead, they now face more due-process and First Amendment suits, she says.

The University of California's Volokh says if zero-tolerance laws are properly written, and the school does not conduct an illegal search or otherwise violate the Constitution, they're perfectly constitutional. Even expulsions for artwork or writings dealing with death may not violate a student's right to free speech, he says.

In *Tinker v. Des Moines School District*, the Supreme Court held that schools can act if they have "reasonable anticipation" that a student's behavior will cause "material disruption" of school discipline, Volokh explains. For instance, if a student jokes about blowing up the school, the government could argue that it reasonably anticipated that such a joke would interfere with discipline because students would be frightened, rumors would get started or other kids might mimic the threat, he says.

"In the current atmosphere of heightened sensitivity, a school might punish something that in a particular context is disruptive, even though in another context it would be protected," Volokh says. For instance, a university recently removed a bulletin board photo of a military-history professor dressed in a mock Roman costume holding a sword. "The school said it creates a climate of violence," he says.

Schools' efforts to ban all images of guns are probably constitutional, he says. But they strike him as "a weird kind of fanatical, militant pacifism — an attempt to deny

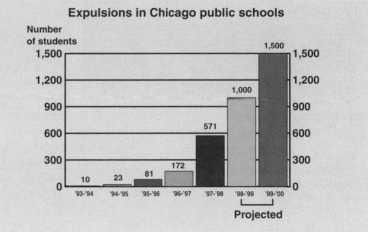

Expulsions in Chicago Rose Sharply

The number of students expelled in Chicago more than doubled in 1996-97, a year after the school board passed a strict zero-tolerance policy. Expulsions tripled in 1997-98 and are projected to keep rising.

Expulsions in Chicago public schools

Number of students

'93-'94	10
'94-'95	23
'95-'96	81
'96-'97	172
'97-'98	571
'98-'99	1,000
'99-'00	1,500

Projected

Source: Chicago Public Schools, "Measuring Progress Towards Goals," 1999

the fact that weapons exist and that sometimes they are useful, and that we pay people to operate them," he says. "Some schools are behaving in ways that are just plain silly," he says. "But silliness is not unconstitutional."

Are zero-tolerance policies fairly and consistently applied?

One of the rationales for zero-tolerance policies both in schools and law enforcement was to remove discretion from authorities and ensure that everyone would be treated equally.

"If you have a policy that clearly articulates what won't be tolerated, what the penalties are and it is consistently applied, that should minimize the extent to which you have discriminatory practices," says Tirozzi of the principals' association.

A discretionary policy allows authorities to consciously or subconsciously treat people from one group differently from those of another, Volokh says. "Zero-tolerance policies theoretically would diminish police discretion and the chance of racist enforcement," he says.

But critics argue that when zero-tolerance policies are actually applied in the real world, blacks, minorities, poor people and disabled students are expelled and suspended at higher rates than whites. Similarly, the

Students attend a prayer vigil in Denver last April following a shooting spree by two Columbine High School students that left 15 people dead. The killings prompted many schools to strengthen their zero-tolerance policies.

critics say, racial stereotyping by police causes a disproportionate number of blacks and minorities to be stopped, frisked or arrested. For example, Strossen says, African-Americans make up 13 percent of the population and 13 percent of drug users. But blacks make up 74 percent of those incarcerated for drug use, she says.

The Decatur case brought this long-simmering controversy to the forefront. Lawyers for the six suspended youths produced statistics showing that 82 percent of Decatur students expelled in the past three years were African-American, although only 48 percent of the student population is black.

In addition, a recent survey of 12 large school districts showed that in some districts black students are three to five times more likely to be expelled than white students are. For instance, in Phoenix, blacks made up only 4 percent of the high school population but received 21 percent of the expulsions or suspensions. By comparison, only 18 percent of the whites — representing 74 percent of the enrollment — were suspended. Similarly, in San Francisco blacks account for 16 percent of the enrollment but 52 percent of the exclusions.[11]

Even the Department of Education's own figures show that in 1997 black students represented 17 percent of public school enrollment nationwide but 32 percent of those suspended — a disparity that has remained consistent since 1975.

"The recent school shootings were done primarily by white kids," Zeidenberg points out. "But African-American kids are the ones being disproportionately expelled and suspended. Is it really fair for them to bear the brunt of America's panic about school violence?"

However, "A numerical disparity does not by itself prove discrimination," Norma Cantu, assistant secretary of Education for civil rights, told the U.S. Commission on Civil Rights on Feb. 18. "It does not tell us the cause of the disparity."

The judge in the Decatur case agreed that disparate statistics alone don't prove discrimination. Judge Michael McCuskey upheld the students' suspensions on Jan. 11 after finding that the school district had not violated their civil rights. "Because the students failed to show that any similarly situated Caucasian students were treated less harshly," he wrote in his ruling, "they failed to establish that race played any role in the School Board's expulsion decision."

Volokh agrees that raw, disparate numbers don't prove discrimination. "There may be a disproportionate amount of improper conduct in certain groups," he says. "For example, a disproportionate number of men are criminally prosecuted, but that doesn't necessarily mean there is an anti-male bias. It may be the case that men commit more crimes than women."

Although he admits that discrimination can occur, "Misbehavior is not evenly distributed among racial and ethnic groups," says Kent Scheidegger, legal director of the conservative Criminal Justice Legal Foundation in Sacramento, Calif. "It's possible they are being punished more because they are misbehaving more."

But researcher Skiba insists, "There's just no evidence of that whatsoever. There is pretty good evidence that this oversuspension is not the result of lower behavioral standards among black students," he says. "There seems to be more going on than that."

In a recent study, Skiba found no difference between the punishments meted out to black and white students once the students are referred to the office. But black students were twice as likely to be referred to the office as white students were. "The real disparity was in classroom referrals," he says.

Black students were referred more often for minor, more subjective behaviors like loitering, disrespect, threats, excessive noise and a catchall category called "conduct interference," he found. Whites were referred for less-subjective behaviors, such as smoking, vandalism, obscene language or using drugs or alcohol. "These things could be culturally bound," Skiba says. "A white female teacher might not be culturally sensitive to the difference in styles of African-American male students."

A study by the Civil Rights Project at Harvard University corroborated Skiba's findings. "African-American and Latino children are constantly being suspended for the more discretionary offenses, such as 'defiance of authority' and 'disrespect of authority,'" it said. "These categories of conduct clearly provide more latitude for racial bias to play a part."[12]

The ACLU's Strossen argues that such "invidious discrimination" is probably occurring in the classroom, when the teacher decides who to refer to the office, just as it does when a policeman decides who to stop and frisk or a prosecutor decides who to prosecute. "Studies have demonstrably shown that with minimum-sentencing guidelines discrimination apparently occurs at the police and prosecutor levels," she says. "I assume the same thing happens in the schools."

Even if the punishment meted out is the same once an offender appears before a principal or a judge, she says, "We'll never know all of the infractions committed by white kids that teachers decide not to treat as an infraction, partly because they know the punishment is going to be so harsh."

"Schools are more willing to recognize mitigating circumstances if they perceive the student as having 'a real future' that would be destroyed by expulsion," said Terry Keleher, program director at the Applied Research Center, in Oakland, Calif., which studies race and social-change issues.[13]

Disparate treatment of disabled students under zero-tolerance policies is more confusing, but no less controversial. Some observers complain that federal law creates a dual system of punishment in which disabled children who bring guns to school are treated less harshly than non-disabled students caught with a weapon at school.

But parents and advocates for the disabled cite statistics showing that, in fact, disabled students are twice as likely as non-disabled students to be expelled or suspended. They say schools use zero tolerance to get rid of disabled students that are difficult to handle or are not performing as well as others.

BACKGROUND

'We Need to Get Tough'

Presidential candidate Richard M. Nixon campaigned on "law and order" issues in the 1960s. Politicians in the '70s bragged of being "tough on crime." Then in the 1980s, as the government's "war on drugs" heated up, "zero tolerance" joined the lexicon.

The term probably first appeared in 1983, when the Navy cracked down on drug abusers. The Marines soon adopted a similar policy, and initiated random drug tests.

A year later, Congress passed the first mandatory-minimum sentencing law, specifying stiff, automatic penalties for drugs and firearms violations. Lawmakers also amended federal forfeiture laws, expanding the government's authority to seize private property suspected of being involved in commission of a crime.

By 1986, with the nation beset by crack cocaine and skyrocketing violence, President Ronald Reagan launched the "war on drugs," and Congress passed the Anti-Drug Abuse Act, which expanded the list of offenses covered by mandatory sentencing.[14]

The same year, Attorney General Edwin Meese III authorized Customs officials nationwide to seize the boats, automobiles, and passports of anyone crossing the border with even trace amounts of drugs.

Within months, angry citizens whose boats had been seized were testifying on Capitol Hill along with Customs and Coast Guard officials accused of trampling the rights and sometimes destroying the property of citizens, some later proved innocent.

But the administration continued on the attack. In May, Education Secretary William J. Bennett asked Congress to withhold federal education money from schools unless they adopted zero-tolerance expulsion policies for students using or dealing in drugs on school grounds.

"We need to get tough as hell and do it right now," Bennett told the House Select Committee on Narcotics Abuse and Control."[15]

Rep. E. Clay Shaw, R-Fla., supported Bennett's proposal, arguing, "We have to quit being bleeding hearts for every kid who's rotten to the core."[16]

But Bennett got little support from the rest of the Democratically controlled committee, which said it preferred drug-education programs to simple expulsion. "Are

CHRONOLOGY

1960s *Illegal drug trafficking skyrockets. Supreme Court recognizes free-speech rights for school students.*

1968 Mandatory drug testing begins for returning Vietnam War veterans.

1969 Supreme Court rules in *Tinker v. Des Moines Independent Community School District* that students' constitutional rights were violated when they were suspended for wearing black armbands to protest the Vietnam War.

1970s *Courts extend due-process protections to students and mandate equal education for the disabled.*

1971 President Richard M. Nixon declares the first "war on drugs."

1975 Supreme Court rules in *Goss v. Lopez* that students cannot be suspended without due process. Education for All Handicapped Children Act requires all children to be educated in the "least restrictive environment" possible.

1980s *Crack cocaine inundates inner cities, and homicide among juveniles, particularly young, black males, reaches epidemic proportions. First mass murders occur on school grounds.*

1982 An article in the *Atlantic* by researcher George Kelling espouses the "broken windows" theory of policing, providing the basis for later zero-tolerance tactics in cities and schools.

1983 Navy and Marines adopt zero-tolerance drug policy.

1984 Congress passes Comprehensive Crime Control Act, requiring a federal commission to develop mandatory-sentencing guidelines for federal judges. Congress mandates stiff penalties for drug and firearm offenses.

1986 President Ronald Reagan launches a second "war on drugs." Congress passes Anti-Drug Abuse Act, doubling the number of federal mandatory minimums in effect. Federal and state governments begin seizing boats, automobiles and homes of drug suspects.

Jan. 13, 1988 Supreme Court rules in *Hazelwood School District v. Kuhlmeier* that school officials can censor student expression for "legitimate pedagogical concerns."

Sept. 26, 1988 A 19-year-old gunman opens fire on a Greenwood, S.C., school-yard, killing two and wounding nine.

1989 On Jan. 17, a man with an assault rifle kills six children and wounds 30 on a Stockton, Calif., playground.

1990s *Congress bans guns from school grounds; mass murders committed by students erupt at decade's end.*

1990 President George Bush signs Gun-Free School Zones Act.

1992-93 Fifty-five violent deaths occur at schools and school functions.

1993 Washington state mandates life imprisonment for repeat felons.

1994 California and 12 other states pass "three-strikes-and-you're-out" legislation. Congress passes Omnibus Crime Bill, which includes mandatory drug sentences, and the Gun-Free Schools Act.

1995 Supreme Court strikes down 1995 Gun-Free School Zones Act and upholds random drug testing of school athletes. Crime reverses its upward trend, except for homicides by teenage boys, which skyrockets.

1997-98 Students commit mass murder five times within eight months in rural schools; 13 students and faculty die and 47 are wounded.

April 20, 1999 Two teenage boys shoot and kill 13 people at Columbine High School in Littleton, Colo., and then commit suicide.

Feb. 29, 2000 Six-year-old Kayla Rolland is shot and killed by a classmate at an elementary school in Michigan.

you suggesting that a junkie kicked out of school is no longer a junkie?" asked Chairman Charles B. Rangel, D-N.Y.[17]

Another section of the 1986 Anti-Drug Abuse Act contained the Drug-Free Schools and Communities Act, the precursor of today's Safe and Drug-Free Schools Act, the federal government's largest drug and violence-prevention activity. The act required schools to have policies prohibiting alcohol and drug use by youths.

"But it did not specify what was to happen once a kid was found possessing alcohol or drugs on school property," says the Education Department's Modzeleski, noting that the term "zero tolerance" does not appear in the act.

In 1990, the U.S. Customs Service discontinued its boat-impoundment program after a marijuana cigarette led to the seizure of a research vessel from the Woods Hole Oceanographic Institute.

Ironically, at about the same time that Customs was easing its policy, zero tolerance was catching on in the public schools. By late 1989, districts in California, New York and Kentucky had adopted zero-tolerance expulsion policies for drugs or gang-related activity. By 1993, schools across the country had cracked down on tobacco, alcohol and disruptive activities, as well as drugs and weapons.

After an American Association of University Women survey showed that 81 percent of students in grades 8-11 said they had been sexually harassed at least once in school, many schools also instituted zero tolerance for sexual harassment.

Zero tolerance was also becoming more popular with local lawmakers and soon was being applied to everything from pollution and trespassing to skateboarding, racial intolerance, homelessness and boom boxes.

'Broken-Windows' Approach

In 1990, President George Bush signed the Gun-Free School Zones Act into law, prohibiting the possession or discharge of a firearm near a public school. The act claimed Congress had the right to act under its power to regulate interstate commerce. But the Supreme Court disagreed, ruling in 1995 that Congress had exceeded its constitutional powers. By then, lawmakers had gone back to the drawing board and enacted the 1994 Gun-Free Schools Act, which tied enforcement to the federal government's spending power.

That prompted state legislatures to begin requiring local school districts to implement zero-tolerance policies for firearms and bombs. Many of the new laws also included anything that could be used as a weapon.

"There is no universal definition of a weapon," Modzeleski says. "A belt buckle is a weapon, a rat-tail comb is a weapon. So are box cutters and baseball bats."

Meanwhile, zero tolerance got a boost from *Fixing Broken Windows*, a 1996 book by George L. Kelling and Catherine M. Coles. They argue that ignoring minor problems in cities, like broken windows or graffiti, eventually leads to an increase in serious crime.

Republican Mayor Rudolph W. Giuliani based his anti-crime program in New York City on the theory, adding panhandlers, graffiti and street peddlers to the proscribed list. His "broken-windows" policy was first outlined in a 1982 *Atlantic* article by Kelling.

After crime in New York declined dramatically, the policy was widely adopted. "Mayor after mayor has rediscovered that disorderly behavior creates fear and leads to serious crime," Kelling said.[18]

Is Violence Declining?

The string of recent school shootings has added to the perception that violence is increasing in schools. Nine mass homicides on school grounds in less than two years have left 29 dead.[19]

But education and juvenile-justice officials continue to insist that children are safer in schools than in their own homes. Except for the recent shootings, overall school violence has been fairly steady for the past 20 years. And according to the NCES survey, the behaviors that school principals list as "serious or moderate" discipline problems were not violent activities but tardiness (40 percent) and absenteeism (25 percent). Twenty-one percent of the principals listed fighting as a serious problem, but only 5 percent considered gangs serious, and 2 percent listed weapons possession or physical abuse of teachers.[20]

"Despite public perceptions to the contrary, the current data do not support the claim that there has been a dramatic, overall increase in school-based violence in recent years," said researcher Irwin Hyman.[21]

But Stephens of the school safety center says that just looking at official statistics on school violence is

Are Students Losing Legal Rights...

In Texas recently, a high school student was sent to juvenile jail for five days without a hearing after writing a Halloween horror story in which a teacher and some classmates were shot.

Constitutional scholar Jamin Raskin cites the "unbelievable and shocking" case as an example of due process being denied to a student because of a zero-tolerance policy.

In the 1970s and '80s, the war on drugs accustomed American students to such anti-drug tactics as warrantless drug testing, locker searches and drug-sniffing dogs nosing around their cars and bookbags.

But student rights eroded even faster in the '90s as schools embraced zero-tolerance discipline policies to address school violence, say legal scholars like Raskin, a professor at American University. Following a recent spate of mass murders at schools, lawmakers and school officials adopted zero tolerance for behavior that even implies violence. Now, students are being suspended for writing about death, suicide or murder or for drawing pictures of guns.

"Discipline codes should discourage some of the negative writing that goes on," says John Mitchell, deputy director of education issues for the American Federation of Teachers. "Schools shouldn't be compelled to display work that isn't uplifting."

Students have always had fewer First Amendment rights than other citizens, says Eugene Volokh, a law professor at the University of California at Los Angeles. "When you're talking about K-12 education, the government has much more authority than it does over private citizens," he says. But in the 1960s, the Supreme Court expanded those rights, a trend that some say has been dramatically reversed in the past two decades.

"From the Warren Court era to the Rehnquist Court era, there has been a progressive decline in constitutional protection for students' rights," says Raskin, author of *We the Students,* a new textbook on students' rights.

Others disagree. "I don't think students' rights have declined," says Edwin Darden, senior staff attorney for the National School Boards Association (NSBA). "There's been an evolution to try to balance the needs of school districts and the needs and rights of the students."

The courts have been "very thoughtful" about how to achieve that balance, Darden says. But constitutional rights don't exist in a vacuum, he says, and the courts have had to weigh schools' need to ensure the safety of all students against the rights of the individual. "The courts have often ruled in favor of the schools."

Raskin says the Supreme Court "aggressively defended" students' First Amendment rights its 1969 *Tinker v. Des Moines Independent Community School District* ruling. The court said students should not be prevented from wearing black armbands to protest the Vietnam War unless it would cause "material and substantial disruption of school activities or invasion of the rights of other students."

As Justice Abe Fortas wrote in the case: "Neither students nor teachers shed their constitutional rights to freedom of speech or expression at the schoolhouse gate."

But by the late 1980s, Raskin says, the reconstituted court's *Hazelwood School District v. Kuhlmeier* ruling upheld the authority of schools to censor student publications "for almost any reasonable purpose."

Raskin says another constitutional right being "violated all over the country by zero-tolerance policies" is the right to due process. In the years before zero tolerance, students had a right to hear and respond to the charges against them before being expelled or suspended. But now, Raskin says, "Students are automatically suspended without a hearing."

The tough, new policies reflect longstanding complaints by politicians that liberal court rulings allowed chaos to reign in classrooms because educators had to jump through procedural hoops to expel disruptive students. Many observers say the current crackdown is a backlash to those procedural excesses.

"The only due process right that the Supreme Court has given students is that they must be given some notice of the charge against them and some opportunity to respond," says Nadine Strossen, president of the American Civil Liberties Union (ACLU). "It can be completely informal, it can be verbal and it can be after the punishment has been meted out, and students have no right to a lawyer. To even call it 'due process' is an exaggeration.

"It's nothing compared with what you would get if you were accused of even a misdemeanor outside of the school," she says. "Yet the life-destroying consequences can be at least as great if you're talking about someone being thrown out of school."

...Or Getting More 'Care' From Schools?

However, students' rights have expanded in two areas, Raskin says. High school students may now sue their school for student-on-student sexual harassment if the school knew about it and did nothing to stop it. And many state courts have ruled in recent years that corporal punishment is unlawful, he points out.

Legal experts predict that the next two frontiers for students'-rights litigation will involve what Raskin calls school "cyber-censors," and efforts by schools to extend their disciplinary authority to off-campus student behavior.

In the aftermath of the shootings at Columbine High School in Littleton, Colo., some schools are cracking down on students who put material on their home Web pages that criticizes or threatens school personnel.

Except for those posting bomb threats, students have generally won their court challenges to such policies, especially if it merely involved the right to criticize the school administration and caused no disruption in classes, Raskin says.

Darden says the courts will also be seeing more challenges of schools trying to discipline students for what they do during non-school hours. "It's the next big wave of school litigation over the next two years."

For instance the Texas legislature recently passed a law requiring the expulsion of any student who commits a felony or an assault, or distributes drugs or alcohol near school property. Many states are requiring that schools be notified when a student runs afoul of the law, even though it was not on school property or during school hours. Some of those students are summarily expelled or suspended.

Darden says these new laws are efforts by the school districts to tell students, "We care about the whole person. When you do things that are dangerous to yourself, like using drugs or alcohol, the school district cares about that and will not look the other way."

But others find them a disturbing trend. "It would be ridiculous for the school to get involved, unless perhaps the student was arrested for rape," says Kent Scheidegger, legal director of the conservative Criminal Justice Legal Foundation in Sacramento, Calif. "You wouldn't want a suspected rapist in the school. But arrested for marijuana possession? That doesn't make any sense. That should be a matter for parents and the juvenile courts. That's what they're there for."

Darden says it is often the parents who are "asking, begging and cajoling" the school districts to impose tough behavior standards off-campus. If the school is randomly testing kids for drugs, it's easier for a student to resist peer pressure, parents argue.

"Except for the most extreme circumstances, schools really have no rightful authority to discipline students for activity off-campus," says Peter Blauvelt, president of the National Alliance for Safe Schools (NASS). "I think you have to make a case that the child's presence in school causes an undue risk of violence to others at school if a student got caught smoking marijuana or drinking on Saturday night and the school wants to expel him, I think that's ridiculous," Blauvelt says.

"It's much easier for politicians to demand a crackdown on the most silly and imagined transgressions," Raskin says. "So we have some kid spending five days in juvenile detention for writing a ghost story."

John Whitehead, president of the Charlottesville, Va.-based Rutherford Institute, a conservative group dedicated to protecting civil liberties, worries about the long-term impact of zero-tolerance tactics. "You're teaching kids that they live in a totalitarian society," he says. "This generation has been raised being searched without a warrant, being strip-searched and having their urine tested without probable cause. You'll have a whole set of people who will be conditioned to promote order over rights.

"You also have a whole segment of society that is being repressed," Whitehead says. "They operate on a subterranean level, because they really don't have free speech. They have secret signals, eye movements and code words."

Further, he says, "Many kids are smoking as a way to rebel. And younger and younger kids are drinking. I think it's a way of shoving it into the faces of the adults."

He says much of the violence erupting among kids already is the result of repressed anger. "Sooner or later they will blow," he predicts.

Whitehead says adults are sending kids the wrong message with zero-tolerance policies. "The message kids are getting is that some crazy adult game is being played here, and that the rules are really stupid," he says. "The adults say they're teaching kids about 'justice' when they say they must treat every infraction the same. But how is it justice to treat someone with a pair of nail clippers the same as you treat someone with an Uzi?"

'Get Tough,' Younger Students Say

Middle-schoolers in Tustin, Calif., advocated tougher policies on alcohol and marijuana than local high school students.

1. **When should students be suspended for marijuana or alcohol violations?**

MS	HS	All		
72	41	55	A.	Always.
24	50	38	B.	In repeat or severe cases.
5	9	7	C.	Never.

2. **When should police be notified about marijuana or alcohol violations?**

MS	HS	All		
63	34	49	A.	Always.
32	53	42	B.	In repeat or severe cases.
5	13	9	C.	Never.

3. **When should counseling be required for students with a marijuana or alcohol violation?**

MS	HS	All		
57	38	47	A.	Always.
36	48	42	B.	In repeat or severe cases.
7	15	11	C.	Never.

4. **Should students be allowed to avoid transfer if they agree to random drug testing?**

MS	HS	All		
33	44	39	A.	Yes.
47	42	44	B.	Sometimes, depending on the circumstances.
20	14	17	C.	No.

Note: All totals do not add to 100 due to rounding.

Source: Tustin Unified School District, Orange County, Calif., February 2000

misleading. "We have redefined deviancy over the last couple of decades," he says. "In some schools, a fight is not reported unless there is blood on the floor.

"There is a disincentive for administrators to report crime in their schools," he says, because principals are afraid they will be blamed for doing an inappropriate job. To get a true picture of school violence, you must look at reported incidents, unreported incidents and under-reported incidents."

"We've seen a tremendous growth in the number of alternative schools at the elementary level, because so many younger children are acting out violent behavior," Stephens says. "Some of the aggression that before was being experienced at the middle school and high school levels is being manifested in the elementary grades."

But Kathy Christie, a policy analyst at the Education Commission of the States, says she has not seen a huge jump in the number of alternative schools being built for elementary-grade students.

CURRENT SITUATION

Alternative Schools

The Clinton administration wants Congress to require all school districts to provide alternative education for any student expelled or suspended for disciplinary reasons. Under current federal law, that's required only if a child is disabled, and the Senate voted last May to rescind that requirement.

"It ought to be a basic American principle that no student should be punished by being denied an education," said Education Secretary Richard W. Riley after a Dec. 9 meeting with Jesse Jackson. Excluded students should receive "appropriate supervision, counseling and educational services so they can meet state [academic] standards."

But, according to the Education Commission of the States, only nine states require schools to provide alternative schooling, and it's optional in 25 states. In 14 states, no laws govern alternative services.

As a result, only 43 percent of the students expelled for carrying a firearm to school in 1997 were sent to alternative schools. Law-enforcement groups complain that by not providing alternative services, schools are dumping their discipline problems onto the streets.

But even when suspended students get alternative education, the quality of the education they receive is sometimes questionable. "Usually they are warehouses — dumping grounds for the worst teachers, administrators and students," says George Washington University's Kingery. "There have been no evaluations of their quality."

An alternative school is defined as any school that addresses the needs of students that cannot be met in a traditional school. Other than that, there is no standard definition of what constitutes an alternative school. The Education Department is preparing a survey of the nation's more than 3,400 alternative schools — which serve 1 percent of the nation's youngsters — to determine their characteristics.

The quality of education in alternative schools "clearly is a civil rights issue if the kids who are there are disproportionately kids of color, and the schools are demonstrably of poor quality," says Mary Frances Berry, chairman of the Commission on Civil Rights.

Witnesses told the civil rights panel in February that some teachers and administrators — pressured by school boards to raise overall test scores or face pay cuts or dismissal — are using zero-tolerance policies to push out low achievers and learning-disabled students who perform poorly.

"The growing popularity of zero-tolerance school-discipline policies during a period of rapidly raised academic standards and high-stakes testing is not accidental," said Joan M. First, executive director of the National Coalition of Advocates for Students. "There are two ways to change standardized test scores. Either children learn more, or the composition of the test pool changes. Zero tolerance effectively accomplishes the latter."

"With the new standardized tests, there's an awfully strong urge on the part of teachers and principals to get rid of students," agreed Cruz Reynoso, a law professor at the University of California at Los Angeles and vice chairman of the civil rights panel. "I've heard that from many sources in California."

NASSP General Counsel Steven Yurek admitted, "It is a very big issue for schools."

Others complained that by escalating the sheer number of minority students excluded from public education,

---

Prohibited in Providence

Brass knuckles. Hand grenades. Mace. Toy guns. Students who bring those or other banned items to school face automatic expulsion in Providence, R.I., which passed a much more restrictive zero-tolerance policy than the federal Gun-Free Schools Act.

Federal law

- Guns
- Explosive devices
- Silencers and mufflers
- Bombs, grenades, rockets, missiles and mines

Providence policy

- Guns
- Explosive devices
- Silencers and mufflers
- Bombs, grenades, rockets, missiles and mines
- Realistic replicas of firearms
- Knives
- Razors
- Gas repellent, mace
- Martial-arts devices
- Objects that could inflict bodily harm: blackjacks, chains, clubs, brass knuckles, nightsticks, pipes, studded bracelets, etc.
- Any object that gives the appearance of any of the above.

Source: Applied Research Center, Feb. 18, 2000

---

zero-tolerance policies are reversing gains made since the Supreme Court's 1954 *Brown v. Board of Education* decision promised equal educational opportunities for all children.

"Zero-tolerance laws are challenging the whole concept of universal public education," says Ruth Zweifler, executive director of the Student Advocacy Center of Michigan. "Instead, we've moved to an, 'If they deserve it, then we'll give it to them' attitude."

Harsh zero-tolerance policies are "sweeping uncounted numbers of our most vulnerable and needy children into the streets," where they remain "uneducated, unserved and unsupervised," she said.

"If we find that what we have heard is verifiable across the board," Berry says, "the Education Department's Office of Civil Rights should investigate the situation in alternative schools. It ought to be taken up as a very serious issue."

The commission will discuss the issue further on April 14. "We don't want chaos and disorder to reign in the schools," Berry says, "but quite clearly there is something going on here regarding how kids of color and disabled kids are dealt with under these discipline policies."

Amending IDEA

If Congress required all expelled or suspended students to be sent to alternative schools, it would resolve the controversy over the disparate treatment of disabled students under zero-tolerance policies.

Under the 1997 amendments to the Individuals with Disabilities Education Act (IDEA), special-education students — whose disabilities can range from stuttering to serious emotional disturbance — have extra protections from zero-tolerance policies. If a disabled child brings a weapon to school, he may be immediately removed from school and suspended for 10 days, during which time the school must determine whether the offense was a manifestation of his disability. If not, the student may be expelled for a year, the same as a non-disabled child. Unlike a non-disabled student, however, he must be given free alternative education.

The protections were designed to prevent schools from expelling disabled students just because they might be more difficult or expensive to educate.

If bringing the weapon to school was a manifestation of the child's disability, the school may let the child back into school after a 10-day suspension, or, if the school determines that the child is a danger to himself or the other students, the school may send him to an alternative school for 45 days. Then, the school can ask an independent hearing officer to determine whether the child is ready to return to school, a procedure that can be repeated indefinitely.

The 45-day reviews were put into the law so schools could not "just kick the student out and forget about him," says Lilliam Rangel-Diaz, a member of the National Council on Disabilities board. But the policy has generated a lot of resentment, especially among parents of regular-curriculum kids expelled without getting alternative education or review hearings every 45 days.

"IDEA overrides state and federal zero-tolerance-for-firearms laws," Lewis says. "They contradict one another. This policy ties the hands of school administrators, and it's creating a lot of problems."

School administrators complain that if a disabled student threatens a student or a teacher, they cannot expel him as they could a non-disabled student. And parents of general-education students are starting to realize that their kids have less protection than a disabled student does. "Now after a kid gets expelled, some parents are asking for retroactive coverage under IDEA," Lewis says.

Educators and parents are also upset about the cost of providing alternative services for expelled disabled students. "When you run alternative schools with an 8-to-1 student-to-teacher ratio, that comes at a cost to the other students who are sitting in bigger classes," said Edward Kelly, superintendent of schools in Prince William County, Virginia. "The good student is shortchanged."[22]

Administrators say their greater responsibility is to the 2,500 other students that attend a typical high school, rather than the one kid who is expelled.

Under the provision approved by the Senate last May, introduced by Sens. John Ashcroft, R-Mo., and Bill Frist, R-Tenn., disabled students who bring firearms to school would be treated the same as non-disabled students, regardless of whether or not the action resulted from their disability. Thus, if the state where the student lives is not required to provide educational services during the expulsion period, neither child would receive services.

"If you bring a gun or firearm to school, you should be treated the same, if you have a disability or no disability," Frist told fellow senators on May 20.

The amendment was attached to the juvenile-justice bill, which is not expected to go anywhere this year. However, Sens. Edward M. Kennedy, D-Mass., and Patrick J. Leahy, D-Vt., are expected to introduce an amendment to the education reauthorization bill this month requiring all expelled students to receive alternative education.

Dozens of advocacy groups support the amendment, including the two major teachers' unions and the National Parent-Teachers Association, as well as the Clinton administration. The bill would require the Education, Justice and Health and Human Services departments to share the cost of the alternative services.

The amendment is also supported by sheriffs, district attorneys and police and law enforcement groups like

AT ISSUE

Should disabled students be disciplined differently under zero-tolerance policies?

YES
Kevin P. Dwyer
President, National Association of School Psychologists

Written for *The CQ Researcher*

Misguided efforts by some Congress members to amend the Individuals with Disabilities Education Act (IDEA) perpetuate the public's erroneous impression that the law creates a dual-discipline system that prevents schools from removing a child with a gun from school. Nothing could be further from the truth.

The law was amended in 1997 so that any gun-carrying child can be removed. Schools can expel a student with disabilities who brings a gun to school for one year — just as they do other students — if the behavior was not the result of the child's disability.

After removal, students also receive continued education in an alternative program. If it is determined that the behavior resulted from a student's disability, the law allows the child to be suspended for 10 days while determining if the student poses a danger. If so, the school can expel the student indefinitely, but the case must be reviewed every 45 days.

Congress included these rights to protect students with disabilities from discrimination. Students with disabilities often present challenges. Without due process, these students would be removed disproportionately by schools that decided providing services was too costly, time consuming or inconvenient. But Congress acknowledged that children with disabilities, like all children, have the right to a free, appropriate, public education.

Now some in Congress contend the alternative-education requirement should be dropped because other students don't receive such services. But withdrawing educational services from any student does not make our schools and streets safer.

Leaving any student free to roam the streets without supervision is a prescription for increasing crime. Research affirms that expelling troubled children without educational and mental-health services increases dropout rates, drug use and overall juvenile crime.

To get this message to Congress, we have developed a Safe Streets, Safe Schools effort — involving 50 education, mental-health, student-services and child-advocacy groups — to support providing alternative education and crisis-intervention for all students.

But that effort cannot fall upon the education community or the justice system alone. States and local jurisdictions must work together to fund and implement services for all students with challenging behavior.

To balance the movement toward zero tolerance for guns, drugs and violence in schools, we must also have zero tolerance for academic failure for all students.

NO
Sen. John Ashcroft, R-Mo.

Written for *The CQ Researcher*

In light of the tragic school shootings, we must ask ourselves if federal education laws do all they can to promote school safety. America's classrooms must be safe and secure for students to get a world-class education.

Our general policy is commendable: Zero tolerance for weapons. Under the federal Gun-Free Schools Act, states receiving federal education funds were required to pass laws mandating an immediate, one-year expulsion for students who bring weapons to school.

Unfortunately, this policy does not apply to one out of every eight students subject to another federal law, the Individuals with Disabilities Education Act. Under IDEA, a student with a weapon typically is returned to the classroom in as few as 45 days. This category includes individuals who have serious emotional disturbances and behavior disorders. Schools have no power to expel these students if their disability caused them to bring a gun to school. If it didn't, schools can expel the student, but still must continue to provide full educational services.

Hence, schools are subject to a dangerous dual-discipline system that handcuffs them from removing violent students. It is deeply distressing that federal law requires that some who bring guns to schools be returned to a classroom filled with kids who want and deserve a safe and secure setting in which to learn.

Missouri teachers, parents, principals and superintendents have told me that we must do something in Washington to end this dual-discipline system that threatens the safety of children and invites a mass tragedy.

In response, I have authored the School Safety Act, which gives schools authority to remove any student who has a weapon at school. Congress voted overwhelmingly to include this provision in juvenile-justice legislation that now awaits conference committee action.

My legislation abolishes the dangerous double standard for weapons and returns control to where it belongs — local schools. Teachers, principals and superintendents care deeply about students with special needs. I trust these individuals to make the right decisions, including making special exceptions on a case-by-case basis. Dangerous and disruptive students are a small minority and pose a threat to all students.

A safe and orderly learning environment is critical to our children's success in school. Local schools must have the authority and flexibility to keep classrooms safe by being able to remove any student with a weapon from the classroom.

After several black high school students from Decatur, Ill., were suspended for two years for fighting at a football game, the Rev. Jesse Jackson and others said zero-tolerance policies unfairly target minorities.

Fight Crime, Invest in Kids, which represents victims of violence.

"Giving a gun-toting kid an extended vacation from school and from all responsibility is soft on offenders and dangerous for everyone else," said the victims' group in opposing Ashcroft-Frist.

Supporters of mandatory alternative education often point to the tragic case of Kip Kinkel, the 14-year-old Oregon boy who was suspended for bringing a gun to school. He was not required to attend alternative classes. He went home and killed his parents, then returned to school later to shoot and kill two students and wound 25.

Zero-Zero Tolerance

The administration also has proposed that Congress require any school receiving federal education funds to have "sound and equitable" discipline policies. Although neither the House nor the Senate has acted on the proposal, school districts across the country are revisiting their zero-tolerance policies anyway, partly after pressure from parents.

"After all of the bad press, people are saying, 'Let's calm our jets a bit and think through this a little more,'" Newberry says.

But while some lawmakers are trying to make their laws less harsh, most are trying to broaden the definition of what is covered. "There has been a tremendous amount of activity in the state legislatures on this subject," says Christie of the Education Commission of the States.

Often legislators try to impose zero tolerance for drug and alcohol sales or consumption on school grounds. But the proposals usually don't make it through the legislature once lawmakers realize how damaging the consequences of long expulsions would be, she says.

"Zero-tolerance policies were initially put into place to ban lethal weapons from school grounds," she says. "Having a beer in your locker probably doesn't rate up there with carrying a weapon that could threaten the life of another student."

Some school districts are extending zero tolerance to cover off-campus behavior, punishing kids who get into trouble with the law on weekends, even for non-violent behavior like alcohol or marijuana use.

More and more schools are moving to ban images of guns on school grounds. Several school districts have taken rifles out of the hands of color guards, and one would not allow students re-enacting a Civil War battle to carry fake wooden muskets.

"Schools are reluctant to glorify guns in any way right now," Tirozzi says. "You're seeing a knee-jerk Pavlovian response when people ban images of guns or weapons."

If a policy oversteps good sense, communities generally let their elected school board know about it, Resnick says. "Ninety-six percent of school board members in this country are elected. So there's a real opportunity for self-correction."

Tirozzi would like to see school boards limit their zero-tolerance policies to weapons, drugs and serious altercations, and return discretion to local superintendents. "Even the federal law mandates that for firearms superintendents should have discretion," he says.

The national associations representing elementary and secondary principals issued a joint statement in January asking school districts to consider three critical areas when reviewing zero-tolerance policies: the age of the child; fitting the punishment to the "crime" and ensuring that educational services are continued.

Blauvelt suggests that school boards should adopt the language in federal and state laws governing illegal drugs and weapons. "An aspirin is not a 'controlled and dangerous substance,'" he says. "Midol is not a 'controlled and dangerous substance.'"

Ferrandino of the elementary school principals association advises school boards to make sure policies are developed with community input and have reasonable penalties and allow for discretion. "There needs to be some sort of rationality and balance brought to the discussion," he says.

The National School Boards Association's Resnick agrees. "Hopefully, when you have a policy that can have as great an impact — positive and negative — on individual children as zero-tolerance policies can have, they are being developed with substantial community input," he says.

Mitchell of the AFT says school boards should be careful not to confuse zero-tolerance policies with discipline codes. Zero tolerance should be reserved for very serious offenses, he says. Less serious infractions should be covered under a discipline code, which allows for graduated consequences proportionate to the offense and punishes repeat offenses more severely than first-time offenses, he says. For instance, "A 'true weapon' should be covered by zero-tolerance policies," Mitchell says. "But a look-alike weapon should be covered by a school discipline policy."

The Rutherford Institute's Whitehead suggests that by relying on student courts for minor infractions, "You can get the decision out of the hands of one guy who's afraid of losing his job."

But most important, he says, zero-tolerance policies should only apply to "real offenses, like carrying real guns, real knives and real drugs — like cocaine — and not Alka-Seltzer."

Schools also should provide adequate due process and alternative educational services for expelled students, others say. "I don't know of any other situation in which an individual can be arrested, or put in jail or punished without some form of due process," Stephens, of the school safety center, says. "After all, we even have an appeal process for traffic tickets."

OUTLOOK

Ebb and Flow

Educators predict that for the immediate future, the zero-tolerance pendulum will continue to swing back and forth. "It's cyclical," researcher Skiba says. "Every time there's another school shooting, you see a new round of ever-tougher zero-tolerance policies, followed in a few weeks by new community and parental outcries about violations of basic rights and common sense."

"Like any other reform issue, these things tend to ebb and flow," the Education Department's Modzeleski says. "Some places are already backing off from zero tolerance. We recommend that policies be reviewed on a regular basis."

George Washington's Kingery hopes that there will be "a little more reason" applied to zero-tolerance policies, and that the quality of alternative education will come under more scrutiny.

If zero tolerance is a backlash to judges and school administrators having broad discretion, says the University of California's Volokh. "Maybe there will be a backlash to the backlash. Maybe we will decide that we can't have a one-size-fits-all rule, and we should return discretion to the individual principals."

"Zero tolerance is now in the court of public opinion," Whitehead says. "All the major magazines have criticized it lately, and now even the teacher groups are saying, 'Let's have some reason.'"

But most agree that schools will not entirely abandon strict discipline, and that the public will continue to support zero tolerance for extreme acts involving guns, violence and drugs.

The NEA has launched a public-education campaign to get school districts to think in terms of a comprehensive, community-generated school-safety program that addresses the entire education system, including physical plant, teacher training, early elementary intervention, effective mental-health programs, crisis intervention and conflict resolution.

"We must move from a knee-jerk reaction to one in which we are willing to invest a lot of dollars over the long term," the NEA's Newberry says. "Until school boards come up with money and creative plans to address these larger issues in a comprehensive way, we're not really going to solve the problem."

Ferrandino of the elementary school principals' group says many school districts are trying to make schools smaller and gentler places. "Since these school shootings began, we have learned that there's much that both the schools and communities can do to create an environment where students can feel they belong and are valued as individuals," he says. Among other things, principals are trying to reduce class size and student anonymity. Other schools have developed community relationships with social-service agencies and are getting parents more involved in the schools.

"I think it is quickly being recognized that smaller might be better," Ferrandino says.

Others advocate more after-school and youth-development programs, both of which are more expensive and require long-term commitments — and time — from adults.

Sadly, two weeks before Kayla Rolland was shot in Michigan, several experts tied the future of zero tolerance to what the nation decides to do about guns. "Handgun availability is part of what is driving this ridiculous response on the part of the schools," Newberry says.

"I would love to say that within 10 years we won't need policies like zero tolerance," Tirozzi says. "By then, I would hope we will have gotten weapons out of the hands of youngsters, parents will be doing a better job in the household and we will have changed the kind of things that are projected onto movie screens. But unless and until this society comes to grips with its love affair with violence, and as long as children can easily obtain weapons, these problems will continue to come into the schoolhouse.

"When society zeroes out violence, we'll be happy to zero out zero tolerance," he says.

NOTES

1. Of the 100,000 students expelled nationwide during the 1997-98 school year, 3,930 were expelled for bringing a firearm to school under the Gun-Free Schools Act. That was a 31 percent drop from the previous year's total, according to Department of Education statistics.

2. The statistics are from an unpublished study by Kingery, "Suspension and Expulsion: New Directions."

3. See *Dothan City Board of Education v. V.M.H.*

4. Quoted in "The Intolerance of Zero Tolerance," IntellectualCapital.com, Aug. 19, 1999.

5. Robert C. Johnson, "Decatur Furor Sparks Wider Policy Debate," *Education Week,* Nov. 24, 1999.

6. "The Fight's Not Over, *The New Republic,* Dec. 6, 1999.

7. "National Survey of Teens, Teachers and Principals," National Center on Addiction and Substance Abuse, Columbia University, 1998.

8. "Violence and Discipline Problems in U.S. Public Schools: 1996-1997," National Center for Education Statistics, 1998.

9. Russ Skiba and Reece Peterson, "The Dark Side of Zero Tolerance: Can Punishment Lead to Safe Schools?" *The Kappan,* January 1999.

10. For details, see Kathy Koch, "Drug Testing, The *CQ Researcher,* Nov. 20, 1998, p. 1014.

11. The unpublished study was conducted by the Applied Research Center, in Oakland, Calif.

12. "Education Denied: The Negative Impact of Zero Tolerance Policies," The Civil Rights Project at Harvard, February 2000.

13. Keleher testified before the U.S. Civil Rights Commission on Feb. 18, 1999.

14. For background, see Margaret Edwards, "Mandatory Sentencing," *The CQ Researcher,* May 26, 1995, pp. 465-488.

15. "Zero tolerance on drugs urged," *Houston Chronicle,* May 21, 1986.

16. James J. Kilpatrick, "Get tough with kids who use, sell drugs," *Houston Chronicle,* June 17, 1986.

17. *Houston Chronicle,* op. cit., May 21.

18. Harry Bruinius, "In Giulianiville, it's a case of law vs. order," *The Christian Science Monitor,* Nov. 9, 1999.

19. For background, see Kathy Koch, "School Violence," *The CQ Researcher,* Oct. 9, 1998, pp. 881-904.

20. Violence and Discipline Problems in U.S. Public Schools, 1996-1997, The National Center for Education Statistics, February, 1998.

21. Quoted in Skiba and Peterson, *op. cit.*

22. Dennis Cauchon, "Zero-tolerance policies lack flexibility," *USA Today,* April 13, 1999.

BIBLIOGRAPHY

Books

Kelling, George L., and Catherine Coles, *Fixing Broken Windows: Restoring Order and Reducing Crime in Our Communities,* Martin Kessler Books, 1996.
The Rutgers University professor and his co-author argue that ignoring minor problems in cities, like broken

windows or graffiti, eventually leads to an increase in serious crime. Kelling first outlined the approach in a 1982 *Atlantic* magazine article.

Raskin, Jamin B., *We the Students: The High School in the High Court, Congressional Quarterly,* 2000.
An American University constitutional law professor outlines precedent-setting Supreme Court cases involving drug testing, locker searches, school newspaper censorship, sexual harassment and free speech.

Articles

"Zero tolerance on drugs urged," *Houston Chronicle,* May 21, 1986.
Education Secretary William Bennett becomes the first official to ask Congress to withhold federal education funds unless schools adopt "zero-tolerance" expulsion policies for drug dealing on school grounds.

Baxter, Bethany, "The Intolerance of Zero Tolerance," Intellectual Capital.com, Aug. 19, 1999.
A consultant to colleges argues that school officials do not model good judgment by setting up zero-tolerance policies that treat all offenses equally harshly.

Cloud, John, "The Columbine Effect," *Time,* Dec. 6, 1999.
Zero tolerance sounds like a good way to treat violence in schools, but experts say it may have gone too far.

Grier, Peter, and Gail Russell Chaddock, "Schools get tough as threats continue," *The Christian Science Monitor,* Nov. 5, 1999.
Educators are struggling with how to implement get-tough safety rules meant to stop student shootings.

Johnson, Dirk, "Schools' New Watchword: Zero Tolerance," *The New York Times,* Dec. 1, 1999.
This overview looks at how zero-tolerance school discipline has replaced more traditional punishment.

Skiba, Russ, and Reece Peterson, "The Dark Side of Zero Tolerance: Can Punishment Lead to Safe Schools?" *The Kappan,* January 1999.
The authors argue that increasingly broad interpretations of zero tolerance have resulted in a near epidemic of suspensions for seemingly trivial events, increasing the likelihood that excluded students will get involved in drugs and gangs.

Wing, Bob, and Terry Keleher, "Zero Tolerance: An Interview with Jesse Jackson on Race and School Discipline," *Colorlines,* spring 2000.
Jackson contends that zero-tolerance polices disproportionately target minority students.

Reports and Studies

Keleher, Terry, Applied Research Center, March 1999.
In a survey of 12 large school districts across the country, the public-policy institute found that black students are three to five times more likely to be expelled than white students in some districts.

Kingery, Paul, "Suspension and Expulsion: New Directions," Hamilton Fish Institute, unpublished 1999 study.
Kingery found that expulsions and suspensions are rising nationwide and that longer and permanent expulsions are at an all-time high.

National Center on Addiction and Substance Abuse, "National Survey of Teens, Teachers and Principals," 1998.
The Columbia University research center found that 85 percent of principals believe zero-tolerance policies keep drugs out of schools.

National Center for Education Statistics, "Violence and Discipline Problems in U.S. Public Schools: 1996-1997," 1998.
This survey of more than 1,000 school principals found mixed and minor improvements in school discipline and drug problems.

The Civil Rights Project at Harvard, "Education Denied: The Negative Impact of Zero Tolerance Policies," February 2000.
A briefing paper prepared for the U.S. Civil Rights Commission argues that zero-tolerance policies are having a disproportionate impact on African-American and Latino children.

U.S. Department of Education, "Report on State Implementation of the Gun-Free Schools Act," August 1999.
This annual report shows that in the 1997-98 school year, 3,930 students were expelled for bringing a firearm to school, a 31 percent drop from the previous year.

For More Information

National Association of Elementary School Principals, 1615 Duke St., Alexandria, VA 22314-3483; (703) 684-3345; www.naesp.org. This association of elementary and middle school principals conducts workshops for members on federal and state policies and programs.

National Association of Secondary School Principals, 1904 Association Dr., Reston, VA 20191-1537; (703) 860-0200; www.nassp.org. This group, which includes college-level teachers of secondary education, conducts training for members and serves as an information clearinghouse.

National School Boards Association, 1680 Duke St., Alexandria, VA 22314; (703) 838-6722; www.nsba.org. This federation of school board associations monitors legislation and regulations affecting public-education funding, local governance and education quality.

National School Safety Center, 4165 Thousand Oaks Blvd., Suite 290, Westlake Village, CA 91362; (805) 373-9977; www.nssc1.org. The center was created by presidential directive in 1984 to meet the growing need for additional training and preparation in the area of school crime and violence prevention.

18

Bullying

Are Schools Doing Enough to Stop the Problem?

John Greenya

AP Photo/Noah Burger

Thirteen-year-old Jacob Rubin, of Oakland, Calif., says students teased him throughout sixth grade because his hair was long and called him "gay," "faggot" and "homo." His mother, background, intervened when she found out he had been beaten up. A third of all students nationwide report being bullied, and an estimated 160,000 children skip school every day to avoid bullying.

From *CQ Researcher*, February 4, 2005.

Bullies made sixth grade a "living hell" for Jacob Rubin, an honor student in Oakland, Calif., but he kept silent. The daily insults gave him stomachaches and affected his grades, but it was only after several boys beat him up that his mother finally realized what had been happening.[1]

- Chris and Kim Brancato also finally realized their 12-year-old son had been suffering in silence from savage bullying at his middle school in Fork Union, Va., when they saw marks around his neck from a suicide attempt.[2]
- At Tonganoxie Junior High in Kansas, bullies who targeted a quiet seventh-grade boy even wrote their taunts on classroom blackboards. After three years of asking school authorities to stop the bullying, his parents sued the school board. The boy dropped out.[3]
- After Brittni Ainsworth, 16, a cheerleader in Plainfield, Ind., told a television reporter that other girls bullied her and damaged her car, she testified last year before state senators considering anti-bullying legislation.

Today, bullying is widely regarded as a serious problem in the United States. Ron Stephens, executive director of the National School Safety Center, calls bullying "one of the most enduring problems" in schools.[4] Up to 75 percent of American children have been victims of bullying, according to the National Crime Prevention Council.[5] On an average school day, three out of 10 American youngsters in grades six through 10 are involved in

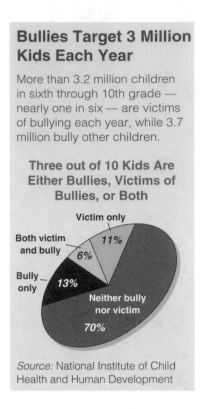

Bullies Target 3 Million Kids Each Year

More than 3.2 million children in sixth through 10th grade — nearly one in six — are victims of bullying each year, while 3.7 million bully other children.

Three out of 10 Kids Are Either Bullies, Victims of Bullies, or Both

Victim only

Both victim and bully

11%

6%

Bully only

13%

Neither bully nor victim

70%

Source: National Institute of Child Health and Human Development

bullying — as perpetrators, victims or both — according to a National Institute of Child Health and Human Development (NICHD) study.[6]

But for many educators — and anguished parents — it took the horror of Columbine to awaken the nation to the seriousness — and pervasiveness — of bullying.

After Columbine High School students Dylan Klebold and Eric Harris massacred 12 students and a teacher and then killed themselves at their school in the affluent Denver suburb of Littleton in 1999, parents told investigators that bullying had been rampant at Columbine.

Shari Schnurr, the mother of a student injured at Columbine, told the Governor's Columbine Review Commission she had discussed bullying at the school with her daughter, who was a peer counselor. "There was just across-the-board intolerance [of others]," Schnurr said.

Several witnesses, including the aunt of slain Columbine student Isaiah Shoels, testified that Principal Frank DeAngelis had discounted their concerns about

bullying. Several parents also testified that students and others were unwilling to come forward with their stories for fear of retaliation.[7]

In fact, bullying was also cited as a factor in subsequent school killings, according to a U.S. Secret Service study.[8] Concern about bullying has prompted at least 16 states to adopt legislation recommending or requiring schools to institute programs to help kids unlearn bullying behavior.[9] At least one such measure was introduced in Congress last year as well (*see p. 414*).

Most bullying begins in elementary school. "The thought of children barely old enough to read singling out and tormenting other youngsters is disturbing and uncomfortable to contemplate," Sandra Feldman, president of the American Federation of Teachers (AFT), wrote recently. "Yet researchers have found that bullying begins among preschool children and peaks in grades six through eight."[10]

During her first year of junior high school, a young woman recalls, "There were a bunch of them, and they were older than me. They took my backpack and kicked it along the ground like a soccer ball, and when I tried to stop them they kicked me. One boy pulled my hair so hard a big clump came out."[11]

Bullying in high school has a different name, says Ralph Cantor, the Safe and Drug Free Schools Coordinator for the Office of Education in Alameda County, Calif. "It's called harassment," particularly when it has sexual overtones, he says, and a "hate crime" if it involves bullying based on sexual orientation.

Indeed, experts say that much bullying revolves around taunts about other youths' sexuality. Gay, lesbian and bisexual youths (GLB) are five times more likely than their peers to miss school because they feel unsafe, according to a recent study.[12] And for good reason: Studies show that one-third of gay students are physically harassed due to their sexual orientation, one in six is beaten badly enough to need medical attention and gay teens are four times more likely to be threatened with a weapon at school than straight kids.

Jaana Juvonen, a psychologist at the University of California, Los Angeles (UCLA) who studies school culture, says bullying "may be particularly problematic in American schools." According to student surveys, she says, U.S. schools rank roughly on a par with those in the Czech Republic as among the least friendly in the Western world.[13]

Some experts say American culture in some ways may condone, or even support, abusiveness as an acceptable way to get ahead — and not just on the playground. Television shows like "Scrubs," "House," and "ER," for instance, feature successful — albeit arrogant and rude — doctors frequently verbally humiliating and abusing underlings. Teen movies portray the most popular kids — cheerleaders and football players — as the most likely to bully. One of the regular cartoon characters on the "Simpsons," Nelson Muntz, is a bully who regularly picks on Bart.

Studies even confirm that school bullies are often star athletes or class leaders, popular with students, teachers and administrators who are often reluctant to discipline them. "Classmates are not keen to affiliate with a bully, but they recognize that these people have social capital and power," Juvonen said.[14]

Others say the enormous size of today's public schools may contribute to the problem by providing long, unmonitored hallways or stairwells where vulnerable students can be victimized with impunity. And some teachers and parents may be reluctant to intervene — perhaps unintentionally encouraging the practice by their inaction — either because they see bullying as a natural part of childhood or because they fear adult intervention will exacerbate the situation. According to Juvonen, teachers intervene only about 10 percent of the time.[15]

The U.S. Department of Education's Office of Safe and Drug Free Schools defines bullying as: "intentional, repeated, hurtful acts, words, or other behavior committed by one or more children against another; it may be physical, verbal, emotional, or sexual in nature."

The National Education Association (NEA) says bullying can be direct — such as teasing, hitting or threatening — or indirect, involving exclusion, the spreading of untrue rumors or psychological manipulation. The NICHD study said "belittling insults about looks and speech" were a common form of bullying, and that girls were more likely to spread rumors or make sexual

Overweight Teens Are Bullied the Most

Overweight children are picked on the most, followed by kids who are gay or thought to be gay, according to a 2002 survey of schoolchildren ages 12 to 17.

How often are the following types of students teased or bullied in your school?

Kids who are:

Percentage of students who answered "all the time," "most of the time" and "some of the time"

Kids who are:	Percentage
Overweight	85%
Gay or thought to be gay	78
Dress differently	76
Have disabilities	63

Source: National Mental Health Association, "What Does Gay Mean? Teen Survey," December 2002

remarks, while boys would slap, hit or push their victims.[16]

But even if bullying doesn't escalate into horrific Columbine-level violence, both the victims and the perpetrators suffer in other, less-obvious ways, along with society as a whole. Bullying not only begets depression and suicide but also serious crime, researchers say, not to mention poor academic performance, truancy and higher dropout rates.

"Parents and schools recognize that bullying is a problem that will not go away of its own choice — it's not a faddish thing," says Ted Feinberg, assistant executive director of the National Association of School Psychologists (NASP). "This is something that has been long overdue in terms of it being addressed by responsible agencies."

"When you and I were at school, mom or dad would say, 'Well, just ignore it and it will go away,' " recalls Rob Beaumont of Safe Schools, Safe Students. "Or, 'Stand up and fight for yourself.' Unfortunately, the level of violence has increased to the point where standing up and fighting back or ignoring it is not really an option," he said. Parents and teachers need to get involved right at the beginning."[17]

Anti-bullying programs are being conducted by schools and nonprofit organizations across the country, including the American Association of University Women (AAUW), the American Psychological Association and the Ford and Kaiser Family foundations.

Many programs say the role of the bystander is crucial. "Bystanders to bullying often play a key role in determining whether bullying will occur and escalate — or be prevented," wrote psychologist and bullying expert Ronald G. Slaby, developer of "Aggressors, Victims and Bystanders," a popular anti-bullying program. Slaby is a research scientist with the Education Development Corp. in Newton, Mass., and a lecturer in the Harvard Graduate School of Education and the Harvard School of Public Health. "Bystanders often directly fuel bullying encounters by setting up or cheering on the aggressor and victim," Slaby adds.[18]

Meanwhile, legislation and anti-bullying programs that seek to reduce sexually oriented teasing are encountering strong opposition from conservative Christians, who claim they promote homosexuality and impinge on Christian students' freedom of speech.

"When harassment based on sexual orientation is explicitly banned, school staff and students are inevitably trained that the reason such harassment is wrong is not because all harassment is wrong or because all people should be treated with respect, but because there is nothing wrong with being gay or lesbian," Peter Sprigg, senior director of policy studies at the conservative Family Research Council, testified before the Maryland House Ways and Means Committee, Feb. 19, 2003.

Although much is being done to reduce bullying, many parents say their children's schools are not responding quickly or aggressively enough. "I called everyone I thought could help me, and I just couldn't get it stopped," said the father of a boy who says he was bullied from the age of 12 until he dropped out of high school at 16. "It's like my son didn't matter."[19]

The boy's father has joined a growing list of parents and students who have sued their schools and school districts for not protecting their children. And in a new wrinkle, in July 2004 a teenager from Fredericksburg, Va., Joe Golden, sued three former high school classmates, alleging they shoved his head into a plastic bag and threatened to kill him; that teachers ridiculed him

and that school administrators did nothing to stop the bullying. He is seeking $450,000 in damages.[20]

Daniel Fisher, 17, a senior at Chancellor High School who played recreational soccer with Golden, said he was picked on because he was "an average kid" — not from a family with a lot of money or part of a "cool" social group. Golden was also very friendly with teachers, Fisher said, something that would immediately make him a target. "He was just the perfect specimen for bullies to pick on."[21]

As legislators, school officials and parents confront the bullying problem, here are some of the questions being debated:

Is bullying a serious problem?

Before Columbine, few Americans would have drawn a connection between bullying and schoolyard massacres. But as Gerald Newberry, director of the NEA's Health Information Network, points out, "The kids who pulled the trigger weren't who we thought they were. They were not the bullies — they were the kids who had been bullied. That's what changed the focus of the schools and the nation."

In the next several years, gun-related school killings occurred in Conyers, Ga., Fort Gibson, Okla., Santee, Calif., New Orleans, La., and Red Lion, Pa. Suddenly a nationwide debate was raging over the causes and consequences of bullying on the victims, perpetrators and even bystanders.

A Bureau of Justice Statistics survey found that 86 percent of high school students said teenagers resort to violence in school because of "other kids picking on them, making fun of them, or bullying them."[22] The Secret Service's National Threat Assessment Center and the Department of Education found that in two-thirds of 37 school shootings over the last 25 years the attackers had felt "bullied, persecuted, or injured by others" before the attack and that the bullying was often "longstanding and severe."[23]

The findings strongly suggested that bullying could no longer be considered just a relatively harmless phase that children must go through to get toughened up for life. "Being bullied is not just an unpleasant rite of passage through childhood," says Duane Alexander, director of the NICHD. "It's a public health problem that merits attention. People who were bullied as children are more likely to suffer from depression and low self-esteem, well into adulthood, and the bullies themselves are more likely to engage in criminal behavior later in life." (*See graph, p. 403.*)

James C. Backstrom, county attorney of Minnesota's sprawling Dakota County, frequently speaks at local elementary and middle schools about bullying in an effort to "get to kids before they move up to a larger school setting." When parents and school officials ask why a county prosecutor is interested in bullying, Backstrom has a simple answer: "Bullying prevention is crime prevention."

Backstrom urges students to be part of the solution. "If they see other children being bullied, the worst thing is to start laughing," he says. Instead, he urges kids to "stand up and be a hero. Do the right thing: Tell an adult."

Yet, there are still those who think adolescent bullying is necessary for children to learn to make it in a tough world. Cantor, the Safe and Drug Free Schools program coordinator in California, says, "I've heard parents — usually the male parents — say, 'People just need to toughen up some. I went through this, and I've just got to teach my kid to defend himself.' "

Parry Aftab, executive director of WiredSafety.org, a group that combats online bullying, agrees that the attitude is common. "You often hear, 'Big deal; all of us were bullied,' " Aftab says. "Americans have this sense that they're supposed to be tougher. The country has a macho mindset."

Ray Lora, a school board member and a former high school teacher, said that Golden — the Virginia youngster who sued his alleged high school bullies — should have been able to get beyond the torment without filing a lawsuit. "I'm sad that he hasn't gotten over that," he said. "Every kid has a rough time, but you have to overcome it."[24]

Estimates of the prevalence of bullying vary widely. The U.S. Department of Education's Office of Safe and Drug Free Schools says 7 million school bullying incidents occur each year.[25] A recent Department of Justice survey found that in any given month a quarter of U.S. students are bullied.[26] The Kaiser Family Foundation found that 55 percent of 8-to-11-year-olds and 68 percent of 12-to-15-year-olds thought bullying and teasing were the "big problems" in their schools — bigger

A kindergarten student adds her name to an anti-bullying poster at Grapevine Elementary School in Madisonville, Ky. Researchers say bullying often begins in preschool and peaks in grades six through eight.

problems than drugs, alcohol, racism, AIDS or pressure to have sex.[27] The study also found that fully 86 percent of youngsters ages 12 to 15 thought that students at their school get teased or bullied.

In April 2001, the first large-scale national survey of bullying in U.S. schools among students in grades six through 10 was published. Conducted before Columbine, it found that bullying was a problem that needed immediate nationwide attention. "This is a serious problem that we should not ignore," Tanja Nansel, an investigator at NICHD and the lead author of the study, said. "In the past, bullying has simply been dismissed as 'Kids will be kids,' but the findings from this study suggest that it should not be accepted as a normal part of growing up."[28]

Effective Programs Stress Adult Intervention

One of the most successful anti-bullying programs used in American schools was developed in the 1980s by a Norwegian educator, Professor Dan Olweus, after three adolescent Norwegian boys committed suicide — probably because of severe bullying by their classmates.

The Olweus [Ol-VEY-us] Bullying Prevention Program, which is used in several hundred U.S. schools, has been found to reduce bullying by 20 percent in U.S. schools where it has been adopted, while bullying increased in schools without the program.[1]

Schools adopting the Olweus program usually first conduct a survey to determine the seriousness of the problem, followed by a training period for teachers, administrators and selected students, parents and other school personnel. Anti-bullying rules — and consequences for rule-breakers — are established before the school year starts. In addition, adult supervision is established in places where bullying is known to occur, and the monitors are charged with intervention, not just supervision.

Intervention — a major component of the process — also includes sessions with individual bullies (and their parents) and their victims. "The goal is to ensure that the whole school, and not just a few teachers, will come together and act to make sure students know that 'bullying is not accepted in our class/school, and we will see to it that it comes to an end.' "[2]

The program has been praised by the University of Colorado's Center for the Study and Prevention of Violence and the federal Substance Abuse and Mental Health Services Administration.

Two other highly regarded programs are LIFT (Linking the Interests of Families and Teachers) and The Incredible Years.

LIFT is a 10-week anti-aggression intervention program that takes place on three levels: the classroom; the home (parents attend six training sessions to learn how to implement the program at home); and the playground, where adults monitor the behavior and reward or warn the students.

According to Fight Crime: Invest in Kids, a national anti-crime group based in Washington, D.C., LIFT's goal is to "instill social coping strategies in the students and to create an environment that surrounds each child with parents, teachers and peers who are working together to help prevent aggression and bullying. The playground becomes the practice field for these new techniques, and the children come to prize their good-behavior armbands."

The Incredible Years was designed initially for dealing with highly aggressive children ages 2 to 8. It trains both parents and their children in "non-aggression social skills."

Carolyn Webster-Stratton of the University of Washington says the program has stopped "the cycle of aggression for approximately two-thirds" of the families in the program. In certain Head Start settings, 80 percent of the kids tested within an acceptable range for problem behaviors within a half hour; only 48 percent of the children not in the program were within the acceptable range.[3]

Several other anti-bullying programs are expected to show good results as soon as evaluations are concluded, including the Aggressors, Victims, and Bystanders program, which the U.S. Department of Education has chosen as a "Promising Program" for its Safe and Drug Free Schools program.[4] It has been shown to significantly reduce "bystander support for aggression."

Operation Respect, founded by the famed folk-singing group Peter, Paul and Mary, also is considered effective with elementary schoolchildren.

---

[1] The program reportedly has been found to reduce bullying by up to 50 percent in Norway.

[2] D. Olweus, *et al.*, "Bullying Prevention Program," in D. S. Elliott, series ed., *Blueprints for Violence Prevention: Book Nine* (1999), Center for the Study and Prevention of Violence.

[3] Webster-Stratton, *et al.*, "The Incredible Years" Parent Teacher and Child Training Series, in D. S. Elliott, *ibid.*

[4] U.S. Department of Education, *Safe, Disciplined, and Drug-Free Schools Expert Panel* (2002).

Nansel and her colleagues found bullying hurts both bullies and the bullied. Victims of bullies are lonely and have trouble making friends; they are five times more likely than their peers to be depressed. Bullied boys are four times more likely than their peers to be suicidal, and girls eight times more likely, according to the study.[29]

The bullies, meanwhile, were more likely to smoke, drink alcohol and get poor grades. Most troubled of all were those who had both been bullied and had bullied others: They not only reported being lonelier and having more trouble making friends but also did poorly in school, smoked cigarettes and used alcohol.

The negative effects of bullying can last a lifetime, Nansel says. "Your junior high and lower high-school years are when you develop your identity," she says. "When people get the message during those very important years that they're not worthwhile, it certainly makes sense that it can have lasting effects. Similarly, for the bullies, if you learn that the way you gain enjoyment or pleasure is by doing something hurtful to another person, that's a very dangerous thing."

Indeed, society at large suffers from bullying. According to the NICHD, nearly 60 percent of boys who were bullies in middle school had at least one criminal conviction by age 24, and 40 percent had three or more convictions.[30]

"Bullying is an early warning that bullies may be headed toward more serious antisocial behavior," says Sanford A. Newman, president of Fight Crime: Invest in Kids, a crime-prevention organization of more than 2,000 police chiefs, sheriffs, prosecutors and crime survivors.[31]

Bullying also can affect school attendance, academic achievement and dropout rates. The National Association of School Psychologists (NASP) found that fear of being bullied may keep as many as 160,000 students out of school on any given day. And those who go to school are often too upset to concentrate.[32]

"He can't learn anything if he's scared to death," said Betty Tom Davidson, a school board member and parent in Orange County, N.C., who sought to pull her son out of class because bullying by an older student made him depressed and caused his grades to fall.[33]

Nonetheless, the NASP's Feinberg says he still sees schools that don't address the problem. "There are still some systems that deny the reality that is all around them," he says. "That's foolish thinking."

Bullies Are More Likely to Commit Crimes

Boys who were bullies in middle school are far more likely to commit crimes as adults than boys who were neither bullies nor victims.

Neither bullies nor victims
Bullies

23%
60%

At least one conviction by age 24

10%
40%

Three or more convictions by age 24

Source: National Institute for Child Health and Human Development

Is enough being done to curtail bullying?

There is considerable resistance to anti-bullying programs in many states and school districts, but nonetheless, many have joined with parents to fight bullying, and some programs have been running for three and four years.

"When I first started working on bullying five years ago, I used to hear from schools and parents that the bullying issue was blown out of proportion, but I haven't heard that in a long time," says Gaye Barker, coordinator of the NEA's National Bullying Awareness Campaign. "Now everyone is talking about the issue, and almost every state — if not every school district — is dealing with it. There are always going to be some groups that are slower to respond than others."

In fact, only 16 state legislatures have passed laws requiring school districts to implement anti-bullying programs, according to the National Conference of State Legislatures. Legislation is under consideration, however, in at least a dozen more states. Not surprisingly, some of the best programs are in schools that have had the biggest problems. In Colorado, for instance, school and governmental officials instituted the multilevel Bullying Prevention Program (BPP). Developed by the University of Colorado's Center for the Study and Prevention of Violence, BPP utilizes comprehensive measures at the student, class and staff levels to ensure that the entire school community is working together to stop bullying.

While many schools have responded to bullying aggressively, experts say an anti-bullying program is only as good as a school administrator's resolve to implement it.

"We tried for years and years to fix this problem, and at every turn this administration has refused to acknowledge the problem or do anything about it," said Patrice Anibal, a parent in Old Greenwich, Conn., who charged in a suit against school officials that they failed to protect her daughter from schoolyard bullies despite five years of parental pleas. "We felt we had no choice. We don't want this to happen to another family."[34]

Davidson finally resigned from the Orange County school board after it refused to deal with her son's bullies. "Complacency is unacceptable," she said. The board later acknowledged it had acted too slowly in her child's case and adopted an anti-bullying policy.[35]

In fact, fewer than one in four schools has any real bullying-prevention programs, says Newman of Fight Crime: Invest in Kids. "It's clear that not enough is being done. There are still 3.2 million kids being bullied each year in America and 3.7 million who are bullying other children."

Moreover, experts say, some schools are trying to "reinvent the wheel" by creating their own programs, rather than adopting proven measures. (*See sidebar, p. 402.*) Others are moving in another wrong direction, Newman says: "They are either blaming the victim — asking the kid why he doesn't just stand up for himself or quit provoking the bullies — or they are merely suspending or expelling the bullies."

Under zero-tolerance programs adopted by many school systems in the mid-1990s, youngsters were suspended or expelled the first time they broke a school disciplinary rule. When gun carrying or drug use were involved, the zero tolerance approach was often federally mandated.[36]

Newman opposes suspending or expelling a bully for two reasons: "It can feel like a vacation or a reward for the bully, and it squanders the early warning we've been given that a kid is headed for trouble later on." Noting that bullies are four times more likely to become repeat criminals later in life, he says that instead of sending the offending child home, schools should "work with the bully (along with his family) in a firm but effective way to get him back on track."

Teachers and administrators, however, are sometimes reluctant to address bullying, Newman says, fearing it will add to their workload and distract from efforts to improve student academic performance, mandated by the federal No Child Left Behind law.[37] But the fear is shortsighted, he says, because eliminating bullying reduces truancy and allows kids to concentrate better in class rather than worrying about being bullied at recess.

"Principals feel that they're under such pressure to deliver on academics that they don't have time to deal with bullying," says psychologist Slaby, who is a senior scientist at Health and Human Development Programs, an educational research organization in Newton, Mass. He has been studying bullying since the mid-1980s and has developed the widely used bullying-prevention program Aggressors, Victims and Bystanders. "[Principals] don't fully understand that academics suffer if you don't have a safe, bullying-free school. Even if you are only interested in academics and not the child's welfare and freedom from violence, you would do well to have bullying-prevention programs in the school."

"You hear from teachers, 'Don't ask me to do one more thing; I have more than I can handle already,' " the NEA's Barker says. "But when we explain that our program will save them time in terms of class disruptions and absenteeism, they are typically very positive."

However, some religious groups, as well as lawmakers and school officials, say that parents — not the government or schools — should be worried about disciplining and training children. And in some states, conservative Christian groups have sought to derail efforts to pass anti-bullying bills, arguing that when schools teach kids to tolerate classmates' racial, religious and sexual-orientation differences, the schools condone homosexuality and infringe on Christian kids' free-speech rights to oppose gay behavior.

Others also worry that basic discipline decisions are being taken out of the hands of the educators and placed in legislatures. Darcy Olsen, president of the Goldwater Institute in Phoenix, and former director of education and child policy at the Cato Institute, a libertarian think tank, says that anti-bullying legislation will undermine the authority of school administrators and teachers. "This is feel-good legislation," she said. "It is worthless. It will only burden them with more paperwork. Administrators and teachers don't need more training. They need to be able to get rid of students if they need to."[38]

Are school anti-bullying programs effective?

A wide range of anti-bullying information has become available over the last five years, including self-help books, parents' guides, teachers' manuals, informational pamphlets, Web sites and even interactive CDs.

Experts say it is important to identify programs that have been sufficiently tested and have shown meaningful results. The most successful anti-bullying programs, experts say, are both well-structured and well-enforced.

"The challenge," said Julie Thomerson, a policy analyst at the National Conference of State Legislatures, "is there is not enough research to point to specific, effective approaches. It's not that programs are bad, it's that many of them are too new to have been evaluated."[39]

Susan Limber, a professor at Clemson University's Institute on Family and Neighborhood Life who studies bullying, says zero-tolerance policies, group treatment, peer mediation and too-simple solutions, such as a single school assembly, are commonly used by schools, but are all ineffective.

Instead, she endorses a sustained, comprehensive effort to change school norms — like the renowned Olweus Bullying Prevention Program developed in Norway, which includes a prevention-coordinating committee, regular classroom meetings on bullying and immediate intervention and incident follow-up. Successful programs might also administer a questionnaire to assess bullying and teacher monitoring of areas where bullying usually occurs. Many of the schools that have used this program have reduced bullying by up to 50 percent and have achieved significant reductions in vandalism, fighting, and theft.[40]

But not all experts are convinced that bullying can be reduced that much, especially among older kids. In a study released in November 2004, Ken Rigby, an associate professor of social psychology at the University of

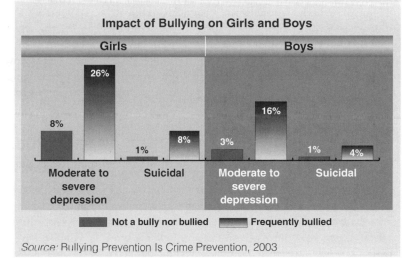

Bullying Linked to Depression, Suicide

Girls who are bullied frequently are eight times more suicidal than other girls. Bullied boys are five times more likely than their peers to suffer depression.

Source: Bullying Prevention Is Crime Prevention, 2003

South Australia, found that anti-bullying programs were less effective than previously had been thought, although still effective.[41] "It is comparatively rare to obtain a reduction in bullying of greater than 20 percent," Rigby says, quickly adding that a 20 percent reduction is still a substantial improvement. Moreover, he notes, nearly all the programs showed some results, especially in schools where the programs had been thoroughly implemented.

"Where there is improvement, it tends to be among younger children; the secondary schools generally show much less," Rigby says.

The American Association of University Women found that while the number of in-school anti-bullying programs and policies had increased, the incidence of sexual harassment and bullying had not declined. "You can change policies, but to actually change the behaviors takes time," says Leslie Annexstein, AAUW's director of legal advocacy. "Research indicates that there hasn't been enough emphasis on training teachers, counselors and administrators on how to deal with this issue."

The most successful programs, Rigby says, stress early intervention, helping potential victims protect themselves (because they are more motivated to change behavior than those who bully) and teaching kids to "problem-solve" — which is at least as effective as punishing the bullies, he says.

Slaby's "Aggressors, Victims and Bystanders" program, among several, focuses on changing the behavior of bystanders. "Bystanders are the most pivotal group of bullying influencers, especially since youth are so heavily influenced by their peers," Slaby says. "If you stand by and watch bullying, then you're letting it happen in your community. But if you stand up, then the bullies don't even have a chance. Bullies wouldn't even consider harassing others if they thought it wouldn't go over well."

Slaby says he has many reports of students who have been trained in the bystander curriculum who have helped defuse threatening situations. "Kids are speaking up to police officers or to teachers when they hear about something that ought to be brought to their attention," he says. "Kids are the best metal detectors. They know when something is happening."

Feinberg says the NASP's two-year anti-bullying program, "Stop Bullying Now and Lend a Hand," has been "an overwhelming success" both in increasing public awareness and preventing bullying because it teaches kids that bullying is not simply a rite of passage. Successful programs teach kids "that there are acceptable codes of conduct and . . . that there are consequences for violating those codes. [But] there will be little or no change in the behavior of school bullies unless the culture within the school is changed."

Experts agree that no matter what program is used, its effectiveness depends on school administrators' level of commitment. "There are a lot of schools with good-sounding programs," says former teacher Derek Randel of Wilmette, Ill., who became a "parenting coach" and specializes in dealing with bullying. "Words on paper are wonderful, but . . . they don't mean anything without a commitment to what they stand for."

For instance, he says, "In some very affluent neighborhoods, the schools take a 'We don't want to get the parents mad at us' approach. Frankly, many of these parents are dysfunctional parents and by bringing that dysfunction into the schools they're ruining the schools. I've seen a number of lawsuits brought by parents whose kids have been disciplined for bullying. You almost have to feel sorry for the schools, which then have to defend themselves."

Faced with confusing data on the effectiveness of various programs and vague anti-bullying laws that don't tell schools what they should do, some administrators resist confronting the problem. Some districts also lack the necessary funds, training and enforcement.

"We have a long way to go and a lot more work to do," Rigby says. "Success is not dependent upon the correct content of the programs. What does seem to make a difference is how thoroughly the program is supported and implemented, and a lot of work is still needed to motivate the schools to address this."

BACKGROUND

Early Research

A major theme of recorded history is the exploitation of the weak by the strong," Rigby writes in his 2002 book, *New Perspectives on Bullying.*[42]

Bullies have long been stock characters in movies, television, books and even cartoons, perhaps because they are so much a part of real life. In the early 18th century, novelist Henry Fielding featured a bully in *Tom Thumb.* On stage, bullies have been featured in works ranging from the intentionally humorous melodramas of the Golden Age to the unforgettable bellowing of Stanley Kowalski in Tennessee Williams's "A Streetcar Named Desire." Popular modern novelists such as S. E. Hinton, Robert Cormier and Walter Dean Myers often feature bullies.

The first scientific paper on bullying was published in 1897, when Norwegian researcher Fredic Burke's "Teasing and Bullying" explored why children bully, what effects bullying had on victims and how bullying could be reduced.[43]

However, bullying did not fully emerge as a field of scientific inquiry for social scientists until the 1970s, when a few articles were published. Then in 1978 came the publication in English of *Aggression in the Schools: Bullies and Whipping Boys*, by Norwegian psychologist Dan Olweus, one of the "founding fathers" of research on bullying and victimization.

In the 1980s, social scientists in Britain and the United States took an active interest in bullying. "Here was an issue that not only intrigued and challenged empirical researchers, counselors and theoreticians in psychology,

CHRONOLOGY

Before 1970 *Researchers pay little attention to bullying.*

1897 Norwegian social scientist F. L. Burk writes the first academic treatment of "bullying and teasing."

1970s-1980s *School bullying remains a low-key issue, although a sprinkling of journal articles discuss the problem. Norwegian school and government officials begin addressing the problem of bullying in schools, but officials in England and the United States begin to focus on the issue only late in the era.*

1978 Norwegian psychology Professor Dan Olweus, widely considered the father of social science research on bullying, publishes the English edition of *Aggression in the Schools: Bullies and Whipping*.

1982 After three unrelated suicides by children in Norway, a Nationwide Campaign Against Bullying is begun in all of the country's 3,500 schools.

1990-2000 *A string of schoolyard massacres in the United States — many committed by victims of bullies — prompts scientists, law enforcement and government officials to study the causes and negative effects of bullying.*

1993 Olweus publishes his landmark work, *Bullying: What We Know and What We Can Do About It*.

Feb. 2, 1996 Barry Loukaitis, 14, kills two students and a teacher in Moses Lake, Wash., later telling officials he was tired of being called a "faggot."

Feb. 19, 1997 Evan Ramsey, 16, kills his principal and another student in Bethel, Alaska, later complaining that school officials had failed to stop the bullying he was encountering at school.

Oct. 1, 1997 Luke Woodham, 16, kills two classmates and wounds seven in Pearl, Miss., after passing a note to friends stating "I killed because people like me are mistreated every day . . . . Push us and we will push back."

Dec. 1, 1997 Michael Carneal, 14, kills three students and injures five others at his West Paducah, Ky., high school. He later says he felt that going to prison would be better than continuing to endure the bullying he was subjected to in school.

Dec. 15, 1997 Joseph Colt Todd, 14, shoots and wounds two students at his Stamps, Ark., high school, later complaining that he was tired of being bullied.

April 20, 1999 Columbine High School students Dylan Klebold and Eric Harris shoot and kill a teacher and 12 students at their Littleton, Colo., school and then turn their guns on themselves; 23 students are wounded. The 18-year-old shooters had been favorite targets of bullies.

2000-Present *Schools across the United States adopt anti-bullying programs; the number of bullying incidents in some districts reportedly decreases by more than 20 percent. At least 16 state legislatures pass legislation requiring schools to adopt anti-bullying programs.*

May 2002 A study of school shooters by the U.S. Secret Service and U. S. Department of Education reveals that in two-thirds of 37 school shootings over the last 25 years the attackers had felt "bullied, persecuted, or injured by others" before the attack.

2004 Parents in Kansas and Connecticut sue their children's schools and school districts for failing to protect students from being bullied despite repeated complaints from the families. Parents in Virginia sue the alleged bullies of their child.

February 2005 Responding to a television report on widespread school bullying, the Indiana Senate is expected to pass a bill calling for statewide anti-bullying programs in schools.

education and sociology but also offered some kind of hope to thousands of people for whom bullying was a grim, everyday reality," Rigby wrote.[44]

When Rigby would tell fellow scientists what he was studying, they thought it "a curious thing to be researching," even though studies on aggression in animals and

Technology Gives Bullies a New Weapon

Hallie Fox, a high school senior in McLean, Va., was in seventh grade when her friends suddenly began giving her the silent treatment. Confused and upset, Fox went online that night to chat with some other girlfriends, who asked her why she had been picking fights through nasty instant messages and e-mails.

In fact, she hadn't. She had been cyberbullied. The culprit was a former friend who had hacked into her e-mail and instant message accounts.

Teasing and bullying are nothing new to youngsters. But modern technology enables bullies to follow kids far off school grounds, into their homes and bedrooms.

Cyberbullying includes sending malicious, sometimes threatening, e-mails, instant messages and cell phone text messages; creating humiliating Web sites that include stories and pictures; posting malicious gossip and comments on Web logs (blogs); and breaking into e-mail accounts to send vicious material to others.

The anonymity of the Internet allows bullies to flourish with increased viciousness and little fear of consequence.

"Kids don't have to look someone in the face when they're cyberbullying; they don't have to take responsibility for their actions," says Kristin Franke, of the Empower program, a Washington-based nonprofit group that works to prevent bullying.

She says that more than 40 percent of kids have been bullied online, according to a 2004 survey by i-SAFE, a nonprofit foundation that educates kids to use the Internet safely.[1] Moreover, as with traditional bullying, kids often bear the burden alone. In 2004, almost 60 percent of kids did not tell their parents or an adult about hurtful online messages, according to i-SAFE.

"Americans are realizing that the issue of kids hurting and harassing other kids is a big one," says Parry Aftab, executive director of WiredSafety.org, another Internet safety group. "We have to teach our kids to be good people when they're online just as we do offline."

A 2001 Department of Justice study found that approximately 14 percent of adolescents admitted to making rude or nasty comments to someone online during the past year.[2] But in 2004, the number increased to 53 percent.[3]

To combat the problem, kids need to be educated about the fingerprints they leave when using Internet, Aftab says, warning that each time the Internet is used, an Internet address is established that can be used to trace all electronic communications on that computer.

While educating kids about the harms and consequences of cyber-harassment is necessary for its prevention, bullying experts say that parents, law enforcers and school administrators also need to be on the alert.

"Schools have to take responsibility for cyberbullying because it can affect a student's ability to concentrate and learn while in class, and that impacts the school just as much as the schoolyard bully does," says

humans were well-established and respectable. "Few, however, had undertaken to study such a 'common' thing as bullying."

Olweus identified the characteristics of both bullies and their victims. In his 1993 book, *Bullying at School: What We Know and What We Can Do*, he found that bullies have a strong need to dominate and subdue other students and to get their own way; are impulsive and easily angered; are often defiant and aggressive toward adults, including parents and teachers and show little empathy toward students who are victimized. If they are boys, he observes, they are physically stronger than other boys in general.[45]

According to Olweus, victims generally are cautious, sensitive, quiet, withdrawn and shy, and are often anxious,

insecure, unhappy and have low self-esteem. They also are depressed and "engage in suicidal ideation" much more often than their peers. "Often they do not have a single good friend and relate better to adults than to peers. If they are boys, they may be physically weaker than their peers. These characteristics are likely to be both a partial cause and a consequence of the bullying."

Another, smaller group of victims, called provocative victims or bully-victims, often has reading and writing problems and attention deficit-hyperactivity disorder characteristics.[46] "The behavior of the bully-victims tends to elicit negative reactions from many students in the classroom, and the teacher often dislikes them also," Olweus writes.

As all the experts have pointed out, the rash of school violence in the 1990s — punctuated by the Columbine

Katy Otto, Empower's director of grants and community outreach.

However, educators and administrators have little jurisdiction over events that happen outside of school grounds, often preventing schools from punishing online bullies, Aftab says. Most cyberbullying cases are not serious enough to warrant police involvement, she adds, further limiting a school's options.

A California-based Web site — schoolscandals.com — showed just how insidious and hurtful online bullying can be. In 2003 parents and school administrators discovered the site had become a breeding ground for hate speech and harassment. Parents and school administrators called for the site's closure, but had little luck. Police were unable to take action. Eventually the site was taken down after a radio station got involved and put enough pressure on the people running the site.[4]

But schoolscandals2.com is already up and running, and kids have already begun using it to cyberbully. "She wears like the same shorts everyday, dresses like a guy and has the ugliest face ever. She has a guy's voice, too! Yuck," wrote a Southern California middle-school student in May 2004.[5]

Similarly, in Chappaqua, N.Y., a wealthy New York City suburb, two senior boys created a Web site with offensive, personal information about students in 2001. Principal Kathy Mason called local police and suspended the boys for five days. But prosecutors said that while the site was "offensive and abhorrent," it did not meet the legal definition of harassment; to widespread community outrage criminal charges against the boys were dropped.[6]

To combat cyberbullying and the limits of school jurisdiction, some schools require students to sign an agreement at the beginning of the year obligating them to use e-mail and the Internet ethically. "Signing a contract is an excellent way to get the point across to the kids," Franke says. "We also recommend that schools get the contracts notarized so that students understand the severity and importance of what they are signing."

Students at Fox's high school must sign a contract each year, and the school monitors its wireless network for cyber offenses. "Last year, about 20 freshman girls were caught spreading rumors through e-mail," Fox says.

In the final analysis, however, most experts agree that fighting cyberbullying isn't that different from standing up to traditional bullying: Teach kids to report incidents to adults and not to respond to the bully's taunts. "If kids are going to have the power of the technology, they have to have the judgment to go with it," Aftab says. "They must learn how to use the filter between their ears to think before they click."

— *Kate Templin*

---

[1] i-SAFE America, www.isafe.org.

[2] David Finkelhor, *et al.*, "Highlights of Youth Internet Safety Survey," U.S. Department of Justice, March 2001.

[3] *Ibid.*

[4] Erika Hayasaki and Jia-Rui Chong, "Parents Rally to Stop 'Cyber Bullying,'" *Los Angeles Times*, April 17, 2003, p. B1.

[5] www.schoolscandals2.com.

[6] Amy Benfer, "Cyber slammed," *Salon.com*, July 3, 2001.

shootings — focused public attention on the problem and prompted a burst of new research on the dangers of bullying.

"In the wake of Columbine and a lot of other high-profile incidents," NICHD's Nansel says, "people wanted to know how much of a problem was posed by [students] who were victimized becoming violent." The study Nansel and her colleagues released in 2003 found that, while bullying victims were slightly more likely than other students to carry a weapon to school and exhibit other risk factors, the bullies themselves showed a much higher rate of violent behavior than either their victims or uninvolved people.

Nansel's group concluded — as have virtually all of the social scientists who've studied the problem in recent years — that bullying is a significant problem that despite all the sound and fury still has not received sufficient attention.[47]

Changing Society

Some experts blame bullying on the changes that have transformed society over the last few generations. For example, the anonymity provided by modern schools — often featuring large, unmonitored common areas — is frequently cited as a major reason bullies feel they can get away with abusive behavior. And the extra demands that education-reform measures have imposed on teachers often keep them too busy to be monitors.

"We used to think teachers stood in the hallway," Nansel says, "but now that doesn't really happen, because

Miss America Erika Harold says that when she was a teenager, teachers and school officials ignored her pleas for help in dealing with bullies. She devoted her reign in 2003 to representing the anti-bullying program Fight Crime: Invest in Kids.

teachers are so stressed about what they need to accomplish in the classroom. It leaves kids a lot of time when [they] are on their own."

Others blame deeper cultural forces, specifically a society that seems to condone or reward rudeness and/or abusiveness by successful people. In some "reality" television shows, for instance, those who shout at their peers and are the most manipulative and backstabbing are often the ones who triumph.

Indeed, teenage bullies are often the most popular kids in school, according to a study published in 2003 in *Pediatrics*. After surveying students and teachers in ethnically diverse urban schools, the researchers concluded that teenage bullies — contrary to some stereotypes — "do not feel depressed, anxious, or lonely" because they enjoy "high social status within their peer collective." But classmates would rather not spend time with them, the survey

found, indicating that perhaps "the social prestige of bullies is motivated in part by fear."[48]

However, the authors continued, "When bullies are considered the 'coolest,' bullying behavior is encouraged" — underscoring the need to address bullying as a systemic problem that involves the entire school community.

Other research has found that comprehensive, schoolwide, anti-bullying programs are most effective when they raise the awareness of how bystanders contribute to the bullying problem and aim to change peer dynamics that encourage the practice. Even when bystanders simply provide an audience of onlookers, they indirectly support bullying by providing the public acceptance that supports its perceived legitimacy and importance," researcher Slaby wrote. In a recent study, bystander peers were present in 88 percent of childhood bullying episodes, but a bystander intervened in less than one-fifth of the cases.[49]

Many anti-bullying programs, such as County Attorney Backstrom's in Minnesota, focus on teaching bystanders the importance of intervening, and how to do it. Many children and adolescents who become bystanders to bullying don't know what to say or do to stop the abuse. Or they may be reluctant to break a perceived "code of silence" or fearful of becoming victimized themselves. In some schools, bullies and their supporters directly intimidate bystanders into silence by stating, "snitches get stitches," according to Slaby.

Recent research has also shed light on how bullying affects those who both get bullied and bully others. Compared with bullies and their victims, bully-victims seem to have the worst of both worlds and a unique risk profile, UCLA's Juvonen and her colleagues have found. "Their high levels of social avoidance, conduct problems and school difficulties suggest that they are a particularly high-risk group," said the study. Other studies have shown that bully-victims are most vulnerable to psychiatric disorders and best fit the profiles of seriously violent offenders.[50]

Learned Behavior

It is now thought — contrary to the beliefs of several decades ago — that bullies are made, not born.

"The majority of bullies come from homes that are abusive and violent, where parents are authoritarian, inconsistent, negative or indifferent," and where there is "too little love and too much rejection," writes Delwyn

Getty Images/Jacob Silberberg

Tattum, an anti-bullying expert at the University of Wales Institute, in Cardiff.[51]

But outside of the home, bullies' "teachers" are everywhere, says Colman McCarthy, a former *Washington Post* columnist and founder of the Center for Teaching Peace, who has conducted classes in non-violent conflict resolution in high schools, colleges, universities and law schools for more than 20 years. "Like all types of violence, bullying is a learned behavior," McCarthy continues. "And there are many types: physical bullying, which people associate with schoolchildren; verbal bullying, which especially occurs in marriages; international bullying, when a powerful, militaristic nation bullies other nations; and there's environmental bullying, when corporations dominate a community. But it's usually associated with schoolyard bullies, who often learn it from a male figure in their lives, at home, and then there are gangs' teaching-the-initiate type of bullying."

But humans are not born with a propensity to bully, McCarthy contends. "I do a lot of death penalty-type work, and I've interviewed many killers. Almost all of them come from highly dysfunctional backgrounds," he says. "They learn how to be violent from all kinds of places, but we teach it in very subtle ways."

Andrea Cohn and Andrea Canter at the National Association of School Psychologists, agree. Bullying is "learned through influences in the environment, such as the home, school, peer groups and even the media, which means that it can also be unlearned or, better yet, prevented," they write.[52]

CURRENT SITUATION

Christian Opposition

Hoping to teach children to reject bullying behavior, at least 16 states have adopted legislation aimed at recommending or requiring schools to institute anti-bullying programs.

Is Your Child Being Bullied?

Children who are bullied often tell no one about their misery out of shame, fear of retaliation or feelings of hopelessness. Experts say parents should be aware of the following signs of victimization:

- Subtle changes in behavior (withdrawn, anxious, preoccupied, loss of interest in school and favorite activities)
- Comes home from school with bruises and scratches, torn or dirtied clothing or with missing or damaged books and property
- Loss of appetite
- Excessive trips to the school nurse
- Inability to sleep, bad dreams, crying in sleep
- Repeatedly loses clothing, money, or other valuables
- Appears afraid or reluctant to go to school in the morning
- Repeated headaches or stomachaches — particularly in the morning
- Chooses a roundabout or strange route to and from school
- Feels lonely
- Sensitive or withdrawn when asked about his or her day
- Big appetite after school (perhaps because lunch or lunch money was taken)
- Reluctant to take the school bus

Source: Tara L. Kuther, National PTA, accessed online Jan. 31, 2005

Besides Colorado, Washington and Oregon were among the first states to react after the Columbine incident, followed by Michigan, Massachusetts and others. Several states have required more adult oversight of lunchrooms and playgrounds, hired "school climate" directors and established procedures for reporting bullying. The "Dignity in All Schools Act" requires New York City schools to get more accurate reporting about the problem.

In the beginning, not all of these efforts went smoothly. Legislators had to deal with the problem that bullying "has been around for a long time and can be defined in a number of different ways," the NCSL's Thomerson said.[53]

In Providence, R.I., for instance, the school board in March 2004 redefined bullying after the American Civil Liberties Union (ACLU) said the school board's original definition was vague and could endanger free speech. The new rule now says: "Bullying occurs when a student, while at school, intentionally assaults, batters, threatens, harasses,

AP Photo/Tom Strattman

Brittni Ainsworth, a high school sophomore in Plainfield, Ind., hopes that proposed state legislation requiring schools to adopt anti-bullying policies will stop the girls who bullied her and others.

stalks, menaces, intimidates, extorts, humiliates or taunts another student; verbal abuse to include teasing, name-calling and harmful gossip; emotional abuse to include humiliation, shunning and exclusion."[54]

Conservative Christian groups, however, have mounted stiff resistance to anti-bullying programs. In northeastern Kentucky, for instance, hundreds of students either refused to attend tolerance training sessions or skipped school the day the program was offered because they felt the anti-harassment workshops were intended to promote acceptance of homosexuality.[55]

Similarly, conservative Christians opposed Washington state's anti-bullying legislation on the grounds that it would promote homosexuality and threatened free speech — specifically students' rights to condemn homosexuality. "[The proposed law] looked like it could be [used against] people who might speak out against behavior," Rick Forcier, director of the Christian Coalition of Washington, said. The legislation might lead to homosexual sensitivity training in schools, he added.[56]

Similar objections were raised when Maryland tried in 2003 to require local school boards to prohibit harassment based on any distinguishing characteristic, including sexual orientation. Supporters — including the Free State Justice Coalition and the Gay, Lesbian and Straight Education

Network — described numerous incidents of taunting, name-calling and intimidation, by teachers as well as students, based on sexual orientation. The legislation, they argued, would make it clear that such activity is wrong.

But the nonpartisan group TakeBackMaryland — which seeks to return Maryland to "biblical foundations" — said the bill went too far. "What are we going to do? Go after every kid who says something some other kid doesn't like?" asked Tres Kerns, the group's chairman.[57]

Maryland Pastor David Whitney argued that such tolerance training "is not the jurisdiction of the government."[58] Republican Gov. Robert Ehrlich eventually vetoed the bill, saying its requirement that county school boards report incidents of harassment and intimidation would create more paperwork for administrators without making schools safer.[59]

Sprigg, at the Family Research Council, says his organization agrees that students should never be subjected to "unprovoked violence or to the use of abusive epithets for any reason — including sexual orientation." Such behavior should be prohibited by school disciplinary codes, which should be strictly enforced, he says. However, explicitly banning harassment based on sexual orientation teaches that "there is nothing wrong with being gay or lesbian," he says. Thus, anti-bullying rules "are being used as a Trojan horse to get to a larger pro-homosexual agenda."

Most anti-bullying legislation, he says, appears to punish thoughts or motivation behind behavior instead of focusing on actions. "An expression of opinion — saying we believe that homosexual behavior is wrong — is treated as a form of name calling or bullying."

For example, he says, one student opposed to homosexuality wore a T-shirt emblazoned with the slogan "straight pride" to school during a week in which the school's gay students were engaging in "gay pride" activities. The boy was punished and forced to change his shirt by administrators who said the slogan was offensive. "That's not an equal treatment of equal viewpoints," Sprigg says. "The words 'straight pride' are not a vulgar epithet, but they were treated as such."

Newman, of Fight Crime: Invest in Kids, defends anti-bullying programs, saying, "It's one thing to engage in legitimate debate. It's another thing to harass other students. Harassment and bullying shouldn't be tolerated regardless of the grounds."

Do anti-bullying programs promote homosexuality?

YES Peter Sprigg
Senior Director of Policy Studies,
Family Research Council

From testimony before House Ways and Means Committee,
Maryland House of Delegates, Feb. 19, 2003.

Pro-homosexual activists contend that our schools have large numbers of students who are gay, lesbian, bisexual or transgendered (GLBT) and are frequent victims of verbal or physical harassment or even acts of violence. They argue, therefore, that victims of harassment or violence targeted for their real or perceived "sexual orientation" should be singled out for specific protection under school disciplinary codes.

Yet there is evidence that harassment of gay teens may neither be as frequent, as severe, nor as disproportionate, as some pro-homosexual rhetoric would suggest. The majority of gay teens (58 percent), according to a Gay, Lesbian and Straight Education Network (GLSEN) survey, reported no incidents of "physical harassment" in the past year (only 15 percent claimed to have experienced this "frequently" or "often").

Pro-family groups such as the Family Research Council agree wholeheartedly that no student should ever be the victim of unprovoked violence (or taunting) — for their sexual orientation or for any other reason. We believe that such behavior should be prohibited by school disciplinary codes, and that those codes should be strictly enforced.

However, singling out "sexual orientation" for special protection cannot be justified on logical grounds, and it could have consequences not clear at first glance. Lumping "sexual orientation" together with "race, color, national origin, sex and disability" for special protection is illogical because the latter qualities are inborn (except for some disabilities), involuntary, immutable and innocuous — none of which is true of homosexuality, despite the claims of its advocates.

Evidence that homosexuality is inborn (that is, unalterably determined by genetics or biology) is ephemeral at best; while same-sex attractions may come unbidden, homosexual behavior and adoption of a "gay" identity are clearly voluntary; the existence of numerous "former homosexuals" proves that homosexuality is changeable; and the numerous pathologies associated with homosexuality demonstrate how harmful it is.

If all forms of harassment are wrong, then all forms of harassment — without distinction — should be banned. When harassment based on sexual orientation is explicitly banned, school staffs and students are inevitably trained that the reason such harassment is wrong is not because all harassment is wrong or because all people should be treated with respect, but because "there is nothing wrong with being gay or lesbian."

NO James Garbarino, Ph.D.
E. L. Vincent Professor of Human
Development, Cornell University

Written for The CQ Researcher, January 2005

About 10 percent of Americans are gay and lesbian, and research shows that other than their sexual orientation there is little or nothing to differentiate them from the other 90 percent. What is more, the scientific consensus is that sexual orientation is a biologically based trait. That alone should be enough to sustain the claim to full human rights for gay and lesbian kids. Anti-bullying programs don't promote homosexuality. What they promote is basic respect for human rights.

Why pay special attention to the bullying of gay and lesbian kids? Research shows that gay and lesbian kids are disproportionately victimized by peers: five times more likely to miss school because they feel unsafe, four times as likely to be threatened with a weapon at school and three times as likely to be hurt so badly in a fight that they need medical treatment, according to a recent study.

The fact that adult bias and religious fundamentalism sustain and validate homophobic attacks is all the more reason to make efforts to deal with them as part of any community's initiative to protect children from harm at school. In fact, they should fall under the No Child Left Behind Act's provisions concerning the right to be protected in "persistently dangerous" schools: Studies of school shooters compiled by the FBI and Secret Service, among others, document that bullying (and particularly homophobic bullying) has been a contributing factor in severe school violence.

As our national consciousness of human rights issues evolves, we naturally include more and more people in our circle of caring. African-Americans were once outside the circle. Now no one but the most retrograde racist will tolerate overt racial discrimination in the form of verbal slurs, exclusionary policies and hateful assault aimed against children and youth.

Currently, gay and lesbian individuals are singled out for special negative treatment in American public life — such as being the target of state and national legislation and constitutional amendments to prevent them from exercising the basic human right of marriage (a right denied on racist grounds in the not-too-distant past when racially mixed marriages were prohibited).

Fifty years from now, we will experience the same regret for opposition to programs protecting gay and lesbian kids that all good-hearted people do now when they consider our racist past.

Kids Call Bullying the Biggest Problem

Two-thirds of the older children and more than half the younger ones say bullying and teasing are the biggest problems at their schools, according to the Kaiser Family Foundation.

Percentage of Children Who Say Each of the Following Is a Big Problem in School

	Ages 8 to 11	Ages 12 to 15
Teasing and bullying	55%	68%
Discrimination	41	63
Violence	46	62
Alcohol or drugs	44	68
Pressure to have sex	33	49

Source: Kaiser Family Foundation, "Talking With Kids About Tough Issues"

James Garbarino, a professor of human development at Cornell University and coauthor of the 2002 book *And Words Can Hurt Forever: How to Protect Adolescents From Bullying, Harassment, and Emotional Violence*, says rules giving special consideration to the bullying of homosexuals are needed because gays are disproportionately victimized by their peers. A student survey conducted by the National Mental Health Association found that gay kids — and those thought to be gay — are bullied more than any other group except overweight kids. Nine out of 10 respondents said they hear other kids use words like "fag," "homo," "dyke," "queer" or "gay" at least once in a while, with 51 percent hearing them every day.[60]

Gay students are also three-to-seven times more likely to attempt suicide; five times more likely to miss school because they feel unsafe; four times as likely to be threatened with a weapon at school, and three times as likely to be hurt so badly in a fight that they need medical attention, according to Garbarino. (*See "At Issue," p. 413.*)

Federal Law

While anti-bullying legislation has been primarily a state and local affair, in summer 2004 Reps. John Shimkus, R-Ill., and Danny Davis, D-Ill., proposed the first federal law to address the problem. Although the bill failed to advance in the last Congress, Shimkus says he will reintroduce it this session.

The bill required schools that receive funds under the Safe and Drug Free Schools Act to create bullying and harassment-prevention programs. Currently, those funds can be used to promote school safety but are not specifically earmarked for anti-bullying programs.

The bill did not authorize any new funds for bullying-prevention programs, but law enforcement officials say anti-bullying programs could be a cost-effective way to reduce school violence because they help nip violence in the bud. "Bullying creates a cycle of violence," says Newman of Fight Crime: Invest in Kids. "Bullies are six times more likely to be convicted of crime later on."

Nearly every school district has a Safe and Drug Free Schools coordinator, Newman's organization points out, each of whom could be trained as an anti-bullying trainer for their school district at a one-time cost of $4,000. By comparison, the group says, every high-risk juvenile prevented from adopting a life of crime could save the country between $1.7 million and $2.3 million.[61]

Other groups, such as the AAUW, are using another federal law — Title IX of the Education Amendments of 1972 — to address bullying. Title IX prohibits sexual harassment of female students, which AAUW calls a "close cousin" of bullying, so the AAUW is encouraging schools to make sure their Title IX coordinators are aware of the connection between sexual harassment and bullying.

"As far as bullying and sexual harassment are concerned, it's difficult to talk about one without talking about the other," AAUW's Annexstein, says. The group views sexual harassment primarily as a college and workplace issue but defines bullying as a K-12 issue. "We're seeing evidence of bullying at very young ages, and that's troubling on a lot of levels."

However, she says, most parents of bullied kids do not yet understand that when bullying has sexual overtones, it becomes sexual harassment — a federal crime.

Lisa Soronen, a staff attorney at the National School Boards Association, thinks increased attention to sexual-harassment issues in the workplace may have made parents less tolerant of sexual taunts directed at their children. "After the sexual harassment debate," she said, "we decided kids shouldn't have to tolerate nasty behavior."[62]

OUTLOOK
Going to Court

As recent lawsuits indicate, parents increasingly are suing their children's schools and school districts, contending they ignored parental complaints about bullies.

"It's every school administrator's nightmare," writes Santa Barbara, Calif., attorney Mary Jo McGrath. "The phone rings and on the other end of is an angry parent threatening to sue because his child was injured in a bullying incident that took place at school."[63]

The NEA's Newberry also expects more suits to be brought against the bullies themselves. "Boys will be boys, but a felony is a felony, and you can't hit someone or beat someone up without facing the consequences," he says. "That's the next step that we as a society have to take."

Barker, of the NEA's National Bullying Awareness Campaign, agrees. "Kids sometimes do things that adults are arrested and jailed for," she says. "If it gets to that point, you have to get the police involved."

Newman, of Fight Crime: Invest in Kids, says if the schools aren't responsive or the bullying amounts to physical assault, it's "perfectly legitimate" to file a lawsuit. "Assault is assault wherever it takes place."

However, he would prefer that the schools deal with the bullying long before the situation reaches that point. "Preventing kids from becoming bullies and intervening to get bullies back on track can not only protect children from the pain that bullying inflicts immediately but also can protect all of us from crime later on," he says. Newman and others believe strongly that education, training and "attitude adjustment" can solve the problem of bullying, even as serious and pervasive as it is.

"There's always more that can be done," says Feinberg of the National Association of School Psychologists. "We need to increase the basic anti-bullying message to every school district in the country, because I'm sure there are some who still believe the mythical notion that bullying is just a rite of passage that everybody goes through.

"But in general the message has been received, and people know that for it to be effective it has to be given to all the stakeholders involved — students, teachers, community leaders, administrators and parents — so they can all work collaboratively to eliminate, or at least reduce, the problem."

As to the future, he says, the biggest problem will be sustainability. "In our society, yesterday's news is old news. We have to make sure that our awareness of the problem doesn't fade because other things come into play."

Newberry hopes the rigorous new academic demands of the No Child Left Behind Act will not cause teachers and schools to lose their focus on social concerns. "That's going to be a kind of Catch-22," he says. "But, if you compare what's being done now with what was being done five or 10 years ago, I think we've made a gigantic leap in the right direction."

He also worries about the major changes occurring in students' home lives. "Twenty or 30 years ago, parents were able to spend two to three times as much time with their kids in the family room and at the breakfast or dinner table than they do now," he says. "We've lost the adult mentor for such things as social etiquette, manners, problem solving and communications skills, and as a result kids are not getting their emotional needs met at home. Look at the growth in gangs, which, by definition, are kids trying to create a family for themselves.

Indiana state Sen. Tom Wyss proposed anti-bullying legislation after seeing a television news investigation on school bullying in his state. "There was story after story of harassment of kids who are gay or effeminate," he recalls; "of kids getting beaten up; of girls saying things on the Internet like so-and-so is sleeping with so and so. I'm 62, and I was sitting there thinking, 'If I had bullied someone when I was a youngster, my parents would have gotten a phone call from school immediately, and they would have read the riot act to me.'"

"So the challenge for all of us is to create a team of parents, relatives, community leaders and schools who work together to help young people face adult responsibility and become adult leaders, and then good parents themselves," Newberry adds.

Davidson, the former North Carolina school board member whose son was bullied, advocates continual vigilance. "There are all sorts of reasons for tuning into this problem, because ultimately we will pay for it in some fashion if we don't. It's just the right thing to do: If a kid reaches out for help, we have to try to reach back."[64]

NOTES

1. Katy St. Clair, "The Bullying Industrial Complex Gets Touchy-Feely with Mean Girls and Boys," *East Bay Express*, June 16, 2004; see also Margie Mason, "Study: Anti-gay bullying widespread in America's schools," SFGate.com, Dec. 12, 2002.

2. Bob Gibson, "Student's suffering spurs two bully bills," [Charlottesville, Va.] *Daily Progress*, Jan. 18, 2005.

3. Heather Hollingsworth, "Parents turn to courts to stop bullying of their children by peers," The Associated Press, May 22, 2004.

4. Quoted in Michelle Boorstein, "In Suit, Va. Teen Accuses Schoolmates of Bullying," *The Washington Post*, Nov. 7, 2004, p. C1.

5. "Are We Safe?" National Crime Prevention Council, 2000.

6. T. R. Nansel, *et al.*, "Bullying behaviors among U.S. youth: Prevalence and association with psychosocial adjustment," *Journal of the American Medical Association*, April 25, 2001, pp. 2094-2100.

7. Jeff Kass, "Witnesses Tell of Columbine Bullying," *The Rocky Mountain News*, Oct. 3, 2000.

8. "Threat assessment in schools: a guide to managing threatening situations and to creating safe school climates," U.S. Secret Service and U.S. Department of Education, May 2002.

9. Linda Lumsden, "Preventing Bullying," ERIC Digest 155, Clearinghouse on Educational Policy Management, College of Education, University of Oregon, February 2002. The 16 states are: Arkansas, California, Colorado, Connecticut, Georgia, Illinois, Louisiana, Nevada, New Hampshire, New Jersey, Oklahoma, Rhode Island, Vermont, Washington, Oregon and West Virginia.

10. Sandra Feldman, "Bullying Prevention," Teacher to Teacher: Issues Affecting the Classroom Teacher, March, 2004, www.aft.org/teachers/t2t/0304.htm.

11. Peter K. Smith and Sonia Sharp, *School Bullying: Insights and Perspectives* (1994).

12. Robert Garofalo, *et al.*, "The Association Between Health Risk Behaviors and Sexual Orientation Among a School-based Sample of Adolescents,"
Pediatrics, Vol. 101, 1998; National Survey of Teens Shows Anti-Gay Bullying Common in Schools," U.S. Newswire, Dec. 12, 2002.

13. Patrik Jonsson, "Schoolyard bullies and their victims: The picture fills out," *The Christian Science Monitor*, May 12, 2004, p.1.

14. *Ibid.*

15. *Ibid.*

16. Nansel, *op. cit.*

17. Quoted on CBS News, "The Early Show," Oct. 17, 2000.

18. Ronald G. Slaby, "The Role of Bystanders in Preventing Bullying," *Health in Action* (forthcoming).

19. Hollingsworth, *op. cit.*

20. Boorstein, *op. cit.*

21. *Ibid.*

22. Bureau of Justice Statistics, www.atriumsoc.org/pages/bullyingstatistics.html.

23. U.S. Secret Service, *op. cit.*

24. Boorstein, *op. cit.*

25. Namsel, *op. cit.*

26. Bureau of Justice Statistics, *op. cit.*

27. Nickelodeon, Kaiser Family Foundation and International Communications Research, "Talking with kids about tough issues: A national survey of parents and kids," March 8, 2001.

28. Nansel, *op. cit.*

29. *Ibid.*

30. *Ibid.*

31. James Alan Fox, *et al.*, "Bullying Prevention Is Crime Prevention," Fight Crime: Invest in Kids, 2003.

32. National Association of School Psychologists, www.nasponline.org.

33. Jonsson, *op. cit.*

34. Jeff Holtz, "Parents File Lawsuit Over Bullying of Daughter," *The New York Times*, Jan. 9, 2005, Section 14CN, p. 2.

35. Jonsson, *op. cit.* (Davidson quote); Carolyn Norton, "Policy Against Bullying Drafted," *The Chapel Hill Herald*, Dec. 27, 2004, p. 1.

36. For background, see Kathy Koch, "Zero Tolerance," *The CQ Researcher*, March 10, 2000, pp. 185-208.

37. For background, see Kenneth Jost, "Testing in Schools," *The CQ Researcher*, April 20, 2001, pp. 321-344.

38. Quoted in Catherine Lee, "Getting Tough on Bullies," www.jrn.columbia.edu/studentwork/children/downlow/bullies.shtml.

39. Quoted in Andrew Baroch, "Legislators Try to Outlaw School Bullies," *Voice of America*, March 28, 2001 truthnews.net/culture/2001_03_bully.html.

40. *American Psychological Association Monitor*, www.apa.org/monitor/oct04/bullying.html.

41. Ken Rigby, *New Perspectives on Bullying* (2002).

42. *Ibid.*

43. Smith and Sharp, *op. cit.*

44. Rigby, *op. cit.*

45. Dan Olweus, *Bullying at School: What We Know and What We Can Do* (1993).

46. For background, see Kathy Koch, "Rethinking Ritalin," *The CQ Researcher*, Oct. 22, 1999, pp. 905-928.

47. Nansel, *op. cit.*

48. Jaana Juvonen, *et al.*, "Bullying Among Young Adolescents: The Strong, the Weak, and the Troubled," *Pediatrics*, December 2003, pp. 1231-1237.

49. Slaby, *op. cit.*

50. Juvonen, *op. cit.*

51. See Delwyn Tattum and Graham Herbert, *Bullying: A Positive Approach* (1990).

52. Andrea Cohn and Andrea Canter, "Bullying: Facts for Schools and Parents," National Association for School Psychologists, 2003.

53. Quoted in Baroch, *op. cit.*

54. Cathleen F. Crowley, "Board adopts new anti-bullying policy," *The Providence Journal*, March 10, 2004, p. C1.

55. Family Research Council, www.frc.org, Dec. 3, 2004.

56. Mary Ann Zehr, "Legislatures Take on Bullies With New Laws," *Education Week*, May 16, 2001.

57. Steven Dennis, "Bullying Bill Turns Into Gay Rights Flap," *The Gazette*, Feb. 21, 2003, www.gazette.net/200308/weekend/a_section/145455-1.html.

58. *Ibid.*

59. Matthew Mosk, "Ehrlich Vetoes Tuition Bill," *The Washington Post*, May 26, 2004, p. B1.

60. "What Does Gay Mean?" Teen Survey, National Mental Health Association, Dec. 12, 2002.

61. M. A. Cohen, "The Monetary Value of Saving a High-Risk Youth," *Journal of Quantitative Criminology*, Vol. 14, 1998, p. 5-33.

62. Hollingsworth, *op. cit.*

63. Mary Jo McGrath, "Capping the Heavy Price for Bullying," www.aasa.org/publications/sa/200304/focus_McGrath.htm.

64. Quoted in Jonsson, *op. cit.*

BIBLIOGRAPHY

Books

Hazler, Richard J., *Breaking the Cycle of Violence: Interventions for Bullying and Victimization*, Taylor & Francis, 1996.
A professor of counselor education at the University of Ohio in Athens looks at the problems faced by bullies and their victims and how these experiences color the rest of their lives.

Juvonen, Jaana, and Sandra Graham, eds., *Peer Harassment in School: The Plight of the Vulnerable and the Victimized*, Guilford Press, 2001.
Two University of California, Los Angeles (UCLA) professors have compiled essays by an impressive list of international contributors focusing on bullies rather than their victims.

Olweus, Dan, *Bullying at School: What We Know and What We Can Do About It*, Blackwell Publishers, 1993.
This definitive work is based on large-scale studies and other research by the author, who heads Norway's Research Center for Health Promotion at the University of Bergen.

Rigby, Ken, *New Perspectives on Bullying*, Jessica Kingsley Publishers, 2002.
An adjunct associate professor of social psychology at the University of South Australia and an oft-cited authority

on bullying draws on his extensive research into bullying in different countries, societies and social settings.

Smith, Peter K., Debra Pepler and Ken Rigby, *Bullying in Schools: How Successful Can Interventions Be? Cambridge University Press,* **2004.**
This collection of studies by leading researchers examines the failures and successes of numerous anti-bullying efforts.

Smith, Peter K., and Sonia Sharp, *School Bullying: Insights and Perspectives, Routledge,* **1994.**
A professor of psychology at the University of Sheffield (Smith) and an educational psychologist provide a good primer for understanding the causes of bullying and the scientific methodology used to study it.

Articles

"School Bullying is Nothing New, But Psychologists Identify New Ways to Prevent It," *Psychology Matters,* **American Psychological Association Web site, www .psychologymatters.org/bullying.html.**
The online newsletter provides a comprehensive overview of bullying and suggests ways to stop it.

Esplanage, Dorothy L., Ph.D., "Bullying in Early Adolescence: The Role of the Peer Group," *ERIC Clearinghouse on Elementary and Early Childhood Education,* **November 2002.**
Peers play an important role in perpetuating — and stopping — bullying, points out a well-known author in the field.

Jones, Adrienne, "Thwarting Bullies Proves Tough Work," *The Age, Ltd.,* **Nov. 22, 2004.**
Most anti-bullying programs achieve only modest improvements.

Makwana, Rachel R., "Bullying Victims Turn More to Courts," *The* **[Conn.]** *Record-Journal,* **July 7, 2004.**
Some parents have begun suing their children's schools, claiming they ignored repeated complaints about bullying and abuse.

Peterson, Karen S., "When School Hurts," *USA Today,* **April 10, 2001.**
U.S. schools, parents and government officials have slowly realized that bullying can cause long-lasting damage to children and bystanders.

Peterson, Karen S., "Net Broadens Reach of Kids' Rumors, Insults," *USA Today,* **April 10, 2001.**
Bullies have taken their vicious practices to the Internet.

Reports and Studies

"Bullying is Not a Fact of Life," *National Mental Health Information Center, U.S. Department of Health and Human Services,* **www.mentalhealth .samhsa.gov/publications/allpubs/SVP-0052/.**
This compact report includes information for parents and schools about bullying and how to deal with it.

"Hostile Hallways: Bullying, Teasing, and Sexual Harassment in School," *American Association of University Women, AAUW Educational Foundation,* **May 2001.**
Bullying is closely related to sexual harassment — a federal crime — if it is sexually based, according to the women's group.

Fox, James Alan, et al., "Bullying Prevention Is Crime Prevention: A Report by Fight Crime: Invest in Kids," **2003.**
Preventing bullying at an early age is a cost-effective way to short-circuit a life of crime, according to this group of police, sheriffs, district attorneys and crime victims.

Nansel, T. R., et al., "Bullying Behavior Among U.S. Youth: Prevalence and Association with Psychological Adjustment," *Journal of the American Medical Association,* **April 21, 2001, pp. 2094-2100.**
This scientific paper based on research done in the two years just before Columbine was updated in 2003.

For More Information

American Association of School Administrators, 801 N. Quincy St., Suite 700, Arlington, VA 22203-1730; (703) 528 0700, www.aasa.org.

American School Counselor Association, 1101 King St., Suite 625, Alexandria, VA 22314; (703) 683-ASCA; www.schoolcounselor.org.

National Association of Elementary School Principals, 1615 Duke St., Alexandria, VA 22314-3483; (703) 684-3345; www.naesp.org.

National Association of School Psychologists, 4340 East-West Highway, Suite 402, Bethesda, MD 20814; (301) 657-0270; www.nasponline.org.

National Association of Secondary School Principals, 1904 Association Dr., Reston, VA 20191-1537; (703) 860-0200, www.principals.org.

National Mental Health Association, 2001 N. Beauregard St., 12th Fl., Alexandria, VA 22311; (703) 684-7722; www.nmha.org.

Parents, Families, and Friends of Lesbians and Gays, 1726 M St., N.W., Suite 400, Washington, DC 20036; (202) 467-8180; www.pflag.org.

19

Cheating in Schools

Are High-Stakes Tests to Blame?

Kathy Koch

Fourth-graders in Canton, Ohio, cheer at an academic pep rally designed to get them ready for five days of state-mandated tests. Elementary schools around the country have been caught in a string of testing scandals in recent years, with teachers under pressure to raise students' scores accused of feeding them answers.

From *CQ Researcher*,
September 22, 2000.

W hen half the students in an honors biology class at Annapolis High School — including five National Honor Society members — were caught cheating on a test last spring, senior Andrew Smith wasn't surprised.

"Cheating is very prevalent among high school students all around the country, not just at our school," says Smith, the nation's only voting student school board member. After he asked the board to take a tough stand on cheating, it decided to do a student survey on the problem.

While cheating isn't new, the scope of the problem is. Throughout the 1990s, studies consistently found that more than 75 percent of college undergraduates had cheated at least once — an all-time high — and 20-30 percent regularly.

The problem is even worse in high schools, where the slackers aren't the only ones cheating. Honor students are as likely as low-achievers to cheat; girls now cheat as much as boys and — alarmingly — medical and engineering students are as likely to cheat as liberal arts students.

In its last annual survey of 700,000 top students, *Who's Who Among American High School Students* found that 80 percent of the high-achievers admitted to cheating, the highest percentage in the survey's 29-year history.

"Perhaps the most startling finding of the studies on cheating is that kids say it isn't wrong," says Josie Plachta, director of media relations at the Washington, D.C.-based Character Education Partnership, which advocates character education in schools. More than half of the students in the *Who's Who* poll said cheating was "no big deal," a victimless crime.

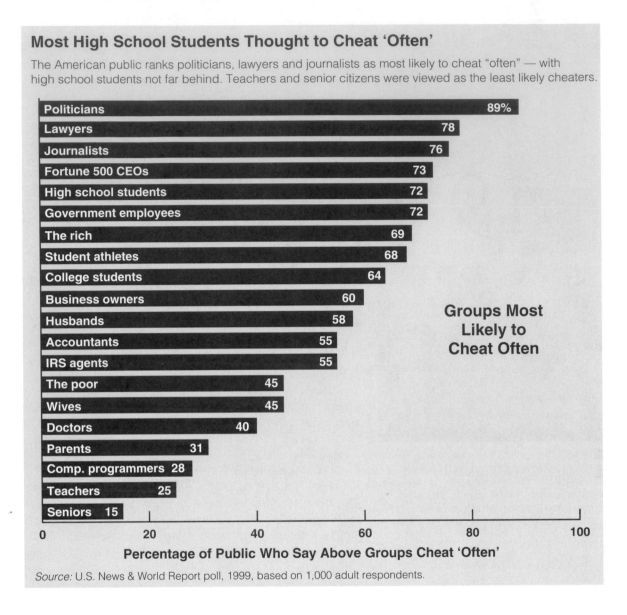

Most High School Students Thought to Cheat 'Often'

The American public ranks politicians, lawyers and journalists as most likely to cheat "often" — with high school students not far behind. Teachers and senior citizens were viewed as the least likely cheaters.

Group	Percentage
Politicians	89%
Lawyers	78
Journalists	76
Fortune 500 CEOs	73
High school students	72
Government employees	72
The rich	69
Student athletes	68
College students	64
Business owners	60
Husbands	58
Accountants	55
IRS agents	55
The poor	45
Wives	45
Doctors	40
Parents	31
Comp. programmers	28
Teachers	25
Seniors	15

Groups Most Likely to Cheat Often

Percentage of Public Who Say Above Groups Cheat 'Often'

Source: U.S. News & World Report poll, 1999, based on 1,000 adult respondents.

But cheating is unfair to non-cheaters when a test is being graded on a curve, and it destroys non-cheaters' incentive to work hard, teachers say. It also undermines the integrity and fairness of standardized tests and threatens the value of degrees and certifications, they say.[1]

The long-term negative effects are even more ominous. "Do you want to go to a doctor who cheated his way through anatomy class, or drive over a bridge built by an engineer who cheated?" asks Donald McCabe, founder of the Durham, N.C.-based Center for Academic Integrity, which promotes anti-cheating campaigns on more than 200 college campuses.

Besides being blasé, some of today's cheaters brazenly show no remorse. "Apologize for what?" asked Jolie Fitch, one of nine students from Chicago's Steinmetz High School who were caught cheating to win a 1995 statewide academic championship. "I would do it again," she said defiantly, after watching a made-for-TV movie last May about the incident.[2]

Perhaps more disturbing, lately it's not just the students who are cheating. In recent years, schools in Connecticut, Florida, Georgia, Illinois, Maryland, Massachusetts, Ohio, Texas, Virginia and other states have discovered teachers or administrators who tried to improve performance by either changing answers or encouraging students to change their answers on statewide tests. In New York City, investigators found 52 educators at 32 schools were cheating.

And today cheating cuts across economic and social strata. In affluent Potomac, Md., the principal at a top school in the horsy Washington suburb resigned in May after allegedly directing students to cheat on a statewide test.[3]

"There's been a general desensitization to cheating on tests, both among students and teachers," says Gregory J. Cizek, a University of North Carolina education professor and author of *Cheating on Tests: How to Do It, Detect It and Prevent It*. Teachers are either ignoring student cheating, enabling students to cheat or changing their answers outright, he says. "That's the most distressing to me. The people you'd think should be the kids' role models are really giving kids the opposite."

Teachers aren't the only poor role models, says Harold J. Noah, professor emeritus at Columbia University's Teachers College and co-author of the forthcoming book, *Fraud and Education: The Worm in the Apple*. In all parts of adult society, he says, "there is a greater emphasis today on winning. In business and in sports, we're seeing an incredible rash of corrupt behavior."

Gerald Tirozzi, executive director of the National Association of Secondary School Principals (NASSP), says schools cannot keep society's degenerating morals from slithering under the schoolhouse door. "Adults cheat, businessmen cheat," he says. "Just about every movie you see these days has someone cheating on something. We're naïve to think kids aren't watching and learning from that."

The problem isn't just pop culture, but the way it's financed, says Theodore Sizer, chairman of the Coalition of Essential Schools, in Oakland, Calif., which promotes the establishment of non-traditional schools and opposes standardized testing. "Pop culture is largely driven by advertising revenues, and advertising is a form of lying,"

he says. Today's kids are subjected to more advertising than any other generation, and "after 500 advertising messages in a day, kids learn that lying is the way the world goes around."

There's plenty of adult blame to go around, says philosophy Professor Lawrence M. Hinman, director of the Values Institute at the University of San Diego. "The ball is being dropped all down the line for the problem to be this extensive," he says.

He says today's large college classes and the Internet make cheating easier. "The larger the class, the greater the potential for anonymity," Hinman says. Similarly, when using the Web, either to download an illicit term paper or to take a distance-learning course, "it's easier to cheat or plagiarize if an instructor doesn't even know your name, and you don't feel any personal responsibility toward him," he says.

He blames weak enforcement by penny-pinching college administrators and ambitious faculty at large, research-oriented institutions, where 500 students can sit in introductory classes taught by graduate assistants unlikely to pursue cheaters.

Not only does the Internet make cheating easier than ever, but so do other new high-tech gadgets, like programmable graphing calculators, pagers and cell phones used to transmit test answers. (*See sidebar, p. 428.*)

Some say kids cheat today because they are too busy and under too much competitive pressure. "You can't just be a good athlete," says Gary Pavela, director of judicial programs and student ethical development at the University of Maryland. "You've got to make good grades and do community service, too. These kids are being asked to do too much."

There's more cheating now because more people are being educated than ever before, so there's more pressure on certain parts of the population than in the past, other observers say. "Once kids dropped out of school to work on the family farm," Noah says. "But you can't get a job as a supermarket check-out clerk anymore without a high school diploma."

The increased pressure is partly internal and partly external, Pavela says. "This generation has higher expectations for itself," he says. And baby-boom parents push their kids more than they themselves were pushed, he says, because they worry about their children's futures in an uncertain information economy where corporate downsizing is commonplace. "They know an education is essential to survive in the new economy," he says.

Politicians have also ratcheted up the stakes — especially regarding performance on new statewide standardized tests instituted as part of education reform, say test critics. Test results often determine whether schools retain their accreditation, whether educators get fired or students graduate — and even whether local real estate values go up or down.

Many think the intense pressure created by high-stakes tests is causing the increase in cheating. Alfie Kohn, a well-known opponent of high-stakes testing, for example, sees cheating not as a sign of deficient character but as a pragmatic response to "an outrageous, heavy-handed, corporate approach to getting tough with kids and teachers."

"Cheating is increasing because the stakes are higher," agrees Cizek of the University of North Carolina. And if students haven't been properly prepared for the tests, the cheating may be part of a backlash against the tests, some critics of the new tests say.

Others say that the definition of cheating has been blurred in an era of high-stakes testing, collaborative learning and cyber research. Students doing research on the Internet no longer view plagiarism as previous generations did, and they are confused about whether sharing notes on a collaborative project is cheating.

But McCabe of the Center for Academic Integrity says some of the fourfold increase in what he calls "unpermitted collaboration" among college students since the early 1960s, is deliberate. "The kids feel it's OK to collaborate, even if the teacher did not authorize it. They argue that the teacher did a poor job of explaining the lesson, that they learn more that way and finish their work quicker," he says.

Sometimes teachers cheat inadvertently when they prepare students for standardized tests, says Peter Sacks, author of *Standardized Minds: The High Price of America's Testing Culture and What We Can Do to Change It.* "There's a fine, unclear line between cheating and teaching-to-the-test coaching," he says, "and school officials are turning a blind eye toward it." For instance, he points out, teachers don't know it's wrong to copy old versions of a test to make workbooks for kids to study.

Rodolfo de la Garza, a professor of government at the University of Texas, asks, "Is it cheating to buy notes from a commercial outlet? Is the student who can afford a tutor competing fairly with students who can't afford such help?"

Others say kids today are just lazier. The average student today spends only seven hours per semester studying for an introductory psychology course, says Stephen F. Davis, a professor of psychology at Emporia State University in Kansas. "Kids tell me, 'Fifteen minutes of cheating is a lot better than three hours of studying,'" he says.

McCabe points out that some kids are not raised with much of a work ethic these days, largely because their parents have made things easier for them. "But, ironically, those same parents have higher expectations for their kids than their own parents had for them," he says.

But Pavela of the University of Maryland doesn't see the problem as laziness but as the "dot-com-instant-gratification phenomenon." Some students think they should be millionaires by age 35, he says, "And to do that they work very hard — in some cases, too hard," but sometimes they take shortcuts.

Davis concedes that perhaps it's not laziness so much as different priorities. "Today's college population has a whole different set of values," he says. "They value acquiring things over getting an education." A third of the students at his university work full time while taking a full course load, and others have children. Spending time with their kids may be more important than studying for a test, he says.

Others care less about the learning experience than about the diploma at the end of the trail, Davis says. "They feel justified to use any means they can to get that piece of paper," because they feel it's necessary to get a good job.

Plus, more people are going to college today than ever before, McCabe says, "many of whom are not as well-qualified to do college work as previous generations." As a result, many have a chip on their shoulder. "They complain that the system is unfair, the tests are unfair and the teachers are too hard," Davis says. "Therefore, they feel it's OK to cheat."

As educators and ethicists wring their hands over the problem, these are the questions they are debating:

Are students today more dishonest than earlier generations?

While at least three separate studies have found that cheating on high school and college campuses is at a historical high, educators and ethicists differ on whether that means that today's kids are more dishonest than previous generations.

One of the studies, conducted in 1998 by the Josephson Institute of Ethics, in Marina del Rey, Calif., found that 70 percent of high school students admitted cheating on exams, compared to 64 percent in 1996 and even lower percentages earlier in the 1990s. Moreover, 47 percent of the students surveyed admitted to stealing something from a store in the last year, compared with 41 percent in 1996.

"Unequivocally, yes, students are more dishonest today," says institute President Michael Josephson. "Kids' internal sense that it's wrong to cheat has been clearly diluted."

And students today are quick to assume the culture's widespread "victim attitude," he says. For instance, the Steinmetz High School students excused their actions by simply declaring that the "system" was unfair because their next closest competitor was a wealthier, better-funded magnet school. "To me, an honorable person would never say, 'You made me cheat,'" Josephson says.

He blames adults for kids' lack of a moral compass. "In the past, we sent a very clear message that cheating was wrong," he says. Today adults themselves are cheating on taxes and campaign finances, he says, and coaches communicate a win-at-any-cost attitude to athletes. "We're sending the clear message to kids that success at any cost is more important than character."

To make matters worse, kids often cheat because punishment is infrequent and more moderate than it used to be, he says. "They cheat because they are allowed to," Josephson says. "There are lots of up sides and very few downsides. We have created an atmosphere of free-crime zones, where all manner of lying and cheating is a very, very safe undertaking."

And it's not only educational institutions that are looking the other way. "Other institutions responsible for enforcing integrity standards have simply caved in," he says, citing recent sports and résumé frauds. "More and more, we are focusing on competency rather than character," he says.

The Center for Academic Integrity's McCabe, who has conducted several long-term studies on cheating, sees a twofold explanation for the increase in cheating: a very real increase in the number of cheaters and an increase in the number of students willing to admit that they cheat. "It might be that cheating is just not such a big deal to kids today," he says.

Kevin Ryan, director emeritus of the Center for the Advancement of Ethics and Character at Boston University, says that when he started teaching in the mid-1950s, he never saw or heard about cheating. "There was such a strong attitude against it. It was clearly shameful," says Ryan, a professor emeritus of education.

Davis of Emporia State, whose ongoing study of student attitudes is now in its 14th year, says today's students are more academically dishonest than earlier generations. He found that 40-60 percent admitted to cheating at least once, compared with only 18-23 percent in a 1941 study, and half of those students are cheating on a regular basis. "That means up to a third of students are cheating their little hearts out," he says.[4]

And even more students, about 78 percent, say they cheated at least once in high school, and 65 percent did so on a regular basis. "I guess you'd have to say kids today are more dishonest," Davis says, but it's perfectly understandable because kids see adults in business, sports and government cheating and not getting punished. "What are they supposed to think?" he asks.

Pavela at the University of Maryland agrees that the failure is not with the students, but with "the people running higher education. For 30 years, we have been reluctant to challenge students to be honest, because a lot of faculty did not want to appear judgmental or dogmatic."

The failure is also with society at large, says Sizer at the Coalition of Essential Schools. "If we re-elect people who play verbal games, then we're sending the message that kids don't have to be honest," he says.

Hinman of the Values Institute says today's students may not be more dishonest, but they clearly haven't gotten the message from adults that cheating is wrong. "These are not bad kids," he insists. "But there is this sort of blind spot for many of them about cheating being wrong."

Larry Nucci, an education and psychology professor at the University of Illinois in Chicago and director of the university's Office for Studies in Moral Development and Character Formation, thinks it's "silly" to call today's kids more dishonest than previous generations. "There's no evidence that they are more dishonest," he says. "In fact, research going back to the early 1920s shows that everyone will cheat under the right conditions."

Today, with easy and sometimes free access to Internet term papers and large, anonymous, overcrowded lecture courses taught by graduate students, the conditions are perfect for cheating, he says. "The teacher doesn't know his students or their abilities individually and students are packed into seats close to one another when they take tests," he says.

He thinks cheating has become more of a pragmatic issue than a moral one. "When students face high-stakes tests perceived as part of an abstract, unfair sorting process, separate from their classroom learning experience, they will cheat," Nucci says. "But if kids perceive a test as a legitimate assessment of what they know, and if they see it as hurting other people if they cheat, then they feel it's wrong and they don't do it."

Should schools adopt honor codes to reduce cheating?

For centuries some schools — particularly Southern colleges and military institutions — have had honor codes requiring students to pledge not to cheat and to report any cheating they observe. Exams at honor code schools are usually unproctored. Allegations of cheating are usually handled by a student judiciary panel, and those found guilty are usually expelled.

Surveys conducted in 1990 and 1995 by the Center for Academic Integrity found that only 57 percent of students at honor code schools admitted to cheating, compared with almost 80 percent at schools without codes.[5] As a result, some educators and ethicists recommend that honor codes be adopted nationwide. "I think every high school across the nation should have in place a very explicit honor code," says Arthur J. Schwartz,

director of character education at the John Templeton Foundation in Radnor, Pa. "It won't reduce cheating to nil, but it is a first step and will send a strong message to students and parents that cheating will not be tolerated."

Honor codes focus everyone's attention on ethical behavior, and make them commit to explicit ideas about how to behave, Cizek says.

And there's an added benefit, Hinman says: At schools with effective honor codes, honesty is not limited to classwork. "People can leave a laptop in their classrooms, and it won't get stolen," he says. "And even the merchants don't worry about bounced checks."

Many educators think that traditional honor codes work better on small campuses than at large public institutions, where the sheer size of classes makes it difficult to generate the same community spirit possible on smaller campuses. But even on small campuses they only work if the students, faculties and administrations are supportive and enforce them, they say.

Honor codes also work best in institutions with a long tradition of honor, in which students are told throughout their school experience, "This is who we are," Josephson says. Without a great deal of moral reprogramming and advocacy on the importance of integrity, today's average student body is not ready yet for traditional honor codes. "Until that occurs, an honor code only advances the cheaters," he says.

"It would be crazy to try to do that now in high schools," he says. "We need more monitoring right now, not less. We need more enforcement right now, not less."

Others agree that an honor code would never work except in a fairly tightly knit community. "I haven't seen any evidence that it would work in a large public university," says Joe Kerkvliet, an economics professor at Oregon State University.

Instituting an honor code requires at least a decade of hard work establishing an environment where honesty is valued, and students and administrators must be on board from the beginning, Hinman warns. "To just

> 'I don't think the existence of an honor code does anything more than a speed limit sign does. It's a reasonable beginning, but it's not an end in itself.'
>
> — *Theodore Sizer*
> *Chairman, Coalition of*
> *Essential Schools*

suddenly adopt an honor code would be courting disaster," he says.

Some say that honor codes are a waste of time because teenagers are not morally developed enough to understand what they are signing. "I don't think the existence of an honor code does anything more than a speed limit sign does," Sizer says. "It's a reasonable beginning, but it's not an end in itself."

Nucci of the University of Illinois thinks the idea of unproctored exams is "stupid and ridiculous." He compares it to putting children alone in a candy story and telling them not to eat any candy. Honor codes only work when students feel a test is related to learning, and in small classes where there is a relationship between the teacher and the students, he says. "And it wouldn't work on high-stakes tests," he says. "That would be crazy."

College Students' Top 10 Reasons for Cheating

When asked why they cheated, college students generally absolved themselves of responsibility, blaming their actions on the instructor or fellow students. Their responses also reflect concern about grades and time pressures.

Rank	Reason for Cheating
1.	The instructor assigns too much material
2.	The instructor left the room during the test
2.*	A friend asked me to cheat and I couldn't say no
4.	The instructor doesn't seem to care if I learn the material
5.	The course information seems useless
6.	The course material is too hard
6.*	Everyone else seems to be cheating
8.	In danger of losing scholarship because of low grades
9.	Don't have time to study because I'm working to pay for school
10.	People sitting around me made no effort to protect their work

* Tied

Source: "College Cheating: Immaturity, Lack of Commitment and the Neutralizing Attitude," *Research in Higher Education*, 1986.

But the NASSP's Tirozzi thinks if the students are involved in developing and implementing them and if the administration supports them, honor codes could work — even in public high schools. And a growing number of state universities have been adopting modified honor codes, which impose modest sanctions but don't have unproctored exams, don't require students to report cheating they observe and don't require automatic expulsion of cheaters.

Public universities around the country are now copying the most well-known modified code, developed at the University of Maryland about five years ago.

"Schools don't have to wait 100 years to create a tradition before they can make a difference," Pavela says. After only five years of experience with the modified honor code, Maryland has 10 percent less cheating than similar schools, he says.

Under Maryland's system, cheaters are not expelled but receive a special "XF" grade for a class if they are caught cheating. The grade, which means the student failed the course due to academic dishonesty, becomes a part of the student's permanent record and can only be expunged if he completes a six-week integrity seminar, and if the student honor council agrees.

Each student applying to Maryland must write an essay about academic integrity and sign an honor pledge, but it does not have a "non-toleration clause," requiring students to report cheating they observe. "When we researched it, we found that the vast majority of students on campuses with strict honor codes simply weren't following the non-toleration clause," Pavela says.

According to a 1999 survey by McCabe, only 6 percent of students at schools with traditional honor codes reported that they cheated repeatedly, compared with 10 percent at schools with a modified honor code and 17 percent at schools without honor codes.

Should educators be more aggressive in stopping cheating?

A *U.S. News & World Report* poll last fall found that 90 percent of college students say cheaters never get punished, and 95 percent of confessed cheaters in the Who's Who poll said they were never caught. Moreover, nearly a third of the 1,000 faculty members from 21 different

Cheating Is Just a Click Away...

Cheating was once a fairly low-tech undertaking — notes scribbled on your palm, a peek at a classmate's paper. But in the age of the Internet, cell phones and graphing calculators, cheating has gone high-tech.

"Video cameras can be concealed in a tie-tack," says Professor Stephen F. Davis of Emporia State University in Kansas, "with a video feed going to someone outside in a van who sends back answers to the test-taker on an alphanumeric pager."

Lazy, immoral or overworked students — depending on your view of cheaters' motivations — also use the vast cyber-library of the Internet, where they can access tests, term papers, foreign-language translators and class notes from major U.S. universities. Students with credit cards can click on the Schoolsucks.com Web page, for instance, and have term papers sent to their e-mail address almost instantaneously.

Technology also allows students to get answers from a friend across the room by simply clicking the screen of a palm pilot. Another popular cheating tool is the graphing calculator, now standard equipment in most higher-math classes. Cheaters program them to display formulas and other information needed during exams. When teachers caught on, they ordered kids to empty the memory of their calculators before taking a test, but some students simply programmed a button next to the actual delete button to say "Memory deleted" when pressed.

"A lot of students are so tuned in to technology...they can create programs teachers aren't aware of," said a spokeswoman for Texas Instruments in Dallas, which makes the most popular graphing calculator. "A lot depends on the teacher and what he knows about technology."[1]

Moreover, high-tech cheating is apparently a global phenomenon, say Harold J. Noah and Max A. Eckstein in their forthcoming book, *Fraud and Education: The Worm in the Apple*. For instance, during military exams in Thailand, soldiers vying for promotion to non-commissioned status hid radio-controlled receivers and batteries in their underwear. And in Australia, frustrated educators have proposed banning students' use of all technological aids, such as preprogrammed calculators, pagers and mobile phones.

Perhaps the most common form of high-tech cheating is the so-called "new plagiarism" — downloading excerpts or entire essays from either legitimate Internet document sources or from scores of Web-based term-paper mills, some of which offer term papers for free. Big spenders can even order customized papers at up to $35 a page.

Advertising directed at college students supports the Web sites. And while dozens of states now make it illegal to knowingly distribute term papers that will be used illicitly, the laws are poorly enforced, and the Web site operators argue they are entitled to free-speech protections. Many of the operators also claim, disingenuously, that their papers are meant only for research and should not be submitted as the student's own work, even as they offer to include the student's name, course name and class period on the cover sheet of custom-ordered papers.

"Some of them will even customize your bibliography to coincide with books in your university's library," says Anthony Krier, the research librarian at Franklin Pierce College in Rindge, N.H., an expert on Internet plagiarism.

In recent years, cyber-cheating has been on the increase at several prestigious universities. In 1997, Virginia Tech registered 280 cheating complaints, up from 80 the previous year, and in 1998 officials at Boston University went to court, unsuccessfully, charging on-line term-paper mills with violating mail fraud and racketeering laws.[2]

Some educators think more cyber-cheating goes on in high school than in college. "High school teachers are generally clueless about Internet plagiarizing," says Donald McCabe, founder of the Durham, N.C.-based Center for Academic Integrity, which promotes anticheating campaigns on more than 200 college campuses. "And the quality of the papers is sufficient to get by in a high school course. But for college, the quality of Internet papers is crap."

But high school teachers are catching on. Scott Underbrink, who teaches French and Russian at Natrona County High School in Casper, Wyo., wised up about Internet cheating after students began turning in translations exceeding even his own abilities. Native French-speakers would have been put to shame by some of the grammatical nuances the students used, he said.

"I can't prove it, but I can stop it....The writing [assignments] are going to be in class from now on," he said.[3]

Krier says students today think information found on the Internet is in the public domain. "They feel that if they

…For Today's High-Tech Students

get it off the Internet, it's different from taking it out of a book," he says.

Lawrence M. Hinman, director of the Values Institute at the University of San Diego, says the Internet makes cheating easier because it's fast and private. "There is no public shame in asking somebody for a paper," he says. And it can be done in the privacy of your own room. "You can download a paper at 2 a.m. and hand it in at 8."

Much of the new plagiarism apparently occurs because students are either overworked, or they procrastinated and got too far behind. "Many students who plagiarize from the Web do so at the last minute," Hinman says. "Five years ago, if they had let an assignment go that long they couldn't have done anything." In the old days, when term papers were offered in tiny ads buried in student newspapers, even plagiarism required planning ahead.

Hinman points out that some cyber-cheating may be unintentional. "With 'drag and drop' capabilities, it's easy to plagiarize if you start gathering data on the Web, and several weeks later you're not sure which of your notes are yours and which came from an on-line source, especially if you forgot to write down the URL," he says.

Fighting back

To help teachers and professors fight digital plagiarism, at least three services now offer to scan papers, like a search engine, for plagiarized passages. Professors at the University of California, Berkeley, developed plagiarism.org and Turnitin.com. A former writing instructor from the University of Illinois, Chicago, offers the Glatt Plagiarism Screening Program, at plagiarism.com.

The programs worked well for two Wyoming teachers who became suspicious about work that did not match their students' styles or abilities. "One of them knew about plagiarism.com, and they ran it," said Natrona County High School Principal Byron Moore. "Sure enough, there were all kinds of matches."[4]

But others say such services aren't foolproof. "I don't think the anti-plagiarism services are that effective," Krier says. "There are just too many sources that can be plagiarized."

Some educators are also fighting back against the newest trend in cyber-cheating — downloading lecture notes from more than a dozen on-line services, like Versity.com and StudentU.com, which pay students for their class notes. Such services allow students who miss (or skip) class to search a data bank, usually for free, containing course notes from a variety of major universities. The operators of Versity.com say their site currently lists course notes for 90 campuses from 4,000 note-takers.[5]

Some colleges have issued cease-and-desist letters to on-line notes companies and warned students that selling lecture notes violates student-conduct rules.

Some educators shrug off the services and even provide their lecture notes to them for free. But others, like Purdue University sociology Professor Mathieu Deflem, argue that the companies violate copyright laws protecting professors' lectures. Deflem's Web page, Free Education Now!, lists case law he says supports that premise. He also blasts on-line companies for their lack of quality control, pointing out that Versity.com, was founded by four 22-year-old college dropouts, "who wanted to have fun, it seems, playing with computers."

Educators fear that unless something is done to nip high-tech cheating in the bud, it will only get worse. "When these junior high and high school kids who've acquired these habits get to college, you will see higher levels of Internet cheating," McCabe says. "Not many schools are using the anti-plagiarism programs, and it's not clear that it is completely effective. I'm not convinced that it will stop it."

In the view of recent Yale graduate John Hickman, the only real solution may be as simple — and expensive — as having smaller classes. "Having spent millions of dollars wiring their students to the Internet, universities may have to invest in smaller classes and a better teacher-to-student ratio," he writes. "That may be the only way to keep on-line plagiarism at the fringes, where it belongs."[6]

---

[1] William Hageman, "E-Cheating Supplants Crib Sheets," *Portland Oregonian*, Dec. 12, 1999.

[2] According to Liz Bailey, "Ctrl-C the key to hi-tech cheating: Education Plagiarism is flourishing at universities, thanks to computers and the Net," *The Daily Telegraph*, Sept. 16, 1999.

[3] "Internet for cheating students and investigating teachers," The Associated Press, May 30, 2000.

[4] *Ibid.*

[5] Stephanie Schorow, "Students take note of these 2 sites," *Boston Herald*, Oct. 19, 1999.

[6] John Hickman, "Cybercheating," *The New Republic*, March 14, 1998.

campuses interviewed by McCabe for his fall 1999 survey admitted that they had observed cheating in their classes and did nothing about it.

"The culture of academic integrity on many campuses seems to have declined," McCabe says, adding that one out of four universities do not have a written academic-integrity policy, or it is not readily available to students.

"Students arrive at college generally ready to follow the rules, believing that the atmosphere will be tougher on cheaters than it was in high school," he says. But the minute the new students see cheating going on and professors ignoring it, they feel that they have to cheat too, in order to compete, he says. "Then cheating spreads like wildfire."

Middle and high school teachers "absolutely should be doing more" to curtail cheating, Josephson says. And he doesn't mince words about why they aren't. "Teachers are not doing more to stop it because they are irresponsible," he says. "Since our first report on cheating in 1990, schools have done virtually nothing about the problem."

Josephson says individual teachers and administrators could do many things that would easily cut the cheating rate in half. "This is not an intractable problem," he says. "We know what works."

Kerkvliet agrees. "We can't blame everything on lazy students with poor morals," he says. "If professors exercise controls, they can have an effect on the amount of cheating going on." In a 1998 study, Kerkvliet found that cheating on exams could be significantly reduced if professors simply used multiple versions of a test, hired additional proctors and warned students that cheating would not be tolerated.

The single most effective disincentive for cheating, he found, was to stop using graduate assistants to teach. "Having courses taught by full-fledged faculty members reduces the probability of cheating by 32 percent," he says. Teaching assistants are less experienced, less likely to want to confront a student, or come from countries with different cultural attitudes about cheating, often with strong cultural taboos against interpersonal confrontations, he explains.

Having smaller classes taught by full professors would reduce cheating to nearly zero, he adds, "but there's been a general reluctance on the part of the faculty and administrators to do anything about this issue." Throughout the 1990s, cost-cutting college administrators have

increasingly hired adjunct and part-time professors to teach students in larger and larger classes.

But classroom teachers point the finger of blame back at cost-conscious administrators or state and county officials. For instance, the NASSP's Tirozzi says, if the state or county provides a standardized test, they alone can provide different versions of the test.

Tom Mooney, president of the Ohio Federation of Teachers, said states actually encourage cheating by refusing to spend money for more test security, like hiring proctors. "They're doing this dirty and cheap and quick because there's a lot of political pressure to get these tests in place," Mooney said. "In what other industry do you have these kinds of stakes put on something and then have them administered by those who will be affected? You're just asking for it."[6]

If administrators were more willing to spend money, Jacobson says, they could make tests as secure as college entrance exams or medical and bar exams. For example, after Florida authorities hired a former FBI agent to help beef up bar exam test security, they began using fingerprints and photo IDs to prevent impersonators from taking the exam for someone else. Then they photographed where everybody was sitting, in case there were similarities in the exams of people sitting near each other.

But Hinman of the Values Institute warns against expelling cheaters for a first offense, and other harsh measures. Such "zero tolerance" techniques could actually encourage educators to ignore cheating, he says. "The teacher may perceive the punishment as too harsh or the administrators may not want to throw out the child of a big donor," he says.

Tirozzi says school officials fear lawsuits by parents if they crack down on cheating. Similarly, fear of litigation or negative publicity often keeps college professors and administrators from pursuing any but the most open-and-shut cases, Maryland's Pavela says.

However, he notes, faculty fear of lawsuits is a red herring. "There hasn't been a single case in which a faculty member was held liable for reporting a case of academic dishonesty," he says. Lawsuits are usually filed against the institution, claiming lack of due process, he says, which is why educators must scrupulously follow proper procedures for reporting cheaters.

Instead of worrying about lawsuits, teachers should make it harder to cheat and make the cost of cheating fairly high, Nucci says. "My students know that if I catch them cheating they get an F in the course," he says.

Others say professors don't pursue cheaters more aggressively because it is too time-consuming. Catching and prosecuting a cheater "is a royal pain in the ass," says Richard Thaler, a professor of behavioral science and economics at the University of Chicago. "Students demand due process, making the time costs of pursuing a cheater very high."

Professors have too many students, too many classes, too many committees, and too many publishing responsibilities and do a lot of advising on the side, explains Bill Chamberlain, a journalism professor at the University of Florida. "Many work more than a 60-hour week, contrary to the common perception," he says.

Prosecuting cheaters takes "a huge amount of time," says Chappell Lawson, an assistant professor of political science at the Massachusetts Institute of Technology. "And spending time playing 'gotcha' with students is not the fastest way to make tenure."

Besides chasing after tenure, professors are chasing after research grants, leaving little time for chasing cheaters, says Daniel Garrison, chairman of the Undergraduate Academic Conduct Committee at Northwestern University. "The more time faculty spends on research and personal career development, the less time they have for writing up fresh exams."

This is particularly true at large state universities and research institutions, where research grants buy relief from teaching duties, he says. "Then classes end up being taught by graduate students and part-time professors, increasing the cheating opportunities."

Schwartz says professors are not rewarded by administrators for catching cheaters. "There is nothing in their contract that says they must produce honest, trustworthy students," he says. "What gets measured is what gets emphasized; and we don't measure whether teachers are taking this issue seriously. So our teachers don't think that we as a society are taking this issue seriously."

Others say they'd rather spend the hours that would be taken up pursuing a cheating allegation helping their honest students who are interested in learning, McCabe says.

Leo Damrosch, a professor of English literature at Harvard, tries to make it hard for students to cheat in his class by giving assignments unique to his courses,

making it harder to use other people's work. "But I'm a teacher, not a policeman," he says.

Similarly, Alessandro Duranti, an anthropology professor at the University of California, Los Angeles, does "some basic things" to make sure students do their own work, "but the atmosphere and spirit I aim for in the classroom is one of intellectual discovery, not fear of being caught."

However, Chamberlain says he doesn't know a single professor who thinks catching cheaters is not his job. "But I know many who care a lot about catching cheaters, and do catch them."

"In my experience," adds Maxwell Stinchcombe, an economics professor at the University of Texas, "professors react quite aggressively to cheating, with the mildest punishment being complete failure of the course, and the worst expulsion."

BACKGROUND

Ancient Crib Sheets

Cheating has been around as long as there have been examinations. More than a thousand years ago, civil service applicants in China were searched for crib sheets before entering the exam rooms. Test-takers, who had to write compositions, were locked into tiny, individual cells with enough food and water for three days. But some were caught smuggling in elaborate "cribbing garments" — rented undershirts inscribed with more than 700 complete compositions, composed of nearly half a million Chinese characters.[7]

In the United States, teaching morals to children in public schools was one way to keep cheating in check. President Theodore Roosevelt supported moral education, declaring, "To educate a man in mind and not morals is to educate a menace to society."[8]

In fact, teaching morals was a major part of children's education in America until the second half of the 20th century. Colonial schools were first established to teach children to read so they could study the Bible. Even as late as the 1920s, the nation's most widely used schoolbooks, *McGuffey's Readers,* were filled with Bible stories and moral lessons.

But attitudes about religion in schools began to change during the 1960s, after the Supreme Court ruled that

CHRONOLOGY

1700s–1800s *Moral education with strong Christian overtones is an integral part of American public schooling.*

1910s *"Progressive" educator John Dewey challenges the use of moral tales to teach students character.*

1918 National Education Association report, "Cardinal Principles of Secondary Education," endorses "progressive" principle of learning by doing rather than memorizing moral lessons.

1960s *In the wake of the antiwar movement, the sexual revolution and struggles over civil rights, American society increasingly views ethics as a matter of personal choice. Attitudes about prayer and moral instruction in public schools begin to change following U.S. Supreme Court ruling on school prayer.*

1962 Supreme Court rules in *Engel v. Vitale* that daily prayer in New York state public schools violates constitutional separation between church and state. Many teachers respond by avoiding discussions of morals.

1966 "Values clarification" becomes a popular method of teaching morals, in which teachers are urged to help students "clarify" their values without being judgmental.

1970s–1980s *Cultural relativism sweeps the country but eventually fades from popularity along with values clarification. Youth violence and school discipline problems skyrocket. Several public school systems resume teaching values, but without religious overtones.*

1982 In Baltimore, a countywide values-education program is established based on 24 common moral values from the U.S. Constitution and the Bill of Rights.

1990s–2000s *Studies show widespread cheating. Teachers and students are caught cheating on high-stakes standardized tests after states begin linking test results to teacher bonuses and student promotions and graduation. Pressure mounts for character education and honor codes.*

1992 A consortium of colleges launches the Center for Academic Integrity to promote academic honesty and honor codes on campuses. Josephson Institute of Ethics convenes educators to draft a statement endorsing character education. It becomes the basis of the Character Counts! program.

Feb. 5, 1993 Education groups form Character Education Partnership to promote character education.

1994 Congress provides money for character education under the Elementary and Secondary Education Act.

1995 Students at Chicago's Steinmetz High School are caught cheating to win a statewide academic championship. Alabama begins requiring at least 10 minutes a day of values education.

Jan. 23, 1996 President Clinton endorses character education in his State of the Union address.

1998 Educators begin acknowledging that students are plagiarizing papers using Internet sources and on-line "term-paper mills." Boston University unsuccessfully sues the services. Study finds various classroom security methods can significantly reduce cheating.

1999 Center for Academic Integrity finds that only 6 percent of students from schools with traditional honor codes cheat repeatedly, compared with 10 percent at schools with a modified honor code and 17 percent at schools without honor codes.

2000 In cheating scandals around the country, teachers are caught helping or ordering students to cheat on statewide, standardized tests.

school prayer and Bible readings were unconstitutional. Many teachers interpreted the ruling as outlawing moral education altogether, and traditional moral instruction began disappearing from public schools.[9]

In earlier eras, Southern American culture — much like contemporary Middle Eastern and Asian cultures — valued the integrity of the family name above all else, Schwartz says. "That's why you didn't cheat in those societies," he says. "In the South, you gave your word as a gentleman. Today shame is no longer a moral motivator in most of this country, and it's a great loss."

There's still a greater sense of honor in the South than in the rest of the country, he says. For instance, he points out, the University of Virginia and the University of South Carolina have a long history of honor codes.

But even the Southern culture of honor was rocked by the radical sociological upheavals of the 1960s — the antiwar movement, struggles over minority and civil rights and the sexual revolution. Those movements shattered public assumptions about what morals were accepted and expected by the community. "The adults lost a sense of certainty about what values the community cherished," says Ryan of Boston University. "There was no longer a collective, clear vision of what was right or wrong."

Values Confusion

Then in the 1970s, the Watergate political scandal "showed that the nation's leadership was equally confused about values," he says. At the same time, "cultural relativism" swept the country, announcing that it was OK to "do your own thing" as long as it didn't hurt others, but that it was not OK to make value judgments about other people's behavior.

In the midst of all this "values confusion," Ryan says, educators "quietly and definitely stepped back from teaching kids what was morally right and became 'information transmitters.' We were there simply to explain mathematics or American history. Any involvement in kids' moral or ethical lives was at our own risk."

An offshoot of "cultural relativism" was the "values clarification" movement, which dictated that teachers were to allow students to determine their own values through guided discussions. But teachers were to act merely as moderators — without declaring what is right or wrong.[10]

"During the '70s and '80s, values clarification was the biggest movement in the education field," Ryan says. "You couldn't go to a workshop or conference without hearing about it."

But when researchers began finding that the programs were ineffective, values clarification lost its appeal. "Parents would go to school boards and say, 'You mean my kids can go through values clarification and still believe in cheating and lying?'" recalls James S. Leming, a professor at Southern Illinois University in Carbondale and an expert on evaluating values-education programs.[11]

Today, even leaders of the movement think it was a mistake. "I'm sorry to say we denigrated the direct teaching of traditional civic values," says Howard Kirschenbaum, who co-authored a values clarification handbook. "History clearly shows that was a very bad assumption," because learning values doesn't happen "unless society consciously works at teaching those values."[12]

But the experiment left in indelible mark on teachers, who became much more timid about telling students that certain values or behaviors were wrong. "It was much easier for young teachers, who had been themselves educated through a values-neutral curriculum, to teach their own students the same way," Ryan says. "As a result, those teachers suffer in schools where children are disrespectful of one another and of school authorities, and the teachers don't have any moral authority."

Thomas Lickona, a professor of education at State University of New York, Cortland, says that the self-esteem movement, which was also popular at the time, helped make teachers reluctant to tell students their judgment about something was wrong. "There was a great deal of fear that any criticism would damage a child's self-esteem," he says.[13]

Feminism and Multiculturalism

Just about the time that public schools began creating a values vacuum, they were inundated with new immigrants — many with very different cultural values about cheating. And many all-male colleges and universities began admitting female students.

In response, educators began stressing multiculturalism and women's rights. "As a result of the stress on tolerance during the past two decades, things are definitely better today than in the 1950s for women and minorities," says Josephson of the Josephson Institute. "But in the rush to teach tolerance, we let the integrity lessons fall by the wayside."

Schwartz agrees. "Today, tolerance seems to trump all other values on college campuses, including honesty," he says. "I'm not one who wants to turn back the clock to the 1950s, when blacks didn't have the right to vote, but we had less cheating. But we sort of threw out the baby with the bathwater, and we have to retrieve it."

Developing Nations Face 'Rampant' Cheating

Academic cheating may seem widespread in the U.S., but it is even worse in many other countries — and sometimes occurs at the point of a gun.

"Indeed, in some countries, cheating during even the most important exams appears to be almost the norm," says Harold J. Noah, a professor emeritus at Columbia University's Teachers College.

Students in countries with civil unrest are often coerced to cheat — sometimes under threat of violence, according to Gregory J. Cizek, a professor of education at the University of North Carolina. In 1990, for example, exam-takers in the Kashmir province in India showed up with AK-47 assault rifles, pistols and hand grenades. "Ph.D.s were doing exams for 16-year-olds, and no one dared complain," said a news report."[1]

In 1997, widespread cheating at three Nigerian universities included concealing source materials in headscarves or skirts, using walkie-talkies to get correct answers from helpers and bribing proctors. In 1998, test-takers in Moscow received answers to essay questions via their pagers.[2]

Noah and Max A. Eckstein, authors of *Fraud and Education: The Worm in the Apple,* found that "fraud in education is absolutely rampant on the Indian subcontinent and in many African countries." And in several countries, including India, Bangladesh, Pakistan, Nigeria and sub-Saharan Africa, "students caught cheating had better not be punished, or the teacher might be beaten up," Noah says.

"Wherever an educational credential is very important economically, the incentive to cheat is greater than when there are many other avenues to success available," he says, especially in countries where teachers and other civil servants overseeing tests may be paid only a few dollars a month.

Cizek reports that, just as in the United States, teachers as well as students in other countries are being caught cheating:

- Ten teachers at the Guiteras pre-university school in Havana, Cuba, were jailed in 1987 for accepting bribes to help students falsify exams.

- Fifty teachers were fired in 1995 after a cheating incident in Bangladesh. A teacher who spoke out against the cheating was hacked to death by angry students.

- During the inaugural national tests for 11-year-olds in Britain in 1995, teachers assigned test questions as homework and wrote answers on the blackboards during the tests. The test results — like many U.S. high-stakes tests — were being used to develop school performance reports.

CURRENT SITUATION

High-Stakes Testing

Recent cheating scandals have renewed the perennial debate about high-stakes standardized tests. Critics have seized on cheating as just another in a long list of reasons to abandon the controversial tests. The stress created by the tests, they say, and the sense that in some cases the tests are irrelevant and unfair, induces both teachers and students to cheat.

"Tying rewards and performance evaluations to student test scores only increases the incentive for teachers to cheat," says Karen Hartke, project director of FairTest, a Boston-based organization that opposes standardized testing. "And students are more likely to cheat if they don't see any relevancy between the statewide tests and what they are doing in the classroom."

Cheating scandals are a "predictable and unfortunate" result of the nation's current overemphasis on raising standardized test scores in a misguided effort to raise educational standards, says Kohn, author of *The Schools Our Children Deserve.*

Paradoxically, high-stakes testing is lowering education standards — not raising them, he says. "The real cheating going on in education reform is by those who are cheating students out of an authentic education by turning schools into giant test-prep centers," Kohn says. Every hour spent drilling students to ace statewide exams is an hour not spent teaching them to become creative, critical and curious learners, he complains.

Rather than focusing on students who cheat, society should be concerned about the whole range of cheating committed by adults in the name of education reform,

Cheating is defined differently in various countries, so international comparisons on cheating rates must be interpreted cautiously, Cizek writes. For instance, because no study shows college students overseas admitting to cheating as much as U.S. students (80 percent or more), "It may be that U.S. students are either the most dishonest in the international community — or simply the most honest about their dishonesty," he writes.[3]

In many other countries cheating is considerably more acceptable than in the United States, Cizek points out, even when it is perceived as wrong. For instance, a 1984 study of Russian student attitudes toward cheating found that "even students who recognize behaviors as inappropriate…nonetheless judge [them] as acceptable."

Thus, as the United States moves toward a more multicultural society, Cizek concludes, those seeking to prevent cheating must understand the various perceptions about cheating held by test-takers from different cultural backgrounds. Otherwise, school administrators could face a situation like that described by educator W.P. Cordiero. At an unnamed U.S. university, he wrote, more than 50 foreign students from the same country were caught passing notes and signaling each other.

The students acknowledged the activities but said it wasn't cheating. In their country, people are viewed as a "brother" in an extended family. "Each 'brother' was expected to assist other brothers," Cordiero writes.[4]

Researchers discovered similar attitudes among American-born minorities. In two different studies, high-achieving black and Hispanic students argued that their actions were justified because cheating was a pragmatic way for poor students to improve their socioeconomic status or because helping other students was their responsibility.[5]

As the U.S. student population becomes more diversified, it is important for educators and administrators to communicate to students that cheating is not OK in American schools, educators say.

It is also important to tighten up security on test-takers. The Educational Testing Service (ETS), which gives millions of college and graduate school entrance exams each year, says it has tightened procedures both here and abroad. In China and India, for example, exams are now given via computers in separate testing carrels. The tests are videotaped, and test takers must present photo IDs before taking a test.

"We have our name and credibility to protect," says Ray Nicosia, head of ETS security. "Our job is to stay ahead of the cheating curve."

---

[1] Gregory J. Cizek, *Cheating on Tests: How to Do It, Detect It and Prevent It* (1999), p. 76-77.

[2] *Ibid.*, pp. 77-78.

[3] *Ibid.*, p. 89.

[4] W. P. Cordiero, "Should a school of business change its ethics to conform to the cultural diversity of its students?" *Journal of Education for Business*, 1995, Vol. 71, pp. 27-29.

[5] A. Hemmings, "Conflicting images? Being black and a model high school student," *Anthropology and Education Quarterly*, 1996, Vol. 27, p. 40.

he says. Administrators "play a variety of games" to raise their schools' scores, he says. They encourage low achievers to drop out of school or stay home on test days, channel poor achievers into special-education classes exempt from high-stakes tests, or ignore meaningful curriculum to drill students on test materials. "It's outrageous," he says. "Even if it works, it compromises the validity of the tests as a measure of what's going on in the school."

Critics claim that in some states, cheating is a backlash to tests perceived as unfair because they are given without first spending money to retrain teachers in the material being tested or to realign the classroom curriculum to match the material on the tests.

Sacks, the author of the book on standardized testing, calls it unconscionable when politicians order students to be tested but don't give failing schools any more money until they improve test scores. Such an approach is tantamount to setting up the public schools to fail, which he says is the real agenda of the testing advocates. If school failure rates can be quantified by test scores, he says, school critics can justify privatizing public education through use of vouchers.[14]

By pushing rote memorization and test-prep, high schools are producing graduates who are more likely to cheat in college, because they are not prepared for college-level work, Sacks says. "Professors tell me students are arriving at college expecting a cook-book approach to education, with everything spelled out for them in worksheets and drills. It's a shock to these kids when they learn that everything will not be spoon-fed to them in multiple-choice tests that review a certain page in the book."

Honor-Code College Students Say They Cheat Less

Twice as many students at colleges without honor codes said they cheated compared with students at schools with codes. But researchers question whether honor codes actually discourage cheating — or just make students less willing to admit it.

% of Students Admitting Cheating

Cheating Behavior	Schools With Honor Code	Schools Without Honor Code
Copied from another student on exam	13%	29%
Helped another student cheat on exam	11	29
Used crib notes on exam	10	25

Source: "Academic Dishonesty Among Males in College: A Thirty-Year Perspective," *Journal of College Student Development,* 1994.

Overreliance on multiple-choice tests also encourages cheating, he says, because they're easier to cheat on. When other countries give rigorous high-stakes tests they generally give essay-style tests, which tends to rule out the kind of easy cheating seen on American tests, he says. Indeed, Sacks notes, "Multiple-choice, machine-scorable tests are known in Europe as 'American-style tests.' "

It all comes down to money, test critics say. It costs less to use computer-graded standardized tests to assess large numbers of kids than to use multiple, hand-graded assessments. It also costs more to have classes small enough so teachers know their students' capabilities well enough to immediately spot a plagiarized paper, says Sizer at the Coalition of Essential Schools. Having students orally defend their papers also discourages cheating, he says, but it takes time, which cost-cutting school boards are reluctant to fund.

But others, like Tirozzi of the National Association of Secondary School Principals, say eliminating high-stakes standardized testing just because some kids cheat would amount to "throwing the baby out with the bathwater." Out of 15,000 school districts in the country, only a tiny number of students and teachers have been involved in cheating scandals, he points out.

Nonetheless, he adds, if administrators or teachers are cheating, "they should be punished and punished severely," especially if the test is fair and aligned with the curriculum and the state standards. Non-aligned tests, however, are "an exercise in futility," and should be done away with, he says. "But under no circumstances is it OK for the teacher to cheat."

If a test isn't fair, "there are other ways to protest than cheating," Tirozzi says. "That's why we have school boards and state boards of education."

Noah agrees that high-stakes tests should not be eliminated just because some teachers are cheating. "After all, the answer to business corruption is not to do away with strict accounting standards," he says.

Defending the Tests

Education reform proponent Chester E. Finn, Jr., president of the conservative Thomas B. Fordham Foundation and a fellow at the Manhattan Institute, says abolishing testing because of cheating would be like abandoning the Olympics just because a few athletes take performance-enhancing drugs. "The remedy is to have secure tests," he says. Any high-stakes test creates temptation to cut corners, he says. "We're all tempted to break the speed limit. That's why we have policemen waiting with radar."

Cheating is not OK even if a high-stakes test isn't aligned with the classroom curriculum, he says. "Sure everybody should have a full opportunity to learn," he says. Tests are one way of "smoking out those schools that lack the necessary instructional resources or procedures," he says. In the meantime, there is bound to be "some fallout," he says, admitting that many states need to both improve their state academic standards and align their curriculums with those standards.

Finn admits that some states erroneously think that education reform will happen automatically without adding funding. "But you have an equal number of states who have been dumping money into their education systems without monitoring the results," he says. "That's also wrong."

The solution is not to throw out the tests, he says, but to institute good standards, aligned curriculums, consequences for both students and adults and tighter test security.

And, just as the anti-test folks think their opponents have a hidden agenda, Finn also thinks his opponents have ulterior motives. "The true agenda is to roll back the standards and accountability altogether," he says.

Should high-stakes tests be abolished in order to reduce cheating?

YES

Monty Neill, Ed.D.
Executive Director, National Center for Fair & Open Testing

Written for *The CQ Researcher*, September 2000

Intense pressures to raise test scores for "accountability" have led directly to increased cheating by teachers and administrators. Why? Because "high-stakes" testing — to decide student graduation or promotion, or to reward or punish schools — sends the message that test scores are the most important goal of education.

Overt cheating, however, is only "the canary in the mine." It warns us of a much greater danger: High-stakes exams are turning schools into little more than test-coaching programs.

Teaching to tests is becoming rampant across the nation. First, schools drop important content areas that are not on state exams. Next, daily instruction comes to resemble testing. Then teachers coach their students with questions that are very close in content and format to those on the test. Finally, some teachers provide the exact questions. We all recognize the last step as "cheating," but each of these steps cheats students out of a rich and meaningful education.

Focusing on exam scores causes the elimination of art, music, recess and physical education, and it can prevent some students from learning to read, write and do math. In Texas, for example, many low-income children who get acceptable test scores in reading cannot really read. They have been trained to hunt for key words in a short passage in order to respond to test questions.

Similarly, writing instruction often is reduced to a five-paragraph canned exercise to fit exam requirements that's useless for any other writing. Meanwhile, history and science teachers are required to provide test preparation in reading and math instead of teaching their own subjects. Students across the nation are being driven out of school, retained in grade or placed in special education solely in order to improve school scores.

Test-driven schooling also cheats the public and fails as accountability. Because teaching to the test creates score inflation — gains from coaching and cheating that do not represent real learning — the public cannot tell how well schools are doing, even by the limited measure of standardized tests.

We could reduce overt cheating by focusing on security, making schools more like jails. A bad solution in its own right, this does nothing to address the larger problem.

Testing has not, cannot and will not induce high-quality education, but it does encourage cheating, both overt and covert. To address these problems, we must radically de-emphasize testing and rethink accountability.

NO

Chester E. Finn Jr.
John M. Olin Fellow, Manhattan Institute

Written for *The CQ Researcher*, September 2000

Should the Olympics be abolished because eager athletes may try to boost their chances by taking drugs? Should elections be done away with because unscrupulous politicians may seek to rig them?

The fact is that every high-stakes human endeavor — one where success brings reward and failure brings unhappiness — carries incentives to finagle the outcome. It's human nature — just like the impulse to slack off where there are no consequences at all. Do we really think world athletics would be taken as seriously — or that athletes would strive as hard as they do — if there were no quadrennial Olympics?

So, too, with education. Where it doesn't matter, it isn't taken seriously. Where learning is not prized, little of it occurs. Where test results don't count, nobody gets worked up about them. Attach consequences, however, and they become important to do well on. And they invite finagling.

We've known this forever. That's why college entrance tests such as the S.A.T. are proctored — and why a lively industry exists to help people do well on them.

As state-level academic standards gain traction, as standards-based education reform begins to get serious and as tests are relied on as key indicators of whether standards are, in fact, being met, we must expect that people will exploit opportunities to rig the results. Does that mean tests should be done away with? Hardly. (A very different question is whether test scores alone should determine high-stakes consequences for youngsters. I think not.)

Keep in mind that standards-based reform — today's main strategy for improving U.S. education, endorsed by governors, business leaders and public opinion — is meant to alter the behavior of educators and students. (If it doesn't affect their teaching and learning, it surely won't change their results!)

A lot of teachers don't like that. Some just don't want to change. Others resist "behaviorist" methods on principle. Some are lazy or unscrupulous. What we're seeing in recent cheating episodes are those people trying to finagle their results in the short run and quash standards-based reform itself over the long run. They're wrong, however, and it would be wrong to throw out the standards baby just because of the dirty bathwater in which he is occasionally immersed. Better test security is the proper response. Plus, of course, good tests aligned to worthy standards!

There are signs that that's just what's starting to happen, at least in some states. In the last year, high-stakes test critics have been heartened by a sprinkling of protests. Wisconsin moved away from using them after parents protested, and in Massachusetts hundreds of students boycotted statewide, standardized tests last spring. Louisiana and Arizona recently delayed their state exam requirements for a year.

"I think policy-makers are beginning to realize that school improvement is more than simply demanding it and enforcing it with a test," says Glen Cutlip, senior policy analyst at the National Education Association.

Preventive Measures

Schools and colleges around the country are cracking down on cheating — tightening security, giving different versions of the same exam, walking the aisles during testing, switching teaching staffs on standardized test days and changing seating arrangements.

Some colleges are requiring students caught cheating to perform community service, and several large state universities — including Penn State, University of Denver, University of California, Davis, and Kansas State — are adopting modified honor codes like the University of Maryland's.

States also are working to align their tests to classroom curriculum. "If the tests are considered a fair evaluation of what the students have actually been taught in the classroom, it'll get rid of a lot of the motivation for cheating," Sacks says.

And some schools and even colleges are switching from relying solely on multiple-choice tests to using portfolios of students' work to make decisions about graduation, promotion and college entrance, Cizek says. And to discourage plagiarism, some teachers and professors are collecting notes, outlines and rough drafts along with finished essays.

Character Education Gains Supporters

Hundreds of school districts around the country are also bringing values-based instruction back into the classroom. For instance, the Chicago school system has instituted a character-education initiative that incorporates 10 values — including honesty, truthfulness, caring, courtesy and courage — into lessons and assignments.

Six years ago, the Josephson Institute launched Character Counts!, a program that started out with 27 organizations agreeing to promote ethical values in a non-sectarian, apolitical way. Today, 422 school districts, sports organizations and YMCAs participate.

"The character-education movement is growing fast," says Plachta of the Character Education Partnership. Forty-eight states now address character education in one way or another, she says, prompted partly by the 1998 mass murder at Colorado's Columbine High School.[15]

"After Columbine, people started clambering for something other than metal detectors, which they knew was only a short-term fix," she says. "Character education is a long-term solution that will get to the heart of the matter." She says schools with character-education programs are seeing declines in violence, disrespect, bullying and cheating.

Ryan of Boston University predicts the movement will continue to grow, and he suspects that much of the push for charter schools, vouchers and home schooling is motivated by parents' desire that their children be educated in a moral environment.

Maryland's Pavela says colleges are also instituting character-education programs. "The whole movement is shifting from middle and high schools to college campuses," he says.

OUTLOOK

More Cheating?

Some educators say cheating on college campuses will probably increase — at least in the short term. "Left unchecked, that's the direction we're headed," says Hinman at the Values Institute.

Garrison at Northwestern is equally pessimistic. "It's not a hopeful picture," he says. "We are in an amoral culture right now, moving away from the right direction."

Others think cheating will increase as the consequences of high-stakes tests go into effect and more kids and schools start failing. "We'll start seeing huge numbers of kids failing to complete high school and probably more cheating in the process," says FairTest's Hartke.

Kerkvliet of Oregon State University says cheating at universities will probably increase as administrators continue to hire adjunct and temporary faculty members, and as they offer more distance-learning courses. "Right now, it's impossible to know who's taking a test in a distance-learning course," he says.

Distance education is merely an extension of the large, anonymous, 500-student undergraduate classes where cheating is common, says Hinman, except that lectures will be available on-line and questions will be handled by e-mail. "The personal relationship will be even more diminished," he says, "because you won't even physically see the students."

Others say cheating will escalate if voucher advocates are successful in establishing programs allowing public school students to attend private schools using public tax money. If education is privatized, parents and students will become consumers, and schools will sell themselves based on their standardized test scores, says Kohn. "Schools will be more inclined to turn a blind eye to cheating if it raises test scores," he says.

In the long run, some observers say, if cheating is not brought under control, both democracy and the fundamental competence of society could be undermined, because people will be unable to trust in the competence of their doctors, engineers, lawyers or merchants. "It will eventually undermine the argument in favor of a democracy run by its citizens," says Sizer at the Coalition of Essential Schools.

Hinman argues that trust is fundamental to the social, political and economic fabric of any successful society. Economists have found that societies where there is no trust outside of the family unit usually hit a developmental glass ceiling, he says. "Without trust in public and business institutions outside the family, an economy stops developing after a certain point," he says.

How to Prevent Cheating — the Students' View

School officials say proctoring is the best antidote to cheating, but college students say scrambled tests and smaller classes work best.

Cheating-Prevention Strategies

Strategy	Percentage
Scrambled test forms	81.6%
Small classes	69.8
Using numerous proctors	68.4
Different make-up exams	68.4
Several distinct test forms	66.6
Provide study guides	54.8
More essay questions	54.6
Make old exams available for review	52.4
Verify student IDs prior to exam	46.9
Give different assignments	42.8
Assign individual term-paper topics	30.2
Put students' names on test booklets	28.4
Assign exam seating	26.9
Fewer take-home tests	26.9
More take-home tests	17.5
Cheating hotline	16.0

Percentage of College Students Who Say the Strategy Is "Effective" or "Very Effective"

Source: "Academic Dishonesty and the Perceived Effectiveness of Countermeasures: An Empirical Survey of Cheating at a Major Public University," *NASPA Journal* (National Association of Student Personnel Administrators), 1996.

Others, like Boston University's Ryan, warn that if public schools don't start teaching character development, the public may abandon the values-free public schools for institutions that place a greater emphasis on morality and good behavior. However, he is optimistic that the public schools will get their act together.

"We are, at heart, a very moral society," he says. "We've just gone through a lot of wrenching changes in the last 30 years. All of us — political leaders, parents and classroom teachers — need to be much clearer about what we expect from students. We've been very confused, so Hollywood and muck sellers have done the teaching for us. We need to take that role back from them."

But it won't happen overnight. "It took us a long time to get where we are," Ryan says. "It will take us a long time to get back to where we were 30 years ago."

McCabe at the Center for Academic Integrity thinks things are already turning around. "All of a sudden," he says, "within the last year you are seeing a lot of schools saying, 'We need to pay more attention to this issue.'"

Josephson, too, is optimistic. "The battle is far from won," he says, "but there's no question the battle is joined. We won't be able to stamp out cheating, but I believe we will be able to reduce the rates of cheating substantially." Society is hungry for a set of moral standards that will level the playing field again, he says. "Because in a world where cheating is rampant, only the best cheaters win."

It's not that people are against curtailing cheating, says Schwartz at the John Templeton Foundation. "It's just that they are not putting the time or emphasis on teaching honesty. We should be as intentional about teaching honesty as we are about tolerating diversity."

People's behavior can change, he says. "A hundred years ago Jews, women and blacks could not go to most colleges and universities in this nation. That has changed. Now we need to tackle this last issue."

NOTES

1. For background, see Kathy Koch, "National Education Standards," *The CQ Researcher*, May 14, 1999, pp. 401-424.

2. Quoted in Dirk Johnson, "Cheaters' Final Response: So What?" *The New York Times*, May 16, 2000.

3. Brigid Schulte, "Evidence of Cheating on MD. Test 'Substantial,'" *The Washington Post*, June 2, 2000.

4. C.A. Drake, "Why Students Cheat," *Journal of Higher Education*, Vol. 12, 1941, pp. 418-420.

5. See the center's Web site at www.academicintegrity .org/Research.asp.

6. Quoted in Kate Roberts, "Proficiency test cheating allegations not closely monitored," The Associated Press, Sept. 2, 2000.

7. Gregory J. Cizek, *Cheating on Tests: How to Do It, Detect It and Prevent It* (1999), p. 75.

8. Quoted in Boston University press release accompanying Character Education Manifesto, April 3, 1996.

9. Beginning in 1962, the Supreme Court issued a series of rulings on school prayer and Bible reading, starting with its decision in *Engel v. Vitale* that the daily prayer in New York public schools violated the constitutional separation between church and state. See Kenneth Jost, "Religion in Schools," *The CQ Researcher*, Feb. 18, 1994, pp. 145-168.

10. For background, see Sarah Glazer, "Teaching Values," *The CQ Researcher*, June 21, 1996, pp. 529-552.

11. *Ibid.*, p. 543.

12. Quoted in Glazer, *op. cit.*, p. 542.

13. *Ibid.*

14. For background, see Kathy Koch, "Reforming School Funding," *The CQ Researcher*, Dec. 10, 1999, pp. 1041-1064; Kathy Koch, "School Vouchers," *The CQ Researcher*, April 9, 1999, pp. 281-304; David Masci, "School Choice Debate," *The CQ Researcher*, July 18, 1997, pp. 625-648; Charles S. Clark, "Attack on Public Schools," *The CQ Researcher*, Aug. 2, 1996, pp. 649-672, and Richard L. Worsnop, "Privatization," *The CQ Researcher*, Nov. 13, 1992, pp. 988-1011.

15. See Kathy Koch, "School Violence," *The CQ Researcher*, Oct. 9, 1998, pp. 881-904.

BIBLIOGRAPHY

Books

Cizek, Gregory J., *Cheating on Tests: How to Do It, Detect It and Prevent It*, Lawrence Erlbaum Associates, 1999.
A University of North Carolina professor takes an in-depth look at cheating in the United States and around the world and offers recommendations on how to stop it.

Noah, Harold J., and Max A. Eckstein, *Fraud and Education: The Worm in the Apple*, **Rowman and Littlefield, 2001.**

Two emeritus professors discuss dishonesty in academia at home and abroad, of, from fraudulent research to faked credentials and fabricated academic papers,

Sacks, Peter, *Standardized Minds*, **Perseus Books, 1999.**

Education researcher Sacks argues that America's over-emphasis on standardized testing does little to improve education but merely punishes the poor and disadvantaged and waters down curricula nationwide.

Articles

Desruisseaux, Paul, "Cheating Is Reaching Epidemic Proportions Worldwide, Researchers Say," *The Chronicle of Higher Education*, **April 30, 1999.**

Two scholars of comparative education report that cheating has become ubiquitous among students, faculty and administrators at all educational levels. They blame competitive pressures and new technology.

Fritz, Mark, "Plagiarism by Internet Now a Staple of College Life," *Los Angeles Times*, **March 4, 1999, p. A12.**

Fritz details a shift in attitudes among today's students, fostered by the vast array of information available on the Internet about what constitutes plagiarism. Cutting and pasting passages from the Web into a school report, he writes, "doesn't seem nearly as nefarious as pilfering a passage from a library book."

Glazer, Sarah, "Teaching Values," *The CQ Researcher*, **June 21, 1996, pp. 529-552.**

Glazer takes an in-depth look at the return to character education in schools after it fell by the wayside during the 1960s and '70s.

Johnson, Dirk, "Cheaters' Final Response: So What?" *The New York Times*, **May 16, 2000.**

Reporter Johnson discusses how the students involved in the Steinmetz High School cheating scandal in Chicago have no regrets about cheating — only about getting caught.

Kleiner, Carolyn, and Mary Lord, "The Cheating Game," *U.S. News & World Report*, **Nov. 22, 1999.**

A cover story on cheating looks at the scope and reasons for the increase in cheating around the country.

Matthews, Jay, "Cheating on the Rise Along With Testing," *The Washington Post*, **June 2, 2000.**

Reporter Matthews links the spate of teacher-cheating scandals around the country with the rise in high-stakes standardized testing.

McCabe, Donald L., and Patrick Drinan, "Toward a Culture of Academic Integrity," *The Chronicle of Higher Education*, **Oct. 15, 1999.**

Saying that colleges and universities haven't done nearly enough to combat cheating, two experts outline areas administrators should address.

Roberts, Kate, "Proficiency Test Cheating Allegations Not Closely Monitored," *The Associated Press*, **Sept. 2, 2000.**

Roberts discusses a recent cheating scandal in Ohio in which the teachers' union complained that states encourage cheating by rushing to impose high-stakes tests without first beefing up test security.

Sacks, Peter, "Tests Carry Too Much Weight," *USA Today*, **June 15, 2000.**

An education researcher argues that high-stakes tests put too much pressure on students and teachers and are a poor substitute for quality teaching and strong curricula.

Schneider, Alison, "Why Professors Don't Do More to Stop Students Who Cheat," *The Chronicle of Higher Education*, **Jan. 22, 1999.**

Many college and university professors turn a blind eye to students who cheat, contending it's not worth the trouble to file formal complaints because school judicial systems are "laborious, even labyrinthine" and punishments rarely match the crime.

For More Information

Center for Academic Integrity, Duke University, Box 90434, Durham, NC 27708; (919) 660-3045; www .academicintegrity.org. This consortium of 200 colleges and universities provides a forum to identify, affirm and promote the values of academic integrity among students.

Character Education Partnership, 1600 K St. N.W., Suite 501, Washington, DC 20006; (800) 988-8081; www.character.org. This nonpartisan coalition of organizations and individuals is dedicated to developing moral character and civic virtue in the nation's youth.

Coalition of Essential Schools, 1814 Franklin St., Suite 700, Oakland, CA 94612; (510) 433-1451; www .essentialschools.org/. A network of 1,000 schools and 24 regional support centers that helps schools through systematic change.

FairTest, 342 Broadway, Cambridge, MA 02139; (617) 864-4810; www.fairtest.org. The National Center for Fair & Open Testing (FairTest) works to end the abuses, misuses and flaws of standardized testing and ensure that evaluation of students and workers is fair, open and educationally sound.

John Templeton Foundation, P.O. Box 8322, Radnor, PA 19087-8322; (610) 687-8942; www.templeton.org. This nonprofit, grant-making organization encourages appreciation for all peoples and cultures; supports studies that demonstrate a progressive approach to learning; and promotes a high standard of excellence in scholastics and character.

Josephson Institute of Ethics, 4640 Admiralty Way, Suite 1001, Marina del Rey, CA 90292-6610; (310) 306-1868; www.josephsoninstitute.org. This nonprofit group established the Character Counts! Coalition, a popular program promoting character education in schools and community groups.

National Association of Secondary School Principals, 1904 Association Dr., Reston, VA 20191-1537; (703) 860-0200; www.nassp.org. The NASSP promote excellence in school leadership to Congress, the administration, the news media and general public.

Supporting researchers for more than 40 years

Research methods have always been at the core of SAGE's publishing program. Founder Sara Miller McCune published SAGE's first methods book, *Public Policy Evaluation*, in 1970. Soon after, she launched the *Quantitative Applications in the Social Sciences* series—affectionately known as the "little green books."

Always at the forefront of developing and supporting new approaches in methods, SAGE published early groundbreaking texts and journals in the fields of qualitative methods and evaluation.

Today, more than 40 years and two million little green books later, SAGE continues to push the boundaries with a growing list of more than 1,200 research methods books, journals, and reference works across the social, behavioral, and health sciences. Its imprints—Pine Forge Press, home of innovative textbooks in sociology, and Corwin, publisher of PreK–12 resources for teachers and administrators—broaden SAGE's range of offerings in methods. SAGE further extended its impact in 2008 when it acquired CQ Press and its best-selling and highly respected political science research methods list.

From qualitative, quantitative, and mixed methods to evaluation, SAGE is the essential resource for academics and practitioners looking for the latest methods by leading scholars.

For more information, visit **www.sagepub.com**.